MW01054594

This copy of

CHARLIE'S CHARTS
WESTERN COAST OF MEXICO
INCLUDING BAJA CALIFORNIA

Belongs to:

Captain:_____

Vessel:_____

Hailing Port:_____

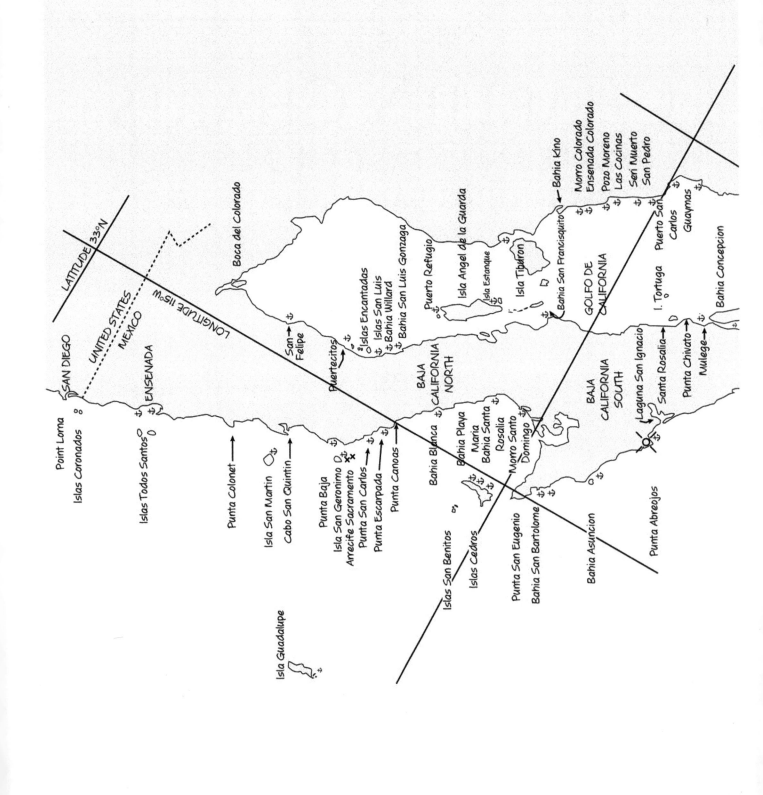

Point Loma
SAN DIEGO
Islas Coronados
UNITED STATES
MEXICO
ENSENADA
Islas Todos Santos

LATITUDE 33°N

LONGITUDE 115°W

Boca del Colorado

San Felipe

Puertecitos

Islas Encantadas
Islas San Luis
Bahia Willard
Bahia San Luis Gonzaga

Puerto Refugio
Isla Angel de la Guarda
Isla Estanque
Isla Tiburon

Bahia San Francisquito

Bahia Kino
Morro Colorado
Ensenada Colorado
Pozo Moreno
Las Cocinas
Seri Nuerto
San Pedro

Puerto San Carlos
Guaymas

GOLFO DE CALIFORNIA

BAJA CALIFORNIA NORTH

Punta Colonet

Isla San Martin
Cabo San Quintin

Punta Baja
Isla San Geronimo
Arrecife Sacramento
Punta San Carlos
Punta Escarpada
Punta Canoas

Bahia Blanca

Bahia Playa
Maria
Bahia Santa
Rosalia
Morro Santo
Domingo

I. Tortuga

BAJA CALIFORNIA SOUTH

Laguna San Ignacio
Santa Rosalia
Punta Chivato
Mulege
Bahia Concepcion

Islas San Benitos

Islas Cedros

Punta San Eugenio
Bahia San Bartolome

Bahia Asuncion

Punta Abreojos

Isla Guadalupe

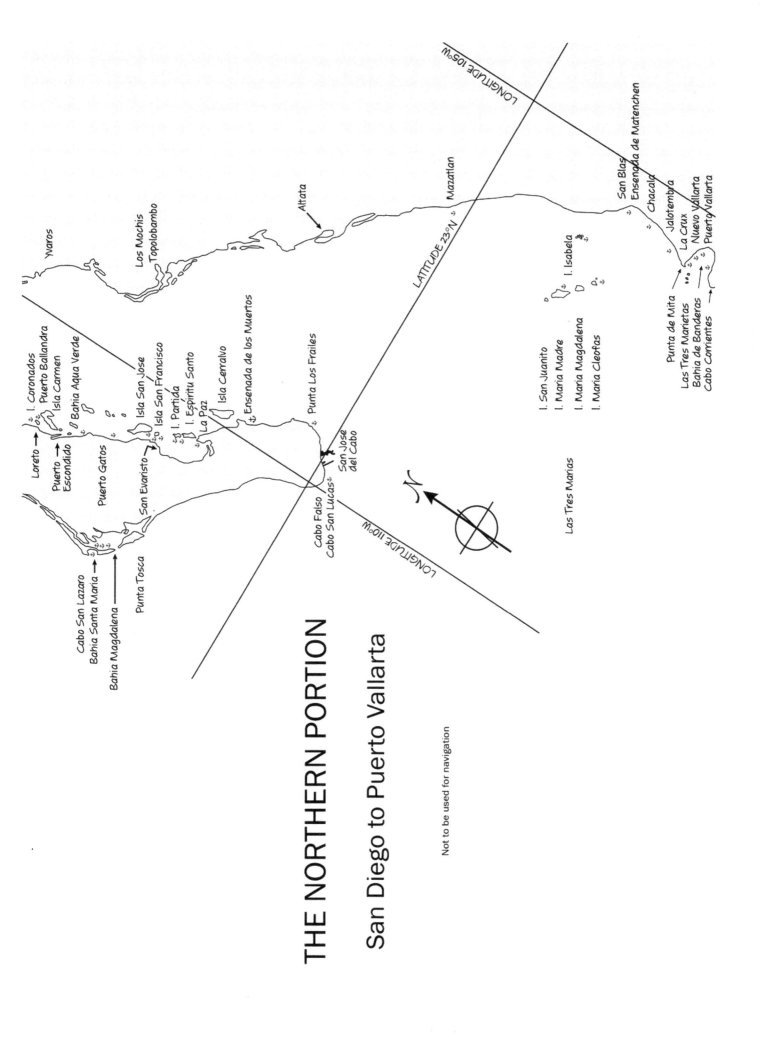

THE NORTHERN PORTION

San Diego to Puerto Vallarta

Not to be used for navigation

LONGITUDE 105°W

LONGITUDE 110°W

LATITUDE 23°N

Yvaros

Los Mochis
Topolobambo

Altata

Mazattan

San Blas
Ensenada de Matenchen

Chacala

Jalotemba

La Crux
Nuevo Vallarta
Puerto Vallarta

I. Isabela

Punta de Mita
Las Tres Marietas
Bahia de Banderas
Cabo Corrientes

I. San Juanito
I. Maria Madre
I. Maria Magdalena
I. Maria Cleofas

Las Tres Marias

I. Coronados
Puerto Ballandra
Isla Carmen
Bahia Aqua Verde

Isla San Jose
Isla San Francisco
I. Partida
I. Espiritu Santo
La Paz
Isla Cerralvo
Ensenada de los Muertos

Punta Los Frailes

Loreto
Puerto Escondido
Puerto Gatos
San Evaristo

Cabo Falso
Cabo San Lucas
San Jose del Cabo

Cabo San Lazaro
Bahia Santa Maria
Bahia Magdalena

Punta Tosca

N

OTHER PUBLICATIONS FROM P&S MARINE, LLC

CHARLIE'S CHARTS CRUISING GUIDES
CHARLIE'S CHARTS of the U.S. PACIFIC COAST
CHARLIE'S CHARTS of the Western Coast of MEXICO Including BAJA
CHARLIE'S CHARTS of POLYNESIA
CHARLIE'S CHARTS NORTH TO ALASKA
CHARLIE'S CHARTS of the HAWAIIAN ISLANDS
CHARLIE'S CHARTS of COSTA RICA

GERRY CUNNINGHAM'S NAVIGATION CHARTS

TO BAJA & the SEA OF CORTEZ
CHART PACKET for the PACIFIC COAST of BAJA
CHART PACKET for LA PAZ
CHART PACKET for CONCEPTION BAY
CHART PACKET for BAHIA DE LOS ANGELES
CHART PACKET for SAN CARLOS
PLOTTING SHEET PACKET for the PACIFIC COAST OF BAJA & SEA of CORTEZ

GERRY CUNNINGHAM'S SEA OF CORTEZ CRUISING GUIDES

CRUISING GUIDE TO THE LOWER GULF
CRUISING GUIDE TO THE MIDDLE GULF
CRUISING GUIDE TO SAN CARLOS
COMPLETE CRUISING GUIDE— Contains all Three Cruising Guides

© Copyright 2013 Charlie's Charts. A Division of P&S Marine, LLC

All rights reserved. No part of this publication may be reproduced or transmitted in any form or by any means, electronic or mechanical, including photocopying, recording or by any other information storage or and retrieval system without the written permission of the publisher.

Illustrated by Charles Wood, Gerry Cunningham and Holly Scott

Photos by Charles & Margo Wood, Gerry Cunningham & Holly Scott
Front cover photo by: Jo Russell
Back cover photo by: Sherry Davis
Other photos as credited.
Design by: Alejandra Cabrera

Publishers Cataloging in Publication Data

Wood, Charles E. 1928-1987, Wood, Margo 1934 - , Cunningham, Gerry 1922-2010, Scott, Holly 1955 -
CHARLIE'S CHARTS OF THE WESTERN COAST OF MEXICO INCLUDING BAJA
Captain Holly Scott with contributions by Charles and Margo Wood and Gerry Cunningham

Library of Congress Control Number: 2013902428
ISBN: 978-0-9833319-5-7
1. Cruising (Boats & Boating) 2. Sailing-Pacific Coast Mexico 3. Sailing-Guidebooks.
VK798 997
797.124

QR CODES AND CHARLIE'S CHARTS

As you can see, there have been many changes to this new edition of our Mexico guide. One change that may need a little explanation is the use of QR codes. You see them everywhere these days... they link a smart phone or tablet to lots of cool things.

In this guide, you will see them linked to videos, maps, interesting websites, Baja Ha Ha information – all kinds of things. Check out the section on cell phones and internet access to be able to use your phones in Mexico, then go to the app store and download the free QR Reader app. Just scan any QR code, and you're ready to go!

Keep in mind that the QR codes are not necessary to make use of this guide, they just add a little extra. Have fun!

Charlie's Charts Website

Charlie's Charts Facebook

Puerto Vallarta

Baja Ha Ha

Turtle Conservation

CHARLIE'S CHARTS
WESTERN COAST OF MEXICO
INCLUDING BAJA CALIFORNIA

by

Captain Holly Scott

with contributions by

Charles Wood, Margo Wood, and Gerry Cunningham

Published by

CHARLIE'S CHARTS

A DIVISION OF P&S MARINE, LLC

PO BOX 352
Seal Beach, CA 90740, U.S.A.
info@charliescharts.com

www.charliescharts.com

ISBN 978-0-9833319-5-7

ACKNOWLEDGEMENTS

At long last, we have a new edition of Charlie's Charts of the Western Coast of Mexico and Baja. This makes the 13th Edition of this guide, it's 2013 – so it has to be full of luck!

Research for this edition began a few years ago, before owning Charlie's Charts. Thankfully, we keep a log and took lots of pictures. The photos in this edition were taken by many different people, during many trips to Mexico. Some were forwarded by crew members at the end of a long trip, and their names have been inadvertently dropped from the photos. Credit for the photos is given whenever possible. Please forgive us if former crew members see their photo without a credit.

Along the way, Charlie's Charts acquired the works of Gerry Cunningham, an avid explorer of the Sea of Cortez. Gerry and his family spent over 50 years poking around in the 'Sea', taking pictures, gathering GPS waypoints, taking notes and recording their findings in his cruising guides and chart kits. He made the first GPS accurate charts of the Pacific side of the Baja, as well as the Sea of Cortez. You will notice that chart plotter positions and the earth don't always agree where things are in Mexico. Gerry's charts are on position and very accurate. Should you want to have them onboard, you may purchase them on our website www.charliescharts.com. Gerry was an amazing man, full of stories, wry humor and inventions. You may remember Gerry backpacks, tents and child carriers – it's the same Gerry. Gerry passed away in 2010. We are honored to be able to offer his life's work, and have included 61 of his charts and many more of his secret spots in this edition. Many thanks to Heather Cunningham and her family for helping us sort it all out.

This 13th Edition has combined Gerry's input, Charles and Margo Wood's previous works, our own experiences, and updates and information into one amazing cruising guide. We owe much appreciation, gratitude and love to our Buddy Boat and her crew. Bob and Sherry Davis on Nirvana, shared two Mexico trips with the crew of Mahalo, and have become our current Field Research Vessel in Mexico, as we have been finishing this guide. They have hosted us, fed us, sent us updates, information and photos, kept us sane(ish), and help us keep one foot in the cruiser's world of Mexico. Guess where we are going as soon as we are done with this one? Yep!

Our Buddy Boat, Bob and Sherry Davis, S/V Nirvana

Reg and Phoebe Wilson on Three Sheets, friends of the Nirvana crew, sent us photos and updates from Topolobampo and Altata. Many thanks to them – we can't wait to see you as well.

A very special contributor to this effort has been Alejandra Cabrera, a Graphic Artist we met in Ensenada. She has spent months digitalizing the charts, formatting the text, cleaning up my ADD messes and turning it all into a book. Many thanks to you Alejandra. She comes highly recommended if you need her services.

As I am a computer dunce, I often hit a brick wall in the process of trying to make this all happen. Two different types of computers, an ornery printer, mysterious programs that eat your work for lunch, websites and Facebook all contribute to my stress levels, which are eased somewhat by my computer savvy friends. To you saviors of my already questionable sanity – I thank you. This could never happen without you.

As always, I want to thank my parents Bud and Betty Scott for taking me sailing as a toddler, for turning me on to maps, charts and navigation at a young age, providing me with a life full of sailing adventures, and the almost uncontrollable desire to get out of here and go sailing! I hope I have passed it along to my daughter, Katie.

Captain Holly Scott

DISCLAIMER

The word, "CHARTS," in the title of this publication is not intended to imply that these hand-drawn sketches are sufficiently accurate to be used for navigation. They and the accompanying text are meant to act solely as a handy cruising guide to anchorages and marina facilities. As a result of marina development and other changes in the areas covered by this book it is inevitable that some of the material is out-of-date and inaccurate by the time it is used.

The use of National Imagery and Mapping Agency (NIMA), British Admiralty, Gerry Charts or Mexican charts are mandatory for safe boating. **DO NOT USE ANY OF THE DRAWINGS IN THIS BOOK FOR NAVIGATION. CHARLIE'S CHARTS and P&S MARINE LLC.** are in no way responsible for loss or damages resulting from the use of this book.

Your choice of method of navigation is entirely your responsibility. If you choose to use the GPS Waypoints or any other material printed in this guide, that is your choice and the publisher is not liable for any consequences of your navigation.

UPDATING MATERIAL

CHARLIE'S CHARTS are constantly being updated as new information becomes available. The material is inserted in each guide and posted on the website where it can be downloaded from the Addenda section of our website: www.charliescharts.com

A WORD OR TWO ABOUT KARMA

Sailors have always been a superstitious lot, and for good reason. How often have we all wondered what we did to deserve the bad things that happen to us as we are sailing around out there 'Just get me out of this storm in one piece and I'll never throw plastic overboard again!' You know what we're talking about...

So be nice to everybody and everything; other cruisers, the local folks, the wildlife with whom you share the land and seas, our planet and especially your boat. And remember that we print these cruising guides for you so you can cruise with some local knowledge, like having a friend onboard. You will want to share your experiences with other cruisers and mark up your guide with changes and suggestions from cruisers who have been there. Perfect!

However, copying these guides and selling or giving them away is BAD KARMA. You don't need any BAD KARMA, you need good karma. We will be happy to mail a brand new copy anywhere in the world, so just pass along our web information and build up some more good karma for yourself and others while you help us keep the presses rolling here at home.

TABLE OF CONTENTS

SKETCH SYMBOLS

- - - - -	Recommended approach	⁄⁄	Range, or leading direction
⚓	Anchorage	⚓	Reported anchorage
✕	Rock or reef underwater	⊗	Dangerous rock
	Shoal area		Shoal dries at low water
	Steep, rocky edges		Sand or pebble beach
	Land area		Underwater patches
⚡ ✕	Navigation light	▪ ▪	Buildings (indication only)
·10·	Depth contour in fathoms	S	Sand bottom
6f	Depth in fathoms	m	Mud bottom
∿∿∿	Surf, where stong (absence does not mean a lack of surf)	r	Rock bottom
		✳✳	Coconut palms
⟨	Kelp		

 GPS Waypoint for Reference Only
Not to be used for Navigation
Always refer to current NOAA charts

NOTE: All depths are given in fathoms, escept where specifically labeled in feet. For conversion to metric measurements:

approximately 1 fathom = 2 meters
exactly 1 fathom = 1.8 meter

INTRODUCTION

Purpose of the Guide

This guide is intended to assist in selecting and identifying small boat anchorages along the west coasts of Mexico and throughout the Sea of Cortez.

Local land form details, depth lines and land contour lines, lights and navigational data are included for each. It is important to remember the sketch charts are hand drawn and are not meant to be accurate surveys.

Where nautical charts of harbors, bays or anchorages are available, they have been used as the basis for sketches and additional detail as may be of benefit to mariners.

The sketches have no other special merit over the nautical charts.

As always, coastal and harbor charts should be used for all navigation; the sketches in the guide are intended as a supplement. This Guide does not relieve mariners of the responsibility to safely navigate vessels.

As in all CHARLIE'S CHARTS Guidebooks, the anchorage sketches, other drawings and information are based on personal visits to and experience with each location contained in the Guide. Every effort has been made to present information that is as correct and current as possible, appreciating that marina developments and new navigational aids are constantly changing.

CAUTION: There is much variation in the scales used for different sketches. It is therefore essential to check the scale indicated and make allowance for different scales.

Scope and Limits of the Guide

The Baja peninsula extends nearly 800 miles southeastward from the U.S. border to its tip at Cabo Falso and Cabo San Lucas. Across the Gulf of California lies Mexico's mainland coast that extends to Puerto Madero approximately 1,300 miles further southeast. To facilitate easy use, the Guide is organized in four regionalized sections.

Section I: South from San Diego down the outer (west) coast of Baja California to Cabo San Lucas
Section II: North from Cabo San Lucas up the inner (east) coast of Baja California to San Felipe
Section III: The mainland coast from Puerto Peñasco to Acapulco
Section IV: The mainland coast from Acapulco to Puerto Madero (Chiapas)

It is possible to travel directly between the end points of each section without stopping or within sight of land. It is assumed that most vessels cruising Mexico's pacific waters prefer to do so in a number of shorter passages. For this reason, anchorages included in the Guide are generally about a day's passage from one another.

Each Section provides a few brief general notes on typical weather, winds, currents and other data that are pertinent to the region covered. For more specific data on these important subjects, mariners are referred to the official Sailing Directions, Pilot Charts or relevant books.

PREPARATION AND ADVICE

When to travel

As hurricanes can be an issue in Mexico, thought must be given to where you want to be and when. Hurricane season is June 15 through November 1. During this time, hurricanes are possible but not a regular event. They are most frequent later in the season. The outer, Pacific side of the Baja can get nailed with a true hurricane, and/or the fringes of a hurricane that has decided to travel up the Sea of Cortez , or a hurricane which is dying, but still packs a punch. The Mainland and the Sea of Cortez can get a real live hurricane in all its glory. Some insurance companies dictate where a vessel must be, or can't be during the summer, so be sure to look over your policy.

Winter months can be quite chilly along the Pacific side of Baja, especially when heading north. There can be some very calm days during the winter however, which is great for the patient skipper waiting for a weather window. Winter is most pleasant on the mainland, and passages can be made with only local weather to worry about. Winter in the Sea of Cortez can be cold and windy when a norther roars down from the States and keeps boats in port, or hunkered down in an anchorage. Keep this in mind when deciding where to spend the night.

The south bound exodus from San Diego begins with the Baja Ha Ha each season, which usually departs during the last few days of October. Non-participants begin on November 1 and continue through the first few months of the new year. North bound vessels try to squeeze as much as they can from their time in Mexico and head north during late spring, which can be some of the nastiest weather of the year.

There is another exodus, which heads north up into the Sea of Cortez in June to escape the hurricanes down south, spending a hot summer in or close to a hurricane hole, then heading south again in November.

VESSELS

Vessels intended for cruising Mexican waters should be sound, well found, and capable of safe open ocean operation in significant winds and seas. Vessels that are exclusively powered must have a range of at least 175 miles between refueling stops (nominally the longest legs between fuel resources along Baja's Pacific coastline).

Trailerable power and sailing vessels will find launching facilities in the northern portion of the Sea of Cortez. These waters are relatively benign compared to the west side of the Baja Peninsula and the mainland, which are exposed to the Pacific Ocean. However, severe weather conditions can and do occur even in the Sea of Cortez.

ENGINES, FUEL AND PROPANE

Diesel fuel and gasoline is available at most marinas and without question in all major port cities and towns. Fuel can almost always be obtained at Pemex stations in smaller towns and anchorages using jerry cans. Occasionally fuel can obtained in an emergency from local fishermen. As a general comment, diesel and gasoline obtained from major marinas is clean and water free, as it is from Pemex stations. If fuel is obtained from other sources, it is highly advisable to filter all fuel with a Baja Filter or equivalent. Charlie's Charts siphons are highly recommended for transferring fuel from jerry cans or barrels to the ship's tanks.

Propane is widely used throughout Mexico. In port cities with marinas, most marinas provide propane refill services on a weekly basis; cruisers take empty propane tanks to marina offices in the morning, which are returned filled later on the same day. Propane is also available in more remote areas and small towns at bulk propane stations. However, these propane stations are generally outside of town, necessitating a taxi ride at considerable expense, to have tanks filled. As a general practice, cruisers will be well advised to have tanks topped off whenever in marinas that offer propane services. Write the vessel name on each tank.

FIREARMS

Leave guns and ammunition at home. The only guns allowed on board are those for hunting, accompanied by valid Mexican Hunting Licenses that must be obtained before you enter Mexico. The authorities are exceedingly sensitive to the gun issue in Mexico and the discovery of an unauthorized gun aboard can lead to forfeiture of the yacht and imprisonment of the skipper.

MEDICAL PREPAREDNESS FOR THE COASTAL CRUISER & OFFSHORE VOYAGER from Captain Denny Emory

Being prepared for a medical illness or injury is an important part of getting ready for any boating activity. Whether day sailing in the bay, making an open water passage or finding oneself in a remote anchorage, being able to cope with a medical emergency may be the most significant factor in contributing to a favorable outcome.

Prior to departure one should evaluate the potential exposure due to distance from or accessibility to professional medical assistance and the level of care that might be available. A vessel should then be properly outfitted appropriately for that exposure and the extent of the intended cruise or passage.

Outfitting should include the appropriate:

First Aid Manual
First Aid Kit
Emergency Medical Equipment (AED, neck brace/Extrication collar, back brace/emergency stretcher, etc)
Prescription Medications (carried in anticipation of need)
Normal Vessel's Medicine Cabinet Consumables
Over-the counter pharmacy supplies

To review the spectrum of product options available, check out the OceanMedix website at www.oceanmedix.com. For further information or advice, contact OceanMedix at information@oceanmedix.com or toll-free at 866-788-2642 (307-732-2642 from outside the U.S.A.). Tell them Charlie's Charts sent you!

In addition to the outfitting of the vessel, one must consider possible training beyond Basic First Aid and CPR classes. Advanced training courses include First Responder, EMT and certified Marine First Aid.

Have a plan in force to allow for communication with medical personnel if need through the U.S. Coast Guard, a 24/7 tele-medical provider or private practitioner via cell phone, VHF, SSB or sat phone.Thinking through an extraction or evacuation plan to transport an injured or critically ill crew member to a facility capable of providing the necessary level of care may prove to be a valuable exercise.

Preparation, training and experience lead to confidence. In a medical emergency situation this may be the most significant aspect in facilitating a favorable outcome.

LANGUAGE

We strongly encourage that cruisers learn some degree of Spanish before sailing for Mexico. English is routinely spoken in all major and medium sized cities; many menus are written in both Spanish and English. However, many Port Captains speak only rudimentary English and Despachos are entirely in Spanish. In small villages little or no English is spoken. If you need help when away from major population centers – location of obscure services, or medical help - some command of Spanish will be of immense benefit. And, if for no other reason, your cruising experience will be far more comfortable and enjoyable if you are able to communicate at some level in Spanish. A Spanish phrase book and English/Spanish dictionary, including one of several such publications that are written exclusively for Cruisers, are mandatory equipment aboard every southbound vessel. Spanish schools are available in most of the larger towns and cities; many cruisers have taken advantage of total immersion Spanish classes in order to expedite or enhance acquiring a reasonable level of fluency. Be sure to include 'Spanish For Cruisers' in your ship's library.

ADVICE FOR FIRST-TIME CRUISERS

The glowing stories you've heard from old-time cruisers about how inexpensive it is to cruise Mexico is a thing of the past. Times have changed and so have the costs of cruising in a country whose currency is closely tied to the US dollar. Many marina slip fees are either equal to or in some cases more than those charged in US facilities. Diesel and gasoline prices are similar to US costs for each. Cost may minimized by anchoring as often as possible.

AWNINGS, DODGERS, BIMINIS, SUN & INSECT SCREENS, DINGHY AND JERRY CAN CHAPS (CANVAS ET AL)

As mentioned in the preceding discussion of dinghies, the intensity of the Sun and UV in Mexico is much greater than that experienced in US and Canadian Pacific waters. In the spring, summer and early fall months, the intensity of the sun is such that unshaded decks are too hot to walk barefoot. It has been our experience, and that our many fellow cruisers, that awnings and open-weave sunscreens, which are easily erected and equally easily taken down are a necessity. Ideally, dodgers, biminis, awnings and sun screens should be designed and carried that will cover all areas of the deck that will be exposed to direct sunlight. These must be designed such that they can be quickly taken down in the event of a Coromuel, Elephante or Chubasco (see Weather discussion), and awnings and sun screens should taken down each afternoon after the sun diminishes. Jerry cans (for extra diesel, gasoline, water, etc.) also need to be shielded from the sun and UV exposure; like unprotected dinghies, these containers will fail after several years, and the fuel they contain is also likely to be adversely affected if not protected from direct sunlight and UV. Similarly, outboard motor fuel lines and fuel squeeze bulbs should be shielded from direct sun exposure for the same reasons.

BUGS

"No SeeUms" (very small irritating flies), flies and occasionally bees (seeking fresh water) are bothersome in some but not all anchorages. Screens for use on portlights, hatches and companion way hatches are well advised. Open weave sun screens will generally keep out all but No SeeUms which penetrate everything but the finest weave screens. We have learned that painting Mineral Oil around the perimeters of screens on portlights and hatches is an effective deterrent to insects, so you should consider taking several bottles of Mineral Oil in your provisions. When going ashore, Skin So Soft original bath oil makes great bug repellent. Bees are drawn to sources of fresh water such as water standing in galley/head sinks, and wet towels and swim suits; if bees are prevalent in an anchorage, take care not to hang wet suits and towels on lifelines, or they may become covered with swarming bees.

Cockroaches (cucarachas) come aboard with the groceries, paper bags and boxes. The best way to avoid them is by constant vigilance. Don't bring aboard cardboard boxes or cases of beer or soft drinks. Empty the cases in the dinghy, spray with bug killer, then stow them away after checking for creepy crawlers. Examine fruits and vegetables; stalks of bananas can be briefly dipped in seawater to eliminate cockroaches. Harris Cockroach Tablets™ which contain boric acid will help to eliminate any that may have escaped your scrutiny.

In summary, Mexico-bound cruisers are advised to think about all of the aforementioned sun shields and insect protection coverings and ideally have them made in the US, or, if unable to do so, purchase and bring Sunbrella or alternative fabrics, zippers, snaps and other associated fittings with them for fabrication in Mexico.

SENDING AND RECEIVING "SNAIL" MAIL

Many cruisers have mail saved and sorted by a friend or relative. Typically, stamped mail sent to a location in Mexico will take at least 3-4 weeks to be delivered from the U.S. or Canada to Mexico, and longer during holiday seasons. To receive mail at a village post office have it labeled "Listo de Correos," followed by your name and the town name and postal code. Many cruisers have mail sent to a Marina with which they have established a relationship. Some marinas and Cruisers' Associations, have a drop-off box for delivery of mail to US or Canadian addresses, which are hand carried by cruisers returning to the US and Canada via land or air. If you plan to take advantage of this practice, bring US or Canadian postage stamps for this purpose.

An alternative solution is engagement of a professional mail scanning and forwarding service. A number of these companies have been in business for years in support of sailors and RV travelers who live away from a land address. Typically, service subscribers pay a modest monthly fee which provides a physical address, mail scanning services, email transmission of scanned mail, and when elected, selective forwarding of physical mail via FedEx, DHL or equivalent to a specified physical address in Mexico. These service providers also offer additional services (for example, automatic submittal of annual US Coast Guard Vessel Documentation renewals, etc.) that can be of real benefit to long term cruisers. (Hint, hint)

GIFTS FROM HOME

Receiving gifts may involve permits from Customs and duty may have to be paid depending on the item. A box of homemade fudge mailed to us for Christmas in Acapulco cost more in duty than five pounds of See's finest. Tell relatives to send money (in money orders, or better yet, keep it for when you return as funny things happen in the Mexican post offices to anything other than ordinary letters).

CHARTERING OUT YOUR VESSEL

Do not plan on earning money by offering charter services aboard your own vessel in Mexican waters. Vessels operating without proper licenses have been seized and/or stiff fines have been levied against offending boat owners. You may get away with it for a while but when the dirt hits the fan... you may not have a boat to stand on! If you are an émigré to Mexico (FM2) you can own and operate a business, but even then it is a very lengthy process to obtain official permission for foreign owned vessels to offer chartering services in Mexico.

LAUNDRY SERVICES

Laundry services (lavandaria), meaning washing and drying but not dry cleaning of clothing, bedding, etc., is available in nearly every village in Mexico, usually for a nominal fee per kilo. Some marinas offer laundromats that require US quarters or tokens needed to operate the machines. In the mid-to-northern Sea of Cortez, where villages are sparse, will you need to do your own laundry on board by hand (two buckets work well-one for washing and the second for rinsing), or by machine if installed on the vessel. Laundry soap will be whatever is available, so if you have issues with soap, provide your own.

CLOTHING

A wise traveler once said, "Take twice as much money as you think you'll need and half as many clothes." Brilliant and true! Sweaters and warm jackets may be needed for the trip from San Diego to Cabo San Lucas which can be chilly, especially during windy or foggy weather. Thereafter, summery clothes (including a light jacket for cool evenings) fill the bill.

Baja in the summer is hot, and cool in the winter; Mazatlan south can be hot at any time of the year. Cotton is more comfortable than polyester but ironing can be a problem, a blend, or no-iron cotton is recommended. Loose fitting, shift-type dresses are comfortable and accepted. Shorts are not completely acceptable except around the beach or in resort areas. Mexicans tend to be conservative in dress and local traditions should always be respected when traveling. The Guayabera, a pleated man's shirt is acceptable for dressy occasions.

Foul weather gear is a problem in the tropics. Light weight gear is not rugged enough to stand up to the rigors of a cruising sailboat and heavy duty gear is too hot. We often wear just the jacket and shorts. Whatever you decide on, take an inexpensive light poncho-type rain cover that will fit in your shopping bag for trips ashore on rainy days, or for use in the dinghy when the spray is flying.

Leather shoes pick up mold easily making canvas or nylon deck shoes and reef-walkers preferable. Good sailing sandals are lifesavers (and toe savers!) A medium jacket and a couple of sweaters are sufficient for winters in the Gulf when storm systems from California and Arizona reduce the temperature.

A wide-brimmed hat which can tied down is essential for keeping you cool and keeping some of the sun's damaging rays directly off your face. Caps just don't do the job. Tilley™ type hats are good and some other designs give even more protection as they have a wider brim.

COOKING

When in Mexico you should learn to use the local foods, such as tortillas. A good Mexican cookbook will also help you with ingredients that may be strange to you. In larger cities, get a group of cruisers together for a cooking class ashore. A bit of asking around will lead to some great experiences and great meals.

EATING ASHORE

You can eat quite well on the street and stay healthy. Try the fresh steamed corn-on-the-cob or some grilled on a charcoal fire. It will be chewy but tasty. Tacos de carne asada (beef bits grilled over charcoal), steaming bowls of birria (goat stew) and whole fish smoked over an open fire are all worth trying. For dessert try churros, — no germs could exist in that boiling oil.

On a restaurant menu "antojitos" are what we think of as "Mexican food." It means tacos, enchiladas, tostadas, etc. Tacos come as either fried (dorados" or not fried as "suaves" (good for dieters). The food will be rather different from the Cal-Mex food we are used to. Enchiladas, for example come with many types of sauces, none of them quite like the typical enchilada sauce of California. Try Enchiladas Suizas for an especially delicate flavor.

Comida Corrida means the "Blue Plate Special" of the day. It is a 3 or 4 course meal which is served from noon to 3 p.m. That's the big meal of the day for Mexicans. Remember, no matter how long you sit at your table you won't get the bill until you ask for it. It is thought to be rude and a hint that you should leave. So learn to say "La cuenta (qwenta), por favor."

DRUGS AND SMUGGLING

Penalties for dealing in drugs and smuggling of contraband are severe. Mexican laws are based on Roman law in which the accused is assumed guilty, is jailed and then must attempt to prove one's innocence. Mexican jails are not a place to visit.

The Mexican Navy periodically patrols anchorages and open waters near major port cities. Their patrol boats are tan/camouflage painted pangas with "Marina" painted on the sides of the vessel, and often manned with four to six heavily armed Navy personnel. When they desire to board, they will typically pull alongside and request that you slow down and request permission for the senior officer to board your vessel. Typically the boarding officer will wish to examine the ship's documentation papers and identification of the Captain. He may or not perform a cursory look in the interior of the vessel. He will also conduct a survey of safety-related equipment carried aboard the vessel (VHF radio(s), SSB radio, radar, GPS, life vests, etc.). Upon completion of the survey, it is a common to invite the Captain of the cruising vessel to complete a survey regarding the experience, indicating whether it was appropriately conducted, satisfactory, etc. Several cruisers with whom we have spoken have had fishing lines out when boarded, but despite that it is within the authority of the Navy to do so, none have asked to see Mexican fishing licenses.

BOATYARD FACILITIES AND REPAIRS

As a general comment, the technical skills that are readily available in reputable American and Canadian shipyards are not as readily available in Mexico. That said, there are full service boatyards that cater to cruisers' needs in Cabo San Lucas, La Paz, Mazatlan, La Cruz de Huanacaxtle (Bandaras Bay), Puerto Vallarta and Puerto Escondido (See Appendix II). Facilities, workmanship and prices vary widely. Labor costs are much less for hauling a vessel but materials (mostly imported) will be more expensive than at home. Always make an agreement on how much everything will cost before committing the boat to the yard and expect to pay about as much in total as you would in the US. Always supervise work being dong by a yard.

There are competent sail makers in La Paz and La Cruz. There is a very competent rigging shop in La Cruz. As a general comment with a concerted effort, cruisers in need of sophisticated repairs can usually locate a shop or individual who can make or repair parts; for example we have found a shop in Turtle Bay that can fabricate custom high pressure oil or hydraulic hoses while you wait at very affordable prices. However, don't expect them to be able to rehab your fuel injectors! But that's another story...

Wages in Mexico are lower than the US and Canada, but not so much so that you are likely to save a bundle on boat repairs or maintenance. This may be the case for something as simple as cleaning and bottom painting but for any other kind of work you should be prepared to pay charges that are comparable to those charged in the US.

Diesel and gasoline engines can be serviced and repaired in major port cities (La Paz, Mazatlan, La Cruz (Puerto Vallarta) region, but replacement parts are not always readily available and workmanship is not always assured. A complete set of routine engine consumable parts - oil filters, primary and engine mounted secondary fuel filters, water pump impellers and associated gaskets, as well as spare spark plugs for gasoline engines, and spare fuel injectors for each type of diesel engine on the vessel is advisable. It is also advisable to carry a spare propeller for outboard engines. (Evil beach landings eat props)

INSURANCE

In the event of an accident in Mexico all parties involved may be held until financial responsibility for any damage has been established. Only insurance issued by a Mexican firm is recognized but few yachts carry Mexican public liability insurance. It is not expensive and any of the agents who handle clearance papers can advise you. American insurance policies vary regarding restrictions on travel and rates, but are required in most larger marinas. Check with friends for recommendations on reliable insurance carriers.

SOUTHERN CALIFORNIA – PACIFIC BAJA PASSAGE PREPARATION

The 750 n.m. passage from San Diego to Cabo San Lucas can be similar in terms of winds, seas and currents that typify the southerly transit from Pacific northwest waters (Canada, Washington, Oregon, and California waters north of Point Concepcion).

In the event that a first time Mexico's cruiser's prior passage experiences have been limited to fair weather trips in local, sedate waters, to every extent possible, make several overnight, extended offshore passages beforehand. When doing so, it will be beneficial, when weary to anchor in an unfamiliar, sloppy bay with the swell from one direction and wind from another.

Travel on Baja's west coast can be a test of seamanship as there are many miles separating anchorages that have limited refuge from the wind, seas and fog. Very good insight into what might be encountered in terms of transiting Baja's pacific waters in terms of seas, micro climates around capes and other associated localized wind patterns and currents, may be gained by reading The Baja Bash, authored by Captain Jim Elfers. He makes valuable suggestions for making the voyage more comfortable.

FOOD AND SHOPPING

Fresh, canned, frozen and pre-packaged meat, poultry, fish, vegetables, fruit and dairy products are available for purchase in just about every small town and village in Mexico, and certainly in larger towns and cities. Food is sold in tiendas in small villages, bodegas in larger villages, mercados and supermercados (akin to major supermarkets in the US and Canada) in towns and cities. Shopping in Mexico requires learning about different cuts of meat, types of cheeses and the multitude of different chili peppers, all of which are in Spanish. There are two kinds of bread in Mexico. Sliced, wrapped grocery store bread is called Pan Bimbo. It is widely available in whole grain (pan integral) and white. Many towns have a bakery where bread is baked daily. Some of it is sweet (pan dulce) and comes in a wide variety of shapes and sizes. Unsweetened bread is baked in a crusty French style, varying in size from small rolls (bolillos) to a long loaf (baguette). It is both inexpensive and of excellent quality. Since preservatives are not used it spoils quickly; it is advisable to purchase only what you will eat in the next day or so.

When you enter the bakery you will see a stack of trays and tongs on the counter. Take one of each and help yourself to the selection you want. The clerk will bag your selection and calculate the bill. You will then pay the cashier.

A limited variety of food and provisions can be obtained in the smaller villages. The larger towns and cities have a wide variety of stores ranging from tiny mini-super mercados to large supermarkets. Imported goods are usually quite expensive; local produce and groceries packaged in Mexico are comparable to US prices.

FRESH WATER

With sufficient capacity and prudent usage, the average cruiser has no difficulty supplying fresh water requirements. Mexican marinas typically proclaim their water to "potable," however, it is wise to use either a ceramic water filter on the hose attachment and/or add drops of Micodyn™ to the tanks. This product is sold in most Mexican markets in small bottles for the purpose of washing vegetables. Water is also sold at a nominal fee, along with a deposit for the container, in 20 liter (five-gallon) jugs in marinas and many village markets. Dedicating a few jerry cans for the transport of water is especially useful in the Sea of Cortez and as a back-up supply, or for deck water. Our siphon hoses are also a useful item when transferring water from the 5 gallon jugs.

It is worthwhile having separate water tanks to prevent contamination of the vessel's entire water supply in case the water-maker fails or water from a particular source has an unpleasant taste. A salt-water pump is a handy fresh-water saver for it provides convenient use of salt water for cleaning jobs not needing fresh water. It should be noted that watermakers will become less efficient in Mexico's saltier seawater and in particular in the Sea of Cortez.

Siphon Video

WEATHER RESOURCES

Each section of the Guide includes a brief description of the average weather conditions that are experienced in the geographical region of coverage. These are generalized comments, but special attention must be paid to remarks on hurricanes, chubascos (summer thunderstorms that generate locally high winds associated with a storm cell), Coromuels (akin to Southern California's Santa Ana winds), Elephantes (unpredicted downslope adiabatic winds such as occur on the eastern slope of the Rocky Mountains) with wind velocities of 50-60 knots that can last for four to six hours and other mini-climes that uniquely affect small regions (particularly around Capes (Cabo San Quintin, Cabo Falso for examples) of Mexico's waters.

Mariners navigating Mexico's waters must be prepared to rely on their own weather knowledge, forecasts available through local Ham and SSB radio nets, and when in range of shore-based internet , (see Communications) weather forecast websites. In general, local forecasts and long range evaluations, such as are continually provided along U.S. and Canadian coasts, are not available in Mexican waters. US forecasts may provide short range forecasts for the northern sections of the Baja peninsula, extending as far south as Cabo San Quintin on the west coast and to Bahia de Los Angeles on the east coast.

If able to receive internet, a number of websites provide forecast winds, seas, and barometric pressure data for the region. They are based on NOAA, Mexican forecasters and real time weather reporting stations at various locations along both sides of the Baja peninsula and Mexico's mainland west coast. Websites for good weather data include: Passageweather.com, Stormsurf.com, Sailflow.com,

Buoydata.com and others.

The hurricane season in Mexico is from June 15th through November 1st. Hurricane activity on the Mexican coast generally occurs south of La Paz on the Baja Peninsula and Mazatlan on the mainland. However, it is not unusual for hurricanes to cross the Baja Peninsula and continue their storm track into and across the Sea of Cortez as far north as Santa Rosalia. Even when a storm is downgraded from a hurricane, it can pack a powerful punch anywhere along the coast. For regions further south, WeatherFax transmissions can be obtained at many marine facilities or from other vessels equipped with proper receivers.

COROMUEL (Pronounced cor-um-well)

This is a local wind condition centering around La Paz but encountered north to San Evaristo and south to about Los Muertos. It blows almost every night from early spring to late summer or fall, arriving with a rush in late afternoon. A southerly wind in La Paz, it acts as an air conditioner changing hot summer days into cool, breezy evenings. It can be a friendly wind when it blows during fair weather conditions, though it can ruin some fine anchorages especially around the Espiritu Santo Islands as local topography can alter its direction. More detailed weather for the Sea of Cortez is discussed in Section II.

HURRICANES

Refer to the guide for general information and notes regarding radio warnings available during the hurricane season. Listen regularly and act sensibly by getting to safe ports early. Baja's Puerto Escondido is a favorite hurricane hole. La Paz/Pichilingue offers protection in the south as do San Francisquito and Puerto Don Juan in the north. Storms are more frequent on the mainland and distances are greater between ports of refuge, which for the most part are crowded commercial harbors, making anchoring during storm conditions difficult. San Carlos Bay, marinas in Mazatlan, Puerto Vallarta, Nuevo Vallarta and Manzanillo make safe head-quarters for summer cruising on Mexico's mainland.

NAVIGATION IN MEXICO'S WATERS

Mexico practices the same Navigation Rules as does the United States. Thus the same lighting, sailing and steering rules, navigation aids (lights, buoys, etc.) methods are practiced throughout. Lights and buoys that mark harbors, harbor entry, fairways, etc., are nominally the same as seen in US waters. However, comparatively speaking with the US and Canadian coastlines, the Baja Peninsula is rather isolated, sparsely populated and there are relatively few navigational aids. Good coastal navigation procedures are necessary in your passage along the coast.

One caution - fishing is a major industry in Mexico. Mariners must be attentive to the presence of long line seiners, offshore trot lines, mobile fish storage pens, lobster buoys, et al, which are prevalent throughout Mexico's waters, often not clearly demarcated (lighted buoys), which can pose navigation hazards (lines wrapped around prop shafts). The bulk of fishing and lobstering is done from ocean going Pangas (open fiberglass outboard-powered boats) used to set and tend lobster traps and trot lines throughout Mexico's waters, frequently at great distances from shore. Many Mexican fishermen carry VHF radios and cell phones, but few are English speakers.

GPS and electronic chart plotters are a boon to navigation, but it must be appreciated that throughout Mexican waters there are many inconsistencies between electronic charts and GPS positions which can be discrepant by as much as two nautical miles or more. Use of paper charts and plotting fixes is highly encouraged when navigating Mexico's waters. Gerry Charts are the only GPS accurate charts available of the Pacific side of the Baja peninsula and the Sea of Cortez. They are available through the Charlie's Charts website at www.charliescharts.com.

ENTERING, CRUISING COASTAL WATERS AND DEPARTING MEXICO

The captain - not the owner, unless he/she is also the skipper - is responsible for the vessel, its crew and all paperwork and clearances.

Requirements for each person cruising aboard a vessel in Mexico's waters

Each person aboard must have a valid passport to enter Mexico. Each person must apply for and be granted one of the following, to stay in the country regardless of how brief the duration (including if flying out of Cabo San Lucas, for example, on the same day of arrival):

1. FMM: a Tourist Permit (Visa) that is valid for 180 days after entering the country. This Visa can only be renewed by leaving Mexico and receiving a new 180 day FMM upon reentering the country. FMMs can be obtained in the U.S. through Mexican Consulate offices, or any Mexican Port of Entry (commercial airports, Immigration Offices in Ports of Entry, etc. station. It should be noted that it is not necessary for your vessel to leave the country each 180 days; only crew members who hold FMM visa must leave Mexico each 180 days. Once having left Mexico, you can return the next day to satisfy this requirement, but as said above, you must pass through an Immigration portal to be issued a new FMM.

2. FM3: a 1-year Non-Immigrant Resident Status which is issued by Immigration Offices (Migracion) located in major cities and Ports of Entry. The application process can be initiated on line (www. inm.gob.mx) but must be completed in person at an Immigration Office. Applicants must present passports, and provide two passport size photographs and copies of the most recent three months of bank statements that reflect a minimum of $2,000USD per month in the account. There is an initial processing fee, and an annual fee (in 2012, $1,292Mx (pesos)). FM3 status is renewable annually. Several benefits accrue to FM3 holders: while there is no requirement to leave the country during the validity period of the FM3, one can come and go an infinite number of times from and to the country,. With an FM3, Mexican companies such as TelCel (see communications) will allow you to enter into contracts for telephone, and internet services, which you cannot do with an FMM. As an aside, these contracts provides these services at considerably less expense than they cost on a month-to-month basis, and, monthly fees can be paid on line with a credit card, thus eliminating the necessity to go to a local TelCel office to renew data or telephone services. FM3 processing takes two to four weeks once initiated at a Migracion Office. It should be noted that Migracion does not process applications during the two week period from the close of business on Friday in the week preceding Christmas until the first business day after New Year's Day. Given that many cruisers make their initial passage to Mexico in early November, if application for an FM3 is desired, it is encouraged that the application process be initiated as soon as practical after entering Mexico. It should also be noted that you must complete the FM3 process at the same office where initiated; subsequent renewals may be done at any Immigration Office, with the same proviso – complete the process at the same office where it is initiated. Renewal can be initiated no earlier than thirty days in advance of its expiration date. It should also be noted that in popular regions of Mexico (Puerto Vallarta, Bucerias, etc.) that processing of applications can take three to four weeks or longer due to processing backlog.

3. FM2: Permanent Immigrant status. Obtaining this status requires five years of residency (as an FM3), and other requirements that are more stringent than required for an FM3. Discussion of FM2 requirements and associated benefits are beyond the scope of this Guide.

Vessel Temporary Import Permit (TIP)

Regardless of the planned length of stay in the country, all vessels entering Mexican waters are required to obtain a TIP. The TIP is valid for 10 years, and permits multiple exits/entries of the vessel in and out of the country, without any further action on the part of its holder. When making application for the TIP you will need all pertinent vessel and major component (engine, generator set, outboard motors, dinghy(ies), etc., information: US state registration or US Coast Guard or Canadian documentation number, engine(s) make, model and serial numbers, etc. The form will also note major electronic equipment that is installed (radios, radars, computers, laptops, etc., so be prepared and have the data with you when making application. The TIP must be renewed at least 15 days prior to its expiration date. When leaving Mexico for the last time then the TIP should be returned to the Banjercito office at a Port of Entry to have it cancelled. The TIP may be obtained in one of three ways:

1. The simplest method is to obtain the TIP on the internet at www.banjercito.com.mx. You will be required to send a photocopy of your passport and boat registration papers. The permit will arrive in less than 20 days with instructions to sign a letter promising not to sell the boat in Mexico (this promise must be strictly adhered to as the authorities may seize the vessel for any infraction). You will be instructed to make copies of the documents you used to obtain the TIP and mail them along with the letter back to the Mexican Aduana (Customs), or take them with you to the Immigration Office at your first Port of Entry. As a footnote, many Mexican marinas and all boatyards where you may have work performed will require a copy of your TIP (as well as your passports, vessel insurance policy, and vessel documentation papers).
2. The TIP is available at Migracion Offices where Immigration Visas are processed.
3. The TIP may also be applied for at a Banjercito office (nearby the Port Captain's Office at your first port of arrival).

Procedure to Follow When Entering Mexico

At the first Port of Entry (most likely Ensenada), the vessel Captain must visit (or hire an Agent to do so) the Capitan de Puerto (Port Captain), Migracion (Immigration Office) and Aduana (Customs) with the following documents in hand:

> Your TIP if you have already obtained one (or apply for one at the Banjercito office as part of these procedures)
>
> Six copies of the Crew List (Despacho) (It is our recent experience that each Port Captain office has its own unique version of the Despacho which they will provide you to fill out upon initial visit to their office)
>
> Passports/copies of the passports for each person on board
>
> Vessel Documentation. If not the Owner of the vessel, proof that you are legally authorized by the owner to act as captain of the vessel.

Immigration will issue each person an FMM. The Port Captain will stamp and provide a copy of the Crew (and Passengers) List showing the Port of Entry (keep this document as you will need it when entering subsequent ports in Mexico, or departing the country with your vessel). The names on the Despacho must agree with the persons on board. So, if and when crew (or passenger) changes occur, a new Despacho must be obtained at the offices of the Port Captain where the crew change occurred before making passage to a subsequent port. As a case in point, upon initial arrival in Cabo San Lucas after a passage from San Diego, crew members from vessels frequently disembark and fly back to the US or Canada. In such case, the Captain should take two versions of Despachos to the Port Captain's

Office: the first reflecting all crew and passengers who are aboard upon arrival in the Port of Entry, and the second reflecting the crew and passengers who plan to remain aboard and continue on to a subsequent port in Mexico.

If entering Mexico from a country other than the U.S., you will have to surrender the Zarpe (documentation issued by the country from which you last departed) to the Port Captain. New vessel entry documents will be issued which, as mentioned above, must be carried aboard the vessel throughout your stay in Mexican waters.

If you are trailering your boat from the US to begin cruising from a port such as San Carlos, for example, you must stop in Nogales at Km21 (or other like portals), to either show or obtain a TIP as described above.

Items Not Allowed for Importation

Mexico does not allow importation of beef products, including those that are pre-packaged. Many vessels that arrive in Cabo San Lucas and in particular in the marina at Cabo will be inspected by personnel from Mexico's Department of Agriculture. All fresh or frozen (with the possible exception of that evening's meal) will be confiscated. Many cruisers stock up with frozen beef products from big box stores in San Diego before heading south. It is wise to provision only as many of these products as you are apt to consume while transiting from the border to Cabo San Lucas if your first port of entry. As a matter of interest, the same big box stores in Cabo San Lucas within an inexpensive cab (or less expensive autobus) ride from the harbor as in San Diego, so you can readily add to frozen beef provisions as desired when in Cabo San Lucas or San Jose del Cabo. There is also a number of Supermercados (Mega, Soriana, etc.) that sell excellent fresh and frozen beef, pork and poultry products in their Carnicerias (meat markets).

Importation of Vessel Materials and Equipment

In association with acquiring the above-described TIP, it is recommended that you complete an AN-EXO 1 at the time of first vessel entry into Mexico. An ANEXO 1 is a list of all accessories (dinghy(ies), outboard motors, watermakers, computers, chartplotters, etc., and equipment (diesel engine(s), generator sets, etc.) that are aboard and/or installed aboard the vessel. When completing the TIP process, or upon initial interaction with an Aduana (Customs) office, have the ANEXO 1 stamped by the Customs office. Later, when importation of any replacement of broken, damaged or failed parts may be required, you will not have to pay Customs duties for the items that are on the ANEXO document. If in the course of your stay in Mexico you install new equipment of significance on the vessel, acquire an updated ANEXO (2) that lists the new items that are being imported.

In order to complete ANEXO 1 you must list the brand and serial numbers of each piece of significant equipment. The form is in Spanish so bring a dictionary although many items are easy to translate such as Purificador de Agua (water maker).

When importing replacement parts and if using local repair businesses or personnel, it will be helpful to present a letter from that local person or repair business vouching for the use of the items. Like many other countries, Mexico is interested in sustaining its industries and economy.

If you find that you need a part from the US or Canada, there is a number of Agents in each country who provide importation (including determination and payment of import duty fees) and intra-Mexico shipping services for delivery to you in your location. It is beyond the scope of this Guide to list such Agents; local VHF nets and many Marina offices can recommend providers of said services.

Procedures When Cruising Within Mexican Waters

When arriving at or departing from a marina or anchorage in locations where there are Port Captain offices you are required to reach the Port Captain by radio or appear in person to inform them of you arrival and complete processing of your Despacho. Departure procedures vary from Port Office to Port Office; some, like La Paz require only that you call on VHF to report your departure-others, like La Cruz, require that you appear in person to have your departure Despacho notated. And in some locations, and Mazatlan in particular, marina offices will take care of your Despacho processing with the Port Captain (Mazatlan is a major international shipping terminal and major fishing port; the Port Captain's office is not concerned with the arrival and departure of cruising sail and power boats). Some cruising hubs, such as Bandaras Bay, have multiple ports/Port Captain offices which require checking in/out, even if moving as few as seven miles; for example, if staying at Marina La Cruz, or anchoring in the free La Cruz anchorage, the La Cruz Port Captain will expect you to comply with arrival/departure registration. If moving from Puerto La Cruz to Puerto Nuevo Vallarta (Paradise Village Marina, or Marina Nuevo Vallarta), you will need to check out with the La Cruz Port Captain and check in with the Nuevo Vallarta Port Captain. This is a relative painless process and there are no fees involved.

In all significant port cities, there is also an API office which has the authority to collect fees for vessels that are anchored out in their port waters. For example, API vessels and officers routinely visit vessels anchored off Cabo San Lucas and charge daily fees for anchoring (reportedly $25USD per day), or the Mogote anchorage in La Paz (newly reinstituted in 2012 and rumored to be on the order of 100 pesos per day).

Procedure to Follow When Leaving Mexico

When leaving Mexico you must obtain a final clearance to leave from all three: Capitan de Puerto, Migracion and Aduana. In addition you must obtain a Zarpe International from the Port Captain at the Mexican Port of Entry from which you are departing. When arriving at the first Port of Entry in the next country being visited report to the quarantine area, hoist a yellow flag and call Customs and Immigration for clearance.

Try to arrange your arrival and visits to officials at any Port of Entry to occur within normal working hours, during weekdays. Otherwise you will have to pay overtime charges of $25 in the U.S. and varies in other countries. Mexican business hours are 8 a.m. to 3 p.m., Monday to Friday.

OFFICIALS

Politeness and friendliness (and an attempt to speak Spanish) go a long way in dealing with Mexican officials. Getting angry will only make any problem worse. Sometimes being cheerful, eager to please and maybe a little dumb seems to help, "Gee Senor Capitania del Puerto, I want to do the right thing. I just didn't realize that I was supposed to have my papers stamped when I arrived in port three weeks ago." If you honestly feel you are being treated unjustly, try to work it out calmly. If there is a language problem, get someone to translate for you. The Department of Tourism is located in most of the major cities and may be able to help solve your problem. However, you must remember that there are rules to be followed and many officials, as at home, can only "go by the book."

MORDIDA

Although it translates as "the bite" literally, it is slang for a bribe. Many who have been doing business in Mexico for years will say that it is an accepted practice, however mordida is becoming less common as time goes by. If you are in a situation where a stale mate has occurred, perhaps the suggestion of a small fee can make things happen to your advantage, or move quicker. If you think of it as a gratuity (propina) or tip for services performed and not as a bribe, it is perhaps more acceptable. Some times a plate of cookies or a cold beer will do the trick.

MONEY, CURRENCY AND BANKING

These days essentially all cash transactions in Mexico are conducted using Mexican currency ($Mx, pesos, etc.). US dollars are only exchanged in larger cities that typically cater to short term vacationers (e.g., Cabo San Lucas, Puerto Vallarta, etc). In major to moderately sized cities and towns (examples, Cabo San Lucas, La Paz, Loreto, Santa Rosalia, Mazatlan, Puerto Vallarta, Bucerias, etc.), ATMs (Cajero Automatico) are prolific; they dispense cash in pesos. Like in Canada and the US, ATM transactions fees vary as a function of the ATM service provider. However, in smaller towns such as Baja's Turtle Bay, San Carlos (Bahia de Magdalena region), etc., there are no banks and no ATMs, although some have Western Union offices to which funds may be "wired" from home, but it's not a quick procedure. There are very few banks and ATMs north of La Paz in the Sea of Cortez, and NONE north of Santa Rosalia, so maintaining a balance of pesos on hand is well advised. As a footnote, a number of Mexican banks have partner relationships with US and Canadian banks and if using their ATM machines, there are no transactions fees if you have an account with that particular bank; some research before departing for Mexico will help preserve the cruising budget.

Before leaving US waters, cruisers are counseled to exchange US or Canadian currency for Pesos including, to the extent practical $20Mx, $50Mx, and $100Mx ($Mx = Pesos) denominations. Many Mexican vendors in small towns do not routinely handle large denomination notes ($200Mx, $500Mx, etc.); thus they have difficulty making change. Be aware that there are few banks with ATM service north La Paz in the Sea of Cortez.

Credit card (Tarjeta de Credito) use for essentially any transaction is commonplace in large cities, moderately sized towns, and occasionally small villages that have good phone services. Mastercard and Visa and most other major cards are accepted everywhere that credit card use is available. Credit cards used for settling marina slips fees and fuel service purchases will usually carry a fee on top of the cost of the services. Be sure to notify your credit card company before you leave the US, that you will be in Mexico for a period of time so that they don't shut down your card. You will avoid some very expensive and frustrating phone calls by doing this ahead of time.

HEALTH CARE

Many North Americans visit Mexico for health care, dental work, surgeries, and cosmetic surgeries as expenses are less, attention from health care workers is often better than 'up north', and the Medical Professionals are well trained. Medicines are available often without a prescription and are much less expensive than in the States. English is spoken in the bigger cities and there is always someone willing to help with translations in an emergency.

There are various types of Mexican medical insurance available to non residents, as well as residents, which lowers the expenses even further. If you will be staying in Mexico for several months or more, it might be worth the low cost of insurance to get that 'trick knee' fixed, that crown replaced, or even a little 'nip and tuck job'!

HEALTH

Immunizations are not required for entry into Mexico at the present time but it is advisable to be immunized against Hepatitis A and B. As to preparation, have your doctor recommend or assemble a good first aid kit; even your pharmacist can help. Most commercial kits don't get past the band-aid/

sunburn ointment/aspirin stage. Carry spare copies of any prescriptions you need and be sure that your Diptheria and Tetanus immunization covers the period you will be traveling. Medicines in Mexico are similar to those that are familiar and are generally less expensive.

Prescriptions are required for only a few medicines. Prices on common medications are government controlled and are comparatively cheap. If you are concerned about the product being identical to what you use at home, travel with sufficient quantities of your prescriptions to last for the duration of your stay or make arrangements for someone visiting to replenish your supplies.

Though it is not approved in the US, a seasickness remedy available in pharmacies is Stugeron™. A dose of 25 mg. every 6 hours is sufficient. It is best taken prior to the onset of seasickness but is surprisingly effective even after the onset of "mal de mer." Since the contents of this remedy are unknown you should not try it if you have any health problems or are taking prescription drugs.

There are people who can eat "practically anything" and never get sick. After one bout of dysentery in high school, we seem to be one of them, (Knock on wood) but a bit of common sense seems in order. We eat broiled meat tacos and fried fish from street vendors, and fresh refrigerated clams or cevice (smell it first!). To gain a bit more safety avoid eating bruised or overripe fruit and vegetables. Soaking vegetables in Chlorox™ treated water bath is another safety precaution; peeling, is recommended rather than scrubbing potatoes, carrots, fruit on the streets etc.

COMMUNICATIONS AND INTERNET ACCESS

Radio

VHF radio is the norm for localized ship-to-ship communication, checking in and out with Port Captains (Capitania de Puerto) and marina Harbormasters to obtain information about availability of marina space and services. Port Captains, Harbormasters and the Mexican Navy all monitor Channel 16. Most mariners monitor Channel 22 for ship to ship communications when in Mexican waters. There are daily VHF radio nets that meet each morning in major cities, marinas, and anchorages (La Paz, Puerto Escondido, Mazatlan, Bandaras Bay (Puerto Vallarta), etc.) that provide local knowledge, regional weather and tidal information, and local assistance with sources for marine goods and services.

Single Sideband High Frequency (SSB HF) and/or Ham radios are highly recommended for long distance communication with fellow cruisers. Users of Ham (amateur radio) frequencies must possess a Ham license in order to talk on these frequencies, except in emergencies when use of these frequencies is authorized. US and Canadian licensed Ham operators are required to register and receive a reciprocal Ham license from the Mexican government (issued by the Secretariat for Communications and Transportation which has offices in major cities such as La Paz, Mazatlan, Puerto Vallarta, etc.); no reciprocal license is required for SSB HF communications. A number of SSB HF and Ham radio nets, managed and controlled by fellow cruising sailors, operate on a daily basis. These nets provide a daily forum for checking in with fellow mariners, getting weather forecasts, and seeking assistance when needed.

Internet

3G internet is widely available throughout the more populated regions of Mexico, including at a number of locations along Baja's pacific coast. The service is operated and offered by TelCel which is Mexico's principal communications provider. Many cruisers have found it highly beneficial to make a one-time purchase of a wireless USB "Banda Ancha Movil" data device, used with a laptop or onboard computer to access the internet. TelCel offices in major cities sell the devices and associated data services. Data services are purchased on a monthly basis (unless you are in an FM2 or FM3 immigration status which enables entering into longer term, less expensive service contracts), at a cost that varies in consonance with the magnitude of data purchased for the monthly period (for example, in one, two or three or more gigabytes of data). Each new month of data services requires a visit to the local TelCel office to pay the fee for the level of data service desired. Unused data services expire at the end of each 30 day period.

If considering purchase of the Banda Ancha Movil data services, it is highly advisable to make a quick trip to Tijuana's main TelCel office before departing from San Diego to acquire the wireless data device and associated data services. Walk across the border at San Ysidro and ask a taxi to take you to the TelCel store next to Starbucks. Between Ensenada and Cabo San Lucas, there are no TelCel offices that offer purchase of this capability. In Ensenada, visit the TelCel store on the avenue just inland from the waterfront. When purchasing the device and services, you will need to present your passport, so be certain to have it with you when initially seeking the services.

Many marinas offer Wireless internet access as part of their slip fee services. It is highly advisable to equip your vessel with a high gain WiFi antenna as signal strength varies widely at the different marinas.

ANCHORING AND GROUND TACKLE

Between Ensenada and Cabo San Lucas there are no marinas. Appropriately sized anchors and durable ground tackle are essential for you will be using them regularly when transiting the Baja pacific coast, and throughout the Sea of Cortez. With exception of the very northern reaches of the Sea of Cortez, tidal effects are relatively minimal. However, many anchorages are exposed and subject to significant winds and seas on both Pacific Ocean and Sea of Cortez exposures (see "Coromuels, Chubascos and Elephantes" comments in the Weather section)..

It is recommended that vessels carry at least several appropriately sized anchors; a number of anchorages warrant deployment of fore and aft anchors. We never leave port without four separate anchors and rodes, (oversized) assembled and ready to deploy. There are chandleries in major port cities and towns (Cabo San Lucas, La Paz, Mazatlan, Puerto Vallarta, etc.) that stock and sell an array of various anchor configurations and sizes in the event that replacement of a lost anchor is needed, but the prices won't be cheap.

Most anchorages are sand bottoms and provide good holding with Bruce, Delta, Ultra, Danforth and other well established anchor designs. Some anchorages between Ensenada and Turtle Bay have extensive kelp beds, so equip accordingly. A number of anchorages have rock or cobble bottoms (Los Frailes, Isla Isabel, e.g.) so integration of length of chain rode is highly recommended. There are no coral reef anchorages on Mexico's pacific coast that will imperil three-strand rodes.

Many of the anchorages described in this guide are in depths of 3 to 6 fathoms (18 to 36 feet) and a few are in deeper water (to 10 fathoms). Anchoring techniques is beyond the scope of this guide, but appreciating the magnitude of seas and winds that are not uncommon, it is strongly encouraged that a 7:1 scope of chain/three-strand nylon rode be available for each anchor.

FENDERS

With exception of marinas there are few opportunities to tie alongside piers and quays. Where there are opportunities for such, the docks are designed for very large fishing vessels and commercial ships and are either concrete docks or rough steel piers, or you may end up tied alongside rusty steel "shrimper" vessels. If your vessel has room to do so, it is advisable to carry Fender Boards a 2" x 6" x 5' piece of wood, with holes drilled vertically in each end to accommodate ropes, tied to hang outside two fenders, which can be very effective. Also, in many of Mexico's marinas, there is a significant degree of current/tidal surge, so fenders, strong and extra-long dock lines and anti-chafe materials are well advised as part of your packup.

DINGHIES AND GOING ASHORE

As previous discussion indicates, there are very few marinas in Mexico, but a plethora of very delightful anchorages. You will need a good durable dinghy of sufficient size to accommodate crew, outboard motor and fuel tank and space for carrying re-provisioning supplies including food and beverages, and propane tanks that require refilling. The election of an Inflatable, RIB or Hard-dinghy is akin to choice of anchors-every sailor has his/her favorite. A factor to be considered in dinghy and outboard motor selection is beaching and departing through breaking surf and incoming waves. Outboard motors should be of sufficient size to accelerate and power through surf, but not so large as to become unwieldy when maneuvering your dinghy. Another consideration in both dinghy and outboard motor selection is transit distances from your vessel to shore, which in some anchorages can be significant and which may present winds and wind chop that must be powered through. If carrying a soft bottom or RIB inflatable, be certain to carry a repair kit with an abundance of patches and glue; there are dinghy repair shops in bigger ports and towns, but they are few and far between. It is highly advisable that you invest in dinghy wheels, and ideally those with larger diameter pneumatic tires, which work well in soft sand that is prevalent in many beach landing locations. It is also recommended that you carry a dinghy anchor as there is considerable tidal ebb and flow in some regions; we have found the use of the dinghy anchor to be beneficial in some locations to secure the dinghy while ashore. In some anchorages, dinghies and outboard motors are very attractive targets for thievery; you should invest in outboard motor locks and very durable security cables, and plan on bringing your dinghy aboard (davits, suspended out of the water abeam with a halyard, or fully aboard) your vessel at night to minimize the possibility of theft. NOTE: this is an issue in only a few anchorages, but replacement of a dinghy or outboard motor in Mexico is challenging and expensive, so taking these precautions each night is well warranted.

The sun is very intense in Mexico and will degrade PVC dinghies in a few years if dinghy surfaces are not shielded from direct sunlight. Accordingly we encourage that you consider having dinghy "chaps" made by your favorite canvas/sunbrella shop. There are very capable custom canvas/sunbrella fabricators in La Paz, Mazatlan and the Puerto Vallarta region who can make dinghy chaps, dodgers, biminis and sun awnings, jerry can covers, etc., (see "Sun and Shade"); they are usually in high demand and as expensive, and perhaps more expensive than having these made in the US or Canada before leaving for Mexico.

Landing a dinghy through the surf can be hazardous; few cruising sailors have found it necessary to do so in US and Canadian waters so it is a technique that will probably be learned in situ. When the surf is high (2 to 3 feet and greater) it may be wiser to postpone going ashore or hire a local to take you to and from shore. In many anchorages, Pangueros (Mexican fisherman in open fiberglass outboard powered pangas (fishing boats) routinely navigate beach departures and landings; look for where the pangas are lined up on shore for they will be near the best landing spots and watch the pangueros come and go before from the beach before making your approach and beach landing. The technique of beaching a dinghy through surf requires waiting for a slack period in the incoming swells and then quickly accelerating in past the breaking surf zone. This also requires quickly pulling up the outboard motor before/while beaching the dinghy, and expediently getting all crew out before the next incoming wave crests and poops the dinghy. Did we mention quickly? Even then it occasionally occurs that dinghies get overturned during a beach landing; all loose items should be securely tied to the dinghy and food, cameras, and etc. should be in waterproof bags (purchased from kayak equipment stores). Be sure to attach the kill switch lanyard to the driver so that a running, unmanned dinghy does not add to your incident. SUNGLASSES are often lost during a dinghy overturning and thus should be secured to wearers with some sort of tether. Available on the Charlie's Charts web store!

FISHING

Fishing Permits are required for each member of the crew. The cost is $25.80 for one week, $37.00 for one month and $48.20 for one year. Even if you do not intend to fish, in the eyes of Mexican Fish and Game Wardens the mere possession of fishing gear aboard can be sufficient reason to require a permit. You can acquire the necessary permits from Mexico's SEMARNAP office at 2550 - 5th Avenue, #101 Fifth Avenue Financial Center, San Diego, CA 92103, Tel: (619) 233-4324 or Fax: (619) 233-0344. Fishing permits are also available in most major port cities. In Ensenada, permits can also be obtained at the SEMARNAP office on Calle Las Medusas, or in the immigration office when you check into the country. You can also hire agents in California and Mexico to obtain licenses (and help with Entry of Crew and Vessel into Mexico (see FMMs, FM3s, FM2s, Temporary Import Permits, etc.); services provided by these Agents can be expensive, particularly when considering that you can do this yourself and particularly so if you speak and read a modest degree of Spanish-something that in our experience will further your enjoyment of cruising Mexico's waters and coastlines.

Be aware that Mexican law prohibits the harvest of shellfish of all types by foreign nationals. The Navy and Fisheries Department officials may periodically board your vessel (a non-threatening and pleasant process in our experience on every such occasion) ascertain to see that this law is obeyed.

Fishing with a trolling line (Charlie's Charts web site store) while making passages is an easy way for mariners to acquire fresh fish for dinner; species that are commonly caught include Dorado (Mahi Mahi), Wahoo, and Yellowfin Tuna, depending on location and time of the year. Trading (cambio) with local fishermen is another way to obtain fresh seafood. Popular trading items include water, children's clothing, radios, toys, playing cards, canned goods and liquor.

INTRA-MEXICO GROUND, FERRY AND AIR TRANSPORTATION

This brief discussion addresses how cruisers may get around the interior of Mexico by means other than their vessels. In major cities and towns (Cabo San Lucas, La Paz, Mazatlan, Puerto Vallarta, Loreto, etc.,) many major car rental companies (Hertz, Avis, National, Fox, Europa, others) offer vehicles for rent. As a general rule, rental costs are considerably higher per day than in the U.S. and Canada. If you plan to rent a vehicle, it is advisable to reserve one a few days ahead of your planned travel, as during high tourism periods (major holidays in Mexico, the U.S. and Canada), the availability of vehicles can become sparse. You will also get the most efficient pricing if you go to a rental car office at an airport, as opposed to other locations-often the local rental car office will have to go to the airport to get the vehicle that you will rent. As a footnote, if you decide to rent a vehicle and drive it from Mexico to the U.S. and back, in 2012 only Europa Car Rentals has vehicles available for this type of travel. A number of cruisers find it advantageous to rent and drive a vehicle from Mexico to the U.S. and back in order to get needed vessel equipment and supplies; there are other means available for doing so, but they can be comparatively more expensive than self-transporting via a rental vehicle.

Taxis operate in all cities, medium and often even small towns and as a general rule are fairly priced for expedient, specific point to point travel to government offices or stores, the specific location of which may not be known. Before embarking in a taxi, be certain to ask and get a quote for the price of the ride. Few taxi drivers have a meter in their vehicle, so negotiating price, assuming you have a sense of how far it is to your destination, is normal and practical. If you have a taxi driver wait for you at your destination, which is not uncommon, be certain to also ask about wait time charges; some drivers would rather have the guaranteed round trip fare and will not add extensive wait charges; others are not so compelled. So, ask before assuming.

Intra-city autobuses run from early morning to late at night and provide inexpensive and reliably service. "Intra-city" extends to regions that are more broad than literal city or town boundaries. For example, in the Bandaras Bay region (Punta de Mita, La Cruz de Huanacaxtle, Bucerias, Nuevo Vallarta, Valle de Bandaras, Compostela, Mescales, and the city of Puerto Vallarta et al) are served by autobuses/vans that transport passengers via different routes that cover the entire region. The same holds for Mazatlan, La Paz, Los Cabo (Cabo San Lucas to San Jose del Cabo) and other cities and regions across Mexico. These autobuses run about every 8 minutes and are very inexpensive – in 2012, $8MX - $16MX (8 to 16 pesos) to be transported a considerable distance (example, Punta de Mita to downtown Puerto Vallarta, a distance of about 30 Km costs 16 pesos, and requires changing buses once to make the trek). The route (ruta) taken by a particular bus is normally painted on the windshield of the autobus/van, which is easy to determine because interim destinations are listed (example, Pta Mita/La Cruz/Bucerias/Mega (popular supermercado)/ Mescales/Walmart/Costco/ Puerto Vallarta). With a little bit of study about a city and its suburbs, as well as major shopping destinations such as Soriana (supermercado), Chadraui (supermercado), Walmart, Sams, Costco (only in Cabo San Lucas and Puerto Vallarta), one can easily navigate around a region for little expense and with only a modicum of difficulty, even if you speak almost no Spanish. Most autobus/van drivers speak a reasonable degree of English and are usually very quick to be helpful. IT IS PREFERABLE to have small change for autobuses and vans. Upon boarding autobuses, you will pay the fare to the driver; he will tell you if you ask what the fare is to your destination. 10 passenger vans are used to supplement the Autobuses, running the exact same routes. It is customary to board the van and upon disembarking hand the driver the required fare through the passenger window. These autobuses and vans do not waste much time at stops, so be ready to board, pay, disembark, pay expediently. Bus stops (Parades) are usually identified by an international Bus sign, but as you will experience, riders often flag down a bus anywhere along its route.

Inter-city (example, Cabo San Lucas to Tijuana with many interim stops such as Todos Santos, La Paz, Constitucion, Insurgentes, Loreto, Mulege, Santa Rosalia, San Ignacio, Ensenada, etc.) autobuses are operated many times daily. These are modern, clean, spacious, comfortable Volvo overroad buses; seating is assigned when you buy your ticket. They often show movies throughout the trip and on some lines the price of your ticket includes a sandwich and drink. Your baggage will be checked when placed in the cargo area on the bus and you will be given a claim check that you must present when reaching your destination. The price for long distance travel is also very reasonable.

There are many intercity flight connections across Mexico. But, some point to point connections that would be thought to be routine are not. For example, there is no established air travel directly between Cabo San Lucas and Puerto Vallarta; travelers often have to fly to Mexico City, change planes, and then proceed on to Puerto Vallarta.

Ferries operate daily between the Baja Peninsula and the mainland. Ferries operate specifically between La Paz and Mazatlan, and La Paz and Topolobampo. Ferries also operate between Santa Rosalia and San Carlos. When taking the ferry it is advisable to spend the additional money to reserve a private cabin as opposed to sitting in an airline-like chair in a large salon area with movies running non-stop. On overnight passages (La Paz to Mazatlan for example), dinner and breakfast meals are available for purchase (or if renting a cabin included in the price of the cabin). The 2012 price for foot passenger passage from Mazatlan to La Paz is approximately $1,000MX (1,000 pesos). Schedules, pricing, reservations, etc., can be made online at www.bajaferries.com, which works very well.

As always, some fluency in speaking and reading Spanish will be of immense benefit to traveling cruisers.

PETS

The law says that dogs and cats should have a current rabies vaccination certificate and a vet's Certificate of Good Health stamped by a Mexican Consulate. To my knowledge this is not enforced, but it is best to have the current rabies certificate in order to satisfy US officials when you return to the US or if you are traveling to other countries. Put your boat's name on a collar tag in case your pet strays. Well behaved dogs on leashes may be allowed in palapa style restaurants in Baja, less so on the mainland. Ask before entering.

There are several restrictions on returning to the US with pet birds. There are also import restrictions on certain furs and ivory, etc. considered as coming from endangered species, so get current regulations from the Dept of Agriculture before you depart. Turtles are protected, thus turtle shells, turtle oil etc. are not allowed out of Mexico or into Canada or the US.
See appendix X for an article on dog customs in Mexico

FLAGS

The Mexican courtesy flag should be flown from the foremost starboard spreader or from the starboard yardarm on powerboats. If the motor vessel is mastless then the courtesy flag is flown alone from the bow staff, thus replacing the club burgee. It should be in proportion to the size of the national flag you fly, not a tiny ragged scrap. Buy several if you plan to stay in Mexico for an extended period.

Canadian and US boats fly their country flag and not the yacht ensign when in foreign waters. The "Q" or quarantine flag is not used in Mexico; it is up to the skipper to go ashore for check in.

GARBAGE

Dispose of wet compost garbage over the side if you are in open seas. Carry sufficient plastic trash bags with ties so that you can carry all trash ashore for deposit in a proper receptacle. Beer and soft drink bottles are returnable for a refund. Bundle aluminum cans separately because some locals collect them to recycle. In extremely remote areas you may burn paper and bury the ashes and sink opened cans and bottles. Most cruisers are within a few days of land and save the trash to take ashore. Plastic is a problem in because it doesn't readily burn. A discouraging sight is the proliferation of trash along the beaches and roadsides; as guests in the country we need to remember to be part of the solution and not part of the problem.

TABLE 1

APPROXIMATE DISTANCES BETWEEN ANCHORAGES OF SECTION I
(San Diego to Cabo San Lucas)

	San Diego	Islas Todos Santos	Ensenada	Puerto Santo Tomas	Cabo Colonet	Isla San Martin	Cabo San Quintin	Punta Baja	Isla San Geronimo	Bahía San Carlos	Punta Escarpada	Bahía Blanca	Bahía Playa María	Bahía Santa Rosalia	Isla Cedros (N. Anch.)	Bahía San Bartolome	Bahía de la Asuncion	Punta Abreojos	Laguna San Ignacio	Bahía San Juanico	Bahía Santa María	Bahía Magdalena	Cabo San Lucas
San Diego	0	53	60	78	118	148	157	184	194	213					279	338	386	431			561	581	733
Islas Todos Santos	53	0	10	25	65	95	104	131	141	160					226	285	333	378			508	528	680
Ensenada	60	10	0	35	75	105	114	141	151	170					236	295	343	388			518	538	690
Puerto Santo Tomas	78	25	35	0	40	70	79	106	116	135					201	260	308	353			483	503	655
Cabo Colonet	118	65	75	40	0	30	39	66	76	95					171	220	268	313			443	463	615
Isla San Martin	148	95	105	70	30	0	9	36	46	65					141	190	238	283			413	433	585
Cabo San Quintin	157	104	114	79	39	9	0	27	37	56					132	181	229	274			404	424	576
Punta Baja	184	131	141	106	66	36	27	0	10	29					105	154	202	247			377	397	549
Isla San Geronimo	194	141	151	116	76	46	37	10	0	19					95	144	192	237			367	387	539
Bahía San Carlos	213	160	170	135	95	65	56	29	19	0					76	125	173	218			348	368	520
Punta Escarpada	220	167	177	142	102	72	63	36	26	7	0												
Bahía Blanca	266	213	223	188	148	118	109	82	72	53	46	0											
Bahía Playa María	282	229	239	204	164	134	125	98	88	69	62	16	0										
Bahía Santa Rosalia	307	254	264	229	189	159	150	123	113	94	87	41	25	0									
Isla Cedros (N. Anch.)	361	308	318	283	243	213	204	177	167	148	141	95	79	54	0	49	97	142			272	292	444
Bahía San Bartolome	410	357	367	332	292	262	253	226	216	197	190	144	128	103	49	0	48	93			223	243	395
Bahía de la Asuncion	458	405	415	380	340	310	301	274	264	245	238	192	176	151	97	48	0	45			175	195	347
Punta Abreojos	503	450	460	425	385	355	346	319	309	290	283	237	221	196	142	93	45	0			130	150	302
Laguna San Ignacio	519	466	476	441	401	371	362	335	325	306	299	253	237	212	158	109	61	16	0				
Bahía San Juanico	563	510	520	485	445	415	406	379	369	350	343	297	281	256	202	153	105	60	44	0			
Bahía Santa María	658	605	615	580	540	510	501	474	464	445	438	392	376	351	297	248	200	155	139	95	0	20	172
Bahía Magdalena	678	625	635	600	560	530	521	494	484	465	458	412	396	371	317	268	220	175	159	115	20	0	152
Cabo San Lucas	830	777	787	752	712	682	673	646	636	617	610	564	548	523	469	420	372	327	311	267	172	152	0

SECTION I: SAN DIEGO SOUTH TO CABO SAN LUCAS

Wind and Weather

The outer coast of Baja California is exposed to the winds and seas of the North Pacific Ocean. The prevailing wind is northwesterly for the greater part of the year (fall to spring). Occasional moderate gales, accompanied by rain, occur during this time. Chubascos are local, fierce winds that are fortunately of short duration, which occur in the fall and affect the southern regions of this section.

In the summer months the northward shift of the Pacific high allows tropical storms and hurricanes to disturb the coast. The summer months are typically a dangerous time to travel on the west coast of Baja. This is reflected in the rider that often accompanies insurance policies, limiting coverage to the northern latitudes of Baja during summer months.

If you are traveling during the summer season (and some cruisers take advantage of the favorable direction of the wind) then choose those anchorages that are considered safe in southerly winds. These are: Bahia Todos Santos, Hassler's Cove on Isla San Martin, Turtle Bay and Magdalena Bay.

The weather is pleasant for most of the year, warmer and clearer as you go south. Fog and haze problems can occur in the northern section of this area almost any time of the year, usually coming in at night and clearing by mid-day. As many of the dangerous passages are in this section it is wise to use caution when traveling here in poor weather.

Waves and Currents

The swell is generally northwesterly with the wind, though refraction occurs to bring the swell in on the coast. The surf can make landing hazardous in many places and as the anchorages of this section are primarily in the lee of capes and points they are only partially sheltered from the swell or wind. In settled weather the anchorages are fairly comfortable but can be rolly.

Coastal currents coincide with the direction of the prevailing winds. There is a strong inshore set along the mid-section of this coast where the lagoons and their entrances affect the flow. This current set should be watched and counteracted by careful navigation. Along the lower coast a back eddy kind of current can be experienced close by the coast, one that can be used to help you on the return passage.

Travel southward down the coast is usually an enjoyable, downwind run. On the return voyage the situation is reversed and it can be a demanding passage against the wind and seas. An average 15- to 18-knot wind that was pleasant going south, can be an apparent 25-knot wind as the vessel pounds her way back against the seas. Though less enjoyable from the standpoint of sightseeing, you may choose to travel at night from 11:00PM to 11:00 AM when the wind is often lighter than during the day. Selecting good times for travel and using routes to suit conditions will help to make the return less onerous. The Baja Bash is discussed in detail in the book titled The Baja Bash II by Jim Elfers.

ENTERING MEXICAN WATERS

Visible from San Diego on a clear day, the **Islas Coronados** (Crown Islands) are 4 miles south of the Mexican border. The islands are a Wildlife Refuge and the waters surrounding them teem with fish, making them a favorite spot for anglers and divers. In settled weather rather rolly anchorage may be taken in about 7 fathoms on the eastern shore of the south island off a conspicuous cut. Landing on the islands is prohibited and the Naval detachment stationed on the southern island sees that this regulation is adhered to. Kelp beds extend southeast from the islands, but they can be passed either to seaward or between the islands and the mainland. Some sailors choose to make the short trip to Islas Coronados as the first leg in their Mexican cruise. Beware of the extensive fish pens anchored at the south end of the Islands. They are not always illuminated.

The conspicuous bullring in the city of Tijuana and the obvious border fence are clear evidence that you have crossed the border into Mexican territorial waters. The coast between San Diego and Ensenada is generally low and sandy with occasional rocky cliffs, backed by hills rising from the beach. The toll-freeway and old highway between the US border and Ensenada run along the shore and are conspicuous from seaward. It is best to leave San Diego shortly after daybreak in order to arrive in Ensenada and spend the night in Mexican waters with the paper work of entry completed. Others prefer to take a longer first step with arrival planned for Turtle Bay, Magdalena Bay or even Cabo San Lucas. Officially, this plan prohibits landing at intermediate points in case of an emergency since entry into Mexico must first be processed at a recognized Port of Entry.

About 10 miles south of Tijuana the Rosarito power plant stacks and storage tanks are prominent. About a mile offshore is a red horn buoy and a number of unlit tanker buoys are closer to shore. Cruisers should transit this part of the coast more than a mile offshore to avoid these hazards. The southeasterly trending coast makes a turn eastward at Punta Descanso and 4 miles to the southeast is Sugar Loaf Rock where there are noticeable currents. The first marina and housing development in Mexico is about 10 miles southeast of this visible rock.

 Maps of town and cities in Baja California

Panoramic view of Ensenada! . Photo: Alejandra Cabrera

Port of Ensenada. Photo: Alejandra Cabrera

MARINA PUERTO SALINA

Is a residential development 33 miles south of San Diego and 27 miles north of Ensenada, with moorage for both property owners and transient cruisers. **WPT 32°30.28', 116°53.20'.** Facilities include 220/110 power, showers, laundry, Internet access, 24 hour security, Immigration services, a new club house, and free shuttle to Ensenada and the US Border. Changes to the breakwater and the addition of an underwater wave deflector (14 ft. under water at low water) have attempted to solve the shoaling problem that occurs at the entrance to the harbor, although it still occurs. We have seen it completely closed to all but the smallest dinghies. You must call the marina office on VHF Ch 6 before entering; office hours are from 7 am to 7 pm. For information call 011-

Marina Puerto Salina can silt in. Call ahead!

52-646-155-4186, and 155-4187. From US 866-365-2562, in Mexico 01-800-824-5164. Email info@marinapuertosalina.com.

Further to the south is Punta Salsipuedes followed by Punta San Miguel, marked by a light. A dangerous submerged rock marked with a light is about 4 miles southwest of Punta San Miguel and 3 miles north of Islas de Todos Santos. Be on the lookout for a proliferation of fish pens that are usually not marked.

Bahia Todos Santos (All Saints) is a large, wide bay, with about 6 miles between the entrance points of Punta San Miguel on the north and Punta Banda on the south. Islas de Todos Santos lie about midway between these two points.

EL SAUZAL

On the northern coast of Bahia Todos Santos lies the fishing town of El Sauzal two miles eastsoutheast of Punta San Miguel. A breakwater protects the enclosed commercial fisherman's harbor that is not available to yachts.

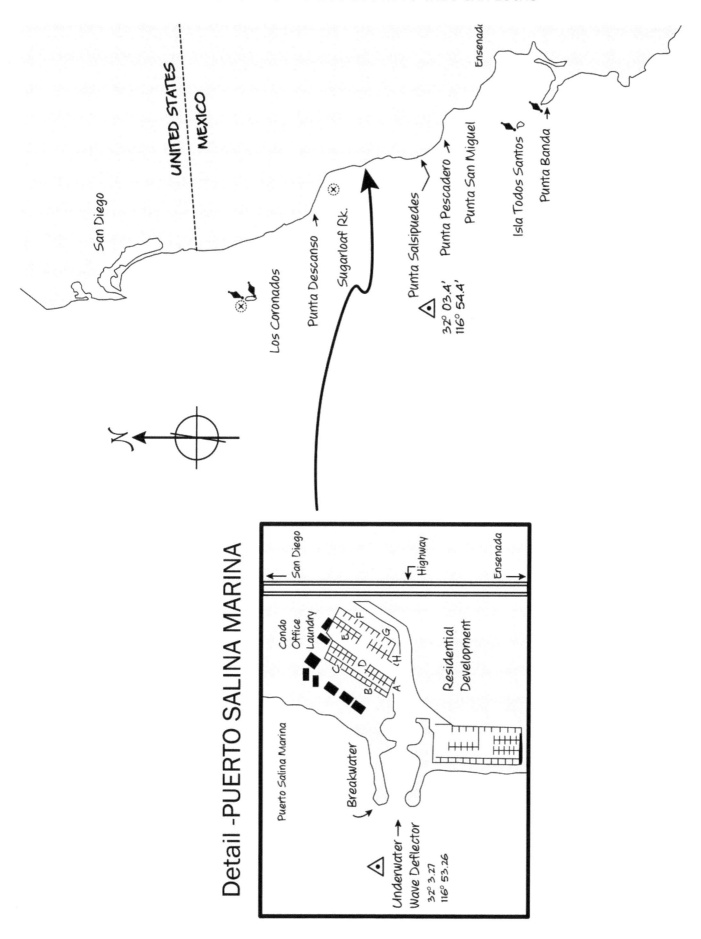

San Diego

UNITED STATES

MEXICO

Los Coronados

Punta Descanso

Sugarloaf Rk.

Punta Salsipuedes

32° 03.4'
116° 54.4'

Punta Pescadero

Punta San Miguel

Isla Todos Santos

Punta Banda

Ensenada

N

Detail - PUERTO SALINA MARINA

San Diego

Highway

Ensenada

Condo
Office
Laundry

E
F
G
C
D
H
B
A

Residential
Development

Puerto Salina Marina

Breakwater

Underwater →
Wave Deflector

32° 3.27
116° 53.26

MARINA CORAL

Three miles southeast of El Sauzal is Punta Morro where a light is located and about ½ mile beyond is the breakwater-protected basin of Coral Marina. A prominent pink hotel fronted by the maze of masts in the basin present conspicuous landmarks east of the Punta Morro light. When approaching the marina keep at least .5 mile off Punta Morro and swing in an arc to avoid the shoal water off the coast. If a south-easterly swell is running care must be taken when approaching the entrance for the vessel will be in the trough of the waves. Approach the entrance from the point shown on the sketch. The entrance is much larger than it appears. Really! Capt. Holly regularly took the 73' schooner Dirigo II with an 8' draft in and out of this basin to get fuel.

Marina Coral, WPT 31°51.67', 116°39.58' is a first-class modern marina with luxurious facilities offering transient and long-term moorage, fuel, chandlery, launching ramp, showers and rest rooms, laundry and fish cleaning stations. The marina has over 350 slips available for vessels from 30' to 60'. Contact the dockmaster on VHF Ch 71 for instructions on moorage. This is a very popular marina and reservations are necessary. They may be made by calling toll free from the US 866-302-0066, from Mexico 01-800-026-3100 or 011-52-646-175-0050, fax 011-52-646-175-0058. Office hours are 8 am to 7 pm. Email: marina@hotelcoral.com, www.hotelcoral.com

Fairways are narrow within the marina. **Extra care** is needed when docking your boat to avoid touching a neighboring vessel. If you are in doubt about your ability to approach your assigned slip, ask for assistance from marina staff who are very helpful. Use sturdy mooring lines protected with chafing gear to allow for surge within the basin.

Fuel is available at the long dock near the pump-out station. A concrete launch ramp is adjacent to the large parking area. The marina will process you paperwork but if you prefer to do it yourself a driver will take you to the Port Captain's Office. Facilities include a marine store, mechanical services, WiFi and use of resort facilities such as a gym, swimming pool and shuttle bus to Ensenada as it is too far to walk. On Wednesdays, the marina provides a van shuttle to Costco, Walmart etc. Sign up in the office.

Fuel Dock at Marina Coral   Photo: Jo Russell

Ensenada is the largest city on the west coast of Baja and has much to interest a first-time visitor to Mexico. Many restaurants, boutiques, souvenir shops and liquor stores line the streets. As in any tourist area check out the shops one or two blocks from the main street to find the most reasonable prices. A bakery is fairly close to the famous Hussongs Cantina and Blanco Supermercado about 2 blocks away. If you plan to stay for a week or so the Spanish language classes at the International Spanish Institute are highly recommended as an excellent way to learn or brush up your Spanish. Bargaining is the norm when dealing in most handicraft and souvenir shops.

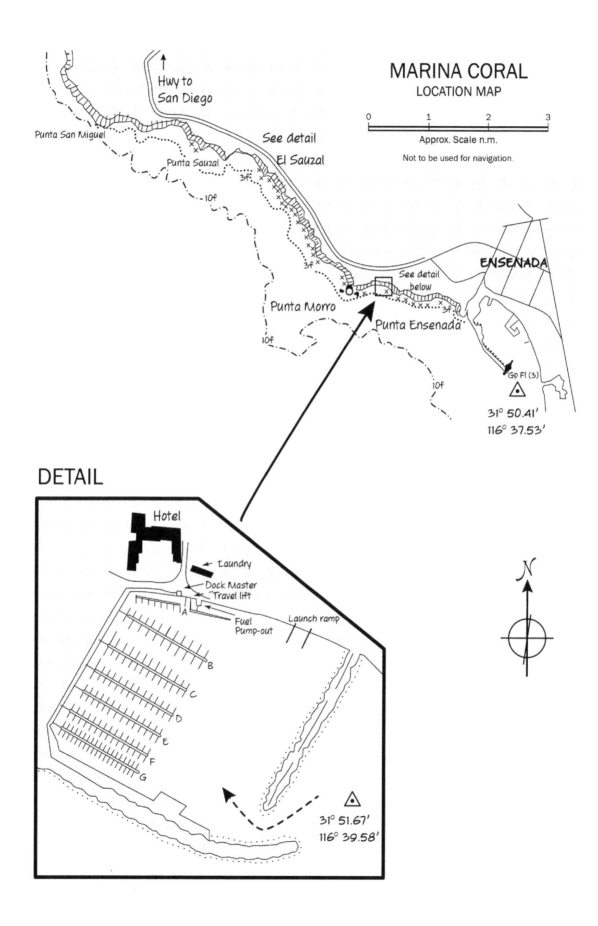

MARINA CORAL
LOCATION MAP

0   1   2   3

Approx. Scale n.m.

Not to be used for navigation.

Hwy to
San Diego

Punta San Miguel

Punta Sauzal

See detail
El Sauzal

3f

10f

3f

ENSENADA

See detail
below

Punta Morro

Punta Ensenada

3f

10f

10f

Gp Fl (3)

31° 50.41'
116° 37.53'

DETAIL

Hotel

Laundry

Dock Master
Travel lift

A

Fuel
Pump-out

Launch ramp

B

C

D

E

F

G

31° 51.67'
116° 39.58'

N

ENSENADA

This Port of Entry is at the head of Bahia de Todos Santos and is about 65 miles from San Diego. Except for those vessels sailing directly for the south from San Diego, most vessels choose to enter Mexico at this port. The city of Ensenada has a population of over 200,000 with the downtown core centered in the harbor area. Located approximately 2.5 miles ESE of Punta Morro, the entrance to the harbor is protected by two breakwaters. **WPT 31°50.42', 116°37.52'**. Anchoring is no longer permitted within the harbor so moorage must be arranged at one of several marina facilities.

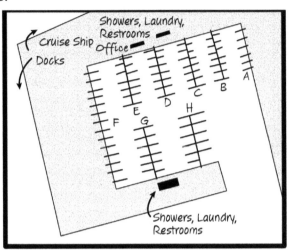

CRUISEPORT VILLAGE MARINA

Ensenada Cruiseport Village Marina, WPT 31°50.39', 116° 38.03' is the newest marina within the harbor and is adjacent to the cruise ship docks. The marina has 200 slips for vessels from 36' to 68' and can accommodate mega-yachts up to 350'. Services include power, water, laundry, rest rooms and showers, and is within walking distance of downtown. The entrance is easy and the basin has been dredged to a minimum of 14' at low low tide. Go to the red buoy and then approach the opening. The basin is protected from the surge that affects the rest of the harbor. The harbor office monitors VHF Ch 12 and 16 from 8 am. to 6:30 pm, Monday thru Friday. Reservations are advised and can be made from the US by calling 1-877-219-5822 or e-mail reservations@ecpvmarina.com

A short distance further is **Baja Naval**, a 50-slip modern marina two blocks from downtown Ensenada. The marina is adjacent to the plaza with the huge Mexican flag. Facilities include fuel, water, power, showers, laundry, telephone (free to the US), Fax, Weatherfax and handling clearance papers. This is primarily a repair facility and their large boatyard has a 75-ton Travelift and provides both full-service and do-it-yourself facilities. They monitor VHF Ch 77 and can be reached by telephone at 011-52-646-174-0020. For reservations email: marina@bajanaval.com. For information regarding work at the boatyard e-mail: diego@bajanaval.com.

A small new marina is being build inside the bay, Marina Ensenada. The docks are healthy looking, with rest rooms and showers, and a restaurant under construction. It is located just west of the larger Baja Naval. Prices are fixed but may be negotiated down a bit. You didn't hear it from us though...

Don't be surprised by the fellows beckoning you from the end of the various docks as they would love your business. Some docks are in poor condition and not strong enough to withstand a good blow. If the weather is settled and you will be staying with your boat, it might be worth bargaining with them to save a few pesos. If the forecast is not good, Cruiseport has very good protection. The most convenient to town Baja Naval and Marina Ensenada.

The immigration office, which you need to visit as soon as possible, is located on the west side of the bay, across the street from the shipyard. See the sketch. The marina where you are staying will help you with your paperwork. This is a great place to check into the country as everything is in one office. Step up to the first window, and continue around the room until you are finished. You can celebrate with a few fish tacos and a Pacifico at the little stands near the fish market. Just follow your nose!

This is also the place to purchase your phone, calling plan, and the Banda Ancha for use with your computer to allow you internet access in Mexico. Ask for Karen in the Telcel office, she speaks perfect English!

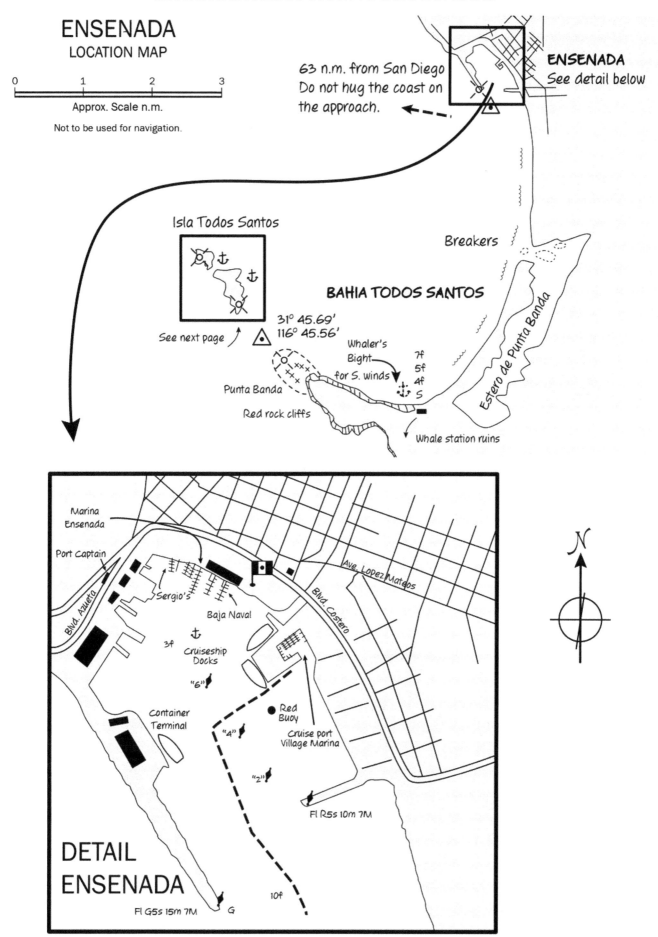

ENSENADA
LOCATION MAP

0   1   2   3
Approx. Scale n.m.

Not to be used for navigation.

63 n.m. from San Diego
Do not hug the coast on
the approach.

ENSENADA
See detail below

Isla Todos Santos

See next page

Breakers

BAHIA TODOS SANTOS

31° 45.69'
116° 45.56'

Whaler's
Bight
for S. winds

7f
5f
4f
S

Estero de Punta Banda

Punta Banda

Red rock cliffs

Whale station ruins

Marina
Ensenada

Port Captain

Blvd. Azueta

Sergio's

Baja Naval

Ave. Lopez Mateos

Blvd. Costero

3f

Cruiseship
Docks

"6"

Container
Terminal

Red
Buoy

Cruise port
Village Marina

"4"

"2"

Fl R5s 10m 7M

DETAIL
ENSENADA

N

Fl G5s 15m 7M   G

10f

Sea Lions take over a dock in Ensenda. Photo: Holly Scott

The flag in Ensenda. Photo: Holly Scott

Ensenda Bay. Photo: Holly Scott

Port Captain's in Ensenda. Photo: Holly Scott

ISLAS TODOS SANTOS

Located 10 miles west of Ensenada, these two small rocky islands lie in the middle of the entrance to Bahia Todos Santos. The northern island is low and fairly flat 55' and the southern is higher, with hills reaching to over 300'. Kelp and some outlying rocks surround much of the islands. A lighthouse marked with red and white bands is above the cliffs on the north side of the northern island and an abandoned lighthouse stands nearby to the east.

Abalone farming is being done in the small coves on the eastern side of the south island. It is reported that there is no longer any space for anchoring within the northernmost cove as a result of congested aquaculture activities. Buoys mark the boundaries of abalone farming activity. Anchorage should not be taken here during easterly winds as the coves are open to the east; immediately vacate if the wind becomes easterly.

Access to the shore is via a narrow passage between the north point of the cove and a large offset rock to a smaller rock-enclosed bight further to the north. A path leads from the pebble beach to flats above where a fascinating, easy hike along the cliffs gives views of the North Island, surf-swept rocks below and nesting seabirds. The abalone farmers and local fishermen are friendly and often want to trade seafood for playing cards, liquor or clothing.

Open roadstead anchorages for large vessels in calm, settled weather can be taken off the eastern side of the north island in about 10 fathoms and in about the same depth off the two coves on the southern island. The passage between the north and south island is foul and should not be attempted as kelp beds and submerged rocks abound.

The channel between Todos Santos Islands and Punta Banda is over 2 miles wide and is free of dangers though adjustments must be made for strong onshore currents that occur in the area. Pass well to seaward of the Punta Banda light located at the end of a reef extending about ¾ mile off the point. **WPT 31°45.69', 116°45.56'.**

Good diving can be enjoyed in the shoal passage between Isla Norte and Isla Sur and off the southernmost cove on the east side of Isla Sur. Many dive sites can be found along the shores of Punta Banda, a very popular area with California divers. About three miles southeast of the Punta Banda light is Bahia Papalote, the site of the spectacular La Bufadora blowhole, a major tourist attraction in the area. Local fishermen use this cove but it is usually thick with kelp.

A WORD OF CAUTION

There are considerable onshore currents of variable strength along the coast of Baja. A prudent cruiser must pay particular attention to maintaining the desired bearing of the next waypoint or point of land to be rounded. Unfortunately many cruisers, and especially single-handed sailors have been swept ashore as a result of preoccupation with preparing meals, trying to sleep or over-confidence. One such vessel was lost during the 2010 Baja Ha Ha. The owner was assisted by many of the participants of the Ha Ha, but the vessel could not be salvaged.

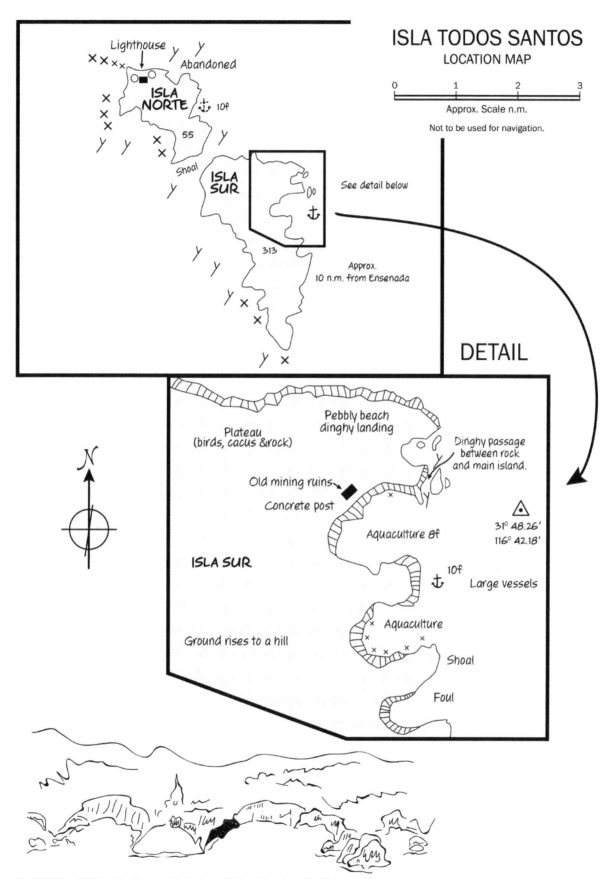

ISLA TODOS SANTOS
LOCATION MAP

0   1   2   3

Approx. Scale n.m.

Not to be used for navigation.

Lighthouse
Abandoned
ISLA NORTE
⚓ 10f
55
Shoal
ISLA SUR
Oo
⚓
See detail below
313
Approx.
10 n.m. from Ensenada

DETAIL

N

Pebbly beach
dinghy landing
Plateau
(birds, cacus &rock)
Dinghy passage
between rock
and main island.
Old mining ruins
Concrete post
31° 48.26′
116° 42.18′
Aquaculture 8f
ISLA SUR
⚓ 10f   Large vessels
Aquaculture
Ground rises to a hill
Shoal
Foul

DETAIL: TODOS SANTOS COVES FROM THE EAST

PUERTO SANTO TOMAS and PUNTA COLONET

The coast from Punta Banda to Puerto Santo Tomas, about 12 miles south, is generally rocky with offlying kelp beds. Inland the land rises quickly to peaks of 3,000' to 4,000' in altitude. Sea fog is often encountered in the summer months so that courses should stay well away from the dangers ashore.

Punta Santo Tomas is a square headland that projects from the generally southerly running coastline. Heavy kelp beds lie around the point. Bahia Soledad, just north of Punta Santo Tomas, is an open bay with only limited shelter, though it can be used as a fair weather anchorage. Rocas Soledad, a group of 20' high, guano-covered rocks that lie about a mile to the west of Punta Santo Tomas, may be passed on either side.

Puerto Santo Tomas, **WPT 31°32.57', 116°40.64** is the anchorage in the southern lee of the point and though affected by swell and surrounded by kelp it is fairly satisfactory. The best spot to drop the anchor is when Rocas Soledad are roughly aligned with the southernmost rocks of Punta Santo Tomas. But many small fishing boats moor here so the only anchorage space is usually available outside of the area with the best protection. (In 1542 Juan Rodriguez Cabrillo was the first Spanish explorer to anchor here. The original Santo Tomas vineyards are located a few miles inland though the well known winery of this name is located in Ensenada.)

Punta China is about 2 miles south of Santo Tomas. A limestone quarry and barge operation is located here. The huge white scar is almost as eye-catching during the day as are its bright working lights during the night. Rocky bluffs with small beaches, backed by mountains near the shore lie along the coast to the south. Anchorage cannot be taken hereabouts.

Punta Colonet, **WPT 30°56.54', 116°17.2'** lies 40 miles southeast of Punta Santo Tomas. This distinctive landmark consists of a great, flat plateau rising in 300' vertical cliffs from a steeply tumbled mass of rocks. Radar returns are good from up to 30 miles distant. A light is located on the cape, but the tower is not easily made out during the day.

Round the cape, keeping beyond the 10-fathom curve, until you can turn into Bahia Colonet, the bight south of the cape. The anchorage lies about 1.5 miles from the point, in line with the deep gorge that cuts through the cliffs. Anchor about 100 yards offshore in 4 to 6 fathoms, sand and shell bottom. Further eastward the bay shoals rapidly; and surf breaks along the shore. A fisherman once advised us to move further out into the bay to avoid a bar, which caused breaking surf right where we were anchored. If a landing is necessary it might be attempted near the fish camp. The light on the point is not visible from the anchorage.

The anchorage is affected by the swell refracted around the point and gusty winds sometimes sweep down the cliffs without warning, (particularly when northwesterly winds are blowing), but the holding is good and a relatively quiet, if rolly, night can be had.

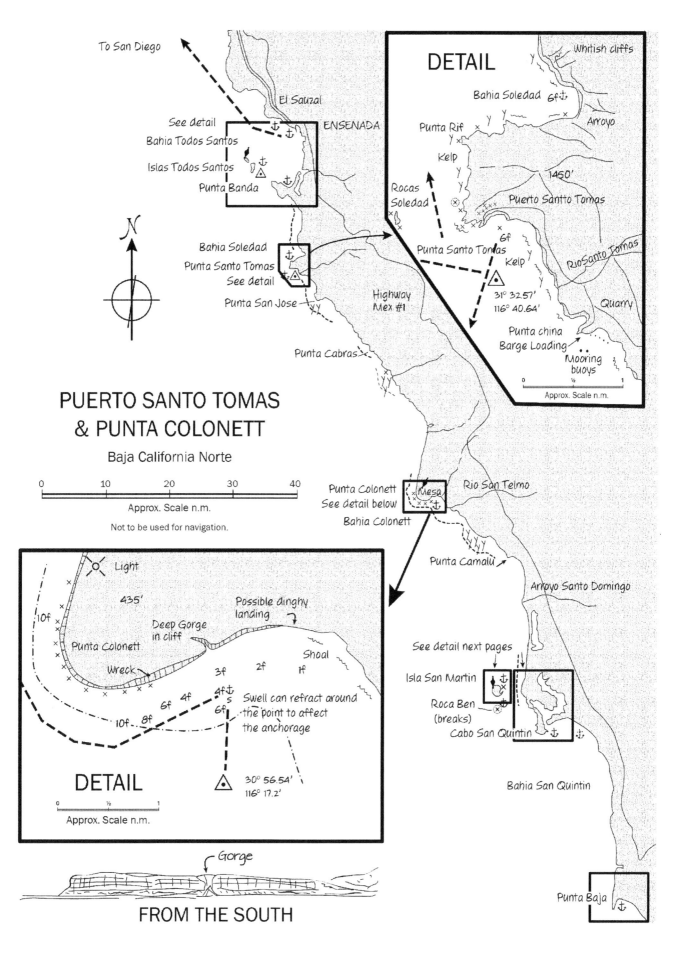

To San Diego

El Sauzal

ENSENADA

See detail
Bahia Todos Santos

Islas Todos Santos

Punta Banda

DETAIL

Whitish cliffs

Bahia Soledad   6f

Punta Rif   Arroyo

Kelp   1450'

Rocas
Soledad   Puerto Santto Tomas

RioSanto Tomas

Punta Santo Tomas   6f   Kelp

Quarry

31° 32.57'
116° 40.64'

Punta china
Barge Loading

Mooring
buoys

0   ½   1
Approx. Scale n.m.

N

Bahia Soledad

Punta Santo Tomas
See detail

Punta San Jose

Highway
Mex #1

Punta Cabras

PUERTO SANTO TOMAS
& PUNTA COLONETT

Baja California Norte

0   10   20   30   40
Approx. Scale n.m.

Not to be used for navigation.

Punta Colonett
See detail below
Bahia Colonett

Rio San Telmo

Mesa

Punta Camalú

Arroyo Santo Domingo

Light

435'

Possible dinghy
landing

10f

Deep Gorge
in cliff

Punta Colonett

Wreck

Shoal

3f   2f   1f

4f
6f   4f
10f   8f   6f

Swell can refract around
the point to affect
the anchorage

30° 56.54'
116° 17.2'

See detail next pages

Isla San Martin

Roca Ben
(breaks)

Cabo San Quintin

Bahia San Quintin

DETAIL

0   ½   1
Approx. Scale n.m.

Gorge

Punta Baja

FROM THE SOUTH

37

ISLA SAN MARTIN

A remnant of an extinct volcano, this island lies about 3 miles offshore and is about 30 miles south of Punta Colnett. Its circular shape and central crater form twin peaks rising about 470', making it an unmistakable landmark. Composed of lava, the island has a thin mantle of desert vegetation. A navigation light is on the western edge of the island.

The natural jetty at Isla San Martin, with San Quintin in the distance.

The island's main anchorage is **Caleta Hassler**, approach **WPT 30°29.3', 116°6.0'**, a small, curved bight on the southeast side. A low arm formed by boulders projects in a curve to the northeast. Within this hook is a small sandy cove, off which anchorage can be taken in about 4 fathoms just within the mouth of the cove. A small fish camp on the beach is usually occupied and lobster receivers (cages for collecting lobsters until they are shipped to market) may be moored in the cove in season. They could present a hazard to boaters since they lie low in the water, are unlit and may have trailing lines attached. Landing is easy on the long sand beach at the head of the cove.

When the prevailing northwesterly winds are strong the anchorage can be uncomfortable and sometimes dangerous, for the circular island does little to affect the wind and swell. During such time the vessel can be taken around to the south lee of the boulder hook, where anchorage can be taken in about 5 to 10 fathoms off a small lagoon. During southwesterly storms good anchorage is reported to be available northwest of the rocky hook. A number of detached rocks are scattered in the thick beds of kelp which surround the island.

Isla San Martin from the south.

A dinghy might be taken into the lagoon, through the opening that is foul but open to the sea at half tide. Landing may be done on the sandy beach within the lagoon that is home to a colony of harbor seals and often elephant seals. It may make more sense to walk from the fish camp landing to see the seals. The island is a sea birds rookery so trips ashore should be done slowly and quietly to avoid unnecessary disturbance of the wildlife. Some rough trails inland from the lagoon are worth taking if you have sturdy footwear for the variety of hardy plants to be seen is amazing.

The peculiar nature of the boulder-strewn hook has led to romantic stories of it being built as a pirate's haven. While pirate vessels could have used the anchorage as a refuge there is little historical evidence to support such stories. The boulders seem to be a natural formation composed of lava rocks. Furthermore, when pirates were active, the Spanish galleons kept well offshore, landing only at Isla Cedros or Cabo San Lucas for water on the way to Acapulco.

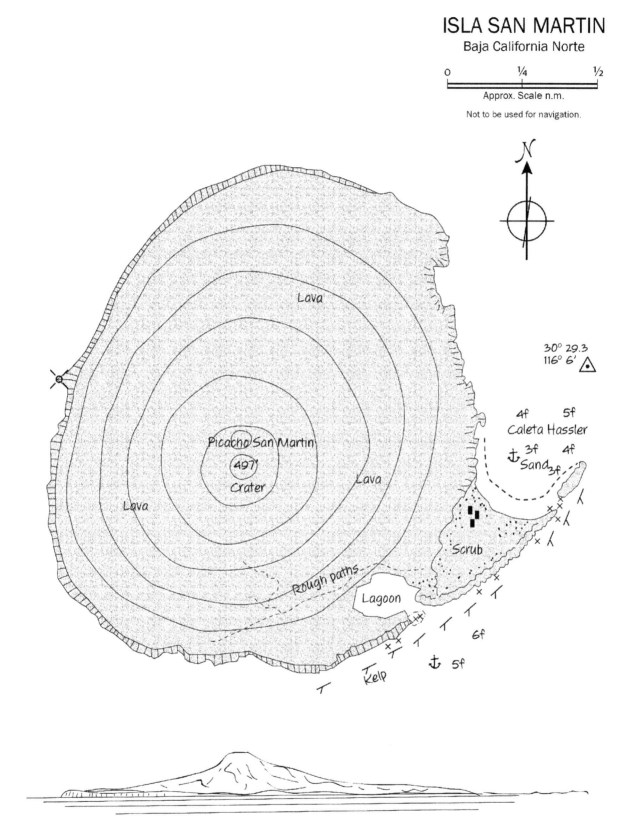

ISLA SAN MARTIN
Baja California Norte

0   ¼   ½

Approx. Scale n.m.

Not to be used for navigation.

N

30° 29.3
116° 6'

Lava

Lava

Picacho San Martin
497'
Crater

Lava

4f   5f
Caleta Hassler

3f   4f
Sand   3f

Scrub

Rough paths

Lagoon

6f

5f

Kelp

ISLA SAN MARTIN FROM SOUTH

BAHIA SAN QUINTIN (Keen teen)

Cabo San Quintin is about 10 miles further to the southeast and there is clear passage (about 10 to 12 fathoms deep) between the island and the Baja shore. No known dangers are in the channel but about 2½ miles south of the island lies **Roca Ben**, a dangerous submerged rock, covered 9', where the sea occasionally breaks. There are reports of vessels lost while fishing in the vicinity of the rock resulting from "rogue" waves rising out of an otherwise calm sea. The normal route followed along the coast to the island and Cabo San Quintin passes well clear of this rock.

The Baja coast opposite Isla San Martin is a bold, rocky bluff that extends south for two miles, ending in a small rocky hill. It then follows a long, low sandy beach, part of a narrow peninsula that is only a few hundred feet wide at the northern end, widening as it continues southward. At the south end it rises, forming Monte Mazo 160' where it is about 1½ miles wide. The rocky end of this peninsula is Cabo San Quintin. A half a mile north and projecting eastward is Punta Entrada.

Reasonably protected, rolly anchorage in 3 to 4 fathoms, sand, can be found outside the bar, abreast of Punta Entrada, a more noticeable feature than the cape itself. **WPT 30°22.40', 115°57.55'.** The bottom shoals slowly for some distance before rising rapidly to the bar where breaking surf usually marks the line of shoals.

A dinghy can be easily landed on Punta Sextante to allow you to wander along the sandy beaches or explore the shore to the south. On these wide beaches there is a wealth of large pismo clams, abalone and other shells. Except for the occasional Mexican fisherman camped in makeshift huts this is a wild and lonely place.

In calm, settled weather, you can anchor about 3 miles ENE of Punta Entrada, opposite the trailer park, keeping well clear of breakers at Playa Santa Maria. Pay attention to your depth sounder as sand banks in the area vary in size and shape. The channel leading into Bahia San Quintin should only be transited with the guidance of a local. It is often too shallow for any vessel with a draft of more than two or three feet. If the channel is clear, anchorage may be taken in the bay where some mooring buoys are also available. However, in talking to the locals, there are vessels in the harbor, which have been trapped for years. Unless a hurricane or other natural event washes the channel clear, entrance is not a good idea. The tidal range within Bahia San Quintin is approximately 16'.

* * * * *

In the 1880's this area was the scene of an enterprising development initiated by American speculators. This land scheme progressed to the point where settlers were brought in, farms developed, a flour mill was built and a railroad was commenced which was purported to link the port to Yuma, Arizona. However, nature did not cooperate, the crops failed and the enterprise died. The remains of these efforts are visible at the village of San Quintin several miles up the lagoon.

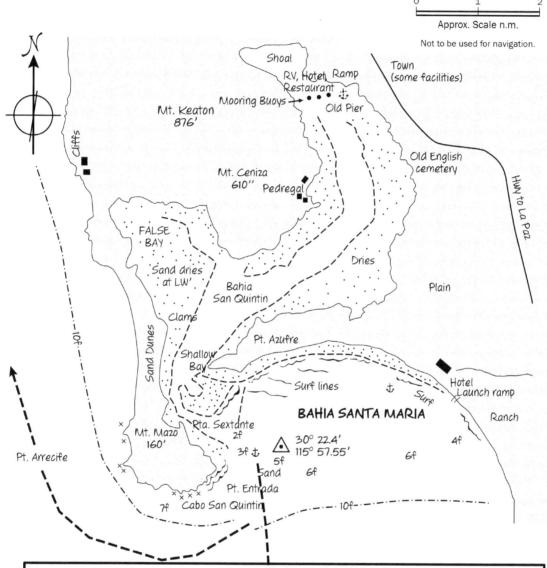

BAHIA DE SAN QUINTIN
Baja California Norte

0   1   2

Approx. Scale n.m.

Not to be used for navigation.

Shoal

Town
(some facilities)

RV, Hotel Ramp
Restaurant

Mooring Buoys → Old Pier

Mt. Keaton
876'

Old English
cemetery

Hwy to La Paz

Mt. Ceniza
610" Pedregal

FALSE
BAY

Dries

Sand dries
at LW'

Plain

Bahia
San Quintin

Clams

Pt. Azufre

Sand Dunes

Shallow
Bay

Surf lines

Surf

Hotel
Launch ramp

BAHIA SANTA MARIA

Ranch

10f

Rta. Sextante
2f

30° 22.4'
115° 57.55'

4f

Mt. Mazo
160'

3f

5f

6f

Pt. Arrecife

Sand

6f

Pt. Entrada

7f   Cabo San Quintin

10f

CAUTION: Constant shoaling along the shores of Bahia San Quintin make it impossible to show the changing extent of shallow areas. Therefore boaters must assume that shoal waters are greater in extent than the sketch indicates. Close monitoring of the depth sounder to avoid grounding is essential when visiting the bay.

Cluster of volcanic peaks

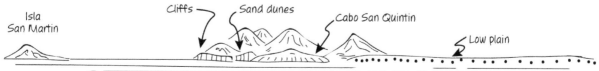

Isla
San Martin

Cliffs   Sand dunes

Cabo San Quintin

Low plain

CABO SAN QUINTIN FROM THE SOUTH

PUNTA BAJA

Punta Baja is 26 miles SSW of Isla San Martin, across Bahia Santa Maria. The coast slowly changes from long, low sandy beaches to bluffs interspersed with beaches. At Punta Baja there are scalloped, low cliffs about 30' high with rocks scattered below them. Kelp is prevalent around the point.

The point is a long finger of land that is less evident as a point when approached from the north than when coming from the south. A reef extends a short distance from the point and other rocks lie to the southeast. The surf breaks heavily on the point and rolls up along the inside of the finger of land. As a result, this area is popular with surfers whose vans and mobile homes are often seen on the flat top near the end of Punta Baja..**WPT 29°56.8' 115°48.7'.**

The village is tucked into the curve of land behind the point, where it swings easterly around the bay. A steep ramp cuts through the cliffs to the beach, a feature readily recognizable from the south. Anchor south of the village, outside the kelp in 4 to 5 fathoms, sand bottom. Surf discourages thoughts of landing and the anchorage can be uncomfortable because the vessel lies in the trough of the swell. Though it is one of the rolliest anchorages in Baja, a bridle on the anchor or fore and aft anchors can help (not eliminate) to ease the motion.

Bahia de Rosario lies between Punta Baja and Punta San Antonio that is about 13 miles SSE. The bay has many kelp patches and a couple of relatively shallow 3-fathom shoals, but most vessels can safely navigate directly across it. The shoreline consists of rock or sand bluffs backed by hills with three major arroyos breaking through to seaward.

ISLA SAN GERONIMO

Isla San Geronimo lies 9 miles south of Punta Baja and about 1/2 mile westnorthwest of Punta San Antonio. Heavy kelp beds surround the island and a long reef extends almost 1/2 mile southwest of the tip of the island. A light is located on the crest of the ridge. Quite comfortable anchorage can be taken east of the island, off the small village, in 7 to 8 fathoms, which may be preferable to Punta Baja. **WPT 29°47.32, 115°47.36'**

The dreaded **Arrecife Sacramento (Sacramento Reef)** lies about 1½ miles south of Isla San Geronimo and about 4 miles west of Punta San Antonio. The reef covers an oval area about 2 miles long and 1 mile wide, where several low, barely visible rocks and many more submerged rocks cause the sea to break and create spume. On relatively quiet days this helps to define the reef, but when there is a good breeze with whitecaps everywhere the reef can be harder to spot. The reef is in the red sector of the San Geronimo light, but night passages in this area are not recommended.

As the sketch shows, a course laid from Isla San Geronimo to Punta San Carlos passes through an inner channel clear of danger. But if on any other course a vessel should stand well out to seaward to clear the dangers of this section of the coast. The courses shown are also useful with radar when summer and autumn fogs often occur. Isla San Geronimo, Punta Baja and Punta San Carlos are good radar targets.

Transient cruisers heave a sigh of relief once this hazardous area has been passed, but it is a favorite spot for fishermen and divers who are amply rewarded by the abundant marine life inhabiting the reef and surrounding rocks.

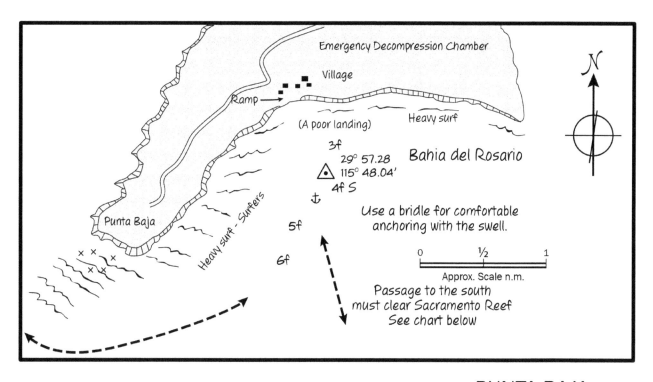

Emergency Decompression Chamber

Village

Ramp →

(A poor landing)

Heavy surf

3f
29° 57.28
115° 48.04'
4f S

Bahia del Rosario

Punta Baja

Heavy surf - Surfers

5f

6f

Use a bridle for comfortable
anchoring with the swell.

0   ½   1
Approx. Scale n.m.

Passage to the south
must clear Sacramento Reef
See chart below

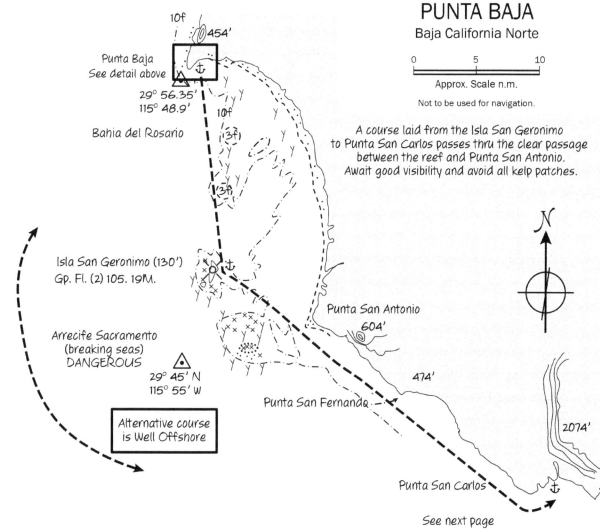

PUNTA BAJA
Baja California Norte

0   5   10
Approx. Scale n.m.

Not to be used for navigation.

10f
454'

Punta Baja
See detail above

29° 56.35'
115° 48.9'

Bahia del Rosario

10f

3f

3f

A course laid from the Isla San Geronimo
to Punta San Carlos passes thru the clear passage
between the reef and Punta San Antonio.
Await good visibility and avoid all kelp patches.

Isla San Geronimo (130')
Gp. Fl. (2) 105. 19M.

Punta San Antonio
604'

Arrecife Sacramento
(breaking seas)
DANGEROUS
29° 45' N
115° 55' W

474'

Punta San Fernando

2074'

Alternative course
is Well Offshore

Punta San Carlos

See next page

BAHIA SAN CARLOS

The coast from Punta San Antonio trends southeast, with a succession of low points and convex curved small bays. Several of these bays offer some protection from the prevailing winds and are useful as anchorages. The first one to be so used is Bahia San Carlos in the lee of Punta San Carlos, about 13 miles southeast of Punta San Antonio. It is a good spot to enjoy the relief of having successfully cleared Sacramento Reef when heading south or when preparing for a passage past it when going north.

A small island lies off the tip of Punta San Carlos, but it is low and not easily made out. Turn into the bay well clear of the island. Anchorage can be taken almost anywhere in the bay in the lee of the land but is most satisfactory off the fish camp in 4 to 5 fathoms, about 400 yds. offshore. **WPT 29°37.38', 115°28.63'.** Though some swell can be felt it is not as objectionable as it is at Punta Baja. Since gusty winds can deflect off the mesa walls or sweep down from the top of the plateau, anchoring some distance out has some merit. Quite often the winds felt within the bay seem to be stronger than those offshore, but the bay provides good shelter from the prevailing northwesterlies. Punta San Carlos is a popular spot for wind surfers because of its reliable, vigorous winds.

San Carlos has been a popular anchorage for both commercial and pleasure skippers for many years, although not one of our favorites. It used to be a coastal stop for taking on cargo or supplying the mining ventures of the interior. It is sometimes used by fishermen and yachtsmen as a jumping off point for the trip to Cedros Island, or as an easily recognizable destination to reach after a bumpy northbound trip. Care must be taken to avoid the lobster receivers scattered within the bay during the lobster fishing season. We have used it during a delivery for a quick stop to transfer fuel from jerry cans to the main tank, but it is too windy and exposed for our taste as an overnight stop.

On the northbound trip, Bahia San Carlos has a basic flaw for sailors for it lies dead to windward of Cedros Island and an easier sailing course can be set to one or other of the bays further south. The sketched chart on page 59 will help in understanding and evaluating your choices in courses and destinations.

The guide continues along the coastal points and bays from Punta Escarpada to Morro Santo Domingo. However, the recommended and most used route crosses directly to Isla Cedros since it provides the shortest overall distance to be traveled. If this route is followed the next anchorage is on Isla Cedros.

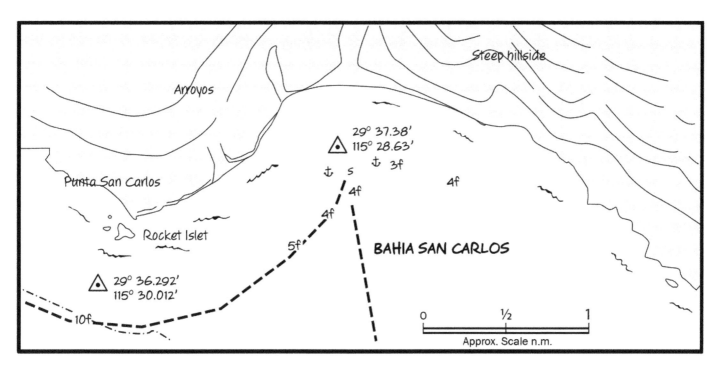

Steep hillside

Arroyos

29° 37.38'
115° 28.63'

⚓ s   ⚓ 3f

Punta San Carlos

4f   4f

4f

Rocket Islet   5f   4f

BAHIA SAN CARLOS

29° 36.292'
115° 30.012'

10f

0   ½   1

Approx. Scale n.m.

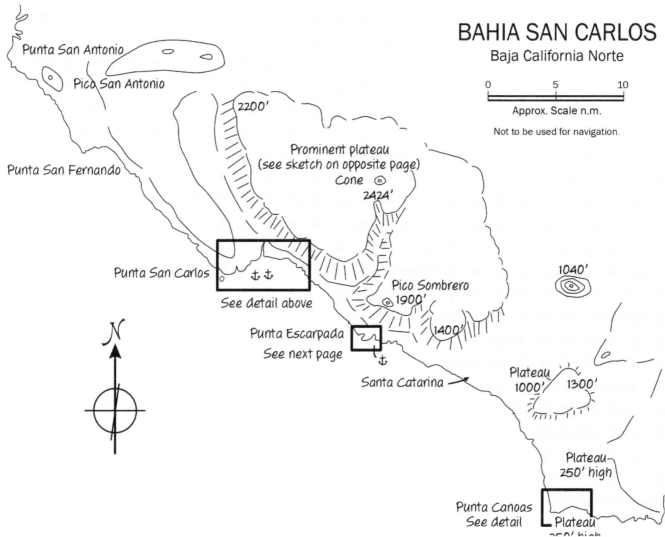

Punta San Antonio

Pico San Antonio

BAHIA SAN CARLOS
Baja California Norte

0   5   10

Approx. Scale n.m.

Not to be used for navigation.

Punta San Fernando

2200'

Prominent plateau
(see sketch on opposite page)
Cone ⊙
2424'

1040'

Punta San Carlos   ⚓ ⚓

See detail above

Pico Sombrero
⊙ 1900'

1400'

Punta Escarpada
See next page   ⚓

Santa Catarina ➤

Plateau
1000'   1300'

N

Plateau
250' high

Punta Canoas
See detail   Plateau
250' high

PUNTA ESCARPADA

This point has been marked on some charts, or known as, Punta Bluff or Punta Acantilado. It lies about 7 miles southeast of Punta San Carlos. Though not a large or apparently definitive lee, its looks are deceiving for though it is not a highly recommended anchorage, it is a better one than the next point to the south, Punta Canoas. What protection it offers is derived from the 100' bluffs that form the point.

The cliffs are brown with streaks of lighter colors from relatively recent rock falls from the vertical section near their tops. Another feature to assist in identification are two arroyos, which cut into the cliffs, one on each side of the point. Anchorage can be taken in about 4 fathoms off the small sandy beach at the foot of the cliffs. **WPT 29°33.50', 115°22.80'.** Though not a fully protected anchorage, the degree of comfort depends on the amount of sea running. Landing ashore is not recommended because of the normally high surf.

A few miles further south is the open roadstead anchorage of **Puerto Santa Catarina**, at the mouth of a large arroyo. This bay was once the site much activity in the transport of ore from copper and iron mines as well as large quantities of onyx from the famous El Marmol quarry. Huge blocks of onyx were hauled over miles of rough road by over-burdened donkeys to the pier which has long since been destroyed, lighters then ferried the ore and onyx to coastal freighters anchored nearby. A graveyard at Santa Catarina with weathered wooden crosses and a few pieces of onyx scattered on the beach are testaments to this period of Baja's history.

PUNTA ESCARPADA
Baja California Norte

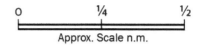

Approx. Scale n.m.

Not to be used for navigation.

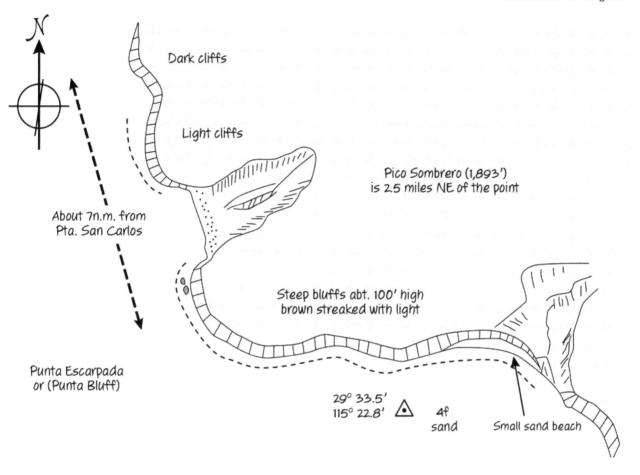

Dark cliffs

Light cliffs

Pico Sombrero (1,893')
is 2.5 miles NE of the point

About 7 n.m. from
Pta. San Carlos

Punta Escarpada
or (Punta Bluff)

Steep bluffs abt. 100' high
brown streaked with light

29° 33.5'
115° 22.8' △   4f
sand

Small sand beach

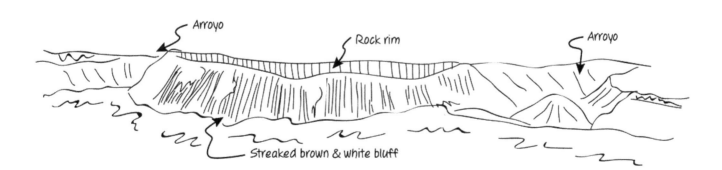

Arroyo

Rock rim

Arroyo

Streaked brown & white bluff

CLOSE-TO FROM THE SOUTH

PUNTA CANOAS

Punta Canoas is about 12 miles southeast of Punta Escarpada. Though it appears to be larger, it is not as satisfactory an anchorage as Escarpada. Somewhat resembling a miniature Punta Colonet, it is a sharply defined cliff backed by high hills, behind which are mountain ranges. In 1542 Cabrillo visited this anchorage and after some unfavorable weather he named it Punta Mal Abrigo (Point Poor Shelter).

If you choose to use this anchorage, do so in about 5 fathoms well within the lee of the cliffs. **WPT 29°26', 115°12'.** A submerged pinnacle with a least depth of about one fathom lies about ½ mile SSW of the point. Care should be taken when entering or leaving this anchorage to avoid this danger. Ocean swells affect this lee to a considerable extent, making it rather uncomfortable.

About 20 miles to the southeast is the small anchorage of **Puerto San Jose**. It is formed by a small headland and reef, as well as by the protection against seas afforded by an offshore rock, **Roca Acme**, which is surrounded by very large kelp beds. The lee of the kelp gives smooth conditions that make this small headland an acceptable anchorage, but it needs care when working your way into it. **WPT 29°16.72', 114°52.62.**

* * * * *

In the 1850's the whaling fleets were attracted to the west coast of Baja by marine animals found in abundance. The gray whales which congregated in the quiet waters of coastal lagoons to give birth to their young were killed by the thousands until international moratoriums signed in 1937 and 1946 prohibited their slaughter. Now numbering in the thousands, their amazing comeback has added to the balance of nature and the enjoyment of cruisers and tourists along North America's west coast.

PUNTA CANOAS
Baja California Norte

Approx. Scale n.m.

Not to be used for navigation.

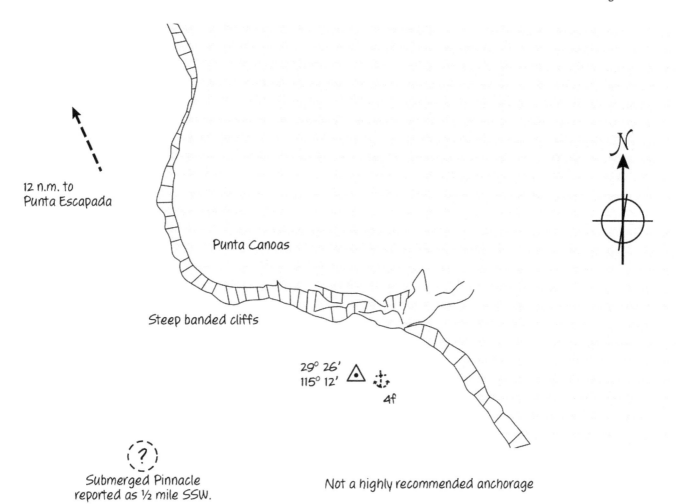

12 n.m. to
Punta Escapada

Punta Canoas

Steep banded cliffs

29° 26'
115° 12'

4f

Submerged Pinnacle
reported as ½ mile SSW.

Not a highly recommended anchorage

APPROACHING FROM THE SOUTH

BAHIA BLANCA

This is a large, open bay about 50 miles southeast of Bahia San Carlos. It is given a lee by the 200' dark sandstone cliffs rising above an equally dark, rocky point. The coastal mountains rise immediately behind this area.

There are two large bights within the bay, separated by an intermediate steep-faced, low bluff with striated markings. Each bight has long arcs of white sandy beaches. A large salt pan lies behind the southernmost beach.

Though an anchorage in the lee of Punta Blanca might seem the most protected, a large shoal area is around the point and the refracted swell makes the anchorage uncomfortable. Thus, though an anchorage in 3 fathoms is available off the first beach, a better location is off the head of the second beach in 4 to 5 fathoms, sand bottom. **WPT 29°06.4', 114°04.5'** The best spot to go ashore is off the fish camp on a small sandy beach east of the point.

The points of land and series of arcs of beaches that form this part of the coast till Morro Santo Domingo do not provide much shelter. However, in settled summer weather with light northwesterlies, the anchorages are adequate. Acting like a pivot causing the swell to refract around the points, the anchorages in their lee share two common features, namely, orientation and shoaling.

* * * * *

After the gray whale became scarce the Yankee skipper, Charles Melville Scammon then turned his sights on killing of elephant seals that inhabited Isla Cedros, Isla Guadalupe and Islas San Benitos and ranged as far north as Point Reyes, in California. By the 1880s these easily killed, docile animals were not to be found anywhere except for a few on Isla Guadalupe which President Obregon of Mexico declared to be a Wildlife Refuge. They now number about 20,000.

BAHIA BLANCA
Baja California Norte

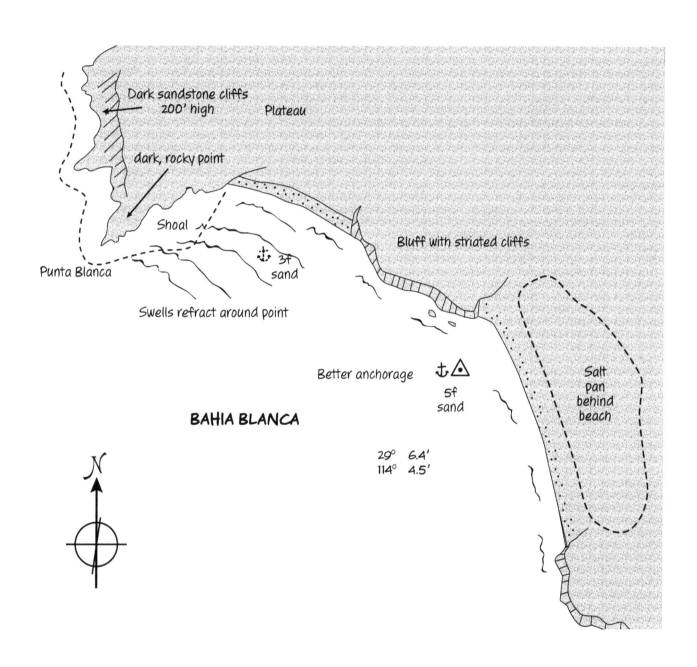

Approx. Scale n.m.

Not to be used for navigation.

Dark sandstone cliffs 200' high

Plateau

dark, rocky point

Shoal

Punta Blanca

3f sand

Bluff with striated cliffs

Swells refract around point

Better anchorage

5f sand

Salt pan behind beach

BAHIA BLANCA

29°   6.4'
114°   4.5'

N

BAHIA PLAYA MARIA

The coast continues as bluffs and sandy beaches for the 10 miles separating Punta Blanca and Punta Cono, to the southeast. The bight of **Bahia Falsa**, continuing around to Punta Falsa, is almost completely lined with a sandy beach. A noticeable arroyo opens midway along the shores of the bay. Anchorage is possible in the bay, but the refracted swell around Punta Cono and shoaling behind the point makes this more uncomfortable than the anchorages in Bahia Blanca and Bahia Playa Maria.

Punta Falsa and Punta Maria (about 1½ miles south) form a low, two-pronged, point of blackish rocks. The bight that is **Bahia Playa Maria** has a number of white sand beach arcs, interspersed with low, rocky points. About 6 miles south of Punta Maria is Punta Ositos, which marks the end of this bay.

Anchorage can be taken near the spots shown on the chart. **WPT 28°55.6', 114°31'.** The preferred anchorage is the one off the beginning of the third beach. The lovely white beaches are very inviting, but are tricky to land on because of the pounding surf. This makes the beaches firmly packed, though sand dunes rise behind Punta Ositos and the southernmost beach.

At one time these beaches were "farmed" for their clams. An enterprising pilot airlifted the clams directly from the beaches to California. Little remains of the "clam farm." The beaches are firm enough to land an airplane on though a small airstrip lies atop a low plateau nearby.

The coast continues for about 4 miles in a series of rocky points and small beaches to Punta Negra, a dark, rocky point living up to its name. A small crescent-shaped beach lies behind the point and in fine weather an anchorage can be taken here. A series of rocky points and small, curved bays line the coast till Punta Rocosa, a steep, 75' cliff marks the end of a ridge extending out to the coast.

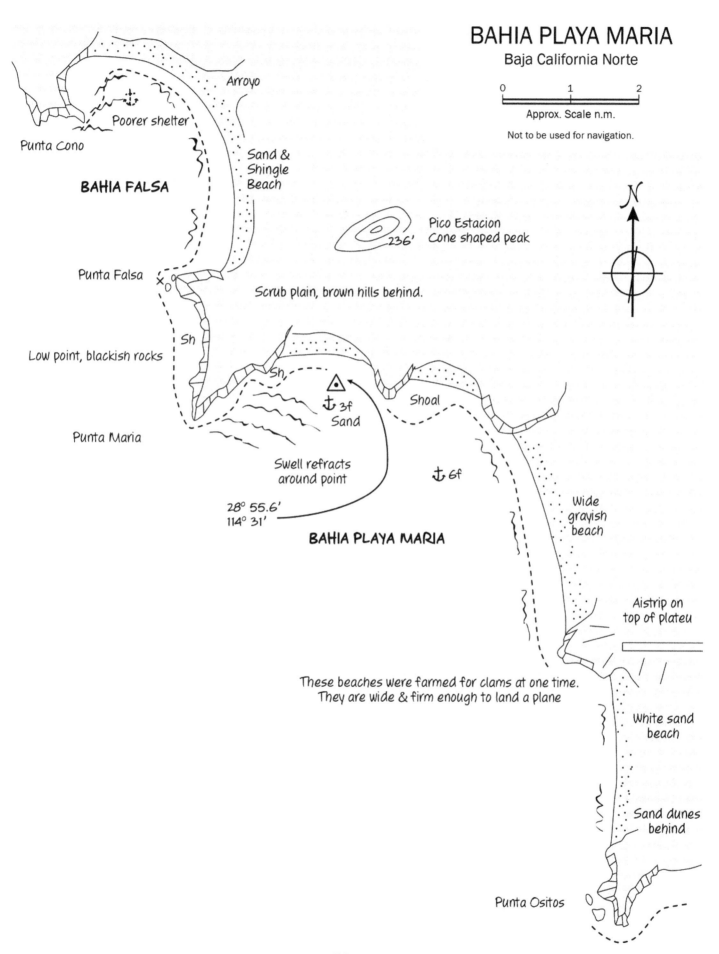

BAHIA PLAYA MARIA
Baja California Norte

0   1   2

Approx. Scale n.m.

Not to be used for navigation.

Arroyo

Poorer shelter

Punta Cono

BAHIA FALSA

Sand & Shingle Beach

Pico Estacion
Cone shaped peak

236'

Punta Falsa

Scrub plain, brown hills behind.

Low point, blackish rocks

Sh

Sh

Shoal

⚓ 3f
Sand

Punta Maria

Swell refracts around point

⚓ 6f

Wide grayish beach

28° 55.6'
114° 31'

BAHIA PLAYA MARIA

Airstrip on top of plateu

These beaches were farmed for clams at one time.
They are wide & firm enough to land a plane

White sand beach

Sand dunes behind

Punta Ositos

BAHIA SANTA ROSALILITA

Punta Santa Rosalilita is a black, rocky point that shelters **Bahia Santa Rosalilita**. A landing strip is located on top of the plateau in addition to parts of an older airstrip. They form a distinctive z-shaped landmark that can sometimes be made out from seaward since the top of the plateau is sloped.

A small islet, Isla Elide, about 40' high and white with guano, lies a short distance off the point. A shoal and sand spit connect the island to the point.

East of Punta Santa Rosalilita is a small, deeply scalloped sandy beach before which a rocky, angular point thrusts sharply south for about half a mile. The eastern side of the point is shoal and swell refracting around the point breaks on the shallow areas. A breakwater encloses a basin off the sandy beach that curves around the bay to end at an arroyo just beneath the upthrust plateau. This is the first construction of a long-standing plan to build a series of marinas along the Baja coast to form a stairway of facilities (escalera). It was intended to be the western terminus of a road crossing the Baja peninsula from Bahia de Los Angeles that would allow vessels to be transported by truck from the upper Sea of Cortez. The plan is presently on hold awaiting final decisions by the Mexican government.

The bay is spacious enough to allow you to find an anchorage spot that is reasonably comfortable and unaffected by the swell. Anchor well out in the bay to avoid the shoals which line the shores; the holding is good in 5 to 8 fathoms, sand. **WPT 28°39.8', 114°14.2'.**

Two arroyos break through the plateau in the northeastern part of the bay. A small fish camp is located where the larger one, Arroyo Santa Dominiquito, opens up on the pebble beach.

A small arroyo to the north ends roughly where the sandy beach curves around to join the plateau. Some of the buildings on the beach are the remains of a meteorological station that has been taken over and used as a fish camp. The bay may have many lobster receivers scattered about in season, necessitating care when maneuvering in the area. Landing ashore can be hazardous unless the weather is calm or you are experienced in landing through surf.

BAHIA SANTA ROSALILITA

Baja California Norte

0   1   2

Approx. Scale n.m.

Not to be used for navigation.

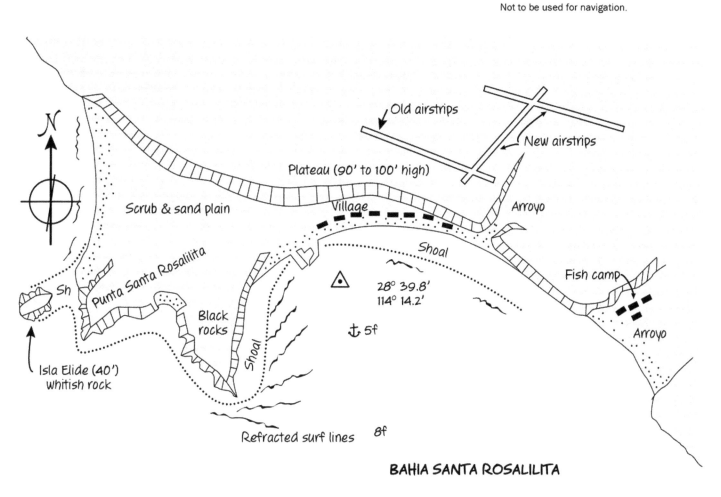

BAHIA SANTA ROSALILITA

MORRO SANTO DOMINGO

The southeasterly trending coast ends at a black, bold, rocky headland that stands out in relation to the otherwise low, sandy shoreline. A light is located on the south tip of this headland, Morro Santo Domingo. There is a small bay sheltered by the point, but shoals limit its usefulness.

Just under the lee of the point an anchorage in about 5 fathoms can be found clear of the outer shoal that begins at the entrance to Laguna Manuela. **WPT 28°14.4', 114°05.3'.** However, the confining shoals to leeward and the windswept bay make this useful only as an emergency or fair weather anchorage.

The openings to the lagoons commence south of Morro Santo Domingo. The lagoons wind into the flat, sandy saltpan section of the peninsula that forms Desierto de Vizcaino.

The northernmost of these lagoons is Laguna Manuela. The opening into the lagoon is between large shoal areas with breaking seas on either side. Tidal currents are strong in the passage leading to a curved and winding route behind the outer shoal. This leads into the lagoon and appears suitable only for shoal draft vessels, dinghies or pangas. Tidal currents are strong in this passage. A low sand spit separates the lagoon from the sea, extending southward into a wide area of sand dunes with high bluffs.

The difficulties of entrance and exit, the numerous shoals and shifting bars, the lines of cresting surf, the lee shores and the swift tidal currents combine to make this section of the coast demand the maximum of caution and are not recommended. The lagoons would be interesting to explore if properly marked, but they are closed to general use since they are a Wildlife Refuge for gray whales, which breed and give birth in the calm, protected waters.

Laguna Guerrero Negro is south of Laguna Manuela. It is a larger lagoon, which can only be entered by pangas at high water for the entrance is blocked by sand at low water. The town of Guerrero Negro lies on the east side of the lagoon, just a few miles off the main Baja Hwy.1. Since Guerrero Negro can be reached both by car and by airplane it is a convenient destination for tourists arriving to view the gray whales in Scammon's Lagoon and to enjoy the marvelous bird-watching that can be had in Laguna Guerrero Negro. Between Guerrero Negro and Scammon's Lagoon is a white sand beach backed by extensive dunes. This is Scavenger's Beach, on which can be gathered an interesting collection of flotsam and jetsam.

Scammon's Lagoon (Laguna Ojo de Liebre) is the largest of these lagoons, the most historic and best known. A marked channel leads to huge salt loading facilities, but since there are no facilities for other vessels, entrance to the lagoon is not advisable. Cruisers are discouraged from entering the lagoon except in an emergency.

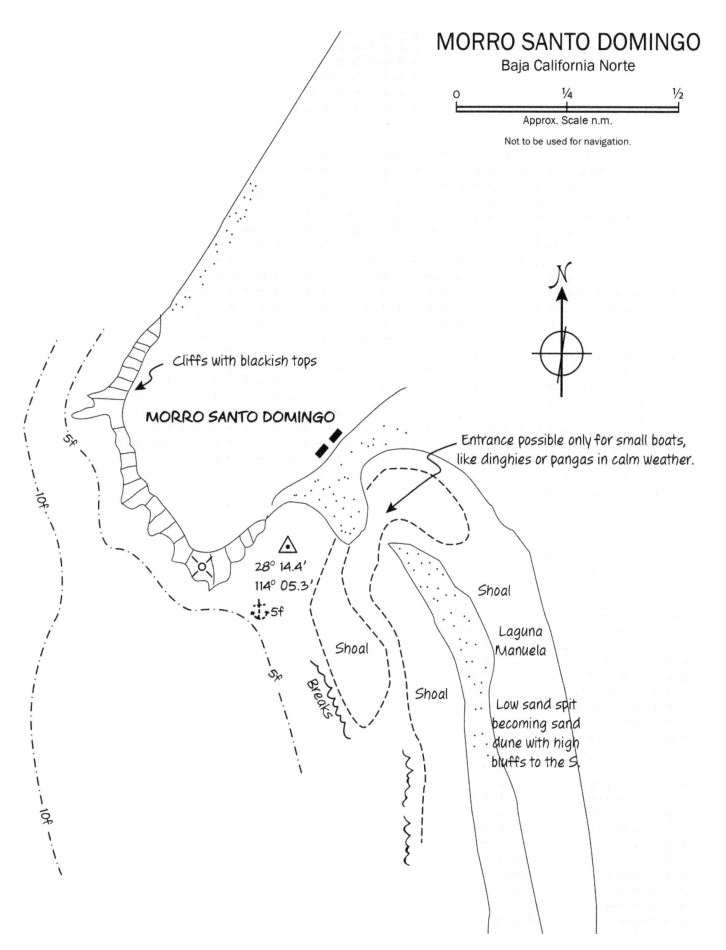

MORRO SANTO DOMINGO
Baja California Norte

0   ¼   ½
Approx. Scale n.m.

Not to be used for navigation.

N

Cliffs with blackish tops

MORRO SANTO DOMINGO

Entrance possible only for small boats, like dinghies or pangas in calm weather.

5f

10f

28° 14.4'
114° 05.3'

5f

5f

Shoal

Breaks

Shoal

Shoal

Laguna Manuela

Low sand spit becoming sand dune with high bluffs to the S.

10f

ISLAS SAN BENITOS

The sketch shows Bahia de Sebastian Viscaino and the relationship of Isla Cedros (and the outlying Islas San Benitos) to the various bays and anchorages on the Baja coast previously described. It will be of assistance when considering a choice of routes when traveling along this coast.

The south shore of Bahia de Sebastian Viscaino continues the low and sandy character found near the lagoons, with shoals running well offshore. At Punta de Malarrimo the coast changes to a series of rocky bluffs and small beaches and the coastal mountains rise close behind the shore. Since much of the southern coast is a lee shore open to swell and winds, there are no anchorages which can be recommended.

Islas San Benitos, 15 miles west of Isla Cedros, are well-known among fishermen who visit the area for its excellent fishing, particularly on Ranger Bank which is about 6.5 miles north of Benito del Este. The group is composed of three main islands: Benito del Oeste, Benito del Centro and Benito del Este (west, central and east) with several small rock outcroppings. Benito del Oeste is the largest of the three islands and is the site of a small fishing village. Benito del Centro and Benito del Este are small, uninhabited, rugged islands.

Two lighthouses are situated on Benito del Oeste, the one on a hill near the west coast can be seen up to 28 miles offshore. A smaller light is located on the south coast of this island.

Canal de Peck separates Benito del Este from Benito del Oeste and Benito del Centro. When northwesterly winds are blowing anchorage can be taken off the village of **Benito del Oeste** in 5 to 10 fathoms. **WPT 28°18', 115°34.7'**. Sometimes this means anchoring in or very near the kelp, the extent of which varies from year to year. During northeasterly weather the best anchorage is in the indentation off the southwestern shore of **Benito del Centro, WPT 28°18.4', 115°34.25'**. The amount of kelp surrounding the islands varies with the prevailing water temperatures, ranging from negligible during El Nino years when the water is warmer, to profuse and extensive during normal periods of cold water.

An elephant seal colony resides on Benito del Centro. Visitors are encouraged to watch them from the water since going ashore will unduly disturb them. Local fishermen are keen to sell or trade their lobster (langosta) to visiting yachtsmen.

The adjoining sketch shows the passage between Isla Cedros and Bahia San Bartolome (Turtle Bay). Canal de Dewey, between Isla Natividad and Punta Eugenia, is 4 miles wide, but the eastern side should be favored. Foul ground and irregular depths with kelp beds extend about 1½ miles southeast of Isla Natividad into Canal de Dewey. A clear passage of at least 1 mile wide beginning 1 mile off Punta Eugenia is available. Currents can be strong through this channel, as well as localized wind. A village with a prominent white church is located in the southern part of Isla Natividad. North of the village is a prominent white light structure on a hill. Indifferent anchorage can be taken off the island but shoals and rocks in the vicinity make use of a detailed chart necessary.

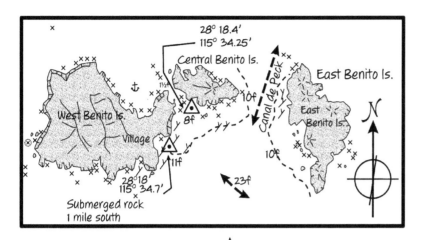

ISLAS SAN BENITOS

Baja California Norte

Approx. Scale n.m.

Not to be used for navigation.

28° 18.4'
115° 34.25'

Central Benito Is.

East Benito Is.

East Benito Is.

West Benito Is.

Canal de Peck

10f

10f

8f

Village

11f

23f

28° 18'
115° 34.7'

Submerged rock
1 mile south

N

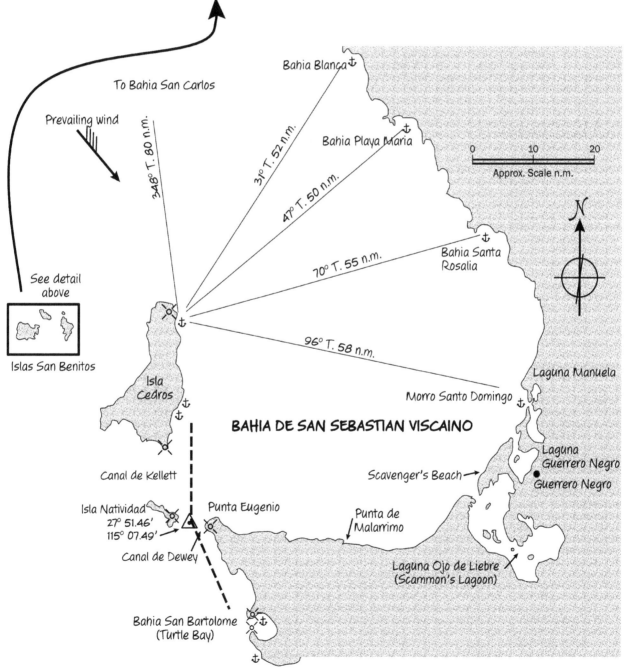

Bahia Blanca

To Bahia San Carlos

Prevailing wind

348° T. 80 n.m.

31° T. 52 n.m.

Bahia Playa Maria

47° T. 50 n.m.

70° T. 55 n.m.

Bahia Santa
Rosalia

See detail
above

Islas San Benitos

96° T. 58 n.m.

Laguna Manuela

Isla
Cedros

Morro Santo Domingo

BAHIA DE SAN SEBASTIAN VISCAINO

N

0   10   20

Approx. Scale n.m.

Laguna
Guerrero Negro

Guerrero Negro

Scavenger's Beach

Canal de Kellett

Isla Natividad
27° 51.46'
115° 07.49'

Punta Eugenio

Punta de
Malarrimo

Canal de Dewey

Laguna Ojo de Liebre
(Scammon's Lagoon)

Bahia San Bartolome
(Turtle Bay)

ISLA GUADALUPE

This is the westernmost part of Mexico, as the island lies about 140 nautical miles WSW of Punta Baja, the nearest land on the coast. Although rarely visited, the island is sometimes of interest to vessels traveling southward on an offshore route and for marine scientists researching its rich and varied marine life. Permission may be needed to go ashore when visiting the island. Ask the Port Captain in Ensenada if paperwork is required.

The barren island is high and of volcanic origin and its red, yellow, rusty brown, black and gold colored cliffs provide a spectacular sight especially when the early morning and late afternoon sun highlights its dramatic colors. It is about 20 miles long and 6 miles in maximum width. Only a few fishermen, some meteorologists and Mexican Navy personnel inhabit it. Clearance to travel to the island should be obtained from the nearest Port of Entry or Consular Office. Permission for landing should be requested of the Naval Commandant when at the island. There is normally no difficulty about either and the isolated inhabitants are always happy to have visitors.

Though there are several anchoring areas the three most important are the Northeast, South and West Anchorages. **The Northeast Anchorage** is within the open bay about 1½ miles south and in the lee of Punta del Norte. Like Isla Cedros, this anchorage is on a shelf, very close to the beach in about 4 fathoms, gravel bottom. It is a good anchorage, usually well protected. **WPT 28°9.5', 118°16.5'.**

The South Anchorages lie in the lee of the great cliffs of Morro Sur in Caleta Melpomene (named after the survey ship which explored it) in 10 fathoms, or in the small cove at the tip of the island at the Meteorological Station. Most shrimpers seem to prefer the former and yachts the latter anchorage. At Caleta Melpomene landing is possible on a small, sandy beach, where elephant seals congregate. **WPT 28°52.9', 118°17.5'** Landing can also be made near the Commandant's office, on the rocky outcrop behind the group of offshore rocks. Passage through the gaps between the point and the islands can be made but the tidal stream is sometimes quite strong. Tuna Alley is the local name given to the area near Caleta Melpomene since tuna are often found in abundance.

On the west side of the island is the **West Anchorage** at Jack's Bay, in the lee of the cliffs and plateau of Punta Oeste. **WPT 28°58.2', 118°17.6'.** A reef and scattered rocks extend southward from the point and should be avoided by approaching the bay from the south. The anchorage is about 1,000 ft. off a small rock slide on the east side and as the bottom is rocky, a chain rode is needed. Although the holding is poorer than elsewhere and there is some swell, this anchorage is the nearest one to the village.

Provisions and water cannot be obtained on the island, though seafood is plentiful. The island is a wildlife refuge, home to elephant seals, sea lions, Guadalupe fur seals and over 100 species of sharks, including great whites and whale sharks. Marine scientists consider this to be one of the richest concentrations of sharks in the world. Wild goats are abundant on the island and have caused problems for vegetation and small fauna because of their omnivorous diet.

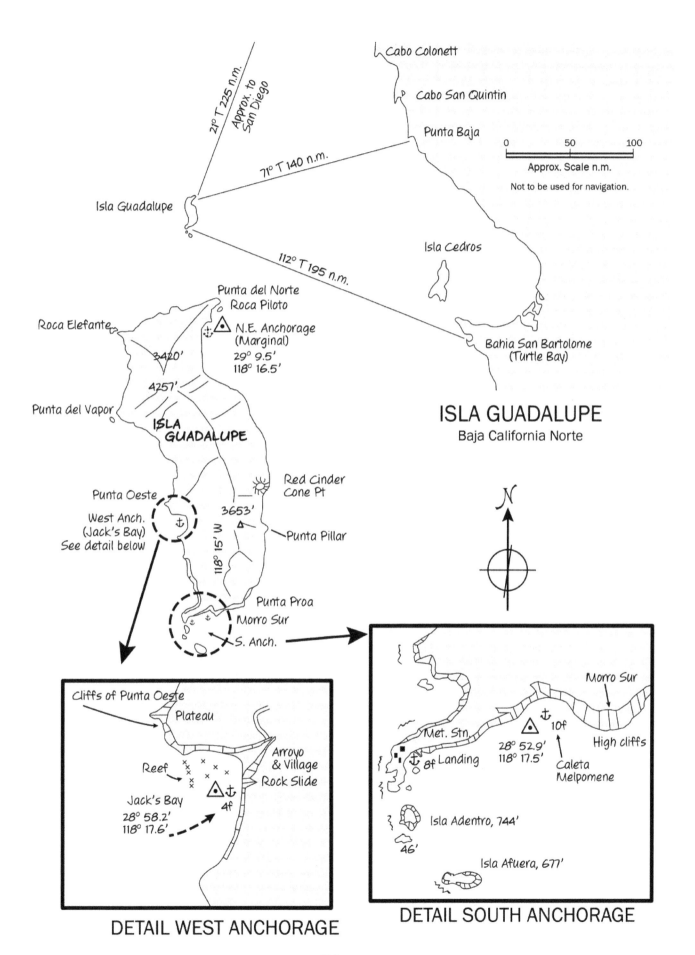

Cabo Colonett

Cabo San Quintin

Punta Baja

0   50   100

Approx. Scale n.m.

Not to be used for navigation.

2º T 225 n.m.
Approx. to San Diego

71º T 140 n.m.

Isla Guadalupe

112º T 195 n.m.

Isla Cedros

Punta del Norte
Roca Piloto

Roca Elefante

N.E. Anchorage
(Marginal)
29º 9.5'
118º 16.5'

3420'

4257'

Punta del Vapor

ISLA
GUADALUPE

Bahia San Bartolome
(Turtle Bay)

ISLA GUADALUPE
Baja California Norte

Punta Oeste

West Anch.
(Jack's Bay)
See detail below

Red Cinder
Cone Pt

3653'

Punta Pillar

118º 15' W

N

Punta Proa
Morro Sur
S. Anch.

Cliffs of Punta Oeste

Plateau

Reef

Arroyo
& Village
Rock Slide

Jack's Bay
28º 58.2'
118º 17.6'

4f

Morro Sur

Met. Stn

8f Landing

28º 52.9'
118º 17.5'

10f

High cliffs

Caleta
Melpomene

Isla Adentro, 744'

46'

Isla Afuera, 677'

DETAIL WEST ANCHORAGE

DETAIL SOUTH ANCHORAGE

ISLA CEDROS

Caution: GPS positions can be as much as 2 miles off in this location.
Isla Cedros is about 21 miles long and varies in width from 2 miles near the northern end to 9 miles at the southern end. Of volcanic origin, it has a backbone of steep mountains culminating in Cerro de Cedros 3,950'. It can usually be sighted from the Baja coast though fog and haze may hide the island till one is close. It is located where wind, waves, fog and other weather patterns often combine to make the crossing from the mainland challenging.

Departure for the crossing should be timed so that a landfall at either end is made during daylight. The island is not abundantly supplied with navigation lights and since some of the anchorages lie close inshore they are difficult to approach in darkness.

The most used anchorages are along the eastern shore of the island. Cabo Norte is the northern point of the island. Somewhat south of the northeastern tip of the cape is a light on a low, sandy point which shelters the village anchorage. South of this is a shelf which runs for some distance along the coast where good anchorage can be found very close to the beach in about 4 to 6 fathoms. This is the **North Anchorage, WPT 29°9.5', 118°16.5',** and it is a popular departure area where many vessels can be accommodated when traveling north or as a landfall when southbound. Northbound vessels can enjoy a quiet dinner and a few hours of sleep prior to departing after the wind settles. Anchorage in the lee of the various rock buttresses is preferred, for gusty winds often blow out of the arroyos as is evidenced by the alternating pattern of calm and whitecaps seen on the water. A colony of sea lions inhabit the nearby shore, providing a nightly cacophony with their barking, while at the same time giving grace and beauty in a phosphorescent underwater ballet as they swim around the boat. This is a memorable anchorage.

About 4 miles south of the North Anchorage is another anchorage off a long arroyo. Here, a trail leads to the island divide from which offshore views in both directions can be obtained. About 7 miles further south is a small beach where palms grow, giving the location the name, La Palmita. Anchorage can be taken on the shelf close to shore where Spanish galleons once stopped to take on fresh water from the nearby springs. This makes a nice day stop to explore the beach and investigate the concrete cistern where fishermen come to supply themselves with fresh water.

The quickly growing, busy town of Cedros is about 3 miles further south. **WPT 28°05.64', 115°10.90'** A breakwater encloses the harbor which is often congested with fish boats. Cruisers who wish to visit the town usually anchor either to the north or south of the breakwaters. Care is needed to avoid fish traps and holding tanks northeast of the breakwater. Landings can be made from both anchorages and since this is a **Port of Entry** you must report to Port Captain if you are anchored in either location. The Port Captain's office (Capitania) is a half mile walk through the town, keeping to the main road when walking up the hill until passing a large liquor store. The Customs office is just to the north of the southern breakwater. Groceries, liquor and basic supplies are available but fuel may be obtained only in an emergency. Be aware that tugs and barges loaded with salt frequent this area.

An isolated anchorage with protection from northwesterly winds is in a notch at the western end of Bahia del Sur, but care is necessary to avoid rocks close to shore. Though the island appears barren, there are remains of its once great groves of pine, oak and junipers, the latter having been identified as "cedars" by early Spanish explorers who gave the island its name. Gold and copper were once mined here. Today the conspicuous salt depot at Morro Redondo and the equally noticeable odors from the town's fish fertilizer plant are evidence of the main business enterprises of this area.

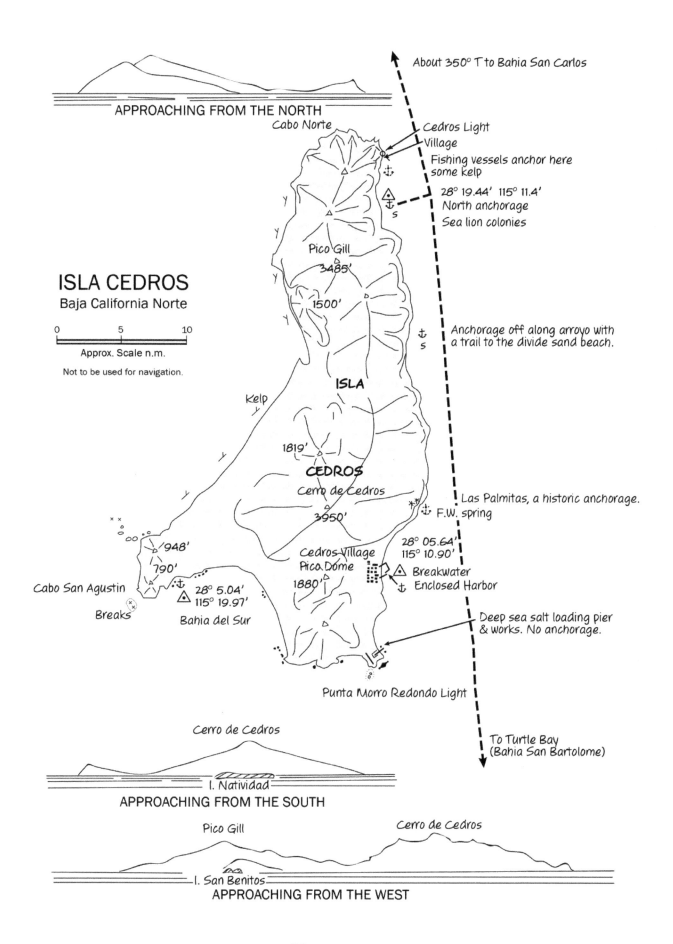

APPROACHING FROM THE NORTH

About 350° T to Bahia San Carlos

Cabo Norte

Cedros Light
Village
Fishing vessels anchor here
some kelp

28° 19.44' 115° 11.4'
North anchorage
Sea lion colonies

Pico Gill
3485'

1500'

ISLA CEDROS
Baja California Norte

0   5   10
Approx. Scale n.m.

Not to be used for navigation.

Anchorage off along arroyo with
a trail to the divide sand beach.

Kelp

ISLA

1819'

CEDROS
Cerro de Cedros

3950'

Las Palmitas, a historic anchorage.
F.W. spring

28° 05.64'
115° 10.90'

948'

790'

Cedros Village
Pico Dome
1880'

Breakwater
Enclosed Harbor

Cabo San Agustin

28° 5.04'
115° 19.97'

Breaks

Bahia del Sur

Deep sea salt loading pier
& works. No anchorage.

Punta Morro Redondo Light

To Turtle Bay
(Bahia San Bartolome)

Cerro de Cedros

I. Natividad
APPROACHING FROM THE SOUTH

Pico Gill

Cerro de Cedros

I. San Benitos
APPROACHING FROM THE WEST

TURTLE BAY (Bahia Tortugas or Port San Bartolome)

There are few turtles seen nowadays in Turtle Bay, a name yachtsmen use for what is labeled as Port San Bartolome on U.S. Hydrographic charts. This is the best all-weather harbor in this part of the coast and it is a popular spot to relax after the open roadstead anchorages that have preceded it. Vessels may be boarded for inspection by members of the Naval detachment.

Punta Sargazo (Kelp Point), an aptly descriptive name, is the northern point of the entrance to the bay. It lies about 16 miles southeast of Punta Eugenia. As detached rocks and kelp beds extend out from and around the point it should be given a wide berth when passing.

The southern point of the entrance is Cabo Tortola, the end of a steep promontory composed of hills rising up to 400 ft. A reef extends NNW from the cape for about 1 mile into the entrance, with four prominent rocks marking its line.

The entrance is almost 3/4 mile wide, though it appears to be narrower. **WPT 27°38.5', 114°54'.** A course through the center of the passage is straightforward and provides depths of about 10 fathoms. A navigation light is located on a small point east of the village where a range of hills terminate at the shore. The large red and white cell tower and its red lights are also good targets. A wide, dry wash extends over a considerable area eastward of this point.

Two main anchorage areas are within the bay. The normal transient anchorage is in the northwest part, off the village and pier in 4 to 5 fathoms, black, sandy bottom. This anchorage has excellent holding, but it is exposed to southwesterly winds and is slightly affected by swell entering around Punta Sargazo. A long pier 400 ft. extends out from a beach on which dinghy landings can be made through gentle surf.

The other anchorage, tucked behind Cabo Tortola in the southern bight, is best in southerly winds but is affected by northerly winds. The bay shoals from some distance, but a good spot is east of and in the lee of the Cape, off the little point with a fish camp ashore. Anchorage can be taken in 4 fathoms, sand bottom and landing be made at a corner or the long, sandy Playa Almejas (Clams). Watch for numerous rows of buoys used for farming scallops and anchor well clear of them.

Don't be surprised if you are approached by pangas as you enter the bay, trying to get your business. Enrique's on the pier has been in business for years and is famous for never having change and over estimating the capacity of your fuel tank. (Really? There are 100 sailboats in the bay during the Baja Ha Ha and you can't make change? How can you fit 55 gallons of fuel in my 50 gallon tank?) Very large vessels will need to med tie to the rickety pier.

Gas may be purchased at the Pemex station in town using your jerry cans. Ask the fuel vendors about filling your propane tanks. They can also arrange water in 5 gallon bottles to be delivered to your boat (a few dollars each) or to the beach (for pennies) where you load up the dinghy, and take it to your boat yourself. Remember to return the bottles as soon as you are done.

Pangas often provide water-taxi service for going ashore to shop or have a meal. Groceries and liquor, are available at numerous markets in town, as well as an auto parts store, hardware, Western Union, internet café, small hotels, clinic, tackle shop. Laundry may be left to be done overnight – ask your fuel vendor. There are many places to get a good meal from evenings-only taco stands, to some rather nice seafood places.

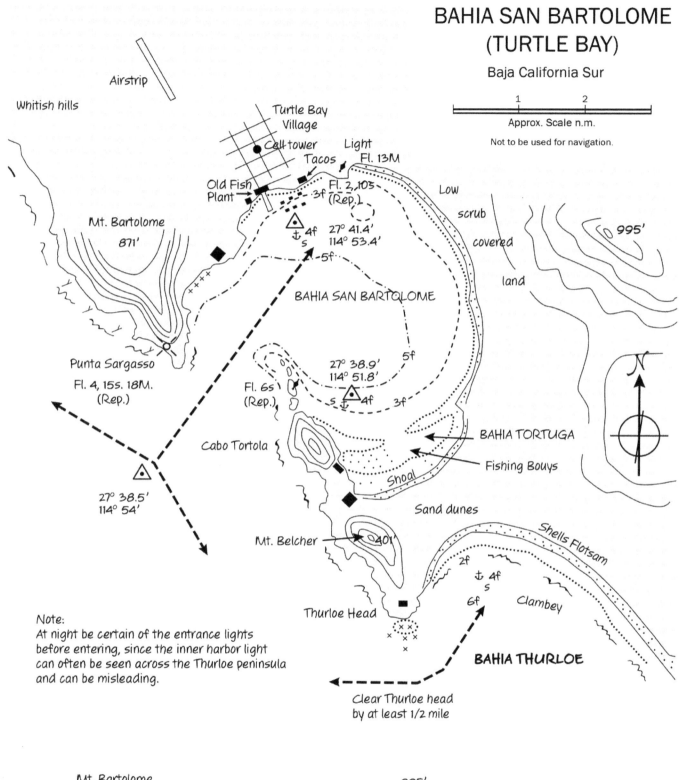

BAHIA SAN BARTOLOME
(TURTLE BAY)
Baja California Sur

Approx. Scale n.m.

Not to be used for navigation.

Airstrip

Whitish hills

Turtle Bay Village

Cell tower

Light
Fl. 13M

Tacos

Old Fish Plant

Fl. 2, 10s (Rep.)

Low scrub covered land

Mt. Bartolome 871'

3f

4f 27° 41.4'
    114° 53.4'
s

5f

BAHIA SAN BARTOLOME

995'

Punta Sargasso

Fl. 4, 15s. 18M. (Rep.)

5f

27° 38.9'
114° 51.8'

Fl. 6s (Rep.)

s 4f 3f

Cabo Tortola

BAHIA TORTUGA

27° 38.5'
114° 54'

Fishing Bouys

Shoal

Sand dunes

Shells Flotsam

Mt. Belcher 401'

2f

Note:
At night be certain of the entrance lights before entering, since the inner harbor light can often be seen across the Thurloe peninsula and can be misleading.

Thurloe Head

4f
s

6f Clambey

BAHIA THURLOE

Clear Thurloe head by at least 1/2 mile

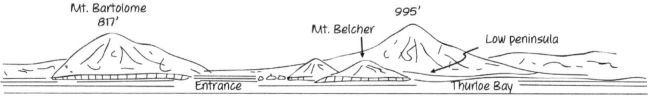

Mt. Bartolome 817'

995'

Mt. Belcher

Low peninsula

Entrance

Thurloe Bay

APPROACHING TURTLE BAY ROM THE SOUTHWEST

Looking out to sea from Turtle Bay.

The cell towers in Turtle Bay are a good landmark.

The Pier in Turtle Bay.

The tackle shop owned by Russ, an expat. Great folks who know everything about Turtle Bay.

BAHIA THURLOE (CLAMBEY)

Thurloe Bay is separated from Turtle Bay by low sand dunes sprinkled with a few grassy tufts. To reach it by boat you should give Thurloe Head a clear offing to avoid the reef that projects about ½ mile south of it. Anchorage may be taken at the head of the bay in 4 to 6 fathoms, sand. This is a worthwhile area to beachcomb on a day trip from Turtle Bay, as there are many interesting shells and bones ashore. Landing ashore can be an educational experience since the surf appears to be less turbulent when viewed from the water. Watch the waves and find a flat spot.

From Thurloe Head the beaches of the bay continue till they end in steep bluffs leading to Morro Hermoso, a high headland. Thereafter the shores of Bahia San Cristoval become low bluffs before being followed by a long, low sandy zone. The dark, high bluff of Morro San Pablo indicates the end of the long bay. Two smaller bays, Bahia de San Pablo and Bahia de San Roque follow, separated by the 500' high, lighter colored bulk of Punta San Roque. The mountains behind these bays show steep, eroded sides with variegated colors. The land looks barren, lonely and rugged, but with a stark beauty.

Isla San Roque is about 4 miles southeast of Morro San Pablo and lies about 2 miles off the coast. It is a long, low, rocky island with the huts of a fish camp near its western end. Strong currents setting east are known to occur irregularly in this area. If your course passes near the island your position should be monitored carefully.

BAHIA ASUNCION

The launching ramp and dinghy landing.

Bahia San Roque ends at Punta Asuncion, a low sandy point ending in a conical hill about 75' high. Isla Asuncion lies about ¾ mile south of this point and is roughly 50 miles southeast of Turtle Bay. Both Isla Asuncion and Isla San Roque blend into the background when seen from seaward and are only clearly made out from certain directions or when nearby.

A shallow bank, with a rocky patch awash lies between the island and the point. Though a passage exists closer to the point it is not recommended. To be on the safe side, continue in a wide arc around the southern end of the island to clear the detached rocks that lie ¼ mile off its tip. **WPT 27°05', 144°16'.** A rock, exposed at times, is about ½ mile west of the north end of Isla Asuncion.

By continuing well up into the lee of Punta Asuncion, good anchorage can be taken near the head of the bay in 4 - 5 fathoms, sand. At times the surf makes landing ashore tricky. This friendly, clean town is built along the waterfront and has a number of stores, restaurants and an Internet cafe. In some eateries, it may be necessary to purchase beer at the deposito to take back to the restaurant. Fuel is available at the Pemex station via jerry cans.

Anchorage in 4 to 5 fathoms may also be taken in the lee of the barren sandstone hump of Isla Asuncion, off an abandoned house on the plateau below the hill. But to drop the hook here you must be a keen bird-watcher, capable of withstanding the stench of mounds of fresh and aging guano, and flies in season. The island is home to thousands of sea birds and the rocky shores are a favorite area for seals and sea lions to haul out for rest and sun bathing.

Cormorants darken the hillsides of Isla Asuncion

VIEW FROM THE NORTHWEST

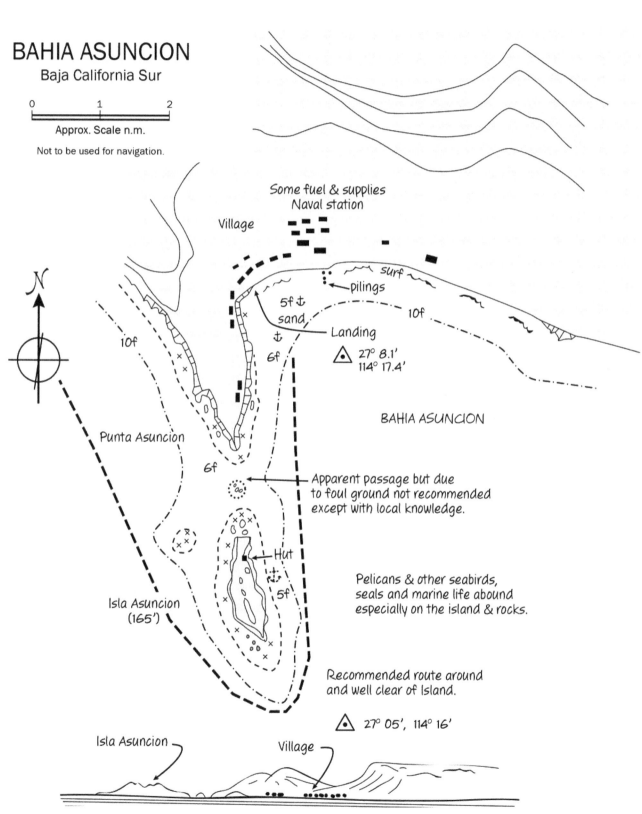

BAHIA ASUNCION
Baja California Sur

0   1   2
Approx. Scale n.m.

Not to be used for navigation.

Some fuel & supplies
Naval station

Village

N

surf

pilings

5f ⚓
sand
Landing
⚓
△ 27° 8.1'
    114° 17.4'

10f

10f

BAHIA ASUNCION

Punta Asuncion

6f

6f

Apparent passage but due
to foul ground not recommended
except with local knowledge.

Hut

Isla Asuncion
(165')

5f

Pelicans & other seabirds,
seals and marine life abound
especially on the island & rocks.

Recommended route around
and well clear of Island.

△ 27° 05', 114° 16'

Isla Asuncion

Village

PUNTA ABREOJOS

The long, narrow bight of Bahia Asuncion is followed by Bahia San Hipolito which is about 19 miles to the southeast. Anchorage may be taken off the village which is reported to vary from fair to good, depending on sea conditions. The next anchorage is an additional 30 miles down the coast at Punta Abreojos.

Most of the intervening shoreline is sandy with several lagoon openings, all of which are dry except for Pond Lagoon. At the north side of the entrance to the lagoon a long reef projects almost a mile southward. When approaching from the north the coast should be given a wide berth to clear the reef and nearby shoals. In moderate weather and good visibility the skipper can choose an inshore passage to turn Punta Abreojos. In any other conditions it is wiser to stand offshore until south of the point before turning to reach it. The Spanish words "abre ojos" mean "open the eyes" and this meaningful label should be taken seriously for this is an area with significant dangers.

Southbound, when the entrance to Pond Lagoon is past the beam, close the coast to the 5-fathom curve then turn to follow it down the coast toward the point. This course will leave Roca Ballena (Whale Rock) and the other offshore reefs about 3/4 mile to seaward. Roca Ballena is generally visible for the sea breaking on it can throw up spume similar to a blowing whale. Breakers indicate the location of other nearby reefs.

Continue along the 5-fathom line and when nearing the point stay just outside the beginning of the large swells that roll in to break on Punta Abreojos. On one occasion we towed three pangas back to the village and the advice of the local fishermen was to follow this line and it kept us clear of Wright Shoal while passing in good water around the point. Though breaking seas are said to be seen over parts of Wright Shoal and Knepper Shoal we have not observed any and this lack of definition of a shoal leaves a skipper very much in doubt of their exact location. Many lobster receivers are scattered in the anchorage areas in season and care must be exercised not to foul them.

Northbound, the entrance is straightforward as long as Bajos Wright and Bajos Knepper are identified and avoided. If approaching from offshore, it must be from the south. Lay a course to pass between Wright and Knepper Shoals to enter directly into the first anchorage. **WPT 26°41', 113° 33'.** A night approach to this area should be by making the most of careful navigation.

A reasonable anchorage is found in the lee of the point off the village, in 5 to 6 fathoms, sand. Wind crossing the low point can sweep the anchorage raising wind waves. With care and good timing, landing can be made through the surf on to the beach near the pangas. A somewhat quieter anchorage further from the village can be taken in the cove to the east of the Abreojos anchorage, in 4 to 5 fathoms, sand.

Ashore, you will find a pleasant town with groceries, fuel at the Pemex station, taco stands etc. Diesel and gas are both available via jerry cans, and the staff at the Pemex have been known to drive your jerry cans to the beach near your dinghy.

Laguna de San Ignacio, opening on the east side of the bay, is a whale refuge and is off limits to non official vessels. Shoal areas, with attendant breakers extend a considerable distance south of the entrance. During the whale season in the winter, a guided panga trip into the lagoon to observe the whales is a 'must do' side trip.

Abreojos. The beach and dinghy landing at Abreojos

It is advisable to check your course constantly when passing this part of the coast en route to Abreojos as there can be a very strong set toward the lagoon.

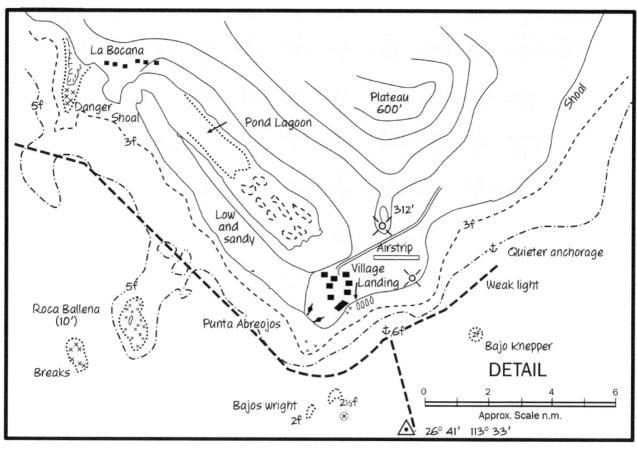

PUNTA ABREOJOS
Baja California Sur

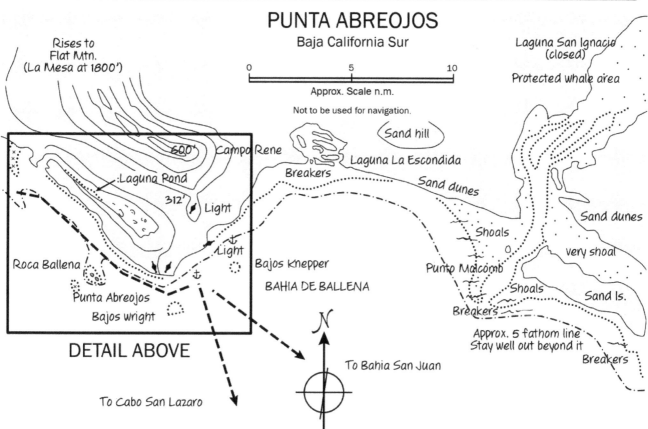

BAHIA SAN JUANICO

From Laguna de San Ignacio the low, sandy coast continues, interrupted by several lagoon entrances, all with shoals and cresting surf before them. At Punta Santo Domingo, about 40 miles southeast, the table-land extends seaward to end in a conspicuous, sharp, dark, rocky cliff almost 175' high. On its northern side the cliff is distinguished by an unusual white, sandy section; on the south side it is dark and continues for some distance beyond the point. Some protection can be obtained in the lee of this point in 6 fathoms, but the heavy swell makes this an indifferent anchorage.

It is better to proceed 10 miles further to **Bahia San Juanico**, in the lee of Punta Pequena. The indentation of bay is greater than at Santo Domingo and good anchorage can be found well into the bay off the village and cannery buildings, in about 4 fathoms. **WPT 26°15', 112°28'.** A light is located at the sandy point west of the village The bay is affected by a heavy ground swell caused by the generally shallow waters found in the area. In southerly weather this becomes a lee shore and should be avoided.

The village has varied in size and fortune and depends on the cannery for its livelihood. There are limited resources for a visiting vessel.

Punta San Juanico is about 15 miles southeast of Punta Pequena. They bear a close resemblance. Do not confuse this with BAHIA San Juanico when approaching from offshore. The cannery identifies Bahia de San Juanico as the good anchorage.

The coast curves in a long arc from Punta San Juanico to end at Cabo San Lazaro, about 75 miles to the south. Depths of 10 fathoms occur up to 3 miles offshore. The low sandy coast is cut through with several entrances leading to dry arroyos and coastal lagoons. Each entrance has a bar, breaking waves and nothing to offer cruising vessels but disaster. There is also a strong onshore current to add to the mix. Stay well offshore during this passage.

The preferred route is to sail directly between Punta Abreojos and Cabo San Lazaro, or at least between Bahia San Juanico and the cape. Though these are long passages and must be arranged to allow approach to land to occur in daylight, they are safe and prudent courses to follow.

BAHIA SAN JUANICO
Baja California Sur

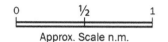

0   ½   1

Approx. Scale n.m.

Not to be used for navigation.

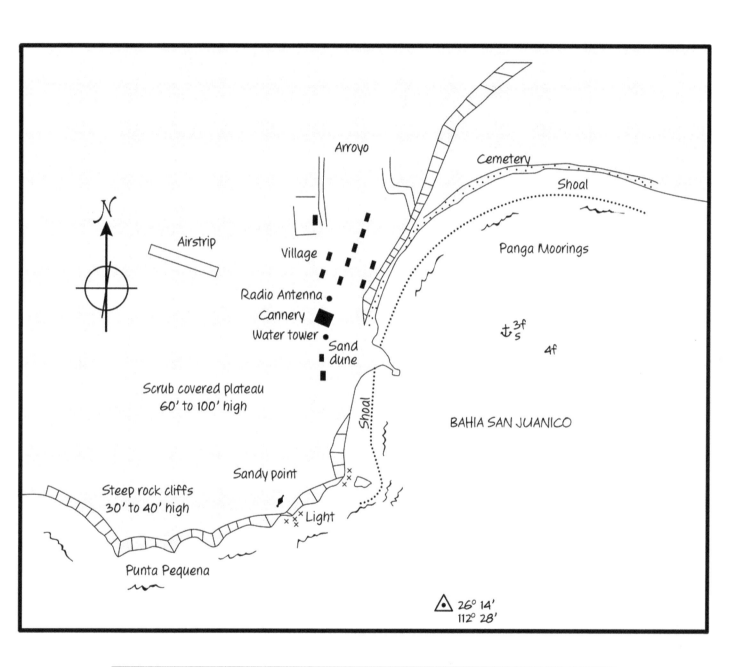

Arroyo

Cemetery

Shoal

Panga Moorings

Airstrip

Village

Radio Antenna

Cannery

Water tower

Sand dune

Scrub covered plateau
60' to 100' high

BAHIA SAN JUANICO

Shoal

Sandy point

Steep rock cliffs
30' to 40' high

Light

Punta Pequena

26° 14'
112° 28'

Note:
Punta Pequena and Punta San Juanico (which is 15 miles to the south) look very similar, but the anchorage shown above in the lee of Punta Pequena is the better spot. The cannery and rock cliffs identify Punta Pequena, while a lagoon opening and attendant surf lines identify the less satisfactory area for anchorage near Punta San Juanico.

BAHIA SANTA MARIA

Cabo San Lazaro is a bold and rocky headland rising quickly to Monte San Lazaro at 1,275'. When approaching from a distance offshore the cape may appear like an island until the high hills of the Baja peninsula show up. The cape gives good radar returns from a considerable distance. A navigation light is shown from a lighthouse situated on a shelf about 200' above the water. The current sets past the cape to the southeast and strong tidal rips are encountered near the cape. Similar to most prominent headlands the area near the cape often has strong local winds and seas.

The extensive mangroves of Bahia Santa Maria

A warning to watch the inshore setting current (during passage from either Punta Abreojos or Punta San Juanico) is underlined by the sight of wrecks, periodically seen high and dry on the beach northeast of the point. Set your course to stand well clear of the cape on your way north or south. Our waypoint to clear the point is **WPT 24°47.4', 112°22.155'.**

From Cabo San Lazaro the rocky formation of the cape continues southeasterly for about 3½ miles to Punta Hughes, the northern point of the entrance to **Bahia Santa Maria**. This lovely, clean and windswept bay is about 4 miles in width and about 11 miles long. The southern entrance point is at Howlands Bluff on Cabo Corso. The bay sweeps back forming a fairly protected bight in the northwest corner where good anchorage can be found. Old sailing skippers loved this bay for it is easy to enter, a relatively quiet place to rest and easy to sail out of again.

Because most yachts are in a hurry to get to Bahia Magdalena, or are rushing by on a return voyage, the lovely bay of Santa Maria is neglected by many cruisers, although it a stop for the Baja Ha Ha. Local fishermen maintain a fish camp near the mangrove lagoon under the lee of the cape. Tuna boats and shrimpers are frequent visitors seeking a few hours of rest in a safe haven before leaving again on their continual offshore sweeps. They usually anchor well out in the center of the bay.

Bahia Santa Maria beach landing

The small boat anchorages are either in the lee of Punta Hughes (midway up the point) on a shallow shelf, or further up near the mouth of the lagoon entrance in 6 fathoms. **WPT 24°46.27', 112°15.41'.** It is recommended that anchorage be taken about ½ mile off the beach to avoid the disturbed waters associated with the heavy surf which breaks on the entire beach within the bay. The beach becomes a narrow spit along part of its middle section. If ventured, a landing ashore is easiest through the surf near the lagoon entrance, where fishermen can sometimes be seen passing through in their pangas. Nevertheless, this is a surf landing requiring care and skill. Be sure to review the surf landing tips in the front of this guide. There are literally miles of unfrequented, pristine and lovely beaches to explore in this bay, and a very worthwhile trip into the mangrove lagoon.

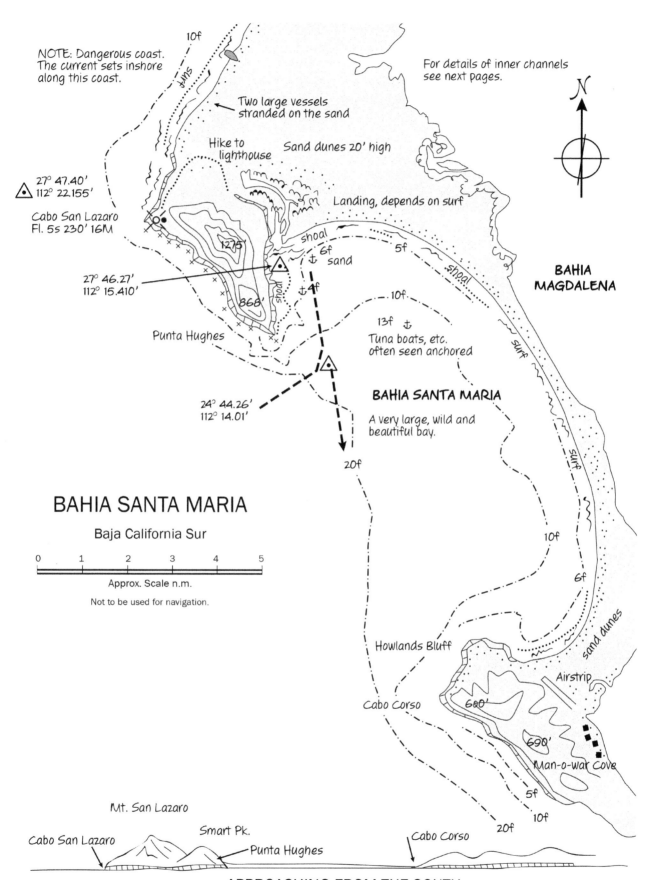

NOTE: Dangerous coast. The current sets inshore along this coast.

10f

Two large vessels stranded on the sand

Hike to lighthouse

Sand dunes 20' high

For details of inner channels see next pages.

N

27° 47.40'
112° 22.155'

Cabo San Lazaro
Fl. 5s 230' 16M

Landing, depends on surf

27° 46.27'
112° 15.410'

1275

868'

Punta Hughes

shoal

shoal

6f
sand

5f

shoal

4f

10f

13f

Tuna boats, etc.
often seen anchored

BAHIA MAGDALENA

BAHIA SANTA MARIA

24° 44.26'
112° 14.01'

A very large, wild and beautiful bay.

20f

BAHIA SANTA MARIA

Baja California Sur

0   1   2   3   4   5

Approx. Scale n.m.

Not to be used for navigation.

Howlands Bluff

Cabo Corso

600'

Airstrip

690'

sand dunes

10f

6f

Man-o-war Cove

5f

10f

20f

Mt. San Lazaro

Smart Pk.

Cabo San Lazaro

Punta Hughes

Cabo Corso

APPROACHING FROM THE SOUTH

75

BAHIA MAGDALENA

This is a large and well protected harbor which includes two spacious bays, **Bahia Magdalena** and **Bahia Almejas**. These bays are fronted on the north by the narrow sandy peninsula that ends in a high hilly section at Punta Entrada and on the south by the volcanic hills and sandy plains of Isla Santa Margarita. The deepwater entrance, which is clear of danger for over 2½ miles, lies on the western side, between Punta Entrada and Punta Redondo. A light is located at Punta Redondo.

Puerto Magdalena, before the hurricane knocked the walls down on top of the Port Captain's jeep.

The actual distance between the two points is 3¼ miles, but some outlying rocks extend about ½ mile beyond each point. At Punta Entrada they include a 20' high pinnacle rock, Roca Vela (Sail Rock), which is a good identifying landmark. The entrance is wide so there is no need to hug the coast. Since wind and current effects act southwesterly toward Punta Redondo and turbulence from the tidal current in and out of the bay is greater near the point, a course favoring the Punta Entrada side of the channel is suggested. Immediately within the entrance and in the lee of Punta Entrada is a small bight where Mexican shrimpers anchor off the

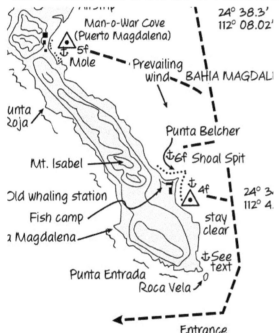

first fish camp. In settled weather it is a convenient spot and is ideal for monitoring weather conditions outside the bay. The anchorages most frequented by transient vessels visiting the bay are those at Punta Belcher and Man-O-War Cove.

Punta Belcher is a low, triangular, sandy point of land under the lee of Mount Isabel. It projects for some distance and a sandspit extends at least ¼ mile beyond the point. Shoal water lies on each side, especially to the south. The colors of the water are indicative of the shoals. Good, if windswept anchorage can be taken on either side of the point in about 6 fathoms. We have felt comfortable anchoring here at night after a passage from Cabo. **WPT 24°34.9', 112°4.3'.** The prevailing wind blows from north to south across the point. The land is sandy and covered with low scrub. On the northwest side are tanks, boilers and other remains of the whaling operations of the last century. Landing is easy, however watch for dogs who live at the fish camp.

Man-O-War Cove is about 5 miles north of Punta Belcher and when traveling to it a course well clear of the spit off Punta Belcher should be taken, watching for permanent fish holding pens. A navigation light is set near the fishing village of Puerto Magdalena. Anchorage in about 5 fathoms with good holding can be taken about ¼ mile offshore from the light. **WPT 24°38.3', 112°08.02'** This spot offers good protection from all except southeast winds. Report to the Port Captain whose home/office is a white building on the low hill overlooking the anchorage. He can arrange for jerry can fuel to be delivered by panga at Turtle Bay prices, but FILTER THE FUEL before putting it in your tanks!

There is a 'farmer's market' in San Carlos on Wednesdays and the Port Captain may be able to arrange transportation via panga for a shopping expedition. Since limited supplies are available from the small tiendas the Port Captain may also take orders for food or items not available in the village when he visits his family in San Carlos on weekends. Donations of school supplies are gladly accepted and badly needed by the local school, the fishermen are always looking for jackets and sweatshirts as they fish offshore.

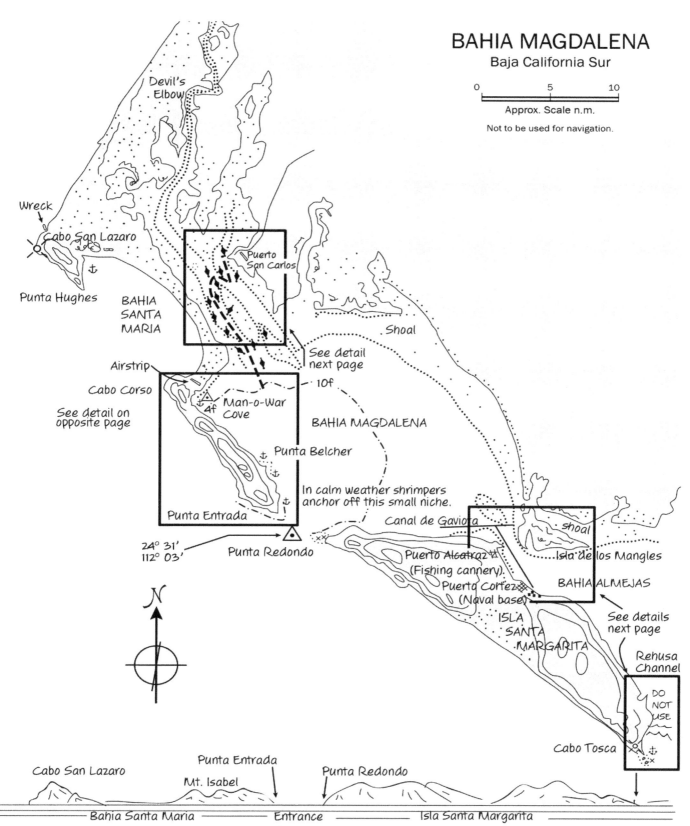

BAHIA MAGDALENA
Baja California Sur

0   5   10

Approx. Scale n.m.

Not to be used for navigation.

Devil's Elbow

Wreck

Cabo San Lazaro

Puerto San Carlos

Punta Hughes

BAHIA SANTA MARIA

Shoal

See detail next page

Airstrip

10f

Cabo Corso

See detail on opposite page

Man-o-War Cove

4f

BAHIA MAGDALENA

Punta Belcher

In calm weather shrimpers anchor off this small niche.

Canal de Gaviota

Punta Entrada

shoal

Puerto Alcatraz (Fishing cannery).

Isla de los Mangles

24° 31'
112° 03'

Punta Redondo

Puerto Cortez (Naval base)

BAHIA ALMEJAS

See details next page

N

ISLA SANTA MARGARITA

Rehusa Channel

DO NOT USE

Cabo Tosca

Cabo San Lazaro

Punta Entrada

Mt. Isabel

Punta Redondo

Bahia Santa Maria —————— Entrance —————— Isla Santa Margarita

VIEW FROM THE SOUTHWEST

BAHIA MAGDALENA (Continued)

A small airstrip lies on the flats northeast of the cove and the long, narrow, sandy spit behind Bahia Santa Maria runs northeast from there. The northwestern part of Bahia Magdalena behind this spit has many shoals and sand banks through which a narrow navigable channel has been marked by buoys leading to Puerto San Carlos. The channel can be used by small craft, taking care to keep out of the way of deep-sea freighters transporting cotton and wheat. The channel is clearly marked with red and green buoys numbered sequentially, with three white

A busy day at the beach.

buoys marking the spots where an abrupt change of direction is required. The channel has depths ranging from 4 to 10 fathoms; monitor the depth sounder as the channel shoals quickly when you approach the outer margins. Good binoculars are vital when navigating the channel.

Puerto San Carlos is a **Port of Entry** and commercial port that is not a recommended stop-over for yachts unless business commitments or fueling in large amounts require a visit. It is necessary to report to the Port Captain to pay a fee for use of the entry channel. The warehouse and loading facilities are visible as you approach and the tall smoke stack from the generating plant can be seen from well offshore. There are no facilities for yachts and broken-down shrimpers and longliners take up most of the dock. Pleasure craft must anchor, either west of the black buoy or to the north of the pier in 4 fathoms. Note the shoal area that extends almost to the edge of the wharf and be sure to allow plenty of scope for the area is windy. A charge is levied for vessels at anchor and someone should be aboard the vessel at all times. A shoal channel that is not recommended leads northward to the lagoon beyond to exit at Boca de Soledad. An airstrip is located beyond the mole and a road connects Puerto Carlos to the main Baja highway. There are no ATMs in San Carlos.

The passage from Bahia Magdalena to Bahia Almejas is via the Canal de Gaviota at the southeast corner of Bahia Magdalena. Range lights on Isla de Los Mangles (Mangrove Island) and another range roughly southeast lead into Bahia Almejas. The least depth in the channel is 6 fathoms.

The fishing village of **Puerto Alcatraz** is south of the spit and bulge of Punta Cisne. Anchorage can be taken northeast of the 350' pier. Tidal currents and occasional gusty winds make fore and aft anchors advisable.

Puerto Cortez is a Mexican naval base in a bight about 2 miles south of Puerto Alcatraz. It is marked by permanent buildings, large oil tanks and naval vessels moored in the bight. Anchorage is possible off the wharf and permission can be requested from the Commandante to go ashore. The naval personnel welcome visitors and it has been reported that they have on occasion been most helpful in solving engine problems. Fresh water is available.

Bahia Magdalena and Bahia Almejas should be exited using the normal entrance channel between Punta Entrada and Punta Redondo. Do not use Rehusa Channel between Isla Santa Margarita and Isla Cresciente at the south end of Bahia Almejas for it is a dangerous, unmarked shoal channel, with shifting bars.

Bold and rocky Cabo Tosca is the southern point of Isla Santa Margarita where a light is shown from a white tower. The seas break heavily on the rocks off the point that extend south for .5 mile. Anchorage for 4 or 5 vessels can be taken about .5 mile east of the point and in its lee. Silting of the channel and bars sometimes reduces the space for anchoring and strong currents run in and out of the channel. This is a rolly anchorage that is affected by surge and swell.

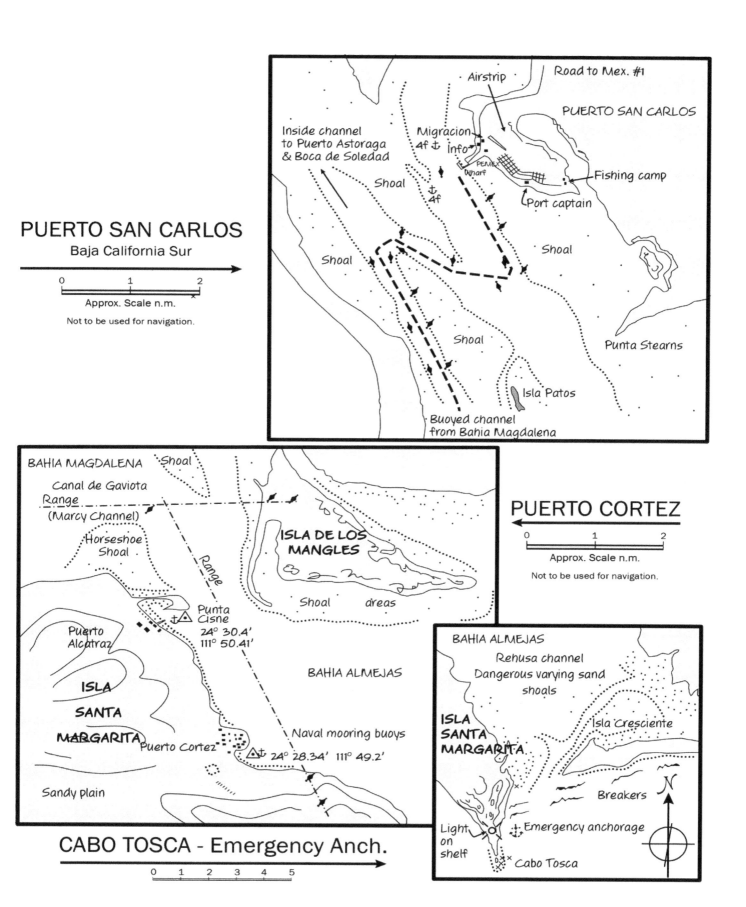

PUERTO SAN CARLOS
Baja California Sur

0   1   2
Approx. Scale n.m.

Not to be used for navigation.

Road to Mex. #1

Airstrip

PUERTO SAN CARLOS

Inside channel
to Puerto Astoraga
& Boca de Soledad

Migracion
4f ⚓ info

PEMEX
Wharf

Fishing camp

Port captain

Shoal

⚓ 4f

Shoal

Shoal

Shoal

Punta Stearns

Shoal

Isla Patos

Buoyed channel
from Bahia Magdalena

BAHIA MAGDALENA

Canal de Gaviota
Range
(Marcy Channel)

Shoal

Horseshoe
Shoal

Range

ISLA DE LOS
MANGLES

Shoal   areas

PUERTO CORTEZ

0   1   2
Approx. Scale n.m.

Not to be used for navigation.

Puerto
Alcatraz

⚓ Punta
Cisne
24° 30.4'
111° 50.41'

BAHIA ALMEJAS

ISLA
SANTA
MARGARITA

Puerto Cortez

Naval mooring buoys

⚓ 24° 28.34' 111° 49.2'

Sandy plain

BAHIA ALMEJAS

Rehusa channel
Dangerous varying sand
shoals

ISLA
SANTA
MARGARITA

Isla Cresciente

Breakers

Light
on
shelf

⚓ Emergency anchorage

Cabo Tosca

N

CABO TOSCA - Emergency Anch.

0   1   2   3   4   5

SOUTHERN BAJA — APPROACHES TO CABO SAN LUCAS

There is no suitable intermediate anchorage in the 150-mile passage between Bahia Magdalena and Cabo San Lucas and so it must be done in one step. When sailing south the direct course between the two harbors is the recommended route.

Cabo Falso is a high hill ending in a rocky bluff. It is the southernmost tip of Baja California Sur and it is clearly identified by the high, white sand drift on its eastern side and the two lighthouses on the point. The old, box-like lighthouse is near the sand drift; the new, red and white banded tower stands at the top of the 656' conical hill just back of the cape. Cabo Falso is a good radar target. An offshore **WPT 22° 49.28', 119° 58.88'**

Cabo San Lucas lies about 4 miles east of Cabo Falso. There is a long stretch of barren, scrub-covered hills behind, followed by the rocky peak of La Virgia and ending in two sharp rocky pillars over 200' high which form the unmistakable landmark for which Cabo San Lucas is known. As you get closer to the cape, more and more signs of civilization are apparent along the coastline. At some point, it becomes almost shocking after the desolate shores you have been passing. Just wait till you pass the tip and turn into the bay at Cabo!

A daily build-up of wind and seas occurs at the two capes and extends for 20 miles or more to seaward. This type of wind pattern often occurs at prominent high points that stand in a prevailing wind stream, as at Point Conception in California, or at Cabo Corrientes on the Mexican mainland coast. Crew aboard vessels moored in the quiet conditions of the lee of the hills can be quite unaware of the rough seas that may be found on the other side of the Cape. Vessels that pass the Cape well offshore are able to avoid these local conditions.

On the return trip northbound you must face this passage, which can test your fortitude. Because the seas sometimes become quiet at night, experienced Baja travelers leave the harbor to pass the Capes just before or at dawn to avoid the daily build-up. Thereafter, a course can be run directly to Bahia Magdalena. But the prevailing wind and swell that was fun at 15 - 20 knots going downwind, can become a bear when beating into an apparent wind in excess of 20 - 25 knots.

Lay a course that rounds Cabo San Lucas well clear of the outer rocks and enter the large and sheltered bay behind. A long, white, curved sandy beach crowded with hotels and condominiums sweeps northward to form an open harbor. You may rent a slip the marina (if space is available, at higher than U.S. prices), or anchor off the beach some distance from town. A deep underwater canyon reaches well into the bay, leaving a narrow shelf along the cape and a slightly broader shelf off the beach. The bottom is sandy and the water is clear so seeing your anchor dig in is easy. Choose a spot near the wash on the beach – there is a gap in the string of restaurants and hotels, in 15 to 20 feet. Set the anchor well. The bay is full of jet skiis and pangas rushing to and fro, so expect a somewhat rolly spot during the day. Night time is quite calm. You may be asked to pay a fee to anchor.

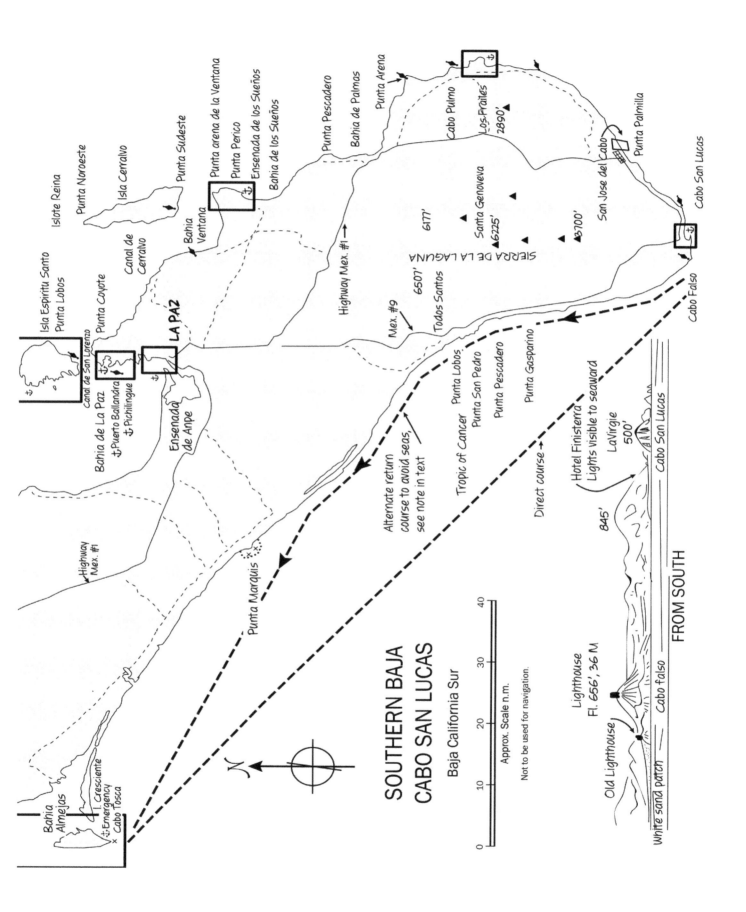

SOUTHERN BAJA
CABO SAN LUCAS

Baja California Sur

Approx. Scale n.m.

Not to be used for navigation.

FROM SOUTH

CABO SAN LUCAS

The harbor is entered by way of a short, dredged channel (marked by lights on either side) at the junction of the rocky hills and the beach. A mid-channel course may be followed into the harbor. The fuel dock will be straight ahead, the marina offices are in the far right hand corner of the basin.

This is a **Port of Entry** and the order of visits is Migracion, Capitan de Puerto and Puertos Mexicanos if this is your entry point to Mexico, or you may have your entry papers processed by the Marina if you have rented a slip there. There is an office near the launching ramp, which will process your paperwork overnight on busy days, or in a few hours on normal days if you start in the morning. Don't be alarmed when you are asked to leave your passports – this is normal.

Neptune's Finger at Cabo

Marina Cabo San Lucas occupies the northern part of the basin. It may have a waiting list for guest slips, you can call the dockmaster on VHF Ch. 88A when approaching the harbor to enquire about temporarily vacant slips. This is a fully modern facility with over 300 slips and a fuel dock. Reservations are advisable and may be made by phoning 624-173-91-40 or Fax 624-143-12-53.

Coast Chandlery Marine Store, a source of boat equipment and supplies is behind the Baja Cantina restaurant located at the base of the fuel dock gate. Items not in stock can be quickly shipped via airfreight from California. There is a laundry service there as well, leave your laundry and pick it up the next day.

This is an informative website on the whales of Mexico.

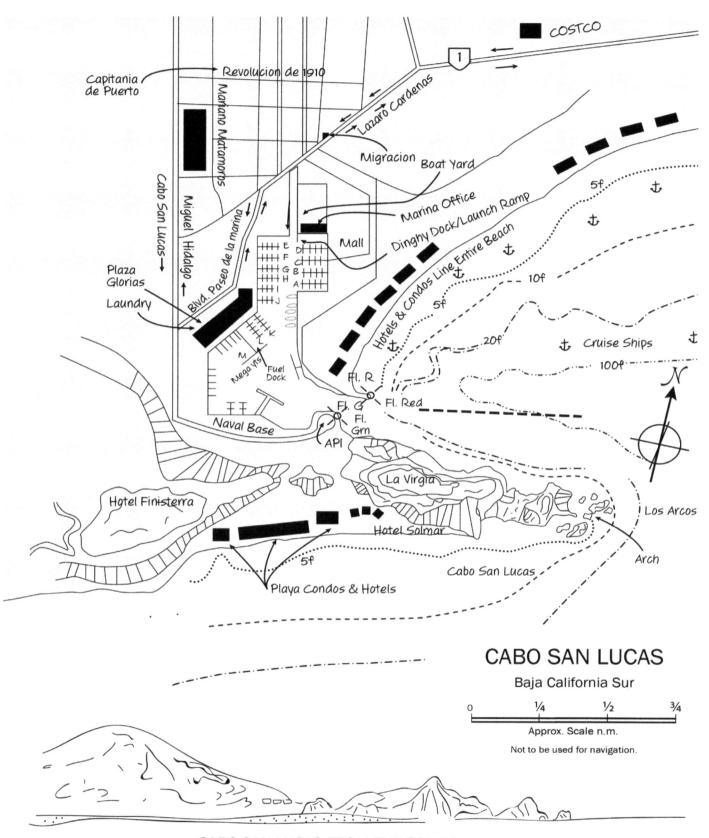

CABO SAN LUCAS

Baja California Sur

| 0 | ¼ | ½ | ¾ |

Approx. Scale n.m.

Not to be used for navigation.

CABO SAN LUCAS FROM THE SOUTH

TABLE 2

APPROXIMATE DISTANCES BETWEEN ANCHORAGES OF SECTION II
(Cabo San Lucas to San Felipe)

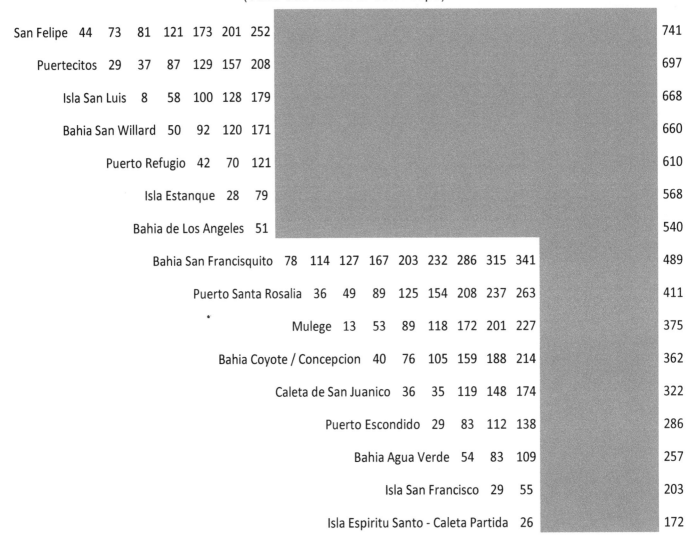

San Felipe	44	73	81	121	173	201	252			741
Puertecitos	29	37	87	129	157	208				697
Isla San Luis	8	58	100	128	179					668
Bahia San Willard	50	92	120	171						660
Puerto Refugio	42	70	121							610
Isla Estanque	28	79								568
Bahia de Los Angeles	51									540
Bahia San Francisquito	78	114	127	167	203	232	286	315	341	489
Puerto Santa Rosalia	36	49	89	125	154	208	237	263		411
Mulege	13	53	89	118	172	201	227			375
Bahia Coyote / Concepcion	40	76	105	159	188	214				362
Caleta de San Juanico	36	35	119	148	174					322
Puerto Escondido	29	83	112	138						286
Bahia Agua Verde	54	83	109							257
Isla San Francisco	29	55								203
Isla Espiritu Santo - Caleta Partida	26									172
La Paz	10	18	58	103						148
Pchilingue	8	48	93							138
Puerto Ballandra	40	85								130
Ensenada de los Suenos	45									90
Los Frailes										45
Cabo San Lucas										

Distances can be added between the groups of this section, e.g. from Los Frailes to Puerto Refugio the distance is: 103 + 341 + 121 = 565 nautical miles.

103 = Los Frailes to La Paz
341 = La Paz to Bahia San Francisquito
121 = Bahia San Francisquito to Puerto Refugio

SECTION II: CABO SAN LUCAS NORTH TO SAN FELIPE

This section covers the southeastern / eastern coast of Baja California which faces the Sea of Cortez and the Gulf of California. There are numerous anchorages, a limited number of marinas, excellent snorkeling and dive sites, prolific marine life and unique scenery which all combine to provide a first-rate cruising area, described by many broadly experienced cruisers as the best in the world.

WINDS, WEATHER, CURRENTS AND TIDAL EFFECTS IN THE SEA OF CORTEZ

Once having rounded Punta Gorda (approximately 30 miles east of Cabo San Lucas) headed north into the Sea of Cortez ("The Sea"), it will become apparent that this region of Mexico and its waters present different weather and sea patterns than are prevalent in open Pacific waters. The Pacific swell that batters the west coast of Baja diminishes in intensity north of Los Frailes. Dinghy shore landings become much less perilous and anchorages somewhat less affected by swell (but not necessarily wind-induced waves). The absence of swells warrants increased attentiveness to detection of shallow/subsurface reefs that in the Pacific would be made readily apparent by swells breaking over them. As described below, local winds can whip up a nasty wind chop that can be very fatiguing; the many good anchorages are located up and down the Sea which can be quickly reached that provide appropriate shelter from short terms winds and seas.

In the northern part of the Sea, pronounced currents are produced by tidal effects and to a lesser extent, seasonal wind flow patterns. From about 28° North Latitude (nominally Santa Rosalia) and northward, the effect of the tidal swing and current velocities becomes increasingly pronounced and vitally important to navigation and anchoring. As a case in point, the tidal range at San Felipe can be 6 to 20' +/-.

This Sea has many distinct weather patterns and associated sea conditions, which can and do vary significantly up and down the region. From a weather forecaster's perspective, the Sea is divided into the Upper, Middle and Lower thirds, each with its own weather and sea conditions.

The Upper 1/3 is generally lies north of a line drawn between Santa Rosalia and San Carlos; the middle 1/3 is lies between Santa Rosalia and the San Lorenzo Channel (north of La Paz); the Lower 1/3 lies south of the San Lorenzo channel and Cabo San Lucas. Forecasters will also speak of the "Northern Crossing", which is the passage between San Rosalia and San Carlos, and, the "Southern Crossing", which is the passage between Ensenada de Los Muertos/Los Frailes and Mazatlan.

Winds in the Sea are generally moderate (10 to 15 knots and frequently less) but can blow at gale force strength during winter and early spring months. The winds generally blow from the north/northwest from early to mid-December through the end of May, and from the south/southwest from early June through early December. During the winter/ spring months, "Northerlies" frequently blow unabated at wind speeds of 15 to 30 knots (and occasionally higher) for three to five days, succeeded by a three to five day period of moderate to light winds. Wind velocities during the Spring/Fall months are generally lower than in Winter/Spring months.

The Arch at Cabo San Lucas   Photo: Jo Russell

The Sea of Cortez is relatively narrow but comparatively quite long, which results in quickly generated steep short period seas that make for unpleasant northbound or southbound passages when encountering these conditions. Most gales are moderate and of short duration. But many regions produce locally strong winds that blow for parts of the day. For example, in the La Paz region and the Islands which lie just to its north, Coroumel winds often come up in the late afternoon and night and can blow at wind velocities of 25 knots and often considerably greater for four to six hours. When anchoring, mariners must anticipate the combined effects of these winds, local terrain features that funnel the winds and local holding characteristics.

The dinghy dock in Cabo, during the Baja Ha Ha Photo: Jo Russell

Elsewhere in the Sea, strong local winds – El Cordonazo - can approach hurricane force for minutes to hours in duration; they occur fitfully at the end of the wet season without much predictability. Mariners should be ready to expediently lift and potentially leave their anchors with a float when an anchorage becomes questionable or unsafe when these winds arise.

From June to November hurricanes are frequently spawned offshore of Mexico's southerly Pacific Coast, and occasionally take a northerly track from open Pacific waters up the western side of the Baja Peninsula; they sometimes bend in a northeasterly direction, crossing the peninsula and proceeding thereafter into the Sea and on to the mainland. Thus, anchorages that serve as reasonable hurricane shelters are specifically mentioned in the guide. Mariners are reminded to be mindful of summer weather forecasts and the need to head for one of these anchorages in the event a hurricane threatens the region.

For most of the year the weather is clear, hot (90s to low 100s during the day), with low humidity and pleasant; in the winter, temperatures range from cool to chilly (high 40s to low to mid 50s at night), particularly when a northerly is blowing down the length of the Sea. The 'dry' season is from December to April. The 'wet' season is not as clearly defined; thunderstorms (Chubascos) with localized microburst winds and rainfall occur between May and November. These storms are more frequent in the north and mid-Sea regions, but can occur anywhere along the peninsula.

The Summer/early Fall months bring fierce sunshine and unrelenting heat. Cruisers are well advised to employ canvas awnings, including side curtains, to shade decks, cockpit and cabin house from direct sunlight. As described, strong winds can and do develop quite suddenly in the summer. Awnings and side drapes must be designed so they can be easily and quickly taken down or stowed. In fact, based on our experience, it is advisable that awnings be taken down or stowed as the afternoon sun begins to diminish in strength. It is also recommended that every night all loose gear on the deck be stowed, dinghy securely tethered to the boat (if not taken out of the water with davits or using a convenient halyard and a plan for quick exit of an anchorage clearly understood and practiced by the crew. It is quite common for cruisers in the Sea to set their anchors and stay in one spot in a favorite anchorage for extended periods of time. It is strongly encouraged after being subjected to these locally strong winds to check and occasionally reset anchors.

LOS CABOS TO LA PAZ

When sailing beyond the Los Cabos region into the Sea of Cotez, until reaching La Paz, there is nowhere to put ashore to reprovision, take on fuel or fresh water, or refill propane bottles. As a footnote, there are several restaurants in Ensenada de Los Muertos that cater to cruisers.

The coast from Cabo San Lucas to Los Frailes (about 43 miles northeast) features several rounded, reddish, rocky points interspersed with large and small bights of brilliant white, sandy beaches. Hotels and housing developments can be seen while passing this part of the coast. Situated in front of several hotels along this coastline are a few small fair weather anchorages such as Santa Maria Cove and Punta Palmilla. Except in the most mild of weather conditions these spots are too exposed to the east and south to be suitable as other than day anchorages.

Bahia de San Jose del Cabo is an open bight that extends from Punta Palmilla to Punta Gorda, about 9 miles further to the northeast. The town of San Jose del Cabo lies along this stretch of the coast, about midway along the sandy beachfront that frequently has heavy pounding surf.

MARINA PUERTO LOS CABOS

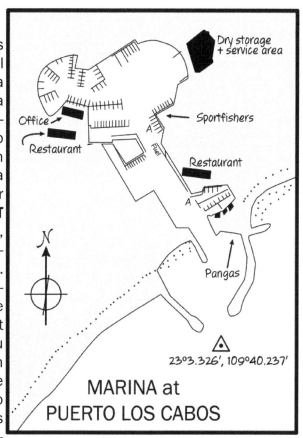

MARINA at PUERTO LOS CABOS

Marina Puerto Los Cabos is located approximately 30 miles east of Cabo San Lucas in Puerto Los Cabos. This new full service marina facility is part of a condominium/marina development located between Punta Palmilla and Punta Gorda in Bahia San Jose del Cabo. This is a well appointed facility that can accommodate vessels from 30 ft. to mega yachts. The harbor is clearly marked with navigation buoys and lights, is easily entered (albeit with a beam sea when making the entrance behind the breakwater under certain conditions), and provides excellent protection. **WPT 23°3.326', 109°40.237'.** In addition to regular services, amenities include wireless Internet, cable TV, several restaurants (on both sides of the marina), and a small tienda. The condominium complex also offers a swimming pool, fitness center, hotel, spa, golf course and tennis courts. The marina is situated approximately 1 1./2 miles (walkable but a long stroll – taxis will come to your slip dock and take you into town) from downtown San Jose del Cabo, a lovely town that is graced with quaint hotels, nice restaurants and like the marina complex, much Mexican artistry. If needing to provision and having bypassed Cabo San Lucas, there is also a supermercado approximately 2 miles from the marina. This marina complex is also very close to the Cabo San Lucas airport. Rental cars are available in town, as are buses that run frequently between San Jose del Cabo and downtown Cabo San Lucas.

The marina office monitors VHF Channels 16 and 22 and the Tel/Fax No. is 011-52-624-1056028. For information or reservations visit website www.puertoloscabos.com or email marinainfo@puertoloscabos.com.

When we last stayed in this marina in late 2011, daily slip rates were surprisingly more expensive than Marina Cabo San Lucas (daily slip fees at IGY Marina Cabo San Lucas have been significantly reduced in the last year). Two rate levels were offered: with or without electricity and water.

LOS FRAILES (The Friars)

Los Frailes is the first anchorage to the north of the San Jose del Cabo region. The anchorage is identified by a prominent, large, gray, rocky hill that is about 750 ft. in height and a bold, rocky east lying headland that drops steeply 410 ft. into the Sea. Located almost on the Tropic of Cancer, it is the easternmost point of land on the Baja peninsula.

In northerly weather, good anchorage can be taken in 4 to 6 fathoms in sand and rock at the northern head of the bay, just off where the white, sandy beach meets the rocks of the headland. **WPT 23°22.78', 109°25.60'.** When anchoring it is recommended to tuck in relatively close to the beach or rocky hill as a deep underwater canyon extends out into the center of the bay and beyond from a point beginning further south along the beach; this canyon quickly plunges to 300 feet and greater. This underwater canyon has undergone significant transformation in 2012 as result of an earthquake and continuing changes in its underwater topography. Cruisers must take care not to anchor too far south of the rocky hill or northerly lying beachfront, and thus in the steeply declining canyon wall.

Scrub-covered sand dunes and an arroyo lie behind the beach, with a small rancho and airstrip to the north. RVs and campers often park along the road beyond the beach. On the south side of the arroyo are a hotel, bungalows and other buildings overlooking the bay; they do not cater to cruisers who are anchored in the bay.

The beach surfbreak in this bay can be as heavy as any on the Pacific side of Baja. If going ashore, the best place to land a dinghy is indicated on the sketch.

During southerly winds anchorage can be taken on the north side of the point. Note the small, 12 ft. whitish rock that lies off the small point of land extending northeast from the Los Frailes massif. Several outlying rocks are scattered along this coast, but by clearing the white rock and sheltering in the sweep of this bay, protection is possible from southerly winds.

When proceeding northward, stand out for at least 2 miles before turning up the coast to clear the reefs and shoals that lie to the north of Los Frailes. Lying about a mile north of Los Frailes is the coral reef "Arrecife del Pulmo", which is also a National Marine Park (spearfishing is prohibited in the Park) known for its spectacular skin and scuba diving. The reef extends out from the shore in a northeasterly direction for a mile or so and ends off Cabo Pulmo. The cape is a sharp point connected to a sand-covered ridge to a hill beyond. Shoal water extends off the cape and large shoal patches on which the sea sometimes breaks lie about 1/2 mile offshore. In order to clear these shoals vessels must stand out when passing this part of the coast.

Anchorage is possible between the reef and the **Cabo Pulmo** in its lee, but the approach is tricky. This anchorage gives good protection form the north. To avoid the reef, position yourself at **23°27', 109°25'.** The outer end of the reef lies about ¼ mile off the point. Keep close to the shore in 20 to 30 feet until you are past Cabo Pulmo. Then swing west and anchor in 25 feet off the beach. **WPT 23°26.63', 109°25.42'.**

As a footnote, many cruisers use Los Frailes as their point of departure or destination when crossing the Gulf of California to and from the Mazatlan.

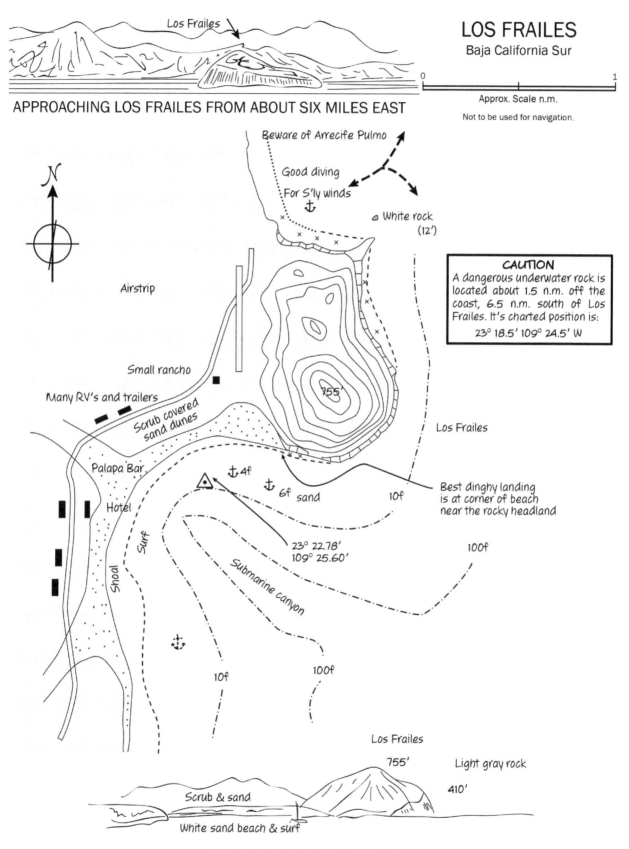

APPROACHING LOS FRAILES FROM ABOUT SIX MILES EAST

LOS FRAILES
Baja California Sur

0   1
Approx. Scale n.m.

Not to be used for navigation.

Beware of Arrecife Pulmo

Good diving

For S'ly winds

⚓

⌀ White rock
(12')

Airstrip

Small rancho

Many RV's and trailers

Scrub covered sand dunes

Palapa Bar

Hotel

Shoal

Surf

755'

CAUTION
A dangerous underwater rock is located about 1.5 n.m. off the coast, 6.5 n.m. south of Los Frailes. It's charted position is:
23° 18.5' 109° 24.5' W

Los Frailes

Best dinghy landing is at corner of beach near the rocky headland

⚓ 4f

⚓ 6f   sand

10f

100f

23° 22.78'
109° 25.60'

Submarine canyon

100f

10f

⚓

Los Frailes

755'

Light gray rock

410'

Scrub & sand

White sand beach & surf

APPROACHING FROM THE SOUTH

ENSENADA de LOS MUERTOS/LOS SUENOS

The coast falls slightly to the west in the 7 miles separating Cabo Pulmo and Punta Arena (sand), the flat, sandy point curves outward almost 1½ miles from the bights found on either side. Two large and slightly indented bays, Bahia de Las Palmas and Bahia de los Muertos, AKA Los Suenos follow as the coast recedes to the northwest. Bahia de Las Palmas ends at Punta Pescadero and Bahia de los Muertos ends at Punta Perico; Punta Arena de la Ventana follows shortly thereafter. The bights are open to the east and southeast. In calm, settled weather temporary anchorage can be found below Punta Arena, or off the village of Buena Vista which lies midway along Bahia de Las Palmas. The only protected anchorage in this area is in the small cove of Ensenada de los Muertos.

Ensenada de Los Muertos/Los Suenos is a small cove about 2½ miles south of Punta Perico and about 47 miles from Los Frailes. The original name meaning Bay of the Dead has been changed to make it sound more welcoming. Los Suenos translates to The Dreams. The cove is formed by a hook of land at the northern end of Bahia de los Muertos. A number of scattered rocks lie off the point of land forming the eastern boundary of the cove. They should be given a wide berth when entering or leaving the bay.

Anchorage may be taken at the head of the bay, well off the remains of a concrete wharf on the east side of the cove. **WPT 23°59.54', 109°49.66'.** The holding is good in 4 to 6 fathoms, sand. The head of the bay is shoal and the remains of an old sunken anchor are reported to lie off the old pier. The beach at the head of the cove consists of pebbles, becoming white sand as you follow the coast to the southwest.

This was once a thriving little port for bringing in supplies and shipping ore from silver mines and later, salt. A large parcel of land surrounding the bay has been purchased resulting in the disappearance of huts of a seasonal fish camp and visiting RVs. Private residences are now located on the western side of the bay. There is a restaurant on the beach, which caters to cruisers and offers very reasonable prices for ice, laundry and showers. Nearby is a road connecting the cove to La Paz.

The Pacific swell has reduced strength this far up the Gulf. As a result, landing on the beaches is much easier since the surf is negligible.

Punta Arena de La Ventana is a prominent, but low, flat, sandy point, which protrudes northward beyond Punta Perico. A conspicuous light is located on the point. Shoal water extends from the tip and surrounds the point. In southerly weather anchorage may be taken off the beach on the north side, about a mile west of the point. **WPT 24°13.12', 109°51.38'**

Cerralvo Channel, which runs between Isla Cerralvo and the Baja, tends to have strong tidal currents making passage at slack water or with a favoring current advisable for slow vessels. In blustery conditions, waiting out the weather may be a better option than bashing.

Isla Cerralvo has two anchorages which may be found on either side of the Viejo spit, a sandy point which forms the southwest corner of the island. The north side offers protection from the southeast wind and swell, the south side from the north. Both anchorages are in 20' sand, close to the beach.

Rancho Las Cruces lies across the channel about 18 miles northwest of Punta Arena de la Ventana and has a beach off which you can anchor in 18' over sand. There is a breakwater at the north end of the beach, which shelters the bay from the northwest. Behind the breakwater, the anchorage is **WPT 24°12.84', 110°5.33'**

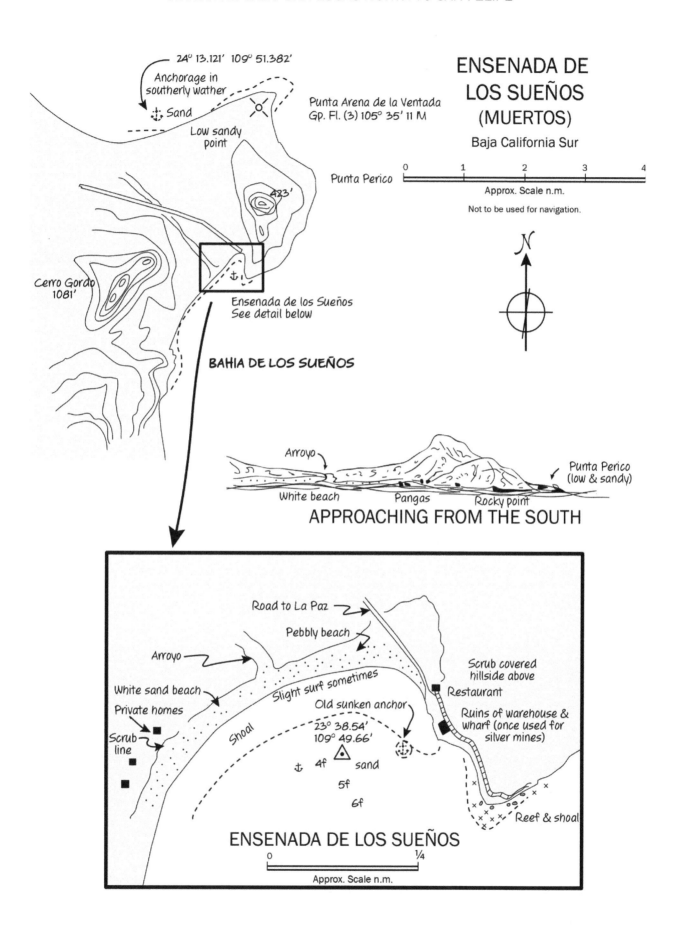

24° 13.121′ 109° 51.382′
Anchorage in
southerly wather
⚓ Sand
Low sandy
point

Punta Arena de la Ventada
Gp. Fl. (3) 105° 35′ 11 M

423′

Cerro Gordo
1081′

Ensenada de los Sueños
See detail below

BAHIA DE LOS SUEÑOS

ENSENADA DE LOS SUEÑOS (MUERTOS)

Baja California Sur

Punta Perico

0   1   2   3   4
Approx. Scale n.m.

Not to be used for navigation.

N

Arroyo

Punta Perico
(low & sandy)

White beach   Pangas   Rocky point

APPROACHING FROM THE SOUTH

Road to La Paz

Pebbly beach

Arroyo

Scrub covered
hillside above
Restaurant

White sand beach

Old sunken anchor

Ruins of warehouse &
wharf (once used for
silver mines)

Private homes

Slight surf sometimes

23° 38.54′
109° 49.66′

Scrub
line

Shoal

⚓ 4f   sand

5f

6f

Reef & shoal

ENSENADA DE LOS SUEÑOS

0   ¼
Approx. Scale n.m.

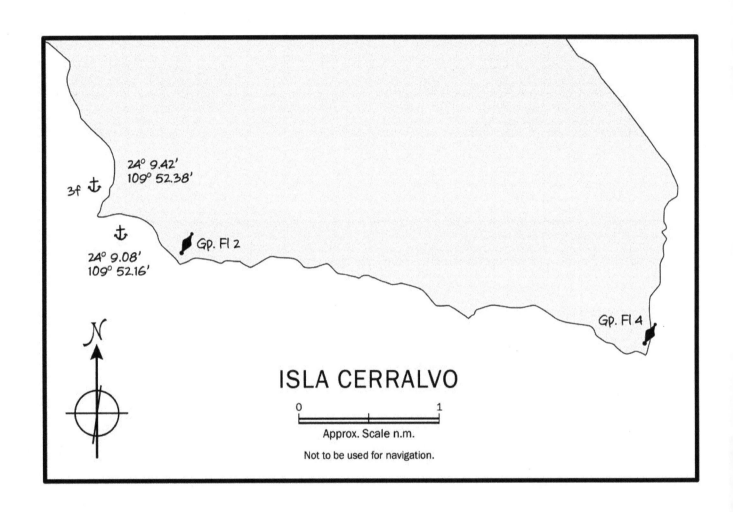

ISLA CERRALVO

24° 9.42'
109° 52.38'

3f ⚓

⚓

24° 9.08'
109° 52.16'

Gp. Fl 2

Gp. Fl 4

N

0   1

Approx. Scale n.m.

Not to be used for navigation.

CANAL DE
SAN LORENZO

Approx. Scale n.m.

Not to be used for navigation.

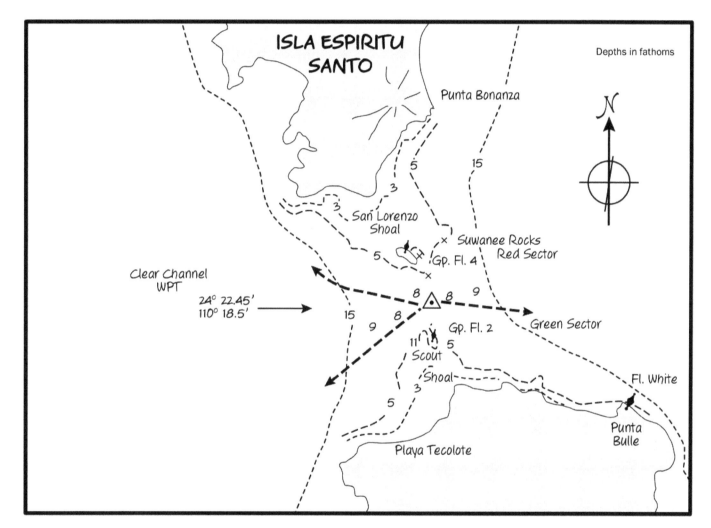

Canal San Lorenzo separates the baja from Isla Espiritu Santo and has plenty of rocks and shoals to keep you focused on what you're doing. At its narrowest point, between Scout Shoal on the south, and Suwanee Rocks on the north, it is about one mile wide, and 8 fathoms deep. Scout Shoal is supposed to be marked by a white navigation light Gp. Fl. 2 with a green sector light visible if you are not heading for the channel. The north side of the channel is supposed to be marked with a white navigation light Gp. Fl. 4 with a red sector light visible when you are not heading the channel. We say supposed because the lights tend to be damaged from storms and not replaced as soon as we'd like. Oh well... The **WPT 24°22.45', 110°18.50'** should put you in the center of the channel and between the lights.

ANCHORAGES IN THE VICINITY OF LA PAZ

Ballandra anchorage. Photo: Robin Richardson Stout

Puerto Ballandra is a very pretty cove where rocky arms encircle a brilliant white, sandy beach with several smaller, inviting beaches tucked into smaller niches. When entering, **WPT 24° 19', 110° 20.8'**, favor the northern point, Punta Tecolote, for there is a submerged reef extending out from the northern part of the south entrance point, Punta Diablo. Off the end of the reef is a **dangerous submerged rock** that is sometimes marked by a breaker during NW winds. Nearby on the ocean floor stands a 10 ft. bronze statue, visible only to divers. Anchorage is good off the first northern most beach just within the mouth of the cove, in 3 fathoms, sand. **WPT 24°19.63', 110°19.96'.** Allow room to swing clear of the shallows in case a southerly comes up. A second spot is near the mushroom rock at **WPT 24°19.31', 110°19.82'** in 3 fathoms, sand. A third anchorage (behind the reef that was avoided on entry) is on the south side off the cliffs above a very small beach. The rear of the cove is shoal, as indicated by the very light colored water and white sand. An extensive shoal area to the northeast is best explored by dinghy. Although the anchorage sometimes experiences gusty winds from the south, it is otherwise well sheltered.

Caleta Lobos is about 1 mile to the south of Punta Diablo. Roca Lobos, about 12' high (on which there is a light), lies ½ mile out from the mouth of a small cove. A detached rock off the north point of the cove reduces the entrance width from about 1,000' to 1,500'. Entry may be made holding a mid-channel course between Roca Lobos and either entrance point. Anchorage can be taken within the cove on its southern side in about 3 fathoms, sand. We have experienced serious numbers of very annoying flies here on occasion, and left. You will know whether or not it is a problem once you get into the cove. The northern part of the cove is shoal and includes two lobes that are filled with mangrove thickets. Check your swinging space to make certain you are clear of the shoal area. Anchorage **WPT 24°17.93', 110°20'.**

Isla Lobos, about ¼ mile along lies only a short distance southeast of Roca Lobos. It must be passed on the western side as it is connected on its east side to Punta Base. A small, but good anchorage can be found tucked under the lee of Punta Base in Playa Pichilingue in 30' sand. **WPT 24°17.02', 110°19.81'.** There is a launching ramp at the north end of the beach and a restaurant at the south end. There is a marina at Club Cantamar, which is a diving resort and doesn't seem to have guest slips. It is a long way to town as well. The only disadvantage of this bay is that the lights from the port and ferry dock across the causeway are very bright all night long.

Isla San Juan Nepomezeino is ¼ mile south of Punta Base and it shelters **Puerto Pichilingue**, an excellent harbor. Give a wide berth to the shoals lining the shores of Isla San Juan Nepomezeino and extending southwesterly from its southern end. At the head of the harbor is the This is the deep water port for La Paz, handling ocean going freighters, truck transports, car ferries to Topolbampo and Mazatlan, and whale watching tour boats. It is well protected, opening directly south onto a short 5 mile fetch. However, Coromuels do come in. The northern end with the wharves is no place fro cruising boats, but between the Port Offices pier, and the old US Navy coaling station on the western side, there is a small cove often used by cruisers. This spot gives Coromuel protection. The bottom is sand in 20 feet. **WPT 24°15.74', 110°19.88'.** Avoid anchoring near the navigation channel that is intended for use by ferries and shrimper

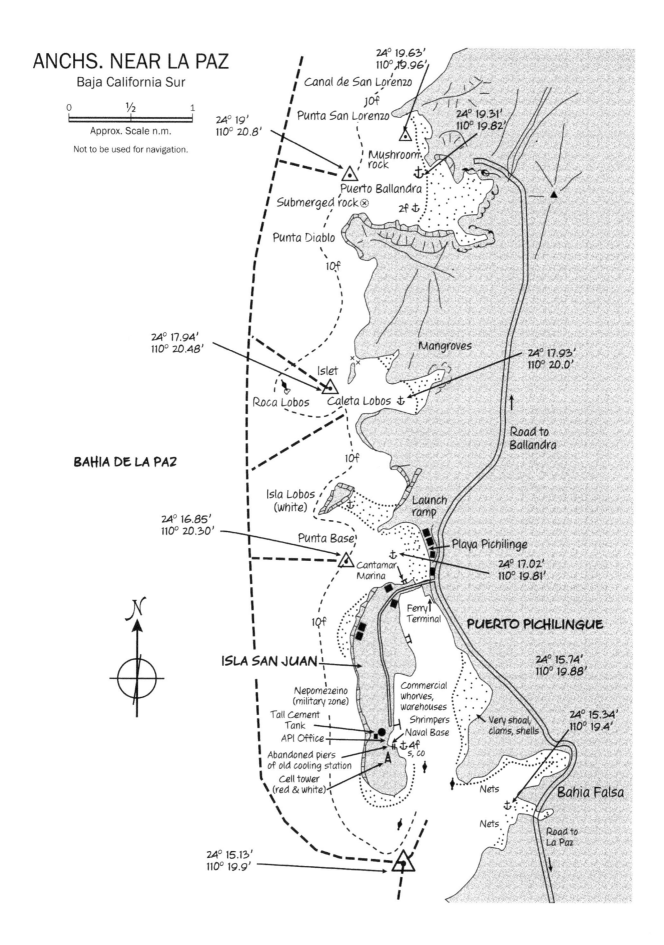

ANCHS. NEAR LA PAZ
Baja California Sur

0   ½   1

Approx. Scale n.m.

Not to be used for navigation.

24° 19.63'
110° 19.96'

Canal de San Lorenzo

10f
Punta San Lorenzo

24° 19.31'
110° 19.82'

24° 19'
110° 20.8'

Mushroom rock

Puerto Ballandra

Submerged rock ⊗

2f

Punta Diablo

10f

24° 17.94'
110° 20.48'

Mangroves

24° 17.93'
110° 20.0'

Islet

Roca Lobos   Caleta Lobos

Road to
Ballandra

BAHIA DE LA PAZ

10f

Isla Lobos
(white)

Launch
ramp

24° 16.85'
110° 20.30'

Punta Base

Playa Pichilinge

Cantamar
Marina

24° 17.02'
110° 19.81'

Ferry
Terminal

PUERTO PICHILINGUE

N

ISLA SAN JUAN

24° 15.74'
110° 19.88'

10f

Nepomezeino
(military zone)

Commercial
whorves,
warehouses

24° 15.34'
110° 19.4'

Tall Cement
Tank

Shrimpers

API Office

Naval Base

4f
s, co

Very shoal,
clams, shells

Abandoned piers
of old cooling station

Cell tower
(red & white)

Bahia Falsa

Nets

Nets

Road to
La Paz

24° 15.13'
110° 19.9'

traffic. Since a military station is on the island, shore trips are prohibited.

The entrance to Puerto Pichilingue is well marked, and if you arrive in the La Paz area after dark, this is a good place to anchor rather than to try to enter the channel to La Paz. At the entrance itself, off the end of the island near the buoy with a light Fl. W at **WPT 24°15.13', 110°10.9'**, start the turn into the bay. There is a rocky shoal inside the buoy, so don't cut the corner. Pass between the red and green buoys, and turn west (left) into the anchorage. The Port Office is well lit, so this is an easy anchorage to make in the dark providing all the lights are working.

Bahia Falsa, this bay is located just south of the entrance of Pichilingue. It offers good Coromuel protection but there may be hazards in the form of fishing nets and pens. Despite these issues, it is a popular anchorage. Enter the bay down the center and anchor in 20 feet, sand. **WPT 24°15.43', 110°19.11'**. There is plenty of room for 5 boats or more.

El Malecon of La Paz   Photo: Jo Russell

Marina Costa Brava in La Paz   Photo: Jo Russell

Marina Palmira on approach Photo: Jo Russell

LA PAZ

The spacious harbor of La Paz is a popular destination for vessels cruising Mexico's west coast. This is a result of a combination of a huge anchorage area, a choice of several modern marinas, complete repair and boat maintenance facilities and the most affordable and best selection of food in Baja. In addition, taking on fuel is uncomplicated and the wonderful cruising on Isla Espiritu Santo and the Sea of Cortez is right at your doorstep. The atmosphere of the town is a comfortable balance between tourism and life in the slow lane. For decades, cruisers have made the pleasant city of La Paz their home base, some almost permanently.

The entrance to the harbor of La Paz begins a scant 2½ miles south of Pichilingue, at Punta Prieta, a gray bluff about 135' high. The oil tanks of the Pemex oil farm, the power plant and its stacks and the tanker wharf on the south side of the wharf clearly identify this point. **WPT 24°13', 110°19'**. A long, sandy shoal extends roughly northeastward of the island of El Mogote, which is opposite the city of La Paz.

Canal de La Paz, the channel leading into the harbor, begins at Punta Prieta and runs behind the sandy shoal to the city's waterfront. East of Punta Prieta is Costabaja Resort and Marina, an extensive resort/ hotel/marina development and home to a charter fleet. Continuing down the channel toward La Paz, fol- low a course south of the tanker wharf and its outlying white drum buoys that are used for securing off- shore cables by tankers. Stay in mid-channel between the white drum buoys and the lighted channel buoy marking the north tip of the shoal. Once past this buoy, the vessel enters a clearly marked channel with red buoys to starboard and green to port. Hug the green buoys, especially the first three, for grounding is possible if you pass into shallow areas between the red buoys. The channel leads past the entrance to the next marina, Marina Palmira, and continues in a southerly direction until a reverse range comes roughly in line astern, just beyond Marina Palmira. A buoy ahead helps to mark the channel's eastern boundary. Channel buoys mark both side of the route though they vary in location as the 2½ fathom controlling depth of the channel is maintained. Proceed down range, between the buoys toward the visible municipal pier. Monitor your depth sounder carefully as shoaling is a constant occurrence.

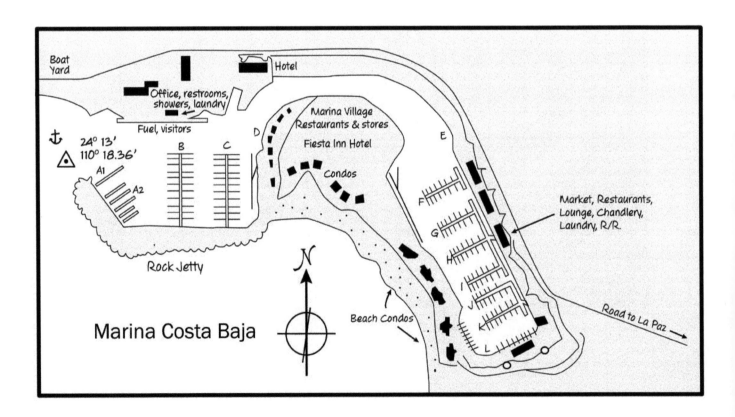

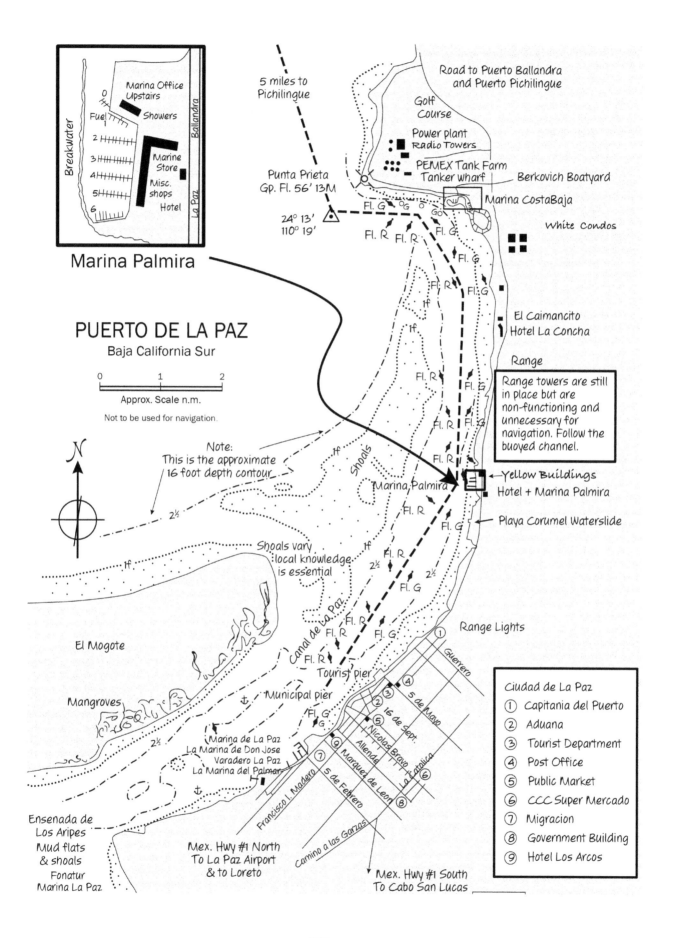

Marina Palmira

Marina Office Upstairs
Showers
Fuel
Marine Store
Misc. shops
Hotel
Breakwater
Ballandra
La Paz

PUERTO DE LA PAZ

Baja California Sur

0   1   2
Approx. Scale n.m.

Not to be used for navigation.

N

Note:
This is the approximate 16 foot depth contour

Shoals vary local knowledge is essential

El Mogote

Mangroves

Ensenada de Los Aripes
Mud flats & shoals
Fonatur Marina La Paz

Mex. Hwy #1 North
To La Paz Airport
& to Loreto

Mex. Hwy #1 South
To Cabo San Lucas

5 miles to Pichilingue

Punta Prieta
Gp. Fl. 56' 13M
24° 13'
110° 19'

Fl. G   O G   O G
Fl. R   Fl. R   Fl. G
Fl. G
Fl. R   Fl. G
1f
1f
Fl. R
Fl. G
Fl. R   Fl. G
Fl. R   Fl. G
Fl. R
Fl. R
Fl. G
Shoals
1f
1f
Marina Palmira
Fl. R
Fl. G
Fl. R
2½
Fl. G
Fl. R
Canal de La Paz
Fl. R
Tourist pier
Municipal pier
Fl. G
Fl. G
2½
Range Lights

Road to Puerto Ballandra and Puerto Pichilingue
Golf Course
Power plant
Radio Towers
PEMEX Tank Farm
Tanker wharf
Berkovich Boatyard
Marina CostaBaja
White Condos
El Caimancito
Hotel La Concha

Range
Range towers are still in place but are non-functioning and unnecessary for navigation. Follow the buoyed channel.

Yellow Buildings
Hotel + Marina Palmira
Playa Corumel Waterslide

Marina de La Paz
La Marina de Don Jose
Varadero La Paz
La Marina del Palmar

Guerrero
5 de Mayo
16 de Sept.
Nicolas Bravo
Allende
La Catolica
Marquez de Leon
Francisco I. Madero
5 de Febrero
Camino a las Garzas

Ciudad de La Paz
① Capitania del Puerto
② Aduana
③ Tourist Department
④ Post Office
⑤ Public Market
⑥ CCC Super Mercado
⑦ Migracion
⑧ Government Building
⑨ Hotel Los Arcos

La Paz is a **Port of Entry** and cruisers must call the Port Captain to report their arrival. The Customs office (Aduana) and Immigration office are on the malecon across from the Municipal Pier. The Port Captain's office is near the intersection of Revolucion and Guerrero. Office hours are usually from 9 a.m. to 3 p.m., Monday to Friday. A stop at the SCT office (a few blocks from the Port Captain's office) is necessary to pay a few pesos for the anchoring fee.

Anchorage may be taken in 3 - 4 fathoms, sand and mud in a large area southwest of the pier **WPT 24°9.4', 110°19.5'** (do not go too close to the city shore as it shoals rapidly) or across the channel at **WPT 24°9.8', 110°19.7'**. Set the anchor securely as tidal changes cause strong currents in the channel and be sure you have plenty of room to swing clear of other vessels at anchor for when the tide changes boats often swing at different angles from their neighbors, nicknamed the "La Paz Waltz." Beware of the shoal mid channel, which may or may not be marked. The open harbor can be windy, building a slight chop that can make shore trips splashy happenings.

If you prefer to moor at a marina there are several choices with varying costs and facilities. They will be described in order from north to south.

Mantas jumping near La Paz. Photo: Robin Richardson Stout

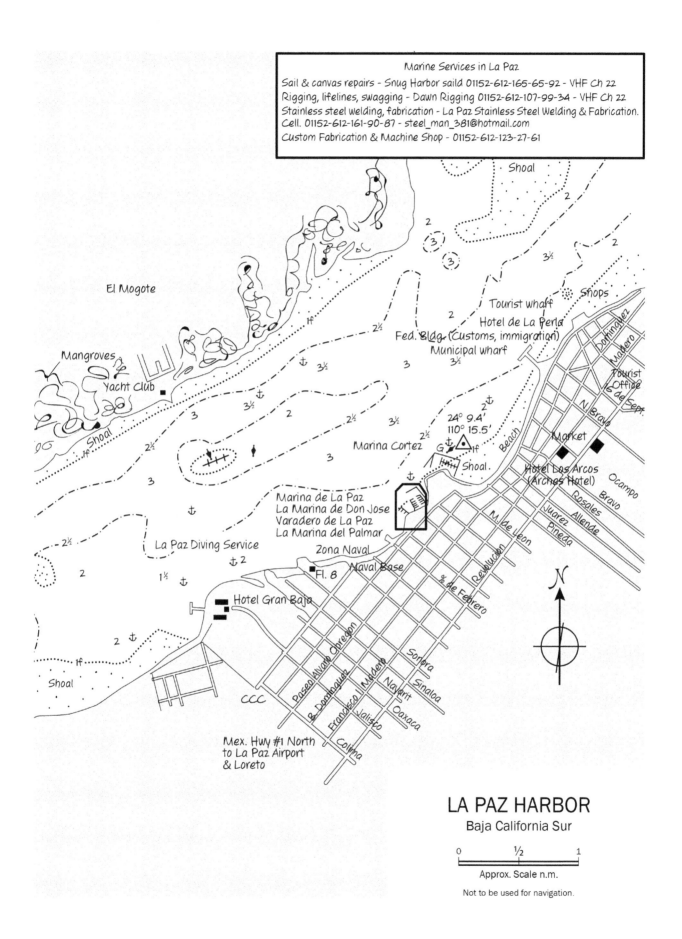

Marine Services in La Paz
Sail & canvas repairs - Snug Harbor saild 01152-612-165-65-92 - VHF Ch 22
Rigging, lifelines, swagging - Dawn Rigging 01152-612-107-99-34 - VHF Ch 22
Stainless steel welding, fabrication - La Paz Stainless Steel Welding & Fabrication.
Cell. 01152-612-161-90-87 - steel_man_381@hotmail.com
Custom Fabrication & Machine Shop - 01152-612-123-27-61

LA PAZ HARBOR
Baja California Sur

0   ½   1

Approx. Scale n.m.

Not to be used for navigation.

MARINAS AND BOAT YARDS IN THE PORT OF LA PAZ (From north to south)

Costabaja Resort and Marina, WPT 24°13', 110°18.36', is a full service facility. It is located about 6 miles from the center of La Paz. The office monitors VHF Ch 16. Amenities include cable TV, WiFi, pumpout and desalinated water on the docks, discounted rates at the hotel, both 110 and 220 power, 24 hour security, a cruiser's lounge and fuel dock, chandlery, restaurants, laundry service and dive shop. Its 250 slips can accommodate vessels up to 200 ft. The full-service marina occupies two connected basins providing all-weather protection. At low low water the depth between the two basins is 6 ft. Deep draft vessels should verify the current depth between the two basins prior to proceeding to the inner basin. For information call (US) 888-866-9394, (Mexico) 011-52-(612)-121-6225 or email the dockmaster at gley@ marinacostabaja.com., www.marinacostabaja.com   800-200-0281

Marina Palmira, WPT 24°11.20', 110°18.24' is a full service marina about 3 miles from the center of La Paz and is just off the channel. It is adjacent to a haul out facility, available for repairs and for dry storage. The marina has a fuel dock and pump-outs are available 7 am to 7 pm. A shuttle to La Paz operates 5 times a day. The marina store arranges for propane refills on Fridays; WiFi is available. Amenities include 24-hour security, 110 and 220 power, restrooms with showers, laundry room,
For information call 011-52-612-121-6159, or (US toll free) 877-217-1513. visit www.marinapalmira.com or email reservations@marinapalmarina.com

Marina Cortez is the new name of the virtual marina known previously as Marina Santa Cruz. At this point, there is one section of nice concrete docks and a breakwater surrounding what will one day be the new marina. Anchorage and moorings are available in addition to the docks, but it is bast to contact them ahead of arrival as things will be changing as work progresses. The good news is that the security is good, it is close to downtown and the malecon, restaurants and chandleries, the down side is the wind and current which run through the marina. This may be less of an issue as the marina is built. Contact the marina on VHF 16, and 22 or at dockmaster@marinacortez.com or ashore at 52-612-123-4101. Entrance **WPT 24°09.42', 110°19.58'**.

Marina de La Paz is a full service facility protected by breakwaters with slips that can handle vessels from 30 ft to 250 ft. The office monitors VHF 16. A small marine supply store and dive shop is next door. Overlooking the marina is the Dock Cafe, a popular meeting place for cruisers. Facilities include free WiFi, video security, dinghy dock for vessels anchored in the bay, restrooms with showers, propane pickup and delivery three days a week. For information call 011-52-612-122-1646, fax 011-52-612-125-5900 or email marinalapaz@prodigy.net.mx, www.marinadelapaz.com. Behind Marina de La Paz is Sea Mar Marine Chandlery, a contact for Mercury repairs and parts, agenciaseamar@gmail.com

La Marina de Don Jose has 40 slips to 130', with friendly management that is a source of local information and history. It is a fifth generation facility that has expanded to include Varadero de La Paz (shipyard and repairs), Marina de Don Jose La Marina del Palmar (repair facility), Materiales and Refacciones Aboroa (marine supply store one block south of the shipyard). For information call 011-52 (612) 122-0808, or VHF 16. The manager is Alejandro Abaroa Gil. Nearby is a dinghy dock for patrons of La Costa Restaurant operated by Martha Cristina Jordan.

La Marina del Palmar has facilities for vessels up to 100 ft., and a 22 ft. beam. It has a 60-ton Travelift and extensive work yard. Monthly moorage include water and electricity. Services include steel, fiberglass and wood repairs, Painting, carpentry, stainless steel welding, and propeller and shaft repairs. For information call 011-52(612)123-4060 or email travel_lift@yahoo.com.mx. Lopez Maine is a marine supply store in Plaza Coral.

Singlar Fidepaz is located quite a distance from town, about two miles further down the channel. A dredged channel about 150 ft. wide with a controlling depth of 9 ft. The channel resembles a trench that

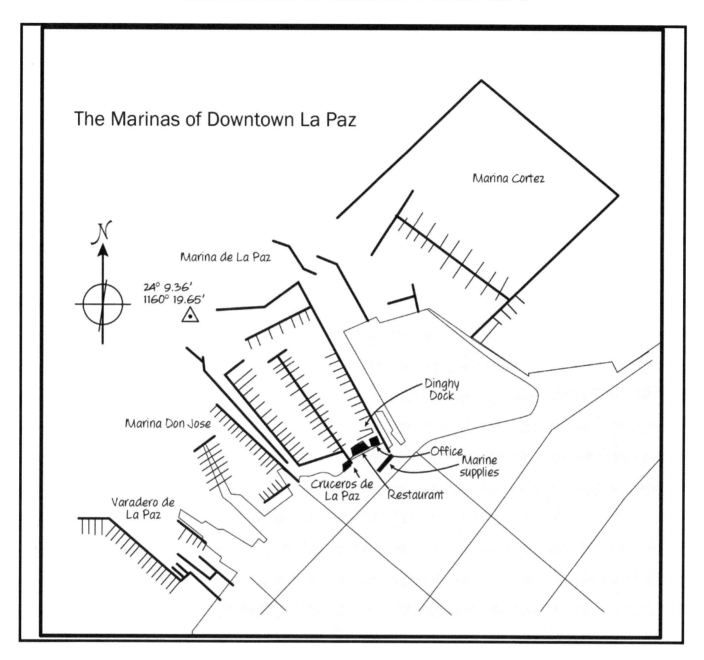

The Marinas of Downtown La Paz

Marina Cortez

Marina de La Paz

24° 9.36'
1160° 19.65'

Marina Don Jose

Dinghy Dock

Office

Marine supplies

Cruceros de La Paz

Restaurant

Varadero de La Paz

has been dug through the shoals making it essential for a vessel to proceed slowly and carefully for any divergence may result in immediate grounding in the mud flats. Skippers of deep draft vessels heading for the marina should call the office on VHF Ch 16 and an escort will be provided to insure safe passage to the marina. After leaving the marinas in downtown La Paz favor the north side (El Mogote side) where the water is slightly deeper than elsewhere until you reach **WPT 24°08.6' 110°22.2'.** This is a newer full service marina in La Paz with 39 slips and a fuel dock. For information visit www.regionmardecortes.com, emailsinglarlapaz@hotmail.com, or call 011-52-612-124-2206.

Varadero de La Paz shipyard has a 40-ton Travelift, a 140 ft. marine railway capable of hauling vessels up to 140 tons, a large work yard and dry storage for vessels up to 40 tons. It is located next door to La Marina de Don Jose. For information call 011-52-612-122-2166. The manager is Humberto Abaroa Diaz. A dinghy dock (Virtual Marina) is tucked between Varadero and Palmar Marinas.

La Paz has all the facilities of any large city, with a great, relaxed feel to it. The latest cruiser's map and the morning cruiser net every morning at 8:00 on VHF 22, will get you tuned into the most up to date events in town. Just ask around of other cruisers for the latest recommendation for sail repair, fabricators, SSB and HAM equipment, groceries, hardware stores, wine store, mail to be taken back home, church services, car rentals, dog sitters, mani-pedi/DayOBeauty fix – you name it. Excellent produce is available at the Public Markets. Two popular supermarkets with American products are CCC (pronounced say-say-say) located at Abasolo and Colima, the other about a mile inland from the waterfront on Isabel la Catolica and Bravo. Aramburo's has a good selection of merchandise and is conveniently located downtown. Two blocks away at Rosales and Ortega is "Karla" Panaderia (Bakery). Other bakeries fairly convenient to the waterfront are: "California Chicken" at 5 de Febrero and Abasolo and "La Colimense" at Revolucion and Morelos.

La Perla is a sizable department store and pharmacy. Visit Thrifty Nieve Americana for large, economical and tasty ice cream cones; it is about a half block north of the east side of the cathedral on 5 de Mayo. LibrosLibros-BooksBooks at 195 Constitucion stocks a few English language books, but go to the Cruceros club house for a book swap. There is much to see in La Paz, with favorite cruiser hang outs, coffee houses, chic restaurants, taco stands – everything you can imagine. Again, just ask on the morning net.

The large, sandy island of El Mogote has endless miles of beaches, a treasure trove of shells, flotsam and a wide variety of birds. An attraction for divers is an artificial reef consisting of three vessels that have been sunk in the area. Information on their location is available at local dive shops. Don't hesitate to try everything here in La Paz. This may be your first chance to relax and enjoy a true Mexican city. Try the food, walk the malecon, visit with the locals, take a cooking class, total immersion Spanish, LP the hull, have a decent sun awning made... relax, you're in real Mexico now. Finally!

Club Cruceros de La Paz (headquartered in their new facility at Marina De La Paz) provides some much needed assistance to children living in poverty in the La Paz area. For many years it has sponsored a Christmas Program for families in the outskirts of La Paz and now their involvement is a year round program. In addition to collecting children's clothes and toys, fund-raising is done to support a breakfast and scholarship program to offset educational costs, medical needs for kids and their families, and a food bank. This is a great way to offset the memories of holidays past and give back to the population of La Paz. For information e-mail: cruceros@baja.com See www.clubcruceros for local goods and services.

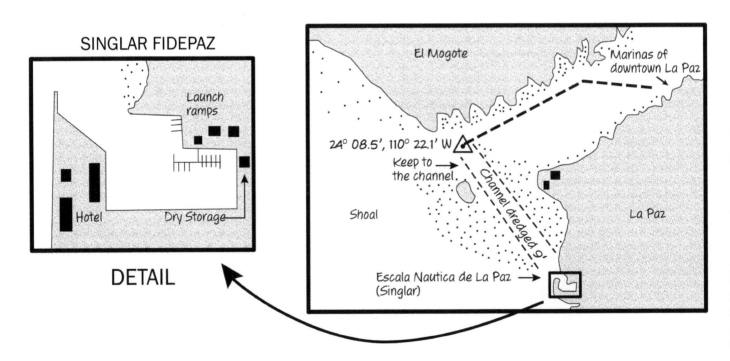

SINGLAR FIDEPAZ

Launch ramps

Hotel   Dry Storage

DETAIL

El Mogote

Marinas of downtown La Paz

24° 08.5', 110° 22.1' W
Keep to the channel.

Channel dredged 9'

Shoal

La Paz

Escala Nautica de La Paz → (Singlar)

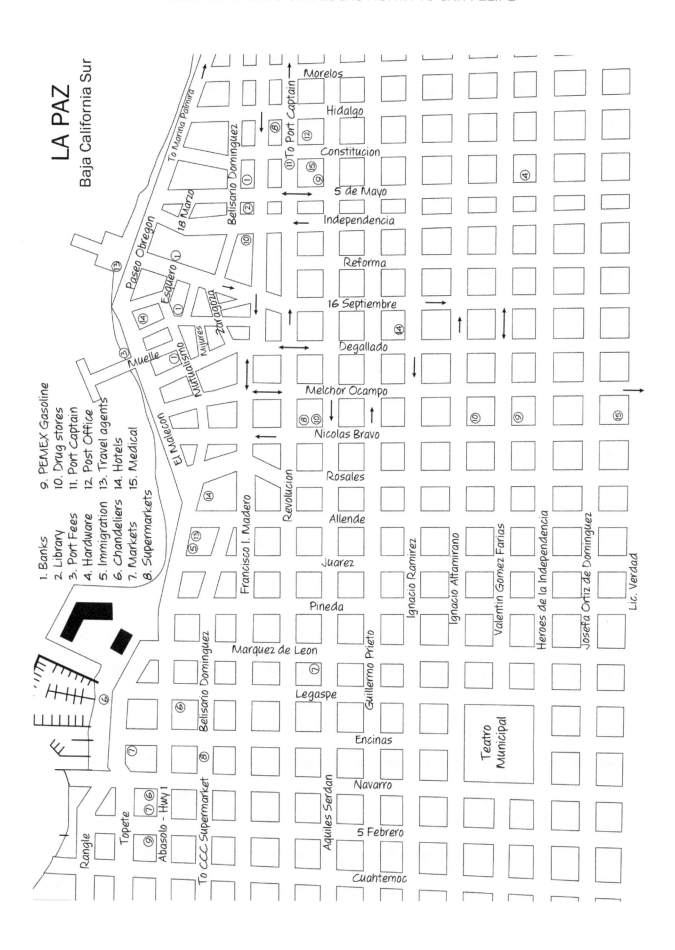

LA PAZ
Baja California Sur

1. Banks
2. Library
3. Port Fees
4. Hardware
5. Immigration
6. Chandeliers
7. Markets
8. Supermarkets
9. PEMEX Gasoline
10. Drug stores
11. Port Captain
12. Post Office
13. Travel agents
14. Hotels
15. Medical

ISLAS ESPIRITU SANTO AND PARTIDA

These scenic islands are close to La Paz and contain a variety of popular and picturesque anchorages in addition to excellent snorkeling and diving. The islands are of volcanic origin, tilted to the east and sloping down in the west to the sea. These islands and surrounding waters are a designated Park where fishing is prohibited up to 1 mile offshore. A wristband to permit landing on the islands may be purchased from park authorities.

Isla Espiritu Santo is the larger of the two islands, being a little over 7 miles long. Close to the north is **Isla Partida.** In the past they were one landmass, but a volcanic crater that formed between them has subsided and been breached open to the sea that now separates them. The tilt of the islands produces almost all the anchorages on the western side. The anchorages are described in clockwise order, beginning with the southernmost, nearest to La Paz.

The western anchorages are open to the west and southwest, making most of them vulnerable to a local wind, the Corumel, which blows off the hot lands to the southwest. It begins in the afternoon, sometimes attaining quite a velocity by evening and continuing through most of the night to die away to a morning calm as the land cools. Thus, some of these otherwise good western anchorages are only useful for daytime visits, requiring a move to better spots for the night.

Punta Dispensa, the southeastern end of Espiritu Santo, lies on the north side of Canal de Lorenzo. It is a low, rock and sand point. Shoals to the south and the very exposed location make this only a temporary daytime anchorage. **WPT 24°24.03', 110°20.03'**

Caleta Gabriel Foyer, WPT 24°24.81', 110°20.88' is a double-bight cove at the entrance to Bahia San Gabriel. The southern bight is a nice anchorage in sand at 15 feet off an inviting beach. This bight is the best protection from a Coromuel for miles around. The northern bight is too shallow for any but the shallowest draft vessels to enter.

Bahia San Gabriel is almost filled with a shoal bank leaving only the eastern and southern corners available for daytime anchorage. **WPT 24°25.4', 110°21.28'**. The beaches are attractive with mangroves and a few remains of abandoned pearling stations at the southern end. This makes for an interesting shore trip if you are able to get the dinghy in to the lagoon. San Gabriel gives only marginal protection from the northwest and is completely open to a Coromuel.

The next cove has three lobes and two small islands, Isla Gallo and Isla Gallina, before them. There is good diving around both islands. The central lobe is **Puerto Ballena.** Two anchorage spots are available, the one behind Isla Gallo offers some protection and the other is off the northern lobe, exposed to Corumel winds. Watch your depths carefully as the area is quite shallow.

Isla Ballena offers little in the way of a protected anchorage, but it's an interesting place to snorkel and dive. It is about ¾ mile long and about 200 ft. high. Three boats have been sunk to create an artificial reef off the west end of the island and they provide an excellent area for snorkeling and diving. On shore, directly opposite the island is Caleta de la Isla, pleasant cove with an inviting beach. It isn't as shoal as most of the other coves in the area. The anchorage is in 10 feet **WPT 24° 29.33', 110°23.12'**. There is a nice hike up the broad valley that backs the beach.

Caleta El Candelero, is next and is a very beautiful bay, named for the candle-like finger of rock which projects from the middle of the cove. This is a popular cove but is completely open to Coromuels. Anchor in the northern lobe, in 15 feet, sand, clear of the shoal water in the bay. The Mexican Navy has an outpost in the hut on the north side of the bay. The only known fresh water supply on the island is a well among the rocks and bushes behind the hut. Water can be obtained from the well; a bucket and 20 ft. of line are needed to accomplish this. Further up the valley is a cave and waterfall, during the wet season.

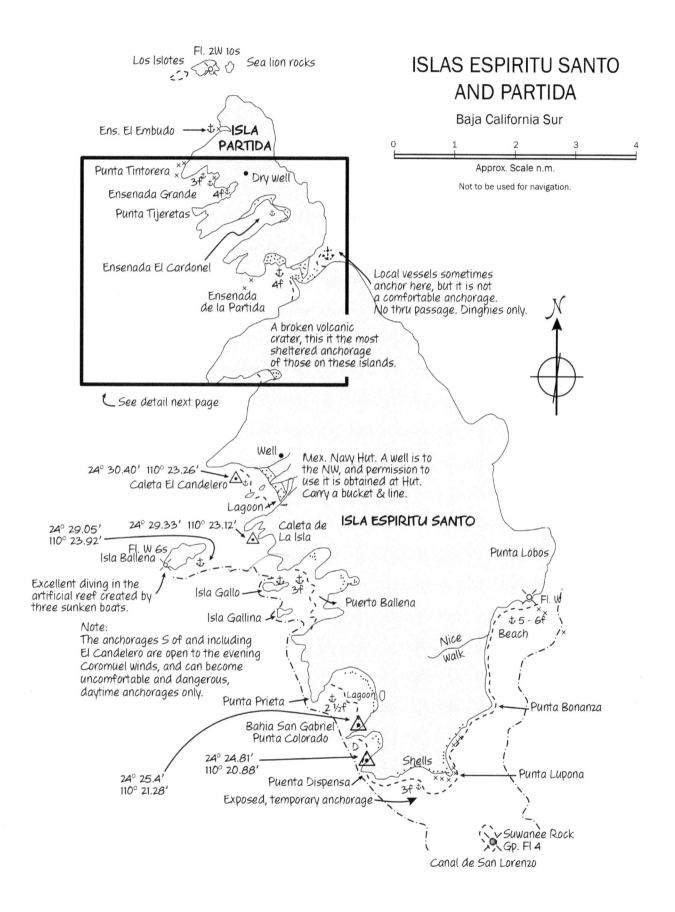

ISLAS ESPIRITU SANTO
AND PARTIDA

Baja California Sur

0   1   2   3   4

Approx. Scale n.m.

Not to be used for navigation.

Los Islotes   Fl. 2W 10s   Sea lion rocks

Ens. El Embudo →⚓× ISLA PARTIDA

Punta Tintorera ××
×
3f ⚓
Ensenada Grande   4f⚓
Punta Tijeretas   ⚓

• Dry well

Ensenada El Cardonel   ⚓ 4f

× Ensenada de la Partida

Local vessels sometimes
anchor here, but it is not
a comfortable anchorage.
No thru passage. Dinghies only.

A broken volcanic
crater, this it the most
sheltered anchorage
of those on these islands.

⤸ See detail next page

N

Well •

Mex. Navy Hut. A well is to
the NW, and permission to
use it is obtained at Hut.
Carry a bucket & line.

24° 30.40' 110° 23.26'
Caleta El Candelero △⚓

Lagoon

24° 29.05'
110° 23.92'   24° 29.33' 110° 23.12'   Caleta de
                                          La Isla   △
Fl. W 6s
Isla Ballena   ⚓

ISLA ESPIRITU SANTO

Punta Lobos

Excellent diving in the
artificial reef created by
three sunken boats.

Isla Gallo   ⚓ 3f ⚓

Puerto Ballena

Isla Gallina

Nice
walk

×
Fl. W
⚓ 5 - 6f ×
Beach   ×
×

Note:
The anchorages S of and including
El Candelero are open to the evening
Coromuel winds, and can become
uncomfortable and dangerous,
daytime anchorages only.

Punta Prieta →   Lagoon ◡
                   ⚓
                   2 ½f

Bahia San Gabriel
Punta Colorado   △

Punta Bonanza

24° 24.81'
110° 20.88'   △

Shells

Punta Lupona

24° 25.4'
110° 21.28'

Puenta Dispensa   ×××
3f ⚓
Exposed, temporary anchorage →

ꜱ Suwanee Rock
× Gp. Fl 4

Canal de San Lorenzo

107

Caleta Enmedia, WPT 24°30.90', 110°23.94', is a diminutive cove with a nice beach around a bend at its head. Back of the beach is another one of the few broad valleys that allow for a hike to stretch your legs. There is possible Coromuel protection in close to the beach. Sand at 15 feet.

Caleta Partida is the best anchorage in the islands, protected from the Corumel winds and situated in a unique setting. It is the breached crater that separates the two islands, The north and east sides show light-colored shoal water areas. Keeping clear of the shoal area, the best spot to anchor is toward the northeast corner in 4 to 5 fathoms, sand. Gusty squalls sometimes blow down from the heights above, but this is usually the quietest location. Another good spot is off the semi-overhang of rock on the western side of the cove. Local boats sometimes anchor off this spot and go ashore to cook their catch.

The eastern portion of the passage between the islands is blocked by low spits of sand reaching out from each island where passage can only be negotiated by dinghy. A little over a mile southeast of the northern tip of Isla Espiritu Santo there is a cave at sea level. A second, much larger cave is a short distance to the south where there appears to be a profile similar to that of Alfred Hitchcock with that of an Indian's face above. By diving under Hitchcock's chin you'll find a spectacular cave that is well worth visiting during settled weather and relatively calm conditions.

The entrance to Caleta Partida is clear. When coming from the north give the northwest entrance point of the bay a wide berth to avoid a reef that extends to a small island and beyond. Swing clear of this reef and enter in mid-channel to avoid all dangers. Good diving is found in the vicinity of the reef. Behind the reef is **El Cardoncito**, a small, narrow cove that may be used when exploring the reef, or as an overnight anchorage in settled weather. There is room for several boats, a small beach and anchorage in 15 feet, sand. **WPT 24° 32.27', 110°23.44'**

The next cove to the north is **El Cardonel** and it is part of a slit that almost cuts across Isla Partida. Though the cove is shoal at its head and is exposed to Corumel winds it can be used as an anchorage. **WPT 24°33.09', 110°23.20'**. The remains of an abandoned oyster farm are visible in the northern part of the bay. A hike of about 1.5 hours on the trail indicated leads to a small fresh water lagoon, and the eastern shore of Partida.

Little Double-Bight is tucked into the point between Cardonal and Ensenada Grande. The head of the larger of the two bights is not a beach, but consists of sheer, smooth rock cliffs. There is anchorage here in 25' right up to the cliffs.

Punta Tijeretas (Frigate-bird Point) projects out for some distance and partially protects the next group of anchorages. **Ensenada Grande** is a large bay with three coves on the northeast side; North Bight, Middle Bight and South Bight. Each of the three small coves provides good anchorage. The North Bight anchorage in 10 feet, **WPT 24°43', 110°24.44'**, the Middle Bight anchorage **WPT 24°33.84', 110°24.16'** in 10 feet, sand, and the most protected spot off Caleta de La Cruz in the South Bight off a small, dark, stoney beach, **WPT 24°33.83', 110°23.90'**. Punta Tintorera provides protection to all three coves from northerly winds. A dinghy trip across the extensive shoal area at the head of the South Bight takes you to a white sandy beach with dry grass and bushes beyond. A dry well marks the spot where Joseph Krutch, the naturalist who did so much to 'discover' Baja, camped in 1959.

The northern point of Isla Partida is 2 miles from Punta Tintorera and only a small indentation, **El Embudo**, lies between. The walls of this cove are steep and rocky, but anchorage can be taken in 15 feet, though it is exposed to the northwest. Off the northern tip of Partida are **Los Isolotes**, 50 ft. islands where a navigation light is located. A sea lion colony inhabits these islands and the uproar they create is so loud that it can be heard in Ensenada Grande. Swimming with sea lions at Los Islotes has an element of danger that can be a special experience. It is best to anchor in Ensenada El Embudo and take the dinghy to the sea lion colony. Male sea lions are quite territorial but females and pups are friendly and seem approachable

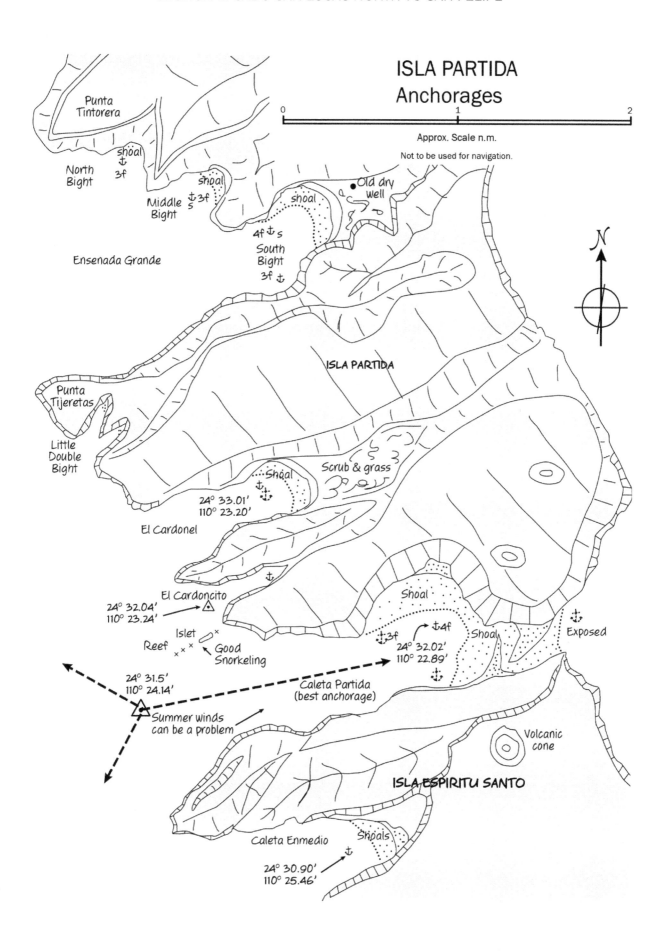

ISLA PARTIDA
Anchorages

0   1   2

Approx. Scale n.m.

Not to be used for navigation.

Punta Tintorera

shoal
3f

North Bight

shoal

Middle Bight
s 3f

Ensenada Grande

shoal

Old dry well

4f s

South Bight
3f

ISLA PARTIDA

Punta Tijeretas

Little Double Bight

Shoal

Scrub & grass

24° 33.01'
110° 23.20'

El Cardonel

El Cardoncito

24° 32.04'
110° 23.24'

Islet

Reef

Good Snorkeling

Shoal

3f

Shoal

4f

Shoal

Exposed

24° 32.02'
110° 22.89'

24° 31.5'
110° 24.14'

Caleta Partida
(best anchorage)

Summer winds
can be a problem

Volcanic cone

ISLA ESPIRITU SANTO

Caleta Enmedio

Shoals

24° 30.90'
110° 25.46'

but do not put your hand out to pet them for if they expect a snack and are disappointed they may give a nasty nip. A tunnel cuts through the easternmost islet of this group. You can pass between the islets and Isla Partida though a safer course is to pass to the north when circumnavigating the islands.

After seeing the numerous coves on the western side of Isla Partida, the run down the eastern side is a complete change, with its high cliffs eroded into colorful formations. Fish camps are located at a gap that leads to Caleta Partida and local boats are seen ashore but this area is too exposed to be a tolerable anchorage.

Punta Lobos, a steep, rocky bluff, is the easternmost extremity of Isla Espiritu Santo, after which the coast then turns southwestward toward Punta Lupona. An extensive reef extends southeast from the point, but anchorage can be found at the head of the bight beyond the reef. This reef is awash at low tide but well covered at high tide. The protection from northern weather is excellent in behind the point, but you must swing clear of the reef before you head northwest and anchor off a hill in sand at 15 feet. **WPT 24°27.26', 110°18.12'.** Beachcombing along the Bonanza beach is exceptional. It is a wide, white 2 mile long beach, littered with great finds.

Further south is **Punta Bonanza**, a rocky bluff, followed by an indentation in the coast forming a bight. Sand dunes back this part of the coast and fishing huts seen ashore are sometimes occupied. A hotspring surrounded by Indian rockwork is a short distance inland.

Los Islotes seem to be covered in frosting. Bird frosting! Photo: Holly Scott

ISLAS SAN JOSE and SAN FRANCISCO

ISLA SAN FRANCISCO is a small island 17 miles north of Isla Partida. At the south end is a curved, rocky ridge connected to the south part of the island by a low, sandy section. Within this comma-shaped tail is a lovely, curved, white sand beach known as The Hook. Good anchorage can be taken in the cove formed by the isthmus and the island in about 3 fathoms, sand. Enter the cove in the center as there are rocks and reefs on either side. Once inside, good protection from northers can be had by snuggling up close to the cliffs on the northwest side of the cove, in 20 feet over sand. The center of the cove is 25 feet, sand at **WPT 24°49.19', 110°34.12'**.

Ashore are salt pans used for drying and collecting salt. Don't taste the salt unless you are having constipation issues – long story, don't ask... There is a well beaten path starting at the lowest spot on the ridge of the hook, which leads to the summit. The view from the top is well worth the climb and the photos of your boat will be classic. Wear closed toe shoes for walks ashore through the scrub weeds of the desert – another story...

There are two other small coves west of The Hook Anchorage. **Caleta Las Cuevas** is just around the hook's western entry point. It has two caves used by fishermen for shelter and provides good shelter from the north. There is a rock reef that comes out of the middle of the cove to separate the two bights. Anchor off the end of the reef at **WPT 24°49.28', 110°34.62'**.

Caleta Dos Playas is the next cove, which is a little larger and has two beaches, but protection form north and northwest is not quite as good as Las Cuevas.
Anchor in 25 feet, sand at **WPT 24°49.54', 110°35'**.

North Anchorage is west of the northernmost point of the island. It is a large area of shallow sand which offers good protection from mild southerly weather. The depth is 12 feet at **WPT 24°50.62', 110°34.38'**.

In settled weather anchorage can be taken in the eastern lee of the island in about 10 feet, sand. There is some foul ground along this section of the coast, with visible rocks, but out from the beach the anchorage is clear. Agates can be picked up on the nearby beach where they have fallen from the steep, colorful rocky cliffs and there are spectacular tide pools at low tide. Gold was found and mined on the island in the 1880's and pearlers also worked the waters of this area for many years.

Two sets of small islets lie off the northern sides of Isla San Francisco. **Rocas de la Foca** (Seal Rocks), is a low outcropping about 5' high, and lie about 2 miles to the northwest at **WPT 24°50.56', 110°36.34'**. The passage between them and Isla San Francisco is clear.

Rocas Del Coyote are a group of rocks and small islands about midway between Isla San Francisco and the low southern extension of Isla San Jose. The largest island, Isla Coyote, is nearly 40' high and is the home of several families of fishermen. The region in the immediate neighborhood of these rocks is dangerous, though there is about 6 to 7 fathoms in the mid-channel passage between the rocks and Isla San Jose. Small vessels can also pass mid-channel between the rocks and Isla San Francisco to the south; an unprotected anchorage can be taken on the west side of Isla Coyote. This tiny island has been inhabited for centuries and continues to be home to a fishing settlement with tidy homes and yards. In settled weather, a trip ashore can be very interesting. Just seeing the whale bones used to decorate may be worth the trip. There is excellent diving in the rocky islets and reefs nearby.

ISLAS SAN JOSE & SAN FRANCISO

Baja California Sur

0   ½   1

Approx. Scale n.m.

Not to be used for navigation.

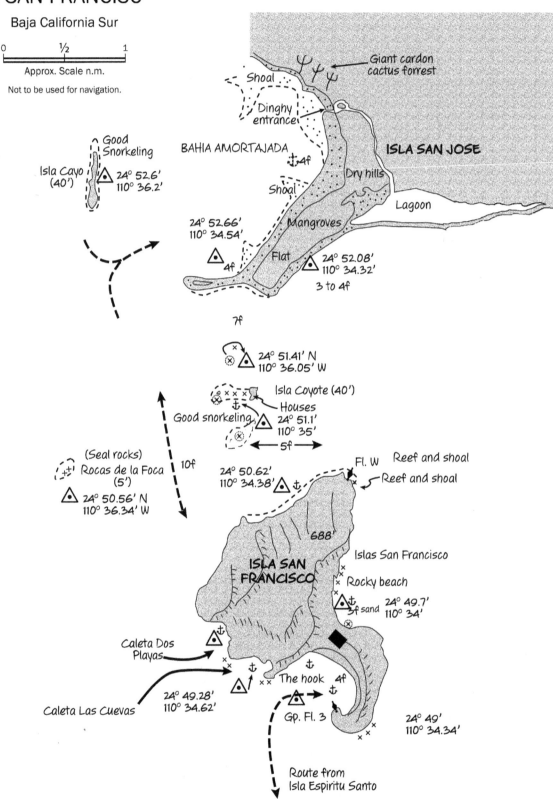

Giant cardon cactus forrest

Shoal

Dinghy entrance

BAHIA AMORTAJADA

ISLA SAN JOSE

4f

Dry hills

Good Snorkeling

Isla Cayo (40')

24° 52.6'
110° 36.2'

Shoal

Lagoon

Mangroves

24° 52.66'
110° 34.54'

Flat

4f

24° 52.08'
110° 34.32'

3 to 4f

7f

24° 51.41' N
110° 36.05' W

Isla Coyote (40')

Houses

Good snorkeling

24° 51.1'
110° 35'

5f

(Seal rocks)
Rocas de la Foca
(5')

24° 50.56' N
110° 36.34' W

10f

24° 50.62'
110° 34.38'

Fl. W   Reef and shoal

Reef and shoal

688'

ISLA SAN
FRANCISCO

Islas San Francisco

Rocky beach

24° 49.7'
110° 34'

3f sand

Caleta Dos
Playas

The hook   4f

Caleta Las Cuevas

24° 49.28'
110° 34.62'

Gp. Fl. 3

24° 49'
110° 34.34'

Route from
Isla Espiritu Santo

ISLA SAN JOSE

This is the third largest island in the Sea of Cortez, being about 16 miles long and 5 miles at its widest. It lies 3 to 5 miles off the eastern Baja coast, about 2 miles north of Isla San Francisco. Both tidal currents and wind can be significant here.

There is a large, low sand spit that extends westward from the south point of the island. This spit ends at Punta Ostiones and marks the south side of **Bahia Amortajada**. A lagoon fringed with mangrove thickets takes up the inner portion of the spit and is home to a great variety of birds. The lagoon has two dinghy openings to the sea. The principal one, a long passage through the mangroves, lies at the eastern end of the north shore beach. The one on the south side is simply a break in the south shore beach and dunes. The lagoon is worth exploring from whichever side provides a safe anchorage for your boat.

Into the Mangroves.

Anchorage on the southeast side of La Amortajada will give you protection from northerly weather although the wind can come over the dunes and lagoon. The holding is good in sand at 20 to 30 feet. Anchor off the low hill that interrupts the flatness of the dunes, and marks the southern dinghy access to the lagoon. **WPT 24°52.08', 110°34.32'.** There is an inoperative light tower on the end of the point.

On the northwest side, shelter from a norther or southeast wind and waves is not as clear-cut. Depths become very shallow for a large area northeast of the elbow in the beach that forms the outer arm of Amortajada, called Punta Ostiones. A decent fair weather anchorage is **WPT 24°52.66', 110°34.54'.** There are other areas farther to the northeast where depths are 45 feet right up to the beach. Ashore, in the northeast part of the bay is an amazing Cardon cactus forest, well worth a stroll.

ISLA CAYO. Proceeding clockwise around Isla San Jose, this long narrow rock is less than a mile northwest of the arm of La Amortajada. There is deep water all around it except off the northern end where the rocky rib extends out under the surface. The south end of Cayo is a solid block of rock about 50 feet high. Good diving and snorkeling is reported at the north end.

Punta Salinas is three miles northwest of Isla Cayo and is another sand spit, much smaller than Amortajada, but large enough to support a salt pan in conjunction with that at Evaristo across the channel. There is a navigation light at its end Gp.Fl.4, as well as an abandoned red and white tower. This point gives a reasonable northwest shelter on its south side, although large swells may refract around the end. **WPT 24°54.84', 110°38.02'** is 20 feet deep in sand. It is open to the south and west. Salinas is another great place for a walk ashore. The beach is beautifully white and uncluttered, the salt operation is interesting as well as the abandoned equipment scattered about, and shelling can be very rewarding.

Bahia Cazadero is the exception to the sand spit anchorages on the western shore of Isla San Jose. This is a broad bay 7 miles north of Punta Salinas. It gives good protection from a norther, and better protection from the northwest than does the Northwest Spit, probably due to the fact that the spit breaks up the swell so there isn't much left by the time it reaches Cazadero. **WPT 25°1.21', 110°41.54'** is a good spot to anchor. The beach is backed by a broad valley with a trail that leads to Rancho Palma Sola on the eastern side of the island.

Northwest Spit offers protection similar to Punta Salinas. A big northwest swell will wrap around the point and the wind will come over the low spit. There is a landlocked lagoon inside the spit which is foul smelling upon close inspection, but not noticeable from a distance. There is a navigation light on the end of the spit which may or may not be operational. Anchorage may be had in 20 feet at **WPT 25°1.79', 110°42.36'.**

Kelton's Coves is one of the few anchorages along the eastern side of the island. There is a navigation light, Fl.Wht., on Punta Colorado, the easternmost bump of the island. North of the point is a series of very small coves with walls of smooth rock on either side, and fingers of rock separating the coves, each of which has a small beach at its head. The northernmost large cove offers protection from the prevailing westerlies, but none for a norther. **WPT 25°1.48', 110°35.22'.** This is a wonderful place to explore by dinghy in settled weather.

Back to the Baja coastline...Across from Isla San Francisco is **Punta El Mechudo**. This is a prominent steep point if you are coasting close in. From offshore to the east, it is not easy to spot although it lies north of the prominent peak after which it is named. As you approach, you can see the little cove **Arroyo Verde** (a beautiful green little valley) south of the point. **WPT 24°47.56', 110°39.66'.** You can also see the point drop away to the north where there is a fine beach and a small cove behind a reef off Punta Mechudo. This is Mechudo Cove, **WPT 24°48.7', 110°39.74,** 15 to 20 feet, sand. Both coves offer protection from the prevailing winds, but anything easterly will not be protected.

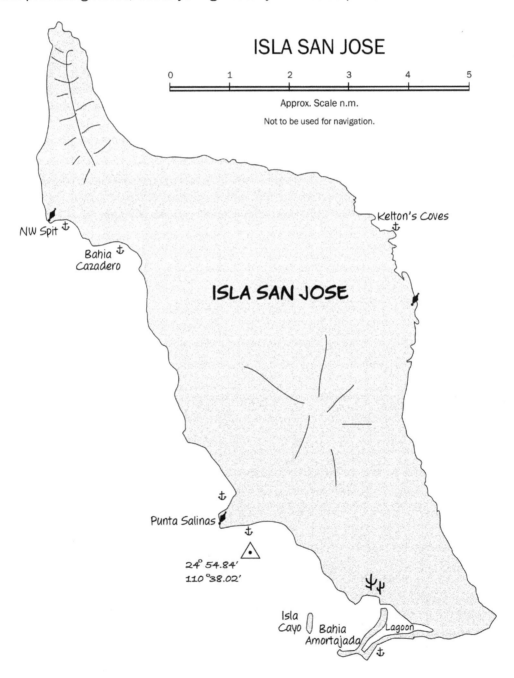

ISLA SAN JOSE

0   1   2   3   4   5

Approx. Scale n.m.

Not to be used for navigation.

NW Spit

Bahia Cazadero

Kelton's Coves

ISLA SAN JOSE

Punta Salinas

24° 54.84'
110° 38.02'

Isla Cayo   Bahia Amortajada   Lagoon

SAN EVARISTO

Canal de San Jose lies between Isla San Jose and the Baja coast north of Cabeza Mechudo. Eight miles north of Cabeza Mechudo is Punta Evaristo, a rocky headland sheltering another excellent anchorage. As it is close to Isla San Francisco, most cruisers choose to visit one of these anchorages when going north and the other when southbound.

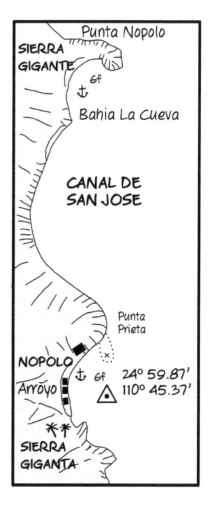

Close under the hook of **Punta Evaristo** is a circular cove about a mile in diameter that provides good protection from all winds. The entrance lies to the east, between the southward projection of Punta Evaristo and the northward curving beach. Enter in mid-channel where it is deep, for both entrance points have dangers that project into the opening. See sketch next .

Good anchorage can be taken within the cove either in the southern bight in 3 to 5 fathoms, sand, **WPT 24°54.7', 110°42.4'** or in the northern part of the cove beneath the point in 4 fathoms, **WPT 24°54.8', 110°42.21'**. The holding is good and the bay is seldom disturbed by wind or seas. Excellent diving can be enjoyed off the point.

Landing on the beach is easy. Punta Evaristo is home to a small community of fishermen and their families. There is a small tienda that is reasonably stocked, a small restaurant, an ice plant and on the south side of the bay, a palapa on the beach that sells very cold beer.

CALETA NOPOLO (Nopolo Cove)

About 7 miles north of Punta Evaristo and 8 miles south of Punta Nopolo is a rocky bluff (sometimes referred to as Punta Nopolo Sur) which protects a small cove between the rocky points. Though there is limited protection from northerly swells, anchorage can be found off the pebble beach in 3 to 4 fathoms, sand. At night the wind sometimes blows offshore from the high mountains behind the settlement on the north side of the bay. **WPT 24°59.81', 110°45.45'.**

The shallow water at the head of the bay maybe a holding area for clams that are collected elsewhere. Clams, calamari and other seafood is taken by panga from Nopolo to Evaristo and from there by truck for shipment to markets and restaurants in La Paz and Cabo. Children often visit vessels at anchor to trade shells for candy or clothes.

The cove to the north of Caleta Nopolo is **Bahia La Cueva**. There is a settlement here and often numerous pangas are either anchored or moored in the bay. At times, there are so many that the depth is 60 feet or more once you are clear of them. The cove is well protected from northerly weather if you are able to get in far enough. Expect strong currents in this area.

SAN EVARISTO

Baja California Sur

0   ½   1   1½

Approx. Scale n.m.

Not to be used for navigation.

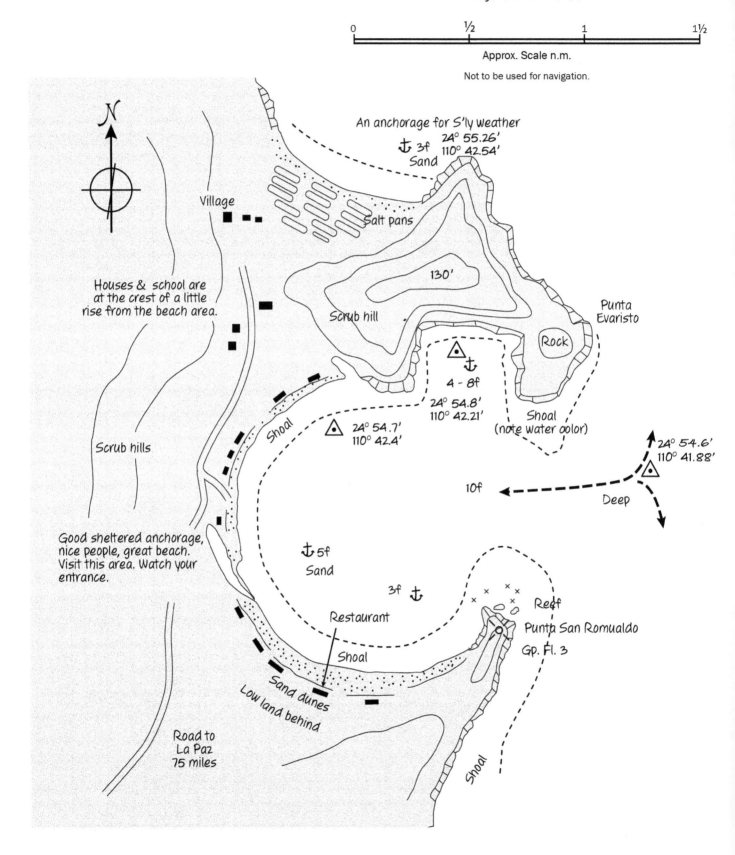

An anchorage for S'ly weather
⚓ 3f   24° 55.26'
Sand   110° 42.54'

Village

Salt pans

130'

Scrub hill

Punta
Evaristo

Rock

Houses & school are
at the crest of a little
rise from the beach area.

⚓
4 - 8f

24° 54.8'
110° 42.21'

Shoal
(note water color)

24° 54.7'
110° 42.4'

Shoal

Scrub hills

24° 54.6'
110° 41.88'

10f

Deep

Good sheltered anchorage,
nice people, great beach.
Visit this area. Watch your
entrance.

⚓ 5f
Sand

3f ⚓

Reef

Restaurant

× × ×
× ×
× ×

Punta San Romualdo
Gp. Fl. 3

Shoal

Sand dunes
Low land behind

Road to
La Paz
75 miles

Shoal

116

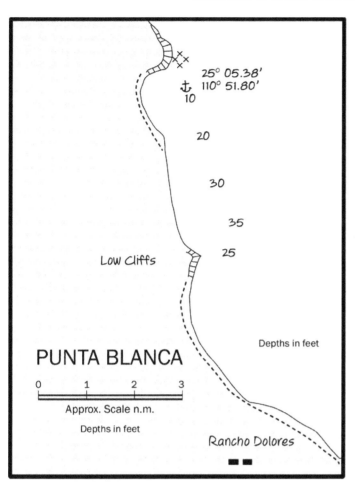

25° 05.38'
110° 51.80'
10

20

30

35

25

Low Cliffs

Depths in feet

PUNTA BLANCA

0   1   2   3

Approx. Scale n.m.

Depths in feet

Rancho Dolores

Bahia Rincon is 2½ miles northwest of Punta Nopolo. It is a well protected cove from southerly weather, however the currents can be strong, it is rather deep close to and it is not protected from northerlies. **WPT 25°1.90', 110°47.72'.**

For the 19 miles between Punta Nopolo Sur and Punta Botella, the coast is a succession of steep, rocky bluffs broken by arroyos that break through to the shore, ending in sandy beaches. The colorful rocks and brilliant light give this desert a stark and dramatic beauty similar to Arizona's Grand Canyon. The commonly followed direct route up the coast stands some distance offshore so that individual features are often not noticed.

Rancho Dolores (Pains) must be an indicator as to the difficulties building a mission in this area. If you wish to visit the Rancho or the ruins of Mission Dolores, this is an open roadstead anchorage. The mission is about 3 miles inland from here. The rancho is large and active, growing citrus, vegetables and cattle with irrigation water from a nearby arroyo. Rancho Dolores is at the beginning of a wide coastal plain that extends north 18 miles almost to Punta San Mateo. **WPT 25°04.73', 110°51.48'.**

If you don't want to leave your boat in the open roadstead for a trip ashore, there is a better and more protected anchorage a little over a mile up the coast at **Punta Blanca**. This cove provides protection from the prevailing northwesterlies, but not much from a real norther. **WPT 25°5.38', 110°51.80'** in 10 to 15 feet, sand. North of Punta Blanca, and south of Timbabichi are 3 offshore rocky islets: La Habana, Rocas Moreno and Roca Negra.

La Habana is the most southerly, and the largest of the islets. It is steep-to except that there is a detached rock at its northeast corner and possibly attendant reefs. Habana is 2¼ miles almost directly north of Punta Blanca, and a mile offshore. **WPT 25°7.7', 110°51.74'** is on the west side.

Punta El Cobre is the mother point for Rocas Moreno. The cove on the south side offers protection in light conditions, but the reefs do little to break down the swell from the north. Anchorage **WPT 25°12.49', 110°55.27'** in 10 to 15 feet sand.

Isla Rocas Moreno is the next islet, about 5½ miles north of La Habana, except that it lies so close to the shore, and is so low and flat that it can be easily missed. Behind it is a good anchorage in the shelter of Punta El Cobre. There is a 20 foot deep passage between the two however, a reef extends off the point 100 yards or so, and a smaller reef off the islet. Passage between them is not recommended.

Roca Negra is the third of the islets. It lies about a mile offshore, almost two miles directly north of Rocas Moreno and two miles southeast of the point at Timbabichi. There is deep water around it except for a reef about the length of the island itself, which extends from the western end toward the shore. **WPT** on the east side is **25°14.8', 110°55'.**

DANGER: East and southeast of the visible Islas Rocas Moreno is a large reef. The northern edge dries at low tide and is visible and avoidable. At high tide, there is an exposed pinnacle near the eastern end. However, the expanse of reef to the southeast is always covered and should be given a wide berth, especially if you are approaching from the north and want to anchor on the south side of Punta El Cobre. A rough **WPT** for the southeast corner of the reef is **25°47', 110°54.77'.**

PUERTO LOS GATOS

Bahia San Carlos opens along the coast northwest of Rocas Negra. It is a rather flat curve that ends at Punta Botella, a rocky, rugged point. Under the hook of the point a narrow lagoon entrance leads to a small, shallow area with some mangroves and green vegetation nearby. Behind the shore south of the lagoon is a two-story stone building that is a landmark seen for miles. It is only a shell, called Casa Grande, but nearby are the lower and smaller adobe houses of **Rancho Timbabiche**. An airstrip lies to the south. Anchorage can be taken in the open roadstead under the point where protection from northerly weather can be found. **WPT 25°16.29', 110°56.41'** in 20 feet, sand. There are several fishing families ashore so buying or trading for fish is no problem.

A mile north of Timbabiche is a bay called **Los Pargos**. This is a good anchorage in prevailing northwest weather, but not so good in a norther. There is a shelf along the north edge from the point to the beginning of the beach. There is a small reef extending out from the southern end of the bay. Enter and anchor in the center of the bay at **WPT 25°17.10', 110°56.23'** in 25 feet sand.

Puerto Los Gatos is a very colorful anchorage immediately north of Punta Botella. Since the bight is not deeply indented it can be identified by its relationship to Casa Grande and Punta Botella. **WPT 25g18.11, 110g56.56'**

Reefs extending from the rocky points of this cove give it some protection but require care to be taken on entry. On the south side of the cove a large, submerged rocky reef extends northward from the black, rocky point. Yellow sand dunes separate this point from a central red rock point, off whose tip there are some submerged rocks. An expanse of white sandy beach reaches to the northern point where the strata run parallel to the shore. Some detached rocks extend seaward off the point and a large reef extends south from the end of the point. Thus the apparently wide opening to the cove is actually restricted to about half its width by the underwater reefs.

Enter the area with care, holding a course well off the bight until the middle point and another sand beach are approximately 240° magnetic before turning into the cove. (See sketch) The clarity of the water is good and the extent of the reefs is usually visible. Depending on weather and sea conditions, anchor off either beach in about 10 feet. The northern beach is the larger of the two; diving is excellent on the reefs.

The setting and the colors make this a beautiful anchorage though it seems isolated since it is somewhat off the route followed when proceeding to Bahia Agua Verde. Water is not available. Some fishermen's huts may still be evident ashore.

Punta San Telmo is also known as Punta Prieta. It lies 1½ miles north of Puerto Los Gatos. The point is essentially a large block of dark rock offshore 100 yards but with an exposed reef connecting it with the shore and thus giving excellent northerly protection. Another short reef extends to the south off its mid-point. There are two beaches on the south side, the southern one is sand and attractive, but anchored off this, you could be exposed to a refracted swell, **WPT 25°19.41', 110°57.37'**. Less pleasant is a cobble beach to the north. Anchored here, you are right up in the corner of the best northern protection, **WPT 25°19.64', 110°57.29'**. The bottom in both locations is sand at about 15 feet, even off the cobble beach.

The north side of the point gives good protection from the south, a rarity in this area. There are rocks awash along the north side of the islet and the point before you come to the end of the long beach. Anchor in 15 feet, sand at **WPT 25°19.81', 110°57.59'**.

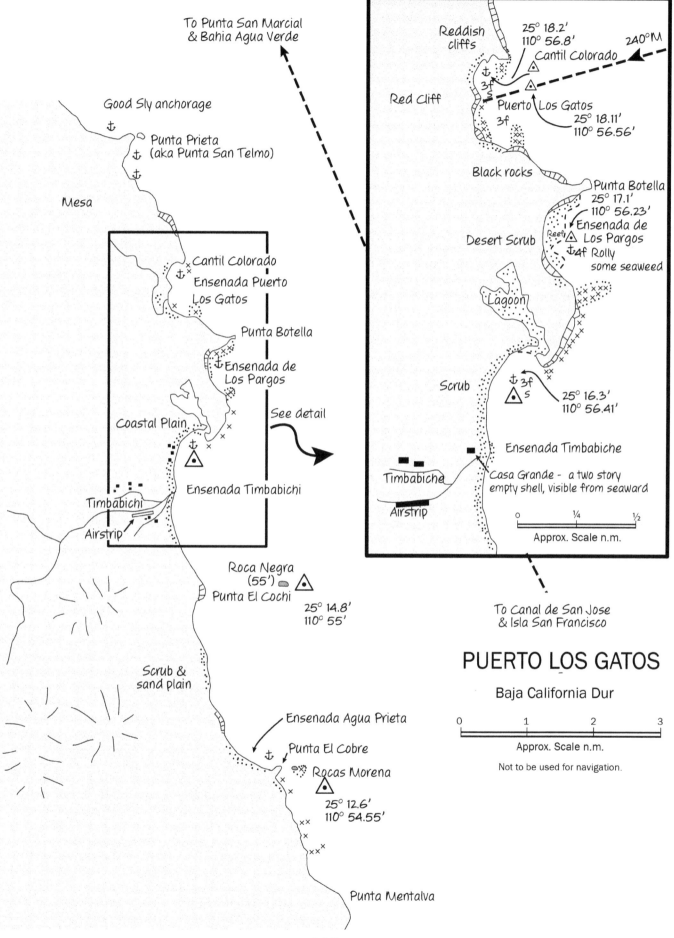

To Punta San Marcial
& Bahia Agua Verde

Good Sly anchorage

⚓

○ Punta Prieta
⚓ (aka Punta San Telmo)
⚓

Mesa

✝ Cantil Colorado
✕✕
⚓ Ensenada Puerto
Los Gatos

Punta Botella

⚓ Ensenada de
Los Pargos

Coastal Plain
⚓
△

Ensenada Timbabichi

Timbabichi

Airstrip

Roca Negra
(55') ▱ △
Punta El Cochi
25° 14.8'
110° 55'

Scrub &
sand plain

Ensenada Agua Prieta

⚓ Punta El Cobre
✿ Rocas Morena
△
25° 12.6'
110° 54.55'

Punta Mentalva

Reddish
cliffs

25° 18.2'
110° 56.8'
240°M
Cantil Colorado
⚓ △
3f
5
Puerto Los Gatos
3f
25° 18.11'
110° 56.56'

Red Cliff

Black rocks

Punta Botella
25° 17.1'
110° 56.23'
Reef △ Ensenada de
Los Pargos
⚓ 4f Rolly
some seaweed

Desert Scrub

Lagoon

Scrub
⚓ 3f
△
5
25° 16.3'
110° 56.41'

Ensenada Timbabiche
Casa Grande - a two story
empty shell, visible from seaward

Timbabiche

Airstrip

0   ¼   ½
Approx. Scale n.m.

To Canal de San Jose
& Isla San Francisco

PUERTO LOS GATOS

Baja California Dur

0   1   2   3
Approx. Scale n.m.

Not to be used for navigation.

See detail

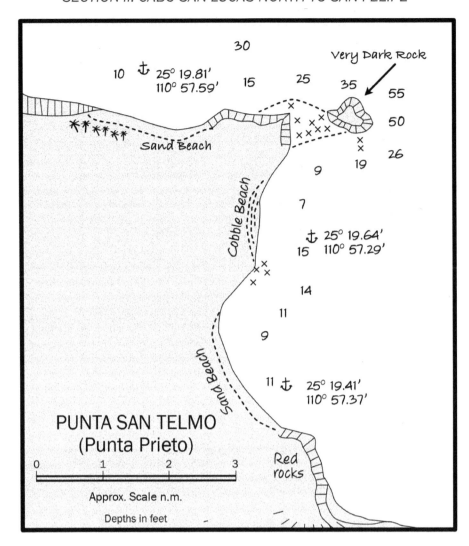

30

⚓ 25° 19.81'
110° 57.59'

10

15

25

35

Very Dark Rock

55

50

26

Sand Beach

9

19

Cobble Beach

7

⚓ 25° 19.64'
110° 57.29'

15

14

11

9

Sand Beach

11 ⚓ 25° 19.41'
110° 57.37'

PUNTA SAN TELMO
(Punta Prieto)

Red
rocks

0   1   2   3

Approx. Scale n.m.

Depths in feet

THE OFFSHORE ISLANDS SANTA CRUZ AND SAN DIEGO

Santa Cruz is 3½ miles long and barren rock, and lies 10 miles east of Timbabichi. There seem to be some possible anchorages here, but the depths are too great, too close to shore.

Isla San Diego, 4 miles south of Santa Cruz is smaller, only about a mile of it above water, but there is anchorage along its western edge. The bottom is best near the northern end and gets gradually more rocky as you approach the navigation light Gp. Fl.3. Spot your anchor carefully, about halfway down the island. **WPT 25°11.98', 110°42.20'**, in 20 feet. The eastern shore is strewn with rocks awash.

Danger: Longer than Isla San Diego itself is a reef extending WSW off its southwestern end near the light.

Punta Ballena is a perfect pyramid at the end of the surrounding mountains. The south side of this point is well protected in the prevailing northwesterlies. There are two beaches where you can land at Ballena, but not much to do once ashore. Ballena is a nice anchorage in 20 feet, sand **WPT 25°28.53', 111°1.10'**. There is an interesting dinghy attraction out at the very end of the point. In a narrow dinghy, or if you are snorkeling, you can enter a deep narrow cave far enough until the light begins to fade.

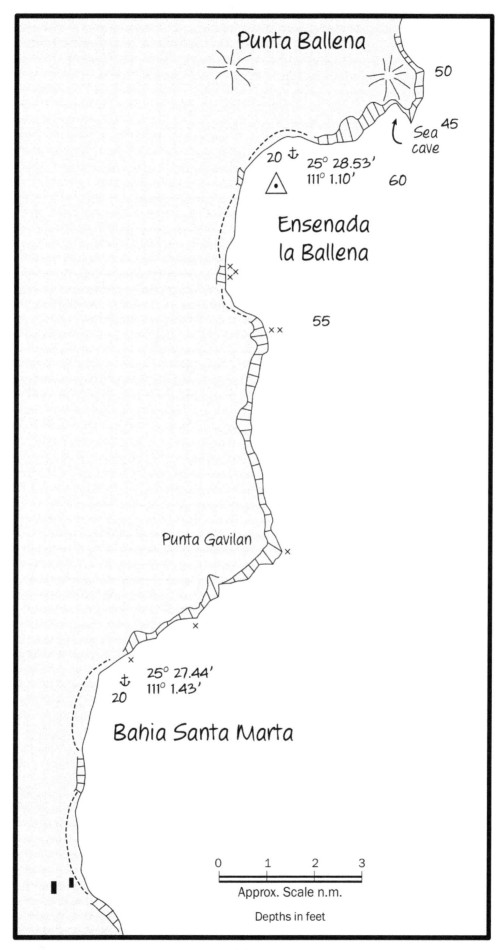

Punta Ballena

50

Sea 45
cave

20 ⚓
25° 28.53'
111° 1.10'   60

Ensenada
la Ballena

55

Punta Gavilan

25° 27.44'
⚓ 111° 1.43'
20

Bahia Santa Marta

0   1   2   3

Approx. Scale n.m.

Depths in feet

BAHIA AGUA VERDE

The anchorages of Bahia Agua Verde rank on a par with Espiritu Santo in popularity among cruising sailors. The spectacular green waters and picturesque setting of this excellent, centrally located anchorage, about 90 miles northwest of La Paz and 100 miles southeast of Mulege, make it a "must" for cruisers.

Approaching from the south, Punta San Marte is a high, rocky cliff beneath a pointed little peak 1,130' high. In the lee of the high peaks and ridges connecting the point to the mountains inland, there is a sweep of beach along the shore of **Bahia San Marte**. This lovely little bay is only 1½ miles north of Punta Ballena, and 3½ miles south of Puerta Agua Verde. It gives better protection from a roaring norther that either of the above. There are three good sand beaches on which to relax. The favored anchorage, giving the best northern protection is off the northernmost beach tucked in behind the knob on the point. If the cove is crowded, good anchorage can be found further down the shore as well. Anchorage is very good at **WPT 25°30.24', 111°1.04'.**

Sunset at Bahia Agua Verde.
Photo: Robin Richardson Stout

DANGER: Two dangerous isolated rocks lie 1 and 1 1/3 miles directly south of the point. An area of danger (approximately 3 miles long and 1½ miles wide) identified by breakers at low tide commences 3 miles SE of Punta San Marte and extends in a ESE direction for about 1½. A short reef lies NE off Punta San Marcial; **Arrecife San Marcial** is 1¼ miles further to the northeast. This extensive reef has one central, large, flat brown rocks and shoal area surrounded by many smaller rocks. Foul ground extends almost ¾ mile to the north and ½ mile to the south of the central rock. See the sketch.

The safest passage for a northbound or offshore vessel, is to stand off the coast by at least 2 miles. Identify Arrecife San Marcial and make a wide turn northward around it, staying beyond the 10-fathom curve, to **WPT 25°30.27', 111°0.81'.** Turn WSW to 240° magnetic, and proceed into the bay. An alternative for northbound vessels is to follow the 5 fathom contour along the shore and it will lead you right into the anchorage. Southbound vessels should head for the same **WPT 25°30.27', 111°0.81',** then turn WSW to 240° magnetic and proceed into the bay.

Punta Pasquel is a 338' rocky point that lies on the northwest side of the bay. It is connected to the shore by a sandy spit; the most popular anchorage is in the small cove formed by this spit. On the seaward side a rock and sand spur from Punta Pasquel end in a rocky pinnacle 100' high which shelters the cove. Some flat rock ledges off the southwest side of this cove lessen its extent. When anchoring, **WPT 25°31.36', 111°4.39',** care should be taken in setting the anchor so that it does not foul an underwater pinnacle adjacent to the 100' rock. The pinnacle is covered by 10' and shows as a brownish patch in the water.

Roca Solitaria, a 115' finger of rock, is the signpost of the Puerto Agua Verde anchorage. It stands about ½ miles off the tip of Punta Pasquel, and is visible for many miles. Apart from rocks ringing its base the passage between the point and Roca Solitaria is clear and vessels approaching from the north have no problems in approaching Agua Verde. Excellent snorkeling and diving can be found around this rock and the reefs in the bay.

An equally attractive anchorage lies across the bay in the southeastern cove. This cove with a fine sandy beach at its head is fringed by rocky walls and a 60' rock pinnacle. Anchor in about 3 to 4 fathoms, well out from the beach. **WPT 25°30.90', 111°3.72'.** Pelicans and other birds frequent the rocks and display their fishing skills, seemingly unaffected by vessels anchored in the coves. Anchorage can also be taken off the main beach of the bay where palms and other trees grow in front of the village of Agua Verde. **WPT 25°31', 111°4.11'.** Cruisers exploring the village will find a Satellite telephone, friendly inhabitants, two little schools, several small markets where fresh produce is delivered several times a week and local goat cheese is sold and a restaurant that is occasionally open. An extremely rough road links the village to Highway 1 and Ciudad Insurgentes, which is to the west.

BAHIA AGUA VERDE
Baja California Sur

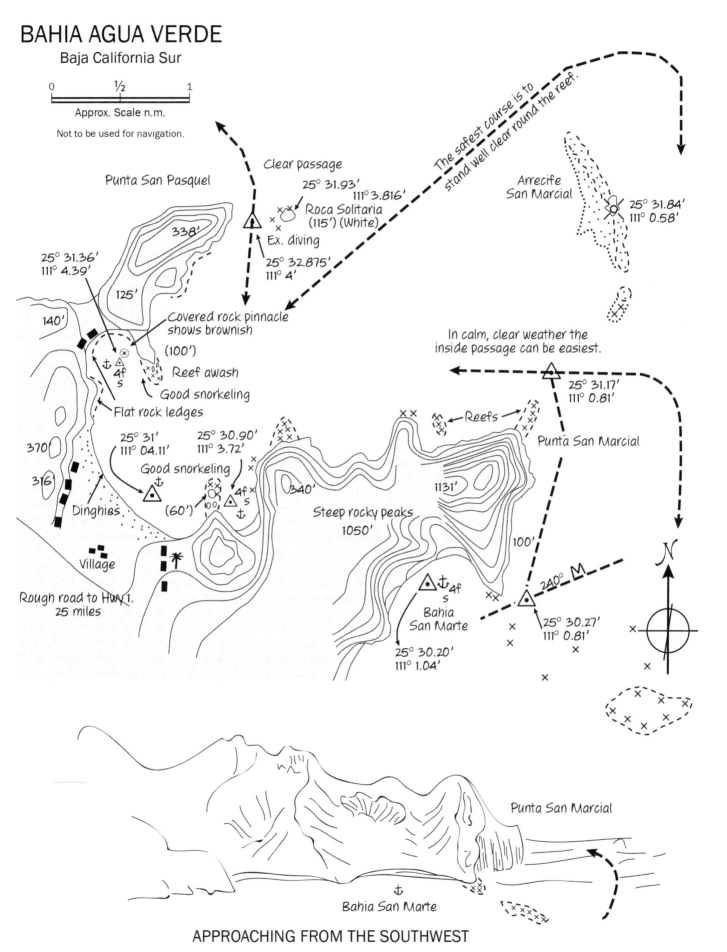

0 ½ 1
Approx. Scale n.m.
Not to be used for navigation.

Punta San Pasquel

Clear passage
25° 31.93'
111° 3.816'
Roca Solitaria
(115') (White)
Ex. diving
25° 32.875'
111° 4'

The safest course is to stand well clear round the reef.

Arrecife San Marcial
25° 31.84'
111° 0.58'

338'

25° 31.36'
111° 4.39'

125'

140'

Covered rock pinnacle shows brownish
(100')
Reef awash
Good snorkeling
Flat rock ledges

In calm, clear weather the inside passage can be easiest.

25° 31.17'
111° 0.81'

Punta San Marcial

25° 31'
111° 04.11'

25° 30.90'
111° 3.72'

Good snorkeling

370'

316'

Dinghies

Village

(60')

4f s

340'

Steep rocky peaks 1050'

1131'

100'

Reefs

240° M

N

Rough road to Hwy 1. 25 miles

Bahia San Marte
25° 30.20'
111° 1.04'

25° 30.27'
111° 0.81'

Punta San Marcial

Bahia San Marte

APPROACHING FROM THE SOUTHWEST

ISLA MONSERRAT

Lying only 8 miles north of Agua Verde, this is a favorite day sail for cruisers laying over at Agua Verde. The south end of Monserrat has two bights in Lighthouse Bay, both with sand at 15 to 20 feet. The eastern bight by the navigation light Fl. Wht. is the smaller and more open of the two. **WPT 25°38.99', 111°01.80'.** The western bight gives better protection from the northwest and north. **WPT 25°39.44'. 111°02.51'**. Either will be good shelter from a norther, but not from the south.

For summer's southerly weather, the north end of Monserrat has a long sandy beach called **Yellowstone Beach** due to the color of the rocks and cliffs ashore. The sand is white. Anchor anywhere along the beach in 20 to 30 feet, sand. **WPT 25°42.56', 111°42.56'.** The west end is protected by a small reef, the eastern end consists of a point, usually with a fish camp on the beach, and an extensive reef off the point to the north.

Around the northeast corner to the eastern shore are several small coves. They offer protection from the prevailing northwesterlies in sand at 15 to 20 feet. The northern cove, **Primero**, is the larger of the two, but reefs constrict the entrance. **WPT 25°42.24', 111°1.87'.** The southern cove **WPT 25°41.84', 111°1.47** is bound by cliffs and has rocks off each entrance point. Fore and aft anchoring will be necessary here.

About 1½ miles north of Isla Monserrat are two low, flat islands, Las Galeras with an extensive reef system between them and to the south. The eastern island has a navigation light. The position between the two islands is **WPT 25° 44.5', 111°2.8'.**

DANGERS: Another 1¼ miles north of Las Galeras is an isolated rock and reef. The rock usually shows, but at night you would be on it before you saw it. **WPT 25°45.69', 111°02.92'.** Between the above rock and Isla Danzante, there is a pinnacle rock with a least depth of 5 feet. **WPT 25°46.18', 111°10.70'.** A third rock lies just north of the east end of the westernmost Galera. It is usually covered.

West Bight has many giant boulders along the beach with white cliffs and a long protruding shelf on the western side. There is good snorkeling and some exploring along the beach. Anchor nearer to the white cliffs.

East Bight is a great place to spend a hot day in the water, exploring the rocks and the sea caves. There are several low ledges along the sides of both caves.

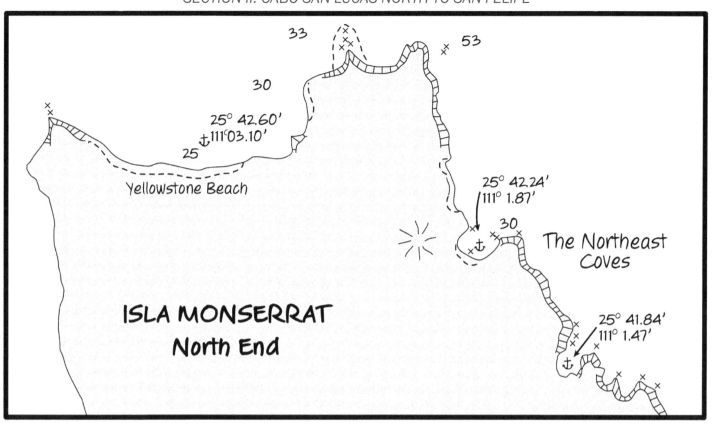

33

53

30

25° 42.60'
⚓111°03.10'

25

Yellowstone Beach

25° 42.24'
111° 1.87'

⚓

30

The Northeast
Coves

25° 41.84'
111° 1.47'

⚓

ISLA MONSERRAT
North End

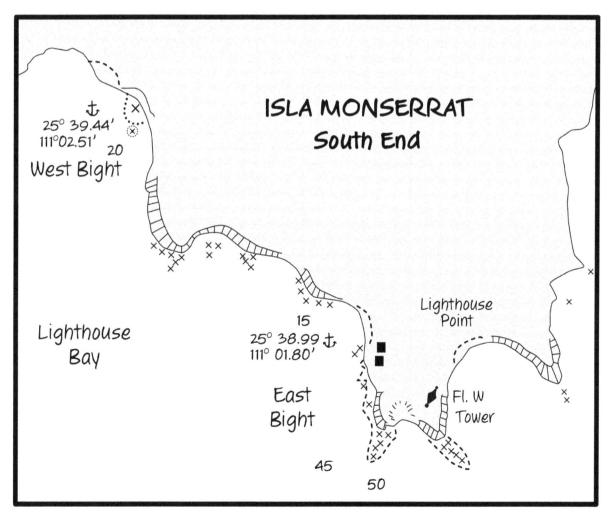

ISLA MONSERRAT
South End

⚓
25° 39.44'
111°02.51'

20

West Bight

Lighthouse
Bay

15
25° 38.99' ⚓
111° 01.80'

East
Bight

Lighthouse
Point

Fl. W
Tower

45

50

ISLA SANTA CATALINA

This island lies about 15 miles ENE of Agua Verde, and is 7 miles long and 2½ miles wide. There are two peaks to 1,300 feet. It doesn't have much to offer cruisers, but there are a few anchorages.

The south end of the island has a good anchorage at its western corner. **WPT 25°36.13', 111°46.76'.** There are large patches of rocks, so watch your anchor as you drop it in sand and set it well in 35 feet. Look for an abandoned water tower ashore. There is another bight just to the east, which is 50 feet deep and rocky as well. Again, set your anchor well, with plenty of scope. These coves are exposed to southerly weather. A navigation light is on the sourthernmost point of the island, Gp. Fl. 3. Further north along the western side of the island is a cove offering protection from easterly weather at **WPT 25°38.27', 110°47.96'.**

Punta San Cosme lies 5½ miles northwest of Agua Verde. It offers nothing in the way of protection, but it does have a dangerous reef extending northeast off its northern point.

ISLAS SAN COSME AND SAN DAMIAN

Isla San Cosme offers a reasonable anchorage on its south side in a little bay. **WPT 25°34.90', 111°09'.** There are sand and rocky patches at 15 feet, but it is tight and both entrance points have reefs, the eastern one is quite extensive. Be sure your anchor is well set. There is a small beach to land the dinghy, but not much to see. At the south end of the beach is a cave used by fishermen.

San Damian is a very small island with no anchorages.

DANGER: A reef, usually exposed, lies midway between these two islands, and slightly to the south. Mid channel on either side carries plenty of water.

A small hotsprings resort is on the Baja opposite San Cosme. It is possible to anchor off with reasonable protection if you wish to relax in its waters.

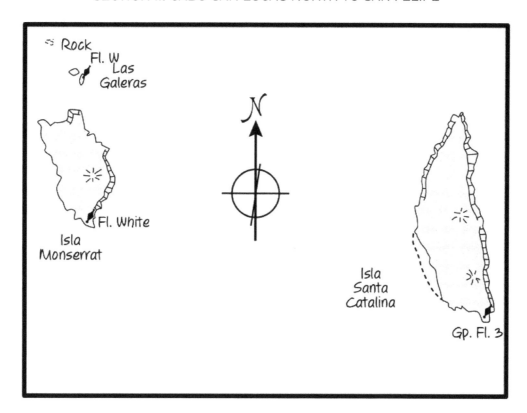

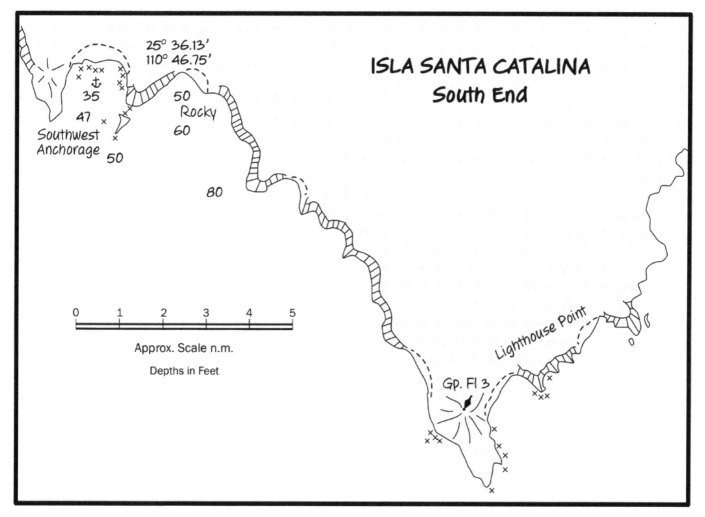

ISLA SANTA CATALINA
South End

25° 36.13'
110° 46.75'

35
47
Southwest
Anchorage
50

50
Rocky
60

80

Gp. Fl 3

Lighthouse Point

0 1 2 3 4 5

Approx. Scale n.m.

Depths in Feet

LOS CANDELEROS AND ISLA DANZANTE (Dancer)

Heading into Candeleros. Photo: Robin Richardson Stout

Roca Blanca is a 127' pinnacle rock about 4 miles southeast of Punta Candeleros, 5½ miles north of Isla San Cosme and 1¾ miles offshore. **WPT 25°38.27', 111°10.4'.** Rising from a base awash with some smaller rocks, it is surrounded by deep water which allows safe passage between the rock and the shore.

Punta Candeleros is a prominent, steep-to-jumbled mass where the coast turns sharply westward in a large bight that terminates to the north at Puerto Escondido. **Candelero Chico**, is a pretty, snug little anchorage 1½ miles south of Punta Candeleros. Though open to the north, it can be affected by easterly winds coming through the gap between the islet and the shore. A sandy beach lies at the head of the resulting niche that can accommodate 1 or 2 vessels. **WPT 25°42.39', 111°12.95'** in 20 feet, sand.

Bahia Candeleros, a bay on the north side of Punta Candeleros, provides excellent protection from southerly winds. The best spot to anchor is off the sandy beach west of the point under the hook of the southeast headland in 3 to 5 fathoms, sand. There is a visible rock to the SW side. A new resort located on the south end of the bay, Villa del Palmar, recently opened and welcomes cruisers. The resort features res-

taurants, a small store, WiFi internet access and a shuttle that runs three times daily to Loreto, a 45 minute drive to the north. Cruisers are welcome to take the shuttle if seats are available after resort guests are accommodated. The resort concierge can also arrange for rental cars if desired. At the northwest end of the bay is a small town that has a very well stocked mercado, "Ensenada Blanca". Cruisers are welcome to beach their dinghies nearby the local fishermen's pangas and walk about five minutes into the village to the tienda.

Mano de Dios. Photo: Phoebe Wilson

Los Candeleros (the candlesticks) are three pinnacle rocks located north of Punta Candeleros, between the point and the southern tip of Isla Danzante. The southern rock Isla Pardo, is about ¼ mile north of Punta Candeleros and the passage has depths of 10 fathoms or more in mid-channel. Isla Las Tijeras, the 100' high middle rock, is about ½ mile further to the north and has a reef extending southwesterly into the passage for about ¼ mile. By holding closer to Isla Pardo, this passage may be used provided that a close watch is kept.

The northernmost rock is 40' high and about ¾ mile north of Isla Las Tijeras and the same distance from the south tip of Isla Danzante. Reefs extend from both sides and

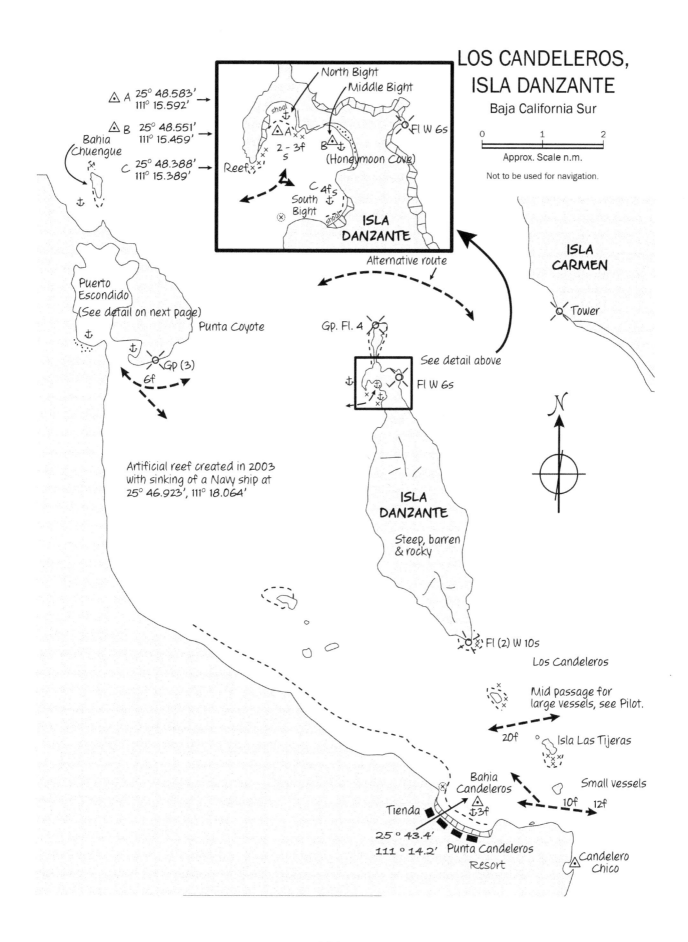

LOS CANDELEROS, ISLA DANZANTE

Baja California Sur

0   1   2

Approx. Scale n.m.

Not to be used for navigation.

North Bight
Middle Bight

△ A 25° 48.583'
111° 15.592'

△ B 25° 48.551'
111° 15.459'

Bahia
Chuengue

C 25° 48.388'
111° 15.389'

shoal

Fl W 6s

△ A

2 - 3 f
s

B △

(Honeymoon Cove)

Reef

C 4 f s

South
Bight

shoal

ISLA
DANZANTE

ISLA
CARMEN

Alternative route

Puerto
Escondido
(See detail on next page)

Punta Coyote

Tower

Gp. Fl. 4

See detail above

Fl W 6s

Gp (3)

6 f

Artificial reef created in 2003
with sinking of a Navy ship at
25° 46.923', 111° 18.064'

N

ISLA
DANZANTE

Steep, barren
& rocky

Fl (2) W 10s

Los Candeleros

Mid passage for
large vessels, see Pilot.

20 f

Isla Las Tijeras

Small vessels

Bahia
Candeleros

10 f   12 f

Tienda

3 f

25° 43.4'
111° 14.2'

Punta Candeleros
Resort

Candelero
Chico

Whale bones are a common decoration pieces Photo: Jo Russell

though the Pilot describes this passage as not to be attempted, a mid-channel course has depths in excess of 15 fathoms. Caution is advised when passing through this area.

DANGER: There is a rock 2 miles east of the south tip of Isla Danzante at **WPT 25°46.18', 111°10.70'.** The least depth is about 5 feet and does not break the water. It is about 100 yards long.

ISLA DANZANTE is a narrow, rugged and centrally ridged island about 3.5 miles long. There are many pleasant little anchorages along the western shore of the island, only about 3½ miles from Puerto Escondito.

Honeymoon Cove is by far the most popular, and has three bights. Tiny **North Bight** will barely hold one boat, but gives protection from all northerly quarters. The bottom is good but shoals half way in to the small sand beach at its head. It is very picturesque. **WPT 25°48.583', 111°15.592'.**

Middle Bight is usually where you end up when there are 4 or 5 other boats in the preferred spots. It has a rough lava rock beach and is quite deep at 30 to 40 feet, with a rocky bottom. It offers good protection from all but southwest. **WPT 25°48.551', 111°15.459'**

South Bight can hold several boats in sand at 20 feet. Two small sand and cobble beaches separated by a rock knob grace the head of this bight. A submerged rock lies off the southern entrance point, so keep well off. **WPT 25°48.388', 111°15.389'.**

Further south, along Danzante are several other anchorages, all open to the northwest, but very pleasant in suitable weather. All have a patch of sand beach, with sand bottom at 20 to 30 feet. Heading south from Honeymoon Cove, they are; Denouement Cove, Pyramid Cove, Tight Bight (small boats only) and off the mushroom rock. Continuing south along the island are many stretches of sand beach off which one could anchor for a swim on a quiet, hot afternoon.

There are endless dinghy exploration possibilities along this area. Some coves are too steep and deep to anchor, but are accessible by dinghy or kayak. This is truly a beautiful area to explore.

Isla Danzante has three navigation lights. Two are on the north end, the NE light is Fl. Wht., the NWGp. Fl.4. One or the other of these you should be able to see when approaching from the north. Neither is on the actual end of the island. On the south end, the light Fl. Wht. Is on the very tip of the island, but Submarine Reef extends ¼ mile SSE from the light, so keep well off.

The ever friendly and helpful fishermen and their pangas.   Photo: Jo Russell

PUERTO ESCONDIDO

This land-locked harbor is also known as **"Hidden Harbor"** as it is one of the few anchorages in the Sea of Cortez that provides reasonable, albeit not assured, refuge from hurricanes. The steep walls of Sierra de la Giganta rising on the west make this a spectacular setting. El Cerro de la Giganta, the highest peak of the range at about 5,800 ft., lies 24 miles northwest.

On the seaward side of the harbor is a hilly peninsula that ends at Punta Coyote. This steep, rocky headland marks the north end of the bay that begins at Los Candeleros. It lies about 2½ miles west of the north end of Isla Danzante. At its northwest end the peninsula is joined to the Baja shore by a narrow isthmus. South of this isthmus the coast projects out to almost meet the peninsula, thus forming the inner harbor and two anchorages ("the Waiting Room" and "the Ellipse") through which vessels pass when proceeding to enter the inner harbor. Shoals at the point reduce the navigable width of the entrance to the inner harbor to about 65 ft. with a reported depth of 9 ft. at low tide. Currents can run at up to 4 knots, making entry best near slack water.

Entrance to Puerto Escondido is made from the south, into and through a cove behind a sandy hook, which extends to the west from Coyote Peninsula. The outer harbor or **"Waiting Room"** is a sheltered anchorage at a depth of 6 fathoms in sand. Deep draft vessels, or those in transit find this anchorage quite satisfactory; space maybe somewhat limited as a result of a number of vessels that have set two or three anchors to maintain their position for an extended period of time. On the west side of the outer harbor is a concrete wharf that serves the surrounding region as a port. A concrete sea wall continues around the point and along the curve of the dredged inner bay (**"The Ellipse"**), culminating in a riprap breakwater at the end of which is a green navigation light that demarks the entry into the inner harbor.

The range markers are a bit misleading as when they are aligned, they lead you through the breakwater. Pay Attention!

Like in other significant harbors in Mexico, there is an API office (Administration Porturia Integradias), located on the west side of the port area that manages the Waiting Room and the Ellipse anchorages. It collects a $7USD each time a vessel enters or leaves the anchorage and a daily anchoring fee of about $1. Check-in and payment is done in the API building southwest of the concrete docks. (2012 prices).

The inner harbor is managed by Marina Fonatur Puerto Escondido. The marina office and Harbor Master are located on the second floor of the three story building adjacent to the concrete seawall. This full service marina has 10 Med-tie slips (which cater primarily to locally operated sport fishing boats) and 117 mooring buoys that are dispersed throughout the inner harbor. The protocol for new arrivals that wish to moor on a buoy is to pick up any open buoy and once ashore check in with the Fonatur marina office; the Harbor Master will redirect new arrivals to a different buoy as necessary. Vessels that prefer to anchor should anchor along the northerly reaches of the inner harbor and away from the fairway in the buoy field. As indicated in the harbor diagram, be aware of a sunken sailboat when anchoring toward the northerly side of the inner harbor; it is not well marked (at last visit, marked with a small water bottle. There are two low-lying sections ("the Windows") along the peninsula, which separates the inner harbor from the Sea of Cortez to the east. It is recommended that cruisers give consideration to local winds that blow through the Windows when making selection of a mooring, or anchoring, particularly if leaving the boat nominally unattended for an extended period or during the hotter seasons.

Depending on planned duration in the marina, charges for mooring on a buoy or anchoring in the inner harbor range from $.30 to $.80 per foot per day, regardless of which is chosen. Mooring/anchoring fees include use of the dinghy dock, bathrooms and showers, laundry facilities, a lap pool and spa, and Wi-Fi internet access. There is also a fuel dock and pump-out facility as well as haul out facility with a 50-ton Travelift, work yard and dry storage area. There is a full service restaurant and bar, and a reasonably well

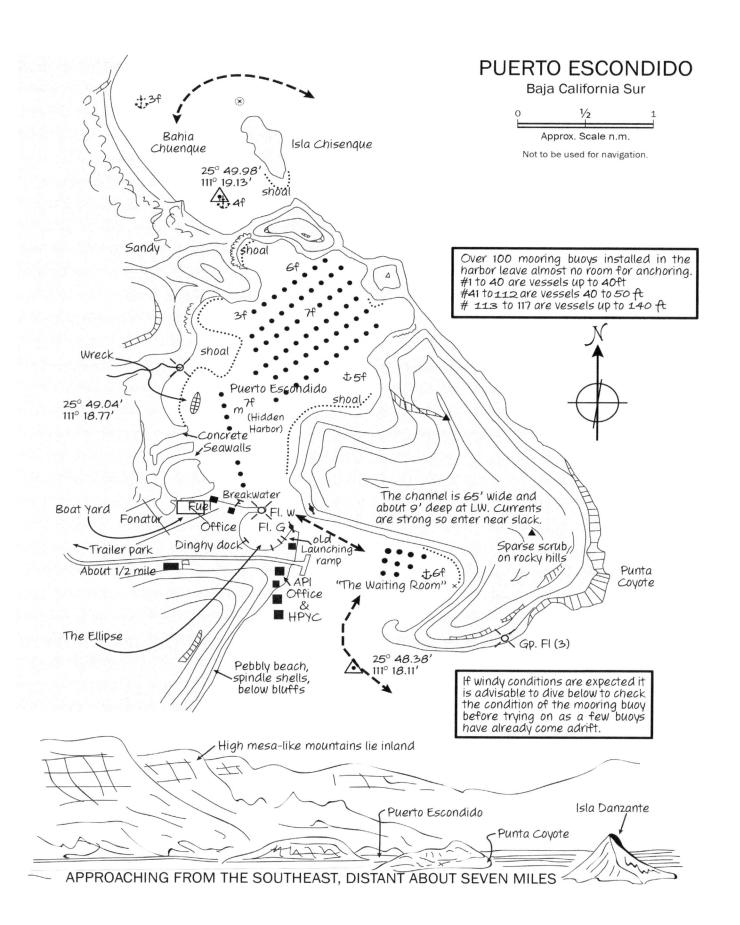

PUERTO ESCONDIDO
Baja California Sur

0   ½   1

Approx. Scale n.m.

Not to be used for navigation.

Bahia Chuenque

Isla Chisenque

25° 49.98'
111° 19.13'

shoal

⚓ 3f

⚑ 4f

Sandy

shoal

6f

7f

3f

Over 100 mooring buoys installed in the harbor leave almost no room for anchoring.
#1 to 40 are vessels up to 40ft
#41 to 112 are vessels 40 to 50 ft
113 to 117 are vessels up to 140 ft

N

Wreck

shoal

25° 49.04'
111° 18.77'

Puerto Escondido

m 7f
(Hidden Harbor)

⚓ 5f

shoal

Concrete Seawalls

Boat Yard

Fonatur

Breakwater

Fuel

Office

Fl. W

Fl. G

old Launching ramp

The channel is 65' wide and about 9' deep at LW. Currents are strong so enter near slack.

Sparse scrub on rocky hills

Punta Coyote

Trailer park

Dinghy dock

About ½ mile

API Office & HPYC

"The Waiting Room" ×

⚓ 6f

The Ellipse

Pebbly beach, spindle shells, below bluffs

25° 48.38'
111° 18.11'

⚑

Gp. Fl (3)

If windy conditions are expected it is advisable to dive below to check the condition of the mooring buoy before trying on as a few buoys have already come adrift.

High mesa-like mountains lie inland

Puerto Escondido

Isla Danzante

Punta Coyote

APPROACHING FROM THE SOUTHEAST, DISTANT ABOUT SEVEN MILES

stocked Mercado nearby the Marina Office. In the marina complex there is a dive service available and small chandlery that stocks limited marine supplies. The chandlery has an association with a larger chandlery in Loreto; marine hardware and supplies that are not normally stocked in Puerto Escondido can be ordered and delivered to the Chandlery, generally on a next day basis. There are also limited marine repair capabilities and boat monitoring services available for those who leave their boats when out of the area. Propane refills (at the propane facility several kilometers south of Loreto) can be arranged through the Mercado; your tank will be taken into Loreto to be refilled and returned the next day (be sure your boat name is on your tank). For information and reservations, telephone 011-52-613-1330-9815 (Fax 011-52-613-1330-189) or email alozano@fonatur.gob.mx.

In addition to the aforementioned facilities and services, the Hidden Port Yacht Club maintains an office in the marina complex of buildings; local information, a book exchange and weather forecasts are available. A Cruisers Net operates on VHF Ch 22 at 0800. www.hiddenportyachtclub.com, hpyc@hotmail.com

The Puerto Escondido complex is situated approximately 9 miles south of Loreto, and approximately 1 mile from Highway 1. Taxi service is available to/from Loreto via telephone call to Loreto, and occasionally by coincidence of taxis at the marina. Located between the port complex and Highway 1, and within a reasonable walking distance of the marina is a full service hotel and restaurant (Tripui), and well stocked Mercado (Modelorama); the mercado owner will often provide transportation back to the marina with purchases.

The Loreto Airport is between Puerto Escondido and Loreto with service to the U.S.

BAHIA CHUENQUE (JUANCALITO)

There is one anchorage immediately north of Puerto Escondido, which is a large and open bay. It has a fine sand beach and a navigation light Gp. Fl.3, fronting a small settlement. Protection is from southern and western quarters. The bottom is sand at 15 to 40 feet. **WPT 25°49.98', 111°19.13'.** On entering, stay clear of Isla Mestiza, which has reefs off both ends and offers good snorkeling. Passage between the island and the mainland is clear in 30 feet in the center.

An amazing video of the release of a humpback whale trapped in fishing nets.

A humpback waves hello. Photo: Phoebe Wilson

Whale shark. Photo: Robin Richardson Stout

LORETO and ISLA CARMEN

The coast north of Bahia Chuenque consists primarily of sandy beaches with intervening rocky points where the ridges run down to the shore. At Punta Nopolo Norte (Nopolo Sur was off Isla San Jose) a rocky knob extends out to cover a shallow lagoon and river mouth. North of the knob the coast curves back in a shallow arc to form Ensenada Nopolo. The luxury Diamond Eden resort is a prominent landmark three miles south the airport (where Immigration Offices are located). The two small basins are for the use of shallow draft resort runabouts and though anchorage can be taken in the bay, it is shallow and open. An extensive sand bank lies south of the basins. **WPT 25°55.34', 111°20.78'**

Loreto. Photo: Robin Richardson Stout

Five miles north of this resort is **Loreto, WPT 26°0.95', 111°20.21'**. The Port Captain's office is a block west of the square, breakwater-formed basin that is always lined with local pangas. A flashing light is shown from a metal structure in the northwest corner of the basin adjacent to the launch ramp. Open roadstead anchorage can be taken north of the breakwater in 3 to 7 fathoms. While adequate in calm weather, it is unsuitable during winds from anywhere between the northeast and southeast. Cruisers often anchor off Loreto in the morning, leave the dinghy at the dinghy dock, provision with fresh water, ice, fuel and supplies and leave before the afternoon northeasterly sea breezes arrive. There is also an excellent Farmers' Market on Sunday mornings, a few blocks south of the Mission, which begins at 7:00 am.

The mission church is symbolic of Loreto, the longest continuously occupied town in Baja, having survived for almost 3 centuries. Loreto is the first of the missions established by Father Junipero Serra. Little of the original building remains; that which does is very old and one of the bells in the tower dates back to 1743. All services and stores are on the main street that is perpendicular to the panga basin and about four blocks to the south.

ISLA CARMEN

Numerous viable anchorages can be found on Isla Carmen, which lies off the coast to the east of Loreto. The island is 17 miles long and from 1½ to 6 miles wide.

Bahia Marquer, WPT 25°52.18', 111°13.21' gives good southeast to northeast protection, but is open to the northwest. The fetch is only 10 miles from that direction, but any appreciable swell coming down the gulf would roll right in. Lying only a short 5 miles from the Escondido entrance, Marquer's sand beach and good holding ground at about 18 ft. make it an attractive anchorage if Danzante is overpopulated.

2½ miles south of Marquer there is a sandspit with a navigation light (Gp.Fl.2). After that, Isla Carmen ends in a mile and a half of low sandy flats culminating in one of the Gulf's many "Punta Bajas" (Low Point). A dangerous reef extends for several hundred meters off this point.

Puerto Ballandra, WPT 26°01.07', 111°10.08', is a pretty little cove, which is located 9 miles due east of Loreto and about 1½ miles south of the northwestern tip of Isla Carmen; it provides excellent protection. The two rocky points forming the ¼ mile wide entrance become apparent only when the coast is closed; beyond them is a circular bay about ½ mile in diameter. Stand in to enter mid-channel where an underwater canyon enters the bay.

Anchorage may be taken on the shallow shelves along the shore. The most popular spot is in the northern part, fairly close to the sandy beach in about 4 fathoms, sand. The bay would be a perfect haven except for the seasonal visitation of flies on the beach, however they pose no problem while at anchor. This

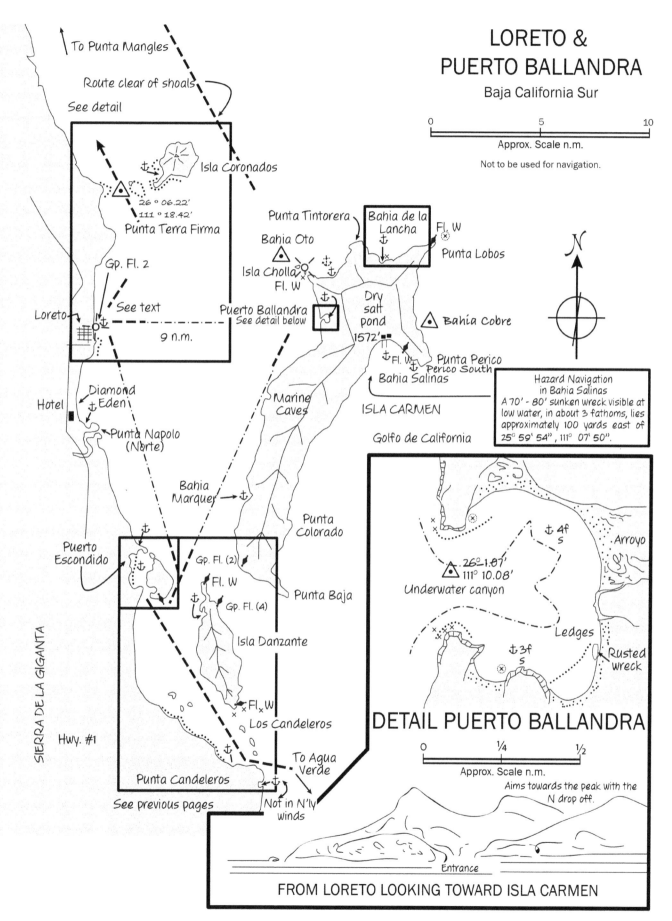

LORETO &
PUERTO BALLANDRA
Baja California Sur

0   5   10
Approx. Scale n.m.

Not to be used for navigation.

To Punta Mangles

Route clear of shoals
See detail

Isla Coronados

26 ° 06.22'
111 ° 18.42'
Punta Terra Firma

Gp. Fl. 2

See text

Loreto

9 n.m.

Diamond
Eden

Hotel

Punta Napolo
(Norte)

Bahia
Marquer

Puerto
Escondido

SIERRA DE LA GIGANTA

Hwy. #1

Punta Candeleros

See previous pages

Punta Tintorera
Bahia Oto
Isla Cholla
Fl. W

Puerto Ballandra
See detail below

Bahia de la
Lancha   Fl. W

Punta Lobos

Dry
salt
pond
1572'

Fl. W
Punta Perico
Perico South
Bahia Salinas

Bahia Cobre

ISLA CARMEN

Golfo de California

Marine
Caves

Punta
Colorado

Gp. Fl. (2)

Fl. W

Gp. Fl. (4)

Punta Baja

Isla Danzante

Fl. W
Los Candeleros

To Agua
Verde

Not in N'ly
winds

Hazard Navigation
in Bahia Salinas
A 70' - 80' sunken wreck visible at
low water, in about 3 fathoms, lies
approximately 100 yards east of
25° 59' 54", 111° 07' 50".

⊥ 4f
s

26° 1.07'
111° 10.08'
Underwater canyon

Arroyo

Ledges

Rusted
wreck

⊥ 3f
s

DETAIL PUERTO BALLANDRA

0   ¼   ½
Approx. Scale n.m.

Aims towards the peak with the
N drop off.

Entrance

FROM LORETO LOOKING TOWARD ISLA CARMEN

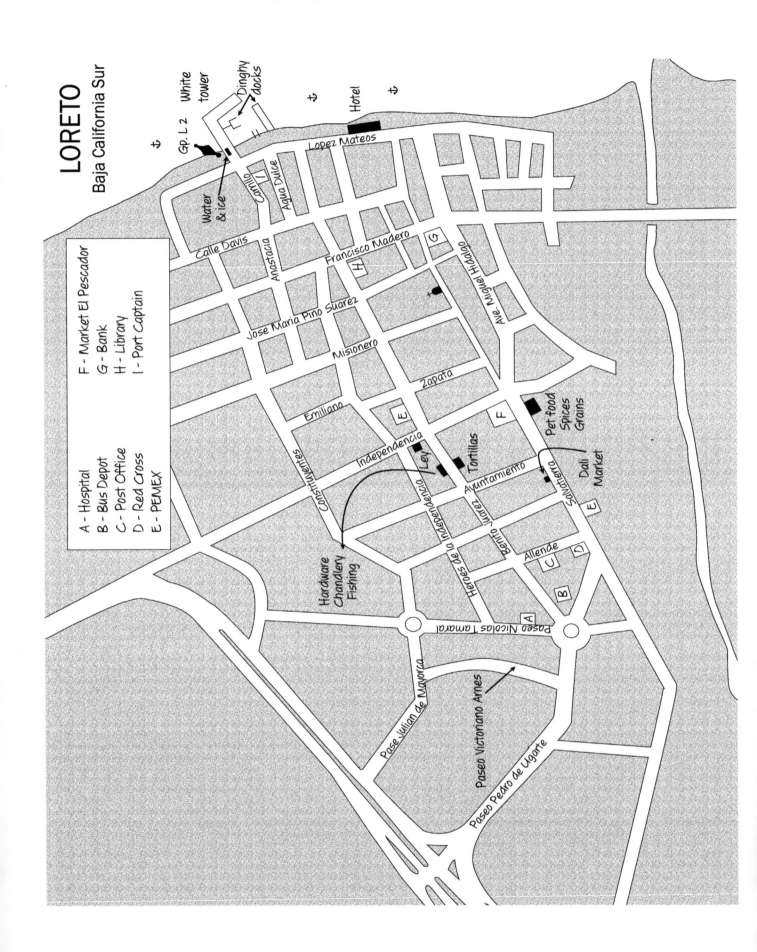

LORETO
Baja California Sur

A - Hospital
B - Bus Depot
C - Post Office
D - Red Cross
E - PEMEX

F - Market El Pescador
G - Bank
H - Library
I - Port Captain

is a beautiful, protected anchorage that shouldn't be missed. The eastern side of the cove is foul with rocky ledges, which makes for a pleasant walk at low tide. Another good anchorage is in the southern part of the cove between the rusted wreck of a grounded barge and the southern entrance point in about 3 fathoms, sand and shell bottom.

DANGER: An extensive reef extends west of La Cholla, the northwesternmost point of the island, and an outlying segment lies a considerable distance northwest of the end of the island. There is NO PASSAGE over the sand bar between La Cholla and the island except for dinghies. Another pinnacle rock has been reported farther out in the same vicinity. **WPT 26°03.33', 111°11.21'** to clear.

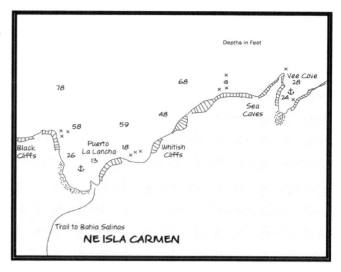

On the north shore of the island between Punta Tintorera and Punta Lobos is the small, open, bay of **Puerto de la Lancha** where anchorage in southerly winds can be found in 4 fathoms. **WPT 26°3.18', 111°06.25'**. Whitish cliffs on each side of the bay help to identify its location; give a good berth to the rocks off the western entrance point. Ashore is a rough black lava beach where a dinghy may be landed and the concrete remains of a building.

Vee Cove, a mile north of La Lancha, is a small Vee shaped cove with white steep-to sides, and a white sand beach at its head, backed by a large dune of the same. **WPT 26°3.45', 111°5.1'**. There are a few submerged rocks that have fallen off the side cliffs, so keep a bow look out as you enter when hugging the sides. Vee Cove is quite tight so fore and aft anchoring may be advisable. The most important features of this cove are two sea caves on the south side. One is the usual size, but the other opens up inside, large enough for several dinghies to enjoy happy hour and cool off a bit. Just north of Punta Perico on the eastern side of the island, lies a bay called **Painted Cliffs** by Gerry Cunningham. **WPT 25°59.87', 111°4.61'**. It gives good protection from the west to southeast. There are reefs extending off the cobble beaches, so head for the canyon between the purple cliffs and the gray cliff on the right. The bottom is 25 feet, mixed sand and rock.

Bahia Cobre is the next bay toward the tip of the point, gives the same protection as painted Cliffs. **WPT 25°58.9, 111°4.17'**. The bottom is sand and gravel at 20 feet, and is worth a shore exploration. The bright aquamarine colored outcroppings at its eastern end give it its name. The bottom is good all along the beach and could hold many boats.

Perico South is the first bay on the south side of Punta Perico. **WPT 25°58.30°, 111°04.53'**. It offers the best protection from northwest to northeast, even better that Bahia Salinas, next door. The bottom is sand and rock mixed, 15 feet.

Bahia Salinas, WPT 25°58.35', 111°4.66', is fairly shallow and anchorage in about 20 feet may be taken about ¼ mile offshore. In strong northerly winds a sharp chop results, making the area uncomfortable; the holding is good provided sufficient scope is allowed. The wreck of a large steel vessel is on her side in the anchorage in about 20 feet, at high tide it is completely submerged. The wreck is located off the end of the loading pier, slightly south.

Punta Colorado forms a small bump in ths shoreline 9½ miles south of Salinas. Stand off while rounding the point as there are tidal shelves off the shore. The anchorage is **WPT 25°51.45', 111°11.66'** in 15 to 20 feet, sand. Be aware the tidal shelves extend out from the shore for 100 yards in some places, so swing wide while exploring the bay. Snorkeling is good along the shelves.

ISLA CORONADOS

Four miles north of Loreto and 6 miles northwest of Isla Carmen, a low, sandy Punta Terra Firma protrudes from the coast. A little northward, an arroyo comes out to the shore just to the south of Punta Baja, identified by a high stone tower. Offshore lies **Isla Coronados.**

There are actually two islands, a large volcanic island with a sandy isthmus and a small, rocky islet between it and the Baja shore. The larger island resembles an irregularly-shaped tadpole with the northern portion composed of volcanic remnants rising to a 928' cinder cone. From the southwest corner of this mass a long, flat sandspit extends about 1 mile southwest. A reef of detached rocks extends for some distance and shoals reach out on either side of the sandspit.

About one mile separates the tip of the sandspit and the bluffs of Punta Baja. The small islet is within this gap, with shoal water surrounding it and extending south for almost ½ mile. Shoaling has occurred in the channel separating the two islands and depths are sufficient only for shallow draft vessels. Caution is urged when passing through this area.

The channel between the small islet and Punta Baja is almost ½ mile wide, but a sand bank and shoal that lie off the bluffs of Punta Baja reduce the navigable part of the passage. A mid-channel course through this passage has depths of 20 to 25 feet. Fishing is usually excellent in this area and cruisers trolling for Dorado often share sushi and fresh fish upon arrival at the next anchorage.

Vessels northbound from Loreto or Isla Carmen must pass these islands. A clear and direct route from Puerto Ballandra on Isla Carmen to Caleta San Juanico may be taken in deep water to the east of Isla Coronados.

Anchorage may be taken on either side of the spit on Isla Coronados, depending on the wind direction. The anchorage on the north side is off a fish camp, 15 to 30 feet, where the shoal water can be clearly seen. **WPT 26°6.81', 111°17.36'.** Ashore are a stone BBQ pit and some palapas. The southeast side of the spit offers good protection from the north in 15 to 20 feet, sand.
WPT 26°6.30', 111°15.92'.

DANGER: Mangle Rock is about 9 miles north of the Isla Coronados anchorage, and about 3 miles south of Punta Mangle at **WPT 26°14.68', 111°22.15'.** It consists of a reef with the pinnacle rock at the southeast end.

Punta Mangles lies on the Baja shore about 12 miles north-northwest of Isla Coronados. It is a 300' bluff, steep and well defined on its northern side. Though a few detached rocks lie about its base, the main danger is a group of rocks awash about 2 miles south-southeast and ¾ miles offshore. They cover an area about 500' in diameter and should be given a clear berth. See above.

Good anchorage may be taken in the bight south of Punta Mangles; shelter from northwest winds is available in the lee of the point in 15 feet, sand. **WPT 26°16.82', 111°23.36'.** Slightly to the west of the anchorage is a large white building project, now abandoned. As the anchorage is open to wind and seas refracted around the point, you may prefer the more protected anchorage at Caleta de San Juanico, which is a short distance further up the coast.

* * * * *

On a clear day when you are south of Punta Mangles the black, box-shaped prominence of Punta Pulpito appears to be an island far up the coast. As you travel northward the "island" grows until the low land joining it to the coast becomes visible and at the same time the profile of Isla San Ildefonso slowly comes into view.

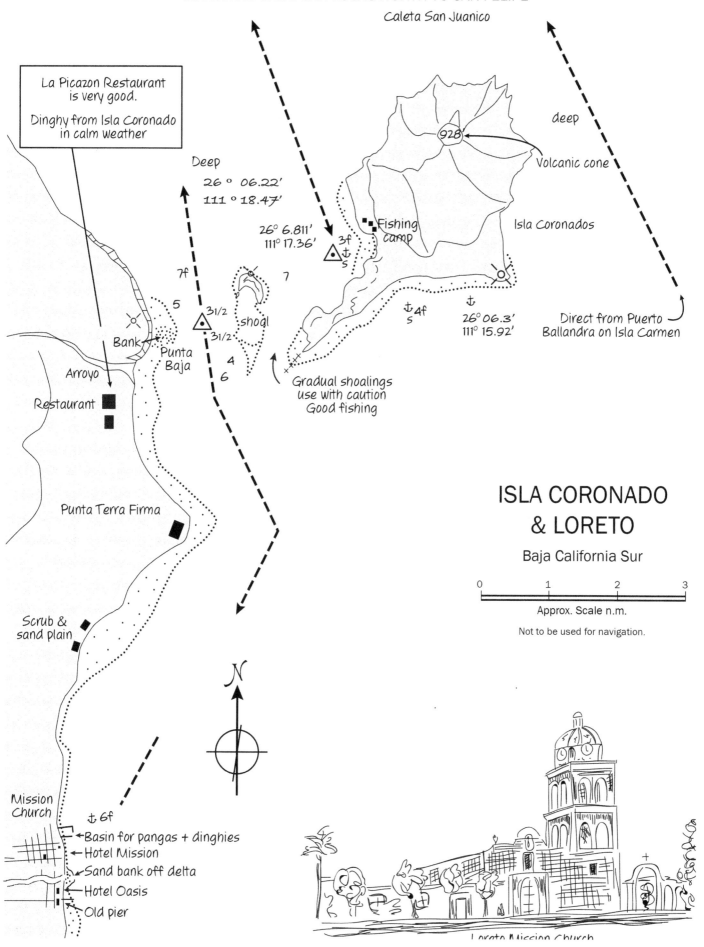

Caleta San Juanico

deep

928

Volcanic cone

Isla Coronados

La Picazon Restaurant
is very good.

Dinghy from Isla Coronado
in calm weather

Deep

26° 06.22'
111° 18.47'

26° 6.811'
111° 17.36'

3f
⚓
s

Fishing
camp

7f

5

3½

31/2

7

shoal

4

6

Bank

Punta
Baja

Arroyo

Restaurant

⚓ 4f
s

26° 06.3'
111° 15.92'

Direct from Puerto
Ballandra on Isla Carmen

Gradual shoalings
use with caution
Good fishing

Punta Terra Firma

ISLA CORONADO
& LORETO

Baja California Sur

0   1   2   3

Approx. Scale n.m.

Not to be used for navigation.

Scrub &
sand plain

N

Mission
Church

⚓ 6f

←Basin for pangas + dinghies
←Hotel Mission
←Sand bank off delta
←Hotel Oasis
←Old pier

Loreto Mission Church

CALETA DE SAN JUANICO

Caleta de San Juanico is a large and open cove that lies roughly 6 miles north of Punta Mangles and 8 miles south of Punta Pulpito, both distinctive points. The cove is not only beautiful but is interesting to explore.

Approached from the south, Punta Los Mercenarios is a prominent landmark at the southern entrance point of Caleta De San Juanico. It is a dark, rocky cliff with a 519' high reddish hill rising from the point. About ¾ mile north a ridge ends in a 50' high, rugged cliff, below which are two small islets, one 30' high, almost triangular in shape and connected to the point by a sandy spit, the other broken into several sections the highest of which is about 10' high. These project out in a northeasterly direction to form the southern point of the cove. An isolated, flat-topped rock about 6' high lies about ½ mile east of the point. There is a clear passage on either side of the rock. See sketch.

The northern point of Caleta San Juanico is **Punta San Basilio** and it is about 1½ miles from the southern entrance point. There are two anchorages within the cove.

The **Southeast Anchorage** is in the bight enclosed by the rocky bluff and islands and the southern shores of the cove. A rocky rib coming down to the southern shore of the cove extends out in a reef that is partly covered at low water. Identify this reef and take anchorage clear of it on either side. The western side has slightly better protection in 25 feet, sand and landing is easy on the beach. Sand sometimes blows off this beach during southerly winds, but otherwise this is a good spot and the beach offers some interesting shells.

The **Northwest Anchorage** lies across the bay. There are several rock bluffs and detached pinnacle rocks and shoals with sand or shingle beaches between the bluffs and the mouths of the arroyos. When close-to these formations help identify the cove, as they are very distinctive. The pinnacle rocks and shoals form several niches, in some of which there is a protected anchorage. The most popular spot is in 10 to 15 feet between the sandy spit and long rock pinnacle and the shoal and isolated islet to the west. Equally good anchorage, with more space is in 25 to 30 feet is outside the line between the islets. **WPT 26° 22.09', 111°25.79'**. Another anchorage lies to the east of the spit and pinnacle. All these anchorages have good holding, sand bottom. The beaches throughout the cove are well worth combing for shells, hikes ashore are rewarded with crystals and fossils as well as a Cruiser's Shrine. For many years, cruisers have displayed items with their boat names inscribed.

Punta San Basilio is a two-pronged, steep-to rocky cliff rising to a hilly peninsula. From a distance it blends into the background hills and is not easy to spot till close. On the north side of the point is a well set-in cove, **La Ramada**, which provides very good anchorage in southerly winds in 10 feet, sand. This is a lovely little cove, large enough for 6 to 8 boats. A white, sandy beach is at the head of the cove. **WPT 26°22.94', 111°25.85.**

Between San Juanico and La Ramada is **False Cove.** This has a good sand bottom at 25 feet, but there is no place to land a dinghy. The snorkeling is good, however.

CALETA DE SAN JUANICO
Baja California Sur

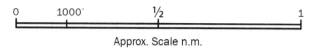

0   1000'   ½   1

Approx. Scale n.m.

Not to be used for navigation.

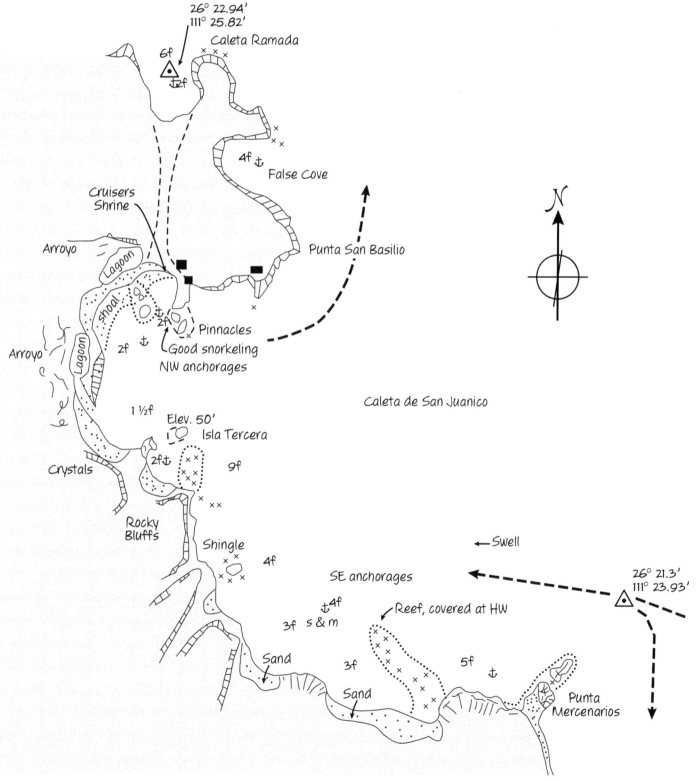

26° 22.94'
111° 25.82'

6f

Caleta Ramada

1½f

False Cove

4f

Cruisers
Shrine

Arroyo

Lagoon

shoal

Punta San Basilio

Arroyo

Lagoon

2f

Pinnacles
Good snorkeling
NW anchorages

Caleta de San Juanico

1 ½f

Elev. 50'

Isla Tercera

2f

9f

Crystals

Rocky
Bluffs

Shingle

4f

← Swell

SE anchorages

26° 21.3'
111° 23.93'

Reef, covered at HW

4f

3f s & m

3f

Sand

Sand

5f

Punta
Mercenarios

APPROACHES TO BAHIA CONCEPCION

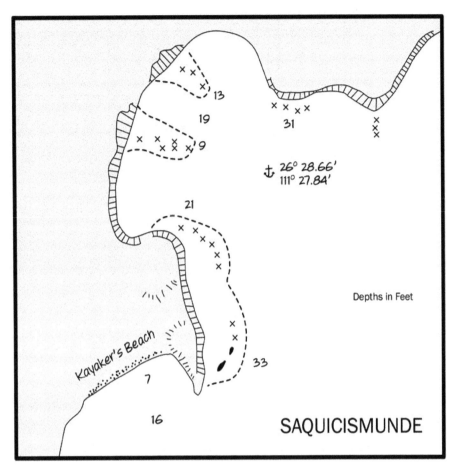

From Punta San Basilio the coast recedes slightly westward in a series of long, shallow, scalloped bays. Four miles north of La Ramada and 2½ miles south of Punta Pulpito is a little bight called **Saquicismunde**. The cove is rimmed with reefs and its south entrance point is well guarded, but there is sand at 20 feet, and enough cobble beach to land the dinghy. **WPT 26°28.66', 111°27.84'.** There is another nice beach around the point to the south, but visit by dinghy as there isn't much water.

Punta Pulpito is a large, steep-ended, appropriately named headland. It projects out about ½ mile from the line of the coast, with a low plain connected to a bulbous rocky lump, 470' high. An anchorage can be found in the southern bight, tucked in toward the sandy beach in 20 to 30 feet. **WPT 26°30.87', 111°26.89'.**

DANGER: Give the point a safe berth to avoid the submerged rock that lies about 650' southeast of the southernmost tip of the point.

Another anchorage, less satisfactory except in southerly winds, lies on the northwest side of **Punta San Antonio,** approximately 1¼ miles north of Punta Pulpito. A reef extends at least 500 yards beyond the point and must be given a wide berth. Surge and winds can affect both of these anchorages, which are used mainly by local fishermen. From Punta San Antonio the coast falls away forming Bahia San Nicolas. The bird sanctuary of Isla San Ildefonso is a rocky, steep-to island lying about 6 miles offshore.

About 7 miles north of Punta Pulpito is the small cove of **Bahia San Sebastian** (or Caleta de Los Puercos/Bay of Pigs), **WPT 26°37.16', 111°33.74'** which offers very snug anchorage for 2 or 3 boats. The cove is only 500 yards wide, with rocks and shoals narrowing it further. Swinging space is very limited, so fore and aft anchors are advisable. Anchor near the head of the cove in 25 feet, sand. There is a spring ashore, as evidenced by the green foliage in this dry, reddish rock and sandy area. A few Mexican and Gringo houses are amongst the trees, but there are no facilities. To distinguish this cove from others, there is a dense grove of palm trees in its valley, and 100' vertical cliffs on both sides.

Punta Santa Teresa, about 5 miles north of Bahia San Sebastian is a rocky point rising to a hill (955') marking the northern end of Bahia San Nicolas.

Medano Blanco is less than a mile north of Punta Santa Teresa, and it consists of a large sand dune behind a point that gives protection from both northwest and southeast, but not east or north. **WPT 26°42.49', 111°34.71'.** Watch for reefs on both sides of the point, to be avoided. There are anchorages

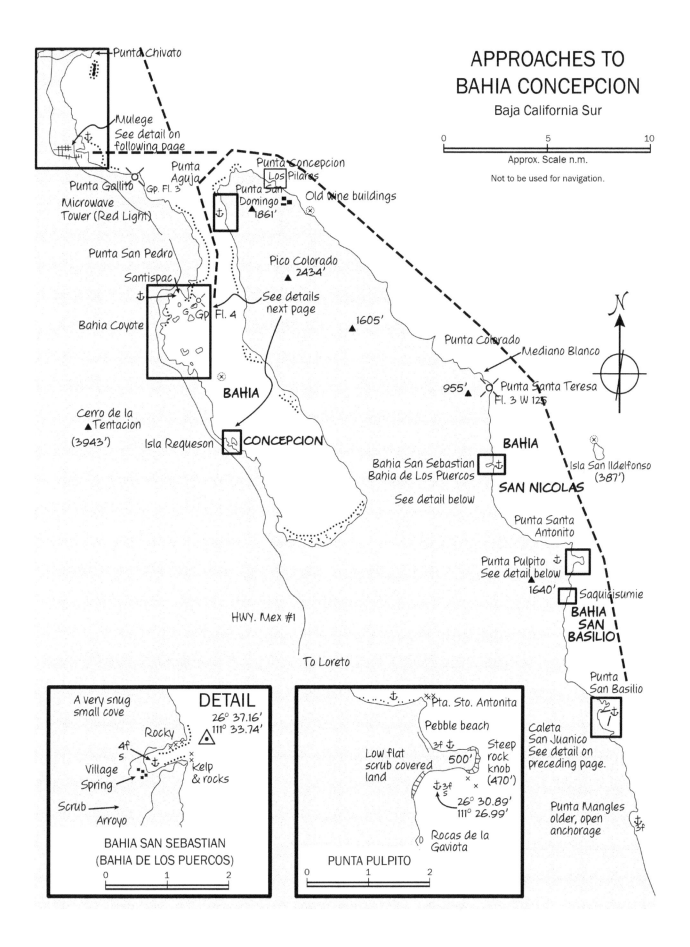

APPROACHES TO BAHIA CONCEPCION
Baja California Sur

0   5   10
Approx. Scale n.m.

Not to be used for navigation.

Punta Chivato

Mulege
See detail on
following page

Punta Chivato

Punta
Aguja

Punta Gallito   Gp. Fl. 3

Microwave
Tower (Red Light)

Punta Concepcion
Los Pilares

Punta San
Domingo
1861'

Old wine buildings

Punta San Pedro

Santispac

Bahia Coyote

GpFl. 4

See details
next page

Pico Colorado
2434'

1605'

Punta Colorado

Mediano Blanco

Punta Santa Teresa
Fl. 3 W 12s

955'

N

BAHIA

Cerro de la
Tentacion
(3943')

Isla Requeson   **CONCEPCION**

Bahia San Sebastian
Bahia de Los Puercos

See detail below

BAHIA

SAN NICOLAS

Isla San Ildelfonso
(387')

Punta Santa
Antonito

Punta Pulpito
See detail below

1640'

Saquigisumie

**BAHIA
SAN
BASILIO**

HWY. Mex #1

To Loreto

Caleta
San Juanico
See detail on
preceding page.

Punta
San Basilio

Punta Mangles
older, open
anchorage

DETAIL
26° 37.16'
111° 33.74'

A very snug
small cove

Rocky

4f
5

Village
Spring

Kelp
& rocks

Scrub

Arroyo

BAHIA SAN SEBASTIAN
(BAHIA DE LOS PUERCOS)

0   1   2

Pta. Sto. Antonita

Pebble beach

3f

Low flat
scrub covered
land

Steep
rock
knob
(470')

500'

3f
5

26° 30.89'
111° 26.99'

Rocas de la
Gaviota

PUNTA PULPITO

0   1   2

on both sides of the point, depending on the weather. The south side has sand at 15 feet close in the corner behind the reefs at the point. **WPT 26°42.32', 111°34.35'.**

Los Pilares, **WPT 26°53.30', 111°48.27' is** a delightful anchorage and the last one on the sea side of Punta Conception, being only a mile south of the point. Coming from the south, before you get to Pilares, you will see the remains of a manganese mining operation. There are many scars on the landscape. The south side of Punta Pilares would give good southerly protection, except that it is a sure death-trap for anchors. The bottom is covered with huge blocks of rock with anchor trapping canyons between them. The north side of Pilares is the anchorage. It has a fine sand bottom at 10 to 20 feet. South and southwestern protection is good. The north end of the cove gives fair northwest protection.

As you near **Punta Concepcion** the colors of the rocky hills explain the attraction this area has long had for prospectors and mining interests. Sometimes the sea seems to be equally colorful, for a curious feature of the area, are reddish patches that may be seen in the water. This is due to the burst of life of millions of tiny sea organisms, which seem to tint the water during certain periods. The extent of these patches caused early explorers to call this the Vermilion Sea. Punta Concepcion is a low and rather poorly defined point. But beyond it, as you turn the rocky coast a series of small points end at Punta Aguja, a sharp, rocky cliff which is the eastern point of the entrance to Bahia Concepcion. Detached rocks and shoals extend out from it, so a course to enter this deservedly popular bay should give the point a wide berth.

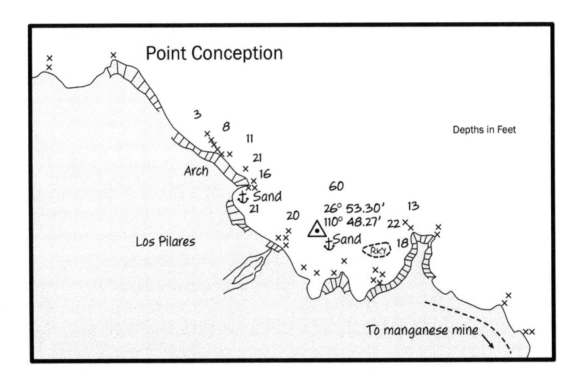

ANCHORAGES IN BAHIA CONCEPCION

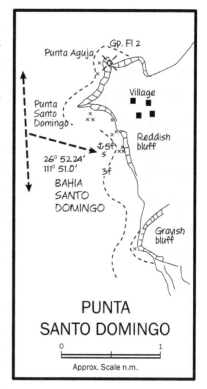

Bahia Concepcion is the largest sheltered bay on the eastern coast of Baja California. It is a long, narrow bay that penetrates south-southeast for almost 22 miles. The bay is 2 miles wide at the narrowest part of the entrance and about 5 miles wide for the remainder. It covers over 100 square miles and has several good anchorages that make it a very popular area for vessels cruising this coast.

The entrance lies between Punta Aguja on the east side and Punta Gallo on the west, some 3½ miles distant and then gradually narrows to about 2 miles. **Punta Santo Domingo** is the SW extension of Punta Aguja, about ½ mile distant. It is a reddish rock bluff, off which a reef extends and a shoal area continues around the point to the northern end of a white sandy beach. When traveling in the area give the point a safe berth. The ¾ mile long beach ends at a gray rocky projection. Anchorage may be taken off the reddish bluff in 3 fathoms, sand. **WPT 26° 52.24', 111° 50.76'**

PUNTA SANTO DOMINGO

Punta San Pedro, on the west shore is the point off which the entrance is narrowest as the shoals extend well into the apparent channel. Shoaling continues making the shallow area more extensive each year. When entering, keep well to the east until you are across from Santispac, before turning in. About 3 miles south of this point a hilly headland projects SSE, connected to the shore by a low sandy spit. Several islands lie scattered to the south. Sheltered behind Punta San Pedro and the islands is Bahia Coyote, the most popular anchorage area which has several coves within it.

Passage into **Bahia Coyote** can be made via any of the channels between the islands, keeping in mid-channel, clear of rocks and shoals that surround each island. During daylight the submerged dangers are clearly seen by the colors in the water. A navigation light (usually not working) is on the northernmost island but a night entrance is not advised.

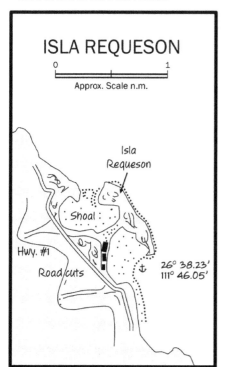

ISLA REQUESON

Santispac, tucked behind Punta Piedrita is a major stopover and meeting place for cruisers. Shoals line the shores, especially off the head of the cove. Vessels can enter on either side of Isla San Ramon to take sheltered anchorage off the long sandy beach in 4 fathoms, sand. Another excellent anchorage lies off the high bluffs on the west side of Santispac, in 4 fathoms, sand, with additional protection afforded by the bluffs and the island.

In the winter, the huge parking area is often filled with RVs that arrive by the dozens. Their presence may add to opportunities for hitching a ride to Mulege for the day. Ana's Restaurant/Bar serves excellent food, is a popular meeting place for cruisers and a book exchange. There are no other services. A hot spring trickles across the beach at the base of the bluffs. Easy landing can be made in either Santispac or **Playa Concepcion**, the cove to the west. In the latter cove shoals almost fill the area and the last part of a trip ashore requires you to tow the dinghy for quite a distance over the flats. To moor here you must anchor quite a distance from shore. Snorkeling for clams and shells is productive.

Geary provides retransmissions of weather on VHF Ch 18, Ham nets , WiFi Service and great information at www.sonrisanet.org. Bertha's Restaurant, also located in Play el Burro, has very good food, possibly the best chile rellenos in the world.

Other very pleasant anchorage spots are found off **Playa Coyote, Playa Santa Barbara** and **Isla Coyote**. While traveling between the various anchorages and setting the anchor you must take care to avoid the numerous shoal areas and make an allowance for possible swinging while at anchor.

Anchorage may be taken off **Isla Requeson WPT 26°38.23', 111°49.65',** in the southern part of the bay during fair weather settled conditions. Avoid Roca Frijol (Bean Rock), covered 6', a dangerous rock about 2 miles north of Isla Requeson at **WPT 26°40.52', 111°50.04'**. The shoal areas here were once famous for clams, but they have been heavily harvested and few remain.

Not to be used for navigation.

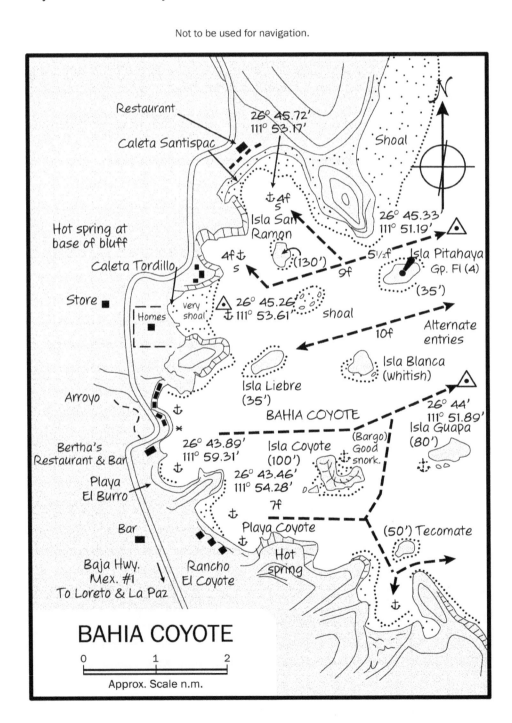

BAHIA COYOTE

0   1   2

Approx. Scale n.m.

Beautiful sunset at sea. Photo: Robin Richardson Stout

Catch me if you Can! Bottlenose Dolphin. Photo: Phoebe Wilson

MULEGE, WPT 26°54', 111°57'

Is a small town along the delta of the Rio Santa Rosalia and it lies just 3 miles northwest of Punta Gallo, which is at the entrance to Bahia Concepcion. A prominent landmark is Punta El Sombrerito, a 119' high cone-shaped, reddish brown rocky point with a flat, round base. It is almost an island, rising on the north side of the Mulege estuary out of a low, sandy spit marked by a navigation light.

The bars and shoals at the mouth of the river prevent deep draft boats from entering. Sports fishing vessels and pangas can enter the estuary where depths of less than 6 feet are found between the shoals. For shoal draft vessels, entry can be made by clearing the reef that extends southeast from El Sombrerito, then favoring the south side of the channel and avoiding the sandbars within the entrance. A launching ramp and small dock are north of the airstrip that runs southward a short distance from the coast. Hotel Serenidad has dry storage for small trailerable boats for short periods as space permits. An experienced, English-speaking fishing guide operates a small charter sportsfishing boat service adjacent to the launch ramp. Another launch ramp is on the north side of the river adjacent to the lighthouse. A concrete wall that affords med-tie to small sailboats is near the white building with a sign "Port Captain" although there is no Port Captain stationed here.

Deeper draft cruising vessels must remain outside the river in the open roadstead, anchoring either to the north or south, as shown. The main anchorage, between Punta El Sombrerito and Punta Prieta to the north is off the shore beyond the shoal area in 3 to 6 fathoms. Prevailing winds and local currents affect this anchorage. It is not a tenable position if the weather turns, and should be vacated for a more protected anchorage. An alternative open anchorage is found in the southern area, well clear of the large shoal that extends from the estuary. From these anchorages take the dinghy up the river to the town where groceries and jerry can fuel can be obtained.

The town of Mulege is well known for the beautiful lush growth of towering palms and greenery that are fed by fresh water springs. Mulege has numerous restaurants, adequate provisioning, ice and bus service. The most unique features of the town are the famous territorial penitentiary and the Mission. The prison stands on a hill to the north of town and its square, white bulk is an excellent landmark. Its relaxed and humane penal system was famous for it allowed inmates to leave the prison each day to visit their families and work at nearby farms and shops, returning on signal to their cells each night. The Mission was founded in 1705. It is on the south side of the river and a short distance west of the bridge. Part of the church is rebuilt and in use; the ruins are more extensive than they appear at first glance. A walk around them will take you to a spot with a great view of the entire valley.

To the north of Punta Prieta is Bahia Santa Ines which ends at **Punta Santa Ines**, some 9 miles distant. About 2 miles southeast of this rocky, flat-topped headland are three low islets, surrounded by shoals and rocks. The passage between the islands and the point has no dangers but is only about 2 fathoms deep. These islets are very difficult to see at night. A luxury hotel, Hotel Punta Chivato, and a residential complex are on the point and an airstrip lies behind the western beaches. A short breakwater extends off the point. Anchorage can be taken in the southern lee at **Playa Santa Ines WPT 27°03.94', 112°57.11'** in 10 to 20 feet. Punta Chivato, about 2 miles north of Punta Santa Ines, marks a turning point of the land as it slants toward Puerto Santa Rosalia.

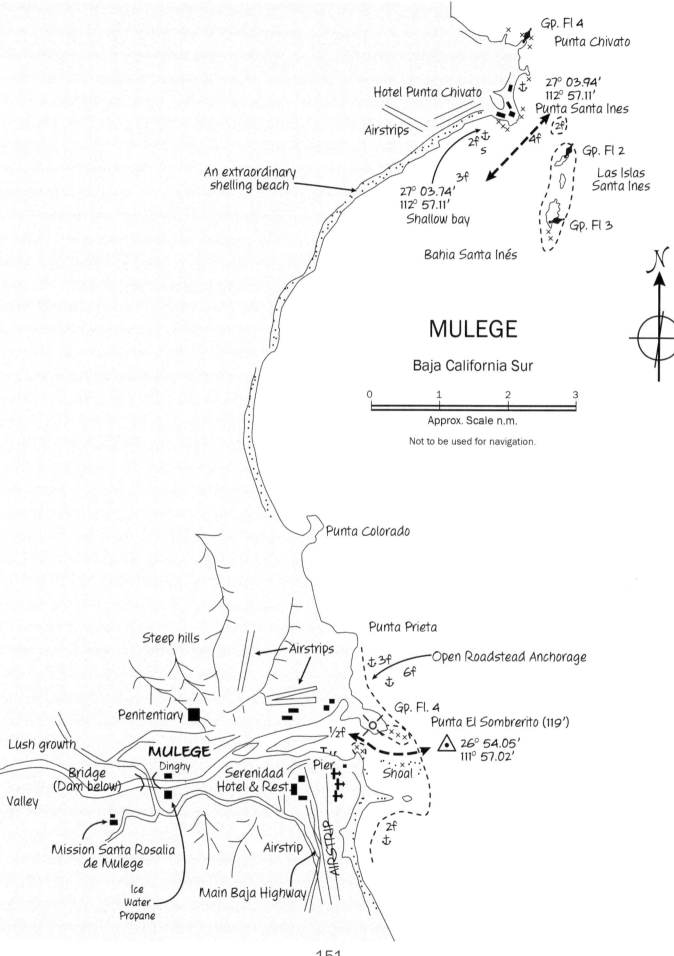

Gp. Fl 4
Punta Chivato

27° 03.94'
112° 57.11'

Hotel Punta Chivato

Airstrips

Punta Santa Ines

(2f)

4f

Gp. Fl 2

Las Islas
Santa Ines

2f ⚓
s

3f

An extraordinary
shelling beach

27° 03.74'
112° 57.11'
Shallow bay

Gp. Fl 3

Bahia Santa Inés

MULEGE

Baja California Sur

0   1   2   3

Approx. Scale n.m.

Not to be used for navigation.

Punta Colorado

Punta Prieta

Steep hills

Airstrips

⚓ 3f   Open Roadstead Anchorage
⚓ 6f

Gp. Fl. 4

Penitentiary

Punta El Sombrerito (119')

Lush growth

½f

26° 54.05'
111° 57.02'

MULEGE
Dinghy

Bridge
(Dam below)

Serenidad
Hotel & Rest.

Pier

Shoal

Valley

Mission Santa Rosalia
de Mulege

2f
⚓

Airstrip

AIRSTRIP

Ice
Water
Propane

Main Baja Highway

ISLA SAN MARCOS

From Punta Chivato the coast recedes westward before resuming its general northwesterly trend. Across Canal de San Marcos (also known as Craig Channel) to the north, lies the high, barren island of Isla San Marcos. A long, shoal bank and reef extend in a southerly direction for almost 1¼ miles from the south tip of the island before reaching Roca Lobos 20' high. The remaining rocks are within ¼ mile of the shore. The navigable portion of the channel between the dangers at the southern end of the island and the mainland is about 1 mile wide and has a least depth of 10 to 12 feet. Because of its shallow depth there are fairly strong currents in the channel.

A red navigation light marks the northernmost rock off the north end of the island, but a reef extending further north from the lighted rock makes it necessary to give a wide berth when passing this end of the island.

A number of peaks dot the 6-mile long island, the highest being roughly in the middle of the island at 891'. White scars on its southern end are evidence of the surface mining of gypsum (calcium sulfate) of which much of the island is composed. For many years this component of plaster of Paris and dry wall has been mined on the island and shipped all over the world, though mainly to the U.S. A processing plant with a dock lies on the southwestern shore where large freighters are often seen loading at the 320' pier. Northwesterly winds usually result in a coating of powdered gypsum on vessels anchored down wind.

Anchorage with good protection from northerly winds can be taken in **Puerto el Viejo, WPT 27°10.85', 112°3.95'** which is the curved bight east of the southern tip of the island, directly north of Roca Lobos. Give safe clearance to reefs on both the eastern and western sides, especially approaching from the north. You will need to swing west almost to the Baja (see sketch). Set the anchor well to avoid dragging in the grassy sand in about 20 feet. A 15-minute walk along a trail leading from the middle of the beach takes you to the village near the pier.

A second anchorage is on the western side of the island tucked behind the pier in about 25 feet, with good holding. Though it is subject to uncomfortable surge, it is closer to the excellent fishing and snorkeling to be had around the reefs off the northern tip of the island. In the village is a beautiful white church made of gypsum that is well worth seeing. Its unique decorations feature fishing nets and various fish. A rock arch on the northern part of the island provides passage for dinghies to a beautiful beach beyond; this spectacular trip should be undertaken only in calm conditions.

Punta Piedra Blanca is the northwest corner of the island. The navigation light Gp.Fl.2 lies on an offshore rock. There are anchorages on both sides of the point, depending on the weather, with good holding in both. There is a fish camp with several families in the northern cove.

Caleta de Los Arcos is approximately ¾ mile north of the point. It is a fantastic place for dinghy exploration and snorkeling. There is a small cobble beach, backed by narrow caves used by fishermen. The name of the cove came from the fact that there is a natural arch at the water's edge.

The main attraction here are two commodious sea caves, one has a large front door, and a smaller side door. The northernmost has a very low front door to swim through, but once inside, the back opens up onto a small beach accessible by dinghy around the end. The cave itself enjoys a large skylight in its ceiling. Not only are caves fascinating, but next to them are narrow canyons penetrating the cliff face. Some of these open up into a wide basin once you squeeze the dinghy through the entrance.

Along the eastern side of the island are a few coves worth exploring. Anchorage may be had at **Bahia El Burro** with protection from any westerly weather at **WPT 27°13.07', 112°2.93'**.

Caleta San Lucas is a shallow lagoon that lies due west of Isla San Marcos and about 15 miles northwest of Punta Chivato. A long, sandy spit encloses a shallow body of water where depths within the lagoon and across the entrance constantly change due to shifting sandbars. Only vessels having a very shallow draft (5' or less) might be able to anchor here. A dinghy should be used to investigate the entrance as well as a possible route to an anchorage spot. Strong tidal currents occur in the shallow waters.

A fishing village is located on the western shore of the bay and a lime mine is located in the vicinity. A road connecting the settlement to the Mulege/Santa Rosalia highway is about one mile away.

ISLA SAN MARCOS

Baja California Sur

Approx. Scale n.m.

Not to be used for navigation.

PUERTO SANTA ROSALIA

Puerto Santa Rosalia is easily recognized by the two tall chimneys of the copper smelting works north of town and many buildings built around the harbor. Protected by a breakwater, the harbor provides facilities for the ferry to Guaymas, commercial ore-loading docks and two marinas. Navigation lights are located at the end of each breakwater and range lights behind the commercial dock lead into the basin. The entry range **WPT 27°20.16', 112°15.61'**.

This is a **Port of Entry** where cruisers may be asked to report to Immigration and Customs in person after calling the Port Captain. The office is located at the ferry dock and the Port Captain's office near the inner end of the breakwater. Anchorage can be taken at the north end of the harbor in 20 to 25 feet, taking care to leave space for commercial traffic.

Fonatur Marina Santa Rosalia is a full service marina located near the Guaymas car ferry dock. The facility has 20 slips and can accommodate vessels up to 80 ft. Moorage charges (2013) of 10 pesos per foot per day include all facilities such as Wi-Fi, a swimming pool and HD TV. Propane is available with tanks picked up and returned on Saturdays. For information call VHF Ch16, Telephone 011-52-615-152-1768 or email alozano@fonatur.gob.mx

Marina Santa Rosalia offers friendly service with water and power on the docks. It is within easy walking distance of grocery stores, an excellent bakery, liquor store and restaurants. The friendly dockmaster will assist in making arrangements for taking on large quantities of fuel at the commercial dock when space permits, or small amounts may be taken aboard in jerry cans.

A telephone is located on the side road near the dockmaster's office, though traffic noises are a nuisance. The renowned hot dog stand, "Equisitos Hot Dogs," is located on the corner of Calle Pedro Altamirano and Avenida Alvaro Obregon near the front of the church and is open only at night. A laundry, bank and several mercados are a short walk from the marinas. See map on page 159

The town has an interesting history, beginning in 1866 when copper ore was discovered in the area. A French syndicate developed the mines and this became a busy port with square-riggers off-loading coal to fuel the copper smelter and taking on refined copper. Iglesia Santa Barbara is a unique pre-fabricated metal church, designed and built by Carl Eiffel (as in Tower) for the Paris Exposition of 1889, re-built in Brussels and subsequently taken down, shipped to Santa Rosalia and re-assembled by its French owners in 1895. Restoration of part of the town to resemble its historic past provides additional interest for this is the only community in Baja attempting to rediscover its roots. Near the hospital on the hill overlooking the harbor is the recently repaired Hotel Frances (1886), where a gallery of fascinating photographs from the early days are on display. In addition to serving excellent food in generous portions, it prepares special lunch packages of Mexican or International food that can be delivered to your boat.

NOTE: The tidal range becomes more significant from here to the head of the Gulf and it should be considered when anchoring, both as to the depth of the anchorage as well as calculating scope.

The journey between Puerto Santa Rosalia and Bahia San Francisquito is a long one, 77 nautical miles. For the most part the crumpled landforms come down to the shore, ending in bluffs or sand and shingle beaches with limited well protected coves or anchorages. Depending on the weather, it may be preferable to make the trip to San Francisquito in one step.

Caleta Santa Maria is about 6 miles north of Santa Rosalia, a working gypsum mine with a 'T' head pier. It offers excellent protection from all northern quarters but is not even close to being remote or wilderness. Anchor in sand in 20 to 25 feet at **WPT 27°26.89', 112°18.98'**. See sketch.

PUERTO SANTA ROSALIA
Baja California Sur

1000'　　　　　　0　　　　　　¼

Approx. Scale n.m.

Not to be used for navigation.

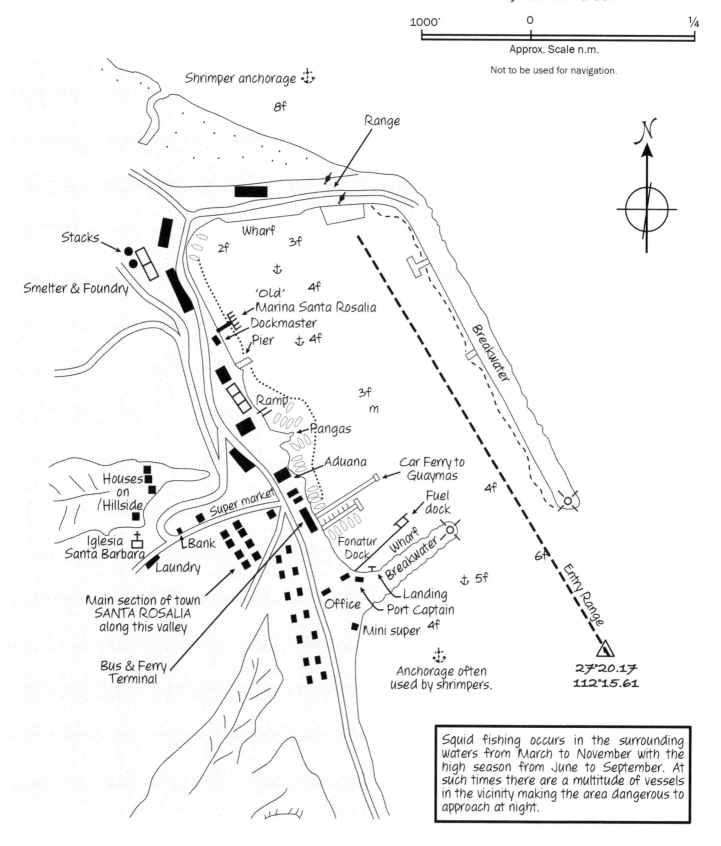

N

Shrimper anchorage ⚓

8f

Range

Stacks

Smelter & Foundry

Wharf

2f

3f

⚓

'Old'　4f
Marina Santa Rosalia
Dockmaster
Pier　⚓ 4f

Ramp

3f
m

Pangas

Aduana

Car Ferry to
Guaymas

Breakwater

4f

Houses
on
Hillside

Super market

Iglesia
Santa Barbara

Bank

Laundry

Fuel
dock

Wharf

Fonatur
Dock

Breakwater

Landing
Port Captain

Office

⚓ 5f

6A

Entry Range

Main section of town
SANTA ROSALIA
along this valley

Bus & Ferry
Terminal

Mini super　4f

⚓
Anchorage often
used by shrimpers.

27°20.17
112°15.61

Squid fishing occurs in the surrounding
waters from March to November with the
high season from June to September. At
such times there are a multitude of vessels
in the vicinity making the area dangerous to
approach at night.

Punta Santa Ana, WPT 27°40.97', 112°37.37' is a fair weather anchorage, but gives very minimal protection from any direction but west. The bottom is sand at about 10 feet. The point is low and hard to find from offshore. There are some cottages and palm trees on shore, and the arroyo behind has considerable greenery. Punta Santa Ana is about 14 miles northwest of Cabo Tres Virgenes.

The 200 foot cliff of Cabo Virgenes lies about 14 miles north of Santa Rosalia. Behind it a high coastal range with the three sharp peaks of Las Tres Virgenes (The Three Virgins) reach almost 6,550 feet. The strong rips and brisk winds that sometimes occur off the cape can make it uncomfortable for small vessels. When passing through this area, either hold an inshore route or stand well out from land.

Punta Trinidad, about 25 miles northwest of Cabo Virgenes (Virgins Cape), offers protection from either north or south of the point depending on the prevailing wind. The south side has several rocky deadheads visible. Enter with caution. The north side gives excellent protection from southerly weather. There is a short reef extending northwest from the point, and the ground shoals gradually so you can't approach the beach very closely. The bottom is sand at 10 to 15 feet at **WPT 27°49.45', 112°43.55'**.

Punta Salina is 5 miles north of Trinidad and is named for the salt pans behind the beach. It is a rather tight anchorage, but offers limited protection from the northwest. There is a reef off the east end of the point, which wraps around to protect the cove. Swing wide to avoid the reef off the southeast end of the point. The bottom is mostly sand at about 15 feet. **WPT 27°53.4', 112°45.85'**.

On the north side of the point lies **Caleta Lobera, WPT 27°54.22', 112°45.86'**. An offlying rock gives this small cove some of its southeast protection, and the home of a colony of sea lions. Behind the rock and a second rock near the land, you can anchor in 13 feet, sand. This cove offers protection from the south and west.

About 50 miles to the north of Cabe Tres Virgenes, and 17 miles south of San Fransisquito, lies **Cabo San Miguel** where several distinctive peaks rise behind the cape. Fair anchorage can be found for small vessels in the second cove south of the cape at **WPT 28°11.36', 112°47.34'**. The north point of this cove is a red, rocky projection off which lie several rocks and a reef. Anchorage may be taken off the cliffs south of this reef in 10 to 15 feet. There are several pinnacle rocks that rise 6 feet from the otherwise flat bottom. Be sure you are clear of them when you swing at anchor.

Just nextdoor to the north, at the foot of a white cliff is a very small cove that may provide anchorage if placed fore and aft. The tide rips past on the flood, so take this into consideration.

If winds are southerly, anchorage on the north side of the cape is better when you are tucked well into the bight northward of the cape off a very nice sand beach, 15 feet, sand. **WPT 28°12.23', 112°47.84'**. There is another very small cove at the north end of the beach in 10' sand, providing protection from the southeast.

Rancho El Barril (Barrel Ranch) is an open roadstead anchorage off this inhospitable coast, just 7 miles north of Cabo San Miguel. A rounded point shelters an indentation where a stream emerges from a large wash and arroyo. Shoals over which seas may break lie between the point and the stream. Anchorage may be taken off the houses, north of the shoal area and the mouth of the stream at approximately **WPT 28°18.63', 112°52.46'**.

When approaching **Punta San Gabriel** and **Bahia San Francisquito** from the south, be aware that the point can generate a 4 to 5 knot current on an ebb tide, so give it a wide clearance.

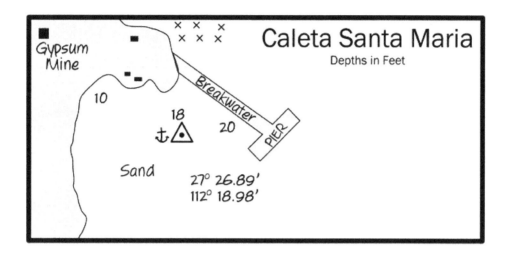

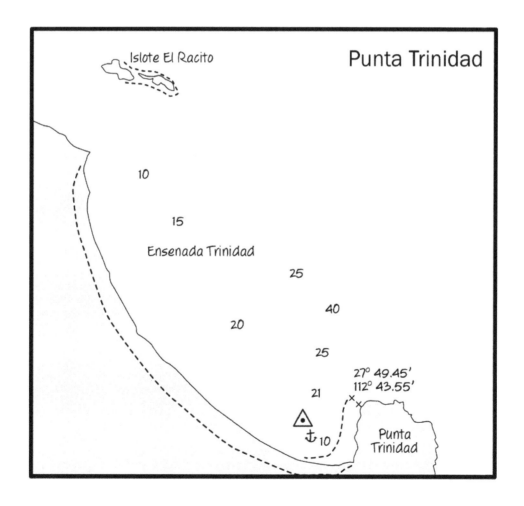

157

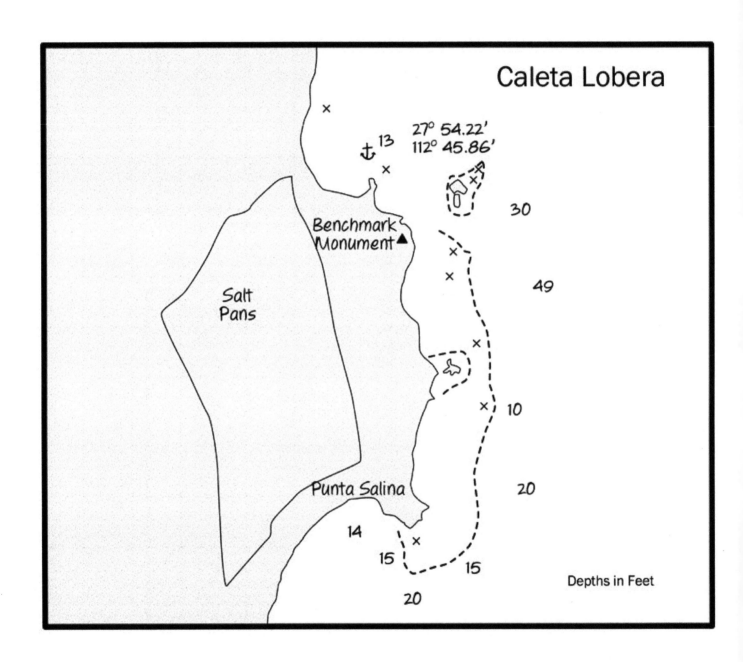

Caleta Lobera

27° 54.22'
112° 45.86'

30

49

Benchmark
Monument ▲

Salt
Pans

10

20

Punta Salina

14

15

15

20

Depths in Feet

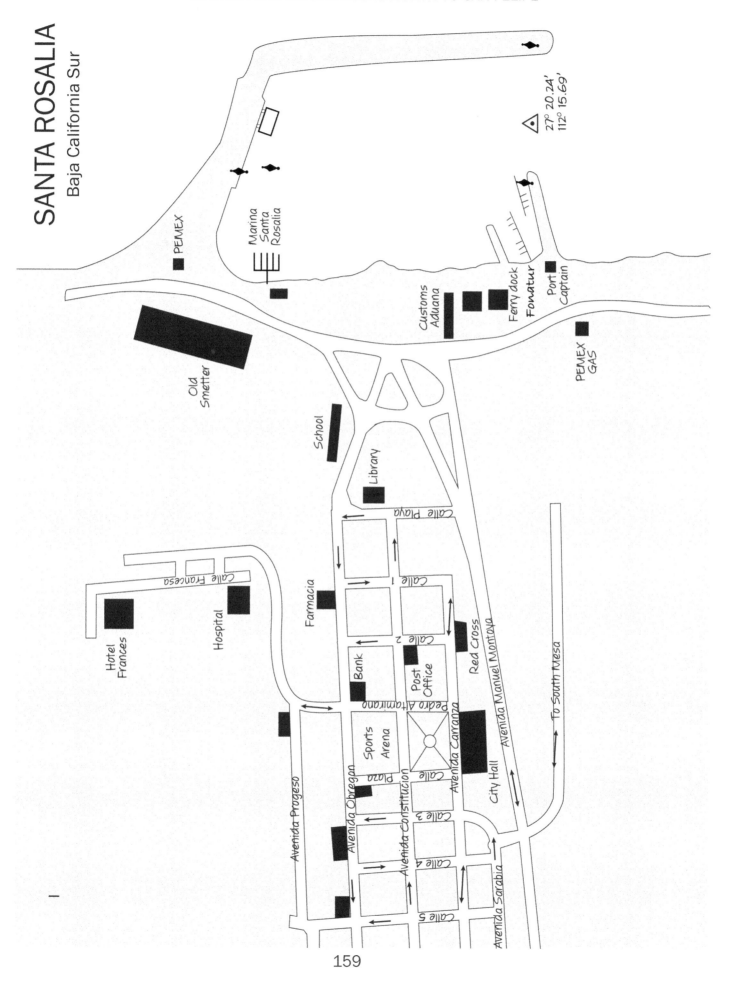

SANTA ROSALIA
Baja California Sur

PEMEX

Marina Santa Rosalia

Customs Aduana

Ferry dock
Fonatur

Port Captain

PEMEX GAS

27° 20.24'
112° 15.69'

Old Smelter

School

Library

Calle Playa

Calle 1

Farmacia

Bank

Post Office

Red Cross

Sports Arena

Pedro Altamirano

Avenida Carranza

City Hall

Avenida Manuel Montoya

Avenida Obregon

Avenida Constitucion

Plaza

Calle 3

Calle 4

Calle 5

Avenida Sarabia

Avenida Progeso

Calle Francesa

Hotel Frances

Hospital

Calle 2

To South Mesa

BAHIA SAN FRANCISQUITO

The popular, protected anchorage at Bahia San Francisquito, **WPT 28°26'8', 112°51.9'**, lies west of and behind a prominent hilly headland, Punta San Gabriel. A long, white, sandy beach on the shore of Bahia Santa Teresa south of the rocky coast culminating in Punta San Gabriel helps to identify it. A beach front resort and airstrip (built on a dry lake bed) are additional landmarks. The bay opens to the northeast and is roughly one mile wide and square in shape. Most vessels anchor in the southwest corner off a sand beach where the influence of northerly winds can make the night uncomfortable, but safe. Shoal areas line the sides of the cove so anchor clear in 20 feet. There are caves to explore up the two valleys that back the beach, swimming is excellent.

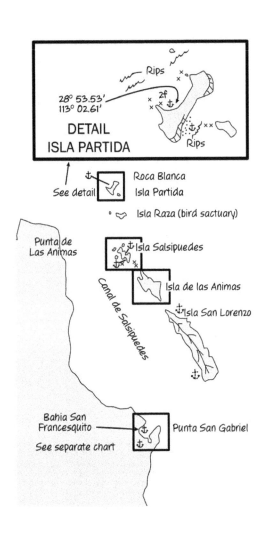

Shallow draft vessels drawing less than 5 ft can find better protection in a small, shoal basin opening off the southeast corner. Pass through the narrow entrance in mid-channel and anchor clear of the grassy patches. Few supplies are available at the resort, though emergency fuel may be obtained if supplies permit.

Caletas Mujeres (Women's Coves) are a pair of pretty coves just to the north of the northern entrance point of Bahia San Francisquito. Though exposed to the north, anchorage in settled weather can be taken in either cove in about 12 feet, sand bottom. An easy hike in the nearby hills is rewarded with excellent views of this picturesque area.

LAS ISLAS DE LA CINTURA, or the **MIDRIFF ISLANDS** as we call them, clog the waist of the Gulf of California, making narrow channels, which compress and accelerate the speed of the 20 foot tides of the northern gulf as they pass through. However, they offer a myriad of wonderful anchorages for the cruiser. They also present an opportunity for those with smaller boats to make a safe crossing of the gulf from Kino to either Bahia de Los Angeles, or Bahia San Francisquito, by island hopping.

When the 20 foot tides of the upper gulf are squeezed through these narrow passages, the speed of their travel is greatly increased, especially around points of land which intrude into the tidal stream. You should either choose a favorable tide for traversing a confined channel, or choose a more capacious channel, or be prepared to fight the current for a few hours. The Salsipuedes Channel, in spite of its name, is the easiest to get through. The San Lorenzo Channel is the roughest, and San Esteban Channel is medium rough. The descriptions of the Midriff anchorages will start at Isla San Lorenzo, the first Midriff Island you will encounter if you are proceeding north along the Baja coast.

There are no good anchorages on San Lorenzo. The island is 9 miles long and 1½ miles wide. It is steep-to all around, and although there seem to be a few, possible coves, the bottom is just too steep to anchor safely.

DANGER: Do not attempt to pass between Isla San Lorenzo and Isla Las Animas. The depth is 6 feet, studded with rocks, and a strong current.

BAHIA SAN FRANCISQUITO
Baja California Norte

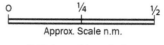

Approx. Scale n.m.

Not to be used for navigation.
Depths in fathoms.

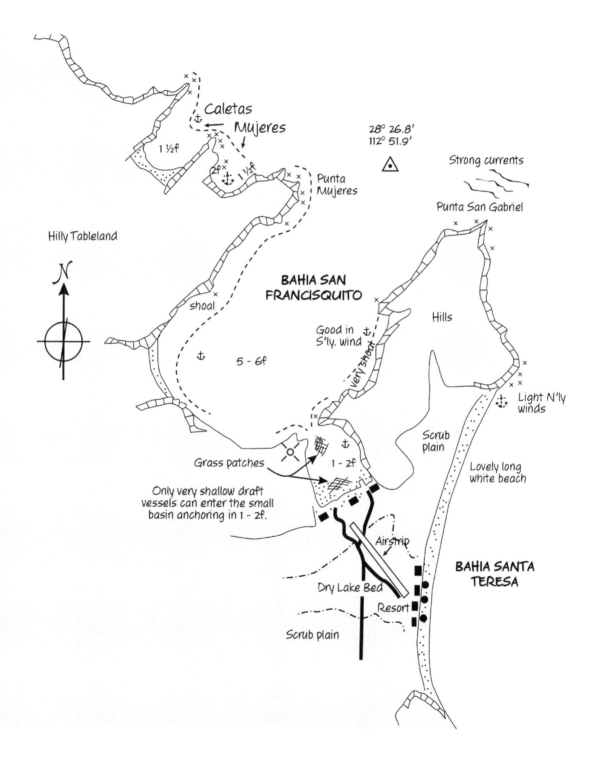

Caletas
Mujeres

1 ½f

2f   1 ½f

Punta
Mujeres

28° 26.8'
112° 51.9'

Strong currents

Punta San Gabriel

Hilly Tableland

N

BAHIA SAN
FRANCISQUITO

Hills

shoal

Good in
S'ly. wind

very shoal

5 - 6f

Light N'ly
winds

Scrub
plain

Grass patches

Lovely long
white beach

1 - 2f

Only very shallow draft
vessels can enter the small
basin anchoring in 1 - 2f.

Airstrip

BAHIA SANTA
TERESA

Dry Lake Bed

Resort

Scrub plain

ISLA LAS ANIMAS

This island has several anchorages. It is 2 ½ miles long and ¾ mile wide.

West bight is near the north end on the southwest side. It is a small cove with a rocky beach, and little attraction for the cruiser except as shelter from a norther if you can't make it to Salsipuedes. The bottom is patchy at 15 feet. **WPT 28°41.80', 112°55.79'.**

Caleta Blanca is at the north end of the island and in good weather is a delightful little anchorage. The bottom, as well as the beach, are both white sand with lots of sand dollars lying around. The beach shoals very gradually, so it is only 5 or 6 feet deep in the actual mouth, but the sand extends out to deeper water. **WPT 28°42.40', 112°56'.**

East Bight too is a marginal anchorage of little interest. It is on the northeast side of the island about half way down. The bottom is patchy at 30 to 40 feet.

DANGERS: The channel between Isla Las Animas and Isla Salsipuedes contains a reef, usually visible, and a pinnacle rock, which never dries out, but which has been seen sending up a 6 ft. geyser in a strong tidal flow. As you can see from a chart, there is a wide and deep passage called Mas Pas (More Passage) between the reef and Las Animas, and another narrow but deep passage called Puedes Pas (You Can Pass), between the pinnacle rock and Salsipuedes

There is a dangerous saw-edged rock, set to cut the bottom out of any boat that hits it. This danger lies centered off Caleta de la Cueva on Salsipuedes, right in the path of boats going in and out of South Slot. It is 3 feet under at zero tide and with high tides running 4 to 8 feet it is safely down most of the time, but the last time Gerry located it, it was only an oar blade under the surface. It is a nasty looking thing. The saw edge is at the eastern end of a small reef, which contains a pocket of sand which shows white when the tide is low.

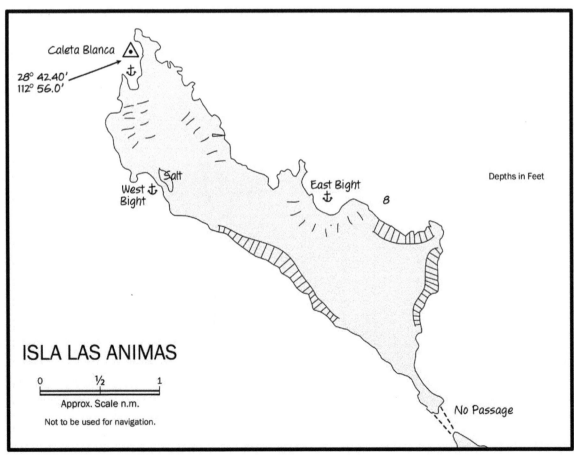

Caleta Blanca

28° 42.40'
112° 56.0'

Salt

West
Bight

East Bight

8

Depths in Feet

ISLA LAS ANIMAS

0   ½   1

Approx. Scale n.m.

Not to be used for navigation.

No Passage

ISLA SALSIPUEDES

This is a favorite island in the Sea of Cortez. It is unique in that it is not a mountainous pile of crumbling rock. "The Peak" almost qualifies as a conventional Baja island, but the rest of the island is fairly flat, smooth, and solid. There are four nice anchorages on Salsipuedes, three on the southwest side.

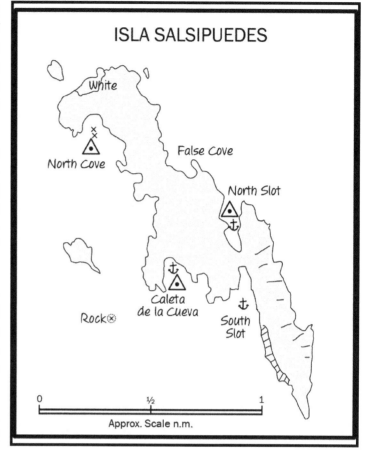

South Slot is the largest. It is possible that at one time this used to be two islands, and then a cobble bar built up through storm action, connecting the two islands, and making long narrow coves on each side. The south side is the most commodious. Its sides are steep-to with a couple of off-lying rocks beneath The Peak.

The bottom is flat sand at 10 to 15 feet. Protection is good from all directions except south, and if a norther came up, the waves wouldn't get to you, but the wind would come over the cobble bar. Under these conditions, it's better to move over into Caleta de la Cueva.

Caleta De La Cueva WPT 28°43.41', 112°57.39', is a wider bay than either slot. There is a small sand beach. The actual cave is too narrow for a dinghy, but makes good snorkeling and usually has a population of red crabs. The shores of this cove are also good snorkeling, being steep-to, with some breakdown, and a flat sand bottom, at about 20 feet. The channel between the island and Sea Lion Rock is deep and clear, but the tide rips through here, worth thinking about when exploring with the dinghy.

North Cove - Watch out for this one. The cove is divided into two halves by a reef. One beach is inviting sand, the other cobble. Perverse nature has made the bottom off the sand beach of cobbles, and the good holding sand at about 15 feet, off the cobble beach. **WPT 28°43.80', 112°57.7'**

False Cove is a nice looking little bight on the northeast side of the island, just north of the North Slot. Great for dinghy trips, but protected by reefs and rocks making it hazardous and too tight for big boats.

North Slot, WPT 28°43.67', 112°57.21', lies across the bar from South Slot. It is considerably smaller than South Slot, both narrower, shorter, and shallower. The sides are steep-to and the bottom flat sand at 10 to 30 feet. However, less than half way inside, the width narrows suddenly. Avoid setting the anchor any further in than this bottleneck, as Northers can come up suddenly during winter months. La Cueva provides the best protection from a norther.

ISLA RAZA

The next island north of Salsipuedes, about 6 miles away, is a bird sanctuary with a scientific observation crew usually in residence in the little stone cabin. The headquarters is on the north side, as are the official anchorage and landing. Since this is open roadstead, there being no coves on Raza, consider leaving an anchor watch onboard unless the weather is very quiet.

The shore trip is worthwhile, but check in with the staff before exploring. There are paths among the nesting birds, which of course you don't disturb. The island is covered with man-made rock structures of uncertain origin.

RAZA ROCK

A mile northwest of Isla Raza is a monumental rock, home of a large colony of Sea Lions. The rock is steep-to, so you can circle it, and enjoy the antics of the curious sea lions. However, there is a **DANGER**. About 200 yards southeast of the rock there is a small reef, usually awash, but covered at high tide. This is Raza Rock's Baby, and can be a danger if you don't know it is there. Don't let the Sea Lions distract you. Bearing from Baby to Rock is 325° True.

ISLA PARTIDA

Five miles north of Isla Raza is the last of the Minor Midriff Islands. From a distance, Partida looks like two islands because the connecting bar is only 30 feet high.

Southeast Anchorage is where you go for protection from the northwest. There is a small patch of sand lying off a Roestte patterned rock cliff below the south hill. With the Rosette bearing 265° True, and about 350 yards off, you should find the edge of the sand at about 35 feet. Approximate **WPT 28°53.18', 113°20.29'**, as you move in closer the bottom has more patches of rock. However, the tidal current that makes the sandbank sweeps the end of it with considerable force. A suitable scope for the depth will allow you to swing into the current. Move in as close as you can and still find a good patch of sand for the anchor. It is also possible to anchor on the south side of Partida Chica (Little Partida). The bottom is definitely not all sand, but the anchor sets well in whatever is down there and the tidal current is minimal.

Crescent Bay, WPT 28°53.53', 113°02.61', on the northwest side of Partida is a much nicer anchorage with a white sand beach, but completely exposed to the northwest, so it is most useful in summer, or very quiet weather. The bottom is sand at about 20 feet. Be careful rounding into this bay from either direction. Give both headlands plenty of room. There is a detached, submerged rock off the northern headland.

Partida Rock lies 3/4 mile north of Crescent Bay. There is deep water between it and the island, but a long reef extends north of the rock with a rock that dries out, near, but not at, the far end. Give it a wide berth. The tidal currents are quite strong in all these passages.

BACK TO THE MAINLAND OF THE BAJA

DANGER: Bernabe Rocks lie 28 miles north of Bahia San Francisquito, and 4 ½ miles south of Punta las Animas (Souls Point). There is some confusion of nomenclature here. The Mexican topo maps ignoring this navigational hazard completely, use this name for a large block of rock 3 miles to the north, which gives Animas Slot its protection. We will stick to the conventional cruisers' nomenclature.

These rocks, and the reef connecting them to the shore are far enough offshore so that at high tide with them covered, you might think yourself a prudent distance off, and come to grief. Even when the highest rocks are showing, there is another rock 100 yards southeast that is usually a couple of feet under. The reef connecting the rocks to the shore may show tidal riffles. From the south, the rocks are in line with a gray lenticular cliff, bearing 286o mag. From the north, they are in line with a gray triangular cliff bearing 205° mag. **WPT 28°47.48', 113°11.38'.**

Puertocitos Del Enmedio lies 3½ miles north of Bernabe Rocks, and a mile south of Punta las Animas. It is a small cove with good protection from the northwest. The bottom is mostly sand at 25 to 30 feet, **WPT 28°50.1', 113°14.5'.**

DANGER: Off the point separating Puertocitos and Animas Slot there is an extensive reef. About 1/3rd of its length off the point is a usually visible rock. Give it a wide berth before rounding into the Slot.

Animas Slot is just around the reef from Puertocitos. **WPT 28°50.27', 113°14.9'.** It is a small cove protected from the northwest by a large block of rock almost 100 feet high, and connected to the shore by an exposed bar. As pretty as this cove is, it may be rolly, so that Puertocitos might be more comfortable.

BAHIA DE LAS ANIMAS

This is a large bay with several good anchorages. It is the last significant bay before Bahia de los Angeles, and all but the two southern coves give good protection from the northwest. **WPT 28°49.7', 113°19.9'.**

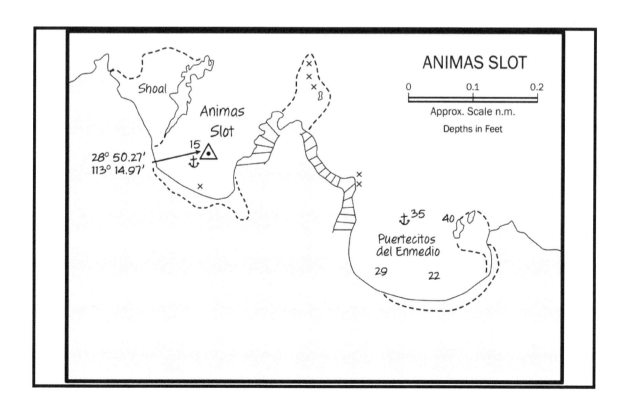

Animas South Anchorages

About 2 ½ miles west of Punta las Animas at the southern end of Animas Bay are two small coves which would give good protection from the southerly quarters. The beaches are gravel and the bottom is sand or gravel at 20 feet.

Playa Las Animas: The entire south end of Animas Bay is a long beach backed by lagoons. It would be possible to anchor anywhere off this beach, weather permitting, for swimming, shelling and possibly clamming in the lagoons.

Punta Islotes: This is a low point which extends out from what could be called the southwest corner of Animas Bay. This location is accessible by road, so you may find RVs along the west end of the beach. There is a more or less permanent fish camp on the south side of the point. The small islets for which the point is named have questionable channels between them. **WPT 28°48.61', 113°21.28'**, in 20 feet, sand.

DANGER: Leland Rock, so named by Jack Williams, lies north northwest of the easternmost islet. It is a sizable reef, carrying only a foot or two and with a single pinnacle rising above it which uncovers only at extreme low tides. The outer reaches of the reef are about 500 yards from the islet, so keep well clear. **WPT 28°49.07', 113°20.94'**

ISLA SANTA ANA

This is a barren chunk of rock a half mile north of Punta Islotes. There is clear passage with three fathoms between it and the mainland.

Punta Soldado: The next point north offers northwest protection on the south side in 25 to 30 feet sand and rock. The northern side offers southerly protection 30 to 40 feet. Be sure to swing wide, north of the Isla Racito when entering the northern cove.

ISLA RACITO

This is the low-lying, exposed north end of a reef about 1/2 mile north of Punta Soldado. Do not pass between this and the mainland.

Punta Alacran: Alacran gives good protection from the northwest. There is a beach to the west of the point with a resort ashore, and lots interesting exploration by dinghy. The bottom is good at 15 to 20 feet, **WPT 28°53.97', 113°22.63'.**

Punta Pescador: The sand beach west of the rocky point used to be wilderness, but now there is a row of palm thatched palapas lining the beach. It is still a very nice beach. The point offers northwest protection, and if you need southeast protection, you can anchor behind the low island. It isn't very deep, only a fathom between island and beach, but the bottom is good sand. **WPT 28°55.3', 113°23.32'.** Several rocky coves along the point and one right at its extreme end are favorite spots for kayakers. The rocks extend offshore all around the point, so don't crowd it.

Ensenada Quemado is named for the point forming its western shore, whose black lava looks burnt. There is a lagoon behind this rocky embankment, and Punta Pescador forms its eastern shore. Anchorage may be taken on the eastern shore under the red hill and off the beach. **WPT 28°55.63', 113°24.49'.**

PUERTO DON JUAN

As you approach Bahia de los Angeles from the south, the first anchorage around Punta Don Juan is a large land-locked bay. It is difficult to see the entrance to Puerto Don Juan, especially after dark, because the channel makes a dog-leg to the right and then left into the bay itself. From offshore you can't see that there is anything there but land. The channel is not very wide, so you enter alongside the west shore of Punta Don Juan (not too close), until you almost hit the shore dead ahead, at which point you should be able to see around the dog-leg to starboard **WPT 28°57.07', 113°26.61'.** Past the Bathtub Bar to port, the bay opens out and could take almost 100 boats at anchor. You may find one or two others there, as this is a popular place. The wind sometimes comes with force over the gravel bar forming Don Juan's northwest comer, but the wave action can't get in around the dog-leg. Puerto San Juan has mostly sand bottom from 15 to 30 feet. Anchorage at **WPT 28°56.66', 113°26.96'**

Don Juan has a great beach for careening your boat for bottom work. For a 5 ft. draft boat you have approximately 5 hours to work during an 11 ft. tidal range. Gerry Cunningham often painted his boat bottom here, and once painted both sides in one day. It's primitive, but it doesn't cost a cent.

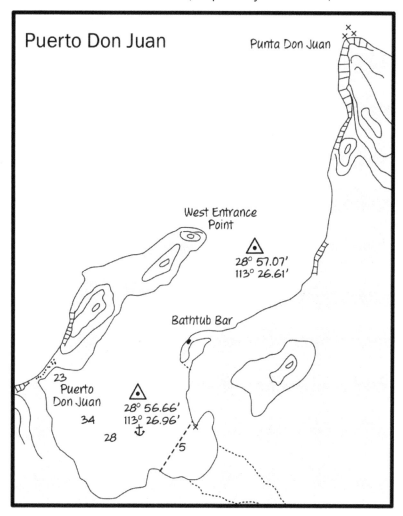

BAHIA DE LOS ANGELES

Bahia de Los Angeles (Bay of the Angels) is a large bay, about 12 miles long from the south end to the tip of its northernmost island. From the town of Bahia de los Angeles, to the outer shore of its outermost island, is about 5½ miles. Within this capacious bay there are 15 islands, 4 dangerous pinnacle rocks, and 10 pleasant anchorages.

Bahia de Los Angeles is about a 10 hour drive, 386 miles of paved road from San Diego. It has 3 launching ramps and there are 30 anchorages within 40 miles of the ramps. This is almost as dense an assortment of anchorages as at San Carlos on the mainland. Going clockwise around Bahia de los Angeles as you leave Don Juan, there first are two deeply indented coves but without beaches or other attractions.

La Mona is a pleasant anchorage at the eastern end of the long beach, which is the south end of Bahia De Los Angeles. The bottom is sand at 15 to 20 feet. In quiet weather, anchorage may be taken anywhere along the beach. **WPT 28°57.8', 113°28.3'.**

The town of BLA has several grocery stores, a liquor store, water and ice. Limited mechanical service is sometimes available. Casa Diez has one of the several restaurants in town and one of the grocery stores as well as rooms for rent. Also in town are a bakery, fresh produce, a motel, and fuel. The town anchorage is in behind Punta Arena with its navigational light Fl.Wht. on a concrete tower. Coming in at night, give it plenty of clearance as it is not on the end of the spit. Channel depth is 15 to 25 feet over sand, but a shoal extends off the point and a large area to the east. **WPT 28°57.2', 113°32.9'.**

La Gringa is the last anchorage on the shores of the bay itself. This is a good sized bay within a real hook of land protecting against any large wave action from all directions except south. Strong winds can sweep across, but is usually safe. The bottom is sand at 20 to 30 feet, with some cobble patches. Set the anchor well. **WPT 29°2.06', 113°32.6'.**

THE ISLANDS OF BAHIA DE LOS ANGELES

There are several islands, which do not have good anchorages, nor do they form part of another island's anchorage. These are: Los Gemelos (The Twins), Cabeza de Caballo (Horse Head), Gravel Island, Piojo (Crab Island), La Calaveras (The Madcap), Coronado Rock, Jorobado (Crooked Island), and Flecha (Arrow Island).

DANGER: Winds resembling Santa Anas occasionally blow out of the canyons west of the town. Because the clouds rolling out of the canyons look like wrinkled elephant trunks, they are called elephantes. They sometimes blow the roofs off buildings! Puerto Don Juan is the only really safe place, although they don't blow offshore much farther than that. These winds should be kept in mind when anchoring for the night.

ISLA VENTANA

This sizable island and its several satellites is the closest to the town of BLA. Ventana has an excellent anchorage at its northwest corner, which gives reasonable protection due to the short fetch to mainland Baja and its neighboring cluster of small islands. The bottom is sand at 20 to 30 feet. **WPT 29°0.03', 113°30.92'.** Climbing the peak affords an excellent view of Bahia de Los Angeles and Isla Angel de la Guarda to the east. Should an Elefante catch you here, you can move over behind Isla Cerraja, less than half a mile away. This would give shelter from the wave action, but the wind would whip right over it. However, the holding is good in sand at about 35 feet. This whole cluster of islands is worthy of a little dinghy exploration.

There is another cove on the south side of Ventana, but the bottom appears rocky. It is not attractive, but would give good shelter from west around to north. Be sure your anchor is set if you have to use it. The "window" for which the island is named lies at its southeast corner.

DANGER: In a southeast direction from the Isla Ventana window there is a reef, well defined, with deep water (100 feet or so) around it, but which covers at most tides and so can be dangerous if you don't know it is there. It is over a quarter of a mile long in the direction of Cabeza de Caballo, and half as wide. There is plenty of room between it and Cabeza.

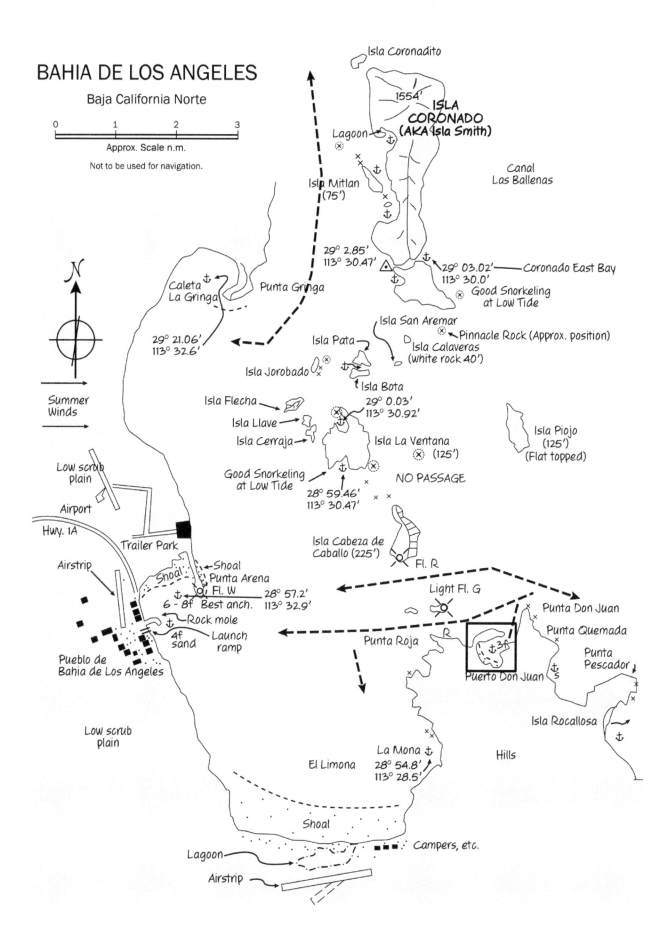

BAHIA DE LOS ANGELES

Baja California Norte

0   1   2   3

Approx. Scale n.m.

Not to be used for navigation.

Isla Coronadito

1554'

ISLA CORONADO (AKA Isla Smith)

Lagoon

Canal Las Ballenas

Isla Mitlan (75')

N

Summer Winds

Caleta La Gringa

Punta Gringa

29° 2.85'
113° 30.47'

29° 03.02'——Coronado East Bay
113° 30.0'

Good Snorkeling at Low Tide

29° 21.06'
113° 32.6'

Isla San Aremar

Pinnacle Rock (Approx. position)

Isla Pata

Isla Calaveras (white rock 40')

Isla Jorobado

Isla Bota

Isla Flecha

29° 0.03'
113° 30.92'

Isla Llave

Isla Cerraja

Isla La Ventana

(125')

Isla Piojo (125') (Flat topped)

Good Snorkeling at Low Tide

NO PASSAGE

28° 59.46'
113° 30.47'

Low scrub plain

Airport

Hwy. 1A

Trailer Park

Isla Cabeza de Caballo (225')

Fl. R

Airstrip

Shoal

Shoal

Punta Arena
Fl. W

28° 57.2'
113° 32.9'

6 - 8f Best anch.

Light Fl. G

Punta Don Juan

Punta Quemada

Rock mole

4f sand

Launch ramp

Punta Roja

Punta Pescador

Pueblo de Bahia de Los Angeles

Puerto Don Juan

Isla Rocallosa

Low scrub plain

La Mona
28° 54.8'
113° 28.5'

El Limona

Hills

Shoal

Lagoon

Campers, etc.

Airstrip

169

ISLAS PATA Y BOTA

Between these two small islands is a tight, sand bottom slot 15 to 30 feet deep. The bar at the east end carries 6 feet, if you need to exit in a hurry. Snorkeling along the shores is good. This makes a very pleasant lunch spot.

DANGER: A pinnacle rock, rising out of 40 to 50 feet about 250 yards off Isla Jorobado directly in line with the slot between Pata and Bota. This uncovers at extreme low tides but is about 1 1/2 feet under at zero tide. It is part of a small reef.

ISLA CORONADO (AKA Smith Island)

This is the largest island in BLA. Its north end is an extinct volcanic cone, distinguishable from afar.

Rada Laguna: Near the south end of Coronado, on the west side, there is an extensive lagoon, excellent for a dinghy trip, but the entrance only carries about a foot. South of the lagoon is a bay with good bottom at 15 to 20 feet. **WPT 29°2.68', 113°30.3'.** This gives excellent protection from the southeast. There is also a shallow bight off to the east of the bay, which might take a small swing-keel boat. Behind this small bight is an extensive, marshy, meadow with a trail over to the East Bay of Coronado, and to the head of the main lagoon.

Coronado East Bay: There is only one decent anchorage on the east side of Isla Coronado. It lies directly across the cobble bar from the lagoon at Rada Laguna. Approach this bay from north of east as the south shore is loaded with rocks and reefs. East Bay gives pretty good protection from the northwest, although the low bar may let the wind funnel through. The south shore is good snorkeling.

Las Rocas Bay: North of the Laguna anchorage about a mile, there is a little bay with two beaches. Two rocks about 50 ft. high mark this spot. The bottom is mostly sand at about 20 feet. **WPT 28°3.63', 113°30.69'.**

ISLA MITLAN

To the north of Las Rocas Bay is an offshore island, behind which you can anchor for some good snorkeling. The bottom behind Mitlan is good at 10 to 15 feet. **WPT 29°4.16', 113°30.87.** Farther to the north, at the foot of the volcano is a low sandy hook, enclosing a large lagoon. It is too shallow to enter in anything but a dinghy, however anchorage may be had outside the lagoon.

DANGER: There are two more pinnacle rocks of which you should be aware before leaving BLA. One is about 500 yards off the southernmost point of Isla Coronado, almost half way to the offshore rock La Calaveras, and slightly west of that line. **WPT 29'2.01', 113°29.91'.** It comes up out of 25 ft. and is awash at low tide. The other rock is a small reef slightly west of north off the end of Isla Piojo. It is 1 ft. under at zero tide.

ISLA ANGEL DE LA GUARDA

Although Angel de la Guarda is the second largest island in the Sea of Cortez, its rugged, steep-to shores, which drop off into hundreds of fathoms on the west side, yield only half a dozen viable anchorages. La Guarda is 41 miles long and 12 miles wide at its widest. We will proceed clockwise around it, starting at the southern tip and quickly moving to the northern tip because there is only one good anchorage on the western side. There is a Navigation Light Gp.Fl.2, on the southern tip of the island.

Este Ton: Within easy reach of Bahia de Los Angeles' launching ramps which are only 16 miles to the southwest, this may be the only anchorage on the west side of Angel de la Guarda, but it is a charmer. It graced the front cover of the 12th Edition of Charlie's Charts. The bottom at 15 feet is sand. The beach is mostly gravel. **WPT 29°09.69', 113°19.86'.**

From offshore, Este Ton is difficult to spot until you can pick out the Three Black Hills to the north of it. When you see the hills, aim to the south of them. Watch for a low gravel bar and a small black knob at its end. The entrance is to the right and behind the knob. Small reefs guard both sides of the entrance, so stay in the center. Este Ton is a wonderful anchorage for a norther, but no place to be caught in a southerly.

Humbug Bay: Eight miles north of Este Ton is a nice looking anchorage on the charts, but it got its name from the fact that it is too steep-to to allow anchoring.

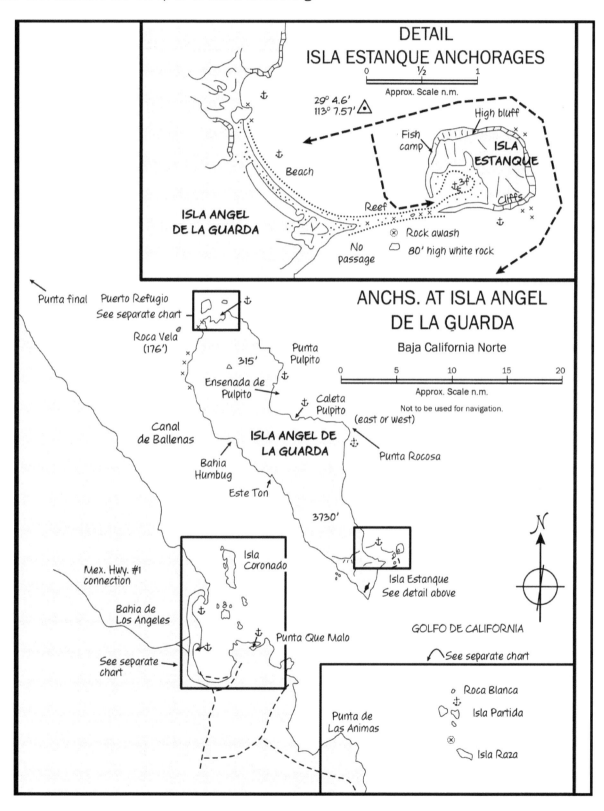

PUERTO REFUGIO

The entire northern tip of Angel de la Guarda is a mass of anchorages, offering protection from any winds somewhere within its scope. It can be approached from three directions, west, north, or east. There are two major bays, each with a selection of anchorages and special features. Study the sketch carefully before approaching this area.

DANGER: Approach West Bay from west and north of Sail Rock (looks like a large sloop under full sail). By keeping Fang Rock in East Bay visible through False Pass, between Isla Division and West Point, on a course 58° to 60° mag, you will miss both the extensive reef to the south, and the pinnacle rocks lying off Punta Monumento on Isla Mejia, to the north. The large reef is usually visible, either dried out, or by conspicuous wave action. There is plenty of deep water on either side of the reef as long as you can see where it is and stay center channel. The pinnacle rocks off Punta Monumento are slightly inside the mouth of the bay, and less obvious than the large reef.

West Bay, WPT 29°32.92', 113°43.15', on **Isla Mejia** is the best protection from a norther. Anchor almost anywhere in 30 to 40 feet. The south side has a cobbled bottom off the two cobbled beaches. There is a large shallow lagoon called **Mejia Cove** at the north end of West Bay. The approach to the lagoon makes a fine anchorage in sand at 10 to 15 feet. However, don't try to get in the lagoon except by dinghy. It carries only about 2 feet at zero tide. To the west of the little rock islet which separates the lagoon from the anchorage, there is a submerged rock which the local fishermen marked with a plastic bottle. They used to have a large fish camp, family style, west of this anchorage. You can get a fine view of the entire Puerto Refugio complex by climbing the peak behind the lagoon.

The Pass from West Bay into East Bay is immediately east of Mejia Cove. It is deep, about 60 feet, and narrow, with steep-to sides.

North Entrance: Coming into Refugio's East Bay from the north, keep well clear of the reef which extends north off the northernmost point of Mejia. The reef extends past the last visible rock as an underwater ridge, creating tidal riffles. A mile clearance isn't too much. There is plenty of water between Mejia and Isla Granita (Granite Island), but rocks extend off both entrance points.

Coming over from Kino, San Carlos on the mainland or from the east side, you will probably enter Puerto Refugio through the EAST ENTRANCE. Because Isla Granita has a Navigation Light, Fl.Wht., this entrance can be made in the dark, but do not attempt the other entrances. In the daytime, you can line up Fang Rock with Sail Rock, through False Pass, and you'll run right down the channel center.

East Bay: The **East Bight** of East Bay is not very interesting. There is a reef, usually visible, and close to the south shore. The bottom is mostly sand at 30 to 40 feet, with good snorkeling along the shoreline.

Isla De Las Cuevas makes an interesting dinghy trip. It has a wide tidal shelf that you can walk around at low tide to explore the many tall narrow lozenge shape caves on its western shore. Some go back into the cliff quite far. There is a little cove to the south of the island which a small boat could probably enter from the north. There is no passage between the island and the shore. Anchor just west of the island in sand at 40 to 50 feet. **WPT 29°32.39', 113°32.22'.**

Middle Bight is a good anchorage with sand at 15 to 20 feet, however, **West Bight** is a better anchorage in East Bay. Come in around a reef extending out from Rocky Point which makes up the east side of West Bight, then avoid a single rock sticking up about 100 yards off this point. Anchor in behind this rock. There is about 10 feet depth between it and the point. Bottom is sand at 15 feet. The beach is gravel as are most of the other beaches at Refugio. From here a broad valley crosses over to Hueso Bay, and the easily climbed hills give a grand view of Puerto Refugio. This bight gives the best protection in East Bay from the northwest, however it is no place to be in a norther. West Bay is preferable.

PUERTO REFUGIO
(ISLA ANGEL DE LA GUARDA)

Baja California Norte

0   1   2

Approx. Scale n.m.

Not to be used for navigation.

Reef

Grey rock point

Isla Granito (281')

Light Fl. 5s

Sea Lions

N

Isla Mejia (857')

3f

West Bay

29° 33.5'
113° 32.9'

(Fang rock)
Roca Blanca
(41')

6f

29° 33.36
113° 30.85

Punta Monumento

Reef

Punta Bluff

Interesting Dinghy
Passage at High Tide

East Bay

29° 32.17'
113° 35.11'

East Bight

DANGER

3f

3f

West Bight

Middle Bight

shoal

shoal

Sail rock

29° 31.89'
113° 35.72'

Fish Camp

ISLA ANGEL DE LA GUARDA

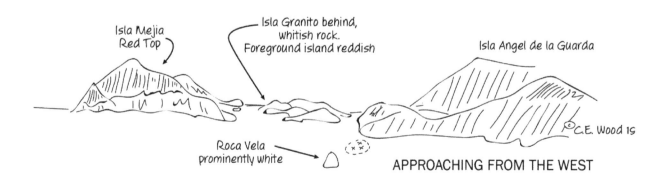

Isla Mejia
Red Top

Isla Granito behind,
whitish rock.
Foreground island reddish

Isla Angel de la Guarda

C.E. Wood 15

Roca Vela
prominently white

APPROACHING FROM THE WEST

ISLA GRANITA

This island forms the north side of Refugio. Unfortunately, although it would give good protection from a norther, there seems to be nothing but big rocks in which to drop your anchor. Granita is the home of a large colony of Sea lions.

Punta Pulpito lies 15 miles south of Bluff Point, the south side of the eastern entrance to Refugio. Anchorage may be taken in the lee of Punta Pulpito in the East Bight by the white rock outcropping. The bottom is sand at about 30 feet. There is a strong tidal sweep so it is not considered a good anchorage. Protection would be good from the northwest, but not from the north. There is an extensive lagoon on the north shore of this bay just west of the point.

South Pulpito Bay, about 7 miles from the north end at Punta Pulpito, consists of three small bays.

Caleta South Pulpito - West Bight, WPT 29°17.37', 113°17.57' is the most interesting, with a fine sand beach which shoals very gradually, so you can't anchor in close. The bay is open to the north and northwest, so use it in quiet weather or in summer's usually southeasterly winds. Anchor in sand at about 10 to 15 feet. There is a large lagoon behind the beach, and a broad flat valley. When approaching from the north or east, this cove can be spotted by the red and white banded cliffs along its western shore.

Caleta South Pulpito – Middle And East Bights both have a cobble beach. Anchor in about 20 feet, in sand.

DANGER: Between Caleta Pulpito East and Punta Rocosa, there is an offshore reef considerably separated from the shore. If it is uncovered, you can see it as you approach either of the Caletas, but it is invisible against the background when you are offshore. The approximate position has been reported at **WPT 29°17.45', 113° 14.85'**.

ISLA ESTANQUE

Thirteen miles south of Punta Rocosa, and 4½ miles northeast of the southern tip of Angel de la Guarda with its Navigation Light Gp.Fl.2, lies a unique island with four good anchorages in the vicinity. When coming down from the north, you will see Estanque protruding out from the shore as you round Punta Rocosa.

DANGER: There is **NO PASSAGE** between Estanque and La Guarda. They are connected by a reef which does not dry out, and over which a considerable quantity of water pours on a full flood or ebb tide. The tidal flow on ebb also makes it difficult to get around Estanque if you are approaching from the south. The current can be 3 or 4 knots around the corner of Estanque.

Approaching Estanque from the north, there is a long cobble beach on La Guarda with a lagoon behind it. You can anchor anywhere off this beach in southerly weather at 20 to 30 feet in sand. At the north end of this beach is a tiny little cove with a white sand beach and dune at its head. In good weather it is a fine anchorage, but beware if a norther starts to blow.

THE POND, WPT 29°40.6', 113°70.57'

Entrance into the pond with its all around protection can be tricky. See sketch. Inside, is a sand bottom at 16 to 18 feet, which offers excellent protection. It may be beneficial to scout the entrance by dinghy before entering. Whether approaching from the west or the north, you must come very close to the reef until you are able to see into the pond at about 36° Mag. Remember, on an ebb tide you will be set toward the reef. Once you can hold this bearing into the pond 100 FEET OR LESS FROM THE GRAVEL BAR ON THE SOUTH SIDE OF THE ENTRANCE, you can proceed in, heading for the tongue of white sand pointing at you in the channel center and which you can usually see. This point of sand marks the shallowest point, 6 feet at zero tide. Once in the Pond you are safe from all weather. The east end of the pond is shallow. When the tide goes out, the far eastern end drains into the western end in a series of small rapids.

South Estanque: The south side of Isla Estanque gives good protection from all northern quarters. The bottom is sand at 20 to 30 feet, with a few rocky patches to be avoided.

DANGER: The area between Piedra Blanca (White Rock) and the Estanque reef as it emerges to become a spur of La Guarda, is full of rocks. There is deep water close to Piedra Blanca, but there would be little reason to pass west of the rock.

BACK TO THE MAINLAND OF THE BAJA

Ensenada Alcatraz: There are three bights here, only 10 miles north of Bahia de Los Angeles. The north-ernmost bight gives protection from the northwest but the bottom is rocky. The middle bight is very shallow, only about 5 feet deep half way in. The southern bight has a fine, white sand beach and makes a pleasant anchorage in good weather. The bottom is sand in 20 feet. **WPT 29°09.73', 113°36.91'.** There is no passage between the small island off the point, and the point.

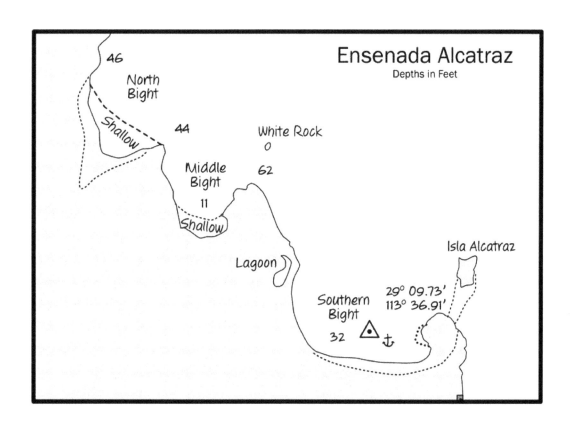

Punta Final is approximately 65 miles up the Baja coast from Bahia de Los Angeles, and 38 miles from Puerto Refugio, and is one of the last interesting cruising destinations on Baja. There is an anchorage in **Paraje de Chencho**, which requires crossing a cobble bar at the entrance, and a careful watch due to extreme tides. **WPT 29°45.82', 114°15.74',** sand. Caleta Las Gatas is to the south, with a rocky shore, and some good dinghy exploring along the shoreline. The two coves off the end of Punta Final both have deep rocky bottoms with nothing but cobble beaches, and very little in the way of protection.

However, Punta la Tijereta hides a bay with two long narrow shallow fingers. With such high tides, if you came in at full flood, you might think the bay was rock-bound and unattractive. When entering at a fairly low tide, (probably around 5 ft.) a series of little beaches tucked in the various bights can be found. Anchor off the first one on the south side and explore the shallow arms by dinghy. **WPT 29°45.25', 114°17.20'.** The center of the bay is about 60 ft. deep and has a cobble bottom, but off the beaches there is enough sand for a good anchorage. Farther to the west is **Snoopy Bay** with lots of sand, but little northern protection. From here six miles north to Isla San Luis Gonzaga, it is all beach.

GONZAGA BAY, BAHIA WILLARD

The south side of Isla San Luis Gonzaga has 3 viable anchorages. Gerry Cunningham named them the **Outer Hook**, the **Middle Bight, WPT 29°48.66', 114°22.84'** (both quite deep at 40 to 50 feet) but unfortunately did not have time to enjoy the most pleasant **Coyote Bay,** so named because he saw a coyote there while taking soundings at 15 feet.

Bahia Willard is very shallow. Good protection can be had off the launch ramp and the small settlement, but with a 13 ft. tidal range, it can too shallow for most boats. Better protection and deeper water is behind the gravel spit off Isla Gonzaga. Waves from a fierce norther have been observed breaking over this spit. The spit is mostly covered at high tide, and at low tide there is a 4 ft. sandy shoal off its end to the northwest.

Anchorages along
BAHIA SAN LUIS GONZAGA

Baja California Norte

0   1   2   3

Approx. Scale n.m.

Not to be used for navigation.

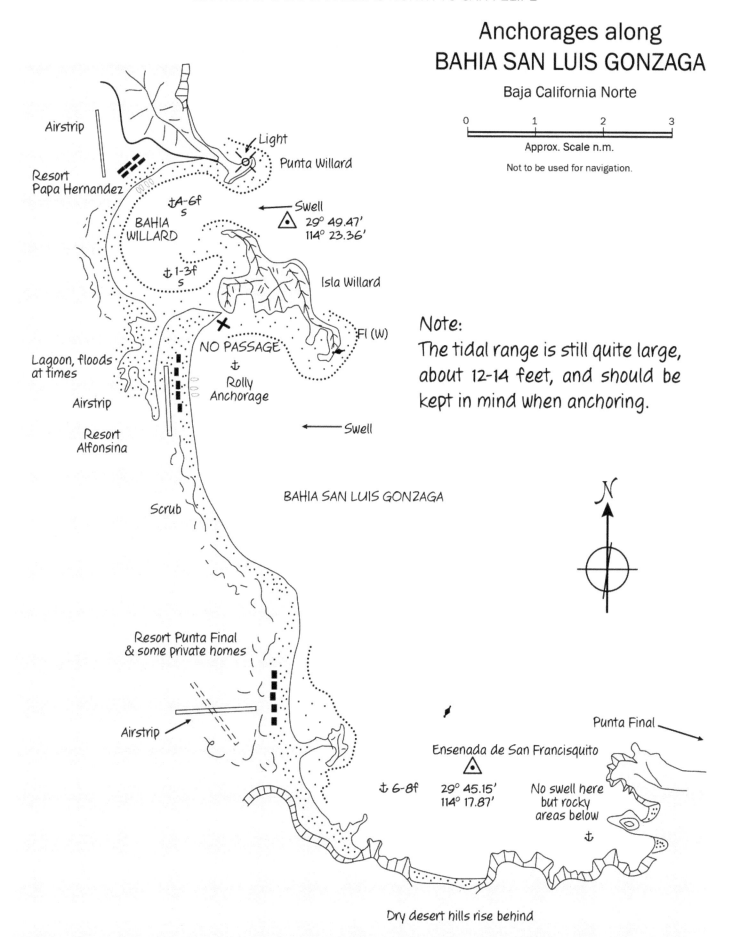

Airstrip

Resort
Papa Hernandez

Light

Punta Willard

⚓A-6f
S

BAHIA
WILLARD

Swell
⊙ 29° 49.47'
114° 23.36'

⚓ 1-3f
S

Isla Willard

✕

NO PASSAGE
⚓
Rolly
Anchorage

Fl (W)

Lagoon, floods
at times

Airstrip

Resort
Alfonsina

Swell

Note:
The tidal range is still quite large,
about 12-14 feet, and should be
kept in mind when anchoring.

Scrub

BAHIA SAN LUIS GONZAGA

N

Resort Punta Final
& some private homes

Airstrip

Punta Final

Ensenada de San Francisquito
⊙
⚓ 6-8f   29° 45.15'
114° 17.87'

No swell here
but rocky
areas below
⚓

Dry desert hills rise behind

ISLAS LAS ENCANTADAS

Punta Bufeo lies about 6 miles north of Punta Willard. It is a rocky point backed by hills and is the north-western end of a large arroyo whose wash extends out between the two points. From Punta Bufeo the land falls west then north again in a sandy beach. Northward of the point lies a large volcanic island, Isla San Luis and a string of smaller islets along about 15 miles of coast. These are shoal waters with 10-fathom depths extending a mile offshore. Tidal ranges are large, but intriguing anchorages are still to be found.

Isla San Luis and the five smaller islands are collectively called **Islas Las Encantadas.** They are truly Enchanted Islands, having many fascinating features: all are of volcanic origin with colorful lava rocks, inhabited only by great flocks of birds and surrounded by prolific marine life. **Isla San Luis** is by far the largest and its volcanic nature is immediately evident in the great crater on the southwest corner, gently subsiding into the sea. The southern cliffs are also collapsing and vessels should not venture too near, for rock falls are common.

Black lava and obsidian cores stand out in the center and northern arm. Many of the beaches are black lava sand, though compacted layers of ash cover much of the lava. A long sandspit, with shoal water on either side, extends for almost a mile and the spit continues to dip underwater to the opposite shore. Amazingly, a clear channel exists beyond the reef, over the dipping spit. **WPT 29°56.74', 114°25.03'.** Good anchorage can be taken on either side of this spit, ½ mile out from the shore to avoid the shoals.

Off the northern end of San Luis Island and about ½ mile to the east is the unique little island of **Isla Pomo**, which is a huge block of pumice. Pieces of rock break off constantly and as pumice is volcanic rock full of air, these 'enchanted' rocks float away on the tidal currents! A reef joins Isla Pomo to Isla San Luis so vessels cannot pass between them. Another reef extends off the north end of Isla San Luis and two dangerous rocks awash are nearby: one to the west, the other is one mile north of the northern tip of the island.

Isla La Encantada is a small rocky island that is remarkably yellow at its northern tip. It lies about 2½ miles northwest of Isla San Luis. A large area of sunken rocks, some awash, lie in a large area about 1 mile east of Isla La Encantada as well as between the two islands. Swing west when passing the area.

Another shoal is south of **Isla Los Lobos**, a very colorful island, with spectacular red lava flows streaking paler, whitish material beneath.

Isla Miramar (El Muerto) is the longest of the smaller islets, rising along its central ridge to 626 feet in height. The hillsides drop down to the sea except in the south where two indentations offer limited shelter and are used by kayakers for access to campsites, on the western shore.

In recent time some of the last remnants of the vagabundos (who lived their lives on the Sea of Cortez) inhabited Isla San Luis, asking for nothing but peace and the chance to live as they pleased.

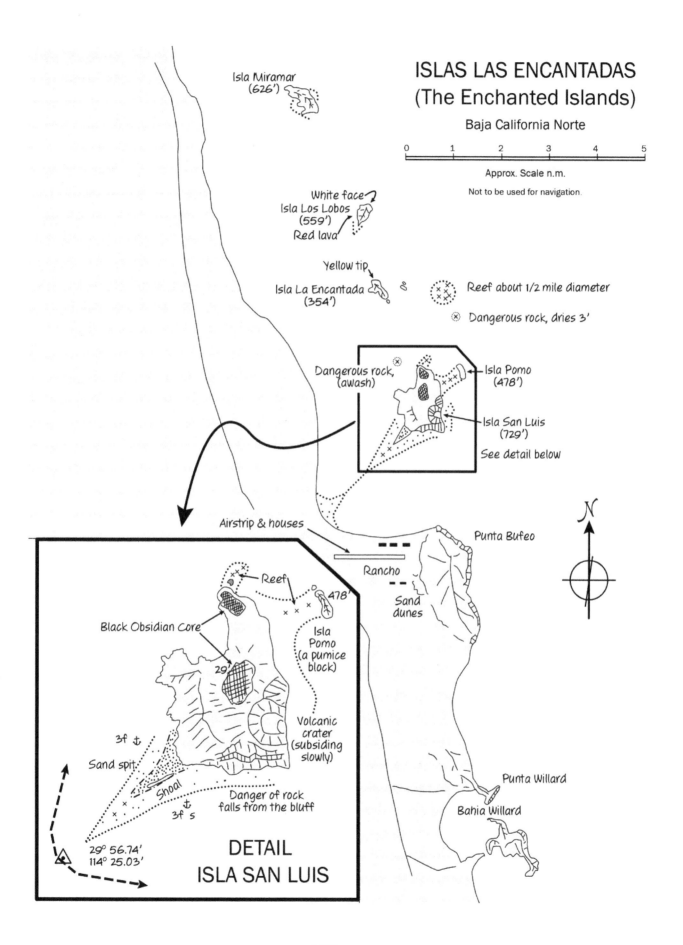

Isla Miramar
(626')

ISLAS LAS ENCANTADAS
(The Enchanted Islands)
Baja California Norte

0 1 2 3 4 5

Approx. Scale n.m.

Not to be used for navigation.

White face
Isla Los Lobos
(559')
Red lava

Yellow tip
Isla La Encantada
(354')

⊗ Reef about 1/2 mile diameter

⊗ Dangerous rock, dries 3'

Dangerous rock,
(awash)

Isla Pomo
(478')

Isla San Luis
(729')

See detail below

Airstrip & houses

Punta Bufeo

Rancho

Sand
dunes

N

Reef

478'

Black Obsidian Core

29'

Isla
Pomo
(a pumice
block)

3f ⚓

Sand spit

Shoal

Volcanic
crater
(subsiding
slowly)

3f s ⚓

Danger of rock
falls from the bluff

Punta Willard

Bahia Willard

29° 56.74'
114° 25.03'

DETAIL
ISLA SAN LUIS

PUERTECITOS

The isolated little island of Isla El Huerfanito (aptly named, the Little Orphan) is a mere lump of rock, 75' high, 5 miles northwest of Isla Miramar and the other Enchanted Islands. It lies a mile offshore and the whitish areas on the steep sides make it a highly visible landmark.

Puertecitos is almost 13 miles north of Isla El Huerfanito. Located almost midway between Bahia San Luis Gonzaga and San Felipe, this cove appears to be an ideal anchorage when seen on a chart. But this is an illusion, for large shoal areas fill the cove and the high tidal range that occurs in the northern Gulf, make it unusable except by shallow draft vessels. Almost any vessel using the harbor will be aground when tide goes out. Temporary anchorage may be taken off the point while visiting the town but a better spot is behind a spur of land about ¾ miles to the south. This spot is also used by commercial fishermen. **WPT 30°20.5', 114°38.2'**.

The cove has several interesting features. It is an unpolished resort area which has attracted many gringos whose bungalows and trailers make up much of the little town. A landing strip lies just behind the sand and pebble beach. Near the tip of the eastern headland is a launch ramp where trailered vessels can be put in the water. Limited supplies can be purchased. The Pemex station and restaurant are sometimes open. As life moves at its own ambling pace, service at the restaurant depends on whether or not the staff have gone fishing!

Perhaps the most unusual and enticing feature of Puertecitos is the hot springs which rise among the rocks at the seaward side of the headland's tip. As they are just within the tide line they are regularly flushed by the tide. There are several natural pools with water of different temperatures in the rocky beach near the point. As the tide falls, you meet most of the town folk at the hot pools. If you have had to ration your bathing, this is an excellent opportunity for a fresh and warm water soak. Arrive on a rising ½ tide for the best temperatures.

On the northern side of the airstrip is a similar but smaller cove opening in the opposite direction with a sandy beach at its head. This cove, open to the north, is even less useful than Puertecitos. Local pangas moor well out at the entrance and even when the tide is in, the cove is seldom used.

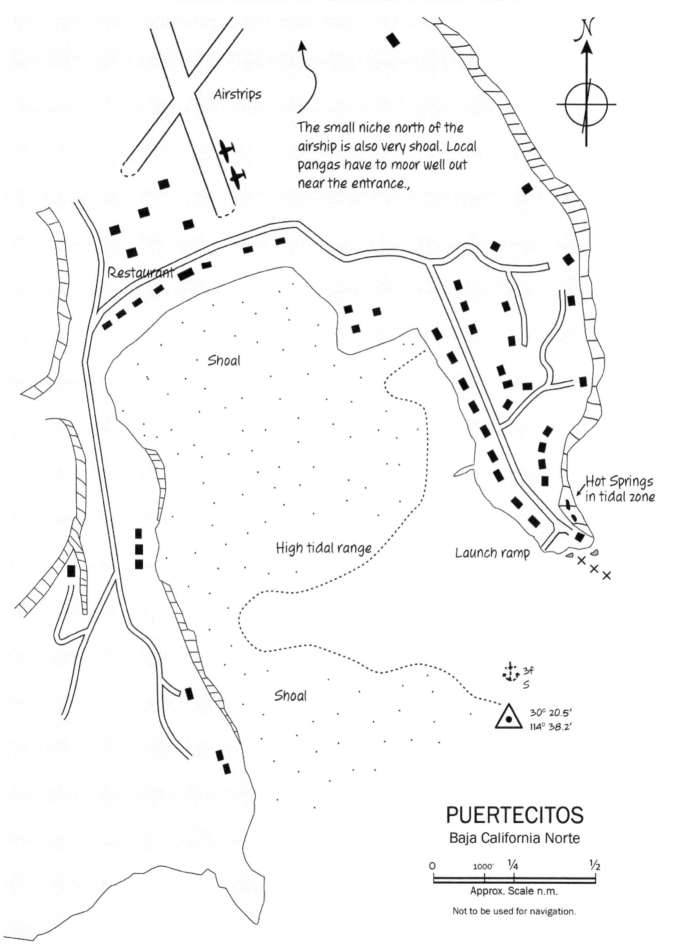

Airstrips

The small niche north of the airship is also very shoal. Local pangas have to moor well out near the entrance.,

Restaurant

Shoal

High tidal range

Hot Springs in tidal zone

Launch ramp

Shoal

3f
S

30° 20.5'
114° 38.2'

PUERTECITOS

Baja California Norte

O   1000'   ¼   ½

Approx. Scale n.m.

Not to be used for navigation.

SAN FELIPE

This city at the head of the Gulf of California represents the end of the line for sea-going craft. Its lovely beaches bring an increasing number of visitors every year. Since it is less than 130 miles on paved roads from Mexicali, on the U.S. border, it is easily reached by visitors driving to the area. Many private homes and condominium developments line the nearby shores and fly-in establishments with their own airstrips are prevalent.

Punta de Machoro (shown on some charts as Punta San Felipe) is the eastern seaward extension of a dark, volcanic hill, Cerro El Machoro. At 940', this mountain marks the north end of Bahia San Felipe and is also the most conspicuous feature on this part of the coast. The beaches and rocky outcroppings of the bay provide a waterfront for the town of San Felipe.

There are numerous motels, RV parks, restaurants, souvenir shops and other tourist facilities. Once the site of a large commercial fishery and excellent sportsfishing, a lack of international conservation policies has resulted in a dramatically reduced number of fish in nearby waters. The main attraction is the miles of lovely beaches stretching along the coast. Many small boats and kayaks are launched here for the 160-mile cruise to Bahia de Los Angeles and the Midriff.

Few large cruising vessels come this far up the Gulf. Contributing factors are the distance between good anchorages, the shallow water that extends well offshore (8 fathoms, 3 miles out) and variable currents. The winds blow vigorously off the desert and boats anchored offshore receive a daily dusting of sand on deck.

At the south end of the bay is a breakwater protected harbor where moorage may sometimes be secured in the commercial harbor. Silting of the harbor is a constant problem and since dredging is not done as often as needed, parts of the harbor dry at low tide. If you anchor within the basin pay particular attention to tidal variation of up to 20 ft.

Anchoring off Punta San Felipe in the center of the bay is in 25 feet, mud. Take care to anchor well out, keeping in mind the state of the tide and its considerable range; spring tides really can exceed 20'. If your cruising plans include the upper end of the Gulf you will be well advised to get the Tide Tables available from: Printing and Reproduction Department, University of Arizona, Tucson, AZ 85721.

Fonatur Marina San Felipe is a new facility with 15 slips and the usual amenities. Follow the range markers when entering the harbor. At low tide the depth of water in the marina is about 10 feet. Vessels up to 90' have moored in the marina. There is a launching ramp and trailer storage available. It is necessary to take a taxi into town to obtain propane. For information call +01-686-5776-394 or email apalomares@ fonatur.gob.mx

* * * * *

The Colorado River empties through a delta into the upper part of the Gulf. It is a tame and humble version of its past wild days, for not only do upstream dams in the U.S. control the flow, but the volumetric flow is also lessened by the large amounts bled off for upstream irrigation. Recently there have been periodic flushing of the river in a meager attempt to alleviate the situation but this cannot result in a long-term solution. Many of the delta flats have been exposed and the wildlife, fish habitat and countless flocks of birds have suffered.

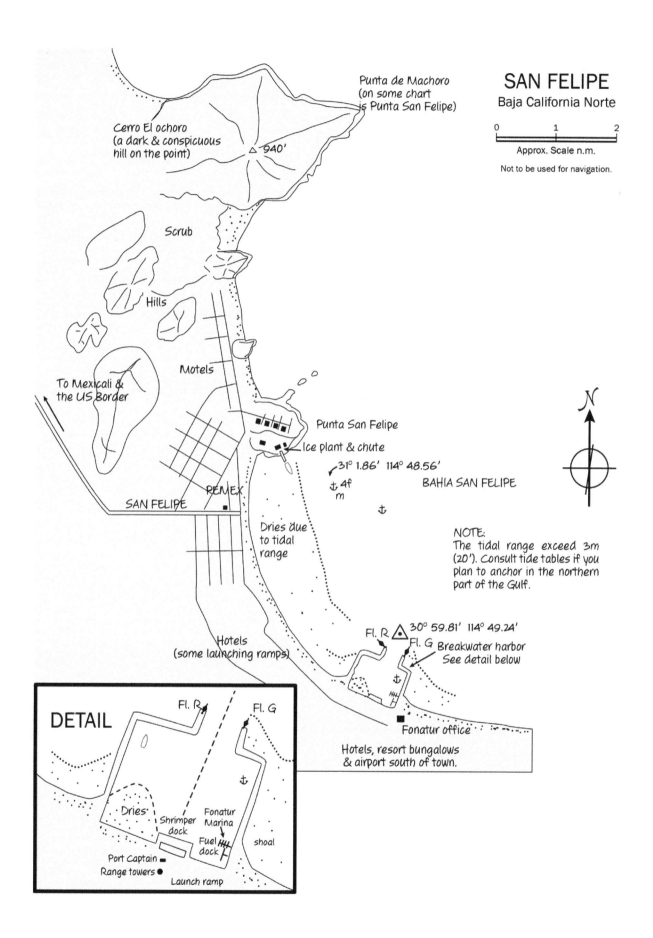

Punta de Machoro
(on some chart
is Punta San Felipe)

SAN FELIPE
Baja California Norte

0   1   2
Approx. Scale n.m.
Not to be used for navigation.

Cerro El ochoro
(a dark & conspicuous
hill on the point)

△ 940'

Scrub

Hills

Motels

To Mexicali &
the US Border

Punta San Felipe
Ice plant & chute
31° 1.86' 114° 48.56'
↧ 4f
m

BAHIA SAN FELIPE

REMEX

SAN FELIPE

Dries due
to tidal
range

NOTE:
The tidal range exceed 3m
(20'). Consult tide tables if you
plan to anchor in the northern
part of the Gulf.

Fl. R △ 30° 59.81' 114° 49.24'
Fl. G Breakwater harbor
See detail below

Hotels
(some launching ramps)

Fonatur office

Hotels, resort bungalows
& airport south of town.

DETAIL

Fl. R   Fl. G

Dries
Shrimper
dock
Fonatur
Marina
Fuel
dock
shoal

Port Captain
Range towers
Launch ramp

SECTION III: PUERTO PEÑASCO TO ACAPULCO

This section covers such a large length of coastline that it is divided into four smaller parts, each having distinctive weather patterns and characteristics. In the first part (San Felipe and the delta of the Colorado to Mazatlan) the conditions are those of the Gulf of California, as described in Section II. Moderate northwesterly winds prevail, generally increasing about noon and decreasing in the evening, with northers common during winter months. The Pacific swell affects the coast from Mazatlan southward.

The mainland shore of the Gulf north of Mazatlan is not as popular a cruising area as the Baja shore, partly because of the long distances between major harbors and also since much of the coast has shoal areas that extend a considerable distance from the shore, and much of the shoreline consists of shallow lagoons and sand dunes with desert beyond.

TABLE 3

APPROXIMATE DISTANCES BETWEEN ANCHORAGES OF SECTION III
(Cabo San Lucas to Acapulco)

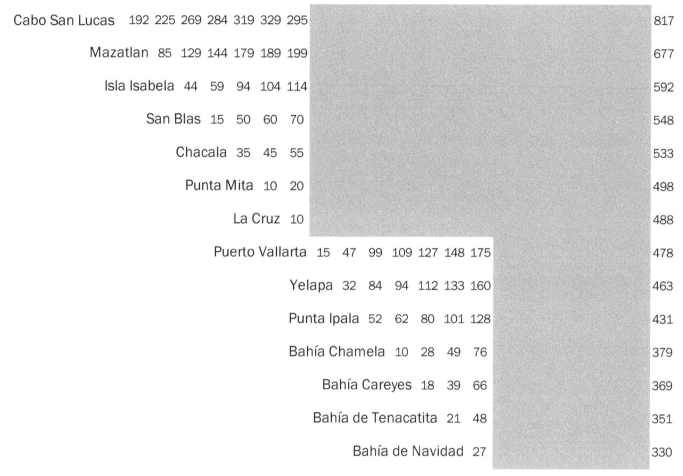

Cabo San Lucas	192	225	269	284	319	329	295			817
Mazatlan	85	129	144	179	189	199				677
Isla Isabela	44	59	94	104	114					592
San Blas	15	50	60	70						548
Chacala	35	45	55							533
Punta Mita	10	20								498
La Cruz	10									488
Puerto Vallarta	15	47	99	109	127	148	175			478
Yelapa	32	84	94	112	133	160				463
Punta Ipala	52	62	80	101	128					431
Bahía Chamela	10	28	49	76						379
Bahía Careyes	18	39	66							369
Bahía de Tenacatita	21	48								351
Bahía de Navidad	27									330
Manzanillo	44	78	118	182	190	228	303			
Punta Cabeza Negra	34	74	138	146	184	259				
Bahía de Maruata	40	104	112	150	225					
Caleta de Campos	64	72	110	185						
Isla Grande	8	46	121							
Bahía Zihuatanejo	38	113								
Punta de Papanoa	75									
Acapulco										

Distances can be added between the groups of this section, e.g. from Puerto Vallarta to Isla Grande the distance is: 175 + 182 = 357 nautical miles.

175 = PV to Manzanillo
182 = Manzanillo to Isla Grande

PUERTO PEÑASCO

This commercial port is dependent on the large shrimp fleet that is based here. It is also a popular spot for small boats to be launched for boaters interested in cruising the upper gulf. Boaters entering Mexico are required to report to the Harbor Master upon arrival. The harbor is fairly shallow with average depths of 12 feet. This area experiences 23 foot tides, so use extreme caution before anchoring. A 65-mile paved road links the town to the U.S. Border at Sonora. Entrance **WPT 31 18.47' 113 33.05'**

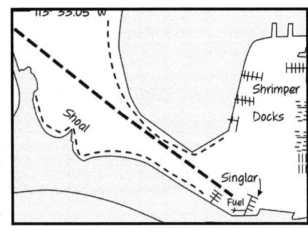

Fonatur Marina Puerto Penasco offers standard facilities and has a dock with 11 slips and a fuel dock nearby. Dinghy landing charges may be charged at the Fonatur dock. For more information call +01-638-3885-599 or email:ejhidalgo@fonatur.gob.mx. Propane is available by taxi or arrangements can be made for tanks to be picked up.

Tepoca Bay, WPT 30°15.79', 112°50.68', is an anchorage protected by reefs off the point, in the bight to the east of Punta Lobos. It lies about 75 miles south of Cabo Tepoca. There is a large lighthouse on the point, visible for miles, and numerous buildings along the beachfront. Avoid the rocky western side of the bay off the point when transiting the area. Anchor in about 25 feet, mid bay. This is well protected from the north.

Puerto Libertad, is obvious from a distance due to the smoke from the local power plant. It's not much of a port however. It offers some protection from the north, and possibly a little from the northwest, but Punta Tepoca, at the northern end, is not a very well defined point. Anchor on the north side of the bay, away from the large T shaped pier, mid bay. **WPT 29°54.47', 112°42.58'.** The small town has a couple of grocery stores, a cantina or two, hardware, and probably other supplies. There is a paved road about 95 miles south to the Hermosillo/Kino highway.

Desemboque is a small town tucked behind a slight bump in the coastline. There is an airstrip here, between the village and the point, where a shallow river drains into the sea. Watch for shallows near the beach. Anchor is 25 to 30 feet **WPT 29°30', 112°23.86'.**

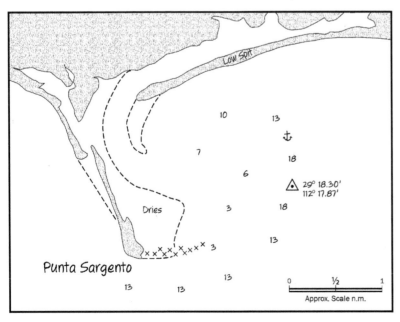

Punta Sargento is a lump of rock about 200 ft. high that and lies at the end of a long narrow and low sand spit, which partially covers at the highest tides. The bay provides decent protection from northerly winds. It is open to the south. The east side of the spit is very shoal. A dangerous reef extends east off the point, about a mile where it carries only about 5 ft. at zero tide. After crossing the end of the reef, proceed east to a **WPT of 29°18.30', 112°17.87,** then turn north heading for the beach. Anchor in about 20 feet, sand.

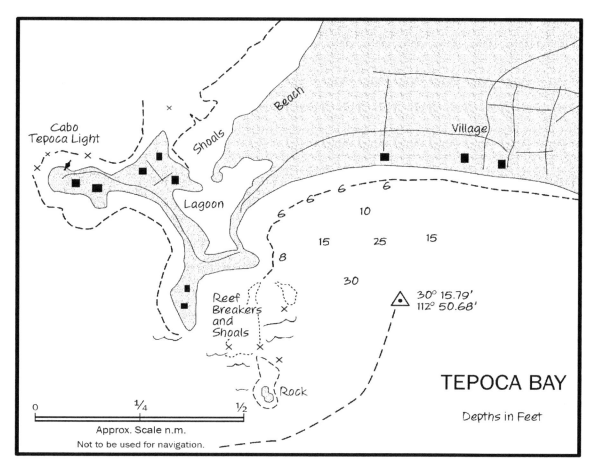

Cabo
Tepoca Light

Beach

Shoals

Village

Lagoon

6 6 6 6

10

15 25 15

8

30

Reef
Breakers
and
Shoals

Rock

30° 15.79'
112° 50.68'

TEPOCA BAY

Depths in Feet

0   ¼   ½

Approx. Scale n.m.

Not to be used for navigation.

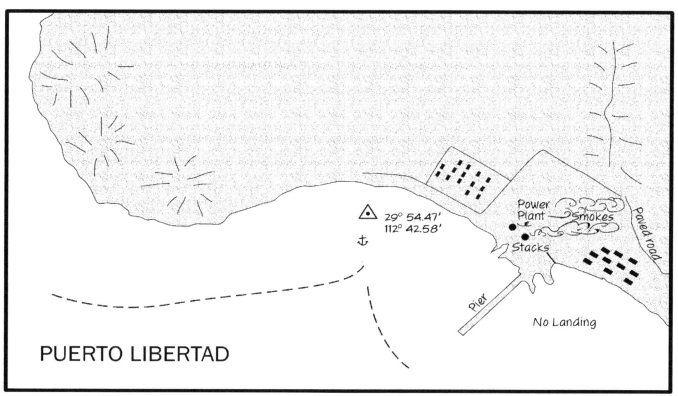

29° 54.47'
112° 42.58'

Power
Plant   Smokes

Paved road

Stacks

Pier

No Landing

PUERTO LIBERTAD

Isla Patos is a tiny island 5 miles north of Isla Tiburon, and 6½ miles east of the spit at Punta Sargento. It has one Navigation Light on a masonry tower and another steel tower lower down which may or may not be working. The southeast shore has a good bottom, a beach, a fish camp, and gives protection from northwest to north. The bottom is sand with rocks at about 30 feet. Another anchorage is on the southeast side, **WPT 29°15.99', 112°27.50'**. The bottom is sand at 20 feet.

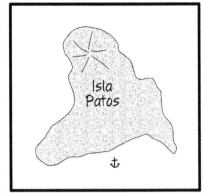

ISLA TIBURON

ISLA TIBURON is the largest island in the Gulf of California, but has the same shortcomings as Angel de la Guarda, being steep-to on west and south. There are very few anchorages. Isla Tiburon is 27 miles long and 21½ miles wide. It is almost rectangular, not long and narrow as are most of the islands. Permits are required to visit the island. They are available in Bahia Kino (Viejo Kino) near the waterfront in the park service's small office building. Permits cost $4USD per day/person. They might also be obtained in Desemboque. Tiburon was originally populated by the Seri Indian tribe which has since been relocated to the mainland. Today only about 2000 Seri survive in a small village, Punta Chueca about 20 miles north of Bahia Kino.

The island was originally established as a refuge in the 1960's to protect large game animals from the dangers of poaching and overhunting which was a problem on the mainland. The Mexican Marines who had bases on the island prevented the Seri Indians from landing or hunting on the island despite the fact that the island had always been Seri territory. By the 70's this changed and the rights of the Seri were recognized. Today, the Seri don't hunt on the islands, instead permits are auctioned off to wealthy tourists and the proceeds are split. Half is allocated to the Seri, the remainder is used to finance conservation efforts.

Bahia Agua Dulce is a large open bay, and is the only anchorage at the north end of Tiburon. **WPT 29°11.75', 112°25.42'**. The bottom is sand at 20 to 30 feet. Protection is nil except from southern quarters. Bahia Agua Dulce is situated at the end of a wide flat valley that penetrates mountainous Tiburon for 12 miles. There are no anchorages on the west side until you reach Punta Willard, 20½ miles to the south.

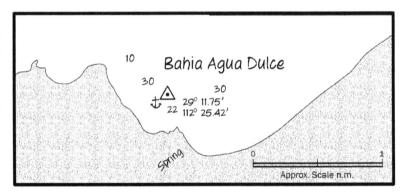

Punta Willard is the westernmost point of Tiburon. It has two anchorages on its north side, and one on the south. There is a Navigation Light Gp.Fl.3 on the western end.

North Willard West is a nice bay **WPT 28°53.01', 112°34.19'**, with a sand bottom at 10 to 15 feet. There are several sand dunes with two sand-filled valleys leading across the point toward the south anchorage. It is possible to walk from the easternmost valley over to the south side. Approaching this anchorage from the west, there is a reef guarding that entrance point. This bay is open to the northwest.

North Willard East is a more open bay than the West Bay, but it gives good western and southern protection, and possibly northwest, although South Willard would be a better anchorage for northwest. North Willard East is not as interesting an anchorage as the West Bay. **WPT 28°53.37', 112°33.63'**, in sand at about 18 feet.

South Willard, WPT 28°52.20', 112°33.73', gives protection from the northwest, but is not much good in a west wind. It usually has a shrimper or two at anchor. The bottom is sand at about 20 feet, but the shores are well supplied with tidal shelves and reefs. There are a couple of beaches good for dinghy landing. Around the corner to the southeast is a unique, tiny pocket of a cove, barely large enough to turn around in. It is surrounded by towering cliffs on all sides that drop right down to a very deep bottom.

HULK. This mountain, about 5 miles from Punta Willard on the south shore of Tiburon, is a landmark useful for navigating in these waters. At its foot is a little spur extending out from the shore, which should give good northwest protection. However, the tide rips past here and can carry a vessel away over the reef.

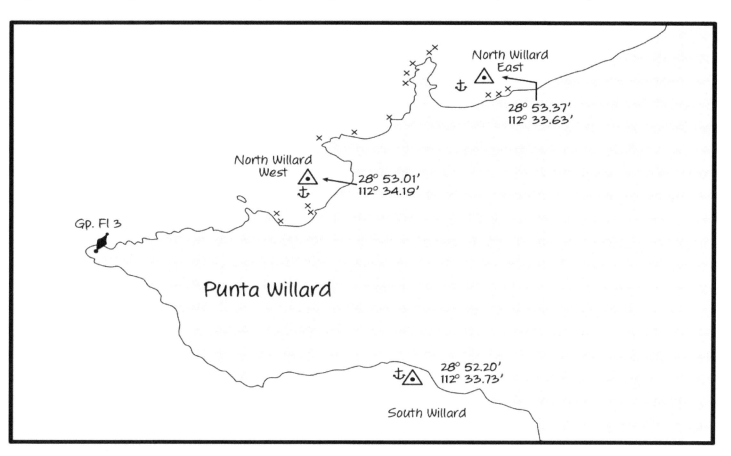

Bahia de Las Cruces: Near the south corner of Tiburon, just before you reach Cactus Pass, is this large bay with several good spots to anchor. **WPT 28°45.38', 112°20.20'**. The best northwest protection is in the west end. You can anchor anywhere along the beach, but beware of the reefs that protrude from the beach in several places. Behind the old Marine outpost is a large valley reputed to have fresh water at its head. For solitude it is possible to tuck into one of the little coves southwest of the Marines.

These coves are separated by reefs and have sand beaches. The prominent feature of Las Cruces is a "Y" shape point with fine beaches. There are rocks off the arms of the "Y". Vessels may also anchor in the eastern bight of Las Cruces. There are rocks on the bottom to be avoided, and a small reef of rocks, which can be covered, so be careful. This bight gives southeast protection, but is open to the south and west.

Isla Turner is a long narrow island, less than 2 miles long, lying off the southernmost corner of Tiburon. There are no good anchorages on it. It does have a Navigation Light Fl.Wht. at its southern end, and there are often tidal overfalls off the southern end.

DANGER: If you have to go around Isla Turner from the west, there is a pinnacle rock, sometimes covered, about ⅝ of a mile southwest of the north end of Turner. It comes up out of 20 to 70 feet of water and dries out at low tide. A reef extends to the north off the otherwise steep-to rock. **WPT 28°43.80', 112°18.93'**.

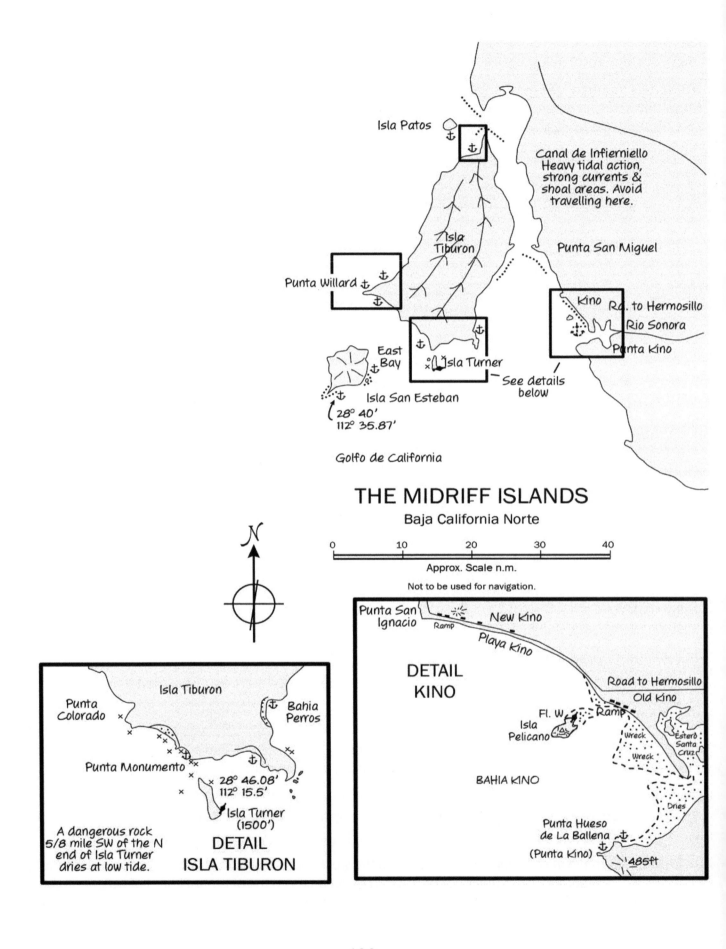

Isla Patos

Canal de Infierniello
Heavy tidal action,
strong currents &
shoal areas. Avoid
travelling here.

Isla
Tiburon

Punta San Miguel

Punta Willard

Kino   Rd. to Hermosillo

Rio Sonora

Punta Kino

East
Bay

Isla Turner

See details
below

Isla San Esteban
28° 40'
112° 35.87'

Golfo de California

THE MIDRIFF ISLANDS
Baja California Norte

| 0 | 10 | 20 | 30 | 40 |

Approx. Scale n.m.

Not to be used for navigation.

N

Punta San
Ignacio   Ramp   New Kino

Playa Kino

DETAIL
KINO

Road to Hermosillo

Old Kino

Fl. W   Ramp

Isla
Pelicano

Wreck

Estero
Santa
Cruz

Wreck

BAHIA KINO

Dries

Punta Hueso
de La Ballena
(Punta Kino)

485ft

Isla Tiburon

Punta
Colorado

Bahia
Perros

Punta Monumento

28° 46.08'
112° 15.5'

Isla Turner
(1500')

DETAIL
ISLA TIBURON

A dangerous rock
5/8 mile SW of the N
end of Isla Turner
dries at low tide.

Cactus Pass: To avoid going way around Isla Turner, en route to Dog Bay, or Kino, you can transit Cactus Pass, but there are DANGERS. Off Punta Monumento (Monument Point) on Tiburon, are several small reefs extending from shore. These are often visible. Running north, off the north end of Cactus Rock is a long reef which is not usually visible. Stay slightly north of the channel center. The tide roars through here at times, making passage difficult if not impossible. **WPT** for the center of the pass is **28°44.67', 112°18.43'.**

Punta Ast Ahkeem is the southeast corner of Tiburon, and has two anchorages. **Monument Bay, WPT 28°46.08', 112°15.5'**, has a good bottom at 15 to 20 feet. This is at the east end of the cobble beach in the wide bay east of Cactus Pass.

The better anchorage is the little bight just inside Punta Ast Ahkeem. It has a good bottom at 15 to 20 feet. It is backed by a low saddle that goes over to the north side of the point and has a large straight Saguaro cactus standing in the center.

Dog Bay (Bahia Perros) is an excellent anchorage, very quiet in most conditions, and only about 17 miles from Kino. The bottom is sand at 10 to 15 feet in the northern bight, **WPT 28°47.31', 112°16.23'**, and slightly less in the south bight. There is a jeep track from here over to Las Cruces, and extending north to the shores of El Infiernillo. This should make a good hike.

DANGER: The channel **El Infiernillo**, between Isla Tiburon and the mainland is shallow, full of shifting sand-bars, swept by strong tidal currents, and a good place to stay out of except in a shallow draft powerboat.

ISLA SAN ESTEBAN

Esteban has two viable anchorages. If en route to San Francisquito on Baja, you might want to shelter at **Southwest Spit** on the east side of the gravel spit at its southwest corner. The anchorage is tucked up in the corner of the spit. The bar extends quite far and in an ebb tide, generates quite a mess of standing waves. It is home to a colony of sea lions. **WPT 28°40.29', 112°35.88'.**

East Bay is the more interesting of the two anchorages. There is plenty of sand, but it takes a little looking around. Toward the north end there is one rock rather close to the surface. Otherwise the rocks are down on the bottom where they belong. Anchor in 30 to 40 feet at **WPT 28°41.4', 112°32.73'.** Strong northwest winds can come down along the shore with little protection in a true norther.

Esteban is part of the ecological preserve, and is home to a large chuckwalla, a large multicolored lizard specific to this particular island. It has a wide central valley that empties out at the East Bay, with a gravel streambed, indicating occasional water flow. On the shore north of the bay is a navigation light, Fl.Wht. that is usually working.

ISLA SAN PEDRO MARTIR

This is the last of the Midriff Islands and lies 21 miles south of Isla Tiburon. It is at the end of a shallow 50 fathom underwater ridge running south from Isla Turner. This unexpectedly shallow ridge rising out of 500 fathoms to the west makes for some pretty messy sea conditions during strong tidal flow.

The conditions can be rough enough to inspire Gerry's crew David Parker to compose the following ditty.

> There was a young man with a yacht
> Who had an ingenious plot
> Stay 20 miles clear
> of San Pedro Martir
> and you'll get where you'd hoped to have got.

Martir is a favorite destination for fishermen and scuba divers. It once held a large guano mining operation, the relics of which are still visible. It is a bird sanctuary, and often has scientific parties camped on the summit. There is no good place to land, and only one decent anchorage on the east side below a large lenticular cliff, in sand at about 40 feet. **WPT 28°22.61', 112°17.95'.** Sperm whales frequent the area near the south edge of Tastoia Shoal.

DANGER: Off the south end of Martir are two large rock islets. These you can see, but between the two of them closer to the farthest one, is a sea mount that does not dry out, but is close enough to the surface to do damage at some tides. If you can see it, there is deep water around it, about 70 ft. between it and the islet closest to Martir. The second DANGER reported but not found is a pinnacle rock off the northwest corner of Martir.

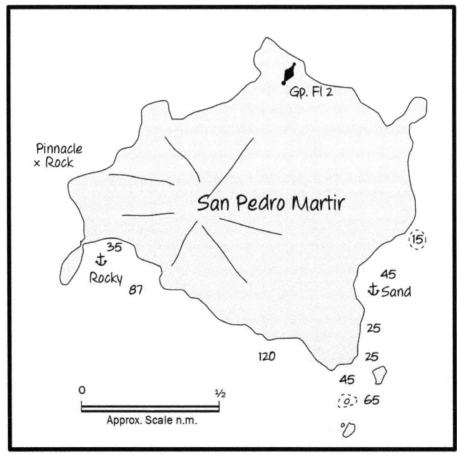

BACK TO THE MAINLAND...

Kino Bay: On the mainland, opposite the south end of Isla Tiburon is Kino Bay, an open bay about 8 miles long, with Isla Pelicano (Pelican Island) in the middle. The east end of the bay is very shoal and much of it dries out at extreme low tides. There is a large estuary, Estero Santa Cruz, behind the beaches at the eastern side. The entrance to the estero is tortuous, carrying only a fathom or two until just inside the mouth, when it shoals rapidly. The tidal range is 6 feet. A friend of Gerry's sailed his 5 foot draft boat in, and had to wait 6 months before he could get out again.

There is shelter here in the south end, from strong southerly storms, usually the peripheral weather from a hurricane. Just inside Punta Hueso de la Ballena, there isn't much storm protection although there is a good bottom at about 20 feet, and this is a very pleasant anchorage. The storm protection is one more point into the bay, **WPT 28°45.83', 111°55.86'.** Here there is good sand at 10 to 15 feet and is relatively quiet in 60 knot winds off the shore. This is the beginning of a beach which stretches for 10 miles around the bay. The disadvantage with the south end of Kino Bay is that although the town is in sight across the way, there is no way of getting to it, or rather of getting back from it, without a powerful dinghy during a southerly storm.

For northwest protection in Kino Bay, about all you can do is anchor in the lee of Isla Pelicano. The whole bay is sand bottom and off Pelicano it is 10 to 20 feet deep. There are often shrimpers anchored here. This is not a comfortable anchorage in a blow, but it is safe. The channel between the island and the mainland is shoal except slightly northeast of the center where it carries about 10 feet. As you can see from the chart, a large shoal extends from the island northeast toward the mainland. Pelicano has a Navigation Light, Fl.Wht. but it is on the shore side, hidden behind the peak until you are almost west of it. If you are east of the light you could be in trouble.

Playa Kino is about 7 miles long from Estero Santa Cruz to Punta Ignacio, and is lined with vacation homes. Anchor anywhere off the beach in quiet weather, paying attention to the shoal spots. Kino has no docks and no harbor, or marina. Vessels must anchor off and take the dinghy through the surf if any.

The Town Of Kino is in two parts. Old Kino, slightly east of Isla Pelicano is where the gas station is. It also has a bank, some stores, and a Trailer park with launching ramp.

The rest of New Kino is a strip town with a couple of motels, restaurants, gift and grocery stores. One trailer park at the end of the beach has a launching ramp, and on the north side of Punta San Ignacio is another ramp. The Seri Indians were removed from their homeland on Isla Tiburon to the village of Chueco, north of Kino.

Approaching Kino from the south, 1155 foot Cerro San Nicolas (Saint Nicholas Mtn.) is the landmark you will spot first, about the same time you begin to see the peaks of Isla Tiburon. It is difficult to sort them out when first sighted, but eventually they sort themselves out and you can see a large sand dune below Cerro San Nicolas. Only 3 miles further north of the dune is Punta Hueso de la Bellena and Kino Bay itself.

DANGER: About 18 miles south of Punta Hueso de la Ballena is Punta Baja, a low sandy point with a couple of light towers. This point is very shoal very far out. Clearing it by 5 miles would not be excessive. Watch your depth sounder.

Along this next stretch of coastline, there is little to offer the cruising vessel in the way of protection for about 35 miles. Keep off the coast by several miles due to bars, shallows, and shoals.

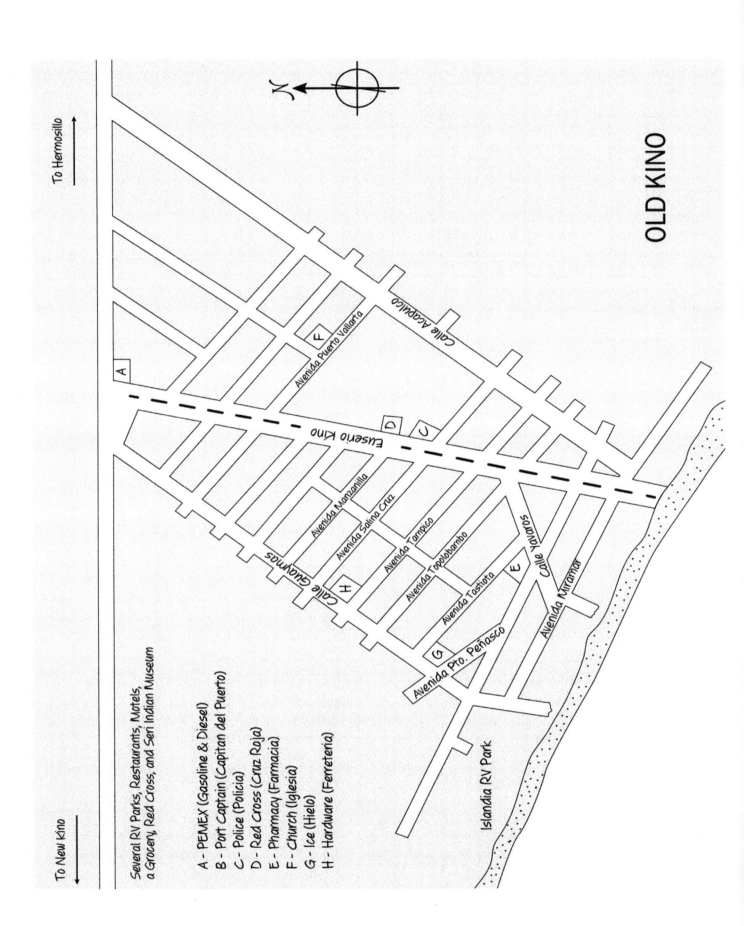

To Hermosillo

To New Kino

Several RV Parks, Restaurants, Motels,
a Grocery, Red Cross, and Seri Indian Museum

A - PEMEX (Gasoline & Diesel)
B - Port Captain (Capitan del Puerto)
C - Police (Policia)
D - Red Cross (Cruz Roja)
E - Pharmacy (Farmacia)
F - Church (Iglesia)
G - Ice (Hielo)
H - Hardware (Ferreteria)

OLD KINO

Calle Acapulco
Avenida Puerto Vallarta
Euserio Kino
Avenida Manzanilla
Avenida Salina Cruz
Avenida Tampico
Avenida Topolobambo
Calle Guaymas
Avenida Tastiota
Calle Yavaros
Avenida Pto. Peñasco
Avenida Miramar
Islandia RV Park

Estero Tastiota

Tastiota is a large, shallow estuary which can be entered only by dinghies and outboards. If you want to explore, anchor up by Corralitos and dinghy over, or walk the beach.

About 9 miles north of Punta Moreno, and just south of Estero Tastiota, the shoreline becomes more indented and coves begin to appear again.

ESTERO TASTIOTA
TO
BAHIA SAN PEDRO

0   5

Approx. Scale n.m.

Los Corralitos: This is a sand spit that extends out from shore, only about 30 ft. high. The south side is not very good for protection from the northwest, but the holding ground is good sand. The north side offers good protection from the south. The bottom is sand at about 6 feet. **WPT 28°20.58', 111°27.62'.** There are reefs extending out from Corralitos, which can usually be detected. Waves from the northwest tend to be very short and steep. If you go in here, watch your depth.

El Choyudo (Los Japoneses) is a small village but there are no supplies. Two bays give fair protection from the south, but not very much from west of south. The first bay is behind a small island that carries a light tower, not working. The bottom is mostly sand at 18 Feet, but rocky shoals extend off the island and adjacent shore.

The second bay lies north of the point that is right in front of the village. There is a rock 100 yards off this point but no known passage between. This bay has a good sand beach where the locals draw up their pangas. The bottom is sand at 18 feet. **WPT 28°19.21', 111°27.29'.** There is no great attraction at either bay.

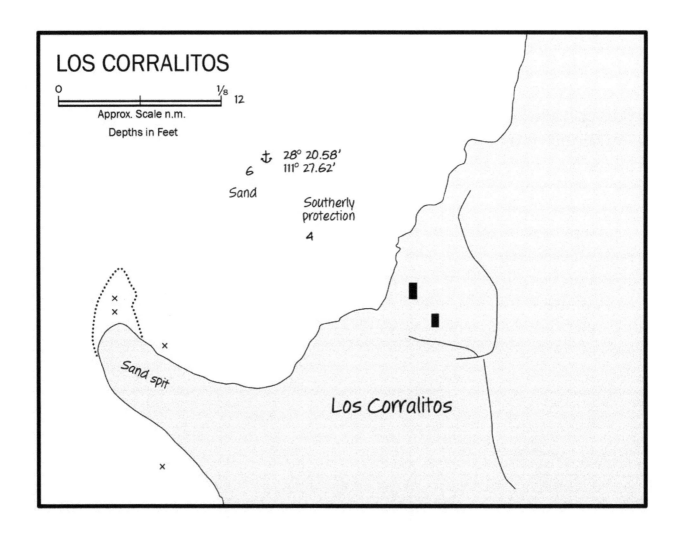

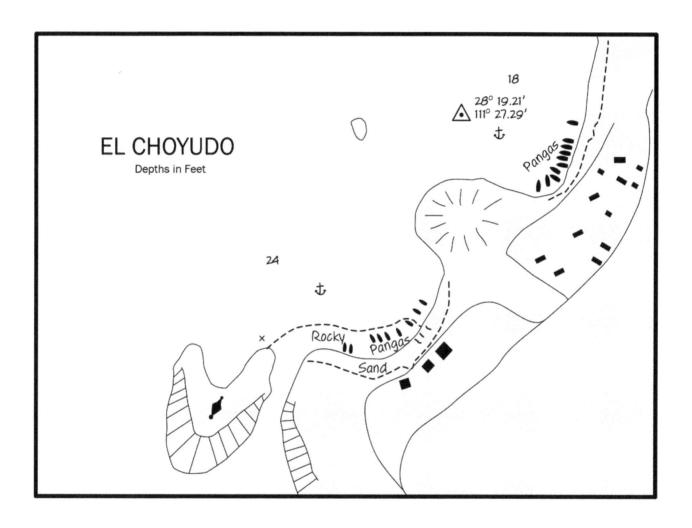

EL CHOYUDO

Depths in Feet

18

28° 19.21'
111° 27.29'

Pangas

24

Rocky

Pangas

Sand

Las Cadenas: Cadenas means chains and refers to the gray chain of mountains behind the two little bays. Either bay can give fair protection from the northwest, but the bottom is rocky at the north end of the north bay. The snorkeling and diving are best at that bay. The south bay is the more pleasant anchorage with a better bottom. Reefs extend off all the points in this area and both the north and south bays have a reef in the middle of their northeast shore. A mid point between the bays is **WPT 28°18.28',**

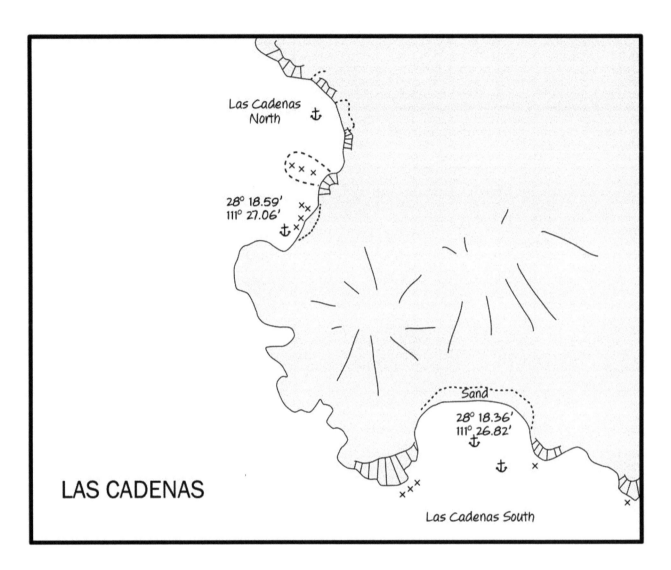

111°27.16'.

Caleta Colorado, WPT 28°17.15', 111°25.14'. Although you will sometimes find half a dozen shrimpers anchored on the south side of Morro Colorado, it doesn't give great protection for small boats. Possibly the shrimpers like it because there is a small village. On the north side of Morro Colorado lies another bay, but this gives even less protection. The bottom is quite rocky at 26 feet. Reefs extend along the eastern

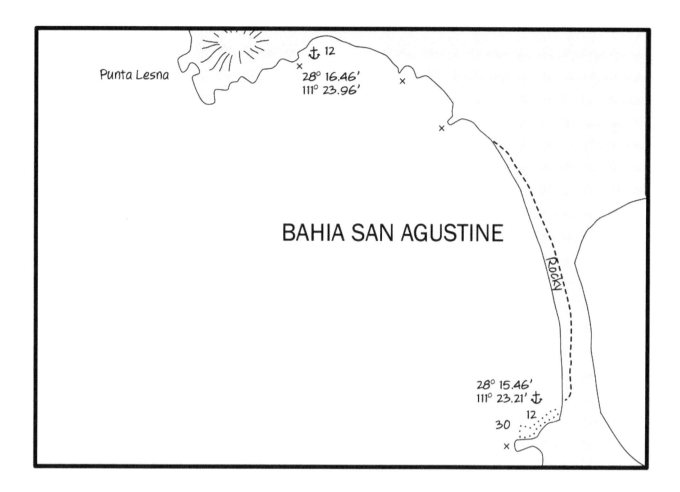

Punta Lesna

⚓ 12
× 28° 16.46'
111° 23.96'
×
×

BAHIA SAN AGUSTINE

Rocky

28° 15.46'
111° 23.21' ⚓
12
30
×

side at the foot of Morro Colorado.

Bahia San Agustin is next and is much bigger. Mid bay **WPT 28°15.73', 111°23.94'.** The south end of this bay gives good protection from the south but there is not much room. It is necessary to tuck in behind the rock islet with its offshore reefs and rocks. The bottom is mostly sand at 12 feet close in, and 28 feet out as far as the rocks awash. There are rocky shoals along the shore between the islet and the end of the beach. One or two boats could swing comfortably, but should the wind veer west of south, it would be time to leave. There is what looks to be a water treatment plant ashore, at the southern end the beach. Watch for possible pipelines on the bottom. At the northern end of San Agustin Bay, behind Punta Lesna, there is good protection from the northwest, in 18 feet over sand bottom. This is a good place to duck into in an emergency. There are few other attractions. For dinghy explorers though, there are interesting little coves at the end of Punta Lesna and around to the north.

Pozo Moreno is a very small cove with a few houses ashore and probably pangas on the beach when you arrive. In settled weather, this is a charming place. A northwestern swell will refract around the rounded headland and come in to rock you to sleep. Mid cove **WPT 28°14.65', 111°22.8'.**

Ensenada Las Cocinas (Caleta Moreno) provides protection in a southerly, tucked in near the beach on the south side.

No matter how rough the swell, Cocinas always seems to be quiet. Here must be the most colorful piece of real estate on the gulf. First there is the azure water over the white sand of the anchorage. Then around the corner are the "kitchens" for which it is named. You can see Morro Colorado, the redish hulk to the north, and the red rock interspersed with yellow and orange, for the sides of the 4 small coves lying between Cocinas and Punta Moreño. Cocinas and Julio Villa are accessible by road from Ensenada Poso

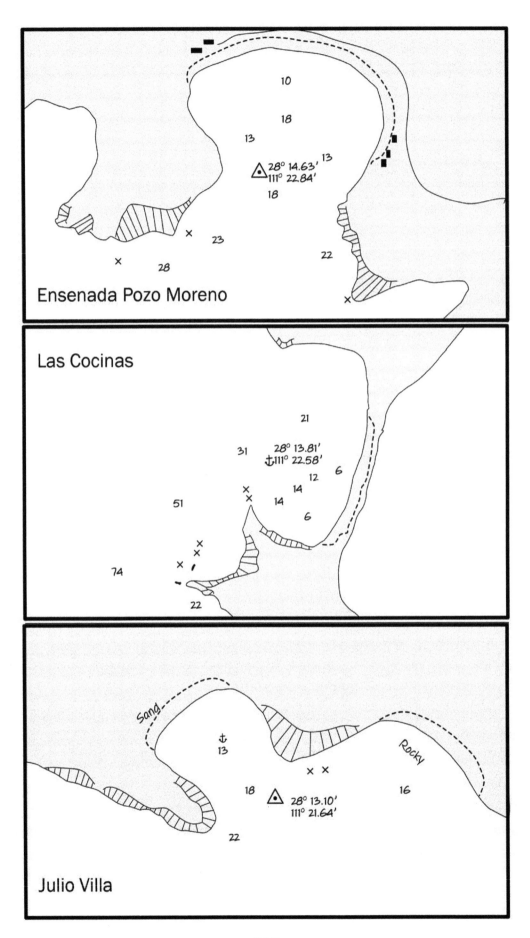

Ensenada Pozo Moreno

Las Cocinas

Julio Villa

Moreño so there are sometimes campers on the beach. **WPT 28°13.82', 111°25.54'.**
DANGER: In rounding Punta Moreño there is a reef about 120 yards off its southern point. There is 27 feet in the channel between, but if the reef is covered and you can't actually see it, give it a wide berth. There are also rocks usually covered off the last 2 points before you round up into Las Cocinas itself.

Behind the point is Ensenada Julio Villa, a small two lobed cove. **WPT 28°13.07', 111°21.57'.** Almost landlocked, this is the perfect textbook anchorage. It gives protection from all points except south. The bottom is good sand at 18 feet, but there is probably only room for one 30 footer to swing, although a larger boat can anchor fore and aft. Around to the north there is a box canyon where you can stretch your legs.

Rada El Pasito: There are three bays here. The first is the most open and susceptible to a northwest swell. There are a few patches of rock to be avoided when setting the anchor, especially to the north off the colorful rock knob that separates this bay from Julio Villa. The beach is pebble, but a good dinghy landing. Opening into the beach is a usually dry stream emerging from a box canyon that is well worth a hike to its upper reaches. When the wash is dry, it provides a smooth highway into the interior. When running it is a matter of bushwacking, but the falls and natural bathtubs are well worth the effort. Take drinking water along on any hikes ashore.

The next bay is a little deeper, 18 feet, and has a better bottom, but it offers less protection.
The third bay gives protection from the northwest. It is a relatively shallow bay and the holding ground deep in where you would like to put the anchor down is rocky. However, the sand at 12 feet begins just in time to make this a secure anchorage. It is accessible by road.

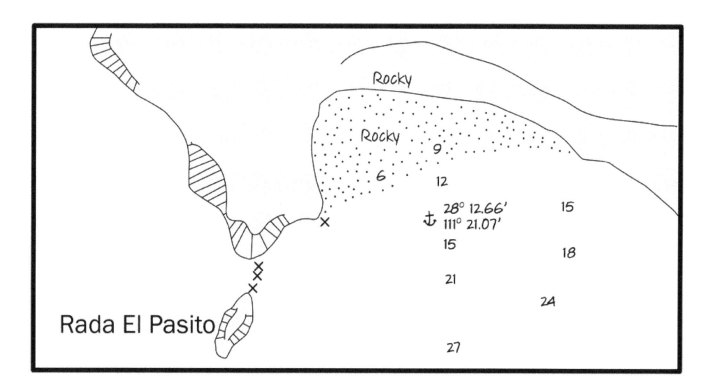

Bahia Jojoval: A whitish offshore rock called Anegado Chico (Little Reef, although it isn't a reef) marks the southern extreme of Jojoval Bay. The northern end is marked by Punta El Moreno (Brown Point). This is a wide bay, giving no protection except at its northern end where there are two good anchorages. There is an abandoned ranch at the southern end and it is accessible by road at this end. The beach is rocky and has no attractions. A rock awash but usually visible, lies about ¼ mile south of the point that divides the bay in half. In the center of the mouth of the bay, about a mile offshore, is Isla el Acerno (Sword Island), aptly named when seen edge-on. **WPT 28°11.50', 111°21.48.** It is all white with guano and is usually the home of a small herd of Sea Lions who will allow you to approach quite close before diving off their perches into the water. The scuba diving is good here, and there is an underwater memorial to the late Tony Corse, a Tucson aficionado of the diving here.

Swing wide around the next point as well. **Punta Molote** has a rock, barely covered, just 150 yards south of the point.

Caleta El Molote: El Molote is an offshore rock islet or peninsula, and the cove on its southeast side give fair protection from the northwest. However, it is very tight and chancy if there is much wind and swell. There is an exposed offshore reef lying to the south of Mollete itself which helps to form the cove, but there are submerged reefs extending out from the point toward this reef, and it is shoal and rocky all along the north side of the cove. There are more submerged rocks along the south side, but these are more steep to and closer to the shore. So you anchor between a rock and a hard place. All of the above notwithstanding, it is a nice place (though accessible by road and sometimes loaded with beach campers). **WPT 28°9.45', 111°19.75'.**

Caleta Venecia: Venecia is another favorite spot. The beach is pebbly but has a nice patch of green grass and trees at its head. Although Ensenada Chica with its fishing village is only a short walk over the hill, and the cove is accessible by road, it is usually deserted. Swimming, snorkeling and scuba are good along the shores and south of the entrance. To the south is also a good place for dinghy trips with many little coves and offshore rocks. On the north corner of the entrance there is a large rocky islet with a wide but shallow sea cave behind it. The bottom in Venecia is mostly sand at 18 feet. The cove is just wide enough to tack out of. Beware of the rocky shoals close to shore on the northwest side, and a reef that extends southwest off the south headland. **WPT 28°7.77', 111°17.92'** is between these two coves.

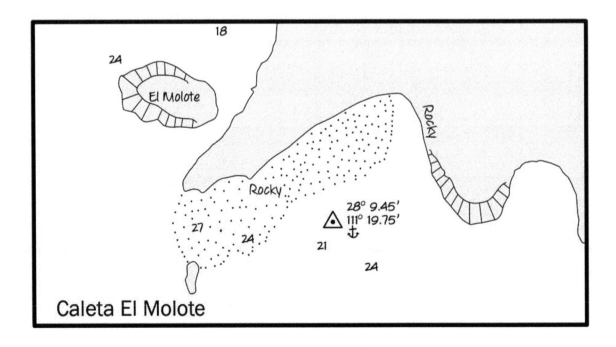

Caleta El Molote

Caleta Himalaya: This is a rather populated bay, accessible by road. There are a couple of houses in the larger northern half of the bay. Himalaya is divided by a mushroom shaped overhanging island. In the narrow southern bight there are a few Mexican fishermen's cabins.

The north half of the bay may be larger, but it is a tight anchorage due to the many reefs. The far northwest bight would be excellent except for the fact that there is a reef awash right in the middle of it. Another reef, submerged, lies off the center of the three little points that adorn the bay. The bottom is mostly sand with patches of rock at about 24 feet.

The southern half is clear of hidden dangers, except around the edges, and a reef that extends off the end of the dividing island. If your boat is small and there is little swell running, you can anchor in here, but protection is not all that good. Neither half of Himalaya has much to recommend it, but it is a favorite spot for scuba diving groups from the states. **WPT 28°8.75', 111°18.89'.**

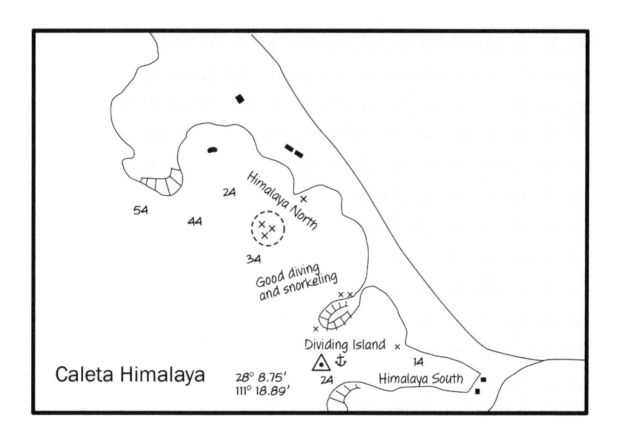

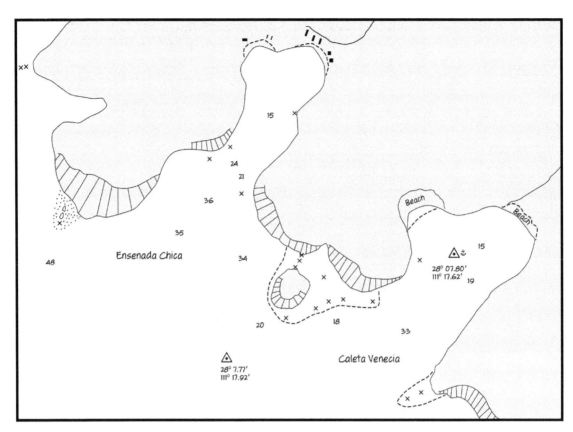

Ensenada Chica: This tiny bay is homeport for a small Mexican fishing panga fleet. It is subject to a surge when the swell is from the south, but it gives good protection from the northwest. However, it is very narrow. When anchoring in Chica, do not drop the hook until abreast the rocky reef that lies off the small point on the eastern shore (to starboard as you go in). Even anchored in that far, it is possible to swing into this reef, so a second anchor may be indicated. The bottom is sand at 12 feet.

DANGER: There are two offshore rocks off the point just west of Chica. They are above water and usually visible, but at night could go unnoticed. There is plenty of water between the outer one and the shore. The other lies close to shore.

Caleta Los Changos, WPT 28°06.11', 111°17.02', is a double cove which offers some protection under some conditions. Since there are other better anchorages nearby, you can swing in, test the action, and if it isn't quiet, head out again. Scuba, snorkeling and swimming are good, and it makes a good lunch spot. The southern bight is a bit tight. The bottom is mostly sand at 18 to 24 feet. There are rocky shoals off the points, and between the southern island and shore. There is plenty of water between the northern islands and shore, but it is a pretty tight squeeze. It is an interesting place but only under quiet conditions.

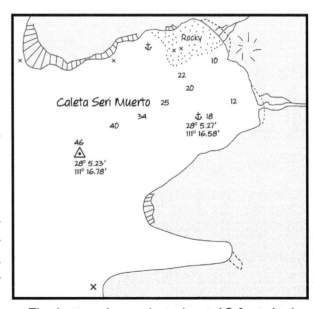

Caleta Seri Muerto, WPT 28°5.23', 111°16.78' is a mitten shaped cove with plenty of room. Swells from the west-northwest can reach into this bay and rock you to sleep, but it is a safe anchorage in storms from that direction. Protection from south to southeast is also good, but it is open to the southwest where a lot of summer weather comes from. The bottom is sand at about 18 feet. At the head of the bay, there are rocky reefs and bottom off the center outcrop and over to the first bight on the north shore. The south bight makes the better anchorage.

A long narrow cove at the entrance, near the south headland is tempting, but not wide enough for any but the smallest boats to swing. Whatever swell there is tends to be magnified at its head. To the south along the shore, there is a whole series of tiny points, bays, and beaches. On a calm day these offer great dinghy exploration. Take your fins and snorkels along too.

Caleta Amarga lies a half mile northwest of **Punta San Pedro**. Being so close to its famous neighbor, it gets little use. It is a fairly tight cove with room for only one or two boats to swing. It is surrounded by cliffs, and has a small rocky beach

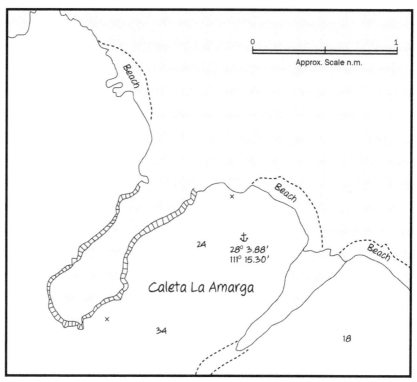

at its head with a single palm tree. A reef off the southern headland helps to break the swell from that direction. Swimming and snorkeling are good. The bottom is mostly sand at about 24 feet. **WPT 28°3.88', 111°15.30'.** The large bay to the southeast, between Amarga and Punta San Pedro has a good bottom but offers little protection except from the southeast quarter.

Palm Grove Beach is a tight little romantic looking spot, but with a big boat, anchor off and dinghy in to enjoy the shade of the palm trees.

Bahia San Pedro, WPT 28°3.16', 111°14.67' is also called Ensenada Grande (Big Bay) by the natives. San Pedro Bay gives good protection from both northerly weather, and southerly, but is open to the west. Anchor in either end, depending on the wind. However, Punta San Pedro is very rounded and swells defract around and can break on almost the entire length of the beach. The sharpness of Punta Amarilla makes a better break for swells from the south and there is room behind it where you can anchor quietly off the end of the beach. Vessels may sometimes share this anchorage with a couple of shrimp boats or other cruisers from San Carlos, but there is plenty of room. A road leads into this bay. The remains of an old farmstead and fresh water spring lie on the slope to the northeast. The beach has stretches of sand and the swimming is good. Several large sea caves and some breakdown canyons with caves along the eastern and outer edges of Punta San Pedro make interesting dinghy trips. The snorkeling and diving are also excellent along here and there is a sunken wreck off the point to lend interest for scuba fans. The bottom of the bay is sand at 20 to 30 feet, except on the north side of the point itself.

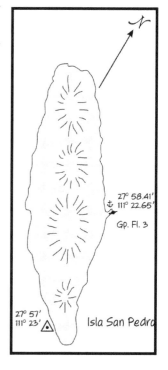

Isla San Pedro is the largest offshore island in the vicinity. It is three miles long and about three quarters of a mile wide, and lies 8 miles southwest of Punta San Pedro. It doesn't have much to offer a vessel seeking an anchorage as it is steep to all around. It is very popular with dive boats from the San Carlos area. A bit of temporary shelter may be found at on the east side **WPT 27°58.41', 111°22.65'**, and north near the light tower.

DANGER: There are NO good anchorages between Bahia San Pedro and Punta Bandito. You can anchor inside Punta Agua Escondido, **WPT 28°1.20', 111°11.51'**, in calm weather and walk up to the ranch where there is a spring of fresh water. About a half mile to the north of Punta Agua Escondido is a very small palm grove tucked in between a couple of cliffs.

Bandito Cove, WPT 27°59.44', 111°10.95' is the last secluded cove along this final stretch before San Carlos. This small, rather open bay, is actually the second bight east of Punta Bandito, and it gives fair protection from the northwest. It is not accessible by road, so its seclusion is good. The coast to the west makes good dinghy exploration country with bays and beaches too small to be entered by a boat.

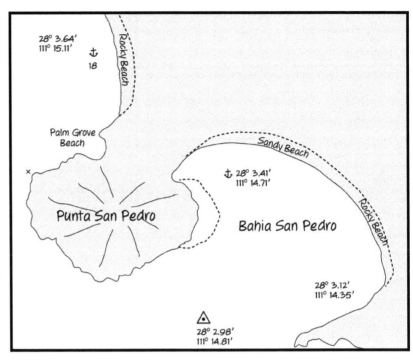

If the swell is heavy, it tends to swing around Punta Bandito and can make for an uncomfortable night. There is a rocky patch off the point to the west, with shallow spots. Otherwise the bottom is mostly sand at 24 feet with rocky patches near the shore.

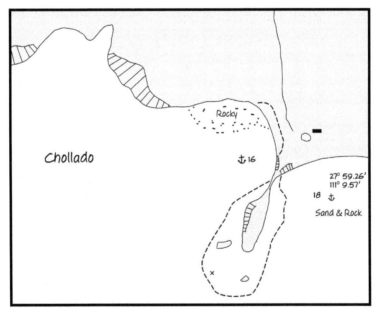

In a very light swell, the west side of **Chollado** gives reasonable protection from the southeast, but probably not for a comfortable night's sleep. This is a rather tight anchorage for a large boat. The bottom is sand with rocky patches at 24 feet . Its attractions are good snorkeling and diving. The eastern side gives protection from the northwest, but the bottom is half rock, so spot your anchor carefully. **WPT 27°59.26', 111°9.57'** in about 18 feet. Chollado is accessible by road.

Bahia Algodones is six miles west of Bahia San Carlos around Punta San Antonio and Punta Doble. Anchorage may be taken at either end of Catch 22 Beach (so named because it was the site of filming part of the movie by the same name) in 15 to 20 feet, sand. Avoid reefs off the rocky cliffs part way down the beach as well as those near Isla San Luis.

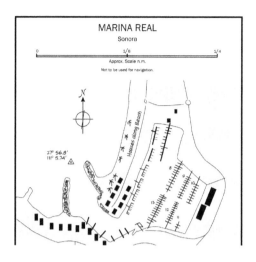

Marina Real is located in the southeastern corner of the bay and has a breakwater protected entrance. **WPT 27°56.8', 111°5.74'.** They have 356 slips to 63 feet, fuel, water, electricity, 24 hour security, launch ramp and dry storage. Contact the marina at marinareal@ prodigy.net.mex A paved, scenic road links the marina to San Carlos.

You can shelter from southerly weather behind **Punta San Antonio** and its offshore rock islet, but it is open to the northwest. In any case it is too open for a good nights sleep except on exceptionally quiet nights. It is fine diving and snorkeling. The bottom is mostly sand with patches of rock at about 30 feet. There is probably no passage between the rock islet and the shore.

Caleta Lalo, WPT 27°56.13', 111°05.45' is a very attractive cove with good swimming and snorkeling, It gives protection only from the northwest or north. There are three pebble beaches. The easternmost is accessible by road and there are usually campers on shore. The bottom is rocky with patches of sand at 15 to 20 feet. Take care in setting your anchor. The much smaller cove to the west of Lalo will hold only the smallest of boats.

DANGER: Anegado Lalo is an exposed reef lying offshore between a sand beach at the foot of the southwest slopes of Tetas de Cabra, and Caleta Lalo. It can usually be seen easily in daylight. There is passage with 28 feet between the reef and shore, but stay in the center of the channel.

Punta Doble is the long headland that protects San Carlos and most of San Francisco Bay from the prevailing west northwest winds. It is called "double" because of the cleft down the center of the end. Deep inside the cleft there is a large sea cave, which makes a fine dinghy trip from Martini Cove when there is no swell running. A shallower cave in the eastern half of the point is more obvious, but less interesting.

Martini Cove is just behind Islote Leon, called Lion Island because it has the shape of a crouching lion, and is one of the nicest little anchorages in the area. **WPT 27°55.90', 111°03.59'.** It is secluded, not accessible by

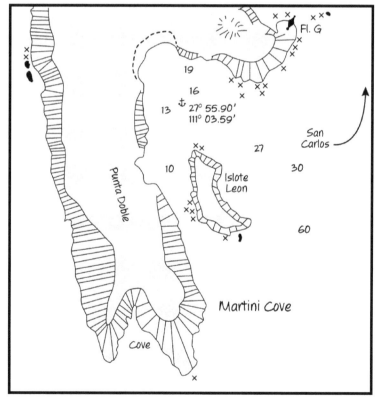

road or even a path. Very few boats spend the night here, yet the lights and sounds of San Carlos are completely masked by the high cliffs. Only the lights of Miramar Beach and Condominios six miles away are visible. During the daytime on a weekend as many as eight boats may be anchored here enjoying the sun, skin diving, swimming, fishing, or barbecuing on the beach, but they all go back to the marina at dusk. In hot weather the steep sides of Punta Doble to the west shield you from the setting sun. This gives the cabin a chance to cool off, and invites an early happy hour, hence the name.

The best scuba diving is on the seaward side of Islote Leon. The most interesting snorkeling is in the narrow channel between the island and Punta Doble, and among the large blocks of breakdown along the north shore of the cove, just east of the beach. There is a large flat submerged rock at the outer reaches of this breakdown. It carries much less than a fathom at low tide and is far enough out to be unexpected. The only other danger within the cove, are a couple of close lying rocks directly off the north end of the island. The narrow channel between the island and Punta Doble is full of rocks along its eastern side, and there are many scattered rocks within the cove guarding the entrance to this channel. Passage is not advised. Within the cove there is good sand bottom at 12 to 18 feet.

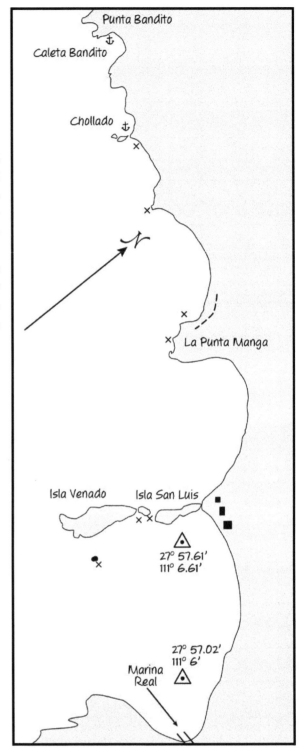

BAHIA SAN CARLOS

Bahia San Carlos is a beautiful inlet boasting marina facilities, private mooring balls and an anchorage area. It is under the jurisdiction of the Port Captain in Guaymas and his office must be called to report your arrival in San Carlos. The spectacular double rocky peaks of Las Tetas de Cabra (Goat Teats Peak) mark the approach to the bay. Below this 1,630' peak Punta Doble extends southward for over ½ mile. Fronting a niche in this peninsula is Isla Leon and to the north, the attractive anchorage of Martini Cove, where anchorage is in 12 - 18 feet, sand. Tumbled rocks and cliffs continue to the east where a rocky pillar and a flashing green light mark the western side of the entrance to the bay. Dan-

Tetas de Cabra. Photo: Phoebe Wilson

gerous rocks line the point and a submerged reef is located northeast of the green light. Two rocks awash lie about ¼ mile further up the entrance close to the west side. Directly across the channel to the north is Nariz Indio (Indian Nose), a low, rocky mound at the southern end of which is a flashing red light. Another rock lies just off this light.

When entering the bay favor the eastern (starboard) side to avoid submerged rocks off the bluff showing a green light. The head of the inlet is shoal. Numerous private mooring buoys are in the area beyond the entrance to the marina that is in a small rectangular bay to the east. The channel to the marina has a least depth of **6 feet** and deep draft vessels must wait until a rising tide to enter and often touch bottom during the very low tides of November and December. Anchorage may be taken in the outer bay, the bight in the southwest being a popular spot. **WPT 27°56.47', 111°3.84'**. Depths are 15 to 20 feet, rather poor holding shingle. Be certain that the anchor is well set and extra scope is let out to allow for possible strong afternoon winds.

The fuel dock is immediately around the corner to starboard at the entrance to the marina. **Marina San Carlos** is a modern, full-service marina that also provides haul-out facilities, hull and mechanical repairs and dry storage. VHF Ch 16 is monitored. For information email info@marinasancarlos.com. Once a week a truck visits the marina to pick up propane tanks for refilling and a fresh produce and seafood truck also stops by regularly. Laundry facilities are available beside the marina office and in town on the main street. Approximately 40 slips with power and water are the northwest side of the entrance to the marina. The pumpout is near the fuel dock and the marina will dispose of used oil and batteries. A large dry storage area is about three blocks inland from the marina where cruisers can work on their own boats. WiFi is available in the café beside the marina and at Marina Terra Hotel. Three marine supply stores are close to Marina San Carlos. The Cruiser net is at 9 a.m., Monday to Saturday on VHF Ch. 72.

Marina Seca San Carlos is next door to Marina San Carlos. This facility offers a work yard and a dry storage area. Boat repair services are available or you can work on your vessel and live-aboard. Vessels are hauled at the marina ramp where boats are floated on to the trailer and hydraulic arms secure the vessel for a short trip to the dry storage area.

For cruisers who lack the time or inclination to return their vessels via the long trip up the Baja peninsula a popular service is hauling boats by truck from San Carlos to Tucson, Arizona where they can be transferred to U.S. based trailers for shipment to other destinations. For information call Marina Seca Transport at 52-622-22-6101 or email marinaseca@marinasancarlos.com

Shangrila Coves: Just east of the entrance to San Carlos lie Shangrila Coves. These two small coves are both open to the south and not at all good in a swell from that direction. The eastern cove is very tight and has a rocky bottom unless you go in far enough. The western cove has plenty of room to maneuver, although there are rocks awash along its western shore. One rock is quite far off and lies at the foot of the

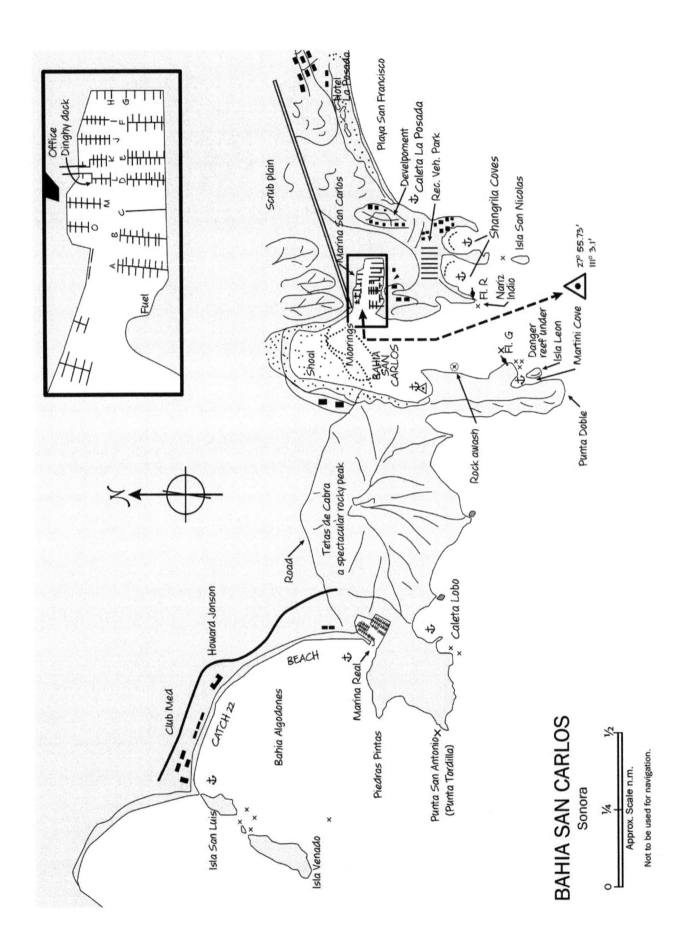

BAHIA SAN CARLOS
Sonora

0   ¼   ½

Approx. Scale n.m.

Not to be used for navigation.

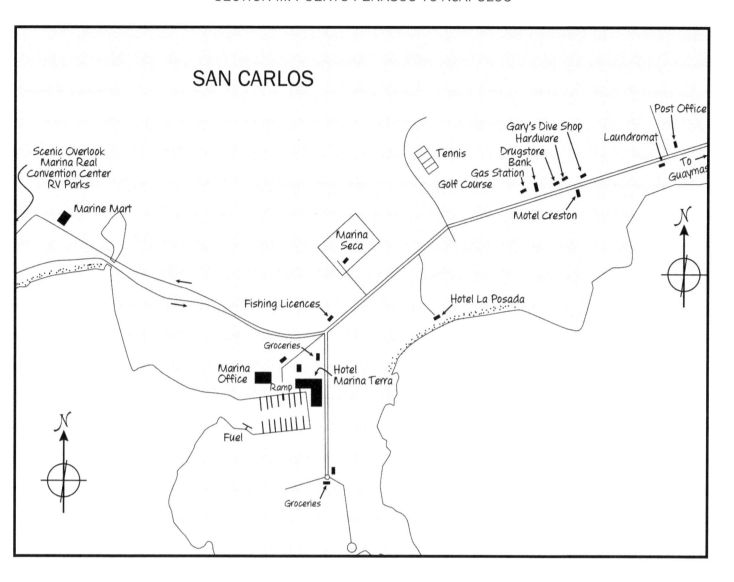

breakdown from the cliff on the west. It is awash at high tide but is usually visible, or makes a disturbance in the swell. We use these coves as a means of fast access to the marina and markets without having to negotiate the narrow entrance all the way in to the marina. The bottom is sand and rock, at 10 to 20 feet, so pay attention to where you set your anchor. **WPT 27°56.39', 111°3.27'.**

DANGER: It is possible to pass to the NORTH of the rock pillar that stands between Isla San Nicolas and Shangrila, with about 6 feet in the center. However, to the SOUTH of this pillar, between it and San Nicolas there are submerged rocks and no safe passage. Otherwise it is steep-to around San Nicolas. There is one large exposed rock off its southern tip. It is best to go around unless you are in the dinghy.

Caleta La Posada: Except in a southern wind or swell, this is a very civilized, but still pleasant anchorage with good sand at 20 feet, located just northeast of Shangrila. You can dinghy in from here for a good dinner at the Hotel la Posada dining room.

Isla De La Raza is also known as Honeymoon Island. This low flat island has an anchorage with a rock and sand bottom at about 10 to 15 feet off its northern end between the sandspit on the west and the rocky reef to the east. The sandspit continues shoal for a considerable distance, so keep clear, or use your depth sounder. There isn't much reason to anchor here except that it is close to San Carlos, and makes a good lunch spot for a day sail.

BAHIA SAN FRANCISCO

Once inside Isla Blanca, the bay is protected by Punta Doble from the northwestern quarter swells and often offers superb sailing in flat water with a stiff breeze coming in over the land. It is a good place for beach cats and sailboards to be sailed off the beach. The passage inside Isla de la Raza is often calm of wave, but enjoys a miniature hurricane coming through the slot from San Carlos Bay. When approaching from Guaymas with a westnorthwest wind, it is often possible to avoid a long beat to weather to the entrance to San Carlos by heading just outside Isla la Ventana on a course that takes you far into San Francisco Bay, almost to the beach. The wind usually bends around and you can then pass inside de la Raza and won't have to tack until you can clear Isla San Nicolas and fight the catspaws into San Carlos.

Playa San Francisco is one of the finest beaches in the area. It is being developed but there are so many miles that there is plenty of pure beach left. There is excellent swimming and sun bathing anywhere along its length. Although open roadstead, the bottom is good sand and when there is not too much swell, it is possible to anchor fairly close and swim or dinghy in.

Isla Blanca is covered in guano, which explains its name. The best anchorage is unfortunately on the lee northeast or northwest sides **WPT 27°56.13', 110°59.5'**, where the bottom is sand at 6 to 12 feet, but the odor of bird poop doesn't encourage long stays. It can also supply you with a boatload of tiny pesky flies, as can any island white with guano if you sail too close. The only attraction of Isla Blanca is the snorkeling on the south side, although you may want to outfit your snorkel with a bit of screen in the end so you don't suck up any flies. The bottom here is foul with rocks and is open to all swells. There is a sand spit, mostly awash, extending north northeast for about 100 yards. Use your depth sounder in this area. Between the end of the spit and the mainland, water remains shoal at about 6 to 12 feet and there are reefs at the shore end of this shallow stretch.

Isla La Ventana one of the landmarks of the area, this pillar of stone with a large hole through its center and painted white by the birds, can be seen for miles around. Extending northeast in line with the hole are two rows of rocks awash, but mostly visible. The canyon between and the area surrounding, especially on the north side is good scuba and snorkeling territory. Anchorage of a sort can be had on the north side in 24 to 30 feet on half sand, half rock. Not a very secure place for a long stay.

DANGER: In the last little bay at the east end of San Francisco Beach, there are several rocks awash, and well offshore toward Isla Blanca. One is exposed and visible. Keep well outside. The water between these rocks and Isla Blanca is only about 6 to 12 feet over sand.

La Reina is an exposed reef with good snorkeling and fishing, but is somewhat picked over. Satisfactory anchorage can be had in the little bay east of the reef, although it is not usually very quiet. The bottom is sand at about 12 feet. The reef is awash at high tides but will identify itself if there is any swell running. Passage between the reef and shore carries about 6 feet, but there may be rocks. One detached rock, sometimes submerged, lies about 100 yards offshore towards the reef. The shoreline between Francisco Beach and Reina has many reefs and should be given a wide berth.

DANGER: La Ahogada (Drowned Rock) is a pinnacle rock and submerged reef. The rock itself just breaks the surface in the troughs of large waves at the lowest winter tides. Otherwise, it makes no disturbance in the water to reveal itself. Keep well clear. Its location **WPT 27°55.32', 110°57.94'**, has a least depth of 1 foot.

Punta Tinajas lies behind Punta Tinajas, and is a little rocky beach with large patches of sand where you can spot the anchor. This is not a good anchorage in rough weather. The snorkeling is picturesque, but picked-over because there is a road and it is a favorite spot for fishermen and picnickers. Rocks lie along the shore and a reef extends out from the high knob at the eastern end.

Playa Miramar, on the south end of this popular beach is the Hotel Playa de Cortez. You can anchor off and dinghy in to enjoy drinks or a good dinner on their tree shaded terrace. A landing here requires quiet water however, as there is no protection from the northwest. The beach offers good swimming except that pollution is always suspect were housing borders the sea. There are a couple of native cantinas and restaurants at the north end of the beach, but this end is very shoal where the estuary empties out. The entire bay is good holding in sand at 6 to 18 feet. There is now a flashing red light on a microwave tower at the north end of the beach, **WPT 27°55.43', 110°56.42'.**

Chencho lies on the north side of Punta Colorado. This is a favorite spot in spite of its accessibility by road from Miramar Beach, and is sometimes the site of experiments by Technologico de Montery Escuela de Ciencias Martimas y Alimentarios. The school is situated on a bluff east of Chencho and they sometimes use the bay for their fish pens. The bottom is mostly sand at 12 to 18 feet, but there are patches of shingle and loose boulders just large enough to jam between the flukes of a 20 lb. Danforth. (Another story) Make sure your anchor is into sand before you sit down to lunch. If you use a plow, you'll have no problem.

Chencho gives excellent protection from the south in summer when the breeze comes over the low neck of land to keep you cool. A northwest swell is robbed of most of its force by Isla Peruano and Punta Colorado. Anchor close enough in to almost close the gap between them. You'll see the lights of Miramar close at hand and those of San Carlos six miles away across the bay. **WPT 27°54.37', 110°57.65'**

DANGER: South of Punta Colorado and Isla Peruano are several dangers. A rock awash lies ¼ mile to the south of the point. This is usually visible, but is submerged at extreme high tides and not obvious unless there is wave action. Seaward of this are three rocks about 50 yds. apart and submerged most of the time. The one furthest out is a pinnacle rock and invisible unless there is a large swell running. Stay well outside of everything you can see. On the inside of the group there is plenty of water and this side is steep-to. South of the rocks a reef with about 6 feet extends about 100 yds. Fishing and diving are good here, but there is no handy anchorage. The tempting cove on the south side of Punta Colorado is open to all swells and winds, and is full of submerged rocks. Close off Punta Colorado lie several obvious offshore rocks. However, well within the pass, but north of the visible rocks, and far enough offshore to be unsuspected, lies a large boulder with less than a fathom over it. North off the eastern end of Isla Peruano a shoal extends about 100 yds. Otherwise the pass is clear. Head for the center.

Bahia Salinitas offers poor protection but it is a good place to anchor for fishing or diving around Islas las Gringas when the water is quiet. The bottom is mostly sand at about 18 feet. There is little scenic beauty. The rocky beach is accessible by road. **WPT 27°53.26', 110°57.18'**

Ensenada La Salada is a large open bay that gives some protection from the northwest quarter, but if the swell is large enough, it sweeps in. It gives no quiet water in a southerly swell. The eastern bight has a sewage disposal lagoon and tank, and a fishermen's village. This makes the western bight preferable, but the bay lacks charm. However, the fishing is good and the snorkeling along the western edge is excellent. A rocky bottom requires careful anchoring if close to shore. The eastern side has many outlying rocks and should be given a wide berth. **WPT 52°52.20', 110°56.02**

Ensenada El Carricito is a double-bight cove that gives good protection from all but the largest west-northwest swell. Under such conditions, its western bight is a little shy. For a southern swell, the eastern bight is best, but protection is not complete and you can experience some motion as the swells diffract around the headland. The bottom is mostly sand at about 18 to 24 feet. Both beaches are rocky, but the eastern one is best and the swimming and snorkeling are great. This is a peaceful and secluded spot. **WPT 27°51,86', 110°54.41'**

Cabo Haro is a high, prominent point on which sits one of the manned lighthouses, giving a group flash of 3 at about 20 seconds. It is 440 ft. high and can be seen for 26 miles if your height of eye keeps it above

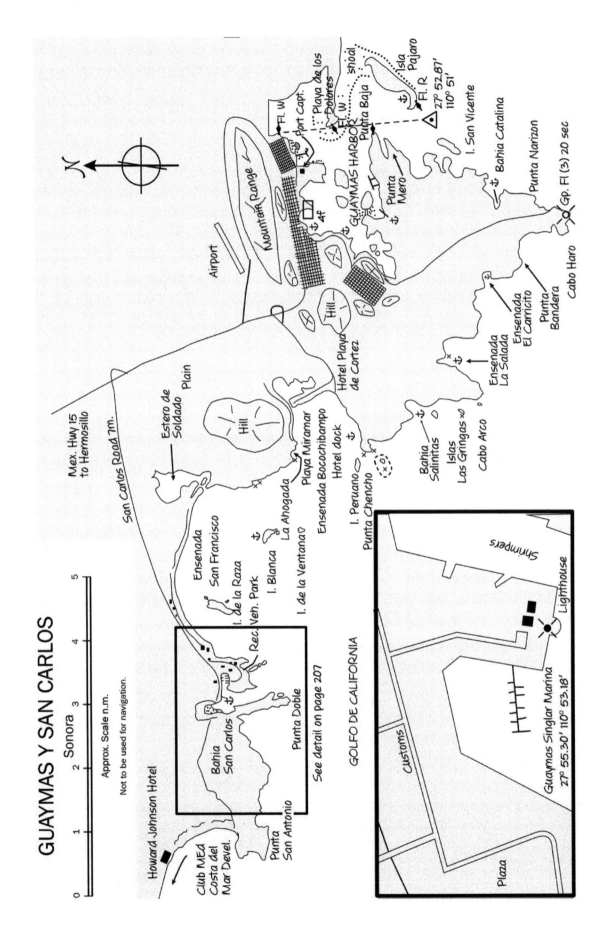

GUAYMAS Y SAN CARLOS

the horizon. Unlike many of the lights shown on charts, this one can be relied on as a navigation aid. Others are often out of service. At the base of Cabo Haro is a tiny cove, home for a herd of sea lions. There can be a strong tidal flow across the point. On its southern corner is a large natural bridge, which you can see through if you are not too far off.

Bahia Catalina is a lovely three part bay. Catalina gives protection from all quarters except southeast. In a southern swell, both ends are too shy to protect from rolling. At 18 feet there is good sand bottom at **WPT 27°51.78', 110°52.75'**. The only hidden dangers lie off the entrance points, especially the eastern one, which has a large area of rocks awash and one obvious 20 foot pinnacle. When the wind is from the northwest quarter, it funnels through the hills and the western bight can be uncomfortably windy. In summer there may be mosquitoes here. You may share this anchorage with a couple of shrimpers, and there are fishermen's cabins on shore, but there is plenty of room for all. Swimming is probably safe here. The west beach is fine white sand. The middle beach has some good snorkeling, but the easternmost beach is not as nice.

Pitahayosa Anchorage is in behind Isla San Vicente is what used to be a very secure and secluded anchorage. However, due to Unidad Industrial Pesquera with its boat yards and fish canneries, it is no longer a place of beauty.

On the west side of **Isla Pajaros**, adjacent to the ship channel, is a cove formed by the island and a long rocky spit. Stay 100 yards. off the end of the spit and there is plenty of water, though you may see suspicious tide rips. If in doubt, keep an eye on your depth sounder, but the shrimpers anchor in here frequently. There is 12 feet with gray mud bottom. This cove gives good protection from all quarters and is secluded except for the ship channel traffic and the industrial development a mile across the way.

Baja/Mero Cove is just west of the entrance to Guaymas Harbor, between Punta Baja (Lower Point) with its green light, and Punta Mero (Sea Bass Point). It is a long, narrow cove. It has nothing to offer except perhaps refuge if you can't make the harbor itself. Halfway in there is 18 feet with gray mud bottom.

GUAYMAS

Guaymas is about 10 miles east of Bahia San Carlos and is a major deep-sea port for this part of Mexico. You must call the Port Captain in Guaymas when stopping in either San Carlos or Guaymas. These two spots are popular with cruisers, in part because of the profusion of anchorages between them. Vessels arrive from Santa Rosalia, about 80 miles across the Gulf from Baja as well as by trailer from Arizona and Texas, making this a busy cruising area.

Entry to the harbor should be made west of Isla Pajaros, at **WPT 27°52.87', 110°51'**. Many shrimp boats and deep-sea vessels anchor in the roadstead and maneuvering in the vicinity of the terminal calls for watchful transit by yachts, which are not given preferential treatment.

Fonatur Marina Guaymas is a full service marina north of the basin providing facilities for cruisers. Facilities include fuel, a 50-ton Travelift, work yard, dry storage, laundry, showers and Wi-fi. The twin spires of San Fernando Cathedral are directly behind the marina and a decorative lighthouse is prominent. The deepest slip has 8 ft. of water at low tide. For information call 52-55-5090-4200 ext. 4697 or jjmartinez@fonatur.gob.mx

Anchorage may be taken across the bay to the south even with the Marina, off the old jail in Las Playitas **WPT 27°53.96', 110°52.81'**. Although this area is a hub of activity for pleasure craft and sportsfishing vessels, it is a fairly quiet anchorage. Patrons of the restaurant may use the pier for landing the dinghy. Leave someone aboard the boat or arrange for a buddy boat to watch your vessel if you go ashore for the evening since uninvited visitors may be possible. As is usual in any commercial port, the water is dirty, often leaving an oily scum on the hull. Further into the basin on the south side there is a dry storage area and work yard. The water is so shallow that the travel lift can only be used at high tide. The neighboring fish boat repair facility will use their travelift to bring your boat into the dry storage yard if your vessel has a deep draft or is very heavy. Dry storage is available at Marina Seca Guaymas, about 5 miles from Guaymas at **27°53.87', 110°53.51'.** The facility is quite basic but has showers, restrooms, security and bus service. Live-aboards are permitted and cruisers can work on their own boats. The route to the facility is quite shallow making it advisable to check with the Manager, Gabriel Larios before making an approach if your draft is a concern. This is one of the few yards that can handle multi-hulls. For information email marinasecaguaymas@yahoo.com

Guaymas is a mixture of old and new, with an actively developing industrial base and until the present time it has retained a Mexican flavor relatively unaffected by tourism. The city offers much in the way of shopping, restaurants and bank machines. The closest ATM to the marina is just across the street at the military bank Banjercito.

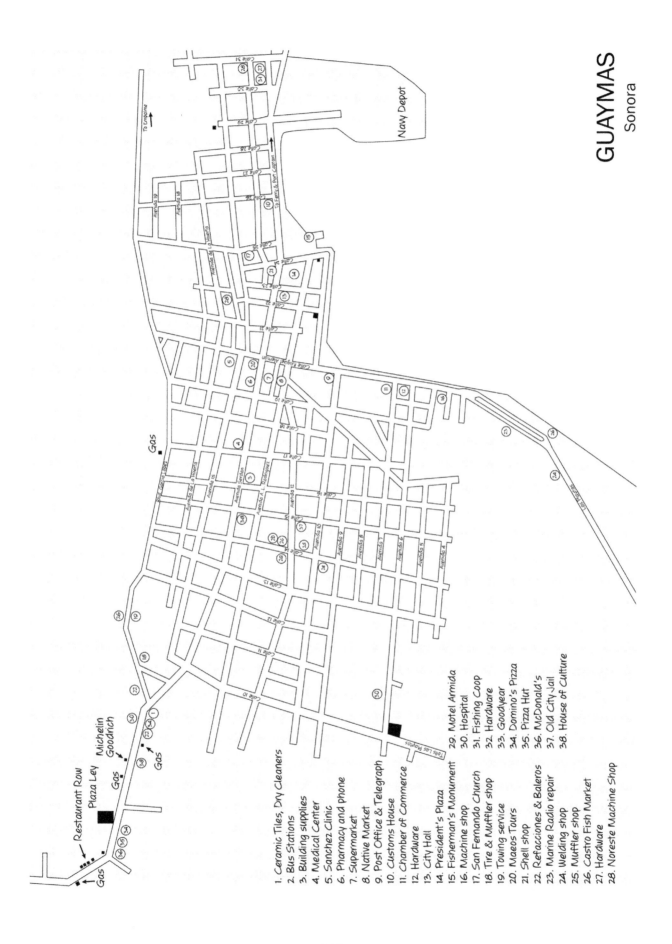

GUAYMAS
Sonora

1. Ceramic Tiles, Dry Cleaners
2. Bus Stations
3. Building supplies
4. Medical Center
5. Sanchez Clinic
6. Pharmacy and phone
7. Supermarket
8. Native Market
9. Post Office & Telegraph
10. Customs House
11. Chamber of Commerce
12. Hardware
13. City Hall
14. President's Plaza
15. Fisherman's Monument
16. Machine shop
17. San Fernando Church
18. Tire & Muffler shop
19. Towing service
20. Maeos Tours
21. Shell shop
22. Refacciones & Baleros
23. Marine Radio repair
24. Welding shop
25. Muffler shop
26. Castro Fish Market
27. Hardware
28. Noreste Machine Shop
29. Motel Armida
30. Hospital
31. Fishing Coop
32. Hardware
33. Goodyear
34. Domino's Pizza
35. Pizza Hut
36. McDonald's
37. Old City Jail
38. House of Culture

GUAYMAS TO MAZATLAN

The coastline between Guaymas and Mazatlan is very different than that of other places in the Sea of Cortez. This is the part of Mexico where agriculture dominates the inland landscape. The terrain is much flatter, rivers and estuaries are common, and the coast is fraught with sand bars, shoals and shallows with few discerning mountains or landmarks.

There are much fewer coves and bays to visit, with long stretches between anchorages. In looking at a map or charts, it makes sense that all the runoff from the rivers would carry sand and silt to the sea and spread out along the bottom making the shallow areas. Once you understand how this works, the whole section of coast is easier to deal with.

Cruisers tend if you cross to the mainland from the Baja without visiting this area, but it is well worth the extra effort to watch your depths and approaches. By now, your crew should be quite confident in the navigation and anchoring of your vessel, Spanish shouldn't be a struggle, and you should feel comfortable with the change of foods, cultures, and scenery. Let's get underway!

The distance between Guaymas and Mazatlan is about 450 miles. Estuaries are very common, but most are too shoal for a cruising vessel. Some offer a town or village with provisions and fuel, some are ports with fishing vessels and ships.

Isla Lobos and the associated sandbars form a prominent point, Punta Lobos, with an enclosed and shallow estuary. A waypoint to clear the point is **WPT 27°17.77', 110°37.56'**. The navigation light on the point is Fl. Wht., with a Racon. An important caution is the long shoal and very shallow water with breaking waves in even modest conditions, extending south of the estuary. One waypoint to clear the end of the shoal may be **WPT 27°15.15', 110°33.10'** however as the configurations of sandbars can change frequently our suggestion would be to give it an even wider berth. Do not relax your watch until well clear to the east of the bar.

Punta Lobos Anchorage, lies about 45 miles south of Guaymas, and is south of Punta Lobos. The anchorage offers protection from the northwest. Anchor at **WPT 27°16.49', 110°28.69'** in 21' off of an attractive sandy beach. It may be necessary to employ a stern anchor to deal with the refracted swell. The entrance to the estuary tends to shoal up, so don't attempt to enter without some exploring first in the dinghy. Surf may break in the entrance.

Bahia Yavaros is east of Punta Rosa, clearance **WPT 26°39.29', 109°39.20'**. Anchorage may be taken outside the bay between the point and the bay. The entrance is **WPT 26°39.50', 109°29.11'**, with a shoal just outside the entrance. Watch for waves or riffling water. The town of Puerto Yavaros is about 2 miles NNW of the entrance. Follow the marked channel to town.

The bay is quite well protected by important sand spits on either side of the entrance. As the entrance channel shifts with the seasons, it is important to call the Port Captain for a guide with the latest information, or follow a shrimper. Anchorage may be taken on either side of the town in 15 to 20 feet, sand. Fuel is available at the fish dock.

Exploring the bay by dinghy is rewarding. Visit the sand dunes on the sand spits, as well the miles of mangroves on the spits and up the river. The open beaches on the ocean side of the spits are beautiful.

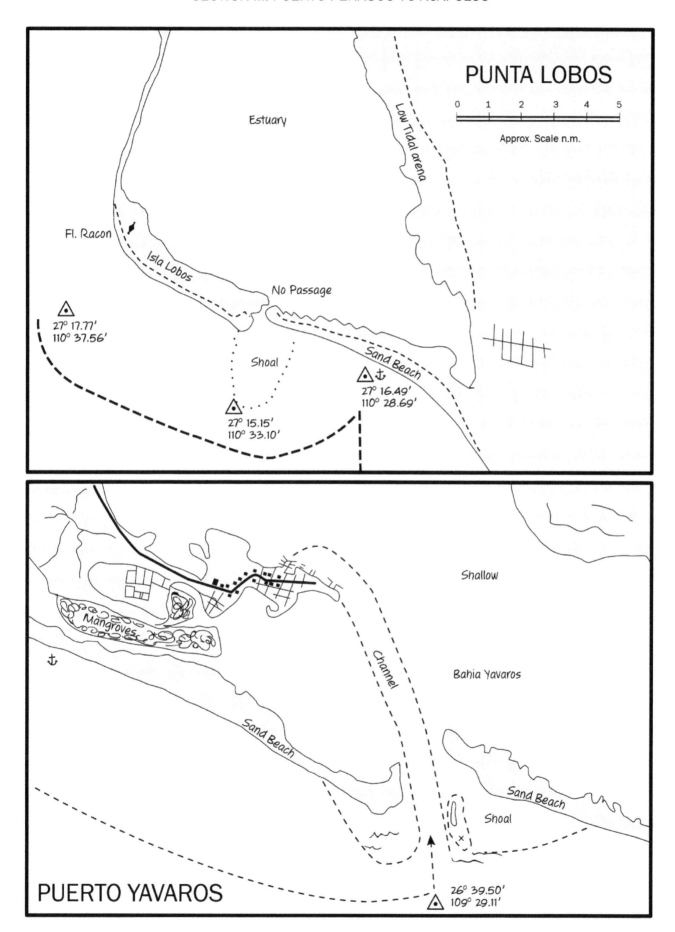

PUNTA LOBOS

0 1 2 3 4 5

Approx. Scale n.m.

Estuary

Low Tidal arena

Fl. Racon

Isla Lobos

No Passage

27° 17.77'
110° 37.56'

Shoal

Sand Beach

27° 16.49'
110° 28.69'

27° 15.15'
110° 33.10'

Shallow

Mangroves

Channel

Bahia Yavaros

Sand Beach

Sand Beach

Shoal

PUERTO YAVAROS

26° 39.50'
109° 29.11'

BAHIA SAN IGNACIO

On the east side of Punta San Ignacio, is the open bay **Bahia San Ignacio**. The point is very shoaly, so stay at least three miles off when rounding and entering the bay. The bay offers protection from northwesterlies along the sand beach. **WPT 25°38.43', 109°19.14'** in 25 to 30 feet, sand. The use of a stern anchor is advised to reduce the roll from refracted waves.

TOPOLOBAMPO

From Bahia San Ignacio, it is a 20 mile run to Marina Palmira with the outer entrance to the shipping channel 10 miles distant at **WPT 25°31.06' 109°12.22'**. The channel is well marked and one range is provided to supplement the buoys. Approaching the town, the channels split with the commercial traffic to the ferry terminal and Pemex facilities to the southeast. The channel to the north of the town passes the navy docks, a private marina, the commercial fishing docks, the fuel dock, another private marina club and eventually **Marina Palmira**. The facilities here are just a few years old, and they are very solid and clean at dockside. There are slips for approximately 40

Photo: Phoebe Wilson

boats in 2012 with plans to expand to over double that including a hotel and improved marina facilities. There is a small variety store with a reasonable selection of marine supplies and maintenance items on site. There is a nice upscale restaurant at the water edge called Pelicanos and one of the staff, Marcos, provides all the English available. All of the staff are very friendly and helpful and the facilities are quite secure, manned 24hrs daily with closed solid gates later in the night. This is a very secure place to leave a boat for the train ride to the Copper Canyon, a major attraction to Topolobampo. Contact the marina for space availability on VHF Ch.72, (668) 862-1544 or contacto_topolobampo@marinapalmira.com.

Topolobampo is primarily a commercial port. It has a well stocked comfortable Santa Fe grocery, hardware store and pharmacia. On Fridays it has the best farmers market we have experienced in Mexico with a great selection of meats, fruits and vegetables from a number of vendors along a three block stretch of the street by the main square. The vendors are very friendly and the freshness and selection are no doubt a result of being within a few miles of the extensive agricultural basins of Sinaloa. The buses run to Los

Photo: Phoebe Wilson

Mochis every 15 minutes, with a stop just across the main road outside the marina, fares of 17-20 pesos. The buses are clean. The taxi stand is across from the main bus station a short walk into the "centro". En-route you will walk past "Cocina Economica" with four very friendly women providing inexpensive and tasty casual lunches and breakfasts. Obviously popular as they deliver, and their driver is the most frequent visitor in the marina, keeping the management and staff nourished.

There is ample information on the train ride, tours and hotels in the area so we will not go into detail, but we encourage cruisers to take the time to see the Copper Canyon. One may start and end the train ride to the canyons in the colonial town of El Fuerte. Enjoy the hospitality at Rio Vista Hotel in El Fuerte, an inexpensive and eclectic facility built and run by the family with excellent views of the river, air conditioned rooms, and great support. They are avid bird watchers and offer river and bird watching tours. There are several other attractive hotels in the town as well, one of which is the childhood home of Zorro. The canyon trip is a great five day experience, and well worth the time and effort with some breath taking views.

Ohuira Bay, to the south of the town past the commercial facilities, offers anchorage. Caution is required again as it shoals quickly. It is bordered on the south and west with high hills and long bays worth exploring by dinghy.

Anchorage may be taken in the lee of the southeastern tip of **Isla Santa Maria** at the entrance to the channel. Head NNE, parallel to the bar at the buoys near the entrance at **WPT 25°33.28', 109°09.17'**. Depths are 25-35 feet until reaching the anchorage at **WPT 25°34.46', 109°09.44'**. This is well sheltered anchorage with limited fetch in any direction. It is a close dinghy ride to the isolated beaches and impressive sand dunes of Isla Santa Maria.

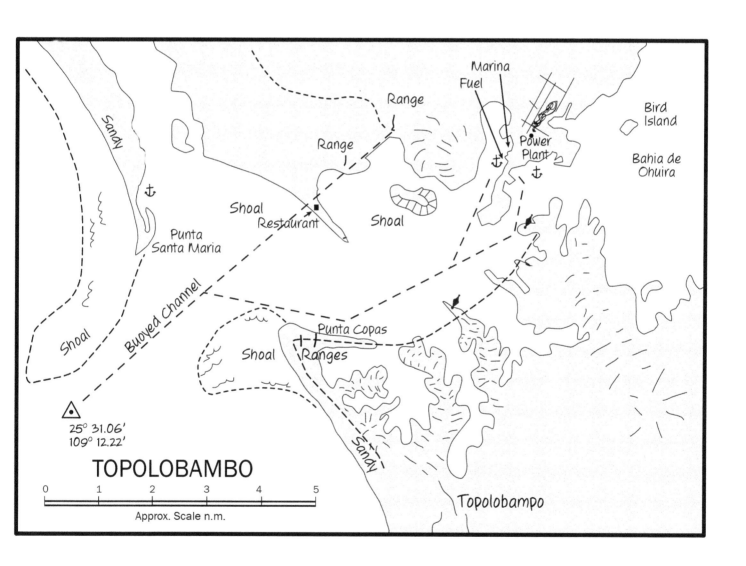

PUERTO ALTATA

From the outer marker of the Topolobampo channel, **WPT 24°31.06' 109°12.22'**, vessels may parallel the coast to the Puerto Altata outer marker. Care should be exercised here as impressive breakers extend south approximately 2 miles from the north side of the entrance channel to the estuary. At the time of writing there was a red buoy, supposedly marking a disused channel according to local advice, at **WPT 24°30.38', 107°51,28'**. Stay offshore from this buoy until you can see a clear approach to the outer buoy of the current channel at **WPT 24°28.98', 107°50.37'**. Heading from this point, parallel the breakers to the north on a heading of 13° M, clearing two lighted buoys at **WPT**

Photo: Phoebe Wilson

24°29.41', 107°50.26' and eventually arrive at the point of entrance to the deeper channel between the two islands bounding the entrance to the estuary. This passage should preferably be attempted at high slack water, as the narrow channel is conducive to standing waves at high tidal flows. In our experience one should cross 2/3 of the distance to the far side of the estuary before turning to the NW and paralleling the mainland shore the 8 miles to **Puerto Altata**. There are a few sandbars along this short passage, one on the port side about five miles inbound, marked with a black and white flag on a tall pole, and a sharp eye should be kept for it and others. Depths are 18-28 feet. You may want to work your way through the fishing fleet whose location is indicative of deeper water.

The fishing fleet is deceptive upon first entering the estuary as they appear like a colorful fleet of dinghies racing with spinnakers. In reality they deploy a fishing net led through blocks to the ends of two 10-12' poles extended fore and aft from their pangas. They then deploy colorful spinnaker like sails and a small dragging anchor amid ships and drift broadside to the wind, raising and lowering the sail to control speed

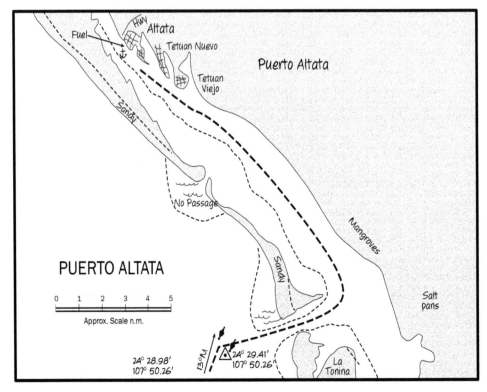

222

depending upon wind strength. Anchorage may be taken at **WPT 24°37.77', 107°55.85'** off the shore of the numerous restaurants on the beach front of town. Mi Charlie is a restaurant owned by Carlos, an English speaking native of the village who also acts as a pilot. He monitors channel 16 and will provide assistance if requested. The Perlas is another well known restaurant on the waterfront.

The beach is very gradually sloped leading from shore then drops off quickly to anchoring depths. The pangas anchored bow and stern, sit on dry land at low tide, the depth varying by 5'.

The local fishermen are very helpful in our experience, for on departure motoring into the sun and too mid channel, a cruiser ran aground. Three fishing boats came to their aid and succeeded in pulling them off the bar.

There is a marina northwest of Altata, about three miles further up the bay, which opened in 2014, called Marina Isla Cortez. The marina, with 43 slips and depths of 8ft+, offers modern concrete docks with electricity and water, free wifi, a fuel dock, pump out, restrooms, showers and laundry services along with a great restaurant, palapa bar and a small store. Also on site are a launch ramp, covered dry storage for small boats and boat trailer parking. A bonus included with your slip is access to the resort's beach club and pool.

To enter the channel, head for **WPT 24°37.90', 107° 36.05'** and proceed up the bay to the entrance of the channel at **WPT 24°38.945', 107°57.337'** where you will see the first of a series of red and green channel markers. The depth in the channel is a minimum of 6 feet, (check with the marina for current channel depths) and becomes quite narrow with shallows on either side, so pay attention as you have some curves to follow. The marina will be on the left just before the bridge. You will see two pointed tops of the palapas as well as a blue and white lighthouse, which is the marina.
Follow the channel markers all the way to the marina! A call to the marina office in advance will bring a panga to guide you through the channel from Altata to the marina.

Contact the marina on VHF 16, at bheimpel@islacortes.com phone 672-854-7371 or 672-854-7157. www.islacortes.com/marina

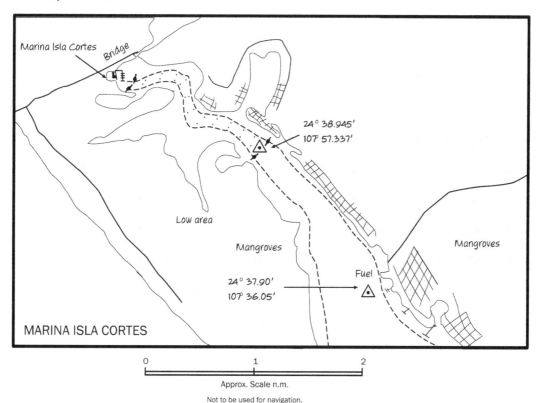

Approx. Scale n.m.

Not to be used for navigation.

MAZATLAN MARINAS AND ANCHORAGES

Tourist, commercial, fishing and transportation facilities have made this natural harbor the most important shipping terminal between San Diego and Panama for many years. The only place for **marina** development was well outside the harbor area in the Sabalo estuary and lagoon that was developed to form the massive El Cid Resort and Marina, Marina Mazatlan, Fonatur Marina Mazatlan and Isla Marina, all of which lie toward the north end of the city. If you are approaching from the north or choose to put in at one of these marinas, the most readily identifiable landmarks are the islands, which lie about ½ mile off the (Gold) Coast, where hotels line the long beach north of the harbor entrance. Isla Pajaros (Birds) is a scrub-covered, rocky island 400' high; about a mile SSE is Isla Venados (Deer), rising to a peak of 499' and joined to nearby Isla Lobos (Wolves) with a peak

Cloudy day in Mazatlan. Photo: Robin Richardson Stout

of 299'. The foul area off the northwest coast of Isla Pajaros should be given a safe berth. NIMA Chart 21301 shows depths between the islands and coast of less than 3 fathoms, with 1.5 fathoms up to 500' off some areas. When awaiting calm conditions to enter the channel a rolly but satisfactory anchorage can be found on the south side of the sand spit located about midway along the east side of Isla Venados.

The channel leading to the **marinas** is northeast of the northern end of Isla Pajaros. **WPT 23°16.05', 106°28.28'.** Punta Sabalo, a rocky headland northeast of Isla Pajaros, is hardly noticeable against the towering Playa Real Hotel that also makes a good landmark. Rock breakwaters protect the entrance channel, however the navigation lights on the tips are difficult to distinguish from background lights ashore at night. Entry into this relatively narrow, curving channel can be perilous on an outgoing tide with an offshore swell of any consequence; a night entrance is inadvisable for a first-time visitor. Although the

Beautiful sunset in Mazatlan. Photo: Robin Richardson Stout

tidal range is only about 2½ feet, tidal currents can run to 4 knots because of the large volume of water inboard of the channel. When inbound and entering the channel, it is advisable to favor the right side. At very low tide conditions, the bar at the channel entrance can be as shallow as 9 feet. Northwesterly winds sweep sand toward the entrance resulting in almost year-round dredging operations to maintain the channel. The dredge is frequently anchored on the northerly side of the channel inboard of the first bend in the channel; a call to Marina El Cid on VHF 16 will determine whether the dredge and associated small tenders are in operation during daylight hours. **Marina El Cid** is just beyond the initial bend in the channel. It is a full service marina with fuel, water, laundry, showers, cable TV, tennis courts and pump-out facilities. The office will arrange for propane pickup and delivery. Marina patrons have access to all hotel facilities and a house doctor is available on site. Moorage fees equal or exceed those charged in the US. Adjacent to the marina is a small convenience store, limited supply store and 5-star restaurant, golf course and hotel. Surge in the marina makes chafing gear necessary on all mooring lines. For information

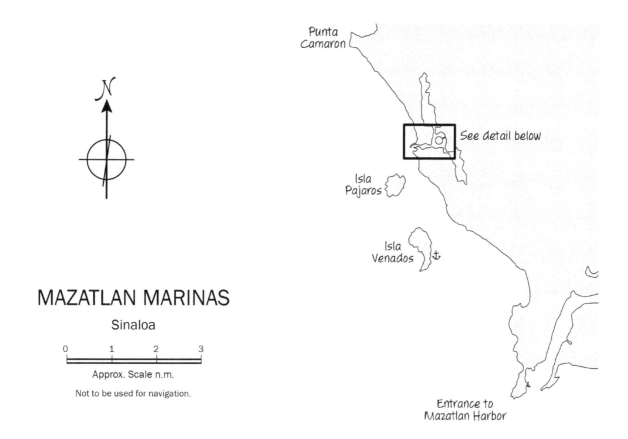

MAZATLAN MARINAS

Sinaloa

0   1   2   3

Approx. Scale n.m.

Not to be used for navigation.

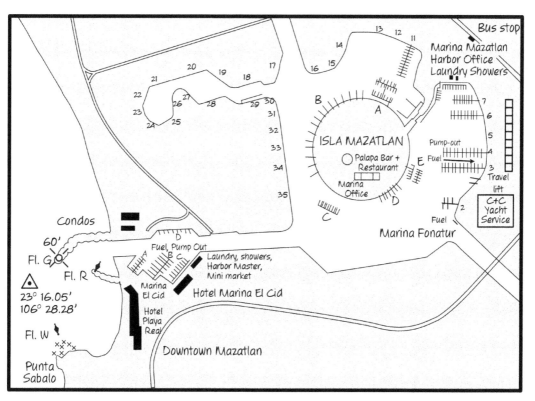

DETAIL: MARINA EL CID, ISLA MARINA & MARINA MAZATLAN

225

call 011-52-669-916-3468 or email marinaelcidmazatlan@elcid. com.mx. The marina also monitors VHF 16 and SSB 8384.4.

Fonatur Marina lies approximately ½ mile beyond Marina El Cid. It offers a limited number of slips, bathroom and laundry facilities, and a fuel dock. It is also located adjacent to a full service boatyard and a number of yacht repair businesses that can handle a variety of repairs.

Marina Mazatlan, a full service facility, is reached by continuing further eastward through a wide channel past the circular man-made island to docks along the far shore. Call the dockmaster Jaime, on VHF Ch 16 for slip assignment. Moorage rates vary depending on length of vessel and length of stay. A small store is next to the marina office. For information call 011-52-669-619-7799 or email Elvira@marina-mazatlan.com or Jaimeruiz@marina-mazatlan.com. A number of private condominium projects are on the island where a large palapa restaurant serves excellent meals in a friendly, casual atmosphere. The cruiser's net operates on VHF Ch 22, Monday to Saturday at 0800.

Marina El Cid. Photo: Robin Richardson Stout

A new well stocked chandlery is located in a small mall that is located just south from Marina Mazatlan across the main thoroughfare and adjacent to the Pemex station. There is also a very well stocked, reasonably priced supermercado in the westerly end of the condominium complex; it is between Marina Mazatlan and Marina Fonatur.

Transportation in and around Mazatlan is readily available by autobus, taxi or pulmonias (open-air taxis resembling over-sized golf carts that are found only in Mazatlan). See discussion on autobuses and taxis in the Introduction of this Cruisers' Guide. There is a Sam's Club, a Home Depot and a Mega Supermercado in Mazatlan, all located within several blocks of one another, and easily and inexpensively reached via autobus; inquire at the Marina Offices for which bus line to take to go to these stores, which are about 2 miles from the marinas. Mazatlan's biggest celebration is Carnival, which takes place the week before Lent. Featuring parades, fireworks, expositions and various cultural events, this 100-year old party rivals Rio de Janiero. Another event of interest is the annual San Diego to Mazatlan International Yacht Race that ends at the Marina El Cid around the middle of February.

In addition to the aforementioned marinas, just inside and to the north of the breakwater entrance to Mazatlan's main shipping harbor, is Old Marina Mazatlan. As mentioned above, Mazatlan is a major shipping port; there is a high volume of commercial shipping and fishing vessels that transit in and out of the harbor and its approaches. If transiting across the shipping lane and harbor approaches when passing north or south, the Port Captain wishes for all vessels to check in and continuously monitor VHF Channel 16. There are no slips or moorings available in Old Marina Mazatlan; cruisers can anchor out and take dinghies into the docks. This is a less secure area than the aforementioned marinas, so if staying in this anchorage, cruisers are advised to ensure that their vessels and belongings are secured when going ashore. As a footnote, the Mazatlan-La Paz Ferry docks are also near this anchorage. An upside to this location is that it is five minutes from Old Mazatlan (which is a 30 or so minute autobus ride from the aforementioned marinas) and its infamous market where multiple vendors sell fresh vegetables, meat, poultry and fish, as well as many other items. There are many restaurants, parks, theaters and musicians performing at night on weekends in Old Mazatlan.

Just south of the entrance to Mazatlan's harbor is Stone Island anchorage. This is a good anchorage and will accommodate many vessels. There are many palapas, bars and restaurants ashore that welcome cruisers and will ensure security of dinghies while frequenting their facilities. It is also possible to take a water taxi from this area to go to downtown Mazatlan. Cruisers who have frequented this anchorage in 2012 report that the anchorage is very pleasant and seemingly secure; however, securing dinghies out of the water each night and locking up outboard motors is imperative as they are very attractive.

Marine services can be handled by a number of firms. The following list is provided as a starting point for firms with a reliable reputation:

Dive service: Mario Diver Service Ph 669982-1951 VHF 16 "MAYA"
Electronic work: Servicio Electronkos Marinos Ph 669-980-6571 VHF 10
General Yacht Repair: RPM Marine – Neil Randle "NOVIA", Rick Cummins "CAPE STARR"
Marine surveyor:
Michael Wilson, Lloyds recognized VHF 72, Ph 669-871-685 e-mail mandmatmex@hotmail.com
Propeller repairs: Kelly Propeller: Ph 669-985-0852 or 669-981-0972
Refrigeration: Mexicolder - Build custom low amp 12/24 volt systems
VHF72, ph 669-871-685 email: mandmatmex@hotmail.com
Stainless and aluminum welding: 669-982-0137
Stainless steel railings, solar mounts, etc. Rosette SS Tel/Fax 011-52-981-0280/0286
Cell 011-521-669-101-0791 (Locally 044-669-101-0791)

MAZATLAN HARBOR

Mazatlan is about 400 miles southeast of Guaymas and 120 miles north of San Blas. Mazatlan is a protected, large commercial harbor that boasts ferry docks, a cruise ship terminal and facilities for the large shrimp fleet based here. It is the nearest mainland harbor to the southern tip of Baja and lies roughly east of Cabo San Lucas. This makes it suitable as a mainland departure point since vessels can lay a course that quarters the prevailing swell and sailing vessels may beat across the Sea of Cortez. The normal destination on Baja is Los Frailes for it provides the shortest distance for crossing the Gulf.

The harbor entrance is between two stubby breakwaters that extend from two islands that form the outer part of the harbor. On the west side of the entrance is Isla Creston, a steep and prominent island about 515' high, with a lighthouse on top. Isla Chivos is on the eastern side of the entrance and is about 240' high. The sea usually breaks on Piedra Negra, a small, black rocky islet about ¾ miles south of the entrance. It has a light on it but in daylight it is not easy to distinguish from the land in the background until you are within a mile or two of it. Approach **WPT 23°10', 106°24.86'**.

Enter between the breakwaters and turn to port off the main channel into the western part of the outer harbor; this is the small boat anchorage area. Just under the peak of Isla Creston is a shipyard where shrimpers and fishing vessels often anchor. Beyond this section you may anchor anywhere in 5 to 10 feet, mud bottom. The water in the harbor is often quite dirty.

Several sport fishing and yacht agencies have docks and buildings lining the western shore. A dinghy dock is located just to the east of the launching ramp and fuel dock. Only bottled water should be put in your water tanks since all else is non potable. The ferry docks lie at the north end of the anchorage where the terminal is prominent on the shore. The main part of the harbor lies further in, along the west side of the dredged channel.

The Port Captain and Immigration offices move frequently. Currently, the Port Captain's office is outside the eastern end of the cruise ship compound near a tall 7-sided structure. The Immigration office is three blocks north near Hotel Atenas. Office hours are 9 a.m. to 2:30 p.m.

Food and other supplies can readily be replenished in the stores and markets in this large city. You can take the Colectivo near Club Nautico to a large supermercado; the bus seems to wander through town but helpful drivers will tell you when to get off. A bus or taxi trip is needed to get to a laundromat. **Club Nautico** can be of assistance when getting beer and ice. You can leave propane bottles at their office and they will arrange for pickup and delivery. A charge of 30 pesos per day allows you to use the dinghy dock, washrooms, showers and the clubroom; Wi-Fi is available in the clubhouse. The fuel dock sells only gasoline. The city sewage plant is across the street from the marina and the odors created are quite objectionable. The world's second highest lighthouse on Isla Creston rewards a hiker with a great view of the city.

Local cruisers' VHF net will aid with local information at 0800 on VHF 22 . Thanksgiving and Christmas are popular times to be in Mazatlan as well as spring departures for Baja Race Week at Partida. Marina reservations are mandatory at these times.

For cruisers needing boatyard services contact:
Betos - cell phone: 0044-669-70013
Servicios Navales Industriales (SENI) at 984-7879, 984-7107 , www.seni.com.mx/ingles
Astilleros Malvinas S.A. de C.V. (Malvinas) at 981-1242
Fonatur Marina Seca at 913-3730 located at Marina Mazatlan
Total Yacht Works or Marine Services Mazatlan at 669-117-0911 or 668-994-8012

MAZATLAN HARBOR

Sinaloa

0   ¼   ½   ¾

Approx. Scale n.m.

Not to be used for navigation.

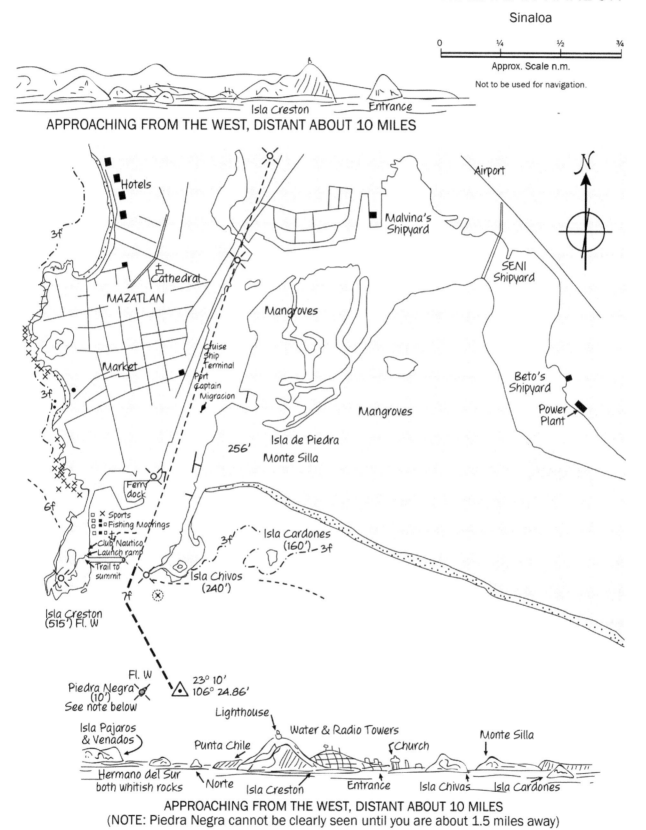

Isla Creston   Entrance

APPROACHING FROM THE WEST, DISTANT ABOUT 10 MILES

Airport

N

Hotels

Malvina's
Shipyard

3f

SENI
Shipyard

Cathedral

MAZATLAN

Mangroves

Market

Cruise
Ship
Terminal
Port
Captain
Migracion

Beto's
Shipyard

Mangroves

Power
Plant

3f

Isla de Piedra
Monte Silla

256'

Ferry
dock

6f

x Sports
Fishing Moorings

Club Nautico
Launch ramp

Trail to
summit

3f

Isla Cardones
(160') 3f

Isla Chivos
(240')

7f

Isla Creston
(515') Fl. W

Fl. W

Piedra Negra
(10')
See note below

23° 10'
106° 24.86'

Lighthouse

Isla Pajaros
& Venados

Punta Chile

Water & Radio Towers

Church

Monte Silla

Hermano del Sur
both whitish rocks

Norte

Isla Creston

Entrance

Isla Chivas

Isla Cardones

APPROACHING FROM THE WEST, DISTANT ABOUT 10 MILES
(NOTE: Piedra Negra cannot be clearly seen until you are about 1.5 miles away)

THE MAINLAND COAST: MAZATLAN TO PUERTO VALLARTA

This section of the mainland coast is the usual departure and/or destination point for crossing the Gulf of California, also referred to by cruisers as the Sea of Cortez, or, affectionately "The Sea." Almost all of this part of the coast is south of the Tropic of Cancer, except for Mazatlan, which is just above the line. Yet the tropical setting is more evident on the mainland than in the dry, desert-like atmosphere of the southern tip of the Baja Peninsula. Tropical forests, birds and animals are more visible and the climate is warmer and more humid.

From November to May the prevailing winds are northwesterly. Since the coast generally trends southeasterly, a crossing to the mainland from Baja has a favorable wind under normal conditions and almost any port in this section can be a suitable destination. The weather is usually mild during these months and the downwind run is comfortable. But during the remainder of the year (June to October), which is the rainy season, southeasterly gales can occur. Radio Costanera on VHF Ch 16 broadcasts weather reports concerning tropical disturbances in the area. In order to take advantage of the prevailing northwesterly wind the trip from the mainland to Baja is usually started at Mazatlan. A sailing vessel can just hold a course with prevailing winds, though powerboats may find themselves in the trough of the waves and may prefer to leave from San Blas.

Currents depend on the wind and season. Information on them is meager. Many vessels crossing the Gulf from Cabo experience strong southerly currents and a short period of steep cross-seas when about 10 to 20 miles out of Cabo, possibly due to an ebb from the Gulf. As you move further into the Gulf this condition is less noticeable.

If a vessel is bound for Isla Isabela or Puerto Vallarta, the route passes near Islas Tres Marias (not to be confused with Las Tres Marietas on page 244). Tres Marias is a group of four high and barren islands of volcanic origin. They are the site of a penal colony which is patrolled by the Mexican Navy. Close approach should not be made and landing is prohibited. Isla Maria Madre (Mother Mary) is the largest and highest at 2,000' and is just southeast of the smallest, Isla San Juanito which is not considered as one of the "Three Marias." Isla Maria Magdalena is the second largest, rising to about 1,500' and Isla Maria Cleofas is the southernmost, almost 1,300' high. A breaking reef extends about 2½ miles east of the northeastern point of this island. In addition to the penal colony prohibitions, the reefs discourage close approach to the islands.

Isla Isabela is a conveniently located stopover for vessels crossing the Gulf. This wild and rugged island, designated as a Bird Sanctuary, is detailed on the next page.

The mainland coast in the vicinity of San Blas is low and sandy, and several miles inland a range of mountains are visible. Near Bahia de Banderas the mountains rise nearer to the coast and provide a good indication of approaching land. Bahia de Banderas lies between two prominent points, Punta de Mita on the north and Cabo Corrientes to the south. This large bay is 20 miles wide at its mouth and 20 miles indented into the land. Puerto Vallarta lies in the inner part of the bay.

The interesting and varied anchorages and villages between Mazatlan and Banderas Bay/Puerto Vallarta make this trip an enjoyable one, especially southbound and traveling with the prevailing wind and current.

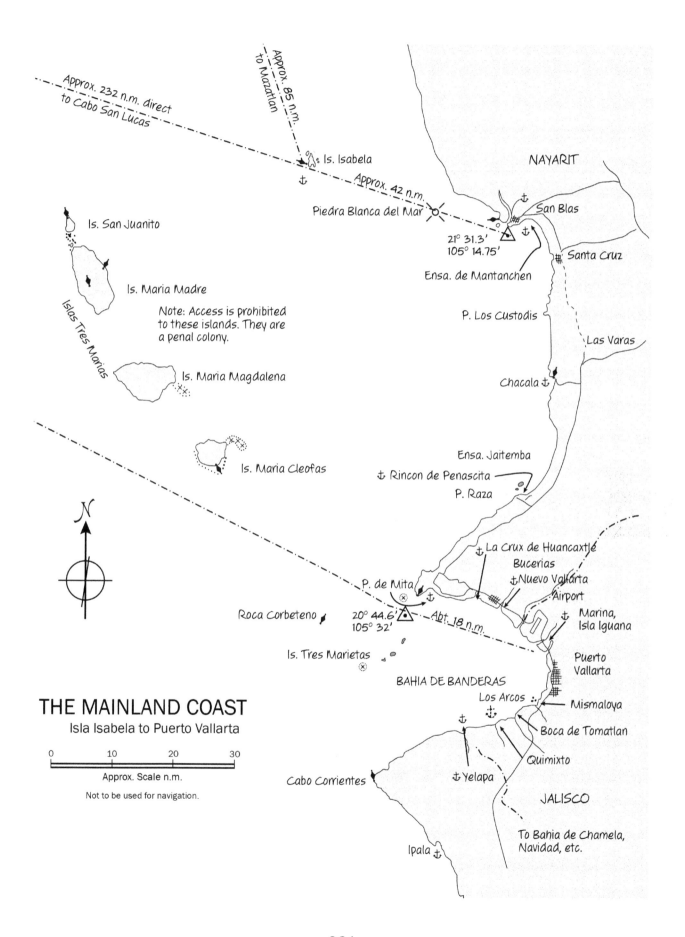

Approx. 232 n.m. direct to Cabo San Lucas

Approx. 85 n.m. to Mazatlan

Is. Isabela

Approx. 42 n.m.

NAYARIT

Piedra Blanca del Mar

21° 31.3'
105° 14.75'

San Blas

Santa Cruz

Ensa. de Mantanchen

P. Los Custodis

Las Varas

Chacala

Is. San Juanito

Is. Maria Madre

Note: Access is prohibited
to these islands. They are
a penal colony.

Islas Tres Marias

Is. Maria Magdalena

Ensa. Jaitemba

Rincon de Penascita

P. Raza

Is. Maria Cleofas

N

La Crux de Huancaxtle

Bucerias

Nuevo Vallarta

Airport

P. de Mita

Marina,
Isla Iguana

Roca Corbeteno

20° 44.6'
105° 32'

Abt. 18 n.m.

Is. Tres Marietas

Puerto
Vallarta

BAHIA DE BANDERAS

Los Arcos

Mismaloya

THE MAINLAND COAST

Isla Isabela to Puerto Vallarta

Boca de Tomatlan

Quimixto

0   10   20   30

Approx. Scale n.m.

Not to be used for navigation.

Cabo Corrientes

Yelapa

JALISCO

To Bahia de Chamela,
Navidad, etc.

Ipala

ISLA ISABELA

This remarkable island is a popular destination when crossing the Sea of Cortez from Baja or traveling between Mazatlan and Puerto Vallarta. It is uninhabited except for the residence of the Warden who oversees this magnificent Bird Sanctuary. Seasonal fishermen frequent the area and their camps line the beach in the southern cove. Though skipped by many cruisers because of anchoring challenges, both the National Geographic and Jacques Cousteau featured the island in television specials as a wonderland of unspoiled nature. Just be sure the weather is settled if you plan to visit.

Crossing from Baja, the island is often difficult to spot because of morning fog or afternoon haze. The island is several miles off its charted position as printed in the US Pilot. Huge flocks of sea birds constantly circling the island can be seen from a distance and are a good indication of its location.

A small, flat, rocky islet lies off the northwest end of the island. On the east side there is a large, whitish rock resembling a gigantic turtle, which separates into two large guano-covered stacks as you approach. Watch for unlit bait traps about 30' in diameter showing about 3' above water northwest of Islotes Las Monas. Roughly ¼ to 1 mile east of the islets are four large yellow buoys marking aquaculture activities. These should be passed either to the east or to the west of the buoys. A shoal lies between the stacks and a beach on the island shore. Anchorage may be taken on the south side of this shoal in 10 feet, sheltered by the island and the stacks. This is generally a more secure anchorage. **WPT 21° 50.9', 105° 52.72'.**

A second anchorage area is in the southern cove where the sea breaks along the ledges and in the caves with a booming roar. Enter along the centerline, aiming toward the highest cliff opposite the entrance. **WPT 21° 50.4', 105° 53'.** Identify the oily slick covering a submerged rock **(21° 50.559', 105° 52.965')** located in the northeast part of the cove, to be sure that your vessel will clear it while swinging at anchor. The bottom is a mixture of sand and rocks with some pinnacles on which the anchor chain grinds and rattles. These obstacles, combined with abandoned ground tackle, can foul your anchor and therein lies the reason that this spectacular anchorage is not the most secure. Dinghy landing may be made in the small western inner cove where pangas are often moored. Local fisherman often trade or sell fish. The large building houses the Warden and various facilities for the study of the numerous birds on the island. **CAUTION:** If strong winds from the south develop, making this a dangerous lee shore you should depart immediately.

An anchorage in 10 to 15 feet, suitable in southerly winds is off the steep cliffs midway along the western coast of the island. Though the rattle of the chain on underwater rocks can be disturbing, sea caves along the shore provide a scenic view. **WPT 21° 50.85', 105° 53.24'.**

Numerous frigate birds nest in the trees surrounding the small lake while blue and yellow-footed boobies nest on the cliff tops and terns and gulls live in the crevices of the cliffs. If you hike up the hill, take care not to scare nestlings away from their nests or disturb the nests. The rich variety of birds and marine animals and the truly wild nature of this unique island are worth seeing in spite of the anchoring challenges experienced by some cruisers.

Photo: Phoebe Wilson

ISLA ISABELA
Nayarit

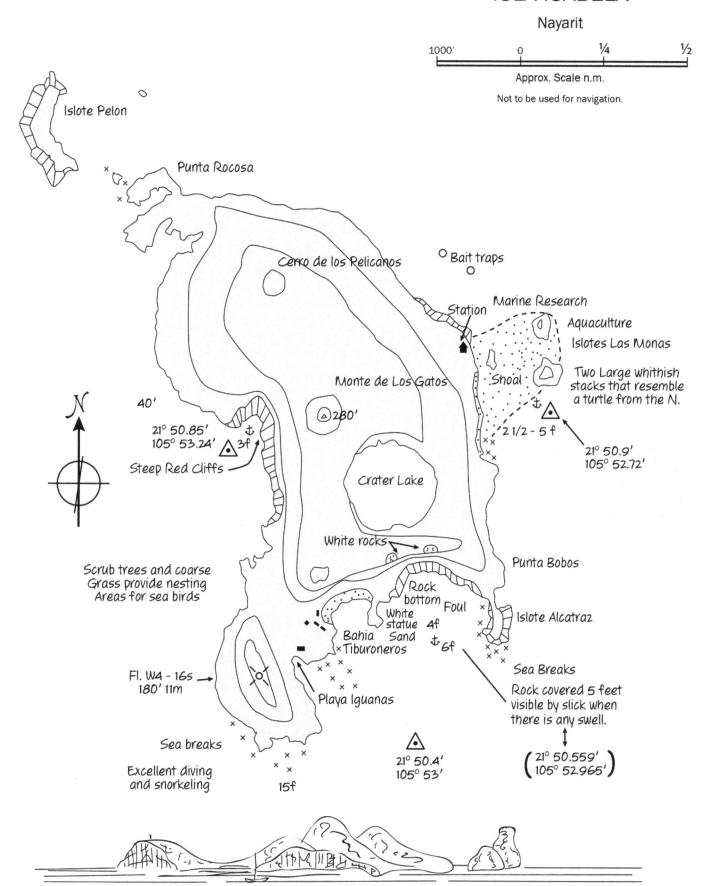

1000'   0   ¼   ½

Approx. Scale n.m.

Not to be used for navigation.

Islote Pelon

Punta Rocosa

Cerro de los Pelicanos

Bait traps

Marine Research

Station

Aquaculture

Islotes Las Monas

Shoal

Two Large whithish stacks that resemble a turtle from the N.

Monte de Los Gatos

40'

△280'

21° 50.85'
105° 53.24'   ⚓ △⦿ 3f

Steep Red Cliffs

⚓ △⦿
2 1/2 - 5 f

21° 50.9'
105° 52.72'

Crater Lake

White rocks

Punta Bobos

Scrub trees and coarse Grass provide nesting Areas for sea birds

Rock bottom   Foul

White statue   4f

Bahia Tiburoneros   Sand   ⚓ 6f

Islote Alcatraz

Sea Breaks

Rock covered 5 feet visible by slick when there is any swell.

Fl. W4 - 16s
180' 11m →

Playa Iguanas

Sea breaks

Excellent diving and snorkeling

15f

△⦿
21° 50.4'
105° 53'

(21° 50.559'
105° 52.965')

ISLA ISABELA FROM SSE. DISTANT ABOUT ONE MILE

SAN BLAS AND MANTANCHEN BAY

Once a major center of Spanish domination of the west coast of the Americas, it was here that Spaniards built the vessels used for exploring the western coast of North America. The overgrown ruins of a large fort, Customs House and cathedral attest to its colorful and historic past. In 1882 Longfellow wrote his last poem, The Bells of San Blas. In October 2002, devastating winds of Hurricane Kenna severely damaged many houses in the town, shredding the palms and toppling countless beautiful old trees that had graced these ancient streets.

The entrance to **San Blas** is protected by two the breakwaters, the western one being the longer of the two. An entry range leads between them and lighted buoys give an indication of a channel leading to the inner harbor. **WPT 21°31.3', 105°17.3'.** Since shoaling in the channel is a constant problem it is advisable to call the marina on VHF 16 or 74 to obtain current information before approaching the entrance. When strong summer southerly winds blow, the bar can be very dangerous as steep, breaking seas sweep across the entrance. A jungle trip by dinghy can be taken for almost 7 miles up the estuary where you may see jaguar, coati, wild boar, Mexican ocelots and a great variety of birds.

Marina San Blas, A Fonatur marina offers 18 slips with 30 Amp power and water, showers, laundry, and Wifi. Contact them on VHF 16 or 74 for slip assignment or the manager at mporras@ fonatur.gob.mx, Phone (323) 285-0033 or (323) 285-0022 The marina site is about three blocks from the plaza and market where excellent and reasonably priced quality fresh produce and groceries are sold.

San Blas is a **Port of Entry** and Mantanchen Bay is under the jurisdiction of the San Blas Port Captain. Normal reporting upon entrance and departure is required. This large bay is quite shallow, with a gradually sloping bottom and it is an excellent anchorage. To avoid the no-see-ums that infest the beach at nightfall, anchor about a mile from shore in 2 - 3 fathoms, sand. Landing on the beach is usually through gentle surf, easier on the northern and western shores, near the numerous palapa food stands that line the waterfront. A short distance north of Punta Camarones at the west end of Mantanchen Bay is "Mantanchen Restaurant." The operator speaks English and is a good source of local information and he can make arrangements for cruisers' tenders to be looked after. Taxi service into town is very reasonable. A visit to the plaza in the center of town in the evening provides a chance to buy beautiful local handicrafts such as weaving, wooden bowls and jewelry. The icehouse uses purified water for the production of ice.

Beautiful spined Venus and small, colorful donax shells can sometimes be found on the beach in January and February. Vendors on the beach sell highly sweetened coconut baked goods. A one-mile walk leads to the main road and the intersection for departure on the "lagoon jungle trip" to San Christoval Creek. This enjoyable day trip includes lunch at the crystal-clear waters in the famous swimming hole at Tovara Springs.

The desperately poor villages of the Huichol Indians are a considerable distance inland. They create beautiful bead art usually in the form of animals that is sold locally and at enhanced prices in tourist destinations. If you have space available to bring used children's clothing to San Blas for these people, it is greatly appreciated.

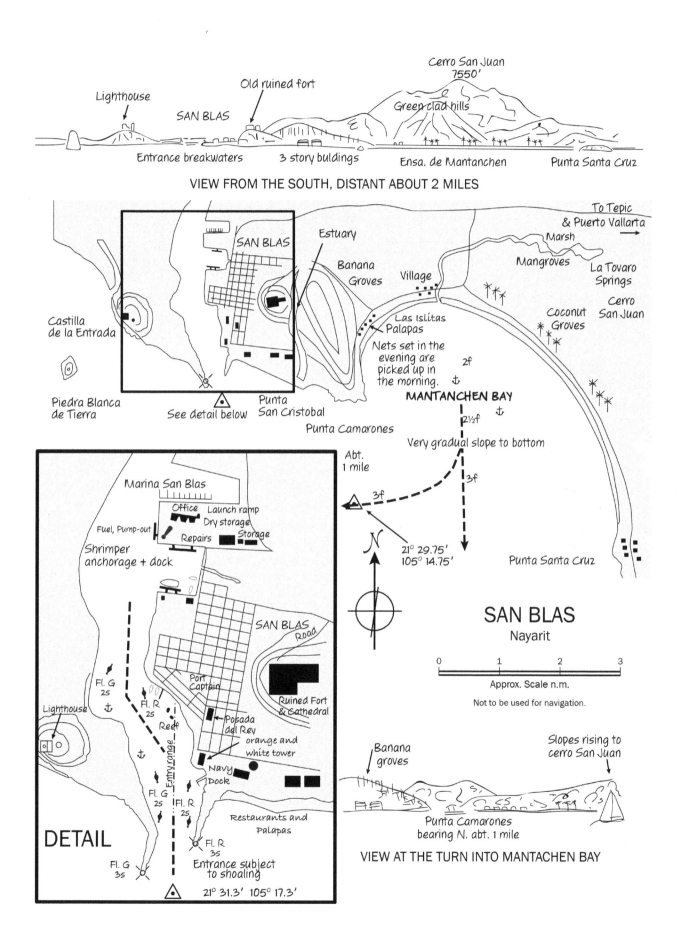

VIEW FROM THE SOUTH, DISTANT ABOUT 2 MILES

SAN BLAS
Nayarit

DETAIL

VIEW AT THE TURN INTO MANTACHEN BAY

CHACALA

The route southward from Mantanchen Bay passes the low, projecting point of Punta Las Custodis, then past a long, white sandy beach. At the end of the beach is a rocky, treed bluff behind which is the small cove of **Chacala**. The rocky bluff has a tall aluminum radio tower visible beyond the palms. A small buoy south of the point also marks this cove about 20 miles south of San Blas. **WPT 21°9.7', 105°13.95'**

Photo: Betsy Crowfoot

Anchorage may be taken in the lee of the point. This is generally a very comfortable anchorage and the swell that affects the cove is typically little more than a "pleasant massage." The use of a stern anchor reduces rolling. Though there is more activity here than in the past it remains a relatively quiet spot away from the hustle and bustle of larger population centers.

A small stone pier at the head of the cove provides a convenient dinghy landing. There is no room at this pier for vessels larger than dinghies or pangas. A small building above the pier is marked "Capitania de Puerto" and cruisers are expected to report to have papers stamped. An official is usually present from 8 a.m. to 3 p.m. capchacala@sct.gob.mx

This cove has a beautiful little beach, where palapa restaurants line the shore in front of towering coconut palms. The area was devastated in 2002 by a hurricane but has been rebuilt to the point where the damage is no longer evident. This has been a popular "eco-resort" for many years. In recent years cruisers have been helpful with the Homes for Humanity project at Chacala. For information on current project assistance needed, ask on a local HAM net. A rough, cobblestone road leads to the coastal highway a short distance inland where extensive mango plantations abound.

Photo: Betsy Crowfoot

A number of small markets that sell basic grocery items and a tortilleria are located one street beyond the beach, about half way up the hill. Numerous RVs stay in the trailer and camping park under the coconut palms along the southern part of the beach during the winter when vendors come daily to supply water, beer, tortillas, baked good and produce. Vendors of coconuts deftly open them on the spot and the coconut milk always seems cool and refreshing. A medical clinic is at the south end of the beach. There is a sports bar where US football games can be watched. A bed and breakfast home on the beach has a book exchange and garbage service for cruisers. Spanish classes are available at the school.

A colectivo (taxi) can be taken to Las Varas, the nearest village several miles distant, where regular bus service is available to Tepic and Puerto Vallarta. Las Varas has a large variety of stores and markets, including hardware stores. About 8 miles south of Chacala is the anchorage at Jaltemba where there is access to a large, busy town with many restaurants, shops and tourist services.

CHACALA
Nayarit

0   ½   1

Approx. Scale n.m.

Not to be used for navigation.

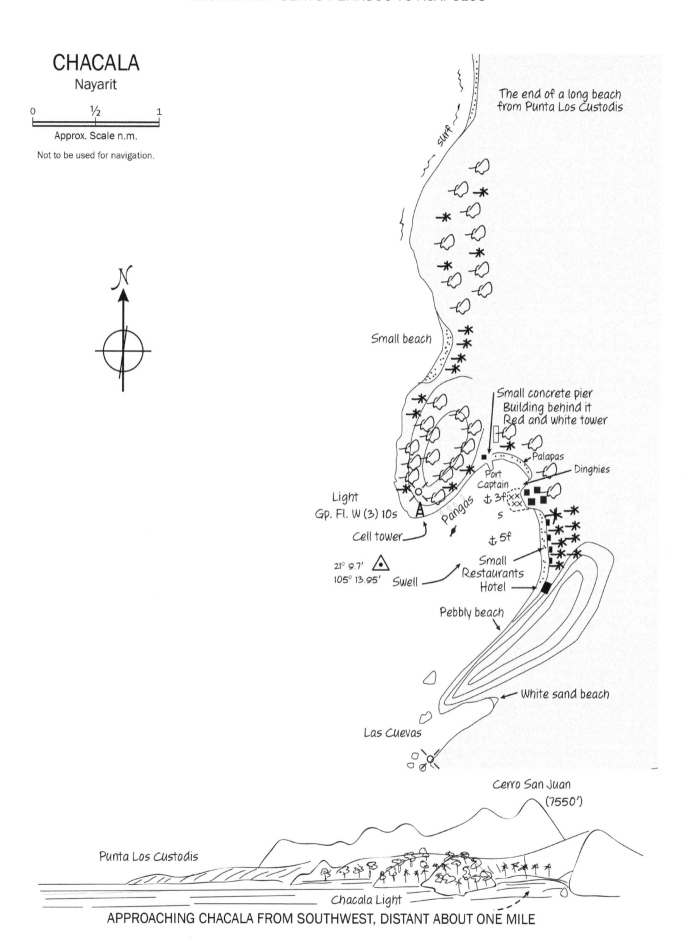

The end of a long beach
from Punta Los Custodis

Surf

N

Small beach

Small concrete pier
Building behind it
Red and white tower

Palapas

Dinghies

Port
Captain
‡ 3f

s

‡ 5f

Light
Gp. Fl. W (3) 10s

Pangas

Cell tower

21° 9.7'
105° 13.95'

Swell

Small
Restaurants
Hotel

Pebbly beach

White sand beach

Las Cuevas

Cerro San Juan
(7550')

Punta Los Custodis

Chacala Light

APPROACHING CHACALA FROM SOUTHWEST, DISTANT ABOUT ONE MILE

*JALTEMBA (La Penita de) & GUAYABITOS (Rincon de)

This usually rolly anchorage is about 8 miles south of Chacala and 25 miles north of Punta de Mita at the entrance to Banderas Bay. Cerro Compostela is a prominent peak 4,262' about 13 miles ENE of Punta Raza that is about 30' high. A lofty range of mountains lies to the southeast, the highest peak being Cerro Vallejo, rising to an elevation of 5,036'. Two islands, one much larger than the other, protect the southern section of a long beach that is interrupted by La Puntilla, a small projection, which creates two niches. At the western end of the beach a rocky section culminates in Punta Raza, a reddish bluff.

Rolly anchorage may be taken in the coves in the southern curve of the bay using both bow and stern anchors, or in the lee of the larger island. Anchorage off the large island should be taken off the panga landing for restaurant patrons. As long as weather and swell from the northwest do not make this anchorage uncomfortable, it is a beautiful but noisy spot, especially on weekends. In settled weather anchorage may be taken part way between the island and the southern part of the bay in 20 to 25 feet, using a bow and stern anchor. During strong northerly winds better protection is found to the south at Punta de Mita.

The gentle surf makes for easy dinghy landing ashore especially in the southwestern corner where the refracted surf is the weakest and the beach is lined with pangas. Good snorkeling can be enjoyed around the offshore islands of El Coral and El Cangrejo.

Rincon de (nook of) **Guayabitos** is a busy Mexican tourist town, with over 70 hotels, in addition to many restaurants, shops, bicycle rental and souvenir shops. There is no dinghy dock but some protection is available at the south end of the beach where tenders may be brought ashore. For information or to arrange a ride call Alterto De Acapulco on VHF Ch 69.

Regular bus service to Tepic or Puerto Vallarta is available, although you have to leave early in the morning in order to accomplish the trip in one day. The winding road through lush greenery may seem tedious to some but a visit to Tepic enables you to visit a small Mexican city which is unaffected by tourism and shows a more realistic glimpse of Mexican life than is seen in tourist-oriented centers. Though only a few of the shopkeepers speak English, a visit on market day is fascinating and often highlighted by seeing some of the isolated Indian hill tribes dressed in their traditional colorful costumes.

*The full name translates to, "The little reef of Jaltemba." The reef is awash at low tide and is located about two miles northeast of Isla El Coral and approximately ¼ mile offshore.

JALTEMBA
Nayarit

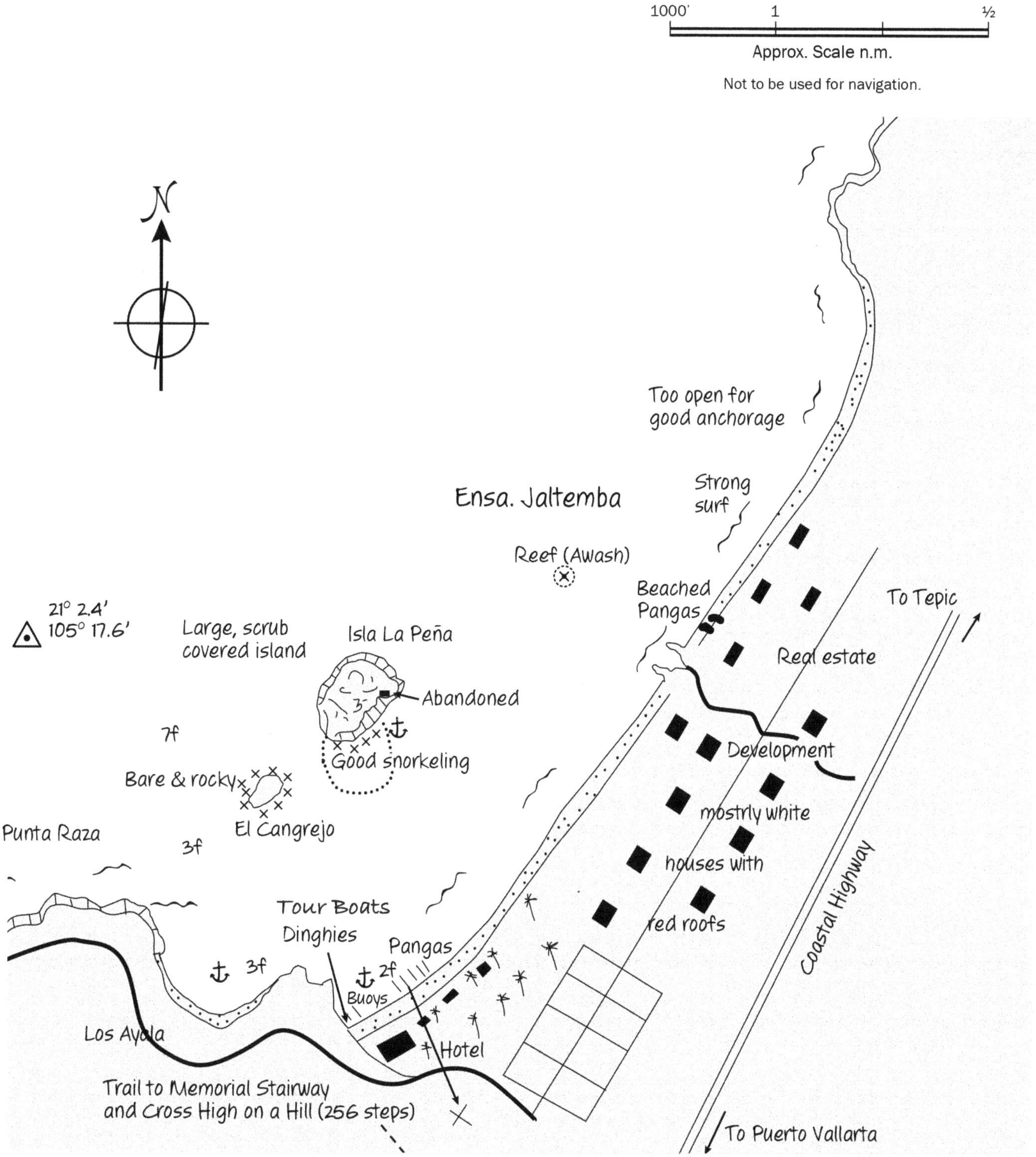

1000'　　　1　　　　　　　½

Approx. Scale n.m.

Not to be used for navigation.

N

Too open for
good anchorage

Ensa. Jaltemba

Strong
surf

Reef (Awash)
⊗

Beached
Pangas

21° 2.4'
△ 105° 17.6'

Large, scrub
covered island

Isla La Peña

To Tepic

Real estate

Abandoned
⚓

3'

7f

Good snorkeling

Development

Bare & rocky

mostly white

El Cangrejo

3f

houses with

Punta Raza

red roofs

Coastal Highway

Tour Boats
Dinghies

Pangas

⚓ 3f

⚓ 2f

Buoys

Los Ayala

† Hotel

Trail to Memorial Stairway
and Cross High on a Hill (256 steps)

✗

To Puerto Vallarta

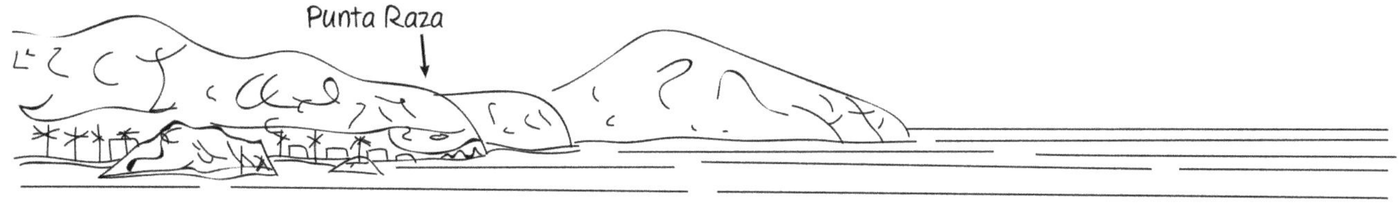

Punta Raza

LOOKING SOUTH FROM OFF ENSENADA JALTEMBA

PUNTA DE MITA (AKA PUNTA MITA)

Punta de Mita marks the northern end of **Bahia de Banderas** and also provides shelter and anchorage on the outside northern edge of the bay. Nearby lie the islands, Las Tres Marietas (The Three Small Marias). The largest in this group is a flat-topped island about located about 4½ miles south-southwest of Punta de Mita, rising to 180'. A lighthouse is located on Roca Corbetena, a steep, whitish islet that lies seaward, about 17 miles west-southwest of Punta de Mita. A dangerous rock awash is about ½ mile west of Roca Corbetena. Currents can be strong in this area so it is wise to give it a wide berth.

On the western side of the peninsula at Punta de Mita are several small islets close to the shore, with a beach and huts behind. (The largest islet is part of the exclusive Four Seasons golf course and is the site of a 196-yard par 3 Hole (#3). When the tide is in #3A is played from its location on shore.) Buoys west of the peninsula should be passed on their seaward side. Breakers some distance off the end of the point reveal the extensive reefs and shoals.

When entering Bahia de Banderas from the north, swing wide of Punta de Mita, **WPT 20°44.6', 105°32'** to avoid a rocky patch located about ½ to ¾ mile west-southwest of the point; it is sometimes demarked by breaking seas. Another rock has been reported about 2½ miles SSW of the point; despite numerous attempts by local boaters, verifiable GPS waypoints have not been determined for these illusive rocks (approximate location **20°44', 105°34'**.

After rounding the point and entering the bay, the sweep of land east of the point and shoals offers shelter from northerly winds and seas, and a good anchorage in its lee. Anchor off the northern part of the beach in sand in about 25 feet with good holding. As the wind blows over the low point of land a vessel tends to ride reasonably comfortably even in a stern-to the swell condition if refracted around the point. There are a number of excellent restaurants and small tiendas ashore in Punta de Mita.

If going ashore in a dinghy, be advised the surf can be fairly strong (excellent surfing and stand up paddle boarding spot) on the beaches adjacent the anchorage. Just south of the village a regular series of cresting lines marks a shoal; landing slightly to the west of this shoal is about the best location. This entails running the surf crests over the shoal, but this area is less perilous than elsewhere along the remainder of the beachfront area. Careful timing is needed to make a dry landing. Several breakwaters provide areas for dry dinghy landings, however most westerly breakwaters provide the driest landing. A green flashing light marks the breakwater for a panga basin east of the point; cruisers' dinghies are NOT welcome in this basin. Local transportation is available to take you to La Cruz and Bucerias.

The Four Seasons Resort with an 18-hole Jack Nicklaus golf course occupies the flat crown of the peninsula. Hotel facilities are for the exclusive use of hotel patrons and cruisers are NOT welcome. Within easy walking distance of the shore establishments is the highway to Puerto Vallarta/Sayulita; autobuses are readily available for expedient and inexpensive transport to La Cruz, Bucerias, and Puerto Vallarta. Taxicabs are also readily available ashore if preferred.

PUNTA DE MITA
Nayarit

Approx. Scale n.m.

Not to be used for navigation.

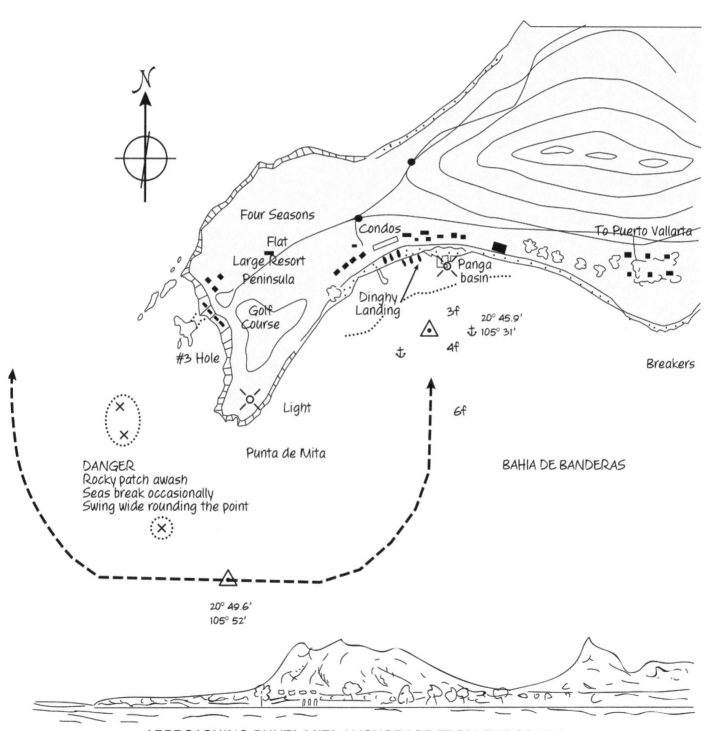

N

Four Seasons

Flat

Large Resort
Peninsula

Condos

To Puerto Vallarta

Golf
Course

Dinghy
Landing

Panga
basin

3f

20° 45.9'
⚓ 105° 31'

#3 Hole

4f

⚓

6f

Light

Breakers

Punta de Mita

BAHIA DE BANDERAS

DANGER
Rocky patch awash
Seas break occasionally
Swing wide rounding the point

20° 49.6'
105° 52'

APPROACHING PUNTA MITA ANCHORAGE FROM THE SOUTH

BAHIA DE BANDERAS (BAY OF FLAGS)

NAVIGATION NOTE
When proceeding south of San Blas and beyond, mariners using GPS for navigation should take note that Latitude and Longitude readings vary from NIMA chart positions by up to 1½ miles. Frequent visual confirmation of your proximity to land and reefs are essential.

Bahia de Bandaras is the largest bay on the west coast of Mexico, indenting the coast more than 15 miles and having an opening to the Pacific Ocean over 25 miles wide. Low-lying Punta de Mita marks the northern entrance to the Bay while rocky and often, windy Cabo Corrientes boldly indicates the southern gateway to this highly developed tourist destination. Less than 5 miles SSW of Punta de Mita is a 5-mile chain of rocky, barren islands, Las Tres Marietas, which is a Bird Sanctuary and favorite spot for divers and snorkelers.

Two different weather and topographical characteristics converge near the eastern end of the bay. The northern shore consists of low, rolling, scrub and grass covered hills that reflect comparatively lower annual rainfall than the southern side of the bay. Numerous homes and condominiums are scattered between the small villages found along the gently sloping shores. The quiet anchorages at Punta de Mita (Anclote) and La Cruz provide good holding in a sand bottom at 20 to 30 feet. In stark contrast, the lush growth covering the steep-sided Sierra Madre Mountains on the southern shore of the bay reflect far greater annual rainfall and tropical jungle climatology. The anchorages along the souther coast are much deeper than along the north shore. The prevailing daytime winds in the Bay are northwesterly, typically reaching 15 – 18 knots in the mid-afternoon; night time winds and seas are typically calm and flat. The northwesterly winds typically produce seas that make anchorages along the southern coastline of the bay quite rolly and potentially unsafe due to very steep subsurface slopes. The tidal range in the Bay is about 6 feet, which creates considerable surge in several of the marinas located around the periphery of the Bay.

From November to April, calm to light winds are experienced in the morning while fresh, warm, 15-knot northwesterly winds conveniently pick up in the afternoon providing ideal sailing and racing conditions for sailors. Consequently it is a destination for sailboat races from Marina del Rey, Newport Beach, and Cabo San Lucas. Regattas held annually in January, March and April make this an active yachting locale.

From mid-May through October, the Bay region is very hot and humid, and receives significant rainfall. Meteorological records that reach back more than 150 years reflect that Bahia de Bandaras is relatively immune to eastern Pacific hurricanes. For that reason several of its marinas (Marina Nayarit in La Cruz de Huanacaxtle, and Paradise Village Marina to name several) were in 2012 declared by marine insurers as safe locations to leave vessels unattended during the summer hurricane season.

The state line that separates the Mexican states of Nayarit and Jalisco lies just north and along the river that flows into the Bay near the Puerto Vallarta airport. Jalisco state is in a different time zone than Nayarit state. However, because of tourism and its impact on the towns around the periphery and located nearby Bahia Banderas, the governments of the two states have established that the area will be on the same time zone throughout, which is nominally the same as the US Central Time Zone (-6GMT). On Monday through Saturday, a VHF Cruisers' net operates at 8 a.m. on VHF Ch 22; it encompasses the anchorages and marinas that are located around Bandaras Bay.

At certain times of the year, especially in early summer, the bay teems with marine life such as whales, large rays, schools of dolphins and poisonous sea snakes. The latter make you hesitant about swimming here, but they are usually seen in the deeper waters of the bay.

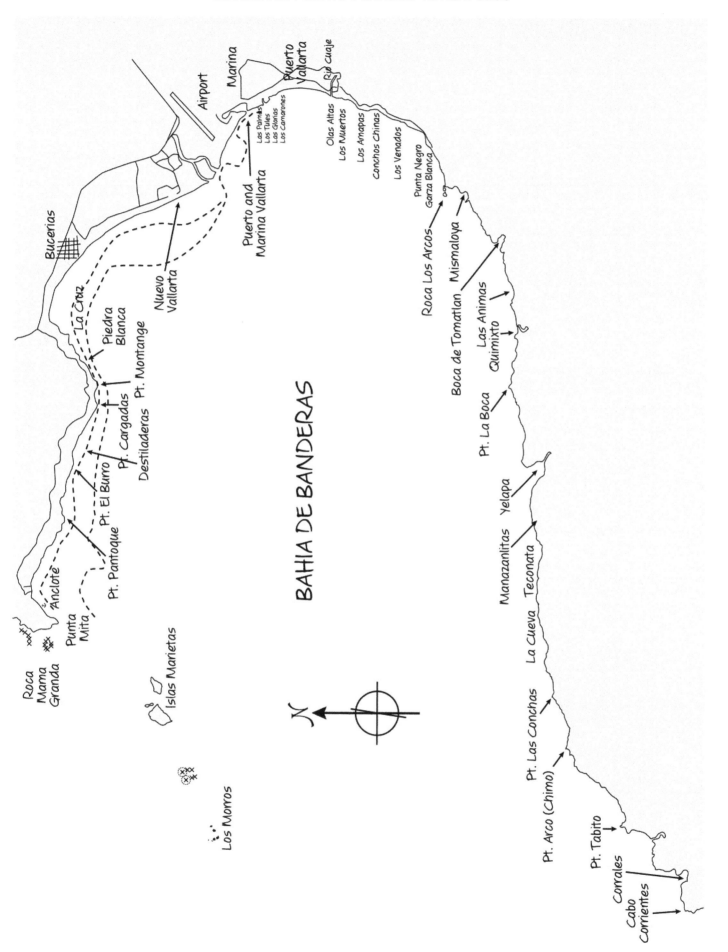

BAHIA DE BANDERAS

Airport

Marina

Puerto Vallarta

Rio cuaje

Las Palmas
Los Tules
Las Glorias
Los Camarones

Olas Altas
Los Muertos
Los Anapas
Conchos Chinas
Los Venados
Punta Negro
Garza Blanca

Puerto and Marina Vallarta

Roca Los Arcos
Mismaloya

Boca de Tomatlan
Las Animas
Quimixto

Pt. La Boca

Yelapa

Manazanlitas
Teconata

La Cueva

Pt. Las Conchas

Pt. Arco (Chimo)

Pt. Tabito

Corrales

Cabo Corrientes

Bucerias

Nuevo Vallarta

La Cruz

Piedra Blanca

Pt. Montange

Destiladeras

Pt. Cargadas

Pt. El Burro

Pt. Pantoque

Anclote

Punta Mita

Roca Mama Granda

Islas Marietas

Los Morros

N

LAS TRES MARIETAS

Long ignored by sailors intent on reaching Puerto Vallarta, the beauty of Las Tres Marietas (the Three Small Marias) is appreciated by cruisers who make Banderas Bay their cruising headquarters. A visit to this National Ecological Park is an enjoyable contrast to the man-made marinas and tourist-oriented businesses in Banderas Bay. The quietest time to visit this area is in the morning before afternoon winds make the anchorage choppy.

This string of small islands located about 4¼ miles south-southwest of Punta Mita forms the southern edge of the route followed when entering Bahia de Banderas from the north. The three islands and adjoining rocks and shoals cover an area of about 5 miles in length, in a curved chain draped in an ENE/WSW direction. Passage between the rocks lying off Punta Mita and Islas Tres Marietas should be made on a course half way toward the islands.

The easternmost and largest island of the group rises in a series of broken white cliffs which rise to a flat-topped summit about 180' high. A mile to the west across an impassable, foul gap is Isla Marieta that rises to 120' with gray, rocky protrusions on its southern side; this area is undercut by numerous coves. A light atop a red metal structure on the island is visible for approximately 14 miles. About 1½ miles to the west is Rocoso Reef on which waves break even on a relatively calm day. The third island of the group, Roca Blanca, lies 1½ miles west of Rocoso Reef and is about 45' high. Another small rock, almost 18' high, is west of Roca Blanca.

Gringos hitching a ride.

The approach to **Isla La Marieta** (the middle island) should be made ONLY from the south on a line from Puerto Vallarta, well clear of the easternmost island. Several moorings are available for day use and overnight, in settled weather. A permit is required and is available in Puerto Vallarta at the Port Captain's office.The variety of seabirds including Blue Footed Boobies, the profusion of fishes, manta ray, dolphins and caves make this a fabulous snorkeling area and a fascinating place to visit. Many tour boats visit with hundreds of passengers daily, so enjoy the islands early in the day.

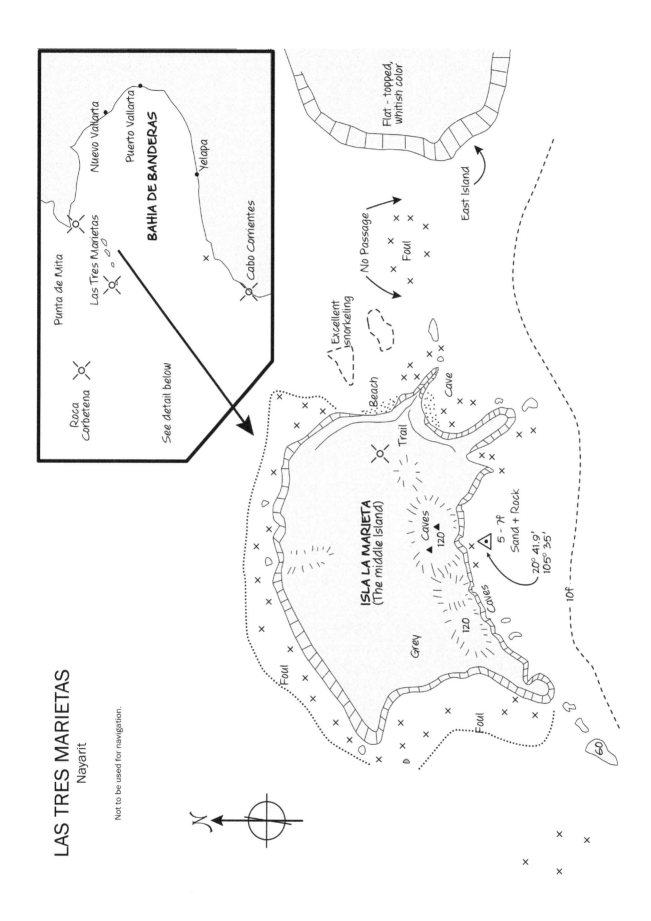

LAS TRES MARIETAS
Nayarit

Not to be used for navigation.

BAHIA DE BANDERAS

Nuevo Vallarta

Puerto Vallarta

Yelapa

Cabo Corrientes

Punta de Mita

Las Tres Marietas

Roca Corbetena

See detail below

Flat - topped, whitish color

East Island

No Passage

Foul

Excellent snorkeling

Beach

Cave

Trail

ISLA LA MARIETA
(The middle island)

Caves

120

120 Caves

Sand + Rock

5 - 7f

20° 41.9'
105° 35'

10f

Grey

Foul

Foul

60

LA CRUZ DE HUANACAXTLE (wanacoxlay)

This town, more simply and better known as La Cruz, is about 8 miles east of Punta de Mita. A forest of masts at **Marina Riviera Nayarit (AKA Marina La Cruz)** and a large cut in the Puerto Vallarta/Tepic coastal highway and are prominent landmarks that identify the approach to the town. This full service marina can accommodate 400 vessels from 30' to 400' with moorage charges that vary depending on the time of year and length of stay. The channel leading into the marina is very well marked with traditional buoys and green and red navigation lights at the ends of the breakwater entrance. **WPT 20°45', 105°22.3'**. It is reported that a rock near the marina entrance has been removed; some vessels have run aground when passing too close to the southern breakwater end, so stay in mid-channel when entering the facility. The marina office is on the second floor of the white two story structure that is on the southern side of the harbor. The office, which is open from 9am to 6pm Monday through Friday and from 9am to 2pm on Saturday and Sunday, will assign slips over the VHF Ch 16. The marina operates a fuel dock and pump out facility, which are on the docks on the north side of the marina. The marina also provides a dinghy dock that is in a secure area for cruisers who are anchored out in the La Cruz anchorage and wish to come ashore. The marina charges $20Mx (20 pesos) per day for use of the dinghy dock; anchoring out cruisers are welcome to dispose of trash. Arrangements can be made through the marina office for propane pickup and delivery. In the same building as the Marina Office is a bar and restaurant facility that is open seven days a week for breakfast, lunch and dinner, as well as a small convenience store that sells a very limited selection of beverages, some food, ice and bottled fresh water. For information call 011-52-329-295-5526 or email: info@marinarivieranayarit.com.

Associated with Marina Nayarit is a full service boat yard. The boat yard has a launch ramp and 150-ton Travelift. Several small fabricators and repair shops are housed in the boatyard facility, and there is a small marine chandlery immediately adjacent the boatyard. Immediately above the boatyard facility on the hillside is a full service sail maker that can repair sails and sells new and a limited selection of used sails. A laundry is located two blocks up the hill and one block east of the marina entrance in the town of La Cruz. La Cruz was, and remains a fishing village. Many pangueros (panga fishermen) operate daily from the harbor. They sell their fresh catch of many different varieties of local fish, shrimp, crabs and lobster in a complex of open air fish markets located along the north side of the harbor complex in front of the panga docks. The catch is fresh, abundant, very fairly priced, and they cater to all comers on a daily basis from early in the morning until the very early afternoon when they typically close for the day.

There is a Port Captain in La Cruz. Arriving and departing cruisers, whether staying in the marina or anchored out in the La Cruz anchorage, are required to check in and out – even if only transiting over to Nuevo Vallarta (where Paradise Village Marina and Marina Nuevo Vallarta are located, and which has its own Port Captain and office) with the Port Captain at his office. The office is located in the complex of two-story building immediately adjacent to the boat yard, and is open on weekdays from 9am to 2pm.

The bay/anchorage immediately to the east of the entrance to the harbor is free of dangers and provides comfortable and safe anchorage for vessels in about 20 to 30 feet, mud bottom. When afternoon winds build, typically to 16 to 20 knots from the northwest, the anchorage often becomes subject to short steep wind waves, which make for very wet shore trips. However, except on very rare occasions, these winds lay down in the late afternoon, and the anchorage again becomes very placid at night and throughout the early to mid-morning. An alternate anchorage in northwesterly weather lies to the east of Punta Montoga and west of the village just off a walled resort (clearly identified by its many archways); however, the shoreline is rocky and there are shoals that extend out from shore, so use care when selecting a spot to anchor when in this location.

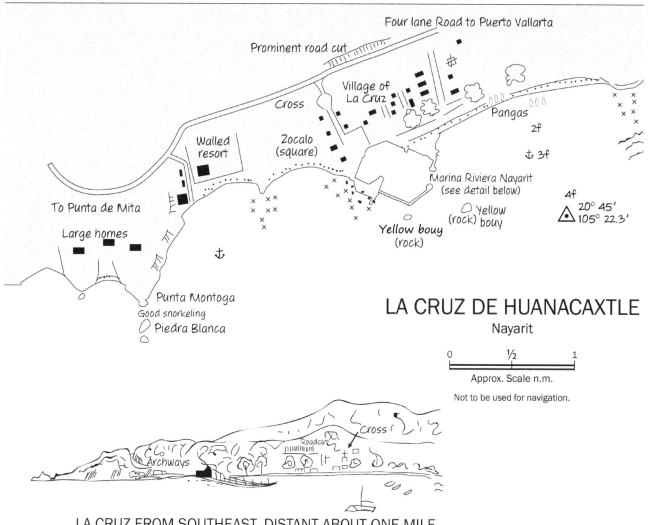

Four lane Road to Puerto Vallarta

Prominent road cut

Village of La Cruz

Cross

Walled resort

Zocalo (square)

Pangas

2f

⚓ 3f

Marina Riviera Nayarit (see detail below)

To Punta de Mita

Large homes

Yellow (rock) bouy

Yellow bouy (rock)

4f

△⊙ 20° 45'
105° 22.3'

⚓

Punta Montoga
Good snorkeling
Piedra Blanca

LA CRUZ DE HUANACAXTLE
Nayarit

0   ½   1

Approx. Scale n.m.

Not to be used for navigation.

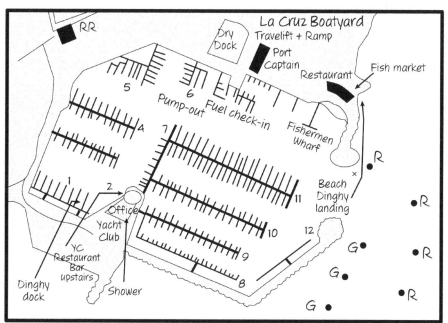

Cross

Roadcut

Archways

LA CRUZ FROM SOUTHEAST, DISTANT ABOUT ONE MILE

RR

La Cruz Boatyard
Travelift + Ramp

Dry Dock

Port Captain

Restaurant

Fish market

N

Pump-out

Fuel check-in

Fishermen Wharf

5

6

4

7

11

Beach Dinghy landing

R

2

Office

Yacht Club

10

12

R

YC Restaurant Bar upstairs

9

8

G

R

Dinghy dock

Shower

1

G

R

G

DETAIL: MARINA RIVIERA NAYARIT

La Cruz is a very safe, neighborly town with cobblestone streets that is delightful. It features a variety of excellent restaurants that range from sit down street taco vendors to full service restaurants. There are several small marine chandleries, a number of different mercados that sell staple goods, breads, beverages, fresh fruits and vegetables, several excellent carnecerias (fresh meat markets), and tortillerias. There is one ATM in the marina/La Cruz area, which is near to the Marina office building; however it only dispenses US dollars versus Mexican pesos. There is an ATM at the OXXO store approximately one mile east along the highway to Bucerias/Puerto Vallarta. From January through late April there is a robust Farmer's Market that operates on the north side of the harbor complex and breakwater; vendors sell everything from jewelry and other craft items made by local artists to fresh vegetables, tamales, and food.

La Cruz is also a music mecca. There is live music performed almost every night in La Cruz by world renowned as well as very talented up and coming local musicians. A popular spot for cruiser's get-togethers is Philo's where there is Wi-Fi, live music every night and pizzas right from the oven. The restaurant serves great meals. Many cruisers participate in local charity activities that are coordinated at Philo's. The Black Forest Restaurant has good food at reasonable prices and sometimes schedules intimate dinner time performances featuring well-known guitarists Latcho and Andrea. There are also several restaurants on the north side of the harbor complex just to the east of the fishermen's open air market.

The cruiser net is on VHF 22 at 8:30 am, Monday - Saturday. Propane can be filled by dropping tanks off 10:00 am Wed. at the marina. Weather advice is available from PV Sailing on VHF 68.

Bucerias is a short bus ride south of La Cruz. It is a quaint town once you walk toward the waterfront, with craft shops, taco stands, Banks, art galleries, nice restaurants and bars. The town square is busy in the evenings with vendors of all kinds. A visit to Buceras is a fun way to spend the day.

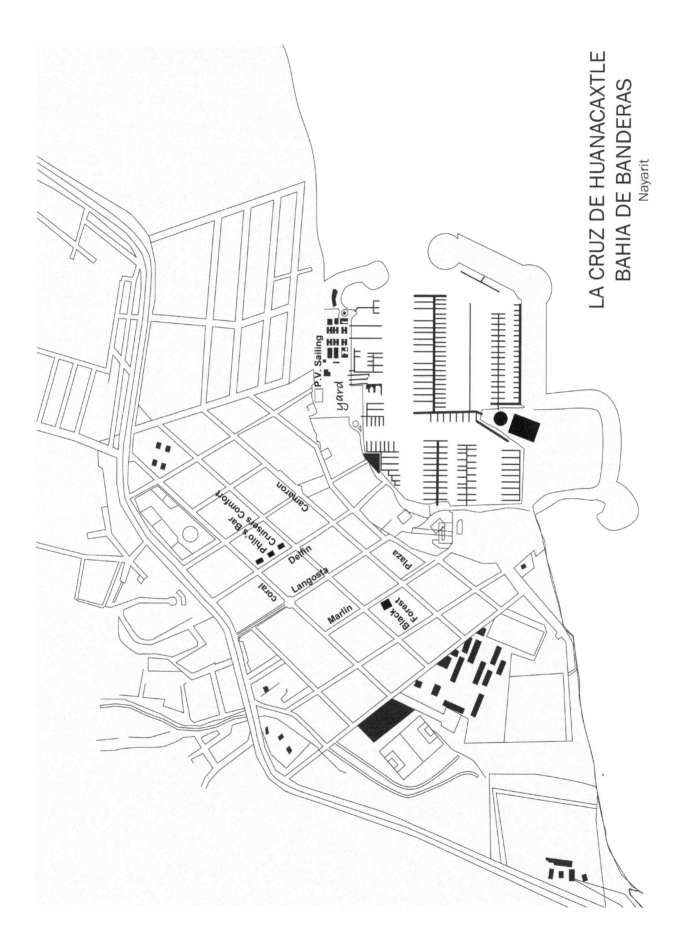

LA CRUZ DE HUANACAXTLE
BAHIA DE BANDERAS
Nayarit

P.V. Sailing

yard

Camaron

Philo's Bar
Cruiser's Comfort

Delfin

Coral

Langosta

Plaza

Marlin

Black
Forest

NUEVO VALLARTA

About 5 miles east of La Cruz de Huanacaxtle and east of the town of Bucerias, a series of large hotels and condominiums and developments line the coast. This marks the location of the tourist destination of Nuevo Vallarta that includes beach-front hotels, the luxury resort of Paradise Village Beach Resort and Spa with a golf course and a luxury marina on the west side of the entrance. The Port Captain's office, Marina Nuevo Vallarta and Marina Pueblo Nautico and are on the east side of the entrance. Do not confuse Nuevo Vallarta with Marina Vallarta, and the city harbor of Puerto Vallarta, 4 miles further along the bay toward the south.

Nuevo Vallarta is the southernmost harbor in the state of Nayarit, and is immediately north of the border between the states of Nayarit and Jalisco. The city of Puerto Vallarta is in Jalisco state. Entry to the harbor is between two breakwaters that have lights at their ends. The channel entrance is at **WPT 20°41.07', 105°17.9'**. (There aren't any breakwaters at Puerto Vallarta so their presence is a clear indication to first-time visitors that you are entering Nuevo Vallarta.) Depths in the entrance channel are a concern for cruisers though regular dredging is done to maintain a controlling depth of 12 to 15 feet at zero tide. Caution is advised during strong southerly winds when swells can break at the entrance. Before entering call Paradise Marina on Ch. 16 to check the depth of the entrance. As was described for La Cruz, it is necessary to check in and register with the Port Captain. His offices are in the white building adjacent the sea wall on the starboard side of the fairway as the harbor is entered.

Marina Nuevo Vallarta has been newly refurbished with modern concrete docks, and good physical security. Inquire locally to contact Radio Rob who offers wireless service for $30 per month. Tourists may swim with dolphins for about US$150 at a facility 100 yards north of Marina Nuevo Vallarta.

On the port side of the entrance is **Paradise Village Marina,** a first-class, efficient, full-service, luxury marina with over 200 slips that can handle vessels up to 240 ft. Additional moorage for low profile vessels capable of passing under the overpass in the northern part of the sketch is under construction. Power at dockside is 110, 220 and three-phase. Also available are a pumpout service, which comes to your boat, potable water, internet at the yacht club and propane drop off for refills. Because of its distance from a population center it is not only a pleasant place to stay but also a safe location to leave your boat when traveling elsewhere in Mexico. Since surge affects boats moored in the outer slips of the dock generous use of chafing gear is essential. For information email: marina@paradisevillage.com or phone/fax 011-52-322-66-728. The marina is ably managed by Dick Markie.

Nearby is a bank, large hospital, shopping center with liquor, groceries, deli, gift shops and boutiques. **Vilma's Yacht Services** is located upstairs at L-1 in Paradise Village Mall and at Av. Las Palmas #37 in Bucerias. She offers a wide range of services including vessel registration and renewal, importation of boat parts, immigration services, clearance papers, insurance, a book store and English, Spanish and German translation. For information call VHF Ch 22, Tel 52-322-297-2274, Fax 52-322-297-2289 or email vilmayachagency@yahoo.com

Regular bus service (less than $1) links the yacht basins to Puerto Vallarta. The bus into town stops near Wal-Mart and to get downtown take a bus marked "Centro" for an additional 4 pesos (about $.50). On the return trip take any bus labeled "Nuevo Vallarta" and it will stop at Paradise Resort before going around the basin to Nuevo Vallarta. Pharmacia Guadalajara is a huge franchise store at the intersection of the north entrance of Nuevo Vallarta and Hwy. 200 and less than 2 miles further north is a very large Commercial Mexicana store with a wide range of items for sale. The Vallarta Yacht Club is an attractive and homey facility open to all cruisers. It features a shower, washroom, meeting room and a restaurant serving good food in a casual atmosphere at reasonable prices.

NUEVO VALLARTA
Nayarit

0 ½ 1
Approx. Scale n.m.
Not to be used for navigation.

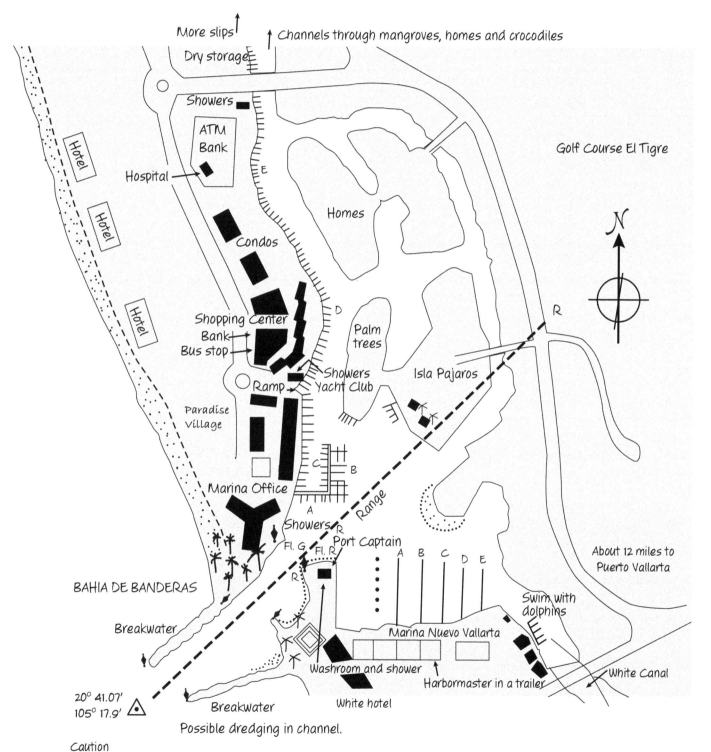

More slips
Channels through mangroves, homes and crocodiles
Dry storage
Showers
ATM Bank
Hospital
Hotel
Hotel
Hotel
Golf Course El Tigre
E
Homes
Condos
Shopping Center
Bank
Bus stop
D
Palm trees
Isla Pajaros
R
N
Showers Yacht Club
Ramp
Paradise Village
C
B
Marina Office
A
Range
Showers
R
Fl. G Fl. R
R
Port Captain
A B C D E
About 12 miles to Puerto Vallarta
BAHIA DE BANDERAS
Breakwater
Swim with dolphins
Washroom and shower
Marina Nuevo Vallarta
White Canal
20° 41.07'
105° 17.9'
Breakwater
White hotel
Harbormaster in a trailer
Possible dredging in channel.

Caution
Strong southwest winds can create a breaking sea across the channel entrance.

THE BLESSING of the FLEET arranged by Paradise Marina
December 12

251

PUERTO VALLARTA

Puerto Vallarta is a **Port of Entry** and the Port Captain's office is adjacent to the cruise ship terminal. If you are entering Mexico from a foreign port your paper work can be done by Vilma Habelloecker whose main office is in Nuevo Vallarta but who also works out of an office in Buceria and another between "I" and "J" dock in Marina Vallarta. She can be reached on VHF 16 or 22 or telephone 011-52-322-221-2752. In the Terminal Maritime is the office of Juan Pablo Arias who also processes papers and can be reached on VHF 16 – answering calls placed to "Paper Man" or telephone 52-322-224-3555. The Customs office is at the airport and Immigration is downtown.

Until Nuevo Vallarta was developed, this was the primary destination for cruising vessels. It can be a base for visiting nearby mainland anchorages, a safe harbor during hurricane season or for long-term moorage and is a convenient spot for replenishing food and supplies or making repairs before traveling on. It is convenient to the airport.

An entry range, **WPT 20°39', 105°15.7'** at the sea buoy, leads past two lit breakwaters where there is a dredged harbor with a large cruise ship terminal. On the south side of the channel leading to marina facilities is the Nautilus Club where a few boats Med-moor to the seawall. There are several sunk and wrecked boats along this sea wall. The channel passes between Isla Iguana (a condominium development with private docks) and Opequimar Marina which has a fuel dock, 85-ton Travelift, mechanical and refrigeration repair facilities, dry storage, stainless steel welding, machinists and a marine supply shop. Just outside the yard gates is an OXXO convenience store and an ATM. A large marine supply store, Ferreteria Zaragoza, is located on the main road into town. They have just about everything you could want and will ship parts to other places in Mexico. They are open 7 days a week from 8:30 till 2:00, except weekends, 8:30 till 7:00.

Hotels and condominiums line the inner basin occupied by **Marina Vallarta**. The marina has 354 slips with all services available. A major renovation is underway. When approaching the harbor call the Harbormaster on VHF Ch 18 for slip assignment. Contacts: 011-52 (322) 221-0275. Pump-out services are carried out by means of portable facilities. Marina Vallarta is a convenient mail drop and correspondence addressed to Marina Vallarta, Apdo Postal 350B, Puerto Vallarta, Jalisco, Mexico. VHF 22 is the hailing channel for this part of the coast as well as the frequency for the 0830 net. Reservations may be made at marina-vallarta.com.mx at least 2 to 3 days in advance. They do fill up in the high season so plan ahead.

Restaurants (some with Wi-Fi), bars, two laundries, an electrical/electronic company, Dive shop, Starbucks, a market, and numerous other services and shops are on the promenade around the marina. Home Depot operates a store north of the airport on Hwy. 200. A Commercial Supermarket is a short distance to the northwest. Sam's Club, Rizzo's and Gigante offer some differences in brands sold and are worth visiting when provisioning. They are located in the hotel part of town, a short bus ride from the marina. Propane (gaz) is available at a facility beyond the airport. For those who plan a long-term stay in the city it is advisable to pick up a copy of Vallarta Nautica, an excellent resource guide for cruisers that has a complete list of local services and contact information.

A popular cruiser's meeting place is Club La Evasion where Dave provides catering, provisioning, boat cleaning services as well as weekly propane pickup and delivery. North Sails, Great American Canvas and Canvas Connections offer sail repair services. Right in front of the latter is Victor's, a popular eatery that serves good food at reasonable prices.

Interactive map of Puerto Vallarta

PUERTO VALLARTA
Jalisco

1000' 0 ½ 1

Approx. Scale n.m.

Not to be used for navigation.

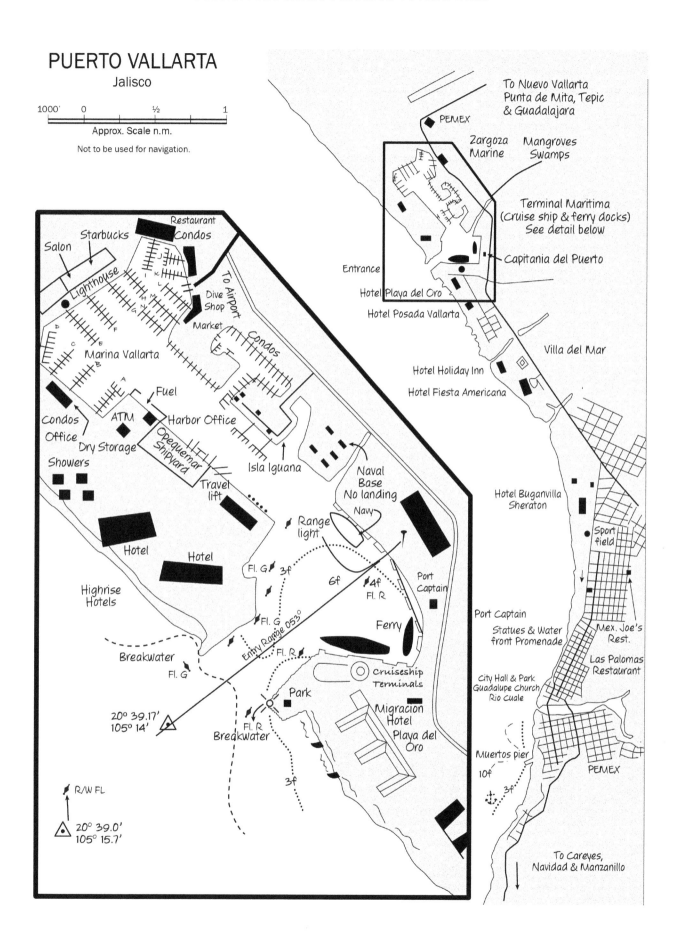

To Nuevo Vallarta
Punta de Mita, Tepic
& Guadalajara

PEMEX

Zargoza
Marine

Mangroves
Swamps

Terminal Maritima
(Cruise ship & ferry docks)
See detail below

Capitania del Puerto

Entrance

Hotel Playa del Oro

Hotel Posada Vallarta

Villa del Mar

Hotel Holiday Inn

Hotel Fiesta Americana

Hotel Buganvilla
Sheraton

Sport
field

Port Captain

Statues & Water
front Promenade

Mex. Joe's
Rest.

Las Palomas
Restaurant

City Hall & Park
Guadalupe Church
Rio Cuale

Muertos pier

10f

PEMEX

3f

To Careyes,
Navidad & Manzanillo

Restaurant
Condos

Starbucks

Salon

Lighthouse

Dive
Shop

To Airport

Market

Condos

Marina Vallarta

Fuel

Condos
Office

ATM

Harbor Office

Dry Storage

Opequemar
Shipyard

Showers

Isla Iguana

Travel
lift

Naval
Base
No landing

Navy

Range
light

Hotel

Hotel

Fl. G 3f

6f

4f

Fl. R

Port
Captain

Highrise
Hotels

Fl. G Entry Range 053°

Fl. R

Ferry

Cruiseship
Terminals

Breakwater

Fl. G

Park

Fl. R

20° 39.17'
105° 14'

Migracion
Hotel
Playa del
Oro

Breakwater

3f

R/W FL

20° 39.0'
105° 15.7'

253

PUERTO VALLARTA TO MANZANILLO

Known as the Gold Coast this section of the mainland has some of the most beautiful and varied anchorages found in Mexico. To leave Bahia de Banderas southbound vessels must pass Cabo Corrientes (Currents) at the southwest end of the bay. It is a steep, rocky headland about 500' high, with the Sierra Madre Mountains behind it rising to an elevation of 2,000'. This cape acts much the same as Cabo Falso in Baja and Point Conception in California. Since Cabo Corrientes projects into the prevailing winds, local winds are accelerated often causing turbulent, disturbed seas accompanied by strong currents.

Passing the Cape in either direction is normally easiest in the morning, becoming more difficult as the day progresses when wind and seas pick up. The passage is easier for southbound vessels traveling with the wind and current. The currents are strong and variable near the Cape, being greatly affected by the wind and built up seas.

Cabo Corrientes also marks the beginning of truly tropical conditions. The weather north of the Cape is generally similar to that in the Gulf of California, whereas south of the Cape it is hotter, with a more pronounced rainy season.

With the high coastal ranges near the coast, much of the rainfall during the wet season (May to November) occurs during afternoon thunderstorms. The amount of rainfall increases as you proceed further south, as is reflected by the greener, more luxuriant vegetation than is seen in northern areas.

The prevailing wind continues to be northwesterly, but because the land also trends in the same direction and combined with the warmer conditions, land and sea breezes become more characteristic. Sea breezes built up during the day from the southwest can be strong. Land breezes at night are less regular in direction and force.

On this coast, Punta Ipala provides a close and convenient terminal for the trip past Cabo Corrientes, followed by a long section of coast without any anchorages until Bahia Chamela. Thereafter, a series of inviting anchorages follow each other closely. They are all attractive and each has its own special charm. Manzanillo, at the end of this section of the mainland, is a commercial port, though there are good anchorages in nearby bays and anchorage as well as dockside moorage is available at Las Hadas.

Photo: Robin Stout

There is a very active sea turtle conservation organization in Nuevo Vallarta called AMA Mexico. Visit their web site to find out how you can volunteer and learn more about the sea turtles of Mexico. www.amamexico.org

 Sea Turtle conservation.

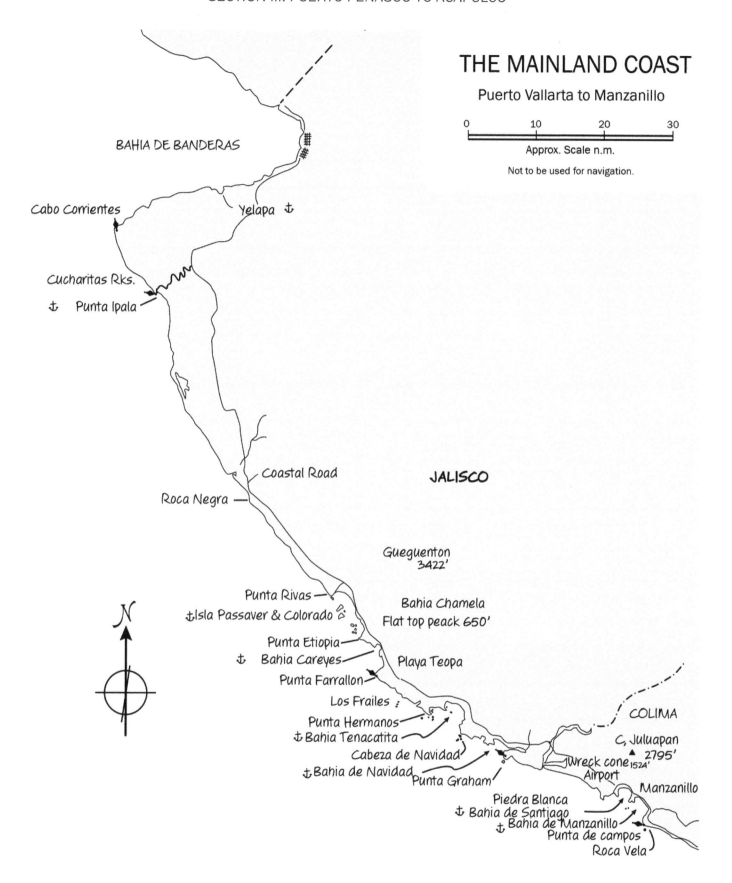

THE MAINLAND COAST

Puerto Vallarta to Manzanillo

0	10	20	30

Approx. Scale n.m.

Not to be used for navigation.

BAHIA DE BANDERAS

Cabo Corrientes

Yelapa

Cucharitas Rks.

Punta Ipala

Coastal Road

JALISCO

Roca Negra —

Gueguenton
3422'

Bahia Chamela
Flat top peack 650'

Punta Rivas —
Isla Passaver & Colorado

Punta Etiopia
Bahia Careyes

Playa Teopa

Punta Farrallon

Los Frailes

COLIMA

Punta Hermanos
Bahia Tenacatita

C, Juluapan
2795'

Cabeza de Navidad

Wreck cone 1524'
Airport

Bahia de Navidad

Punta Graham

Manzanillo

Piedra Blanca
Bahia de Santiago
Bahia de Manzanillo
Punta de campos
Roca Vela

YELAPA

The south side of Bahia de Banderas offers less in the way of anchorages, but the few available are spectacular, if not very secure.

Mismaloya is a few miles southwest of Puerto Vallarta, next to Los Arcos, a trio of rocks, the largest being about 290' high. **WPT 20°29.15', 105°21.73'** Anchorage in the bay is not suitable for an overnight stay but is acceptable for a scenic day trip. The movie "Night of the Iguana" was filmed here.

Boca de Tomatlan is a possible anchorage in calm conditions. **WPT 20°31.69', 105°20.25'** is 1/4 mile off the beach.

Quimixto is a small bay about 5 miles further along the coast past Boca de Tomatlan. This small cove has a white beach with an open anchorage suitable only during calm weather. There is a restaurant ashore. Be sure to see the waterfalls! There may be horse back riding.

For most cruising sailors the cove at **Yelapa, WPT 20°29.9', 105°27.13'** is the most popular and scenic choice for anchorage. It is about 15 miles southwest of Puerto Vallarta and makes a convenient point to begin or end the run around Cabo Corrientes. However, it can be a less than satisfactory anchorage.

The cove is deep, but has two 10-fathom shelves on each side where vessels can anchor. One spot lies off the thatched and bougainvillea-covered hotel at the northern end of the curving sandy beach. You can land a tender at the small rock jetty on the rocky outcrop beyond, where tourists are brought ashore from charter vessels sailing out of Puerto Vallarta. A narrow bridge leads from the pier to the hotel. The other anchorage is across the cove off the village. Landing is through the surf but it may be done in drier fashion by hiring a Mexican panga to take you ashore for a nominal fee.

In both anchorages make sure your anchors are well set, setting bow and stern anchors, both for safety and to reduce swinging in the limited space. The beaches are close and since the cove faces northward it is open to the prevailing wind and swell. With any storm or heavy seas running the anchorage can be dangerous because the swell comes directly into the cove. During a thunderstorm we saw every vessel in the anchorage drag their anchors and one drifted seaward before being retrieved after an interesting chase. So set your tackle with care and leave someone aboard for emergencies, especially during unsettled weather.

Yelapa has become a major destination for tourists from Puerto Vallarta. There are multiple palapas along the beach serving drinks and snacks. A walkway leads through the village to the foot of a waterfall. Few large rosewood and mahogany trees remain in the surrounding forests; long ago canoes and pangas made from these trees were among the best on the coast.

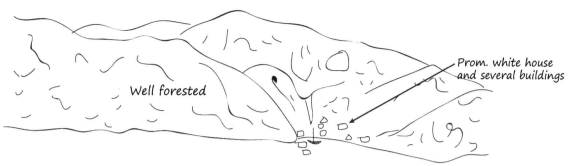

APPROACHING YELAPA FROM PUERTO VALLARTA

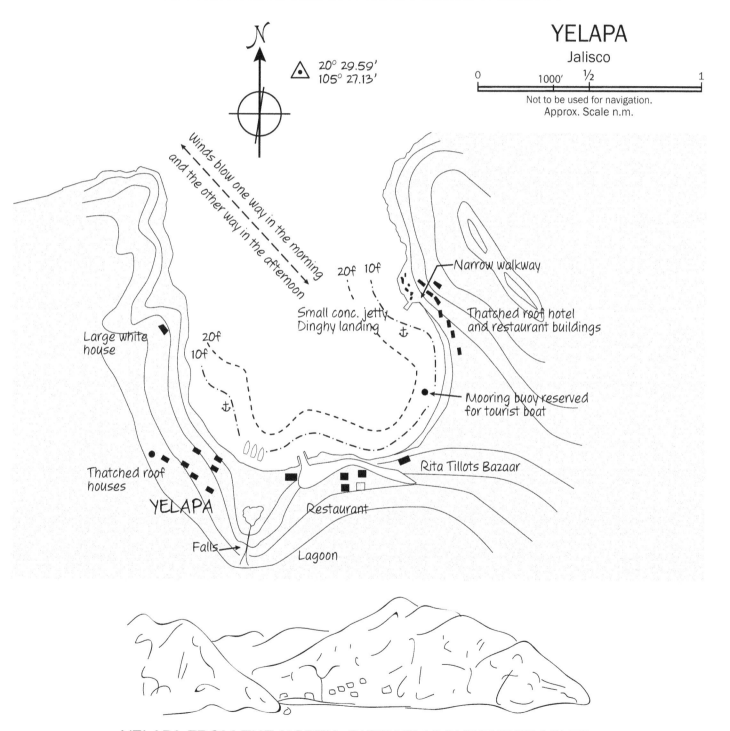

YELAPA
Jalisco

Not to be used for navigation.
Approx. Scale n.m.

YELAPA FROM THE NORTH, DISTANT ABOUT THREE MILES

Punta Ipala is a prominent, gray, rocky bluff, with a roomy bay having sandy beaches at its head, tucked around the corner north of the peninsula. The location once made it a convenient departure or destination point for vessels making the run around Cabo Corrientes. Unfortunately fish farms and fish traps occupy much of the bay and anchorage space is very limited. Punta Ysatan, 3 miles south of the Cape, appears to protrude more than does Cabo Corrientes, especially when coming from the south. It marks the beginning of the disturbed conditions that continue to the Cape itself. A long sandy beach runs some 3 miles south of Punta Ysatan. The reefs of Rocas Cucharitas extend about ¼ miles seaward and are clearly visible as the seas break over them; a beach continues south of these rocks.

Punta Ipala is reasonably evident when approaching from the north, because of its steep, rocky face. **WPT 20°14.1', 105°34.25'.** From the south, the point and its cove are much more obvious. There is a light on top of the point, on a white metal tower 36'. A restaurant is located in the cove.

Some rocky outcrops lie off the end of the point and along the western side of the cove, so the point should be rounded at a clear distance. Depths in the cove reduce slowly from 7 to 3 fathoms before shoaling to the beach at its head. A rock, covered 2 feet has been reported about 80 yards off the slight bulge in the cliff on the northeastern side of the bay. A heavy swell offshore can affect the cove.

Ipala was once a popular overnight stop for migrating cruisers and often became crowded with the addition of shrimpers and commercial fishing boats. Few vessels stop here as it is not a great anchorage unless you anchor quite some distance off and consequently gain little protection from wind and swell.

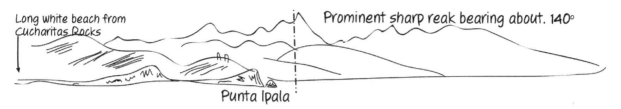

APPROACHING IPALA FROM NORTHWEST, DISTANT ABOUT THREE MILE

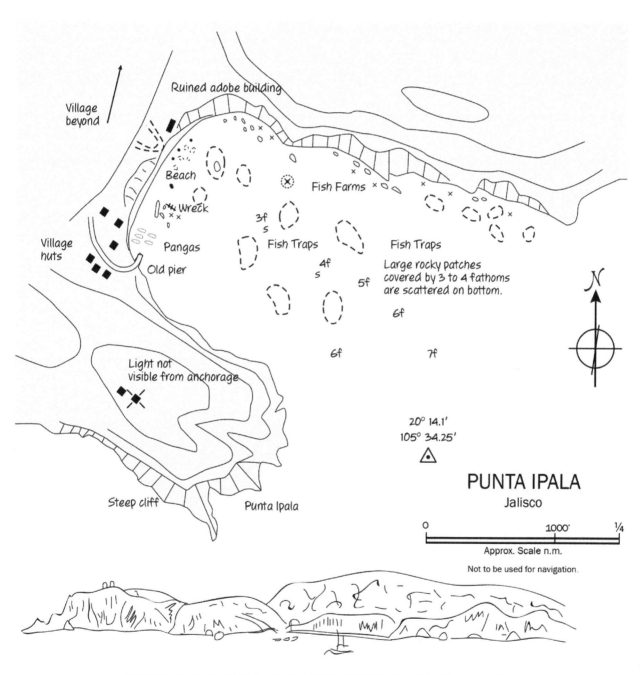

APPROACHING IPALA FROM SSE, DISTANT ABOUT ONE MILE

BAHIA DE CHAMELA

From Punta Ipala it is about 52 miles to Bahia de Chamela, the next good anchorage. The coast between is steep, interspersed with sandy beaches. Tree-covered hills rise behind the shores rising to mountain range in the distance. The dark knob of Punta Roca Negra, about two-thirds of the way is a prominent landmark and Roca Negra is about 1 mile west of the point. The northern entrance to Bahia de Chamela is about 18 miles to the southeast of the point.

Bahia de Chamela is a beautiful, large bay that provides several good anchorages. Two peaks of Punta Rivas make good landmarks. They are 3,422' and 4,675' about 11 and 16 miles ENE respectively. Guegueton, the westernmost one has a peculiar shape and can be identified at a distance during clear weather. On the south side of the bay a cone-shaped, flat-topped volcanic hill with a large white building on the hillside, the residence of a tycoon, is another good landmark.

When approaching from the north the colorful red cliffs of Punta Rivas and the white cliffs of Isla Pasavera mark the entrance to the northern bight and anchorage. **WPT 19°34', 105°8'.** A long reef extends southeast from Punta Perula that is 1/2 mile from Punta Rivas. You must enter clear of this reef, favoring the south side of the opening. The navigable section is over a mile wide, so it is easy to use. A number of islands are scattered along its central and southern part, sheltering this otherwise more open part of the bay.

The northern anchorage, providing the best protection when northwesterly winds prevail, is at the head of the bay in the bight north of Punta Perula. Anchor off the junction of the rocky cliff and sandy beach, staying clear of the rocks along the west side. The holding is good in 25 feet, sand. This corner is the least affected by wind and refracted swell. Landing can be made on the beach at the northwestern corner where a small village is located. Numerous hotels, restaurants and small stores line the beautiful beach. Warning signs are posted to watch out for crocodiles.

An alternate anchorage, usually better in southerly winds, can be taken among the islands in the middle of the bay. One spot is in the southern lee of Isla Passavera, but the best location is off a small beach at the northeast corner of Isla Colorado. Here the water is so clear that in 20 to 25 feet the ridges on the sandy bottom can easily be seen. The islands provide protection from wind and sea and good fishing is found around the nearby reefs. Southerly gales in autumn can send heavy seas into the bay, refracting around the islands and making these anchorages uncomfortable.

In the southern section of the bay are several smaller islands that provide less protection from wind and sea. Fair anchorage can be taken in about 25 feet near the rocky bluff south of the huts off the fishing village of Chamela that is located east of Isla San Augustin. The least disturbed area is easy to see but it is not large enough to accommodate more than 2 or 3 vessels. The surf is strong along most of the beaches on the east side of the bay that is not recommended for anchorage.

Gueguenton, 3422'
(prominent peak)

Flat top peak
Large white bldg

Punta Rivas
(red cliffs)

Isla Colorado (red cliffs)
Isla Passavera (whitish cliffs)

APPROACHING CHAMELA BAY FROM WNW, DISTANT ABOUT FIVE MILES

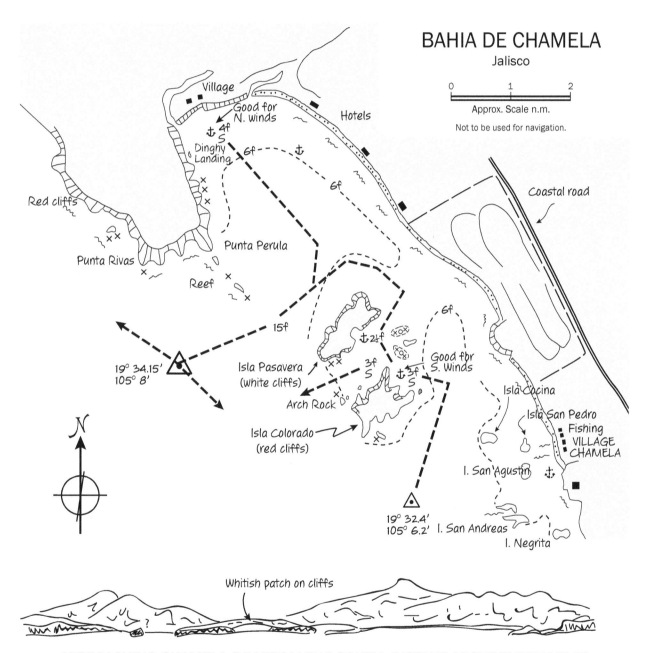

BAHIA DE CHAMELA
Jalisco

0   1   2
Approx. Scale n.m.
Not to be used for navigation.

Village

Good for
N. winds

Hotels

4f
S

Dinghy
Landing

6f

6f

Red cliffs

Coastal road

Punta Perula

Punta Rivas

Reef

15f

19° 34.15'
105° 8'

6f

Isla Pasavera
(white cliffs)

3f
S

Arch Rock

Good for
S. Winds

2½f

Isla Cocina

N

Isla San Pedro
Fishing
VILLAGE
CHAMELA

Isla Colorado
(red cliffs)

3f
S

I. San Agustin

19° 32.4'
105° 6.2' I. San Andreas

I. Negrita

Whitish patch on cliffs

APPROACHING CHAMELA BAY FROM THE SOUTH, DISTANT ABOUT THREE MILES

PARAISO

This pleasant cove is just a short distance from Bahia Chamela. Protected by several large islands, it is located at the bend in the coast which is found before you reach Punta Etiopia. A whitish patch is evident on the larger of the two islands which front the cove. A few visible rocks lie close to the shores of the two islands. **WPT 19°28.52', 105°4.17'.**

Anchorage may be taken in 15 to 20 feet, sand and rock bottom. The cove is somewhat affected by northwest winds and swell, making it better suited to southerly weather.

A large, luxurious estate is on the northern end of the beach and a caretaker resides on the property. LOBO is printed with white rocks on the lawn adjacent to the beach beyond which is a palm plantation.

* * * * * *

In 1977 Charles Wood wrote a two-part article which appeared in CRUISING WORLD. It consisted of a few sketched anchorages on the Mexican mainland along with a brief description. This was the first of many articles he subsequently wrote for various boating magazines in the U.S. and Canada. The response from cruisers was so positive that a few years and several trips later, he decided to complete a cruising guide to Mexico; CHARLIE'S CHARTS of the WESTERN COAST of MEXICO was born! (There were prolonged discussions as to what the guides should be called. Charles preferred the self-explanatory, down-to-earth title of A Cruiser's Guide to Anchorages on the Western Coast of Mexico while Margo felt it was too long and unwieldy and that Charlie's Charts of Mexico was more easily remembered.) She was right – Thanks Margo!

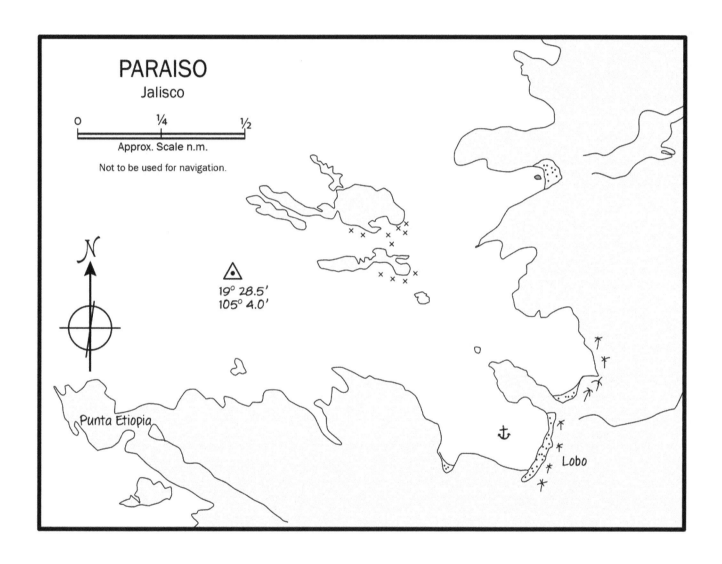

PARAISO

Jalisco

O   ¼   ½

Approx. Scale n.m.

Not to be used for navigation.

N

19° 28.5'
105° 4.0'

Punta Etiopia

Lobo

BAHIA CAREYES

South of Paraiso the coast ends in a dark point, Punta Etiopa, before it falls away again in several small, rocky coves and indentations. Beaches interspersed by rocky bluffs continue until the long beach of Playa Teopa is passed where the land curves westward again to end in a long, low, point, Punta Farrallon. This coastal section is the resort area of Costa Careyes.

Midway between Punta Etiopa and Punta Farrallon, there is a small triple-lobed bay with several islands before it marking Bahia Careyes, the heart of the area. Each of the three lobes of the bay has its own hotel or condominium development, while the high cliffs that extend from the west side of the bay have several large villas and residential structures, some of which are visible from the sea. Newly nicknamed the "Mexican Riviera," huge mansions cling to the rocks.

Two big, rounded, rocky islands lie before the cove and a rocky peninsula is connected by a small spit to the cliffs and bluff on the western side of the bay. The southernmost, outer island has a steep west face, arched over a sea cave forming below. A rock awash marked by a red buoy is west of this island and roughly ½ mile southwest of the rounded northern peninsula. Other rocks and islets are shown on the sketch.

When approaching, enter the bay from the south. **WPT 19°26.44', 105°2.28'**. Follow a course closer to the island with a sea cave; ranges on shore also indicate a safe route. When coming from the south there is clear passage when taking a mid-channel course between the island with the sea cave and the detached rocks visible off the point, as shown on the sketch.

Anchorage was once available in the two northern coves. Unfortunately, local vessels permanently anchor in the available space making it almost impossible for a cruising vessel to find a spot for anchorage. Each hotel is very possessive of their share of the beach and their facilities though they are usually glad to have cruisers patronize their restaurants and bars. The north cove is occupied by private homes.

The middle cove has a permanent fishing skiff mooring for Club Playa Rosa and private bungalows are located behind the beach. You might be able to find a spot to anchor in a niche on the east side of the island.

The last cove has the largest structure, the El Careyes Hotel, a horseshoe-shaped colonial village style. Between these last two beaches, the pink and white buildings of a condominium complex, Casita de Las Flores, is built above the rocky bluff. High above the bluffs the El Mirador restaurant and disco are active during the winter tourist season.

In the next bay to the south, Playa Cayaritos (also known as Playa Careyes) is a high-end palapa restaurant, Cocodrilo Azul. The owner speaks English and is a good source of local knowledge. Dinghy landing in this little bay can be made at the north end of the bay provided the surf is not too high.

About a half mile south of the rocky coast shown on the lower part of the sketch is a closely monitored reserve for the protection of a nesting site for turtles.

BAHIA CAREYES
Jalisco

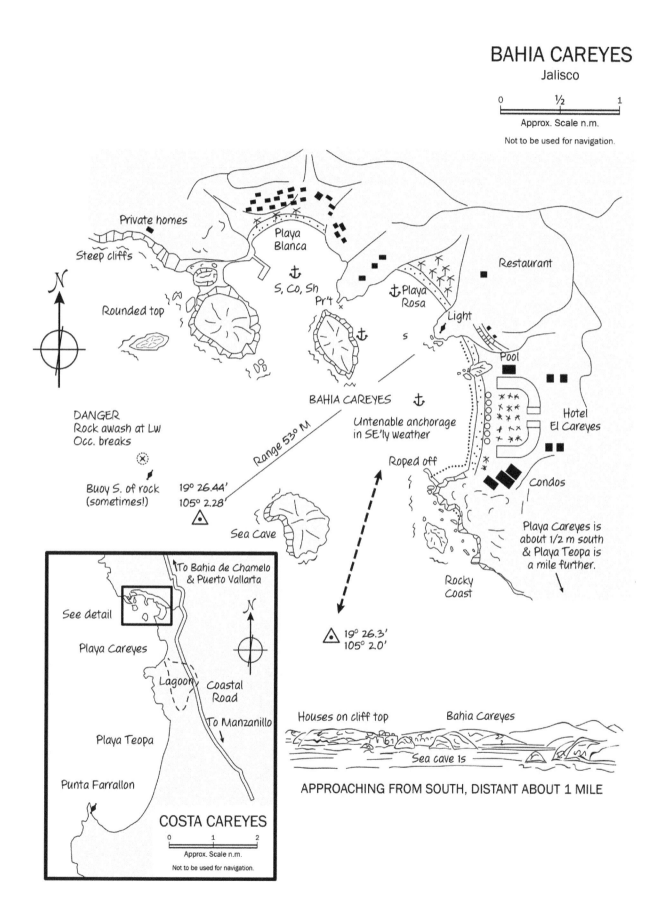

0   ½   1
Approx. Scale n.m.

Not to be used for navigation.

Private homes

Steep cliffs

N

Rounded top

Playa
Blanca

S, Co, Sh

Pr't

Restaurant

Playa
Rosa

Light

Pool

BAHIA CAREYES

Range 53° M

Untenable anchorage
in SE'ly weather

Roped off

Hotel
El Careyes

Condos

DANGER
Rock awash at Lw
Occ. breaks

Buoy S. of rock
(sometimes!)

19° 26.44'
105° 2.28'

Sea Cave

Playa Careyes is
about ½ m south
& Playa Teopa is
a mile further.

Rocky
Coast

19° 26.3'
105° 2.0'

See detail

To Bahia de Chamelo
& Puerto Vallarta

N

Playa Careyes

Lagoon

Coastal
Road

To Manzanillo

Houses on cliff top

Bahia Careyes

Sea cave 1s

Playa Teopa

Punta Farrallon

COSTA CAREYES

0   1   2
Approx. Scale n.m.

Not to be used for navigation.

APPROACHING FROM SOUTH, DISTANT ABOUT 1 MILE

265

BAHIA TENACATITA

The coast from Punta Farrallon to Bahia Tenacatita is low and sandy. Midway along, the steep, pointed rocks of Los Frailes stand close together about 1 mile offshore; other rocky islands lie off Punta Hermanos (Brothers Point), and the entrance to Bahia Tenacatita. To avoid these dangers the course should be at least 1½ miles offshore. Isla Pajaros, a blocky, steep-sided 150' rock lies southwest of Punta Hermanos. A reef continues along the line of the point, necessitating a wide swing when entering the bay. The 4½ mile wide entrance is between Punta Hermanos and Cabeza de Navidad. **WPT 19°15', 104°51.6'**

Cool mangrove tunnel. Photo: Holly Scott

Bahia Tenacatita is one of the most interesting and popular anchorages in this part of the coast. The rocky bulk of Punta Chubasco divides the bay into two anchorage areas. The outer anchorage is in the north west corner, behind the lee of Punta Hermanos. Here you can anchor off a curved, sandy beach in about 25 feet, sand. The small fishing village of Revelcito is at the head of the beach. It has palapa bars, cafes and produce and beer trucks call regularly. Acceptable in calm weather, the anchorage can be disturbed by swell refracting around Punta Hermanos. A short walk across the neck of land takes you to the Pacific side to an isolated surf-washed beach.

The most popular anchorage is in the inner bay behind the bluff at Punta Chubasco. **WPT 19°17.9', 104°50.3'**. Center Rock, about 12' high and ½ mile east of Punta Chubasco is a prominent landmark. **WPT 19°17.406', 104°49.695'.** There is a submerged rock midway between Center Rock and the rocks off Punta Chubasco. Though its exact position is not known, a vessel struck it recently and sustained considerable damage. To be on the safe side, follow a course south of Center Rock before rounding it on the east side when entering the inner bight.

Good, sheltered anchorage in 15 to 40 feet, sand can be taken near the head of the bay, off a small beach. A reef, the entrance to a lagoon and a long sandy beach lie north of the anchorage. There is good diving at the reef and along the rocky shore of Punta Chubasco. A fascinating jungle trip can be taken up the stream through mangroves to a large lagoon. The best time to start is at high tide and when there is little surf. Since the current can run to 4 or 5 knots, a reliable motor is needed. Beach the dinghy at the end and it's a short walk to palapa cafes mentioned above. Fish rolls are the local specialty.

At the end of the long beach is a large hotel with multistory condominiums beyond. The Blue Bay Lagoon Hotel sometimes allows cruisers to patronize the restaurant and enjoy the swimming pool. Their guests may kayak to visit the boats at anchor. On the east side of the bay is the village of La Manzanilla where landing through surf requires skill and very good timing. Landing is easiest at low tide. This is an excellent spot for obtaining basic provisions as well as fresh poultry, produce and fresh tortillas. Gasoline and jerry jug diesel is available about a mile out of La Manzanilla at Abarrotes "El Emporeo". Boats staying overnight in settled weather should also use a stern anchor.

Trailing off from the southernmost part of the bay are a number of rocky islands, the largest of which is Cabeza de Navidad, a 400' pyramid-shaped rock. Some smaller rocks lie beyond it, including Piedra Blanca, a 100' rock with a dark top and whitish midsection. Breakers are usually seen over the two dangerous, barely submerged rocks that lie off this group, one to the south, the other one, near the eastern side. El Tamarindo golf course is visible from sea.

BAHIA TENACATITA
Jalisco

0   ½   1

Approx. Scale n.m.

Not to be used for navigation.

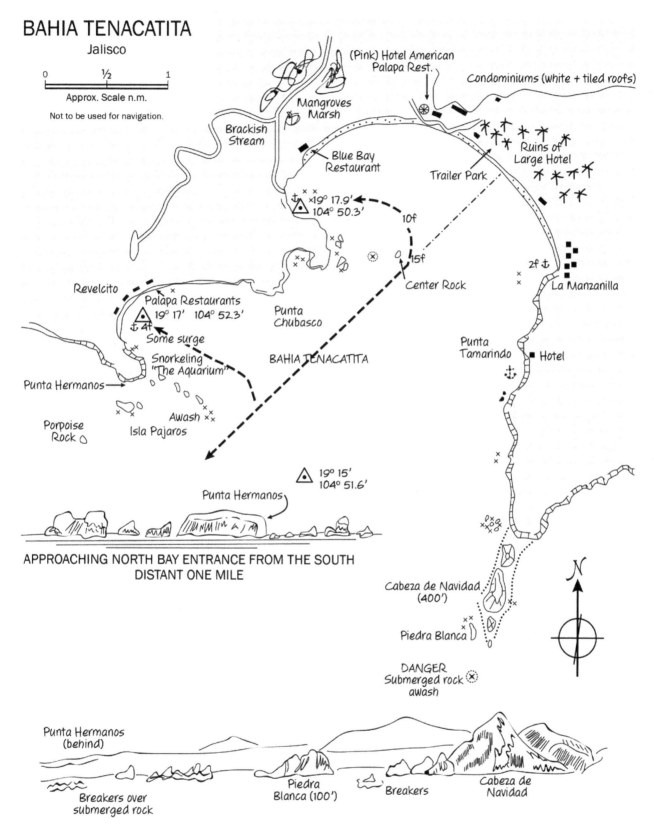

(Pink) Hotel American
Palapa Rest.

Condominiums (white + tiled roofs)

Mangroves
Marsh

Brackish
Stream

Ruins of
Large Hotel

Blue Bay
Restaurant

Trailer Park

×19° 17.9'
104° 50.3'

10f

15f

Center Rock

2f ⚓

La Manzanilla

Revelcito

Palapa Restaurants
19° 17'   104° 52.3'
⚓ 4f
Some surge

Punta
Chubasco

Punta
Tamarindo

Hotel

Snorkeling
"The Aquarium"

BAHIA TENACATITA

Punta Hermanos

Awash

Porpoise
Rock

Isla Pajaros

19° 15'
104° 51.6'

Punta Hermanos

APPROACHING NORTH BAY ENTRANCE FROM THE SOUTH
DISTANT ONE MILE

Cabeza de Navidad
(400')

Piedra Blanca

DANGER
Submerged rock ⊗
awash

N

Punta Hermanos
(behind)

Breakers over
submerged rock

Piedra
Blanca (100')

Breakers

Cabeza de
Navidad

APPROACHING CABEZA DE NAVIDAD FROM THE SOUTHWEST, DISTANT ONE MILE

BAHIA de NAVIDAD/MELAQUE

The coast from Cabeza de Navidad to Punta Bahia at Bahia de Navidad is a series of rocky bluffs backed by wooded hills. When rounding Piedra Blanca give it a wide berth to clear the rocks and reefs that extend about 1½ miles off the mainland. After leaving Bahia Tenacatita it is only a 6-mile passage along the coast before you reach the entrance to Bahia de Navidad. **WPT 19°12.3', 104°42.2'.** This has become one of the best-liked stopovers on the mainland because of the secure anchorage within the lagoon, the first-class marina, ease of shopping, a variety of restaurants, a relaxed atmosphere and the natural beauty of the area.

Punta Bahia is the northern point of the entrance to **Bahia de Navidad.** It is a high, rocky ridge at the end of which is a chain of several large, isolated rocky islands continuing to the southwest. A tall, cone-shaped rock is followed by a group of columnar pinnacles and numerous smaller rocks lie scattered on all sides. The reefs continue some distance underwater as evidenced by breakers beyond.

Anchorage can be taken off the town of Melaque in the lee of the point, off the sandy beach at the head of the northern bight of the bay. Swell often refracts around the point, making this a rolly anchorage; fore and aft anchors can be used to enable a vessel to face into the swell. The holding is good in 15 to 30 feet, sand. Hotels, RV parks, excellent fresh produce, a bank and laundry facilities are reasons to visit. Cobblestone streets, a charming village with a quiet pace, crashing surf and a bus ride to Barra de Navidad entice some cruisers stay in the area for a long time. Dinghy landing through surf on to a sandy beach can be done at cruiser-friendly "Los Pelicanos" restaurant.

The Port Captain's office has jurisdiction over boats anchored off Melaque as well as those in the lagoon anchorage and in the **Marina Puerto de la Navidad.** The only bank in the two communities is Banamex in Melaque. An ATM machine is located in the lobby of the Isla Navidad Hotel complex where Marina Puerto de la Navidad is located. Several other ATM machines are in Barra. A map of Barra de Navidad and Melaque is in circulation.

The local cruiser net is on VHF 68 at 0830. A favorite spot for socializing is Beer Bob's Bookstore that has two rooms of books. Melaque is the best place to buy produce: Wednesday and Saturday at the market behind "Pirata" and Thursday and Sunday at "Hawaii" on the main street. Maria at Maria's Tienda (VHF Ch 77) will deliver to your boat (in the Lagoon or Marina) meat, groceries, water, beer and wine from her tienda near the lagoon on the Colimilla side. She takes orders for a variety of items for weekly trips to Sam's Club and Costco in Guadalajara. A fee is charged for fuel; tipping is appreciated. The French Baker makes announcements on VHF Ch 22 from 8–10 am when deliveries of fresh baguettes, croissants and tartlets are available to vessels in the Lagoon and Marina.

Net Repairs on the Beach at Melaque. Photo: Betsy Crowfoot

Strong surf pounds the beaches in the southern half of the bay; often it is sufficiently high to attract surfers. Beyond the lagoon entrance the land rises with rocky edges to Punta Graham, a 705' bluff. The lighthouse and residences perched right on the edge of the cliff are almost lost atop its massive bulk. Punta Graham, with Roco Cono close below it is a prominent landmark when approaching Bahia de Navidad from the south. Note the small rock that lies about ½ miles southwest of Punta Graham when laying a course to or from Bahia de Navidad.

APPROACHING BAHIA DE NAVIDAD FROM NW, DISTANT ABOUT FOUR MILES

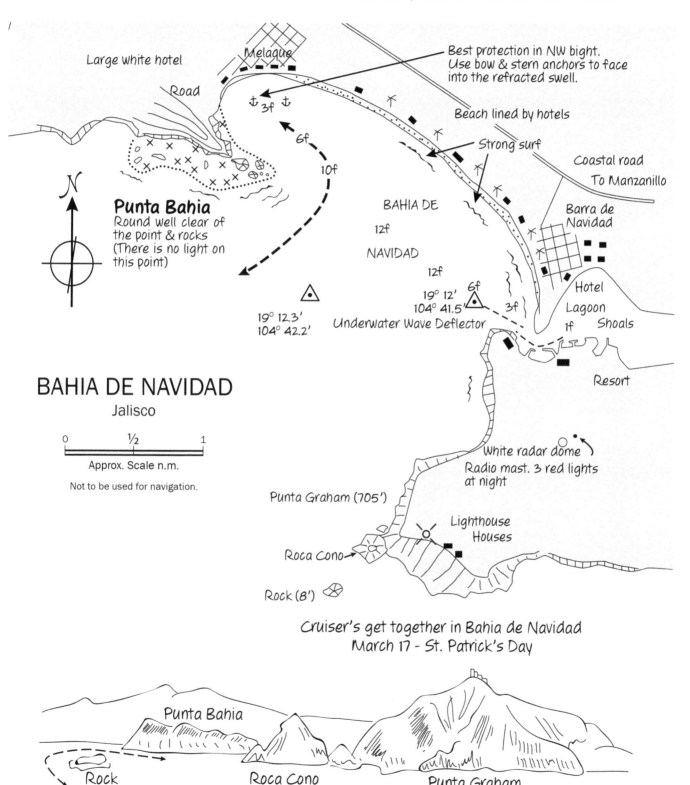

Large white hotel

Melaque

Road

⚓ 3f ⚓

Best protection in NW bight.
Use bow & stern anchors to face
into the refracted swell.

Beach lined by hotels

Strong surf

6f

10f

Coastal road
To Manzanillo

Punta Bahia
Round well clear of
the point & rocks
(There is no light on
this point)

N

BAHIA DE

12f

NAVIDAD

Barra de
Navidad

12f

19° 12'
104° 41.5'   6f

3f

Hotel

Lagoon

Shoals

1f

19° 12.3'
104° 42.2'

Underwater Wave Deflector

Resort

BAHIA DE NAVIDAD

Jalisco

0   ½   1

Approx. Scale n.m.

Not to be used for navigation.

White radar dome
Radio mast. 3 red lights
at night

Punta Graham (705')

Lighthouse
Houses

Roca Cono

Rock (8')

Cruiser's get together in Bahia de Navidad
March 17 - St. Patrick's Day

Punta Bahia

Rock   Roca Cono   Punta Graham

APPROACHING BAHIA DE NAVIDAD FROM THE SOUTH, DISTANT ABOUT ONE MILE

LAGUNA DE LA NAVIDAD, Marina Puerto de la Nacidad and Barra de Navidad

In the southeastern end of **Bahia de La Navidad** a shallow channel leads into Laguna de La Navidad. Beyond the lagoon entrance the land rises to form the 705' high bluff of Punta Graham. The lighthouse on the edge of the cliff and Roco Cono close below are prominent landmarks when approaching Navidad from the south. Two dangerous rocks are in the area, one about ½ mile southwest of Punta Graham, the other, awash at high water is a short distance north of the point at the entrance to the lagoon.

Take care when approaching the entrance to the channel leading to the marina and into the lagoon. A high rip-rap breakwater topped by a lighted walkway extends in a northwesterly direction from the end of the peninsula; it forms the northern edge of the channel. The cement works on the breakwater suffered considerable damage during the earthquake of 1995. A yellow marker indicates the western end of the concrete wave deflector that extends another 50 yards beyond the end of the breakwater in a northwesterly direction. Barely awash at the seaward end at low water, this is a dangerous construction. An orange buoy marks a rock near the southwest end of the deflector. It is best to enter at high tide. **WPT 19°12', 104°41.5'.**

Access to the marina and lagoon is south of the breakwater, staying on the starboard side of the channel continuing to the entrance of the large marina basin. Though a night entrance is not advised for first-time visitors, the entrance is well lit. **Marina Puerto de la Navidad** is a full service marina with over 200 slips that can accommodate vessels from 20' to 180'. The marina does not monitor the radio so just pull in and find an empty slip, then walk to the office to check in. Facilities include fuel, laundry, showers, a dinghy dock and tennis courts. Marina guests can open an account at the Grand Bay Hotel in order to use the pool, 27-hole golf course and the three restaurants. Wi-fi can be purchased in the hotel lobby. Propane is available from a station that is a 20-minute taxi ride towards Cihuatlan. Water taxis from Barra to the marina run 24 hours a day charging 15 pesos per person, round trip. Even though you plan to stay less than a month it is understood that it is cheaper to pay moorage on a monthly basis than for two or three weeks at the daily rate. Things like this change often, so ask questions! The golf course clubhouse serves excellent breakfasts and lunches at reasonable prices. When taking on large quantities of fuel record the time and number of each reset of the fuel pump to prevent being charged for extra fuel. Each reset represents over $600 worth of fuel!

Entrance to the lagoon requires taking a bearing to the port side of the island directly off the bow when the marina is hard to starboard. Steering a course slightly to port of the shellfish storage pens until abreast of the island, anchor anywhere to port in the large lagoon. The bottom is soft mud making it easy to drag unless extra scope is allowed. When anchored, do not leave the outboard motor on your dinghy in the water at night and if the dinghy is not stowed on board be sure to secure it to your boat with cable. As a result of the fetch in the spacious lagoon, dinghy trips to town or the marina can be wet when afternoon winds pick up. This huge lagoon was once a natural fish hatchery and one of the few nesting sites for roseate spoonbills.

Vessels moored at the marina or anchored in the lagoon are required to report to the Port Captain. The only banking facilities in the area are in Melaque: the bank is on Calle Gomez Farias (the first street inland from the beach) and an ATM machine is near the bus stop.

Barra De Navidad is a quaint town, well worth exploring. Many small shops in the village sell fresh produce and other groceries, some shops sell crafts and other odds and ends. A good butcher is next to the bus station. There are numerous bars and restaurants where cruisers congregate but since names of establishments change so frequently, none will be listed here.

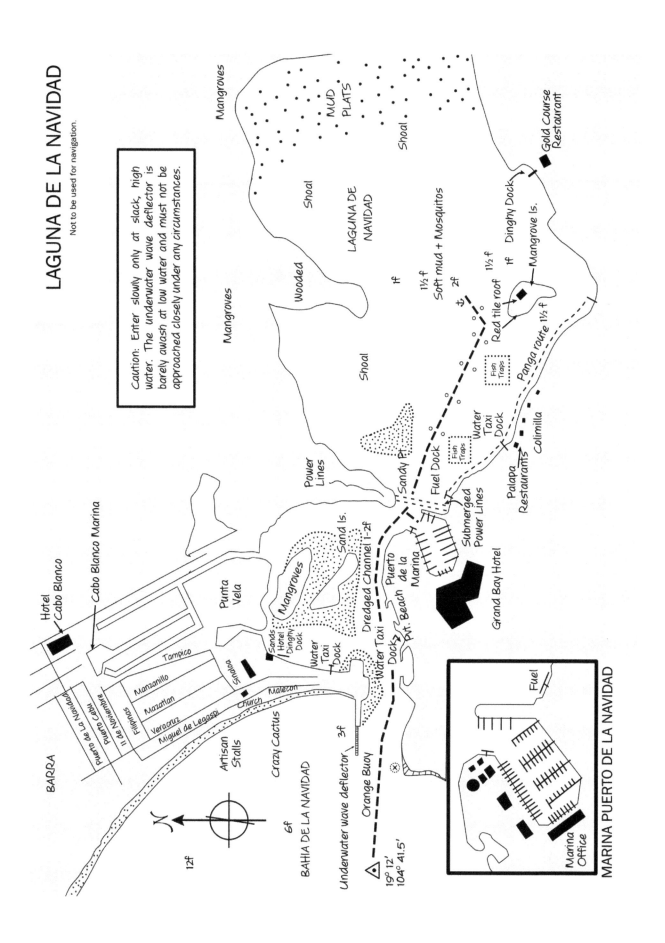

LAGUNA DE LA NAVIDAD

Not to be used for navigation.

Caution: Enter slowly only at slack, high water. The underwater wave deflector is barely awash at low water and must not be approached closely under any circumstances.

Mangroves

Mangroves

MUD PLATS

Shoal

Shoal

Gold Course Restaurant

Woodea

LAGUNA DE NAVIDAD

Shoal

Soft mud + Mosquitos

Dinghy Dock

Mangrove Is.

1f

1½ f

1½ f

1f

2f

Red tile roof

Panga route 1½ f

Colimilla

Fish Traps

Fish Traps

Water Taxi Dock

Palapa Restaurants

Sandy Pt.

Fuel Dock

Power Lines

Submerged Power Lines

Grand Bay Hotel

Mangroves

Sand Is.

Dredged Channel 1-2f

Puerto Beach de la Marina

Pvt.

Water Taxi Dock

Punta Vela

Cabo Blanco Marina

Hotel Cabo Blanco

Tampico

Manzanillo

Sands Hotel Dinghy Dock

Water Taxi Dock

Sinaloa

Mazatlan

Filipinas

Puerto Cebu

11 de Noviembre

Puerto de La Navidad

Veracruz

Miguel de Legaspi

Church

Malecon

Artisan Stalls

Crazy Cactus

BAHIA DE LA NAVIDAD

BARRA

N

12f

6f

3f

Underwater wave deflector

Orange Buoy

19° 12'
104° 41.5'

MARINA PUERTO DE LA NAVIDAD

Fuel

Marina Office

271

MANZANILLO

The coast between Punta Graham and Manzanillo consists of a long, low, sandy beach until the airport towers and buildings indicate the proximity of Bahia de Santiago and Bahia de Manzanillo. A large, prominent whitish island, Piedra Blanca, 260' high and a mile offshore is a landmark visible from a great distance. The rest of the coast is a series of rocky bluffs and interposed bays. Piedra Blanca is steep-to and can be passed on either side. It is a sea bird nesting site, the most spectacular being the Tropic Bird with its two long, white tail feathers.

Punta Carrizal marks the beginning of the bays near Manzanillo. See Sketch. Two small open bays are in the 2½ miles that separate Carrizal from Punta Juluapan (the eastern end of Bahia de Santiago). The first is **Carrizal**, anchor in 15 to 30 feet, sand. The second is **Higueras**, which is less protected. Anchor in 30 to 35 feet, sand.

During northwesterly winds anchorage may be had in the bay to the north of Punta Carrizal. The distinctive features of this part of the coast are Cerro de Juluapan (Table Mountain) a flat-topped peak (2,707') northwest of Manzanillo and Wreck Cone, a flat, conical volcanic peak (1,522') nearer the coast to the southwest. They can be recognized from almost any angle of approach to Manzanillo. In clear weather the 13,000' volcanic peaks of Volcan de Colima and Nevado de Colima are visible among the peaks far behind Manzanillo.

Bahia de Santiago lies between Punta Juluapan and Punta Santiago, an intermediate headland. On the west side of this bay are the exclusive residential estates of Club Santiago. Anchorage can be taken in the western corner off the lagoon entrance, but it can be affected by swell. Otherwise, anchorage is possible in the little cove beneath Punta Santiago, on the east side of the bay. There is heavy surf on the beaches lining the bay.

Punta Santiago is a high headland separating Bahia de Santiago and Bahia de Manzanillo. It is covered with residences and condos. Draped over the top and on the eastern side of Punta Santiago are the white, Moorish arches, towers and buildings of **Las Hadas** hotel, famous for being the film set for the movie "10." It has a small breakwater-protected **Marina Las Hadas** where 70 yachts moor stern-to Med style. There is a fuel service inside the marina, launching ramp, laundry, security gates, market, Wi-Fi pumpout service and clearance paperwork. **WPT 19°6', 104°20.7'.**

Cruisers can also anchor just outside Las Hadas Marina, between the hotel swimming area and the breakwater in relative protection in 10 feet, sand. A daily fee for use of the dinghy dock inside the marina includes all paper work, garbage and oil disposal, use of the fabulous pool and access to the hotel and bus/taxi service for provisioning at Supermercado Commercial or downtown Manzanillo.

Manzanillo, in the southern end of the bay, is a **Port of Entry** and you must register with the Port Captain, Customs and Immigration, or have your paperwork done at the marina. Office hours are 0830 to 1530 and it is important to report that the vessel has entered the area during office hours, otherwise an additional charge may be made. Avoid interfering with commercial boat traffic in the marked channel, maneuvering areas and docks. Smaller vessels congregate at the concrete jetty on the east side of the harbor. Anchorage is adequate and the best access to shore is a ladder near a Chinese restaurant. Economical, clean diesel is available at a fuel pier on the northern side of the inner harbor beyond the Navy base. This facility is designed for large ships making it advisable to enter at high tide to avoid tangling the rigging in protruding rubber fenders on the dock. Fender boards are helpful since the vessel is side-tied to wooden pilings. Be prepared to wait.

This busy commercial port has much radio traffic, VHF Ch 16 should only be used in emergency situations. Weather broadcasts in Spanish are given at noon on VHF Ch 16 and every 3 hours during stormy conditions.

APPROACHING FROM THE NW, DISTANT ABOUT SIX MILES

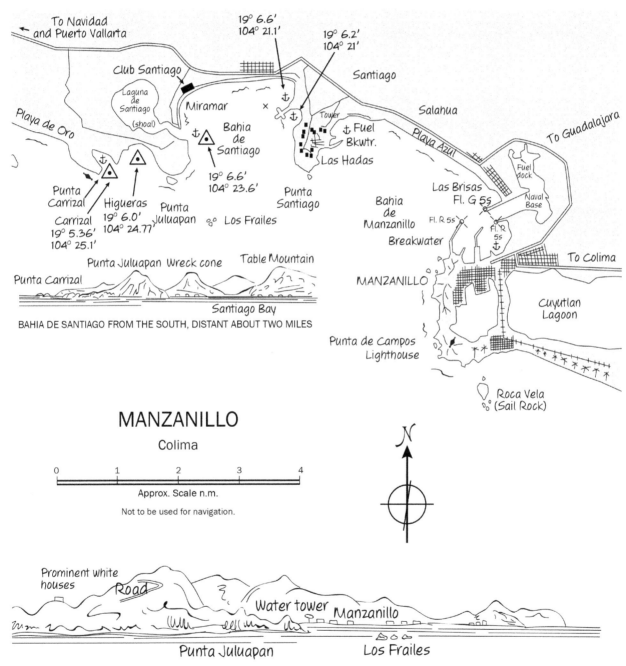

BAHIA DE SANTIAGO FROM THE SOUTH, DISTANT ABOUT TWO MILES

MANZANILLO

Colima

0 1 2 3 4

Approx. Scale n.m.

Not to be used for navigation.

APPROACHING MANZANILLO, FROM THE WEST, DISTANT ABOUT TWO MILES

THE MAINLAND COAST FROM MANZANILLO TO ACAPULCO

Though this section of the coast lies between two immensely popular resort centers, attractive bays and anchorages are infrequent. However, the anchorages that are available are quite suitable and adequate for yachts traveling up and down the coast. Many vessels bound for the South Pacific leave Mexico from Manzanillo or Puerto Vallarta. By using such departure points, they avoid having to make up additional miles in light airs, which would result by leaving the mainland from more southerly ports.

This part of the coast continues its generally southeasterly trend. For the most part, the prevailing winds continue to be northwesterlies, which parallel the coast with a greatly reduced strength. Land and sea breezes are characteristic and are more important considerations. Tropical conditions are pronounced, as sea water temperatures increase and in any absence of wind, the heat can be intense. But since Manzanillo lies at the same latitude as the Hawaiian Islands these conditions can be expected.

The rainy season is from May to November and the annual rainfall increases as you move further south. This is evidenced by green vegetation growing in profusion as coconut, mango, banana and pineapple plantations are a common sight beyond the coast.

Tropical disturbances show some increased activity during the rainy season and afternoon thunderstorms bring much rain. Often the cloudbursts reduce visibility to less than 30 yards and can continue for an hour or more. In the dry season sea breezes are more marked, commencing near noon from the southwest, increasing in the afternoon, then diminishing in the late evening. Land breezes occur at night, but they tend to be irregular in direction and force.

The coast along this section generally consists of long sandy beaches with pounding surf separated by a series of steep, bold, rocky bluffs with small beaches between. In some areas the mountains rise closely behind the coastal areas. The termination of mountain ridges at the coast occasionally ends in rocky points that provide sheltering anchorages useful for cruising this part of the coast.

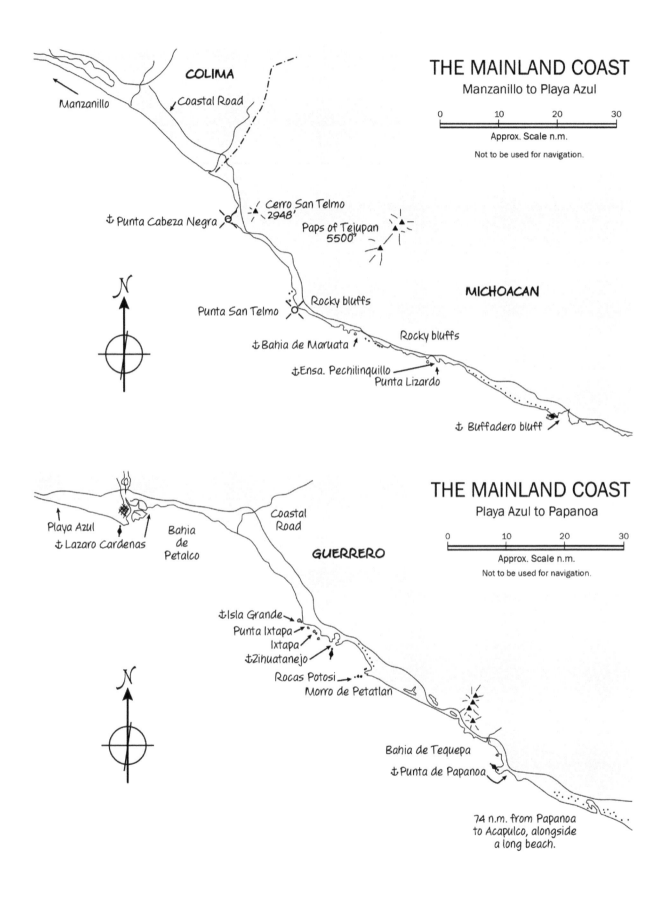

THE MAINLAND COAST

Manzanillo to Playa Azul

0   10   20   30

Approx. Scale n.m.

Not to be used for navigation.

COLIMA

Manzanillo

Coastal Road

Cerro San Telmo
2948'

Paps of Tejupan
5500"

⚓ Punta Cabeza Negra

MICHOACAN

Punta San Telmo

Rocky bluffs

⚓ Bahia de Maruata

Rocky bluffs

⚓ Ensa. Pechilinquillo

Punta Lizardo

⚓ Buffadero bluff

THE MAINLAND COAST

Playa Azul to Papanoa

0   10   20   30

Approx. Scale n.m.

Not to be used for navigation.

Coastal Road

Playa Azul

⚓ Lazaro Cardenas

Bahia de Petalco

GUERRERO

⚓ Isla Grande

Punta Ixtapa

Ixtapa

⚓ Zihuatanejo

Rocas Potosi

Morro de Petatlan

Bahia de Tequepa

⚓ Punta de Papanoa

74 n.m. from Papanoa
to Acapulco, alongside
a long beach.

PUNTA CABEZA NEGRA

Leaving Manzanillo harbor, the high bluffs and hills on the western side of the city end on the south at Punta Campos where there is a lighthouse. Close to the south of the point is Roca Vela (Sail Rock), a triangular rock 112' high. From Punta De Campos to Punta Cabeza Negra the coast consists of a sandy beach on which the surf crashes heavily. These are the "Ola Verde" or giant green waves that reach striking proportions at the time of the full moon in May. Laguna de Cuyutlan is huge lagoon that lies behind the beach. The only known danger is a rock about ½ mile off the beach about halfway down the coast, but as a general rule vessels should not stand in close to shore when passing the coast so it should not present a problem.

Punta Cabeza Negra is a headland 560' high that has a low section where it joins the mainland, so that from any distance it often appears as an island. Some rocks lie around the point, the largest being a whitish islet, Roca Pelicano, off the northwestern side. Coconut palm and banana plantations fill the low area between the hills of the point and the coast.

Good anchorage is available on the northern side of the point, off the sheds and huts visible behind the sandy beach. Anchor about ½ mile northeast of the point in 35 feet, good holding sand. **WPT 18°36.35', 103°42'**. Since swell and surge may be experienced, fore and aft anchors set so that the vessel faces into the swell, may be needed for comfort. However, during normal winter weather when yachts are likely to visit this area, the wind and seas are calmer than at other times of the year, thus making this quite an acceptable spot to anchor.

There is another small beach on the south side of the point, followed by a rocky bluff. In strong northerly winds some shelter can be found here, but the surf pounds heavily on the beach and the bight is too exposed for shelter otherwise.

Punta Tejupan is 18½ miles southeast of Cabeza Negra and about a mile NNW of Punta San Telmo. A marginal anchorage, **Bucerias**, lies southeast of the three small islets off the point in a cove backed by a sandy beach. At the south end of the beach is an almost detached rocky bluff, which is about ½ mile north of the light located at Punta San Telmo. Almost three miles southeast of Punta San Telmo is a remarkable sugarloaf rock 75' high. Because of the rocks and currents along this and the following section of the coast, vessels should stay well to seaward and not travel closer than 2 miles.

PUNTA CABEZA NEGRA
Michoacan

0   1   2

Approx. Scale n.m.

Not to be used for navigation.

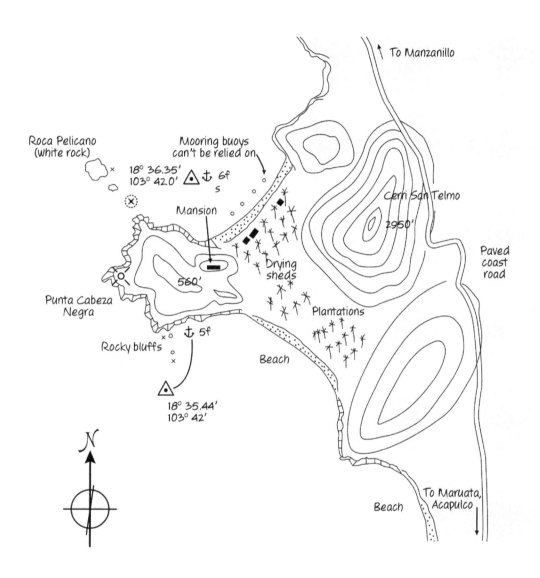

To Manzanillo

Roca Pelicano
(white rock)

Mooring buoys
can't be relied on

18° 36.35'
103° 42.0'

⚓ 6f
S

Mansion

Cerri San Telmo

2950'

Drying
sheds

Paved
coast
road

560'

Punta Cabeza
Negra

Plantations

⚓ 5f

Rocky bluffs

Beach

18° 35.44'
103° 42'

N

To Maruata,
Acapulco

Beach

Punta Cabeza Negra

APPROACHING FROM THE SOUTH, DISTANT ABOUT FOUR MILES

BAHIA DE MARUATA

From Punta Cabeza Negra the coast changes from mainly sandy beaches to rocky cliffs with small beaches scattered along the way. From Punta San Telmo the rocky coast trends in a more easterly direction.

A prominent white rock over 100' high, Piedra Blanca, is a good landmark, for the open bight of Bahia de Maruata. Behind Piedra Blanca are high, distinctive, whitish cliffs, which are the best landmark for identifying the approach to Bahia de Maruata from the north. South of the cliffs is a group of four large and several small islets. A curving, white, sandy beach encircles the bay, ending at another high, steep, rocky face with numerous rocks scattered at its base. Although there is a conical hill of 2,140' three and a half miles north of the bay, it is better used as a landmark when approaching from the south. **WPT 18°16', 103°20.5'**

The best anchorage is in the northern part, about ½ mile from the rocky islands and the same distance from the beach, in about 35 feet. Occasionally a fish net is strung across the bay, forcing one to anchor in a rather exposed position. When a heavy southeast swell is running the anchorage can become dangerous for the swell seems to split near the islets at the western end of the bay and increase in height where the water is relatively shallow as it approaches the coast. Though the surf is heavy, landing can usually be made in the extreme corner behind the islands where a stream empties into the bay and pangas are often seen ashore.

Tall coconut palms fill the flat land north of the bay and a small, quiet, isolated village is next to a paved landing strip that angles off behind the beach. The coastal road passes behind the airstrip and is deeply cut into the southern rocky ridge near the coast.

The coast beyond Maruata continues in a series of steep, rocky cliffs followed by a sandy beach three miles long. Thereafter, another series of steep cliffs leads to the small cove of Pechilinquillo, which is about 15 miles distant.

BAHIA DE MARUATA
Michoacan

0   ½   1

Approx. Scale n.m.

Not to be used for navigation.

ENTERING BAHIA DE MARUATA FROM THE SOUTH

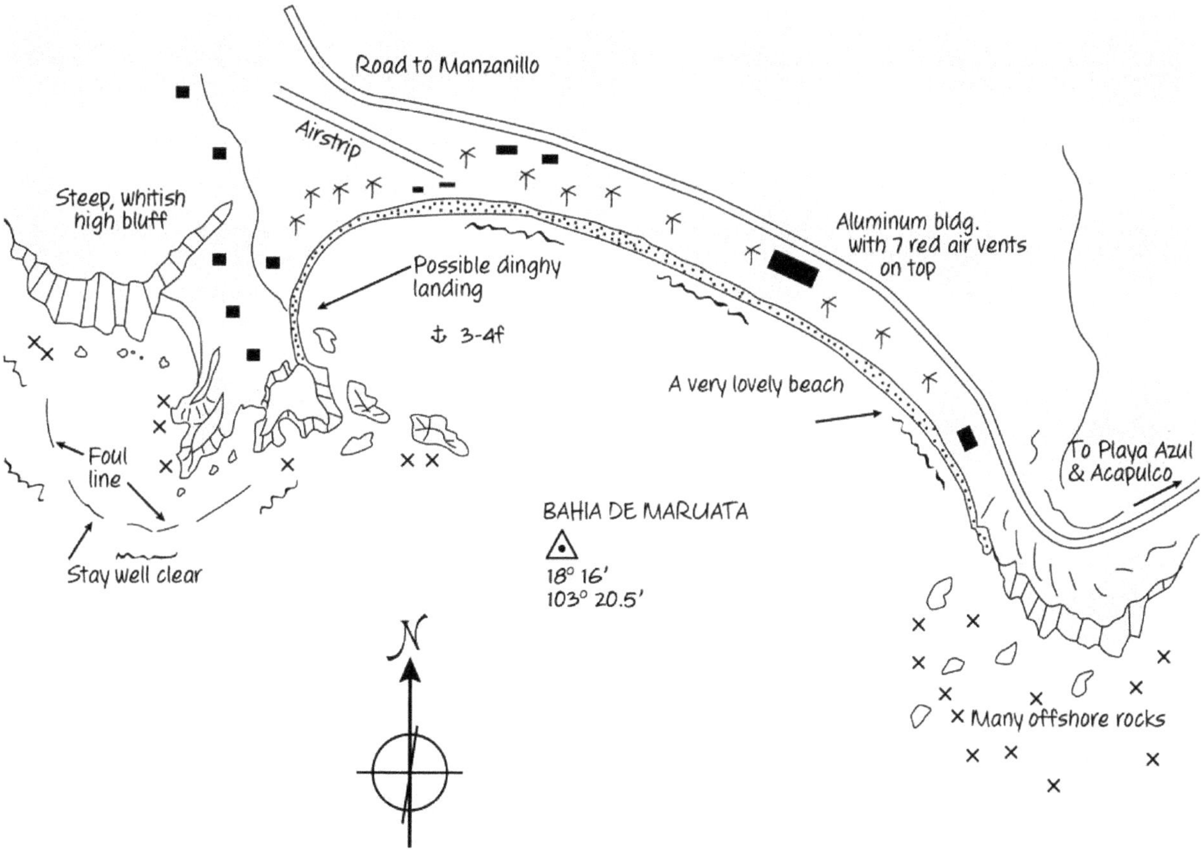

Road to Manzanillo

Airstrip

Steep, whitish
high bluff

Possible dinghy
landing

⚓ 3-4f

Aluminum bldg.
with 7 red air vents
on top

A very lovely beach

To Playa Azul
& Acapulco

Foul
line

Stay well clear

BAHIA DE MARUATA
18° 16'
103° 20.5'

N

Many offshore rocks

Two whitish
rock islands

Steep whitish rock face

UNIQUE CLIFF FACE TWO MILES SOUTHEAST OF ENTRANCE TO BAHIA DE MARUATA

279

ENSENADA DE PECHILINQULLO AND CALETA DE CAMPOS

These two anchorages are presented together, though they are about 23 miles apart, for the choice between them is usually made to suit current conditions. At times when swell and surge are uncomfortable in one anchorage the other may be better.

Ensenada de Pechilinquillo, WPT 18°11.7', 103°7.5', is an open, west facing bay with a small pebble beach separating two rocky points. It is a marginal anchorage. Morro Chino, a large rocky island 98' high, lies off the western bluffs and is separated from them by a foul area. Though it is sometimes difficult to make out against the rocky background, Morro Chino is a good radar target for up to 10 miles. Punta Lizardo, a dark, thickly wood bluff about 98' high, marks the eastern side of the cove.

Anchor within the entrance just inside the line between Morro Chino and the tip of Punta Lizardo, about 1/4 to 1/3 mile from shore. Though it appears more protected further into the cove, the swell seems to be affected by the bottom configuration as it rushes in to break on the beach. A small village with no services is behind the beach.

It is important not to confuse this cove with the next one, which is a mile to the southeast. It has a dangerous rock in the middle of the cove and is readily differentiated, as it does not have a large island on its western side.

Caleta de Campos, WPT 18°04.22', 102°45', is about 23 miles further to the southeast, and faces south. A 13-mile long, sandy beach follows the rocky cliffs after Ensenada de Pechilinquillo, followed by a continuation of the rocky coast with red cliffs ashore contrasting with a milky hue to the nearby waters. Within this rocky section, Caleta de Campos is a sandy cove wedged between Buffadero Bluff and a rocky projection north of the end of Punta Corolon.

A small rock breakwater extends to the east from Buffadero Bluff where a light is located. Two small, flat-topped islands lie before this point but since they blend into the higher cliffs behind, they may not be visible until closer in. A village is on the bluff above the point and a series of palapas are on the small beach below.

The eastern point, consisting of reddish rocks, has two sharply indented sections, one of which has a "blow hole" that is smaller than the one near Buffadero Bluff. (Buffadero means 'snorter' in Spanish.) A paved runway, not usually seen from seaward, lies above the shore and the coastal road runs close behind this section of the cliffs.

Anchor just inside a line between the end of the breakwater and the rocky outcropping in the middle of the beach. Though the anchorage can be quite rolly, fore and aft anchors holding the vessel headed into the swell can make it more comfortable. Similar to Ensenada de Pechilinquillo, close approach to the shore finds you in waters more disturbed by the surf. As usual, landing can best be made where pangas are seen ashore. Facilities in the village include a medical clinic, pharmacy, dentist, laundry services and restaurants, Pemex station and bus service.

ENSA. DE PECHILINQUILLO
Michoacan

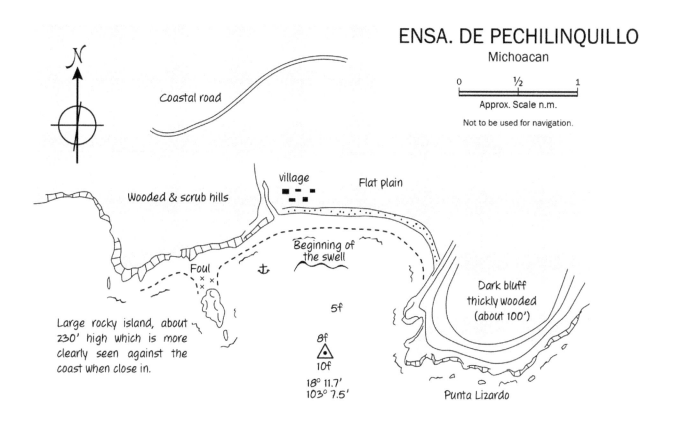

CALETA DE CAMPOS
Michoacan

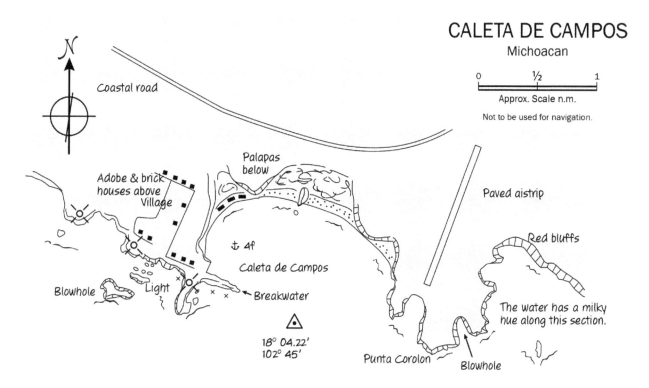

Do not turn into the bay until the breakwater is clearly seen.

LAZARO CARDENAS

The rocky cliffs beyond Buffadero Bluff continue for about 16 miles before the coastal mountains recede inland from a lower coastal strip that is the long, lovely beach of Playa Azul. This beach is about 16 miles long and ends at Punta Mangrove, a low, palm-treed point beyond which the delta of Rio Balsas exits into Bahia Petacalco. Rio Balsas is one of the longest and largest rivers in Mexico and hydroelectric dams on it control the river's discharge. In the rainy season the discharge of silt is seen for several miles at sea.

Lazaro Cardenas is a large commercial port at the delta of Rio Balsas and is an important railway terminus. It is not Cruiser Friendly. Development began in the early 1970s with the dredging of river outlets and construction of breakwaters that resulted in a port that now employs over 15,000 people. The towers, furnaces, boiler plants and large warehouses clearly identify this port. Approach to the port is confirmed by locating a sea buoy near **WPT 17°55.2', 102°09.3'.** The entry range of 330°T leads you through the breakwaters into the harbor entrance. A flashing red buoy is off the end of the northern breakwater.

Though there are no small craft facilities, this is an excellent harbor of refuge during tropical storms. Commercial traffic has the right of way in the channels and visiting yachtsmen are advised to give way to deep-sea traffic at all times when approaching and maneuvering in the area. There are often several large deep-sea ships anchored in the vicinity of the entrance to the channel. Before entering the channel into the harbor call Marina Traffic Central Control on VHF Ch 16 and they will then switch to Ch 14. Cruising vessels must check in with the Port Captain but at present it is not necessary to visit other officials.

The only anchorage is in the Rio Balsas channel in front of the Port Captain's building, across from the Naval Base. It is a convenient spot for checking in with the Port Captain or shopping. Keep a mid-channel course for almost half a mile before setting the anchor in about 12 feet. Anchor close to the Port Captain's building to leave room for Naval ships to turn around in the channel. When the valves in the upstream dam are opened for generation of electricity there may be a slight increase in the river's current, which is otherwise negligible.

Shore access is at the dinghy dock leading to the Port Captain's Office. There is a gate in the fence where a short sidewalk leads to the yard where the Port Captain's office is located. Cruisers are required to report to the Port Captain and have papers stamped, office hours from 8 am to 5 pm. There is a Customs office here. It is a short walk or taxi trip from the Port Captain's office to the main part of the town. Lazaro Cardenas is a busy, no-nonsense city which is unaffected by tourism. The downtown area has many shops where groceries and various supplies can be obtained and jerry can fuel is available from Pemex stations. All purchases must be ferried to your anchored boat.

Bahia Petacalco is an open bay with an uneven bottom. It is affected by the silting discharges of the river and unless you are entering the port, passage near the coast is inadvisable because of disturbed seas found in the shallow spots.

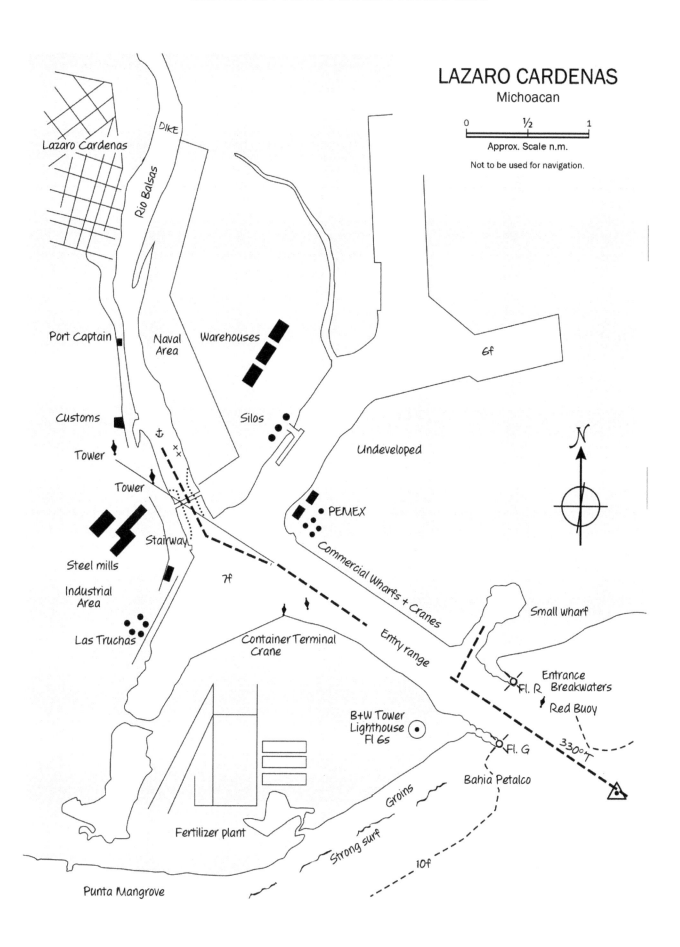

LAZARO CARDENAS
Michoacan

0   ½   1

Approx. Scale n.m.

Not to be used for navigation.

Lazaro Cardenas

DIKE

Rio Balsas

Port Captain

Naval Area

Warehouses

6f

Customs

Silos

Undeveloped

N

Tower

Tower

PEMEX

Steel mills

Stairway

Industrial Area

7f

Las Truchas

Container Terminal Crane

Commercial Wharfs + Cranes

Entry range

Small wharf

Entrance Breakwaters

Fl. R

Red Buoy

B+W Tower Lighthouse Fl 6s

Fl. G

330°T

Fertilizer plant

Bahia Petalco

Groins

Strong surf

10f

Punta Mangrove

ISLA GRANDE (IXTAPA ISLAND)

This popular island anchorage lies northwest of Punta Ixtapa and is just around the corner from the modern facility at Marina Ixtapa. Many large resort hotels and condominiums line the shores north of Punta Ixtapa and those of Bahia del Palmar, south of the point.

The island now has tourist facilities for visitors transported from the mainland by the boatload. Though the pre-development attraction of isolation and peace has been compromised, the anchorages are still secure and attractive, and the snorkeling is excellent. Tourists leave the island by 6:00 pm and the anchorages are peaceful overnight.

When approaching from the north, Isla Grande may appear to be part of a headland, for the bulk of Punta Ixtapa extends some distance offshore behind it. The island has an irregular shape consisting of three hilly sections and many surrounding rocks close to shore. **WPT 17°41', 101°40'.** The preferred anchorage is off the northern cove in 20 to 25 feet, sand. Larger vessels can anchor further out in 30 feet in **Bahia de Isla Grande** that is relatively open. The normal swell is from the southwest, thus the northern side of the island is relatively calm.

A dangerous rock covered by about 5 feet lies about ½ mile north of the north point of the island is marked by a red, lighted buoy. Do not pass close to the buoy for it is placed a short distance from the rock. Take a course clear of the buoyed rock, only turning into the anchorage when well clear of it.

A shoal with foul ground is located between the eastern side of the island and the shore, though small local boats bringing tourists to the island cross over it. Playa Linda, the long beach along the coast, has been a favorite holiday spot for Mexicans for many years. Some palapa restaurants are located north of Hotel Linda and its trailer park. Other large tourist developments line the beaches.

Alternative emergency anchorage, suitable for strong northwesterly winds is on the south side of Isla Grande off the central cove in about 20 feet. Because much damage has occurred to the coral formations in this area, it is recommended that cruisers avoid anchoring in this spot to prevent further damage. Rocks and shoals lie to the east and southeast. Once conch and other shells could be found in these shoal areas, but the heavy influx of tourists has taken its toll.

Isla Apies (Isle of Birds) is an island about 200' high that is connected to the mainland by a sandy bar at low water. Punta Ixtapa is the outermost point of the island. Continuing southward is Bahia de San Juan de Dios where several visible islets and unmarked Sacramento Reef must be avoided when traveling to Marina Ixtapa or Zihuatanejo. Rocks can be seen on the east side of Sacramento Reef but submerged rocks to the west must be given a wide berth.

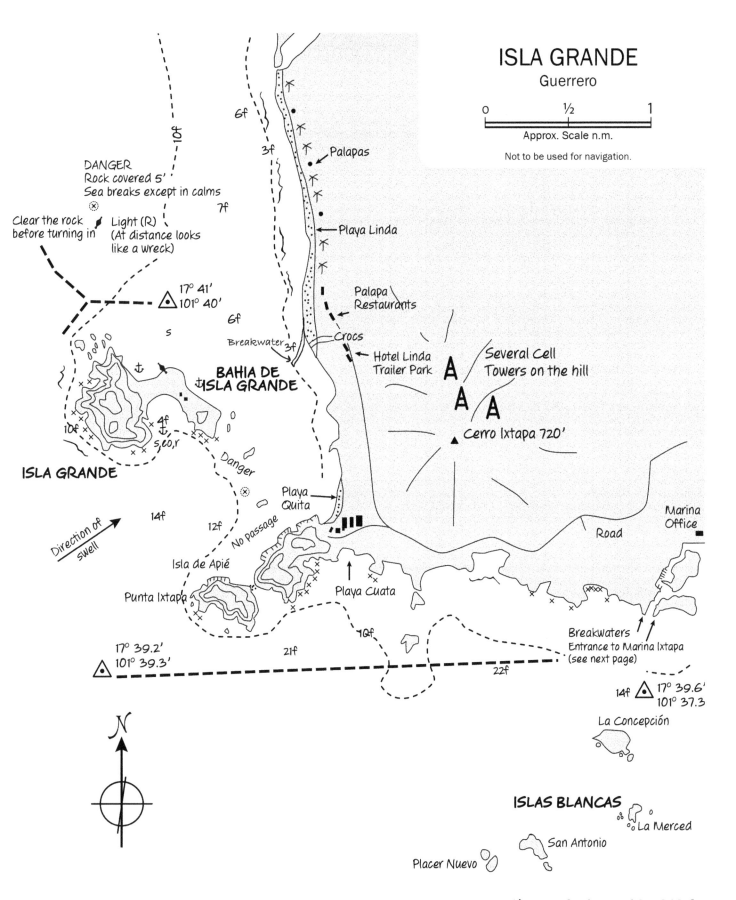

ISLA GRANDE
Guerrero

0   ½   1
Approx. Scale n.m.
Not to be used for navigation.

6f

3f

→ Palapas

→ Playa Linda

10f

DANGER
Rock covered 5'
Sea breaks except in calms
⊗

Clear the rock
before turning in   Light (R)
                     (At distance looks
                     like a wreck)

7f

17° 41'
101° 40'

Palapa
Restaurants

6f

s

Breakwater 3f

Crocs

BAHIA DE
ISLA GRANDE

⚓

Hotel Linda
Trailer Park

Several Cell
Towers on the hill

A A A

Cerro Ixtapa 720'

4f

ISLA GRANDE

10f

s,co,r

0

Danger

⊗

Direction of
swell

14f

12f

No passage

Isla de Apié

Playa
Quita

Playa Cuata

Road

Marina
Office

Punta Ixtapa

10f

21f

22f

Breakwaters
Entrance to Marina Ixtapa
(see next page)

17° 39.2'
101° 39.3'

14f   17° 39.6'
      101° 37.3

La Concepción

N

ISLAS BLANCAS
La Merced

San Antonio

Placer Nuevo

BAHIA DE SAN JUAN DE DIOS

285

IXTAPA AND ZIHUATANEJO

Bahia de San Juan de Dios lies to the east and south of Punta Ixtapa. Rocky bluffs inset with small isolated beaches are in the lee of the point. The mile-long curving beach is lined with luxury high-rise hotels, while a skein of small islands lies offshore. Ixtapa is under the jurisdiction of the Port Captain in Zihuatanejo. Ixtapa is a five-star tourist center, with two 18-hole golf courses, shopping centers, high-priced restaurants and a modern marina. Limited provisioning is possible in the market, "Scruples," but fresh meat is hard to find in Ixtapa. Taxis and inexpensive buses run frequently to Zihuatanejo.

Two short breakwaters protect the channel that is frequently dredged. The stated depth is 15 feet, however, depths of 6 feet have been reported on occasion. Call the marina to check the current depth before approaching. **WPT 17°39.2', 101°39.3'.** The entry channel leads to what was once a large lagoon that was a natural fish hatchery and home to crocodiles. Stay exactly in the middle of the channel to avoid grounding, and transit only at high tide. The fuel dock closes at 2:00 PM on Sundays, and has even shorter hours on holidays. A key is needed to get off the docks and out of the marina, so try to plan your arrival when the office is open. **Marina Ixtapa** is a full-service, modern marina providing showers, power, water, and pump-out facilities. To arrange for moorage when approaching the marina call the harbormaster on VHF Ch 16 which is monitored from 0900 to 1400 and 1600 to 1900. For information email administracion@marina-ixtapa.com. A swimming pool on the beach is available to marina guests. Caution: Do not swim in the marina area or leave small pets unattended for crocodiles can periodically be seen in the water looking for a tasty morsel!

Bahia de Zihuatanejo, WPT 17°37.15', 101°34', is about 6 miles southeast of Punta Ixtapa. Roca Negra is an isolated, lit rock about ½ miles southeast of the entrance to the bay. This is a lovely bay, with an entrance about ½ mile wide and large enough for over 100 boats to co-exist comfortably. Since the bay faces the southwest, the swell rolls straight in. Anchoring in the southeast corner is restricted by a number of snorkeling and swimming buoys that keep boats away from Los Gatos beach. Vessels anchored off La Ropa beach are in clean water, which is a plus for those with water makers, but dinghy landing through the surf can be difficult. The shortest dinghy ride to Zihuatanejo is in the lee of the inner point just outside the panga moorings, however, the town's sewer system empties into the bay here. The concrete dock at the northwestern corner of the bay is for fishing vessels.

When checking in, report first to Migracion near Zihuatanejo's central market, second to the Port Captain (at the head of the public dock), third to the specified bank to pay a port fee and finally report back to the Port Captain with the receipt. The Harbormaster will do the paper work for a reasonable fee. Asking other cruisers on the VHF is always a good way to find out the latest requirements.

Fuel can be delivered via panga from Ismael and Hilda who charge 100 pesos for their services. They also deliver propane, beer, ice and water. Laundry service is available. Landing is usually easy on the beach. Propane may also be obtained from Gas de Guerrero located about a block north of the central market.

The daily net on VHF Ch 22 at 0830 helps newcomers become familiarized with the town. Shops provide a practical mix of services with tourist-oriented stores not overpowering the village atmosphere. A low foot bridge to the west of the bay's pier leads to restaurants and the hotels. Provisioning is convenient at a large Commercial Mega that is within walking distance of the bay or by taking a bus to the Bodega market, between Zihuatanejo and Ixtapa.

Medical Note: Favorable reports have been received about the care given by Dr. J. Arturo Hernandez Montejano at Hospital Guadalupano in Zihuatanejo.

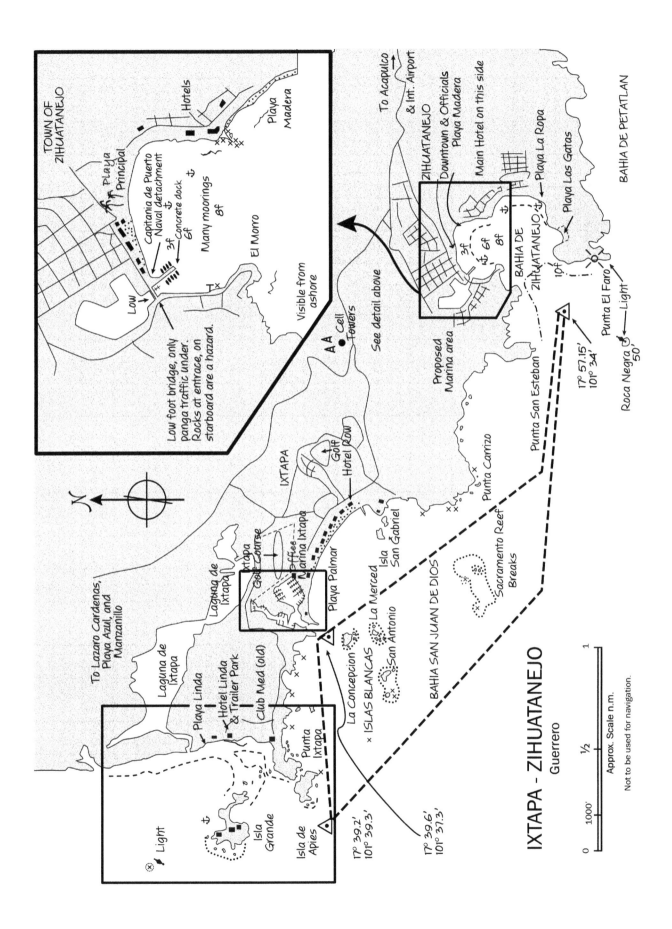

IXTAPA - ZIHUATANEJO
Guerrero

0   1000'   ½   1
Approx. Scale n.m.
Not to be used for navigation.

Stock up in the main market place. Photo by Betsy Crowfoot

In Zihuatanejo, pull your dinghy up on the beach next to the pier.
Photo by Betsy Crowfoot

Interactive map of the city of Zihuatanejo

Rocas Potosi AKA Los Frailes Blancos. Photo by Betsy Crowfoot

PUNTA DE PAPANOA

Bahia de Petatlan is just to the south of Bahia de Zihuatanejo. At its southern end is Morro Petatlan, a 650' hill, the western extremity of which is Punta Gorda. A group of Islets, Rocas Potosi (AKA Los Frailes Blancos), lie about 1½ mile off this point, two of which are large, white and prominent when approaching from the north or south. They are excellent landmarks assisting in identifying your position and lie approximately 7 miles south of Zihuatanejo and about a mile off Punta Gorda (Morro de Petatlan). **Potosi Anchorage** is a beautiful anchorage off the south end of a long beach where the land begins to rise, leading to Morro de Petatlan. It offers good protection from the east and south, but is exposed to northwesterlies. **WPT 17°2.33', 101°27'** for the anchorage in 20 feet, sand. Inland from the beach is Laguna Potosi, an extensive swampy area, complete with crocodiles and bugs, although an interesting place to explore by kayak.

South of Morro de Petatlan the coast is a long stretch of sandy beach, broken from Punta Japutica to Morro de Papanoa by a rocky projection of the coastal mountains. Morro de Las Animas is a large guano-covered rocky island is which is about 3½ miles north of Morro de Papanoa. However, Morro de Papanoa at 527', is a striking protrusion from the coast and identification of Morro de Las Animas is merely confirmation of your approach to Bahia de Tequepa. The knoll (morro) is the westernmost of a series of bluffs which are covered with dense brush (with some rocky edges breaking the pattern) and it is connected to the mainland by a low neck of land.

The northern tip of Morro de Papanoa is Punta de Papanoa. In the cove on the north side, two breakwaters form the protected little harbor of Puerto Escondido. **WPT 17°16.7', 101°3.5'.** Pangas usually line the shore at the head of the cove. A naval dock is at the head of the western breakwater and an army base is on the shore further into the bay. Army personnel often check the papers of cruising vessels. Transient vessels may anchor inside the harbor in about 25 to 30 feet.

Limited provisions may be purchased in the small, rather run-down village of Puerto Escondido on the south side of the harbor. A building labeled 'Marine Laboratory' is located in the town. Another small village is on the beach, about a mile north of the town, which is a short distance from the main coastal highway. There is another open cove on the south side of Punta de Papanoa, which has a foul bottom. From Papanoa the coast to Acapulco is an almost continuous stretch of steep sandy beach for about 70 miles. The rocky projection that marks the entrance to the harbor at Acapulco is the only interruption in this beach, which continues thereafter from Puerto Marques another 60 miles to Punta Acamama, far to the south. Though the land is low behind the coast and often backed by lagoons, mountain ranges rise to 12,000' within 40 miles of the coast.

PUNTA DE PAPANOA
Guerrero

0   1000'   ¼   ½

Approx. Scale n.m.

Not to be used for navigation.

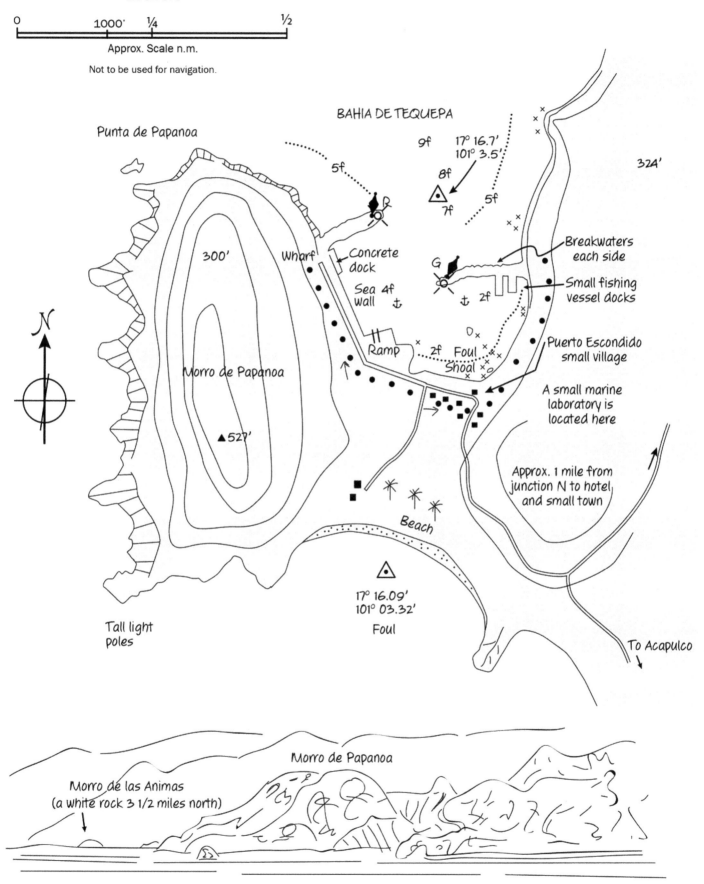

BAHIA DE TEQUEPA

Punta de Papanoa

9f   17° 16.7'
101° 3.5'

8f

7f

5f

5f

324'

300'

Wharf   Concrete dock

Sea 4f
wall

Morro de Papanoa

Ramp

▲527'

Breakwaters
each side

G

2f

Small fishing
vessel docks

2f   Foul
Shoal

Puerto Escondido
small village

A small marine
laboratory is
located here

Approx. 1 mile from
junction N to hotel
and small town

Beach

17° 16.09'
101° 03.32'

Tall light
poles   Foul

To Acapulco

Morro de Papanoa

Morro de las Animas
(a white rock 3 1/2 miles north)

ACAPULCO

One of the world's finest natural harbors and a **Port of Entry**, Acapulco is easy to identify. Not only is the major rocky projection from the long beach distinctive, but the numerous buildings and developments on shore are a clear indication of approach to this sprawling city. Isla Roqueta lies off the western side of the entrance and is separated from the mainland by Boca Chica (Small Mouth). Vessels can pass through this deep, narrow channel or pass around the island to enter the harbor through Boca Grande, a 1¼ mile wide entrance. The harbor within occupies an oval about 3 miles wide. The east side of the harbor is a naval base and cruise ship, commercial and fishermen's docks are on the west side. Small boat facilities are in the southwestern bight, tucked behind Punta Griffo.

Two marinas operate in the bay and mooring fees vary from time to time, but are generally comparable to those charged in U.S. marinas. The **Club de Yates de Acapulco** provides first-class facilities such as laundry (pickup and delivery), showers, washrooms, children's play area, portable pump-out, Wi-fi, tennis courts, swimming pool, children's sailing school and rescue center. The marina caters primarily to Yacht Club members but non-members are welcome if space is available. It is advisable to call ahead to ascertain the availability of space and services offered to cruising vessels. When anchored, a rather stiff fee be charged for use of the dinghy dock and access to the pool. Moorings are also available. They may be reached by telephone at 011-52-744-482-3859/60, Ext.109, via Fax at 011-52-744-482-2836 or email: nanegacion@clubdeyatesaca.com.mx. Fuel is available at the Club de Yates and arrangements for propane pickup and delivery can be made at the Club office. A 25-ton Travelift, small workyard and stackable small boat storage are available for vessels up to 33'. A marine supply store is located near the driveway.

The fuel dock in Acapulco. Photo: Betsy Crowfoot

La Marina is located near the prominent tower a short distance from the Yacht Club. **WPT 16°50.35', 99°54.28'** For information call 011-52 74-83-7498, www.lamarinaacapulco.com. The marina offers electricity, potable water, amenities at the club house, security etc.

Provisions can be purchased from local shops but a better variety can be found at the market. An ATM is about a half a block from the main gate. Bus service to the center of the city is frequent and very cheap; taxis are readily available but be sure to agree on a price before getting in the car.

A tourist information center is conveniently located on Hornos Beach. You can use the blue-tiled domes of a church as a landmark when looking for the main plaza. Two blocks away on La Costera is the Post Office Building where you may do your own paper work if Acapulco is your first port of entry, (or if you are departing Mexico) if you haven't had your entry papers handled by the marina office. On the north side of the bay is the famous Hotel Row with its well-known profusion of nightclubs, discos and restaurants.

Puerto Marques is the smaller bay opening to the east of Boca Grande. Anywhere else this would be a spectacular harbor, but it suffers by comparison and close proximity to Acapulco. The beach at the eastern end is a crowded collection of palapa restaurants and the remaining shores are filled with condos. The safety of a vessel in this anchorage is questionable and security concerns discourage leaving your dinghy on the nearby beaches. Anchor in 25 feet off the panga moorings in sand. You can drop off and pick up at the public dock.

Interactive map of the city

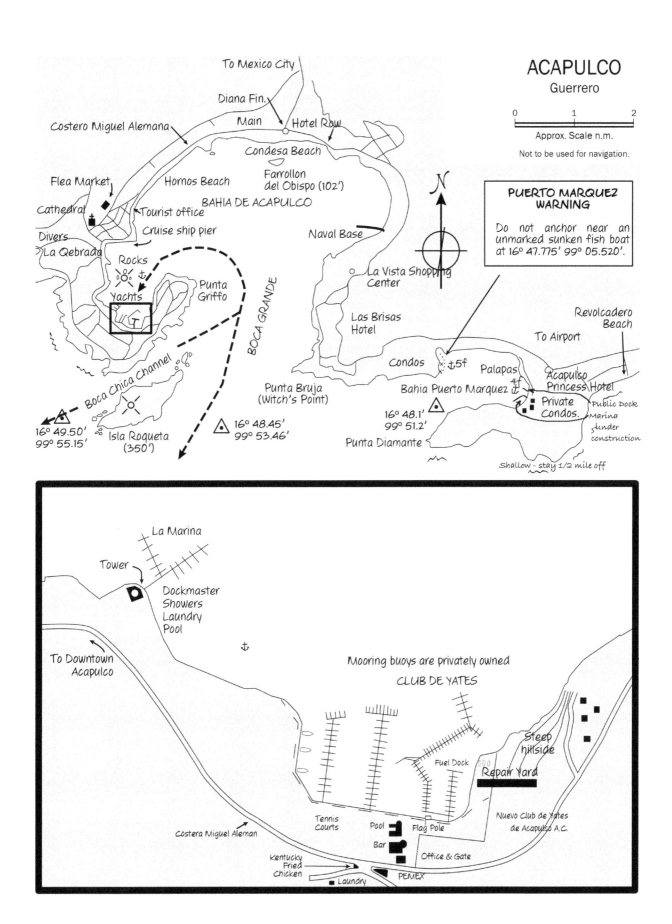

To Mexico City

Diana Fin.

Main

Costero Miguel Alemana

Hotel Row

Condesa Beach

Flea Market

Hornos Beach

Farrollon
del Obispo (102')

Cathedral

BAHIA DE ACAPULCO

Tourist office

Divers

Cruise ship pier

La Qebrada

Rocks

Naval Base

Yachts

Punta
Griffo

Boca Chica Channel

BOCA GRANDE

Isla Roqueta
(350')

16° 49.50'
99° 55.15'

16° 48.45'
99° 53.46'

Punta Bruja
(Witch's Point)

N

ACAPULCO
Guerrero

0   1   2

Approx. Scale n.m.

Not to be used for navigation.

**PUERTO MARQUEZ
WARNING**

Do not anchor near an
unmarked sunken fish boat
at 16° 47.775' 99° 05.520'.

La Vista Shopping
Center

Las Brisas
Hotel

Condos

↨5f

Palapas

Bahia Puerto Marquez

16° 48.1'
99° 51.2'

Punta Diamante

Revolcadero
Beach

To Airport

Acapulso
Princess Hotel

Private
Condos.

Public Dock

Marina
under
construction

Shallow - stay 1/2 mile off

La Marina

Tower

Dockmaster
Showers
Laundry
Pool

To Downtown
Acapulco

Mooring buoys are privately owned

CLUB DE YATES

Steep
hillside

Fuel Dock

Repair Yard

Nuevo Club de Yates
de Acapulco A.C.

Tennis
Courts

Pool

Flag Pole

Costera Miguel Aleman

Bar

Office & Gate

Kentucky
Fried
Chicken

PEMEX

Laundry

SECTION IV: ACAPULCO TO PUERTO CHIAPAS

This section of the mainland covers approximately 500 miles of coastline of which about 250 miles border the Gulf of Tehuantepec that stretches from Puerto Angel to Puerto Madero. Because of the long distances between the few harbors available, and the intimidating and well deserved reputation of the Gulf of Tehuantepec, few cruisers sail these waters for pleasure. Those who pass this way do so because they are heading to or from the Panama Canal or are sailing for other offshore destinations.

Except for the Gulf of Tehuantepec, sea breezes generally commence near noon, increase in the afternoon, then diminish in the late evening; land breezes occur at night, but they are variable in strength and direction. The rainy season is from May to November, with most of the precipitation falling during afternoon thunderstorms. During these months, tropical disturbances such as chubascos, tropical cyclones (tropical storms and hurricanes) show increased activity.

In the Gulf of Tehuantepec, winds average force 6 throughout the year. Violent gales, known as Tehuantepeckers, normally occur from October to April but they can happen at any time. Lasting from a few hours to as much as several days, their Force 8 or 9 winds raise treacherous, short, high seas which can be experienced as much as 100 miles offshore. Forecasts can give up to 12 hours notice of the beginning of a Tehuantepecker. A Vessel Traffic Control center and Weather Reporting Station for the Gulf of Tehuantepec has been established. This high-tech facility has taken much of the guess-work out of choosing a time for passing through the area. Prior to departing Huatulco you should contact the Port Captain to get the latest weather report as he can obtain the most accurate and up-to-date information available.

Because of the intensity of the winds in the Gulf of Tehuantepec this is rarely an easy passage and if caught by a Tehuantepecker it can be truly dangerous. It is essential to keep informed of weather forecasts, wait out storms in a safe anchorage or port, then make a run for it. Two schools of though exist regarding crossing the Tehuantepec. One is to sail "with one foot on the shore," the other is to travel 500 miles offshore. Whichever route the cruiser selects, prudent skippers will wait for a weather window before heading out across the Gulf.

From Acapulco to Puerto Angel the coast consists of long stretches of sandy beaches backed by lagoons or low, rolling hills covered with dense foliage. In the distance the Sierra Madre del Sur mountain range can be seen and the shoreline is punctuated by prominent cliffs and high bluffs. Forming a gap between the mountain ranges to the west and east is the Isthmus of Tehuantepec through which the strong northerly winds are funneled with accelerated strength. Further south, the high Sierra Madre mountains with their lush foothills and flat coastal plain are separated from much of the sandy coast by numerous lagoons

TABLE 4

APPROXIMATE DISTANCES BETWEEN ANCHORAGES OF SECTION IV
(Acapulco to Puerto Chiapas)

Acapulco	175	212	236	289	538
	Escondido	37	63	126	426
		Puerto Angel	26	86	146
			Huatulco	60	300
				Salina Cruz	240
					Puerto Chiapas

PUERTO ESCONDIDO

The 175-mile coast from Acapulco to Puerto Escondido is predominantly one long, sandy beach interrupted by a few silt-laden rivers and several rocky points and headlands. Variable currents close inshore, detached rocks and dangers such as Tartar Shoals, discourage hugging the coast too closely. Maintaining a safe distance offshore means giving Punta Maldonada a berth of at least 8 miles.

The first anchorage beyond Acapulco is 140 miles distant at **Bahia de Chacahua**. Breakers are evident, though rolly anchorage may be taken between the rocks east of Punta Galera and the sandy beach to the north **WPT 15°58', 97°40'.** Two breakwaters have been built to access the lagoon, but the entrance is shallow and no facilities are available here.

About 35 miles further east are the steep, gray, tumbled rocks of Acantilados de Escondido, beyond which is Bahia Escondido. A range of low hills overlooks the bay, the southeastern end of which is marked by Punta Escondido. A prominent white cross on the land beyond the point is a good landmark. **WPT 15°51.2', 97°03.7'.**

Though the bay is open to the southwest, good, though somewhat rolly anchorage can be taken in the northeastern part of the bay in 35 to 50 feet, sand. Watch the depth sounder when picking a spot, as an underwater canyon lies between the two rocky areas on each side of the northern end of the bay. Many pangas tied to private moorings mark the edge of the shallow water. Landing is easiest on the western end of the beach where native craft are scattered ashore.

You must report to the Port Captain whose office is next to the naval detachment. Office hours can fluctuate but from Monday to Friday you are expected to check in; otherwise, report to the senior officer at the naval detachment upon coming ashore.

The town of Puerto Escondido is north of the bay. Fuel (available at a Pemex station on the highway) and water must be ferried to the boat in jerry cans or water bottles. Groceries and other basic supplies are found a good walk or taxi-ride up the hill to Avenida 16 de Septiembre where there are the variety of shops and the main grocery store, "Super Che." About a half a block down the hill on the opposite side of the road is a bakery called, "Panificadora: Reyna Del Valle." It is easy to miss it among the numerous small shops that line the street. Propane is available at Gas de Oaxaca, which is a taxi ride away on the highway; call ahead at (958) 2-03-46.

Catering to the ever-increasing tourist traffic, many hotels, restaurants, bars, discos and craft shops line Avenida Alfonso Perez Casca. The palapa-lined beach backs on to the thoroughfare where it becomes a pleasant, wide pedestrian mall and meeting place for the local population. The town has a slightly Mediterranean charm as a consequence of a book and movie based here that attracted many Italians who eventually settled, bringing a touch of their lifestyle.

A lovely, secluded beach lies at the head of Puerto Angelito, which is a pocket bay located a short distance northwest of Acantilados de Escondido. In the opposite direction, Playa Zicatela is reputed to be one of the four best surfing beaches in the world. Caution: a dangerous undertow is present in these waters.

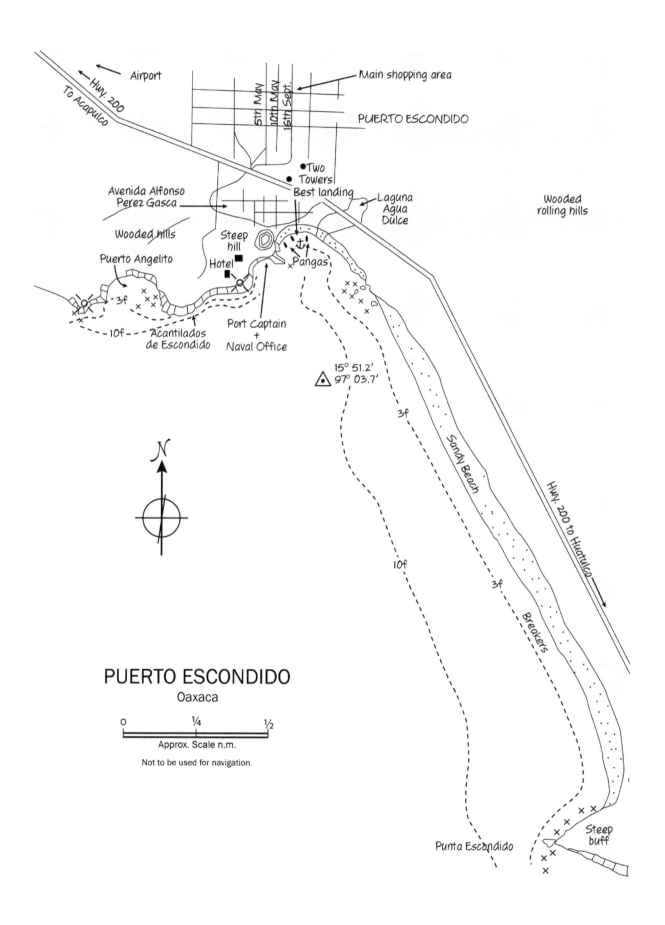

Airport

Hwy. 200

To Acapulco

Main shopping area

5th May
10th May
16th Sept.

PUERTO ESCONDIDO

● Two
● Towers
Best landing

Laguna
Agua
Dulce

Wooded
rolling hills

Avenida Alfonso
Perez Gasca

Wooded hills

Steep
hill

Hotel

Puerto Angelito

Pangas

3f

10f — Acantilados
de Escondido

Port Captain
+
Naval Office

15° 51.2'
97° 03.7'

3f

N

10f

3f

Sandy Beach

Hwy. 200 to Huatulco

3f

Breakers

PUERTO ESCONDIDO

Oaxaca

0   ¼   ½

Approx. Scale n.m.

Not to be used for navigation.

Punta Escondido

Steep
buff

297

PUERTO ANGEL

In Puerto Angel, the east side of the bay is overrun by pangas.
Photo: Betsy Crowfoot

The next anchorage is an easy 37-mile run to beautiful Bahia de Puerto Angel. Most of the coastline consists of white, sandy beach marked by the flying spray of breakers. These sometimes extend some distance offshore, giving an indication of shoal waters that should be given a clear berth.

The western approach to the bay is indicated by Puerto Angel Light which is mounted on a 46' stone tower located on Punta Izuca, found about ½ miles west of Bahia de Puerto Angel. About 2½ miles west of the entrance to the bay are two rocks, Roca Negra and Roca Blanca, which are about ½ mile offshore. North of these is a small, foul bay which should be ignored.

Entrance to Bahia de Puerto Angel is between a rocky islet on the west and a conspicuous 290' bluff on the east side. **WPT 15°39.497', 96°29.53'.** A short distance beyond the entrance, visible rocks on the western side reduce the channel to about 200 yards opposite the bluff headland of Bufaderos.

What a treat! This picturesque anchorage gives excellent protection from all but southerly winds. The best area is in the northwestern part of the bay in 25 to 40 feet, sand; a cemetery on the steep hillside makes a good landmark for the anchorage. Landing ashore is usually through gentle surf though occasionally a heavy swell disturbs the bay. Surge in the vicinity of the concrete pier discourages any approach to the landing platform that is a popular fishing spot.

Puerto Angel is a **Port of Entry** and the skipper must report to the Port Captain whose office is in a white, clearly labeled building a short distance east of the pier. Office hours are 0800 to 1500, Monday to Friday; otherwise report to the senior office at the Naval Detachment that is marked by two large flagpoles further along the beach. Sometimes the Harbormaster or Port Captain will fill in a form for southbound vessels that is to be turned in to officials in Huatulco. At present there is neither a Migracion, or an Aduana office located here.

Fuel must be trucked to the pier from the city of Pochutla, 10 miles inland. Arrangements can be made by a telephone call in Spanish to Gasolinera San Pedro at 40270. If only a small amount is needed you can take a taxi to the station to fill up your jerry cans.

Puerto Angel is a tourist town with houses and hotels perched on the steep hillsides with convenience stores, fast food outlets and souvenir shops crowded on to the street facing the beach. A bank is located on the main road near the center of town. By following the road around the bay you can take a short, steep walk up the hill to the hotel overlooking the bay for some memorable photographs. A laundry, pharmacy and grocery store can supply most of your needs but for major provisioning better selection and prices are in Pochutla, an interesting town to explore that may be reached by taking a 10-mile taxi trip.

Puerto Angel. Anchor just around this rock on the west side.
Photo: Betsy Crowfoot

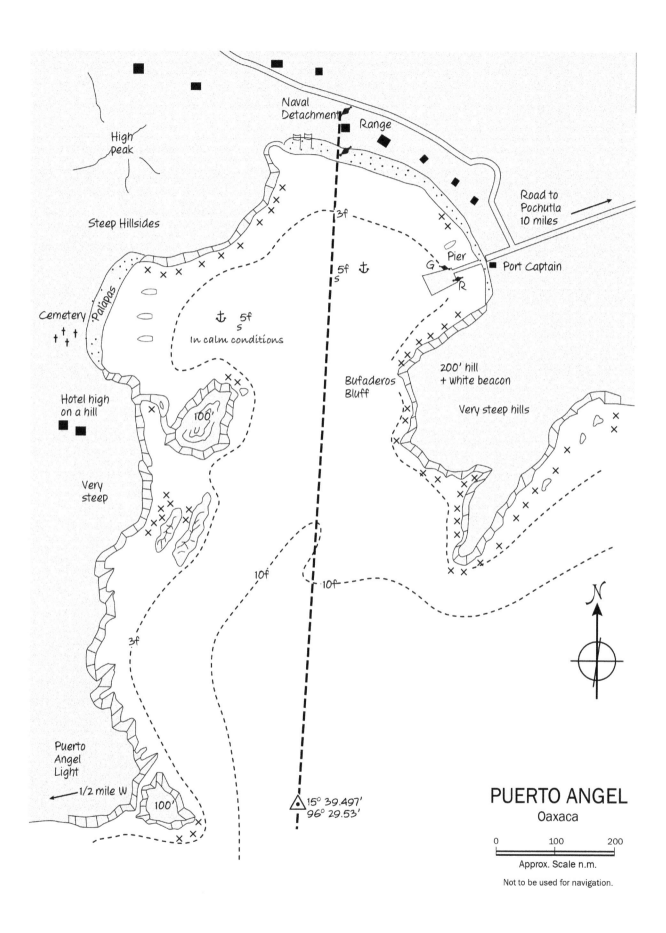

Naval
Detachment   Range
High
peak
Steep Hillsides   3f
                                    Road to
                                    Pochutla
                                    10 miles
Palapas   Pier
                              5f ⚓
                              s   G   Port Captain
Cemetery   R
        † † †   ⚓ 5f
        †   s
                    In calm conditions
Hotel high   200' hill
on a hill   + white beacon
        ■ ■   100'
                                    Very steep hills
Very
steep   Bufaderos
                                    Bluff

                                              N

                        10f
              10f   10f

        3f

Puerto
Angel
Light
    ← 1/2 mile W
              100'   ⚠ 15° 39.497'
                          96° 29.53'

PUERTO ANGEL
Oaxaca

0   100   200
Approx. Scale n.m.

Not to be used for navigation.

BAHIAS DE HUATULCO (pronounced wah-tool-koh)

Proceeding from Puerto Angel the coast follows an easterly direction with sandy beaches alternating with rocky bluffs and a few rocks close to shore. Some 15 miles from Puerto Angel is the first notable landmark of Punta Sacrificios, standing out from the eastern edge of a well defined bay having the same name. **WPT 15°40.35', 96°13.87'**. This marks the beginning of a series of 12 spectacular bays and coves along the rocky coast known as Bahias de Huatulco.

The 12 bays, from southwest to northeast are: Puerto Sacrificios, Jicaral and Rescalillo, Manglillo, Isla Chachacul, Isla Cacaluta, Maguey and Organo, Bahia Santa Cruz (Huatulco Bay), Chahue, Tangolunda and Conejo. A total of 36 sandy beaches are found in this convoluted stretch of coast that is backed by heavily wooded, rolling hills. Scattered rocks and reefs make some of the bays inaccessible and only for exploration by dinghy, but these hazards for boats are one of the main reasons that this area is a diver's paradise. There is something for everyone, good snorkeling and diving to view beautiful coral and several wrecks that can be explored.

After leaving Puerto Angel, the next distinctive landmark is Isla Cacaluta that is 4½ miles east of Punta Sacrifios and lies ¼ mile offshore. A little over 3 miles beyond is Punta Bufadero where there is a light on an aluminum tower. A blowhole in one of the rocks makes a sound resembling a blowing whale. The 4 mile stretch from Punta Bufadero to the east contains 4 fairly deeply indented bays separated by tree-covered hills with rocky shores. Many of these anchorages are for day use only, as they are exposed to wind and swell when the weather is up. Overnight anchorage and moorings are available in several coves, depending on the weather conditions.

The most popular small craft anchorages are in Puerto Huatulco (Bahia Santa Cruz) and Bahia Tangola (Bahia Tangolunda). Details for these anchorages are given in the pages that follow. At the present time the only **Port Captain's** office in Bahias de Huatulco is located in the basin of what is called Puerto Huatulco in the U.S. Pilot, but has been known locally for many years as Bahia de Santa Cruz.

Puerto Sacrificios is just east of **Punta Sacrificios**, and is tricky to get into. It is exposed to the south and east, and has several rocks to avoid. There are two anchorage spots within the bay. Enter the bay from the **WPT 15°40.80', 96°14.00'**, on a straight course heading north toward the break in the sand beach where a tree topped cliff divides it into two beaches. There are many rocks on both sides of this course, some awash and some exposed. The first anchorage is just past the point on your port, even with the island (Isla Sacrificios) on starboard. The second is further into the bay, following the northerly bearing. Depths in both are 25 to 30 feet. See the sketch.

Jicaral and Rescalillo are two coves which are side by side, just east of Sacrificios. Swing wide before entering, as there is a large white rock with surrounding smaller rocks awash, just south of the cove. Jicaral is a pretty cove, **WPT 15°41.67', 96°13.40'**, with a sand beach, and no roads. Anchor in 25 feet, sand. Rescalillo is next door to the east and is very narrow deeper into the cove. It is another roadless cove with an interesting bit of exploring ashore. Watch for the submerged rocks about 100 yards outside the cove, south of the eastern point.

Manglillo is a two lobed cove, which is foul on the eastern side. **WPT 15°41.90', 96°12.82'**. It is located a few hundred yards northeast of Rescalillo. Anchor off the beach on the western side in 20 feet, sand.

CHACHACUAL AND LA INDIA

Again, swing wide, away from the shoreline when approaching these coves, due to outlying rocks and reefs. Enter from **WPT 15°41.96', 96°12.02'**, and head due north into the cove. Anchor in either side, with the swell as a determining factor. Avoid the rocks on the west side (breaks) and the reef on the east side (breaks). Both coves are sand.

Isla Cacaluta is a small island that lies just off the pointed beach of Bahia Cacaluta. Anchorage may be taken on the northwest side in the lee of the island. **WPT 15°43.17', 96°9.80',** in about 35 feet, sand. The south side is rocky. Anchorage may also be taken in the eastern part of the bay.

Bahias Maguey and Organo are two coves that look a bit like Mickey Mouse on a chart. They are separated by a small wooded headland, and both offer different protection. Maguey has a road and houses on the beach, and is less protected from the southeast. Organo has no houses or road, and offers more protection, especially further into the cove. An entrance **WPT 15°43.85', 96°8.56',** serves both coves.

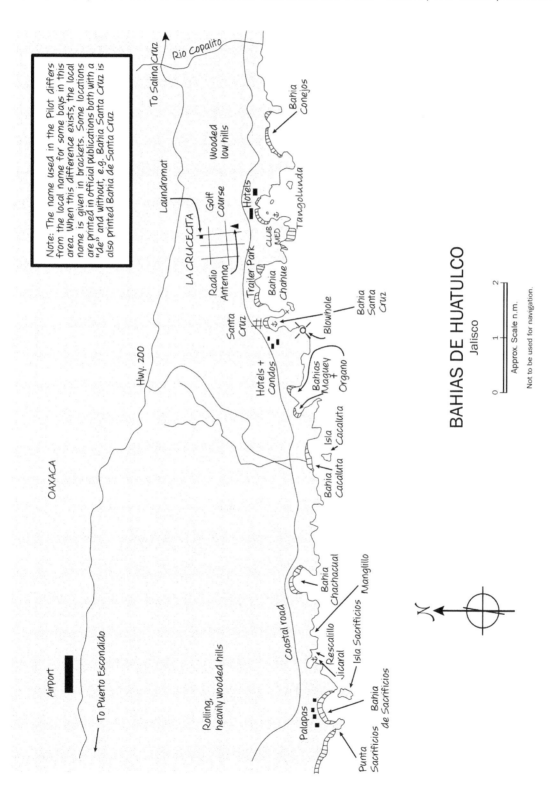

Note: The name used in the Pilot differs from the local name for some bays in this area. When this difference exists, the local name is given in brackets. Some locations are printed in official publications both with a "de" and without, e.g. Bahia Santa Cruz is also printed Bahia de Santa Cruz

BAHIAS DE HUATULCO
Jalisco

Approx. Scale n.m.
Not to be used for navigation.

BAHIA DE SANTA CRUZ (PUERTO HUATULCO) AND BAHIA CHAHUE

A wide point approximately 2½ miles north east of Isla Cacaluta, marks the westerly side of the entrance to **Bahia Santa Cruz**. There is a light on the highest part of the point. The entrance to Bahia Santa Cruz **WPT 15°44.72', 96°7.33'**, is between Punta Manzano and Punta Rosas, which lies almost ½ mile to the NNE. Piedra Blanca, a 90ft high patch of rocks, is 400 yards southeast off Punta Rosas. This area should be avoided because reefs extend southeast of both Punta Rosas and Piedra Blanca and the waters between these two patches are also foul.

Extending in a dogleg fashion into the center of the bay is **Muelle Santa Cruz**, a large concrete cruise ship dock capable of handling two 900 ft. passenger vessels. Visiting yachts should anchor to the east of the dock, out of the channel. In the northeast corner of the bay, behind the Muelle are two rock breakwaters protecting a channel into a dredged basin lined with a concrete seawall. **Santa Cruz Marina** is usually occupied by shallow draft charter vessels that cater to tourists. The Port Captain's office is in a clearly marked building just inside the west corner of the basin in front of the cruise ship dock. This is a Port of Entry where you may obtain a Zarpe before leaving Mexico for points south. Just around the corner from Bahia de Santa Cruz is the larger wide open bay of **Bahia de Chahue**.

Marina Chahue is a safe port with services, and close to town while you wait out the Tehuantepeckers. Photo: Betsy Crowfoot

When leaving Bahia de Santa Cruz, give a wide berth to Punta Rosas and the rocks and reefs extending out from Piedra Blanca and enter the center of Bahia de Chahue between Piedra Blanca and the exposed rocks seen ½ mile to the northeast. The clearly marked approach to Marina Chahue lies in a north-northwesterly direction.

Marina Chahue is an excellent place to stop before or after crossing the Gulf of Tehuantepec. The entrance is at **WPT 15°45.61', 96°07.21'**. The well marked channel, with a depth of 12 ft., is between a rock jetty and the face of a small mountain ridge. The marina has 86 slips for boats up to 70 ft. in length and six for yachts up to 180 ft. Thirty slips with no services are available on a secondary channel. At times, surge in the marina necessitates the use of chafing gear on mooring lines. Fuel is no longer available at the fuel dock. A small building at the head of the main dock houses the marina office. Across from the

Marina Chahue entrance. Photo: Betsy Crowfoot

office are bathrooms with showers attached to the outside of the building. Free Wi-Fi is provided and laundry is picked up in the office and delivered back to your boat. A dry storage yard is available for trailerable boats. For information and Tehuantepic advice contact the helpful English and French speaking harbormaster Enrique Laclette who monitors VHF Ch. 16, Tel/Fax, 52 (958) 587-2652 or e-mail, marinachahue@hotmail.com. He can arrange for pickup and delivery of propane as well as transportation to the Pemex station for jerry can fuel until diesel is available at the marina. However, the marina does not allow transfer of fuel from jerry cans in the slips. You must go to the closed fuel dock to transfer fuel. Welcome to Mexico! A large Che Supermercado is a short walk up the road towards La Crucecita. For banking, provisioning, medical needs, and a wide range of restaurants and shops, walk or take a taxi to the nearby town of **La Crucecita** (Little Cross).

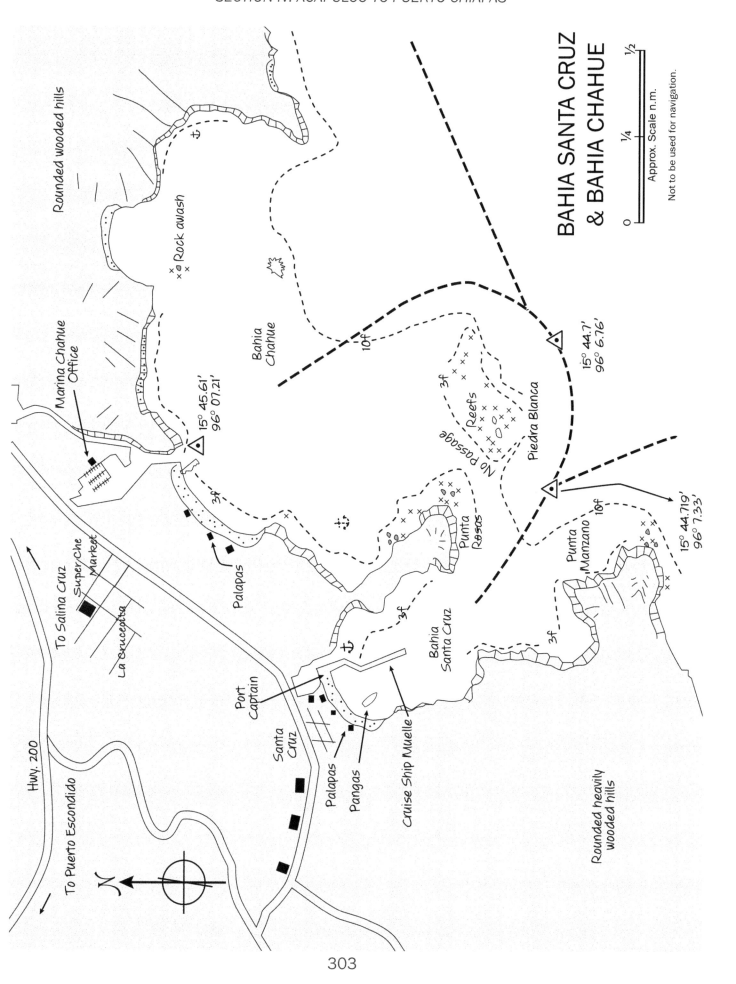

BAHIA SANTA CRUZ
& BAHIA CHAHUE

Approx. Scale n.m.

Not to be used for navigation.

0   ¼   ½

Rounded wooded hills

Rock awash

Bahia
Chahue

10f

15° 44.7'
96° 6.76'

3f

Reefs

Piedra Blanca

No Passage

Marina Chahue
Office

15° 45.61'
96° 07.21'

3f

Palapas

Punta
Rosas

Punta
Manzano

10f

15° 44.719'
96° 7.33'

To Salina Cruz

SuperChe
Market

La Crucecita

3f

3f

Port
Captain

Bahia
Santa Cruz

Hwy. 200

To Puerto Escondido

N

Santa
Cruz

Palapas

Pangas

Cruise Ship Muelle

Rounded heavily
wooded hills

303

BAHIA Tangolunda

The last big bay of Bahias de Huatulco is separated from Bahia Santa Cruz (Bahia Chahue) by a wooded, rock-lined peninsula that is about 1 mile wide. This bay is easily identified by the colorful tanks and sprawling structures of Club Med perched on the western end of the bay. The large, wooded island of Isla Tangola Tangola that is located outside the eastern end of the bay, has a shoal, rocky area separating it from a smaller island northwest of it. Within the bay are two other treed island groups and a rocky islet that should not be closely approached since detached and underwater rocks are close by. Huge hotels such as the Barcelo Hotel (formerly, Sheraton) and Royal Maeva, are built near the beach and serve as artificial landmarks. Further hotel development in the area continues to take place.

When approaching from the west, a safe berth should be given to the wooded peninsula separating Bahia Chahue from Bahia Tangola Tangola to avoid the patch of detached rocks and reefs, which extend seaward. Entry to the bay from the east is safest by rounding Isla Tangola Tangola as there may be some uncharted rocks in the canal separating the numerous rocks and shallower areas from the shore. **WPT 15°45.30', 96°5.26'.**

Bahia Tangolunda provides good, but often, rolly anchorage in 30 to 60 feet, sand in the western end of the bay near the Club Med. The use of facilities at Club Med is at the discretion of the staff.

Landing ashore is easy through gentle surf. For those who want to enjoy a game of golf, an 18-hole golf course lies beyond the Sheraton Hotel. As part of the complex is a typical shopping center featuring jewelry, sportswear, quality handicrafts and five-star restaurants. For banking services, take a taxi to La Crucecita where a multitude of shops and a variety of services satisfy shopping needs. ATMs are widely available.

Bahia Conejo is a three lobed bay. **WPT 15°46.36', 96°4.15'.** The westernmost is the smallest, with a large hotel ashore. Anchor in sand in 25 feet, sand. You might go ashore to make use of the spa services.

The center lobe of the bay has a long stretch or beach with no development ashore. It is exposed to any southeasterly wind and swell. Anchor on the northwestern side, behind the exposed rocks.

The northeastern lobe is more protected than the others. There is a large hotel ashore. Enter mid bay to avoid exposed rocks, and anchor off the beach.

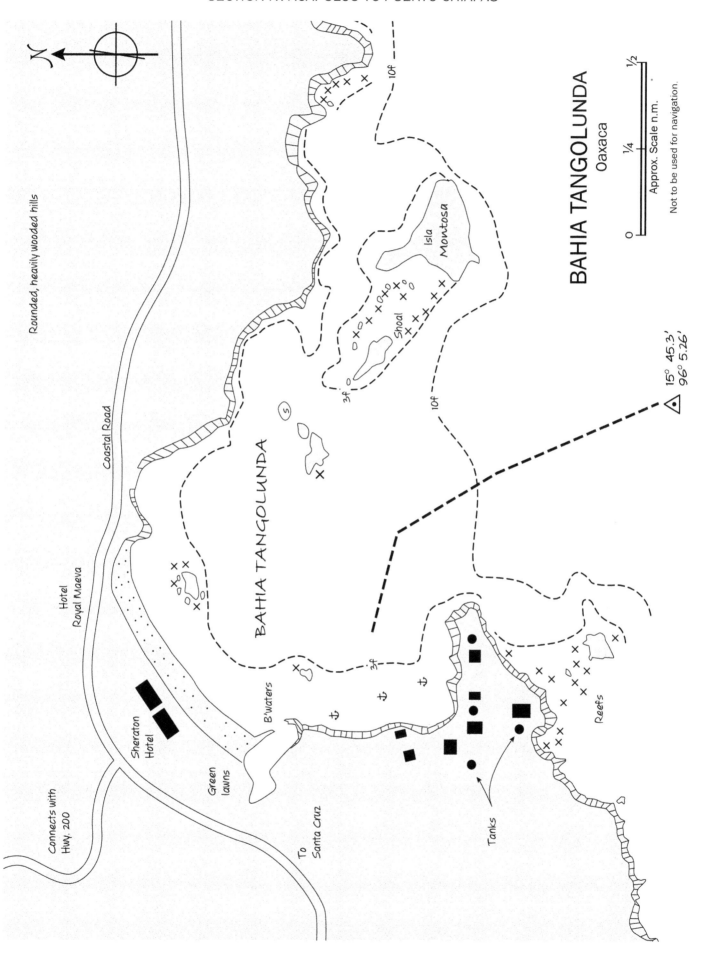

Rounded, heavily wooded hills

Coastal Road

Hotel
Royal Maeva

Connects with
Hwy. 200

Sheraton
Hotel

Green
lawns

To
Santa Cruz

B'waters

BAHIA TANGOLUNDA

Tanks

Reefs

Shoal

Isla
Montosa

3f

10f

10f

3f

3f

10f

S

15° 45.3'
96° 5.26'

BAHIA TANGOLUNDA
Oaxaca

0   ¼   ½

Approx. Scale n.m.

Not to be used for navigation.

SALINA CRUZ

The next leg of the trip along this coast is a crucial passage that may be difficult. The formidable reputation of the Gulf of Tehuantepec is well deserved since the winds sweeping over the Isthmus maintain a yearly average of Force 6 on the Beaufort Scale and at times exceed Force 8 (especially from October to April). Added to the problems of heavy winds and seas felt over 100 miles offshore are strong currents which vary in direction and rate depending on the wind's intensity. Northwest or northeast currents of over 2 knots on either shore of the Gulf of Tehuantepec are a result of the wind being so strong at times that it actually lowers the water level at the head of the gulf.

A program for Port Control and Weather Reports has taken much of the guess work out of forecasting Tehuantepeckers. Official weather forecasts are available from the Marine Control Center, which is strategically located in the hills overlooking Bahia de Salina Cruz. The station monitors UHF 8242.8 and transmits on UHF 8792.8. In addition, they monitor VHF Ch. 06, utilizing a range of 70 miles. They can be called from Huatulco for a report on wind speed and trend and thus give information regarding the existence or likelihood of a Tehuantepecker. Vessels not equipped with SSB or Ham have on occasion placed a call to a freighter at sea and asked them to call the Port Controllers for a weather report and relay it to them. If you intend to enter the harbor, call the Marine Control Center on VHF Ch.16 and when traveling in the vicinity keep a sharp lookout for deep-sea traffic, yielding right-of-way to them.

Entrance to the outer harbor is between a breakwater (about .4 mile long) built out from the northern side of Bahia Salina Cruz and a sandy point to the west from which a mile-long, angled breakwater reaches toward the south, then southwest. A dredged channel leads to the inner harbor through a gap in the two moles built out from each side. Entrance **WPT 16°09', 95°11.60',** then follow range lights 346°T. Do not confuse the smaller harbor entrance, with the much larger port entrance to the southwest.

Though Salina Cruz is a large, industrial port with no small craft facilities; the people are friendly and helpful to cruisers who stop by. The only place pleasure craft may anchor is outside the outer harbor off the beach and this involves a long dinghy trip to check in. See sketch. To have shore access in the inner harbor get permission to tie alongside a shrimper, preferably one not leaving port for a couple of days. In this way you can avoid frequent line adjustment necessary because of the 6' tidal range. The fishermen are friendly and keep a careful eye on your boat while you are away. This is a **Port of Entry** and to clear with the port authorities you must use a ship's agent whose fees can be as much as $50. An agent can be recommended by the Port Captain, whose office is just beyond the shrimper's dock; office hours are from 0800 to 1500 and 1800 to 2200.

Fuel is controlled by Portuarios del Istmo de Tehuantepec; office hours are 0800 to 1730. Forty-five gallon drums of fuel can be brought to the dock but for small amounts, a Pemex station is only a few minute's walk for transporting fuel by jerry cans. Arrangements for engine repairs may be made at the embarcadero and since this is a major deep-sea port and fisherman's base, a wide range of repair services are available. Bus and taxi service are available for going to the downtown markets to replenish supplies. As with many towns and villages seldom visited by tourists, few of the local inhabitants speak English and the people are very friendly. There have been a number of reports of local individuals going to considerable lengths to find someone who could speak English in order to help cruisers in need.

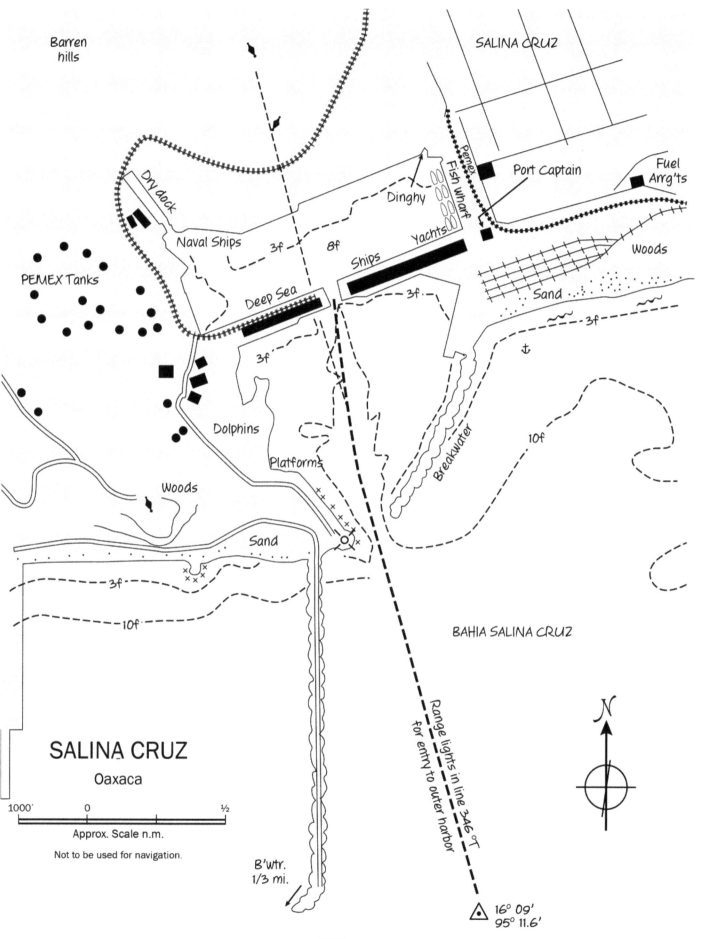

Barren
hills

SALINA CRUZ

Dry dock

Naval Ships

3f

8f

Dinghy

Pemex Fish wharf

Port Captain

Fuel Arrg'ts

Yachts

PEMEX Tanks

Ships

Woods

Deep Sea

3f

Sand

3f

3f

3f

Dolphins

Platforms

Breakwater

10f

Woods

Sand

3f

10f

BAHIA SALINA CRUZ

SALINA CRUZ

Oaxaca

Range lights in line 346 °T
for entry to outer harbor

N

1000'   0   ½

Approx. Scale n.m.

Not to be used for navigation.

B'wtr.
1/3 mi.

16° 09'
95° 11.6'

PUERTO CHIAPAS

The southernmost Mexican **Port of Entry**, Puerto Chiapas, is 190 miles beyond Salina Cruz but only 14 miles from the Rio Suchiate which generally marks the boundary between Mexico and Guatemala. This man-made port was built in 1975 with the hope of becoming a major commercial port. This dream did not materialize and it remains a small town, which can be a stop over either before or after tackling the Gulf of Tehuantepec.

The coast from Salina Cruz to Puerto Chiapas generally consists of low, sandy beaches fronting large lagoons with the foothills and mountains of the Sierra Madre and Sierra Soconusco ranges rising beyond. A few lights are scattered along the coast, which is generally free of dangers except for the mouths of two lagoons where shoals and breakers extend almost a mile offshore. These hazards are located at 27 miles and 75 miles east of Salina Cruz. Otherwise, by keeping fairly close to shore the seas raised by Tehuantepeckers are less onerous.

Entry to the port facilities is between two rock breakwaters extending from the sandy beach about a mile southeast of the coastal village of Puerto Chiapas. **WPT 14°41.55', 92°25.30',** then follow range lights at 38°M. The turning basin has two channels, the one to the north leading to commercial facilities and access to the Port Captain's office, Customs and Immigration; the one to the east leads to a fisherman's wharf, naval pier and the marina. Call the Port Captain on VHF 16 before entering and request permission to enter(Spanish Only). This is a **Port of Entry.** The Port Captain and Navy will come to the Marina to check you in and inspect the vessel shortly after you arrive. The Immigration office requires a taxi ride to the office at the airport. If you are checking into the country or need a zarpe, the marina staff is very helpful and will provide transportation to the Port Authority, Port Captain and Aduana. Allow all day.

The marina opened in 2012. Email marinachiapas@hotmail.com for reservations. There is a restaurant but no other services nearby. However, there is a Sam's, Walmart, Home Depot and Auto Zone in Tapachula, about 30 minutes away. The marina manager often provides transportation there and back.

A fuel dock is in the eastern basin as shown. The dock is meant to service the shrimpers and the rough concrete dock is protected by large tractor tires. It is not suitable for vessels with low freeboard. The marina has jerry jugs and will take you to the fueldock by truck, without charge if you need fuel.

Bus and taxi services connect Puerto Chiapas to Tapachula, a city where food and other supplies are readily available. Few people speak English here so keep your Spanish-English dictionary handy.

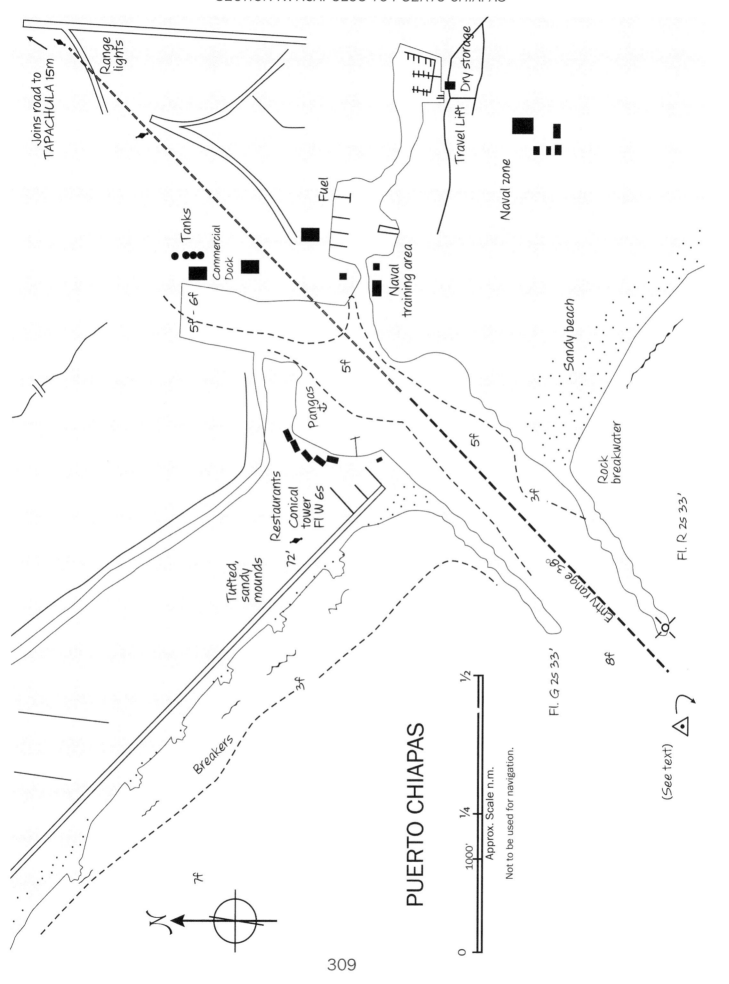

Joins road to TAPACHULA 15m

Range lights

Dry storage

Travel Lift

Naval zone

Fuel

Tanks

Commercial Dock

Naval training area

Sandy beach

Rock breakwater

Fl. R 2s 33'

5f - 6f

5f

5f

3f

Pangas

Entry range 38°

8f

Restaurants

Conical tower Fl W 6s

72'

Tufted, sandy mounds

Breakers

3f

Fl. G 2s 33'

(See text)

7f

N

PUERTO CHIAPAS

0   1000'   ¼   ½

Approx. Scale n.m.

Not to be used for navigation.

309

APPENDIX I: WAYPOINTS

CAUTION: A waypoint list can be a handy tool, but please refer to the appropriate chart and sketch before entering waypoints into your GPS. You may have to round a point, dodge a reef, or enter from an odd direction to get to the waypoint. Plot your courses and waypoints carefully! There may be discrepancies in these waypoints. Please double check before relying on them. Use care and caution when navigating in these waters.

The Pacific Coast of Baja

Marina Puerto Salina entrance	32° 30.28'	116° 53.20'
Marina Coral entrance	32° 51.67'	116° 39.58'
Ensenada entrance	31° 50.41'	116° 37.53'
Ensenada Cruiseport	31° 50.39'	116° 38.03'
Todos Santao anchorage	31° 48.26'	116° 47.18'
Punta Banda passage	31° 45.69'	116° 45.56'
Punta Santa Tomas	31° 32.57'	116° 40.64'
Punta Colonet	30° 56.54'	116° 17.20'
Isla San Martin	30° 29.30'	116° 6.0'
Bahia San Quintin	30° 22.40'	115° 57.55'
Punta Baja	29° 56.35'	115° 48.90'
Isla San Geronimo	29° 47.32'	115° 47.36'
Sacramento Reef (outside)	29° 45'	115° 55'
Bahia San Carlos(approach)	29° 36.29'	115° 30.01'
Punta Escarpada	29° 33.5'	115° 22.80'
Punta Canoas	29° 26'	115° 12'
Punta Blanca anchorage	29° 6.4'	114° 40.5'
Bahia Playa Maria anchorage	28° 55.6'	114° 31'
Bahia Santa Rosalilita anchorage	28° 39.8'	114° 14.2'
Morro Santa Domingo anchorage	28° 14.4'	114° 05.3'
Isla San Benito west anchorage	28° 18'	115° 34.7'
Isla San Benito central anchorage	28° 18.4'	115° 34.25'
Isla Guadalupe NE anchorage	29° 9.5'	118° 16.5'
Isla Guadalupe S anchorage	28° 52.9'	118° 17.5'
Isla Guadalupe W anchorage	28° 58.2'	118° 17.6'
Isla Cedros N anchorage	28° 19.44'	115° 11.4'°
Isla Cedros harbor entrance	28° 05.64'	115° 10.90'
Isla Cedros south anchorage	28° 5.04'	115° 19.97'
Turtle Bay entrance	27° 38.5'	114° 54'
Bahia Asuncion anchorage	27° 8.1'	114° 17.3'
Bahia Asuncion clearance	27° 05'	114° 16'
Punts Abreojos entrance	26° 41'	113° 33'
Bahia San Juanico entrance	26° 14'	112° 28'
Cabo San Lazaro	27° 47.40'	112° 22.15'
Bahia Santa Maria entrance	24° 44.26'	112° 14.01'
Magadalena Bay entrance	24° 31'	112° 03'
Belcher anchorage	24° 34.9'	112° 4.3'
Man o War Cove	24° 38.3'	112° 08.02'
Cabot Falso clearance	22° 49.28'	109° 58.88'

Cabo San Lucas to Canal San Lorenzo

Cabo San Lucas harbor entrance	22° 52.88'	109° 54.30'
Punta las Palmillas anchorage	23° 00.80'	109° 42.30'
Cabo Los Frailes South	23° 22.78'	109° 25.60'
Cabo Los Frailes North	23° 24.41'	109° 25.43'
Cabo Pulmo, south side	23° 26.63'	109° 25.42'
Punta Arena, safe off	23° 34.55'	109° 28.61'
Ensenada de los Suenos	23° 59.36'	109° 49.73'
Montana Rock, 15 ft.	24° 7.82'	109° 47.97'
Viejo Spit, Isla Cerralvo N	24° 9.42'	109° 52.38'

Rancho Santa Cruz	24° 12.86'	110° 5.27'
Rosario Rocks, N side	24° 15.15'	110° 9.37'
Scout Shoal light (rough)	24° 21.98'	110° 18.40'
Canal San Lorenzo	24° 22.45'	110° 18.50'

La Paz Area

Entrance to La Paz Channel	24° 13'	110° 19'
Costabaja Marina entrance	24° 13'	110° 18.36'
Marina Palmira entrance	24° 11.20'	110° 18.24'
Marina Vista Coral entrance	24° 9.42'	110° 19.58'
Anchorage off the malacon	24° 9.4'	110° 19.5'
Anchorage near mogote	24° 9.8'	110° 19.7'

North of La Paz and Isla Espirit Santo

Bahia Falsa anchorage	24° 15.34'	110° 19.11'
Puerto Pichilinque	24° 15.74'	110° 19.88'
Playa Pichilinque	24° 17.02'	110° 19.81'
Caleta Lobos anchorage	24° 17.93'	110° 19.99'
Balandra off Mushroom Rock	24° 19.31'	110°19.82'
Balandra off north beach	24° 19.63'	110° 19.96'
Punta Lupona, west side	24° 24.03'	110° 20.03'
Bahia San Gabriel, E. side	24° 25.54'	110° 21.14'
Isla Ballena, SE corner	24° 29.05'	110° 23.91'
Caleta de la Isla anchorage	24° 29.30'	110° 23.12'
Caleta Candelero anchorage	24° 30.40'	110° 23.26'
Caleta Enmedia anchorage	24° 30.90'	110° 23.46'
Partida Cove, west end	24° 32.02'	110° 22.84'
Partida Cove, east end	24° 32.01'	110° 22.51'
El Cardoncita anchorage	24° 32.27	110° 23.44'
El Cardonal off north beach	24° 33.09'	110° 23.20'
Ensenada Grande South bay	24° 33.64'	110° 23.90'
Ensenada Grande Middle bay	24° 33.83'	110° 24.16'
Punta Lobos, Santo	24° 27.26'	110° 18.12'

Isla San Jose Area

Isla San Francisco, Hook	24° 49.19'	110° 34.12'
San Francisco, Cuevas	24° 49.28'	110° 34.62'
San Francisco, dos Playas	24° 49.54'	110° 35.00'
San Francisco, north side	24° 50.62'	110° 34.38'
Coyote N.W. rock	24° 51.41'	110° 35.05'
Seal Rocks	24° 50.56'	110° 36.34'
Amortajada, south side	24° 52.08'	110° 34.32'
Amortajada, north side	24° 52.66'	110° 34.54'
N.end Isla Cayo main block	24° 52.60'	110° 36.20'
Punta Salinas S. side	24° 54.84'	110° 38.02'
Evaristo entrance cove	24° 54.80'	110° 42.21'
Evaristo	24° 54.68'	110° 42.38'
Evaristo, North side of point	24° 55.33'	110° 42.81'

Playa Piton anchorage	24° 58.26'	110° 44.92'
Nopolo Cove anchorage	24° 59.81'	110° 45.45'
Bahia Gacetero	25° 1.21'	110° 41.54'
San Jose NW Light anch.	25° 1.81'	110° 42.53'
San Jose SE corner (rough)	24° 53.05'	110° 31.39'
Kelton's Coves, north	25° 1.48'	110° 35.22'
Punta Colorado anchorage	25° 4.32'	110° 50.80'
Punta Blanca anchorage	25° 5.38'	110° 51.80'
Punta Cobre, south side	25° 12.49'	110° 55.27'
Roca Moreno Reef, SE	25° 12.47'	110° 54.77'
Punta Cobre north side	25° 12.69'	110° 55.43'
Roca Negra, E end (rough)	25° 14.86'	110° 55.24'
Timbabichi anchorage	25° 16.29'	110° 56.41'
Bahia Pargos	25° 17.10'	110° 56.23'
Puerto Gato N. anchorage	25° 18.20'	110° 56.81'
Punta San Telmo sand	25° 19.41'	110° 57.36'
Punta San Telmo gravel	25° 19-64'	110° 57.30'
Punta San Telmo, N. side	25° 19.81'	110° 56.81'
Isla Santa Cruz SE corner	25° 15.58'	110° 43.05'
San Diego middle W. side	25° 11.98'	110° 42.20'
San Diego S. end of reef	25° 10.86'	110° 43.04'

Agua Verde Area

Bahia Santa Marta N	25° 27.44'	111° 1.43'
Punta Ballena anchorage	25° 28.53'	111° 1.10'
Bahia San Marte anchorage	25° 30.24'	111° 1.04'
Marcial Reef S. end 15 ft	25° 31.55'	111° 0.30'
Marcial Nav. Lite	25° 31.98'	111° 0.34'
Marcial Outlier (dries at 0 tide)	25° 32.17'	111° 0.50'
Marcial Reef, N. end 34 ft	25° 32.32'	111° 0.55'
Playa con Grava anchorage	25° 31.04'	111° 2.50'
Agua Verde Entrance	25° 31.52'	111° 3.90'
Agua Verde SE bight	25° 30.90'	111° 3.72'
Agua Verde Center off beach	25° 31.00'	111° 4.11'
Agua Verde NW bight	25° 31.36'	111° 4.39'
Isla Monserrat So-Nav.lite	25° 38.99'	111° 1.80'
Isla Monserrat SW anchorage	25° 39.44'	111° 2.51'
Monserrat NE Cove (middle)	25° 41.84'	111° 1.47'
Monserrat NE Cove (northern)	25° 42.24'	111° 1.87'
Monserrat, Yellowstone Beach	25° 42.56'	111° 3.12'
Las Galeras Nav. Lite (rough)	25° 44.54'	111° 2.66'
Galera Rock (rough)	25° 45.69'	111° 2.92'
Isla Catalina W anchorage	25° 38.23'	110° 48.00'
Isla Catalina SW anchorage	25° 36.13'	110° 46.76'
Isla Cosme, south cove	25° 34.90'	111° 9.00'
Westhaven	25° 40.53'	111° 12.52'
Candelero Chico	25° 42.47'	111° 12.89'
Bahia Candelero	25° 43.39'	111° 14.39'
Escondido entrance	25° 48.38'	111° 18.11'

Puerto Escondido Area

Candelero Chico anchorage	25° 42.47'	111° 12.89'
Bahia Candelero anchorage	25° 43.39'	111° 14.39'
Danzante Reef, least depth 5 ft. at zero tide	25° 46.18'	111° 10.70'

Honeymoon Cove, entrance	25° 48.41'	111° 15.55'
Escondido Waiting Room ent.	25° 48.38'	111° 18.11'
Bahia Marquer	25° 52.02'	111° 13.18'
Balandra Entrance	26° 1.17'	111° 10.33'
Puerto Balandra, N. end	26° 1.17'	111° 9.84'
Punta Perico, S. side	25° 58.30'	111° 4.53'
Loreto roadstead	26° 1.07'	111° 20.31'
Isla Coronados, S. by lite	26° 6.30'	111° 15.92'
Isla Coronados, N. of spit	26° 6.81'	111° 17.36'
Mangle Rock	26° 14.68'	111° 22.14'
Punta Mangle anchorage	26° 16.82'	111° 23.36'
San Juanico, N end anchorage	26° 22.09'	111° 25.79'
La Ramada anchorage	26° 22.89'	111° 25.85'
Saquicismunde anchorage	26° 28.66'	111° 27.84'

Conception Bay Area

Punta Pulpito anchorage	26° 30.87'	111° 26.89'
Punta Pulpito - safe distance off	26° 30.86'	111° 24.96'
San Sebastian offshore	26° 37.18'	111° 33.71'
San Sebastian anchorage	26° 37.09'	111° 33.95'
Punta Santa Teresa safe distance	26° 42.00'	111° 32.93'
San Lino anchorage	26° 44.06'	111° 37.49'
Punta Santa Rosa, south side	26° 46.80'	111° 39.03'
Los Pilares anchorage	26° 53.30'	111° 48.27'
Santo Domingo anchorage	26° 52.03'	111° 50.79'
River Mouth Rock	26° 54.01'	111° 57.05'
Frijol Rock	26° 40.52'	111° 50.04'
Santispac anchorage	26° 45.82'	111° 53.10'
Playa Santa Barbara, center	26° 42.08'	111° 52.81'
Mulege	26° 54'	111° 57'

Santa Rosalia Area

South Isla Santa Inez	27° 1.80'	111° 55.10'
North Isla Santa Inez	27° 3.79'	111° 54.49'
Punta Chivato Resort,	27° 3.94'	111° 57.70'
Isla San Marcos	27° 10.87'	112° 3.99'
Santa Rosalia Harbor	27° 20.24'	112° 15.69'
Punta Trinidad anchorage	27° 49.82'	112° 43.77'
Punta San Gabriel	28° 12.30'	112° 46.68'

Bahia de Los Angeles

Bahia San Francisquito W	28° 26.22'	112° 52.75'
Bahia San Francisquito Harbor	28° 25.71'	112° 51.98'
Bahia San Francisquito E	28° 26.13'	112° 51.67'
Isla San Lorenzo W Side S	28° 38.56'	112° 51.80'
Isla San Lorenzo W Side N	28° 38.83'	112° 52.00'
Animas Island:Caleta Blanca anchorage	28° 42.42'	112° 56.00'
Salsipuedes, South Slot	28° 43.40'	112° 57.11'
Isla Partida,	28° 53.53'	113° 2.61'
Bernabe Rocks	28° 47.48'	113° 11.38'
Animas Slot anchorage	28° 50.27'	113° 14.97'
South Animas Bay East	28° 49.27'	113° 17.18'

CAUTION: A waypoint list can be a handy tool, but please refer to the appropriate chart and sketch before entering waypoints into your GPS. You may have to round a point, dodge a reef, or enter from an odd direction to get to the waypoint. Plot your courses and waypoints carefully! There may be discrepancies in these waypoints. Please double check before relying on them. Use care and caution when navigating in these waters.

Ensenada Alacran anchorage	28° 54.02'	113° 22.62'
Puerto Don Juan, off entrance	28° 57.19'	113° 26.67'
Puerto Don Juan anchorage	28° 56.66'	113° 26.96'
Bahia de los Angeles village anchorage	28° 56.84'	113° 33.32'
Jorobado Rock,	29° 0.72'	113° 31.33'
Ventana Rock	29° 0.2"	113° 30.95'
Caleta Ventana anchorage	29° 0.01'	113° 30.86'
Coronado Rock, dries at low tide	29° 2.01'	113° 29.91'
Rada Laguna anchorage	29° 2.66'	113° 30.30'
Las Rocas Bay anchorage	29° 3.63'	113° 30.69'
La Gringa anchorage	29° 2.10'	113° 32.58'
Ensenada Alcatraz, S Beach anchorage	29° 9.73'	113° 36.91'
Paraje de Chencho anchorage	29° 45.82'	114° 15.74'
Beach #1, Caleta Tijireta	29° 45.25'	114° 17.20'

Isla de la Guardia Area

NOTE: The Puerto Refugio chart grid, taken from the old 1873 surveys, is off station. It is 1.6 minutes too far east, and 0.15 minutes too far north.

Este Ton anchorage	29° 9.69'	113° 19.86'
Sail Rock	29° 31.89'	113° 35.86'
Puerto Refugio W. Entrance	29° 32.55'	113° 34.32'
Puerto Refugio E. Entrance	29° 33.45'	113° 31.69'
East Bay, West Bight, off sand beach	29° 32.20'	113° 33.56'
Puerto Refugio N. Entrance	29° 34.11'	113° 33.50'
Caleta Pulpito West	29° 17.10'	113° 17.50'
Caleta Pulpito East	29° 17.24'	113° 16.35'
Isla Estanque, entrance to the tank	29° 3.73'	113° 6.12'
Isla Estanque, south side anchorage	29° 3.63'	113° 5.55'

Islas Encantadas Area

Paraje Chencho anchorage	29° 45.82'	114° 15.74'
Beach #1, Caleta Tijereta	29° 45.25'	114° 17.20'
Isla Gonzaga, outer hook anchorage	29° 48.54'	114° 22.31'
Isla Gonzaga, middlebight anchorage	29° 48.64'	114° 22.59'
Bahia Willard, inside entrance to N	29° 49.47'	114° 23.82'
Punta Bufeo, northwest side	29° 54.64'	114° 26.24'
Isla San Luis, northwest cove	29° 58.46'	114° 25.11'
Luis Rock Channel, center	29° 59.05'	114° 25.40'
Pomo Rock	30° 00.71'	114° 23.44'
North Reef	30° 01.6'	114° 25.5'
Isla Miramar, northwest anchorage	30° 05.33'	114° 33.09'

Puertecitos to San Felipe

Puertecitos	30° 20.5'	114° 38.2'
San Felipe harbor entrance	30° 59.81'	114° 49.24'
Punta San Felipe	31° 1.86'	114° 48.56'

Puerto Penasco To Kino Area

Puerto Penasco	31° 18.27'	116° 33.05'
Tepoca Bay	30° 15.79'	112° 50.68'
Puerto Libertad	29° 54.47'	112° 42.58'
Desemboque	29° 30'	112° 42.58'
Isla Patos, south side	29° 15.99'	112° 27.50'
Punta Sargento, 18ft depth past end of reef	29° 18.30'	112° 17.87'
Punta Sargento, possible anch.sand 13ft	29° 19.2'	112° 18.7'
North Willard W. anchorage	28° 52.99'	112° 34.26'
Bahia de las Cruces, W end anchorage	28° 45.82'	112° 20.98'
Isla Esteban SW spit E. side corner 48ft	28° 40.10'	112° 36.15'
Roca de Foca (off station to E on the chart)	28° 43.63'	112° 18.97'
Cactus Pass center	28° 44.67'	112° 18.43'
Dog Bay, anchorage, N end	28° 47.31'	112° 16.23'
Isla San Pedro Martir	28° 22.61'	112° 17.95'
Kino Bay anchorage	28° 45.83'	111° 55.86'
Punta Baja (S of Kino), 50 ft. depth	28° 24.50'	111° 45.50'

Kino to San Carlos

Los Corralitos	28° 20.58'	111° 27.62'
El Choyudo	28° 19.21'	111° 27.29'
Las Cadenas North	28° 18.59'	111° 27.05'
Bahia San Agustin, N end	28° 16.46'	111° 23.96'
Bahia San Agustin, S end	28° 15.42'	111° 23.21'
Pozo moreno	28° 14.63'	111° 22.84'
Ensenada Las Cocinas anch.	28° 13.81'	111° 22.58'
Julio Villa entrance	28° 13.10'	111° 21.64'
Rada el Pasito	28° 12.66'	111° 21.07'
Caleta Venecia	28° 7.80'	111° 17.62'
Caleta Los Changos, north	28° 6.11'	111° 17.02'
Seri Muerto	28° 5.27'	111° 16.56'
Caleta Amarga	28° 3.88'	111° 15.30'
North Side San Pedro Point	28° 3.64'	111° 15.11'
San Pedro Bay Entrance	28° 2.98'	111° 14.81'
San Pedro Bay, N end	28° 3.41'	111° 14.71'
San Pedro Bay, S end	28° 3.12'	111° 14.35'
Caleta Bandito	27° 59.54'	111° 10.09'
Club Med. anchorage	27° 57.61'	111° 6.61'
Off Marina Real Entrance	27° 57.02'	111° 6.00'
Mirador Cove	27° 56.22'	111° 5.65'
Caleta Lalo entrance	27° 56.18'	111° 5.48'
Lalo Reef, outer end	27° 56.03'	111° 5T29'
Martini Cove anchorage	27° 55.90'	111° 3.59'
Martini Rock, 5ft. least depth	27° 55.91'	111° 3.47'
Marina Real entrance	27° 56.8'	111° 5.74'
San Carlos Bay Entrance	27° 56.13'	111° 3.34'

San Carlos South to Mazatlan

Bahia San Carlos entrance.	27° 55.73'	111° 3.1'
Shangrila Coves	27° 56.39'	111° 3.27'
San Carlos Reef, outer end	27° 56.02'	111° 3.41'
La Ahogada, least depth 2 feet.	27° 55.32'	110° 57.94'

CAUTION: A waypoint list can be a handy tool, but please refer to the appropriate chart and sketch before entering waypoints into your GPS. You may have to round a point, dodge a reef, or enter from an odd direction to get to the waypoint. Plot your courses and waypoints carefully! There may be discrepancies in these waypoints. Please double check before relying on them. Use care and caution when navigating in these waters.

Chencho anchorage	27° 54.38'	110° 57.69'
Punta Colorado reef, outer end	27° 54.10'	110° 58.03'
Carricito, north bight	27° 51.97'	110° 54.37'
Bahia Catalina entrance	27° 51.79'	110° 52.26'
Bahia Catalina, west bight	27° 51.79'	110° 52.72'
Las Playitas anchorage	27° 53.85'	110° 52.93'
Guaymas entrance	27° 52.87'	110° 51'
Punta Lobos anchorage	27° 16.49'	110° 28.69'
Bahia Yvaros entrance	26° 39.50'	109° 29.11'
Bahia San Ignacio anchorage	25° 38.43'	109° 19.14'
Topolobampo entrance	25° 31.06'	109° 12.22'
Puerto Altata	24° 28.98'	107° 50.37'
Mazatlan Marina (El Cid) entrance	26° 16.05'	106° 28.28'
Mazatlan Harbor entrance	23° 10'	106° 24.86'

Isla Isabella South to Puerto Vallarta

Isla Isabela Stacks anchorage	21° 50.9'	105° 52.72'
Isla Isabela S anchorage	21° 50.4'	105° 53'
Isla Isabela W anchorage	21° 50.85'	105° 53.24'
San Blas entrance	21° 31.3'	105° 17.3'
Mantanchen Bay entrance	21° 29.75'	105° 14.75'
Chacala	21° 9.7'	105° 13.95'
Jaltemba	21° 2.4'	105° 17.6'
Punta Mita clearance	20° 44.6'	105° 32'
Punta Mita anchorage	20° 45.9'	105° 31'
Las Tres Marietas middle island anchorage	20° 41.9'	105° 35'
La Cruz entrance	20° 45'	105° 22.3'
Nuevo Vallarta entrance	20° 41.07'	105° 17.9'
Puerto Vallarta entrance	20° 39.17'	105° 14.9'
Puerto Vallarta buoy	20° 39'	105° 15.7'

Yelapa South to Acapulco

Yelapa	20° 29.9'	105° 27.13'
Punta Ipala	20° 14.1	105° 34.25'
Chamela N entrance	19° 34	105° 8'
Chamela S entrance	19° 32.4'	105° 6.2'
Paraiso entrance	19° 28.52'	105° 4'
Bahia Careyes W entrance	19° 26.44'	105° 2.28'
Bahia Careyes S entrance	19° 26.3'	105° 2'
Tenacatita entrance	19° 15'	104° 51.6'
Bahia De Navidad	19° 12.3'	104° 42.2'
Laguna de la Navidad entrance	19° 12'	104° 41.5'
Carrizal	19° 5.36'	104° 26'
Higueras	19° 6'	104° 24.77'
Bahia De Santiago anchorage	19° 6.6'	104° 23.6'
Manzanillo Marina entrance.	19° 6'	104° 20.7'
Punta Cabeza Negra N anchorage	18° 36.35'	103° 42'
Punta Cabeza Negra S anchorage	18° 35.44'	103° 42'
Bahia de Maruata	18° 16'	103° 20.5'
Ensenada de Pechilinqullo	18° 11.7'	103° 7.5'
Caleta De Campos	18° 04.22'	102° 45'
Lazaro Cardenas entrance	17° 55.2'	102° 09.3'
Isla Grande	17° 41'	101° 40'
Marina Ixtapa approach	17° 39.2'	101° 39.3'

Marina Ixtapa entrance	17° 39.6'	101° 37.3'
Zihuatanejo	17° 37.15'	101° 34'
Acapulco N entrance	16° 49.58'	99° 55.15'
Acapulco middle entrance	16° 43.45'	99° 53.46'

Acapulco South to Puerto Madero

Puerto Escondido, Oaxaca	15° 51.2'	97° 03.7'
Puerto Angel entrance	15° 39.49'	96° 29.53'
Puerto Sacrificios	15° 40.80'	96° 14'
Jicaral and Rescalillo	15° 41.67'	96° 13.40'
Manglillo	15° 41.90'	96° 12.82'
Bahia Chachacual entrance	15° 41.96'	96° 12.02'
Isla Cacaluta anchorage	15° 43.17'	96° 9.80'
Bahias Maguey and Organo entrance	15° 42.85'	96° 8.56'
Bahia Santa Cruz entrance	15° 44.71'	96° 7.33'
Santa Cruz Marina entrance	15° 44.16'	96° 07.11'
Bahia Chahue approach	15° 44.7'	96° 6.76'
Marina Chahue entrance	15° 45.61'	96° 07.21'
Tangola Tangola approach	15° 45.3'	96° 5.26'
Salina Cruz approach	16° 09'	95° 11.
Puerto Madero approach	14° 41.55'	92° 25.3'

CAUTION: A waypoint list can be a handy tool, but please refer to the appropriate chart and sketch before entering waypoints into your GPS. You may have to round a point, dodge a reef, or enter from an odd direction to get to the waypoint. Plot your courses and waypoints carefully! There may be discrepancies in these waypoints. Please double check before relying on them. Use care and caution when navigating in these waters.

APPENDIX II: MARINAS

MARINA	LOCATION	HARBOR MASTER	PHONE	FAX	WEB SITE
Baja Naval & Baja Naval Boatyard	Ensenada, Baja California	Gregg Rogelio	011-52 (646) 174-0020	011-52 (646) 174-0028	www.bajanaval. com
Club de Yates de Acapulco	Acapulco, Guerrero	Jose Marquez	011-52 (744) 482-3859 or 60 or 70	011-52 (744) 482-2836	www.clubdey-atesdeacapulco. com
Costa Baja Resort & Marina	La Paz, Baja California Sur	Gabriel Ley	(888) 866-9394 or 011-52 (612) 121-6225	011-52 (612) 121-5764	www.costabaja. com
Ensenada Cruiseport Village	Ensenada, Baja California	Jonathan Cervantes	(877) 219-5822 or 011-52 (646) 178-8801 x3303	011-52 (646) 173-4151	www.ecpvmarina.com
Marina Cabo San Lucas	Cabo San Lucas, Baja California Sur	Agusto Cachòn Guty	011-52 (624) 173-9140	011-52 (624) 143-1253 or 54	www.cabomarina.com.mx
NEW! Marina Chiapas	Puerto Chiapas, Chiapas	Enrique LaClette			
Marina Coral Ensenada	Ensenada, Baja California	Arnulfo 'Fito' Espinosa	(866) 302-0066 or 011-52 (646) 175-0050	011-52 (646) 175-0058	www.hotelcoral. com
Marina Dársena Santa Cruz	Bahia de Huatulco, Oaxaca	Capt. Eduardo de la Raya Foruezan	011-52 (958) 587-0726	same as phone	-
Marina de La Paz	La Paz, Baja California Sur	Mary G. Shroyer	011-52 (612) 122-1646	011-52 (612) 125-5900	www.marinadelapaz.com
Marina El Cid	Mazatlan, Sinaloa	Gerónimo Cevallos	011-52 (669) 916-3468 x6598	011-52 (669) 916-6294	www.elcid.com
Marina Ixtapa	Ixtapa/Zihuatanejo, Guerrero	Lic. Elsa Zuñiga	011-52 (755) 553-2180	same as phone	
Marina Las Hadas	Manzanillo, Colima	Adrián Sánchez	011-52 (314) 331-0101	011-52 (314) 331-0125	www.mexonline. com/lashadas. htm
Marina Mazatlan	Mazatlan, Sinaloa	Jaime Ruiz	011 52 (669) 669-2936	011-52 (669) 669-2937	www.marinamazatlan.com
Marina Nuevo Vallarta	Nuevo Vallarta, Nayarit	Juan Sebastian Estrada	011 52 (322) 297-7000	same as phone	www.marinanuevovallarta.com
Marina Palmira	La Paz, Baja California Sur		(877) 217-1513 or 011-52 (612) 121-6159	011-52 (612) 121-6142	www.marinapalmira.com
Marina Puerto de La Navidad	Barra de Navidad, Jalisco	Ing Secundino Alvarez	011-52 (314) 337-9008	011-52 (315) 355-5974	www.islanavidad.com

MARINA	LOCATION	HARBOR MASTER	PHONE	FAX	WEB SITE
Marina Real	San Carlos, Sonora	Isabel Escobar	011-52 (622) 227-0011	same as phone	
Marina Riviera Nayarit	La Cruz, Nayarit	Rafael Alcántara Luarte	011-52 (329) 295-5526 x102 or 104	-	www.marinarivieranayarit.com
Marina San Carlos	San Carlos, Sonora	Kiki Grossman-Krueger	011-52 (622) 226-1230	011-52 (622) 226-0565	www.marinasancarlos.com
Marina Vallarta	Puerto Vallarta, Jalisco	Sergio Bernal	011-52 (322) 221-0275	011-52 (322) 221-0722	-
Marinas de Baja	Cabo San Lucas, Baja California Sur	Juan Pablo Montes	011-52 (624) 143-6522	011-52 (624) 143-6523	www.marinadebaja.com
Paradise Village Marina	Nuevo Vallarta, Nayarit	Dick Markie	011-52 (322) 226-6728	same as phone	www.paradisevillagemarina.com
Puerto Los Cabos	Cabo San Lucas, Baja California Sur	Enrique Fernandez	011-52 (624) 105-6028	same as phone	www.marinapuertoloscabos.com
Puerto Salina La Marina	Tijuana, Baja California	Antonio Palacious	(866) 365-2562 from U.S. or 011-52 (646) 155-4186 or 87 or 88	011-52 (646) 155-4109	www.marinapuertosalina.com

Dry Storage

MARINA	LOCATION	HARBOR MASTER	PHONE	FAX	WEB SITE
Marina Real	San Carlos, Sonora	Isabel Escobar	011-52 (622) 227-0011	same as phone	
Marina Seca	San Carlos, Sonora	Kiki Grossman-Krueger	011-52 (622) 226-1061	011-52 (622) 226-1061 x116	www.marinasancarlos.com
Marine Group Boat Works	San Jose del Cabo, Baja California Sur	Michele Kiely	(619) 600-5539 or 011-52 (624) 105-6500	011-52 (624) 105-6506	www.marinegroupboatworks.com
Opequimar Marine Center	Puerto Vallarta, Nayarit	Coral Aruecga	011-52 (322) 221-1800	011-52 (322) 221-1978	www.opequimar.com

APPENDIX III: GLOSSARY OF SPANISH TERMS

For The Gringo Yachtsman
Compiled by Dix Brow, Kay Boylen, and Chris Caswell

We've all seen it: the American tourist trying to ask for something in the non-English-speaking shop. The face gets redder, the voice gets louder, and the charade of descriptive gestures gets more convolute. Compound that problem by making the American into a yachtsman trying to buy a shackle (el shacklo?) and the result is often total frustration.

For the benefit of SEA readers who venture below the border, we've put together a basic list of boating terms that probably won't be found in your average English Spanish dictionary. We haven't included the more common words, so be sure you take the basic dictionary with you. One point to remember: language is a tenuous thing and varies from one area to the next. What a North American calls a boom vang is a kicking strap to an Englishman. So if our word draws a blank when you use it, don't blame us. If all else fails, try the last phrase on this list. It should get action.   Practice your Spanish!!

Sailing
Sloop	El balandro.
Yawl	La yole
Kech	La queche
Schooner	La goleta
Sail	La vela Genoa
Jib	El genoves
Jib	El foque
Mainsail	La Mayor
Mizzen	La mesana
To Reef	Rizar
Reef Points	Los puntos de tomar prizos
Spinnaker	El balon

Spars
Boom	La botavara
Bowspirit	El baupres
Gooseneck	El zuncho de la botavara
Mast	El palo
Spinnaker Pole	El tangon del balon

Engine Terms
Spark plug	La bujia
Belt	El cinturon
Hose	La manguera
Pump	La bomba
Starter	El arranquedor
Points	Los platos

Anchors
Anchor	La ancla
Anchor chain	La cadena de la ancla
Anchor line	La cuerda de la ancla
Capstan	El cabrestante
Sea Anchor	La ancla flotante

Deck Gear
Cleat	La abrazadera
Life lines	Los guardamancebos
Stanchion	El candelero
Steering Wheel	El volante
Tiller	La cana
Winch	El torno

Rigging
Chainplate	El endenote
Stay	El estay
Forestay	Estay de proa
Backstay	La burda
Shackle	El grillete
Halyard	La driza
Block	El moton
Sheet	La escota

Hull
Anti-fouling paint	La pintura anti-incrustante
Beam	El pantoque
Bulkhead	El mamparo
Cabin	El camarote
Cockpit	La banera
Companionway	La escotilla
Deck	La cubierta
Draft	El calado
Centerboard	La orza
Bow	La proa
Stern	La popa
Frame	La cuaderna
Hand rail	La barandilla
Keel	La quilla
Hull	La brusca
Rudder	El timon
Outboard motor	El motor fucra de borda

Accommodations

Bunk......................	La litera
Forecastle..............	El castillo
Head......................	El vater
Mahogany..............	La caoba
Oak.......................	El roble
Teak......................	La teca
Spruce..................	El abeto de Canada

Terms Underway

Ahead....................	Avante por la proa
Astern...................	Atras por la popa
Amidships..............	El medio del barco
Closehauled...........	Barloventeado
Jibe......................	Trasluchar
In irons.................	Proa encantada
Leeward.................	A sotavento
On the bow............	Por la amura
On the quarter........	Por la aleta
Reaching................	Descuartar
To reef..................	Rizar (Tomar rizos)
Running.................	Viento en popa
To tack..................	Virar
Watch....................	La guardia
Windward..............	A barloveto

Phrases Underway

Turn left (right).......	Doble a la izquierda (derecha)
Straight ahead.......	Directo de frente
Stop!.....................	Para! (alto)
Faster (slower).......	Mas rapido (despacho)
Can you tow us?....	Puede remolcarnos?

Navigation Terms

A fix......................	Una situacion
A sight..................	La observacion
Compass...............	La brujula (el compas)
Dead reckoning.....	La situacion de estima
Dividers.................	Los compases de puntas
Lead line..............	El escandallo
Offshore...............	Alta mar
On shore...............	El la costa (cerea de tierra)
Parallels................	Las reglas paralelas
Sextant.................	El sextante
Depth sounder.......	El sondador mecanico
Speedometer........	El velocimetro
High tide...............	La marea alto
Low tide................	La marea baja
Hand bearing compass	Brujula acimutal de mano

Miscellaneous

Oars......................	Los remos
Oarlocks...............	Las chumaceras
Dinghy..................	La ponga
Life preservers.......	Las salvavidas
Binoculars.............	Los binoculaes (los prismaticos)
Flashlight..............	El foco de mano
Deep.....................	Muy hondo
Not deep..............	Poco honto
Dock.....................	El muelle
Knot (in rope)........	El nudo

Fishing Terms

Rod......................	La cana
Reel......................	El carrete
Line......................	La piola (linea)
More drag..............	Mas freno
Leader..................	El empate
Swivel...................	El destorcador
Hook.....................	El anzuelo
Gaff......................	El gancho
Bait......................	La camada
Fishing chair..........	La silla de pesca
Troll......................	Trolear
Fish following........	La pez viene
Strike!...................	Esta jalando!
Birds working.........	Pajaros trabajando
Tangled.................	Enredado
A jump..................	El salto
Slack.....................	Floja
Coming up.............	El sube
Bad hookup...........	Mal anzueliado
Too bad.................	Que lastima!
Turtle....................	Caguama/Tortuga
Shrimp..................	Camaron
Lobster.................	Langosta
Whale....................	Ballena
Shark....................	Tiburon
Marlin...................	El marlin
Sailfish..................	La pez vela
Dolphin.................	Delfin
Yellowtail..............	El jurel
Porpoise...............	La tonina
Grouper................	La garropa
Rock bass.............	La cabrilla
Skipjack................	El bonito
Carp......................	El cangrejo

We also recommend Kathy Parsons' book Spanish for Cruisers to provide valuable Spanish boat terms and phrases for concise, accurate communication whenever needed... and check out her website as well at www.spanishforcruisers.com/.

APPENDIX III: GLOSSARY OF SPANISH TERMS

a bordo	aboard	hondo/bajo	deep/shallow
aduana	Customs	hundiendo	sinking
aeropuerto	airport	huracan	hurricane
agua	water	isla(s)	island(s)
arrecife	reef	islote(s)	islets(s)
arroyo	stream, gully	laguna	lagoon
ayuda	help	llegada	arrival
bahia	bay	mar	sea
baja	lower	marea	tide
bajo	shoal, shallow	mecanico	mechanic
banco	bank (sand or money)	mercado	market
barco/lancha	boat	mesa	mesa, plateau
boca	mouth, entrance	montaña	mountain
bomba	pump	morro	headland, cliff
bucear	dive	motor	engine
cabo	cape	niebla	fog
cabeza	head	norte	north
caleta	cove	nube, nublado	clouds, cloudy
camino	road	oceano	ocean
canal	channel, strait	oeste	west
cañon	canyon, ravine	panga	fishing craft (sm)
capitan (a)	captain	pescado	fish
cerro	hill, mountain	picacho	small peak
claro	clear	pico	peak
colina	hill	piedra	rock
datos	data, information	piloto	pilot
diesel	diesel	playa	beach
ensenada, ensa.	cove, small bay	puerto	port, harbor
entrada	entrance	punta	point
escolar	aground	remolcar	tow
este	east	rio	river
estero	inlet, estuary	roca(s)	rock(s)
farallon	cliff	santa	saint
farro	lighthouse	sierra	mountain range
gasolina	gasoline	soga/cuerda	rope
gas	propane	soldadura	welding
golfo	gulf	vela	sail
grasa	grease	viento	wind
guantes	gloves	yate	yacht

APPENDIX III: GLOSSARY OF SPANISH MECHANICAL TERMS

Acid	Acido	Companionway	Escotilla
Adhesive	Adhesivo	Compass	Brujula
Ahead	Adelante	Copper	Cobre
Alignment	Alineacion	Cord	Cordel
Aluminum	Aluminio	Cotter Pin	Pasador de una chaveta
Amidships	Medio del barco	Deck	Cubierta
Ammeter	Ampetimetro	Deep	Hondo
Anchor	Ancla	Not Deep	Poco hondo
Anchor chain	Cadena del ancla	Depth Sounder	Sondador mecanico
Anchor line	Cuerda del ancla	Dinghy	Panga
Anchor, sea	Ancla flotante	Dividers	Compases de punta
Angle	Angulo	Dock	Muelle
Anti-fouling Pant	Pintura anti-incrustante	Draft	Calado
Armature	Inducidos	Fire Extinguisher	Extinguidor
Astern	Por atras	Flashlight Bulb	Linterna
Awl	Lesna	Galvanized	Galvanizado
Axe	Hacha	Garbage	Basura
Axle	Ejes	Gasket	Empaquetaduras
Backstay	Burda	Gasoline	Gasolina
Bad hoockup	Mal anzuelado	Gear	Engrane
Bait	Carnada	Genoa	Genoves
Battery	Bateria	Generator	Generador
Beam	Pantoque	Gloves	Guantes
Belt	Banda, Correa, Cinturon	Grease	Grasa
Binoculars	Binoculares	Grease Gun	Pistola de grasa
Blacksmith	Herrero	Grommet	Arandela de cabo
Block	Moton	Hacksaw	Segueta
Block & Tackle	Moton y aparejo	Hacksaw Blade	Navaja de segueta
Blower	Soplador	Halyard	Driza
Boat	Barco	Hammer	Martillo
Boat, Motor	Barco de motor	Hand Pump	Bomba manual
Boat, Sail	Velero	Hand Rail	Barandilla
Boat, Ketch	Queche	Hardware Store	Gerreteria
Boat, Schooner	Goleta	High Tide	Marea alta
Boat, Yawl	Yole	Hook	Anzuelo, gancho
Boat, Yacht	Yate	Hose	Manguera
Bolt	Perno	Hose Clamp	Abrazadera de manguera
Bolt Cutter	Cortador de pernos	Hose Nozzle	Boquilla de manguera
Boom	Botavara	Hull	Brusca
Bow	Proa	Heavyweight Oil	Aceite lubricante pesado
Bowsprit	Baupres	Hydraulic	Hidraulico
Bronze	Bronce	Ignition	Ignicion
Brush	Brocha	Impeller	Impulsor
Bucket	Cubeta	Jib	Foque
Bulckhead	Mamparo	Keel	Quilla
Bunk	Litera	Key	Llave
Bushing	Bujes	Knife	Cuchillo
Cabin	Camarote	Knot (rope)	Nudo
Cable	Cable	Lifelines	Guardamancebos
Capstan	Cabrasante	Life Preservers	Salvavidas
Caulking	Calafa	Lightweight Oil	Aceite Lubricante ligero
Centerboard	Orza	Lobster	Langosta
Chain	Cadena	Lock	Cerradura
Chainplate	Endedonte	Low Tide	Marea baja
Cleat	Abrazadera	Lubricating Oil	Aceite lubricante

Magnet	Iman	Rubber glove	Guantes de goma
Mainsail	Vela mayor	Rudder	Timon
Mast	Mastil	Sail	Vela
Master	Maestro	Sander	Lijadora
Measure	Medida	Sandpaper	Lija
Micrometer	Micrometro	Saw	Serrucho
Milter	Inglete	Scraper	Raspador
Miter Box	Caja de inglete	Screw	Tornillo
Mixer	Mezcladora	Screwdriver	Desarmador
Mizzen	Mesana	Sealant	Sellador
Motor	Motor	Seam	Rebordes
Oitboard Motor	Motor fuera de borda	Shaft	Tubo
Motor oil	Aceite de motor	Shackle	Grillete
Nail	Clavo	Silicon Lubricant	Lubricante de silicon
Nut	Tuerca	Silver solder	Soldadura de plata
Oak	Roble	Sledgehammer	Martillo macho
Oars	Remo	Socket	Tubo
Oars Locks	Chumaceras	Socket set	Set de tubos
Obstruction	Obstaculo	Socket Wrench	Llave de tubo
Offshore	Alta mar	Sparkplug	Bujia
Ohmeter	Ohmiometro	Sparkplug socket	Cubo de bujias
Oil	Aceite	Sparkplug wrench	Llave para bujias
Oil Pressure Gauge	Indicador de presion de aceite	Speedometer	Velocimetro
On the bow	Por la amura	Splice	Union
On the Quarter	Por la oleta	Spot Weld	Punto de soldadura
Paint	Pintura	Spray gun	Pistola rociadora
Paint scraper	Sacapintura	Spray nozzle	Boquilla rociadora
Paint sprayer	Rociador de pintura	Stainless steel	Acero inoxidable
Pallet	Palet	Stanchion	Candelero
Pattern	Patron	Staple	Grapa
Pedestal	Pedestal	Staple gun	Engrapadora
Pencil	Lapiz	Starter	Arrancador
Pilot	Piloto	Steering wheel	Volante
Pipe	Tuberia	Stern	Popa
Pipe Wrench	Llave de tuberia	Straight ahead	Derecho
Piston	Piston	Tack (fastener)	Tachuela
Pliers	Pinzas	Teak	Teca
Plumber	Plomero	Template	Plantilla
Plumber's friend	Amigo de plomero	Test	Prueba
Plumber's snake	Vibora de plomero	Tester	Probador
Points	Puntos	Tiller	La cana
Polish	Pulir	Tin	Estaño
Polisher	Pulidora	Torque (Wrench)	Llave de torsion
Porpoise	Tonina	Tow	Remolque
Power Winch	Potencia del cabrestante	Tow rope	Soga de remolque
Preheat	Precalentar	Tube	Tubo
Pulley	Polea	Tube bender	Doblador de tubos
Pump	Bomba	Tube cutter	Cortatubos
Quarantine	Cuarentena	Varnish	Barniz
Reef points	Puntos de arrecife	Welding	Soldadura
Reel	Carrete	Winch/Windlass	Torno
Regulator	Regulador	Wind	Viento
Repair	Refaccion	Wire	Alambre
Rivet	Remaches	Wood	Madera
Rock	Roca	Wrench	Jurel
Rod	Caña		
Rubber	Goma, caucho		
Rubber cement	Cemento de goma		

APPENDIX IV: VESSEL AND CREW PREPARATION

Charlie's Charts believes that one of the most important parts of the adventure you're about to undertake is preparation. A well prepared boat and crew can deal with almost any situation and ensure the safety of both. From our many experiences cruising, both coastal and passage-making, as well as information and suggestions from our friends and fellow cruisers, we would like to provide the following suggested list of gear and equipment.

IMPORTANT: Along with the gear in each of the categories, we strongly recommend you have an owner's manual, service manual and parts list (along with part # if available) for all equipment and electronics you routinely use or need onboard. At a minimum, you should make your own operational check list for equipment such as watermakers, generators, etc... so that any member of the crew will know how to operate it properly.

SAFETY

1. A.I.S. to track commercial vessels' speed & course for collision avoidance.
2. Ham Radio with Marine SSB and Pactor E-mail capability, even if there is no licensed Ham Operator on board. In a medical or vessel emergency, Ham Operators will talk to anyone. In addition, by monitoring the maritime mobile Ham Nets you can get up-to-date news and weather even when there is no satellite coverage. (Optional but highly recommended)
3. Jack Lines installed on both port and starboard sides running the entire length of the boat
4. An inflatable offshore PFD with harness for each person on board
5. Personal strobes and whistles on lanyards for each person
6. USCG registered EPIRB
7. Man Overboard pole with 20' of floating line attached to a horseshoe buoy that is equipped with a sea anchor and man overboard strobe
8. Boarding ladder, swim step or other means to get back on board
9. Masthead strobe light. Remember these are not legal to use except in an emergency
10. Radar reflector / detector
11. Flashlight for each area of the boat, with extra batteries and bulbs securely stored nearby. Battery-less (hand crank) flashlights are handy to have on board as well
12. Powerful spotlight / beam gun
13. One rigid bucket per person, in case a bucket brigade needs to be formed
14. Air Horn and refill cans
15. A Comprehensive First Aid Kit, including easy to read First Aid Manual and Emergency Dental supplies.
16. Tow line, 100 + feet
17. Anchors, chain, rode, chafe gear, extra shackles, seizing wire, swivels, anchor buoy and lines – in multiple sets. NOTE: Your anchor system is your best insurance. Be sure to take different types of anchors and anchoring gear on board, not only for different conditions but in the event you may have to leave one or two behind in a hurry you will still have enough left to securely anchor again. Knowing where each type of anchor is stowed and in what conditions to use them is imperative. Having one monster "storm hook" is advisable, but make sure it is not too big for any crew member to carry on deck and deploy.

MAINTENANCE AND DAMAGE CONTROL

1. Extra electrical wire of all gauges used on the boat as well as connectors for each gauge wire, solder and electrical tape
2. Tri-Flow, Lanocote silicone spray and starting fluid
3. Fins, masks, snorkels, wet suits and weight belts
4. Tubes of silicone caulking (use silicone on plastic / glass only). Sikaflex and Dolfinite for bedding hardware
5. Underwater "poxy-putty", both slow and fast cure types
6. Spare fuses and / or circuit breakers. Both if needed
7. Plywood (as large as you can stow) for emergency hull and cabin side repair, and large nails (and don't forget the hammer!)
8. Extra squares of canvas large enough for use as a collision mat
9. Longest 2x4's that can be stowed on boat and large hose clamps for splinting
10. Assortment of nuts, bolts, screws, etc
11. Emergency marine SSB / Ham & VHF antenna
12. Tapered plugs or bungs for all thru-hulls (best if attached at each thru hull)
13. Expanded inflatable dinghy repair kit, including glue, material, valves, chemical, etc.

RIGGING FOR SAILORS

1. Extra blocks, shackles, thimbles (wire rope) and clevis pins
2. Spare line for sheets, halyards and preventer
3. Spare piece of rigging wire or spectra equivalent, at least as long as your longest stay
4. Cable clamps (Bulldog) for every size wire on board
5. Nicopress tool and assortment of Nicopress sleeves
6. Cable cutter, capable of cutting largest diameter wire on boat
7. Rigging tape, duct tape, chafe tape
8. Seizing wire
9. Rigging knife with shackle key for each crew member
10. Bosun's chair or harness and tackle
11. Sail repair kit containing sail repair tape, sail thread, needles and FIDS, marlin, whipping twine, sail palm, spare hanks, slides, etc
12. Marlin spikes
13. Cotter pins and rings
14. Spare winch handles

MECHANICAL

Check with your engine maker or its distributor for a recommended list of spare parts to maintain on board.
1. Spare kits for all pressure, hand and bilge pumps on board.
2. Spare kit for engine raw water pump, extra impellers and a complete backup pump.
3. Spare burner and / or parts for stove
4. Spare kit for head, extra joker valves and packing (we like to have at least two of these)
5. Spare bulbs for running lights and cabin lights plus a switch or two. Try replacement LED bulbs in your fixtures!
6. Spare chimneys, wicks, mantles and burners for oil lamps
7. Batteries for everything using them
8. Water-separating fuel filter funnel
9. Cartridges for in-line water filters.
10. Fuel additive for algae prevention and water absorption.

GALLEY

1. Environmentally safe cleaners and scrubbers for heads and sinks
2. Environmentally safe soap and hand cleaner
3. Fiddles on all counters and tables
4. Latches on all drawers, doors and cupboards
5. Secure stowage for cutlery, dishes, etc
6. Safety belt in galley
7. Sea rail on stove
8. Pot clamps
9. Pressure cooker
10. Deep cooking pots and pans with lids
11. Fresh and saltwater pumps (if you have an electric water pump, consider installing manual for both fresh and salt water in the galley sink)
12. Non-skid mats for counters
13. Heavy apron to protect cook from burns
14. Kitchen timer

COMFORT

1. Foul weather gear and boots to fit everyone
2. Brimmed, vented hats, cap keepers, UV protected sunglasses, croakies, spare glasses (especially if prescription) as needed
3. Sunscreen for face, lips, nose and ears
4. Deck shoes with toes for days, warm shoes / boots for nights
5. Sun awning if you're planning on cruising Southern California
6. Solar water showers
7. Good dodger and weather cloths
8. Lee cloths on bunks
9. Cockpit cushions
10. Reliable auto-pilot
11. Thermos bottles – 2 or more
12. Non-skid matting for lockers, drawers, carpet bottoms, etc

MISCELLANEOUS

1. Extra set of oars and / or paddles
2. Extra jugs for diesel, gas and water. Make sure these are well secured at all times, full or empty!
3. Waterproof bags of various sizes, especially document bags. Waterproof cases for electronics such as cell phones and cameras
4. Net bags and hammocks
5. Sparker lighters for stove, waterproof matches
6. In-line fresh water filters and spare elements
7. Extra dock lines and chafe gear
8. Canvas bucket (or 2)
9. Funnels to fit everywhere you might need them
10. Small whisk broom, dust pan and 12 volt vacuum
11. Deck brush and synthetic chamois
12. Sponges, rags, etc

13. Saltwater soap or Joy dish washing soap (good in saltwater) for dishes, shampoo, deck – plus hair rinse
14. Environmentally friendly laundry soap
15. Personal moist wipes
16. Paper towels and toilet paper
17. Assorted fishing gear and a fishing license!
18. Fishing gaff and / or net
19. At least 2 sharp knives – 1 large for filleting fish – and a filet board
20. Machete for cutting kelp
21. Boat hook(s)
22. Shock cord, different diameters and lots of it, with plastic hooks!
23. At least 250 ft. of 1/8" or larger line for miscellaneous tie-downs
24. At least 2 pair of heavy duty gloves, preferably one waterproof and one full finger
25. Kerosene lamp oil (can also use as paint brush cleaner, shroud cleaner, etc.)
26. Folding shopping cart.
27. Light(s) in engine compartment.
28. Amp (or Amp hour) meter on ship's main battery bank plus Amp meter for alternator.
29. Fire extinguishers in multiple, marked locations, with current tags and / or an automatic fire system.
30. Smoke and Carbon Monoxide detectors with functioning batteries.
31. Hand-held VHF radio(s)

AND THE LUXURY ITEMS....

1. Water maker and salinity tester for this.
2. Portable generator, wind / trolling generator and / or solar panels.
3. Folding bicycles
4. Deck wash down pump.

APPENDIX V: CHARTS and PUBLICATIONS

BAJA CALIFORNIA: West or Pacific Coast

Gerry Cunningham's GPS accurate Navigational charts, available from the Charlie's Charts website. www.charliescharts.com

Coastal Charts

18000	Point Conception to Isla Cedros (OMEGA)
21005	Cabo San Quintin to Punta Eugenia (OMEGA)
21011	Punta Eugenia to Cabo San Lazaro (OMEGA)
21014	Cabo San Lazaro to Cabo San Lucas (OMEGA)

(Alternatively, you can order slightly larger scale coastal charts

21140	Point Loma, California to Punta Colnett (Loran-C)
21160	Punta Colnett to San Jose (Loran-C)
21200	Punta Eugenia to Punta Abreojos (Loran-C)
21100	Punta Abreojos to Cabo San Lazaro (OMEGA)
21120	Bahia Magdalena to La Paz (OMEGA)

Detail Charts

21021	Bahia de Todos Santos (Ensenada)
21121	Bahia Magdalena including Bahias Santa Maria, Almejas & Sta. Marina
21122	Port of San Carlos (Bahia Magdalena)
21126	Bahia San Lucas
21159	Punta Colnett to San Jose (OMEGA) including Bahia de San Quintin plan
21199	Punta Eugenia to Punta Abreojos (OMEGA) (Pto San Bartolome/Turtle Bay)
21661	Islas Revillagigedos, Guadalupe & Escollos Alijos

BAJA CALIFORNIA: East or Gulf of California Coast

Gerry Cunningham's GPS accurate Navigational charts, available from the Charlie's Charts website. www.charliescharts.com

Coastal Charts

21008	Golfo de California - Northern part
21014	Golfo de California - Southern part: Cabo San Lazero to Cabo San Lucas

Detail Charts

21125	La Paz and approaches (includes harbor plan)
21161	Punta Pulpito to Isla San Marcos, including Bahia Concepcion
21141	Golfo de California - Western Shore, including Bahia Agua Verde

MAINLAND MEXICO: West Coast

Gerry Cunningham's GPS accurate Navigational charts, available from the Charlie's Charts website. www.charliescharts.com. Available as far south as Guaymas'

Coastal Charts

21008	Golfo de California - Northern part (see above)
21014	Golfo de California - Southern part (see above)
21017	Cabo San Lucas to Manzanillo (OMEGA)
21020	Manzanillo to Acapulco (OMEGA)
21023	Acapulco to Puerto Madero (OMEGA)

Detail Charts

21182	Guaymas and approaches
21301	Mazatlan and approaches
21338	Puerto Vallarta
21342	Bahia de Manzanillo and Bahia de Santiago
21384	Lazaro Cardenas and approaches
21401	Acapulco
21441	Salina Cruz and approaches
21478	Puerto Madero

Publication 153: Sailing Directions (Enroute) for the West Coasts of Central and South America
Publication 111: List of Lights, Radio Aids and Fog Signals: The West Coasts of North and South America (excluding continental U.S.A and Hawaii) but including Australia, Tasmania, New Zealand and the islands of the North and South Pacific Oceans.

APENDIX VI: Recommended Books and Publications

Spanish for Cruisers by Kathy Parsons
(Great help when discussing boat repairs, maintenance, and shopping.)

Madrigal's Magic Key to Spanish by Margarita Madrigal M.D.

Where There Is No Doctor by David Werner
Donde No Hay Doctor by David Werner (Translation in Spanish - good to have in tandem with the English version.)

The Cruising Woman's Advisor by Diana Jessie

Cruising Cuisine by Kay Pastorius

The Cruising K.I.S.S. Cookbook by Corinne C. Kanter

The Cruising Chef Cookbook by Michael Greenwald

MexWX: Mexico Weather for Boaters by Captain Pat Rains

Cornish & Ives: Reed's Maritime Meterology and Burch: Modern Marine Weather

The Baja Bash II by Capt. Jim Elfers
The West Marine Catalog

Comprehensive Guide to Marine Medicine by Eric Weiss, M.D. & Michael Jacobs, MD

Advanced First Aid Afloat by Peter Eastman, M.D

West Marine Catalogue

The Charlie's Charts Log Book by Captain Holly Scott and Jo Russell

APPENDIX VII: ATTENTION AMATEUR RADIO OPERATORS

Unlike what is offered already by Canada and the USA in reciprocal ham radio privilege to many countries, Mexico still has no interest in establishing a process to automatically recognize non-Mexican amateur radio operator licenses. For a foreign technician to join in Mexican Ham nets or operate a ham radio legally in Mexican waters, a provisional (reciprocal) operator's permit is required by the Mexican government (aka. XE2 Permit or Mexican Ham License). This permit costs $95.00 (US-2012) and is valid for 6 months or for the length of your visa and can be renewed with each new visa you obtain. There must be a minimum of 5 months remaining on your visa at the time of application for this permit.

Reciprocal Mexican Ham Radio Licensing is a service provided by the Mexican government through the SCT (Secretaria de Communicaciónes y Transportes) under the Comisión Federal de Telecomunicaciones ("CoFeTel") that has headquarters in Mexico City. To obtain such permit you will need to complete an application form at an SCT Center that is authorized to process such licensing and provide 3 copies each of your current Amateur Radio License (US or other), Passport, and your Mexican Tourist Visa obtained through the Mexican immigration services whose offices are located at most places of entry into Mexico. Note that you will be instructed to pay fees through the nearest bank (Banamex) – just follow the directions you are given to the bank you are instructed to visit – it will usually be very close by, i.e. within walking distance.

Used to be your Tourist Visa and XE2 Permit could be obtained in one trolley trip to Tijuana from San Diego, or upon check in with your boat entry at the Port of Ensenada. SCT centers at these locations however no longer issue radio licences that are authorized by "CoFeTel". We have been informed that the only official places where amateur radio licensing can be handled are at the SCT centers in the state capitals, along with "CoFeTel" headquarters in Mexico City. (The state capital of Baja Norte is Mexicali, and in Baja Sur the capital city is La Paz.) SCT centers forward all paperwork and correspondence related to amateur radio licensing to CoFeTel for processing, and then CoFeTel sends back any paperwork to those SCT offices – SCT and CoFeTel now use the Internet for a lot of their correspondence, except for issuing the permits. Those are still sent through the Mexican postal system from Mexico City to the SCT centers like the ones in Mexicali and La Paz.

If your destination is no farther than Baja California, or in fact you plan to venture to the mainland, we recommend if you need an XE Permit that you first reach La Paz where you can expediently file your application for reciprocal ham license. The SCT Center in La Paz is located blocks from the harbor and there, with (3 copies of) your visa in hand from your first port entry into Mexico, you can easily fill out an application for an operator's permit, provide the 3 copies each of your documents, and again run off to the nearest Banamex to pay the radio license fee (@$95.00 US). Upon returning to the SCT with the fee receipt (Recibo de la Cantidad) you will receive a stamped permit from the Comisión Federal de Comunicaciónes that entitles you to put an XE2 prefix in front of your US or other foreign Call Sign and legally operate your radio within Mexico for the period of your visa.

Port cities on the Pacific Coast of Mexico with SCT Centers include: La Paz, Mazatlán, Manzanillo, Acapulco, Zihuatenejo.

Although we have heard recently that not all of these SCT centers will process ham radio permits, cruisers tell us both Acapulco and Mazatlán offices do expediently process them – we just don't know for sure, or if true, for how long. Other than La Paz, none of these cities are state capitals, which in all cases along the west coast of Mexico are far from a port city, For those traveling directly to the mainland, we recommend that you check with "radioactive" cruisers on the local area nets for advice on which port would be best to engage in this process. Check the online version of this Guide too for updates in Ham radio activity in Mexico or subsequent permitting issues if any should occur. Note that the process fees above are established for years but of course any are subject to change at any time.

For more information visit the SCT and/or the CFT websites (these change often but can offer direct help) at www. sct.gob.mx and www.cft.gob.mx/. Better yet, with consistent updates in English for Amteur Radio in Mexico

APPENDIX VII: AMATEUR RATIO OPERATORS PERMIT

There you will fill out an application for an operator's permit. That, along with your copies of the above, your stamped visa and 95 pesos, you will receive a stamped permit that entitles you to put an XR2 prefix in front of your US Call Sign and legally operate within Mexico for the period of your permit.

BAJA NET
7238 KHZ
Daily 1600 Z

SOUTHBOUND NET
4054 KHZ
Daily 0200 Z

AMIGO NET
8122 KHZ
Daily 1400 Z

CHUBASCO MARITIME
MOBILE NET
Daily – 14:45 – 0000 Z

MEXICAN NAVY MONITORS
2182 KHz
12.392 KHZ

SINGLESIDEBAND NETS
North Sea of Cortez 0230 Z

HAPPY HOUR NET
3968.0 KHZ
Daily at 0000 Z

WORKING FREQUENCIES
4.366 KHZ
4.419 KHZ
8.768 KHZ
8.780 KHZ

PAPAGAYO NET: 0430 Z
4030 KHZ – 4024 KHZ

Westbound Pacific Net: 1600Z
8104 KHZ

APPENDIX VII: CHUBASCO/MANANA NET GUIDELINES

Wait until Net Control asks for check-ins. Then, if you have traffic, speak slowly and phonetically. You will be called when it is your turn. Have a frequency in mind where you can meet your other station.

In the following examples the "suffix" should be YOUR Mexican call (if within 12 miles of Mexican territory) or US call (if in International or U.S. waters). ALWAYS USE YOUR SUFFIX WHEN COMING INTO THE NET. USE YOUR COMPLETE CALL WHEN RECOGNIZED BY THE CONTROLLING STATION. USE ITY PHONETICS FOR YOUR SUFFIX. The suffix is the group of letters within (before/after the number) in your call.

DEFINITIONS

NOTE: These frequencies have been allocated for the exclusive use of the Mobile Maritime Service. The frequencies 4125kHz,

Contact: Used upon hearing a station you need to talk to that is talking to Net Control.

Ex: "**Contact**" suffix of station you want followed by your suffix.
Recheck: You were unable to make/maintain contact with another station leaving net frequency.
Ex: "**Recheck**" suffix.
Short Time: You must leave your radio very soon and need to pass a (some) traffic before leaving.
Ex: suffix "**Short Time**".
Re-Entry: Used when a station returns to the net and It is necessary for another station to know they are back .
Ex: "**Re-Entry**" suffix
Re-Entry With/Without: Reserved for use by Relays and 2-way stations and may also be With/Without: used when di-

rected by Net Control. This denotes whether the re-entering station does or does not have further traffic.
Ex: "**Re-Entry**" suffix "**With**"
Info: Used to signify that you have information pertaining to the current traffic subject.
Ex: "**Info**" suffix
Check Out: If you have checked into the Net and have traffic pending or another station has reason to expect to be able to contact you, always officially "**Check Out**" with net control when leaving.

List: If you are unable to contact a station on the Net but still want to try again, tell the net control that you want to remain "Listed". You will be periodically given an opportunity to call your station again.

HIGH SEAS SSB MARINE CHANNELS
All Frequencies Upper Side Band Mode

SIMPLEX Ship/Ship Ship/Shore		SIMPLEX Ship/Ship Ship/Shore	
Channel	Designator	Channel	Designator
4A	4.146 (KHz)	12C	12.359
4B	4.149	16A	16.528
4C	4.417	16B	16.531
6A	6.224	16C	16.534
6B	6.227	22A	22.159
6C	6.230	22B	22.162
8A	8.294	22C	22.165
8B	8.297	22D	22.168
12A	12.353	22E	22.171
12B	12.356		

6215kHz, 12290kHz, and 16420kHz are used for calling, as well as distress and safety purposes and the carrier frequency 8291kHz is used exclusively for distress and safety purposes. The frequencies listed below, may be used for intership simplex (single frequency) and cross band operation. Appendix 16, Sections C 1 and C 2:
4 MHz: 4000, 4003, 4006, 4009, 4012, 4015, 4018, 4021, 4024, 4027, 4030, 4033, 4036, 4039, 4042, 4045, 4048, 4051, 4054, 4057, and 4060.
8 MHz: 8101, 8104, 8107, 8110, 8113, 8116, 8119, 8122, 8125, 8128, 8131, 8134, 8137, 8140, 8143, 8146, 8149, 8152, 8155, 8156, 8161, 8164, 8167, 8170, 8173, 8176, 8179, 8182, 8185, 8188, and 8191.

Comment: Note that the frequencies 4417kHz (4 Charlie) and 6516kHz (6 Delta), which are often used by ship stations for simplex intership transmissions and the 6215z Caribbean Net, have been specifically allocated solely to Coast Stations under Appendix IC-Section A - Table of Single-Sideband Transmitting Frequencies for Duplex Operation under the new Band Plan.

APPENDICES

WWV & WWVH – Time Ticks And Adverse Weather Conditions

WWV	5,000	(10 min. after each hour for N. Pacific east of 140W.)
Fort Collins	10,000	
	15,000	
WWVH	5,000	(48, 49, and 50 min. after each hour for Hi. No. & So. Pacific.)
	10,000	
	15,000	

CH	SHIP TX	SHIP RX (freq. KHz)	CALL
402	4068	4360	
405	4077	4369	WLO
406	4080	4372	
407	4083	4375	
408	4086	4378	
409	4089	4381	
413	4101	4393	
414	4104	4396	WLO
415	4107	4399	
418	4116	4408	
419	4119	4411	
420	4122	4414	
421	4125	Distress - Band HF4	
424	4134	4426	U.S.C.G.*
425	4137	4429	
426	4140	4432	
450	4149	SIMPLEX SHIP Distress	
451	4146	SIMPLEX SHIP	
452	4149	SIMPLEX SHIP	
453	4417	SIMPLEX SHIP	
601	6200	6501	U.S.C.G.*
602	6203	6504	
603	6206	6507	
604	6209	6510	
605	6212	6513	
606	6215	6516	DAY ONLY
607	6519		WLO
650	6215	SIMPLEX SHIP Distress - Band HF6	
651	6224	SIMPLEX SHIP	
652	6227	SIMPLEX SHIP	
653	6230	SIMPLEX SHIP	
654	6516	SIMPLEX SHIP	
801	8195	8719	
803	8201	8731	
806	8210	8734	
807	8213	8737	
812	872	8752	
813	8731	875S	
816	8240	8764	U.S.C.G.*
817	8243	8767	
818	8246	8770	
819	8249	8773	
820	8752	8776	
821	8255	8779	
823	8261	8785	
824	8264	8788	WLO
827	8273	8797	
828	8276	8800	
829	8279	8803	
830	8282	8806	WLO
832	8288	8812	

CH	SHIP TX	SHIP RX (freq. KHz)	CALL
850	8291	SIMPLEXSHIP Distress – Band HF8	
851	8294	SIMPLEX SHIP	
852	8297	SIMPLEX SHIP	
1204	12239	13086	
1205	12242	13089	U.S.C.G.*
1207	12248	13095	
1212	12263	13110	WLO
1213	12266	13113	
1214	12269	13116	
1216	12275	13122	
1217	12278	13125	
1218	12281	13128	
1219	12284	13131	
1220	12287	13134	
1221	12290	13137	
1222	12293	13140	
1224	12299	13146	
1225	12302	13149	
1226	12305	13152	WLO
1227	12308	13155	
1231	12320	13167	
1232	12323	13170	
1250	12290	SIMPLEX SHIP Distress – Band HF12	
1251	12353	SIMPLEX SHIP	
1252	12356	SIMPLEX SHIP	
1253	12359	SIMPLEX SHIP	
	12362	SIMPLEX SHIP	
1604	16369	17251	
1606	16375	17257	
1607	16378	17260	WLO
1608	16381	17263	
1609	16384	17266	
1612	16393	17275	
1613	16396	17278	
1614	16399	17281	
1615	16402	17284	
1617	16408	17290	
1618	16411	17293	
1619	16414	17296	
(1621	16420	17302)	
1650	16420	SIMPLEX SHIP Distress – Band HF16	
1622	16423	17305	
1623	16426	17308	
1625	16432	17314	U.S.C.G.*
1627	16438	17320	
1628	16441	17323	
1629	16444	17326	
1630	16447	17329	
1632	16453	17335	
1633	16456	17338	
1634	16459	17341	
1635	16462	17344	
1636	16485	17347	
1637	16465	17350	
1638	16471	17353	
1639	16474	17356	
1640	16477	17359	
1641	16480	17362	WLO
1651	16528	SIMPLEX SHIP	
1652	16531	SIMPLEX SHIP	
1653	16534	SIMPLEX SHIP	
2202	22003	22699	
2203	22006	22702	
2204	22009	22705	
2206	22015	22711	
2207	22018	22714	

CH	SHIP TX	SHIP RX (freq. KHz)	CALL
2208	22021	22717	
2209	22024	22720	
2211	22030	22725	
2212	22033	22729	
2213	22036	22732	
2217	22048	22744	
2218	22051	22747	
2219	22054	22750	
2220	22057	22753	
2221	22060	22758	
2224	22069	22765	
2225	22072	22768	
2226	22075	22771	
2227	22078	22774	WLO
2228	22081	22780	
2230	22087	22783	
2231	22090	22786	WLO
2232	22093	22789	
2233	22096	22792	
2234	22099	22795	
2235	22102	22798	
2237	22108	22804	WLO
2238	22111	22807	
2239	22114	22810	
2240	22117	22813	
2251	22159	SIMPLEX	
2252	22162	SIMPLEX	
2253	22165	SIMPLEX	
2252	22168	SIMPLEX	
2255	22171	SIMPLEX	

*USCG Working Channels

WLO – Ship to Shore Contact via Big "A" antenna in Mobile Alabama

Other Ship Services
Ship Tx & Rx

2065	Ship/Coast
2079	Ship/Coast
2082.5	Ship
2093	Ship/Commercial Fishing
2095.5	Ship/Coast
2142	Ship: Pacific S. of 42' N DAY ONLY
2182	Safety & Calling
2203	Ship: Gulf of Mexico
2638	Ship
2670	Ship / U.S.C.G.
2738	Ship
2830	Ship: Gulf of Mexico
3023	Search & Rescue, Inc.
5680	Search & Rescue, Inc.

For updates see Marine SSB Frequencies at:
www.yachtcom.info/MarineSSB/index.html

MARITIME MOBILE/RADIO NET LIST

Time (UTC)	Freq. (MHz)	Net Name	Days	Coverage	Details	Contact/Web (Some Update Needed!)
0000/0100+	3.968	HAPPY HOUR UN-Net	Dly	Baja, W/Mex.	MM.Soc.	XE2/WP2F
0000	14.320	SEA MM Net	Dly	S/Pac, W/Pac	SEA MM	
0025	14.323	MOBILE MAR SE ASIA	Dly	HongKong to Aus	MM	
0055	14.323	MOBILE MAR SE ASIA	Dly	HongKong to Aus	WX	
0100	3.925	Gulf Coast Hurricane Net	Dly	G/C USA	WX. TFC	WD5CRR
0100+	3.855	BR. COL. BOATER'S Net	Dly	Sts. Of Geo.	Summer MM	VE7-
0100>0300+	14.305	Cal.-Haw. Cocktail Hr.	Dly	Cal/Haw/Pac	MM OK	KH6DEH
0130>0300+	28.313	10 METER M/M NET	Dly	E/PAC-Haw.	Novice OK	N6URW
0200/0100+	21.492	GERRI'S HAPPY HOUR M/M	M-F	Pac/Baja	MM/Social	K7YDO
0200	14.334	Brazil/East Coast Net	Dly	E/C Atl.	WX. TFC	K3UWJ
0200	3.932	Great Lakes Emerg. lfc	Dly	G/L	WX. TFC	WD8ROK
0200>0400+	14.300-14.313	PACIFIC SEAFARER'S NET	Dly	Pac., W/C	MM	14300.net/
0300+	14.116	Traveler's Net	Dly	Aust,W/Pac-I/OTFC	MM	VK6BO
0330/0230+	7.294	Sandia Net	Dly	W/C, Baja	Soc/Trivia	KA6HFG
0400+	3.856	Taco Net	Dly	Baja	Social	
0400+	14.115	CANADIAN DDD NET	Dly	PAC	W/U 0330	VE7JY
0400+	14.318	ARNOLD'S NET	Dly	S/Pac	MM, WX	ZK1DB
0430	14.118	Le Reseau Du Capitaine Net	Dly	ATL, CAR, PAC	MM, WX	
0500/0400+	14.313	PAC MARITIME NET	Dly	PAC	W/U	KH6UY
0500	21.200	UK/NZ/AFRICAN NET	Dly	PAC, I/O	MM	VK3PA
0500	8.101/12.353	Radio "Peri-Peri"	Dly	East Africa	WX at 8.101	
0530/0430+	14.313	PACIFIC MARITIME NET	Dly	PAC	MM, R/C	KH6UY
0630+	14.316/7.045	SO AFRICAN MAR NET	Dly	S/ATL, S.AFR, I/O	MM	ZS5GC
0630	14.313	INTERNATIONAL MM NET	Dly	ATL, MED, CAR	also 1700	DK0MC
0700>0800+	7.085	MED SEA CRUISER'S Net	Dly	MED SEA	MM	
0715+	3.820	BAY OF ISLANDS NET	Dly	NZ, Aus, PAC	MM	ZL1BKD
0800>0830+	14.315	Pacific Inter-Island Net	Dly	S/PAC, W/PACTFC		KX6OU
0800+	14.303	UK MARITIME NET	Dly	MED, PAC	also 1800	G4FRN
0900	14.313	MED SEA MM NET	Dly	MED	MM	5B4MM
1000	14.313	German MM Net	Dly	ATL, MED	MM	DK0MC
1000+	14.320	South China Sea Net	Dly	S/PAC		
1030	3.815	Caribbean WX Net	Dly	CAR	WX also 2230	VP2AYL
1100/1000+	3.770	Mar Provinces WX Net	M-Sa	NE Canada	WX	VE1AAC
1100>1200+	7.241	CARIBBEAN MM NET	Dly	CAR	MM	KV4JC
1100>1600+	14.300-14.313	Intercon Net (MM)	Dly	N/S/C/Am	TFC/MM	14300.net/
1100+	14.283	Carribus Traffic Net	Dly	E/C, CAR	TFC	KA2CPA
1110	3.930	Puerto Rico WX Net	Dly	PR/VI	WX also 2310	KP4AET
1115+	14.316-14.341	INDIAN OCEAN MAR NET	Dly	W/PAC, I/O		VK6HH
1130+	14.316/7.045	SO AFRICAN MAR NET	Dly	S/ATL, I/O	MM	ZS5MU
1130	21.325	So Atlantic Roundtable	Dly	S/ATL	TFC also 2330	PY1ZAK
1200+	28.380	MARITIME MOBILE NET	Dly		Novice OK	
1200+	14.320	So/East Asia Net	Dly	SEA, S/PAC		WB8JDR
1200>1400+	7.233	E/C WATERWAY NET	Dly	E/US	RV TFC	KB1Z
1220+	7.096	Bahamas WX Net	Dly	Bah/Fla	WX, MM	C6AGG
1230	7.185	Barbados Info Net	Dly	CAR	TFC	BP6DH
1245/1145+	7.268	E/C WATERWAY NET	Dly	E/C, CAR	MM	NU4P
1245	14.1225	MISSISSAUGA MM NET	Dly	E/MED, ATL,CAR	VE Relay, MM	VE3NBL
1300>1400+	21.400	TRANS ATL MM NET	Dly	N/ATL, CAR	R/C, WX	BP6OM
1300>1400+	3.963	E/C Recreational Vehicle Net	Dly	E/C US	TV TFC	KB1Z
1300+	7.085	C/A BREAKFAST CLUB	Dly	C/A	MM Social	TI7MEG
1430+ (I-1330 +)	3.968	SONRISA NET	Dly	Baja, So Cal	MM, WX	sonrisanet.org/
1400>1600+	7.263/8	Rocky Mountain RV Net	Dly	Mid West	RV TFC	K5DGZ
1415+	7.192	CHUBASCO NET	Dly	Baja, So Cal	MM	XE2/N6OAH
1500	8.101/12.353	Radio "Peri-Peri"	Dly	East Africa	WX at 8.101	
1600/1500+	7.238	PST - BAJA CAL MAR NET	Dly	Baja, So Cal	WX-0815	N6ADJ
1600+	7.200/268	Taco Net	Dly	Baja	Social	
1600>0200+	14.300-14.313	MAR MOBILE SERV NET	Dly	ATL, CAR, PAC		mmsn.org/
1600>1800+	7.263/8	PAC RV Service Net	M-F	W/US	RV TFC	K6BYP
1630/1530+	3.865	PT. LUDLOW BOATER'S NET	Dly	Wash	MM, WX, R/C	WO7O
1630	14.303	SWEDISH MAR NET	Dly		MM 0530, 2030	
1630	14.313	GERMAN MAR NET	Dly	Worldwide	MM	intermar-ev.de/
1700>1800+	14.308	RV Service Net	Dly	US	RV TFC	KB1Z
1700+	14.323	US/Canada Power Sqdn.Net	Sat	US/Canada	Boat TFC	W7LOE

Net List continued next page ⊠

Please contact us with <u>any</u> discrepancies you find so we can help cruisers maintain this list.

APPENDICES

Time (UTC)	Freq. (MHz)	Net Name	Days	Coverage	Details	Contact
1700+	7.240	Bejuka Net	M-F	C/A	TFC	HP3XWB
1700	14.313	INTERNATIONAL MM NET	Dly	ATL/MED	MM also 0630	DK0SS
1700>1900+	14.280	Inter-Mission RA Net	M-Sa	C/A, S/A, CAR TFC		WA2KUX
1700	14.118	Le Reseau Du Capitaine Net	Dly	ATL, CAR, PAC	MM (WX AT 0430)	
1800+	14.303	UK MARITIME NET	Dly	ATL/MED	MM also 0800	G4FRN
1800*	7.076	SO PAC CRUISING NET	Dly	S/PAC	MM, WX, informal	
1830/1730+	14.340	MANANA NET - WARM UP	M-Sa	W/C, E/PAC	MM	KB5HA
1900/1800+	14.340	MANANA NET	M-Sa	W/C, E/PAC	MM	reocities.com/TheTropics/3989/
1800+	14.283	KAFFEE KALTCH UN-NET	MWSa	HAW/Tahiti	Social, news	FO5GZ
1900/1800	14.305	Confusion Net	M-F	PAC, ATL	TFC	W7GYR
1900+	7.285	Hawaii AM Net	Dly	Hawaii	TFC, WX	KH6BF
1900>2000+	21.390	Halo Net	Dly	N/A, S/A	TFC	WA4FXR
1900+	14.329	BAY OF ISLANDS NET	Dly	NZ, S/PAC	MM	ZL1BKD
1900/2000	14.297	ITALIAN MM NET (Ital/Eng)	Dly	ATL (AFRICA-BRAZIL) WX		IK6IJF
2000+	7.080	NEW ZEALAND WX NET	Dly	NZ	WX, MM	ZL1BTQ
2000>2200+	21.390	Inter-American Traffic Net	Dly	N/A, C/A, S/A	TFC	WD4AHY
2030	14.303	SWEDISH MAR NET	Dly	ATL	MM 0530, 1630	
2030+	14.315	TONY'S NET WARM UP	Dly	NZ, AUS, S/PAC	MM, W/U	ZL1ATE
2100+	14.261	Ben's Friends MM Un-Net		E/C	MM Social	K3BC
2100+	14.315	TONY'S NET	Dly	NZ, AUS, S/PAC	WX-VK9JA	ZL1ATE
2100+	14.113	MICKEY MOUSE CONNECT.	Dly	S/ATL, S/PAC	MM	CX9ABE
2200>2230+	3.963	E/C Recreational Vehicle Net	Dly	E/C, US	RV also 1300	KB1Z
2200+	21.402	PACIFIC MAR NET – 15 mtr.	M-F	PAC, C/A, BAJA	MM	KB7DHQ
2200+	21.412	MAR MOBILE SERVICE NET	M-F	PAC/Worldwide	MM	KA6GWZ
2230	3.815	Caribbean WX Net		CAR	WX also 1030	VP2AYL
2310	3.930	Puerto Rico WX Net	Dly	P/R, V/I	WX also 1110	KP4AET
2330	21.325	South Atlantic Roundtable		S/ATL	TFC, social	
24/7 All Year	14.300-343	MARITIME EMERGENCY NET				14300.net/
AS NEEDED	14.325	Hurricane Net	A/R	ATL, CAR, PAC	Hur. Track	K0IND

LEGEND:
ATL = Atlantic, CAR = Caribbean, C/A = Central America, EC = East Coast, E/Pac = East Pacific, G/C = Gulf Coast, I/O = Indian Ocean, MED = Mediterranean, MM = Maritime Mobile, R/C = Roll-Call passage maker positions taken, TFC = Traffic, W/C = West Coast, W/Pac = West Pacific, W/U = Warm Up session check-ins, WX = Weather, "+" = Net information checked recently, "*" = No current information, may be outdated, ">" = Net operates from/to times listed, "/" = Net time changes from/to for daylight savings or summer to winter.

Footnotes:
1. Credits: Many thanks to the dozens of people, both cruisers and base stations, who have provided this information. Cruisers "out there" and dedicated base stations are often the only source of updated information. All updates are appreciated. Thanks also to those hard working Net Managers, Net Controls, and Relay/ Two-way Stations. We all appreciate all your efforts! Please contact Downwind Marine with any changes or additions to this list at (619)224-2733 or email to ▓▓▓▓▓▓▓▓▓▓▓▓▓▓▓▓▓▓▓ .

2. Amateur Nets:

MM Nets above are shown in capital letters. Other nets listed above provide information or services useful to cruising hams. MM Nets are active nearly worldwide 24 hours a day, between 14.300 - 14.320MHz.

Traffic Nets in the U.S. include many state and regional Traffic Nets that exist on 75 and 40 meters, normally above 3.900MHz on 75 and 7.225MHz on 40. Most are active in the early evening. Cruisers may find them useful for phone patches and message traffic.

VHF/2 Meter Nets are run in popular cruising grounds and often provide check-ins, WX and sometimes wide area linked systems. The B.C., Straits of Georgia, system has several repeaters linked together covering the entire straits area. It runs daily MM Nets in the late afternoons during the summer months. The Chesapeake Bay 2 Meter Net provides check-ins and WX during the summer months.

3. Operators are **strongly** cautioned to check appropriate band allocations, operator privileges, reciprocal licensing agreements, third party traffic agreements, and net protocols before transmitting .

4. Nets often vary over time and frequency, based upon conditions and QRM. If nets are not found when or where listed, listen around plus or minus any listed frequency/time. Quick list also provided on page 10 of this Guide.

5. Marine Band Nets: Marine VHF Nets are frequently run in popular cruising areas. Examples are the Downwind Cruisers Net on Ch 68, 0830 M-F in San Diego; and the Cruisers Net in La Paz, Baja, Mexico on Ch 22.

Marine HF Nets are often run for regional areas. Popular examples include the:
Keri Keri Net (New Zealand), Western S PAC on 2480/ 4417/ 4445 KHz, WX at 1925/2000L, Position Reports taken at 0800/1900L.
Caribbean SSB Net on 6.215 MHz at 1200/2300Z.
Herb's WX Net (Southbound II) on 12A, 12.353 MHz at 1900/2400Z for E/C and CAR passage makers (also on 6A).
VNN555 Net (NSW Australia, by VK4NN), 2000Z, ITU Channel #608/6221T/6522R, #1234/12329T/ 13176R, #1642/16483T/17365R.

Informal nets are often held during popular passage making times. Examples include the 8A, 8.294 or 12B, 12.356 MHz nets for boaters heading south from San Diego to Baja and vice versa. WX information is often provided. Additions to the Marine Band Net List are requested.

6. Information: Photocopying of this MM Net List for free distribution is authorized, as long as credit is given and the list is published including the legend and all footnotes. Entering the list into a computer database or any other use requires written permission.

Please contact us with any discrepancies you find so we can help cruisers maintain this list.

APPENDIX VII: Radio Fax Time Schedules & HTTP: Addresses

Locate updates and transmission contents for worldwide schedules at www.nws.noaa.gov/om/marine/rfax.pdf

PT. REYES, CALIFORNIA, U.S.A.

CALL SIGN
NMC

FREQUENCIES
4346 kHz   8682 kHz   12786 kHz
17151.2 kHz 22527 kHz

TIMES
0140-1608 CONTINUOUS CONTINUOUS
CONTINUOUS 1840-2356

EMISSION POWER
F3C 4KW F3C 4KW F3C 4KW F3C 4KW F3C 4KW NMC
Coast Guard San Francisco (Pt. Reyes), North Pacific- weather.noaa.gov/fax/ptreyes.shtml

NEW ORLEANS, LOUISIANA, U.S.A.

CALL SIGN
NMG

FREQUENCIES
4317.9 kHz   8503.9 kHz 12789.9   kHz
17146.4 kHz

TIMES
CONTINUOUS CONTINUOUS CONTINUOUS 1200-2045

EMISSION POWER
F3C 4KW F3C 4KW F3C 4KW F3C 4KW
NMC Coast Guard New Orleans, Gulf of Mexico &
Baja California - weather.noaa.gov/fax/gulf.shtml

HONOLULU, HAWAII, U.S.A. Call Sign Frequencies

CALL SIGN
KVM70

FREQUENCIES
9982.5 kHz   11090 kHz   16135 kHz

TIMES
0533-1630 CONTINUOUS 1733-0437

EMISSION POWER
F3C 4KW F3C 4KW F3C 4KW
KVM-70 DOD Honolulu, Central & South Pacific -
http://weather.noaa.gov/fax/hawaii.shtml

Additional Pacific Basin Radio FAX Schedules: CHARLEVILLE, AUSTRALIA

CALL SIGN
VMC VMC VMC VMC VMC

FREQUENCIES
2628 kHz   5100 kHz   11030 kHz
13920 kHz   20469 kHz

TIMES EMISSION POWER
0900-1900 F3C 1KW CONTINUOUS F3C 1KW
CONTINUOUS F3C 1KW CONTINUOUS F3C 1KW
1900-0900 F3C 1KW

TIMES EMISSION POWER
1100-2100 F3C 1KW CONTINUOUS F3C 1KW
CONTINUOUS F3C 1KW CONTINUOUS F3C 1KW
2100-1100 F3C 1KW

TIMES EMISSION POWER
0945-1700 F3C 5KW CONTINUOUS F3C 5KW
CONTINUOUS F3C 5KW CONTINUOUS F3C 5KW
2145-0500 F3C 5KW

WILUNA, AUSTRALIA

CALL SIGN
VMW VMW VMW VMW VMW

FREQUENCIES
5755 kHz   7535 kHz   10555 kHz
15615 kHz   18060 kHz

WELLINGTON, NEW ZEALAND

CALL SIGN
ZKLF

FREQUENCIES
3247.4 kHz 5807 kHz 9459 kHz 13550.5 kHz
16340.1 kH

APPENDIX VII: RADIO FAX TIME SCHEDULES & HTTP: ADDRESSES

(Updates and worldwide schedules are available at www.nws.noaa.gov/om/marine/rfax.pdf)

Point Reyes, California, U.S.A.

Call Sign	Frequencies	Times	Emission	Power NMC	4346 kHz	Night
F3C	4 KW					
	8682 kHz	Continuous	F3C	4 KW		
	12786 kHz	Continuous	F3C	4 KW		
	17151.2 kHz	Continuous	F3C	4 KW		
	22527 kHz	Continuous	F3C	4KW		

NMC Coast Guard San Francisco (Pt. Reyes), North Pacific http://weather.noaa.gov/fax/ptreyes.shtml

New Orleans, Louisiana, U.S.A.

Call Sign	Frequencies	Times	Emission	Power
NMG	4317.9 kHz	Continuous	F3C	4 KW
	8503.9 kHz	Continuous	F3C	4KW
	12789.9 kHz	Continuous	F3C	4KW
	17146.4 kHz	1200-2045	F3C	4KW

NMG Coast Guard New Orleans, Gulf of Mexico & Baja California website
http://weather.noaa.gov/fax/gulf.shtml

Honolulu, Hawaii, U.S.A.

Call Sign	Frequencies	Times	Emission		Power
KVM70	9982.5 kHz	0533-1630	F3C	4KW	
	11090 kHz	Continuous	F3C	4KW	
	16135 kHz	1733-0437	F3C	4KW	

KVM-70 DOD Honolulu, Central and South Pacific website
http://weather.noaa.gov/fax/hawaii.shtml

Voice Radio Weather Broadcasts (LSB)
NMC: 04:30Z and 10:30Z 4426 8764 13089 kHz
16:30Z and 22:30Z 8764 13089 17314 kHz
Baja Net: 07:45 PST 7238 kHz Net weather forecast
          08:15 PST 7238 kHz radio traffic

Mexican Weather (in Spanish): 09:30 15:30 21:30 CST 8242.8 kHz

The above material is available courtesy of Downwind Marine, San Diego.

APENDIX VII: MARITIME RADIO NETS

We hope these are current but all could be significantly changed.Please get back to us with updates!

HAM NETS: BAJA NET

7238 kHz - LSB Daily @ 16:00Z

CHUBASCO MARITIME MOBILE

7192/7294 kHz - LSB Daily @14:30Z

SONRISA NET

3968.0 kHz - LSB
Daily @ 13:30Z
Weather at 14:45Z (13:45 in summer)

BAJA CA MARITIME SERVICE

7233.5 kHz - LSB Weekdays @ 15:00Z

PACIFIC SEAFARER'S NET

1430 kHz - LSB Daily @ 03:00Z 2182 kHz

MARITIME EMERGENCY NET

14300 kHz (COVERAGE ALMOST 24/7)

MEXICAN NAVY MONITORS:

8257 kHz
12392 kHz

USE WORKING FREQUENCIES:
4366 kHz, 4419 kHz
8768 kHz, 8780 kHz

MARINE SSB NETS:

AMIGO NET

6.212 USB/6.227 USB kHz USB
Daily @ 14:00Z (then goes 4B)

NORTH SEA OF CORTEZ NET

4051 kHz – 4060 kHz - USB Daily @ 02:30Z

PAPAGAYO NET

4030 kHz / 4024 kHz – USB Daily @ 04:30Z

PAN PACIFIC NET

8143 kHz - USB Daily @ 22:00Z

WESTBOUND PACIFIC NET

8104 kHz - USB Daily @ 16:00Z

SOUTHBOUND NET

Primary Freq. 4054 kHz - USB Daily @ 01:15Z

BLUEWATER NET

6516 KHz - USB Daily @ 02:00Z

PICANTE NET

6214 kHz - USB Daily @13:30Z

Also check these websites for current updates on Ham and SSB nets at www.docksideradio.com/Cruising%2 0Nets.htm and www.made-simplefor- cruisers.com/communications. APE

APPENDIX VIII: TELEPHONING IN MEXICO

Mexican Dialing Codes
Refer to the Telephone Dialing Codes Table for Mexico for a list of codes for cities and towns in Mexico.

Calls to and From Mexican Phones (Land Lines)
Local Calls - To make local calls, drop the 011 52 and dial direct, just as you would do at home. Note that major city's numbers have eight numbers and other places have seven numbers.

National Calls - Dial 01 is the prefix for all non-local calls in Mexico, followed by the area code, followed by telephone number.

International Calls - To access a number outside of Mexico, you need to prefix the number with 00 (the international access code) then the country code, then the national area code (omit the first zero if there is one), then the local no.

Dialing to Mexico From Overseas - Dial the International access code (in most cases this is 00, in the USA it is 010) followed by Mexico's country code (52), the area code in Mexico (see National Calls, above) and then the seven or eight digit local number.

Calling Toll-Free Numbers in the USA from Mexico:
If you are in Mexico and you want to contact someone in the USA who is advertising a toll-free number, you will need to dial "001" then the 10 digit 800 number; for example: 001-800 123 4567 or, e.g. 001-880-123 4567.

Calling Cell Phones From a Land Line in Mexico
When calling a cell phone from a land line within Mexico, the number will be preceded by a 3 digit access code, thus: For calls to a local cell phone (that is, a cell phone with an area code that is the same as the land-line's), dial 044 then the 10-digit number of the mobile phone. The caller will be charged for the full cost of the call.

For calls to a non-local domestic cell phone (that is, a cell phone with a Mexican area code which is different from the land-line's area code) dial 045 followed by the 10-digit mobile number, and the entire cost of the call will be charged to the caller if the mobile phone is in its home area. For the latest prices on telephony in Mexico connect to the Mexico Price Index on Mexperience.

Calling Cell Phones From a Mexican Cell Phone in Mexico
If you are calling a cell phone phone from another cell phone, just dial the area code followed by the mobile number.

Calling a Cell Phone in Mexico from Outside Mexico
Dial your country's international access code, followed by Mexico's country code (52), then add a "1", then the mobile phone's area code and its number. The cost of the call will be charged to the caller.

For example, if the cell phone number in Mexico is listed as 044 55 1234 5678, ignore the "044" or "045" (see notes above about these codes), and place a "1" in its stead. Then dial the area code (55) and then the number (1234 5678). So, from the USA, you would dial: 010 52 1 55 1234 5678

If you plan on cruising in Mexican waters or leaving your boat for some time it is advisable to complete ANEXO 1 and have it stamped by the Customs officer at the time the vessel is imported into Mexico. This will avoid paying import duties on any replacement parts that are needed in the future.

APPENDIX IX: SHORE TRIPS of INTEREST by Christie Gorsline

ALAMOS:
From Mazatlan, travel north through Los Mochis and continue to Navojoa. It's difficult to get to (53 kilometers east of Sonora Hwy. 182) at the end of a dead end but it is a delightful town, one of the oldest in northern Mexico. Don't miss: Hotel Mansion de la Condesa Magdalena on Obregon, Iglesia de la Purisima Concepcion and the Museo Costumbrista de Sonora (open weekdays: 9-1 and 3-6).

COPPER CANYON AND CHIHUAHUA (Prices and exchange rates vary over time.)
Day 1: Mazatlan to Los Mochis bus leaves every hour from the Mazatlan terminal. The cost is $100 pesos each - 5 hours. In Mochis, 3 block walk to change buses. $13 pesos buy tickets on bus, 1 hour to El Fuerte. Walk to Hotel San Francisco on Obregon St. $200p for two. Take a walk to the zocalo, church and fort. Have dinner at Meson a General.

Day 2: Take the bus ($2p each) or taxi ($35p) to train (4k). The train leaves at 0730. Get a seat assignment on right side, the cost is $75p each to Creel (7 hours). Pack a picnic or buy food at stops (burritos, etc.). In Cree. stay at Hotel Korachi, 90m (100 yds.) from train stop (across tracks from town with a view of the church).

Day 3: Walk through town to the Indian cave/lake and hike up to the statue. Hire a driver to take you to the waterfall at Basaeachi or to the rim and hike to hot springs. Suggestions for hikes are shown on a wall at Casa Margarita's across from the Zocalo.

Day 5: The train to Bahuichivo departs at noon; sit on left side. The bus from Hotel Paraiso del Oso meets the train at 1600. Cash/cruiser price is $250p for two and includes breakfast. Walk or ride horses to the burial cave. Visit the town of Cerocahui and mission.

Day 6: Take the 1600 train to Los Mochis and a taxi to the bus station. The 2000 bus to Mazatlan arrives at 0300. Take a taxi to the marina.

NOTES: The total expenses for the above six-day trip are $1760p (approximately $235US) includes transportation and rooms. Food, gifts and tips are extra. The cost of drivers in Creel is $50p per person, each day and is not included in the $1760p total.

Some prices and times are close estimates. The room rental at Hotel Paraiso del Oso of $120US is a cash special for cruisers. NOTE: It's just as interesting to stop in Bahuichivo first and then go on to Creel. An additional overnight is possible at Divisadero. The train stops for 15 minutes going each way. Temperatures in April/May were cool in the morning and evening and comfortable. Creel gets occasional snow during the winter. If your desire is "VIEW," visit the Grand Canyon in Arizona instead. Copper Canyon is interesting primarily because of the Indians and the hiking.

Concordia and Copala: In the foothills east of Mazatlan, these two towns are an easy day trip with return to your boat. Concordia is 45 minutes from Mazatlan and known for its artisans: wood, leather, furniture and pottery. Overlooking the zocalo is the 18th century Iglesia de San Sebastian and the only baroque church in the state of Sinaloa. Twenty-four kilometers past Concordia is Copala, with cobblestone streets, colonial homes and a quaint atmosphere.

Near Manzanillo: Colima, a state capitol, is less than an hour from Manzanillo. It is best explored on foot. You can peer through the gates of colonial residences at luxury living, Mexican style. Visit Jardin Libertad, the Museo Regional de Historia, the cathedral and Palacio de Gobierno. Fifteen minutes north of Colima is the village of Comala where all the houses are white adobe with red tile roofs.

Guadalajara, Ajijic, Guanajuato and San Miguel de Allende: These towns are readily accessible by bus or car from either Manzanillo or Puerto Vallarta. They are well worth at least two weeks of inland exploration.

Inland to Cuernavaca and Taxco: Cuernavaca is a one-hour drive south of Mexico City and in addition to being a historical city in its own right, is a vacation or second home paradise for wealthy residents of Mexico City. Must see places are: Jardin Borda, Palacio de Cortez (Diego Rivera mural) and Catedral de la Asuncion. Around the corner from the cathedral is the Casa de Robert Brady, an American art aficionado whose home is open to the public.

Cuernavaca is known for its numerous Spanish language schools. One that is recommended is the Spanish Language Institute. Its address is: Bajada Pradera #208, Col. Praera, Cuernavaca, Morelos 62170, MEXICO; Telephone: 73-11-0063, Fax: 73-177-52-94, US#1-800-552-2051.

Day trips out of Cuernavaca are: Tepotzlan and Zochicalco. About 30 minutes from town is Piramide de Zochicalco, a Mayan ruin. Tepotzlan is 1 hour NE of Cuernavaca and is believed to have supernatural powers. Visit the convent, church and the vendors market (open Wed and Sun). There is a lovely view of the valley and the tip of an unexcavated pyramid at the top of a cliff, a slippery and difficult 45-minute climb.

Taxco: Two hours from Cuernavaca, Taxco is a silver mining town of twisting cobblestone streets that wander up the side of a steep hill. One full day and one or two nights is sufficient to explore the town, buy silver and tour the cathedral.

Near Zihuatanejo: From the local bus depot (between the bay and the mercado) take a bus to Bara de Potosis. Transfer to a pick-up truck that doubles as a bus and school bus..

Oaxaca: Sights include many Roman Catholic churches, convents and monasteries dating from the colonial period. A short walk from the zocalo is a church with an Italian bronze altar and giant gold and silver crucifix that has survived all the insurrection of hundreds of years. The zocalo, markets and south side streets are famous places where Zapotec vendors peddle their wares. Restaurants surround the zocalo and make a wonderful location from which to observe the action.

Oaxacan artisans are famous for their work and the Saturday market is the largest indigenous run market in Mexico. For a unique experience in buying alebrijes (brightly painted wooden animals you can go directly to the artisan's homes, in the villages of Arazola and San Martin Tilcajete. Senor Don Manuel Jiminez is the most famous and pieces are gallery priced. Along the road to Mitla, detour to visit "Mezcal Pensamiento" and taste locally produced mezcal with the proprietor. Also detour at Teotitlan Del Valle and visit "LIIS LAAH DI"rug making operation. In the village of San Bartolo Coyotepec you will see the famous shiny black pottery being crafted. Don't miss the Thursday only market in the village of Zaachila. Zapotecs inhabited Mitla and Mt. Alban in 500 - 800 BC. These archaeological sites are an inspiring look into an ancient culture.

Oaxaca is a one-hour flight from Mexico City, or five-hour first class bus ride, or a 5 - 6 hour bus ride from Salina Cruz. There are lots of choices of hotels near the zocalo, clean, spacious and convenient was Hostal Santa Rosa at $220 pesos for double rooms (#15, 16, and 17) have a patio).

APPENDIX X: PETS IN PARADISE

I suppose there are hundreds of articles out there about the "best" way to live with your pets. They cover just about everything from food, feedings and dishes, barf, pee, poop, mats, cat boxes, litters and potty training, shipboard security officers, pet security underway, beds, hair management, fleas, shots, passports, PFDs, dinghy do and don'ts, to leashes and sunscreen. But I have never read an article about teaching your dog to speak a foreign dog language, or learning foreign dog customs.

Gracie is my Border Collie mix rescue dog. Her hair is a bit shorter that a pure bred, she is about the same size at 40 pounds or so. She's very devoted, quite smart, not too hyper, tolerates the cat but hates big trucks. The vet's guess was that she was about three years old when we brought her aboard. The whole boat thing was new to her and it took a few days to get the hang of it, but she settled in pretty quickly. She only walked off the dock once.

Then we went to Mexico. Just for the record, the cat never noticed. The first time we went ashore for a potty run, was in Turtle Bay, which is about half way down the Pacific side of the Baja peninsula. It is a small town as opposed to a village, with dirt streets and lots of seemingly stray dogs. Big dogs. With scars on their heads. Running loose along the beach and very interested in the new girl in town. Sheesh! Poor Gracie had her tail clamped down tight – which is tough when you REALLY have to go potty on dirt, after three days at sea. We finally found an appropriate place to get her business done, and then had to deal with the other dogs.

They don't have and never have had leashes. It made Gracie look like the dorky kid on the playground, except it made her feel a bit more secure. There was a mad rush for the sniffing of everyone's goods. Maybe frenzy is a better word. Then, the play posture by the locals. Did we dare? Would she be mauled as soon as she was off the leash? Somebody threw a stick toward the water and off they went. The next time she flew by, I took off the leash and she joined the pack. Some kids showed up and chased the dogs and the dogs chased them, laughing and rolling in the sand. Life off the lease is grand!! They finally exhausted themselves and trotted back to the shade of the palapa where the humans were visiting and enjoying a Pacifico or two. Big happy dog grins. Oops, no water anywhere – note to human for the next shore trip. The kids couldn't pronounce Gracie, so called her Crazy instead. This happened everywhere.

It turns out that the local dogs guard their houses/territories without visible fences. Each dog is resting but also keeping watch in the front yard, and has decided where the boundries of their yard stop. They just watch as long as you don't cross their 'line'. If you get too close, they stand up, and if you enter their territory they bark or come to ask you to leave. They possibly rip your leg off if you don't listen, but we're pretty sharp like that. Of course, this was all news to Gracie, who didn't speak dog OR people Spanish, and didn't know the customs. We had a few minor mishaps till we caught on. Very few dogs just wander around, most are guarding something and stay close by.

There are a few exceptions however. Now and then, some big scary looking dog decides to follow you. Or maybe lots of little ones. You quickly leave his territory but he continues to follow, maybe even with his hackles up. Your mouth starts to go dry and your heart speeds up a bit. Your dog looks at you for advice. Now what? Here is how the locals advised us.

All Mexican dogs are scared of being hit by a thrown rock. All you have to do is fake them out. Here are the steps to be used - in order. Work through the steps only until you get the proper results. There is no need to actually throw a rock or proceed to any unnecessary steps except in cases of extreme emergency.

1. Stop walking, turn and face the dog – it's all about posture. Make eye contact and look like you are in charge. Possible "Git!" in a deep forceful voice if needed.

2. Bend over as if picking up a rock. Maintain eye contact.
3. Cock your throwing arm back and take a step forward as if you are about to let that rock fly. More meaningful words to the dog – English is fine.
4. Go ahead and 'throw' your imagined rock, by making a throwing motion. Scan the area for a real rock.
5. Quickly grab a real rock or two and repeat the above steps. Assure the bad dog that you are serious – perhaps some cuss words in English. Avoid the F bomb. (Ugly Americans etc.)
6. Throw the real rock in the general direction of the big scary dog. Make some noise!!!
7. Grab a big fat rock, take aim and throw it right at the devil who is about to attack you and your dear dog. Scream/yell for help in any language you want. The locals will know how to deal with that dog. Really bad dogs don't last long in a town full of kids and nice dogs.

We never had to go past step 6, but it can happen. The really bad dogs go to the big yard in the sky as most towns don't have shelters or pounds. They either catch on and learn some manners or disappear.

Once you get back to the boat, grab a wet rag and clean your dog's feet. The dirt and sand will get every-where if you don't!

Yes, they sell dry dog food in Mexico. Canned too. Fish and rice work fine between shopping trips.

Gracie says "Come on down!"

This article appeared in Living Aboard Magazine.

INDEX

INDEX

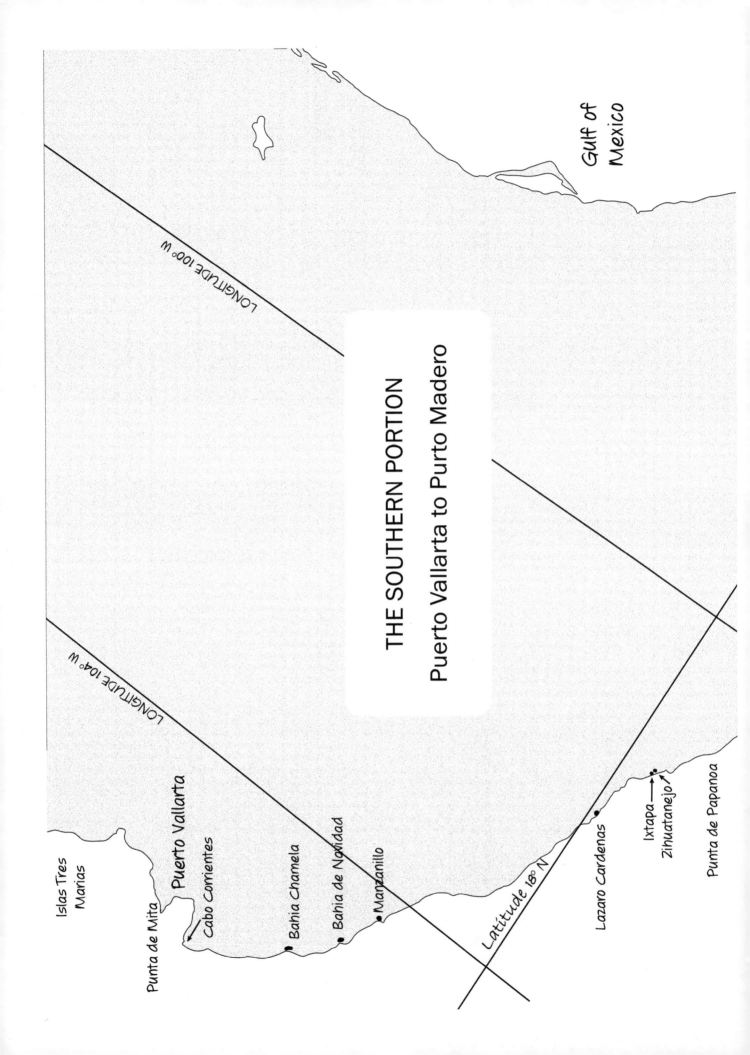

THE SOUTHERN PORTION

Puerto Vallarta to Purto Madero

Gulf of
Mexico

LONGITUDE 100° W

LONGITUDE 104° W

Islas Tres
Marias

Punta de Mita

Puerto Vallarta

Cabo Corrientes

Bahia Chamela

Bahia de Navidad

Manzanillo

Latitude 18° N

Lazaro Cardenas

Ixtapa
Zihuatanejo

Punta de Papanoa

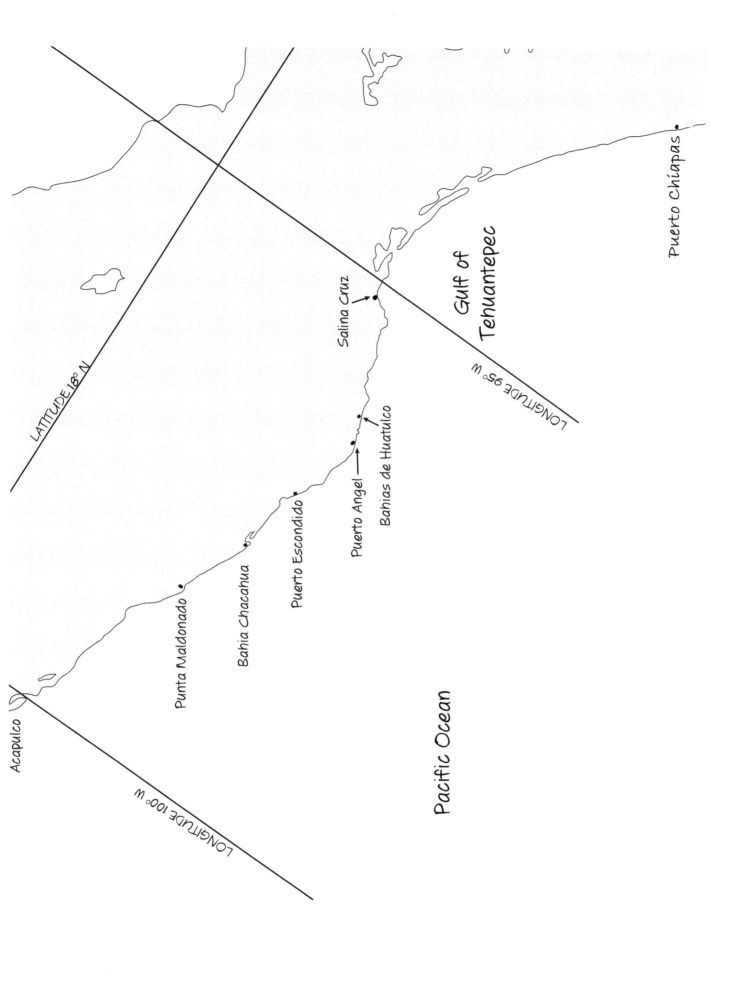

CPSIA information can be obtained
at www.ICGtesting.com
Printed in the USA
BVHW021003081021
618337BV00003B/75

9 781937 196356